THE

Vampire

COMPANION

THE

Vampire

COMPANION

The Official Guide to Anne Rice's
The Vampire Chronicles

KATHERINE RAMSLAND

BALLANTINE BOOKS · NEW YORK

Copyright © 1993, 1995 by Katherine M. Ramsland, Ph.D.
"Interview with the Vampire" copyright © 1995 by Anne O'Brien Rice
Maps and illustrations copyright © 1993 by Laura Hartman Maestro

All rights reserved under International and Pan-American Copyright Conventions. Published in the United States by Ballantine Books, a division of Random House, Inc., New York, and simultaneously in Canada by Random House of Canada Limited, Toronto. Originally published in different form by Ballantine Books in 1993.

THE VAMPIRE COMPANION is the title of Innovation
Publishing's fan-oriented support title to its adaptions of
Anne Rice's Vampire Chronicles. TM 1993 Innovative Corp.
All rights reserved. Used with permission.

Grateful acknowledgment is made to Anne Rice and Alfred A. Knopf, Inc.
for permission to reprint from the following works by Anne Rice:
Interview with the Vampire: Copyright © 1976 by Anne O'Brien Rice,
The Vampire Lestat: Copyright © 1985 by Anne O'Brien Rice,
The Queen of the Damned: Copyright © 1988 by Anne O'Brien Rice,
Tales of the Body Thief: Copyright © 1992 by Anne O'Brien Rice,
Memnoch the Devil: Copyright © 1995 by Anne O'Brien Rice.

Library of Congress Cataloging-in-Publication Data
Ramsland, Katherine M., 1953–
    The vampire companion : the official guide to Anne Rice's The
vampire chronicles / Katherine Ramsland. — Rev. ed.
        p.   cm.
    ISBN 0-345-39739-8
    1. Rice, Anne, 1941–   Vampire Chronicles—Dictionaries.
2. Vampires in literature—Dictionaries—.   3. Horror tales, American—
Dictionaries.   I. Rice, Anne, 1941–   Vampire chronicles.
II. Title.
PS3568.I265V28   1995
813'.54—dc20   95-10620
                                                                            CIP

Text design by Holly Johnson

Manufactured in the United States of America

Second Ballantine Books Edition: September 1995

9 8 7 6 5 4

For Jim Kerr, who supported my vision

And for Ruth Osborne and Donna Johnston, for their enthusiasm

CONTENTS

ACKNOWLEDGMENTS

Many people contributed ideas and material and helped with illustrations. I wish to thank one and all: Lloyd Arback, Diane Arlington, Murray Berman, Helen Brown, Patricia Byrne, Steve Cook, Frank Corey, Joe Cornish, Tom Cruise, Sabrina Cuttler, Donna Daley, Eric DeBruyn, Dave the Driver, Nancy Diamond, Phyllis Galde, David Geffen, Christopher Golden, Alvin Guthertz, Lee Anne Haigney, John Heyer, Barbara Johnston, Donna Johnston, Mike Johnston, Russell Leaf, Joanne Leary, Peggy Lynch, John Macarty, John Maclay, Danny Manning, Gigi McBrien, Janny McBrien, Leslie McNair, Sonny Mehta, Susie Miller, Troy Moss, Ruth Osborne, Nancy Pontier, Sue Quiroz, Steve Ramsland, Allen Reubens, Martin V. Riccardo, Stan Rice, Susan Roberts, Marlo Rodriquez, Audrey Scharmen, Robert Spates, Michelle Spedding, Kevin Steiner, Eileen Sullivan, Mary Sutton, Joel Sweimler, Lorna Toolis, Robert Wall, Shallah Weiss, Pelli Wheaton, Victoria Wilson, Bob Wyatt, and Gail Zimmerman.

Thanks also to editorial assistant Phebe Kirkham; my agent, Lori Perkins; and my editors, Joanne Wyckoff and Elizabeth Zack, whose sophistication and enthusiasm contributed to my motivation.

Most of all, I want to thank Anne Rice, whose patience and assistance with this project was immeasurable, and without whom this guide could not be what it is.

INTRODUCTION

Anne Rice began her popular series, *The Vampire Chronicles*, out of a desire to know what it was like to be a vampire. What if someone had the chance to find out, she wondered; what would a vampire say? Her curiosity prompted her to write a short story about a reporter interrogating one of these creatures of the night. Rice called it, appropriately, "Interview With the Vampire." Years later, the story became a novel by the same title, in which the vampire protagonist, Louis, related his fruitless search for redemption and for escape from grief and suffering. His tale of angst was a metaphor of the age, and when it was published in 1976, the enthusiastic reception demanded a sequel.

The Vampire Lestat emerged nine years later. Told by another vampire, Lestat, it connected Louis's experience to a broader mythological base, deepening the meaning of the nocturnal figure and freeing it from scenarios typical of the genre. Lestat's story was too long for one volume, so the *Chronicles* grew into a trilogy with the 1988 publication of *The Queen of the Damned*. Then Lestat had another story to tell, so Rice added yet a fourth book to the series, *The Tale of the Body Thief*. Finally, in 1995, Lestat described his ultimate encounter with God and the Devil in his fifth narrative, *Memnoch the Devil*.

Each of Rice's novels has found a widespread and diverse audience because vampires have a multifaceted appeal: they are seductive, sensual, hypnotic, and immortal—the epitome of what we'd all like to be. Unfortunately, they have to drink blood in order to survive. Thus, they exhibit a dark, dangerous side and their allure, coupled with their destructive potential, makes for a complex psychology. For over a century, popular fiction represented vampires as evil creatures that should be destroyed. Then Rice stepped in with Louis, a humanized vampire who resisted his dark nature. He felt guilty, he offered compassion, he wanted love, and he feared isolation. He was an intricate blend

of good and evil, body and spirit. Vampire fiction has never been the same since.

The first time I read *Interview with the Vampire,* I was impressed with its literary and philosophical themes. Then I noticed the same qualities in Rice's other novels. I wanted to know more. I looked for a biography of its author but none existed. I then took the rather bold step of deciding *I'd* like to write her biography. This way I could explore in my own way the creative process of a woman of obvious intelligence and education who had chosen to work with supernatural images. I approached Rice and she agreed to cooperate.

For two and a half years I focused on Rice's work exclusively. My philosophical and psychological training allowed me a unique perspective that went beyond what Rice herself was consciously aware of about her novels. She does not analyze the images and ideas that come to her; she simply expresses those that seem to be most clearly an authentic representation of her own inner life.

"I am swimming in an atmosphere when I write where there is a deliberate balance between the specific and the evocative," Rice explains. "Things are suggested. I do not keep detailed notes. I do believe, however, that all things in a book have meaning."

As a biographer, I discovered that Rice prefers to tap into a process she calls "the essential dream," and to let the subconscious do its work. "You write a novel with your whole being and you know a lot of things that you're not aware that you know. I trust to that. When I say I'm accessing the subconscious to write, it means I'm trusting to feelings of authenticity that what I'm saying has a deeper meaning. It never lets me down. I do whatever I can to make that state occur."

In addition, Rice imbues her work with a strong mythological framework. "Myths fascinate me," says Rice. "I feel like I'm going into them. It's like a burrowing. For example, when I was trying to discover a plausible origin to the vampires, I happened upon the Osirian myth and thought, 'This is it. It's perfect.' I see myself exploring the relationship between popular vampire fiction and the vegetation gods of ancient times. I feel like I amplified the connection."

As a biographer, I was fascinated with how all these elements came together in Rice's novels, but as I worked on the biography, I sensed that my ideas were taking two different tracks: one was biographical and the other was thematic and interpretive. It became clear that I would not be able to include all that I wanted to in the biography. I was frustrated. There was so *much* material in the novels that I wanted to address, yet to do so in the biography would mean losing focus. I toyed with the idea of writing a book on the literary themes in Rice's work but put that idea aside until I finished the biography, *Prism of the Night.*

Shortly after the biography was published, Rice asked me if I'd like to work on an interpretive guide to *The Vampire Chronicles*; she had been approached to do it herself but preferred to concentrate on writing novels. I nearly jumped out of my chair. Yes, of course! What could be more wonderful than to go back to those themes and interpretations I'd left behind? I'd be able to write about the novels in a much fuller way, and I was already many steps ahead with all the work I'd already done. The faxes flew back and forth as Rice and I developed a vision of what this guide would be: it would have pictures, of course, and maps. I should enable readers to see such things as the paintings in the Subterranean room in the Theater of the Vampires, the cathedral where Louis killed the priest, and the town house that inspired the French Quarter home where Louis, Claudia, and Lestat lived for sixty-five years. Readers might want to know what the QE2 looks like, or see the mountains of Nepal where Pandora met with Azim.

We decided that the entries should provide more than a plot summary, so Rice agreed to provide deleted material from early drafts of her novels and to talk about background influences, like the kind of art that inspired her when she developed the Theater of the Vampires, and why she chose Divisadero Street in San Francisco as a setting for her first novel. In addition, the entries should offer readers such things as the meaning behind Stan Rice's poetry in *The Queen of the Damned* and explanations for allusions to historical events, films, and literature.

Thus was born *The Vampire Companion: The Official Guide to Anne Rice's The Vampire Chronicles*. This book is intended as a supplement to *The Vampire Chronicles*, and even though parts of plots are summarized in places, the *Companion* should not be seen as a substitute for reading the novels. Consisting of over twelve hundred entries, the *Companion* also includes a chronology of events that begin with the vampire origins, maps of significant locations, cross-references, and over one hundred drawings and photographs. I organized the entries in encyclopedic fashion and added background material, expanding the significance of key events and ideas. I categorized the contents of Rice's novels according to characters, places, themes, literary allusions, symbols, famous quotes, and vampire-related terminology. Page numbers are given in each entry to help readers find the first or primary reference and are not intended to be exhaustive. The texts referred to throughout the *Companion* are Ballantine mass market paperback editions, except for *Memnoch the Devil*, which has just been published in hardcover.

Anne Rice elaborated on many of the entries and also served as a consultant to the entire project. But although she commented freely throughout the *Companion*, she prefers that some things remain a

mystery, kept open-ended for possible elaboration in future books. For example, I have not tried to explain Louis's mortal love, the fate of the musician vampire, or Claudia's ghostly appearance to Jesse.

My interpretations throughout the *Companion* are informed by the theories of Swiss psychiatrist Carl Jung and by existential philosophy, which, like the *Chronicles*, deals with free will and the personal quest for meaning. According to Jung, the human psyche is divided into conscious and unconscious realms. The ego is the center of consciousness, but the unconscious contains energy that motivates many behaviors. It also includes a universal aspect—the collective unconscious—that consists of deeply ingrained patterns of thought and behavior called archetypes. These patterns are expressed in symbols and metaphors that have strong emotional appeal, such as the Hero, the Wise Teacher, the Great Mother, the Trickster, and the Shadow. The vampire characters in the *Chronicles* show clear connections to archetypal material.

Although Rice has not read Jung, she agrees that her books provoke a strong response in readers. "It's not hard for me to create these characters," she says, "because they all represent longings and aspirations in myself." Her first novel echoes the grief of losing a daughter, and the other four trace her spiritual quests.

Early in her career, Rice felt pressured by friends and teachers to write the "slice-of-life" novels that were gaining popularity in the late sixties, but her first attempts at realistic settings failed to express the deep and profound feelings she experienced: "For years, two forces warred in me. As a young writer, I tried to force myself into a mold of writing about my life, but I couldn't work with it. I couldn't make my life believable in novels. I didn't know how to use it. It was when I abandoned that struggle and wrote *Interview with the Vampire* that it came together for me. I have entered the dark world of the imagination, a country traveled by the Brontës, Mary Shelley, Hawthorne, James, Melville, and Dickens, and I have found that imagined realms and characters work well for me as images of truth."

Although Rice works with supernatural images, she weaves them into actual settings and includes historical facts and literature that make the vampires seem more real. "The vampire image," Rice points out, "is a mythic image that we use to talk about being human. Vampires are not literal evil. They enable me to talk about ideas that go beyond them. You can make a vampire character talk about anything that concerns you. I don't think there's any moral, psychological, or aesthetic limit to supernatural fiction.

"For example, *Macbeth* has characters that are larger than life; it has mythic battling forces. Aristotle said that tragedy works best when you have great men, heroes. What we have today is a theory about fiction that claims the opposite—that the most important, truth-filled

fiction must deal with very ordinary, middle-class individuals who have no distinction whatsoever. This is deeply embedded in our culture. It's a belief that truth lies with the familiar. Fantasy gets a bum rap. People today argue that writing about real situations is somehow superior to fantasy, but I always argue that it isn't.

"For thousands of years fantasy has been the medium for people talking about the meaning of life. We know that the works of imagination survive. *Faust* is a household word, and so is *Macbeth* and *Moby Dick*. Dickens's characters have a shimmering life in the minds of people who have never actually read his books.

"I think people are hungry for imagery and for the deeper truths that fantasy and myth give them," Rice says. "They crave the flamboyant characters and flights of imagination, the chills you get when you watch a great performance of *Faust* or Shakespeare. They want the intensity. People are passionately concerned about good and evil. They're passionately concerned about living a moral life and about living every minute—not letting the intensity of life slip away."

The Vampire Companion offers readers a means for exploring how Rice's supernatural fiction addresses human concerns. Her intent as a novelist is to provide a way to look at life from a unique angle, and my hope for this *Companion* is to help readers probe the works more deeply.

Note to readers of this revised edition:

In order to provide full descriptions for entries from *Memnoch the Devil*, some entries from the previous edition of *The Vampire Companion* have been deleted. For the most part, these entries focused on symbols or minor characters or events. A few entries were merely cross-referenced, without loss of content. Every effort was made to retain entries that readers were likely to look up or from which readers gained valuable background information not found in the novels. In some cases, where *Memnoch the Devil* involved characters, settings, or themes already addressed, new information has been provided in the relevant entries. One map and several photos and drawings have also been added.

ABBREVIATIONS

The following abbreviations are used throughout for references to Anne Rice's novels:

IV   *Interview with the Vampire*

VL   *The Vampire Lestat*

QD   *The Queen of the Damned*

BT   *The Tale of the Body Thief*

MD   *Memnoch the Devil*

WH   *The Witching Hour*

THE

Vampire

COMPANION

Abandonment   The fear of being rejected or left alone without resources; symbolic of death. The theme of abandonment portrays a psychological struggle on the part of an individual, as his or her own inner power battles with the compulsion to depend heavily on the will and presence of others.

In the *Chronicles*, abandonment becomes an issue for several vampires. Louis is the most prominent example, since he possesses the personality of a victim: passive, blaming, weak, and resentful. Vulnerable to the ebb and flow of circumstances, he wants others to make his life better. He craves someone to dominate him. Thus, when Lestat appears, Louis becomes dependent on him. Although he eventually comes to despise Lestat, he is so frightened of being abandoned that he cleaves to Lestat for over half a century. He can break away only if someone else fills Lestat's role for him. *(VL 499)*

So, when Claudia joins them, Louis becomes dependent on her. They leave Lestat and go to Paris, where Louis transfers his dependence to Armand. Claudia believes that Louis will leave her, so she demands that he make Madeleine a vampire guardian for her. Yet he is wary of performing the requested task, because he fears abandonment by her. This fear of abandonment is so pervasive among vampires that Armand, perceiving that Louis might remain with Claudia instead of joining with him, pressures him into making Madeleine. Thus, the triumvirate cling to one another in a symbiotic dependency that results in all of them being abandoned in one tragic act: the destruction of Claudia. *(IV 288–290)*

Similarly, in VL, Lestat fears being abandoned by Magnus when Magnus says he will jump into the fire and annihilate himself. However, Lestat survives Magnus's destruction and comes to rely on inner strength rather than dependence. *(VL 96)* Conquering the fear of abandonment is necessary to attain true independence. Lestat shows he has

achieved this when he metaphorically abandons Louis by refusing to be his teacher; he wants Louis to find answers through his own experience. *(VL 498)*

For many characters, though, the terror of being left alone remains primal. It forces them to face their own vulnerability, alienation, and emptiness. Drinking blood—the source of life—then becomes an addiction, since it offers them warmth and the illusion of comfort.

See also Teacher, Victim Psychology.

Absinthe   A yellowish green alcoholic beverage containing wormwood and anise. Absinthe can destroy the nerve centers of the brain.

Claudia uses a mix of absinthe and laudanum to poison Lestat. She drugs two mortal boys with it, and presents them to Lestat as victims. When he drinks from them, he grows weak enough for her to attack and overcome him. *(IV 137)*

See also Claudia, Estrangement, Laudanum, Lestat de Lioncourt, Violence.

Accident   The theme of random causality grows out of the aforementioned notion of an absurd universe that lacks absolute or coherent meaning. That vampires exist at all is said by the oldest of them to have been an accident that should never have occurred. *(VL 431)*

If there is no Supreme Being and no ordained order, then anything can happen. There is no immutable right or wrong, and good and evil are malleable concepts. Marius learns this from the vampire Elder who had been Akasha's guardian. He discloses his knowledge to Lestat, who finds the idea that there may be no reason for what he is repugnant. The idea removes from Lestat a buffer of illusion, and requires him to face the tenuousness of existence and the absence of a larger plan. Two centuries later, as Lestat thinks back to his fight with the wolves, he recognizes that his survival was a mere accident as well; no divine protector had watched over him. *(BT 42)*

"We live in a world of accidents finally," Lestat says, "in which only aesthetic principles have a consistency of which we can be sure." *(QD 6)*

Lestat's sentiments echo Rice's own beliefs. "I think it's important," she says, "not to build false systems around things that happen. Our tendency is to think that things have meaning and inevitability, but usually they don't."

Actaeon and Adonis   Gods from Greek mythology to whom Gabrielle refers when she describes for Lestat ancient deities who were dismembered. Actaeon's dogs tore him apart, while a wild boar killed Adonis. *(VL 330)*

Addiction   The experience of clinging to something in desperation even though it may be harmful to oneself. Addiction is often associated with the search for feelings that have been anesthetized by religion, family conditions, and/or social propriety. It mixes pleasure with guilt, a combination that can seduce the addict by being more alluring than pleasure alone. Addicts are caught in a trap of circularity: not attaining so much pleasure that they can override their feelings of guilt, and simultaneously not suffering so much that they can choose to end the pleasure. The loss of self-control they experience often leads them to lives of secrecy and denial.

"The vampire metaphor," claims Rice, "is about addiction, about sensual satisfaction." She knew about addiction firsthand from her mother's dependence on, and decline from, alcohol. Her mother seemed to believe that addiction was caused by something in the blood, and Rice later captures this idea when Marius says, "It made sense that something was in my blood impelling me to drink more blood." (VL 445)

Vampires are overwhelmingly attracted to the joy of the swoon. They need blood to survive, but such a survival requires accepting themselves as killers. Those with a conscience must deceive themselves about, or attempt to buffer, the negative aspects of what they are really doing, just as addicts might do. For example, when Akasha, the first vampire, is told by Mekare how she can stop drinking blood—by exposing her body to the sun, thereby destroying it as a vehicle for the spirit Amel—she cannot fathom doing such a thing. Although she does not want to kill and dislikes being unable to go out in daylight, she is addicted to survival at all costs. She chooses to remain in a disturbing situation in order to feed her need. (QD 405)

Yet some vampires are torn by the situation in which they find themselves and take dramatic action to end their existence. Magnus and Nicolas jump into the fire to destroy themselves, and Lestat exposes himself to the sun. Although Lestat's suicide attempt fails, he knows that he has within himself the power to escape his existence. Since he chooses not to do so, by the end of BT he has stopped deluding himself with the notion that he is trying to do good and has accepted exactly what he is: the embodiment of evil, addicted to survival at all cost. (BT 406, 433)

See also Blood, Swoon.

Adventure   See Hero, Quest.

Aegean Sea   The Aegean is an arm of the Mediterranean Sea and is bordered by Greece, Turkey, and Crete. The island on which Marius has built a fortress for Those Who Must Be Kept is located in this body

of water. Marius takes Lestat here from Egypt, shows him the vampire King and Queen, then tells him the story of the vampire origins. *(VL 367)* (See Vampire Atlas)

See also Those Who Must Be Kept.

Aesthetic choice

The idea that guides Louis's early years as a vampire. After he describes in IV how he killed animals rather than humans for four years, the boy reporter asks if this was an aesthetic choice rather than a moral one. Louis answers that they are the same. The artist may break social codes of morality, but that does not make his choice, when it is in the name of art, immoral. Louis had enacted this mode of killing partly because he wished to understand death in stages; he wanted to begin with the lower species, saving the experience of human death for when he had a more mature understanding. For him, the process served a higher spiritual principle, and was thus a moral choice. *(IV 72)*

Armand lives by a similar concept, although he defines it as spiritual rather than aesthetic. *(VL 303)*

See also Animal Blood, Armand, Louis de Pointe du Lac, The Spiritual.

Aesthetic principles

See Savage Garden.

Agents

Well-paid lawyers, bankers, and merchants who make it possible for the vampires to carry out human transactions, be outfitted with fine clothing, transfer funds, purchase property, and, in Lestat's case, set up a career as a rock star. Lestat's first such agent is Pierre Roget, who distributes Lestat's newfound vampire wealth among Lestat's friends and family and takes care of everything with which Lestat cannot or does not want to deal. Lestat's lawyer, Christine, hires producers and directors for making his rock videos. She also procures for him a fake birth certificate, a Social Security card, a driver's license, and bank accounts, so that he can "pass" as a mortal. *(VL 14, 118)*

See also Christine, Roget (Pierre).

Age of Enlightenment

The eighteenth century, during which Newtonian methods of science were applied to the study of human beings and philosophers believed in reason and the senses. During this time, Lestat, Louis, and Claudia were made into vampires. Lestat refers to the era as the Age of Reason, and he is influenced enough by its emphasis on the rational mind to crave the company of a sophisticated vampire like Marius after his encounter with Armand's coven, which acts as if it were from the Dark Ages.

Age of Innocence   One of Lestat's twelve rock music videos, designed to reveal to mortals what vampires really are. *(VL 540)*

See also Music Videos, Rock Music, Rock Star.

Aging   Growing older is a central issue throughout the *Chronicles*. Lestat describes most clearly what it means for mortals: with age, they become creatures governed by their thought and will, with only an insubstantial body to support them. *(BT 22)*

After Lestat forms a friendship with a mortal, David Talbot, he grows concerned as the ravages of age encroach on David's body and spirit. He then tempts David with immortality, which David fleetingly considers as he reaches his final years and acknowledges that he did not achieve all that he had wanted to in his lifetime. *(BT 61)*

Sooner or later, all of the vampires understand that the process of aging in mortals affects their connections with them. After Louis watches his mother and sister grow old and die, he realizes that no relationship with a mortal comes without the pain of inevitable loss. *(IV 169)*

The issue of aging affects Claudia and Armand in a unique way. Claudia agonizes over her mental and emotional maturation because she is trapped in the body of a child. She will never know what it is like to have the form of a woman. Similarly, as Armand had been made as an adolescent, he realizes that he lacks worldly understanding because he doesn't know what it is like to have a significant number of mortal years behind him. *(IV 264, QD 89)*

Aging, however, also has a positive side for vampires. Their powers increase the longer they exist, although their mental ability to sustain and utilize those powers may decrease if boredom undermines their motivation to endure. *(BT 223, QD 4)*

See also Armand, Change, Claudia, Immortality, Talbot (David), Vampire Powers.

Akasha   An ancient Egyptian queen who became the first vampire, she is part of the vampire couple known in legend as Those Who Must Be Kept. Her name was inspired by a place name Rice had seen on a map in the book *Lost Cities of Africa*.

Becoming a queen upon her marriage when she was a mortal, Akasha, with her husband King Enkil, turns her people away from cannibalism and encourages the eating of grains. In all things Akasha disregards the beliefs of others and demands that everyone practice hers. Her dark, nihilistic side compels her to seek evidence of the supernatural and, as a result, she has the twin witches, Maharet and Mekare, brought to her court. They perceive that she throws a moral cloak over her evil deeds, so that these deeds become a mix of good and evil that is actually more dangerous than pure unadulterated evil. Aka-

sha has no true morality but is driven to continually create meaning. *(QD 330)* When the twins demonstrate to her what the spirits can do, she is caught between fascination and rage. She needs elegant beliefs to fill up her inner emptiness, but the presence and power of these spirits confirm her nihilism. When she scorns the spirits, one of them—Amel—attacks her, prefiguring a future attack that will result in a bizarre and disastrous bond. *(QD 333–341)*

Akasha humiliates the twins by making them undergo a public rape, then sends them away. By attacking the perpetrator, Amel avenges the twins. Akasha and Enkil then attempt to learn more about

Kali, an ancient blood goddess and a model for Akasha

this spirit and consequently put themselves at risk. Those mortals who wish to lead the people back to cannibalism use the occasion for an assassination attempt. Akasha and Enkil are both seriously wounded, and as Akasha's soul ascends, Amel joins with it and reenters her body through her wounds, fusing with her heart and brain to produce a new entity: the vampire. Akasha then saves Enkil by making him a vampire and goes on to give the Dark Gift to Khayman, who gives it to the twin witches. (QD 344, 382–388, 412–413)

As her progeny proliferate, Akasha's need for blood diminishes. Eventually she becomes a living statue, kept safe for centuries by guardians who know that she is the source of their existence and immortality. After one of these guardians, the Elder, tires of the task, he places Akasha and Enkil in the sun. Akasha draws Marius to her and urges him to take her and Enkil out of Egypt. Marius does so and protects them for nearly two thousand years. During that time, Akasha projects her soul from her body and watches the world through the eyes of mortals and immortals. At one point, the witch Maharet, now a vampire, stabs Akasha in the heart. As Maharet feels the energy leave her own body, it confirms the legend that to kill Akasha is to annihilate the vampires. Akasha, however, does not react to the attack. (VL 434, 462, QD 260, 418)

"She was too catatonic," Rice explains, "utterly indifferent. After all those thousands of years she doesn't give a damn. People can do anything, but it's not going to hurt her."

When Lestat first sees Akasha, he wants to touch her immobile face. That she seems to be alive inside an inert body upsets him; it is like being buried alive. Marius urges him to talk to her, and Lestat tells her that she is beautiful. He kisses her and she reveals to him her name. Later he plays the violin for her, waking her from her trance. She allows him to drink her blood while she drinks from him; they remain locked in this intimate embrace until Enkil, too, wakes up and, in a rage, separates them. (VL 388, 485)

Marius then sends Lestat away, but not before Marius has made an ominous statement that becomes a prediction: "Who knows what Akasha might do if there were no Enkil to hold her?" (VL 472)

In 1985, Lestat again wakes Akasha with his music—this time rock music in which he mentions her name and the legends about her. She rises, and upon realizing that Enkil no longer has power to keep her with him, kills him. She then leaves the shrine and becomes a relentless destroyer, killing most of the vampires. She leaves a few, including Maharet and Khayman, to be immortal witnesses and to join with her in her plan for a new world order: to kill ninety-nine percent of the world's men and to set up a new Eden in which women, with Akasha as the goddess, reign. While Akasha insists this is for the benefit of mortal women, in truth she wants to dominate and be worshiped, to

once again subject everyone to her will. The surviving vampires form a plan to stand against Akasha, aware that the witch Mekare, also a vampire, is moving to join them.

Akasha abducts Lestat to be her apprentice and prince; he participates for a brief time, then stands against her with the surviving vampires. Their rebellion enrages her, but before she can attack them, the witch Mekare shoves her into a glass wall. The broken shards cut off Akasha's head. Maharet immediately grabs Akasha's heart and brain, and gives them to Mekare to eat. As Mekare does so, she takes into herself the source of the spiritual fusion with Amel and becomes the new life force of the vampires. *(VL 428–487, QD 306–352, 378–390)*

"Akasha is the villain of QD," Rice explains, "because she is subordinating everything to a pure idea."

See also Akasha's Plan, Amel, Enkil, Heart, Inanna, Lestat de Lioncourt, Marius, Moral Dilemma, *The Queen of the Damned*, Symmetry, Those Who Must Be Kept, Vampire, *The Vampire Lestat.*

Akasha's plan

While Akasha lies dormant over six thousand years, she realizes the evil of what vampires and men are doing worldwide. She devises a plan to create a paradise on earth—a new Eden in which she will reign as the goddess. She will define the concept of goodness on her own terms, as she revamps the world myths that worship the Great Mother and her lover. She wants to free women from injustice, poverty, war, and crime. Doing so entails ridding the world of ninety-nine percent of the men. When the women take over, they then will learn to limit men through gender selection of babies. They will teach the few boys who survive new ways of participating in the world, without violence and crime. Once this is accomplished, they will then increase the male sex gradually.

Akasha rises when technology has become advanced enough to perpetuate what she wants to accomplish. Although she tells Lestat that she wants him to assist her, she also betrays him by using him as an example of what is wrong with all things male: hatred, aggression, and eloquent excuses for violence.

Akasha's first act is to destroy vampires and their meeting places around the world. Some resist her, like Khayman and Maharet, and others she saves because Lestat loves them or so that they can serve as immortal witnesses. Then Akasha abducts Lestat from Carmel Valley and takes him to the Auvergne, in France, to prepare him to join her. He is part of her design; he woke her and he mirrors her in his vision to use evil for good. Lestat recognizes the ambiguity of Akasha's plan: either it can mean tragedy or it can be something magnificent that could lift them out of irrelevance and provide a form of redemption.

They continue on to Azim's temple in the Himalayas, where

Azim becomes the first martyr to Akasha's cause. She commands Lestat to kill the mortal men in the temple—the henchmen of this blood god. He is horrified but obeys.

Akasha calls their actions a divine war; they are killing for a righteous cause. She then takes Lestat to Sri Lanka, representative of hunger, petty war, and miserable conditions all over the world, to show him what the reign of men has created. Through visions of the end of hunger and poverty, she inspires the women there to turn on the men. She promises perfection, security, and serenity, and is careful to minimize challenge by selecting places as primitive as she is.

She then goes to a Greek island, Lynkonos, and repeats these atrocities. Lestat is overwhelmed and decides that he cannot stand with her. In Haiti, he asks to see the other vampires and she takes him to them, ready to command them to join her or die. But they stand against her.

The resistance erodes her confidence and magnifies her loneliness. Her plan ends abruptly at the Sonoma Compound with her death, but not before she wavers in her conviction when she fails to find disciples. *(QD 249–263, 286–305, 353–377, 391–398, 435–457)*

See also Eden, Haiti, Lynkonos, Moral Dilemma, Sri Lanka, Symmetry, Truth, Violence.

Alchemy   A process devised in the Middle Ages as a means of producing a "philosopher's stone," which could turn base metals into gold and prolong life. Alchemy symbolizes illumination, salvation, purification, and immortality.

Magnus was an alchemist who stole the immortal blood from a vampire, but in a larger sense, Rice views all vampires as symbolic alchemists who can transform blood into spiritual, eternal substance. *(VL 88)*

See also Magnus, Transformation.

Alcohol   A metaphor of the vampires, for it, too, seems to mix incompatible opposites—in this case, fire and water. It is also a substance that, when enough is ingested, surpasses the will and invites surrender. The vampires are connected with alcohol in a variety of ways.

Louis first meets Daniel Molloy in a bar, and as he tells his story, he urges the reporter to drink from his flask to get warm. (The vampires themselves find warmth by drinking blood.) Daniel later becomes an alcoholic in his pursuit of elusive immortality.

In QD, vampires gather in the back rooms of vampire bars. While they themselves do not drink alcohol, the mortal patrons out front imbibe drinks named for aspects of vampirism.

See also Addiction, Molloy (Daniel), Vampire Bars.

Alex   The drummer in the band, Satan's Night Out, with whom Lestat becomes a famous rock star. *(VL 13)*
See also Satan's Night Out, *The Vampire Lestat.*

Alexander Stoker   See Stoker, Dr. Alexander.

Alexander the Great   Born in 356 B.C., Alexander was king of Macedon and considered the greatest general of ancient times. By the age of thirty-two, this magnetic, willful leader had founded an empire that stretched from India to the Adriatic Sea.
In QD, Marius compares Lestat to Alexander, who wept when there were no more worlds to conquer. Marius wonders if Lestat will feel the same when there are no more rules to break. *(QD 472)*
See also Lestat de Lioncourt.

Alexandria   An ancient city of Egypt where Marius discovers the reason why vampires worldwide have been burned or destroyed. It is the home of the largest library in the Roman Empire, making Alexandria a symbol of enlightenment—the place where Marius learns all that he needs to know, and where he discovers Akasha and Enkil. *(VL 426)*
See also Marius, Those Who Must Be Kept.

Aliases   Names used by various characters to disguise their identity. Some such names have symbolic meaning. *(VL 66, BT 81, 85, 139, 162, 200, 298, 299, 313)*
See Blackwood (Sheridan); Gregor (Lestan); Hamilton (Jason); Van Kindergarten (Baron); Melmoth (Sebastian); Oddbody (Clarence); Potter (Lionel); Renfield; Rummel (Isaac); Sampson (Eric); Stoker (Dr. Alexander); Valois (de); Wilde (Stanford).

All of Me   A 1984 film by Carl Reiner starring Steve Martin and Lily Tomlin, it tells the story of a millionaire spinster who wants to live forever. When she dies, her soul transmigrates into the brain of a lawyer. The lawyer then controls the right side of his body, while she controls the left.
Raglan James gives a videotape of this film to Lestat in Paris to communicate his intentions of exchanging bodies. *(BT 91)*
See also Body Switching, James (Raglan).

All Saints' Day   See Feast of All Saints.

Altar   The place in a church where the sacraments are dispensed and where holy books are kept. In some religions, it is also the place of

Altar in a Catholic church

sacrifice. Symbolically, the altar serves as the sacred space of death and rebirth.

Louis experiences the emptiness of his religious beliefs as he looks at the altar in St. Louis Cathedral. He kills a priest before he leaves. *(IV 144)*

Lestat and Gabrielle hide beneath an altar in a country church when Armand's coven pursues them. That they can gain entrance to the church, go right up to its most sacred place, and even sleep beneath it, is a sign of the impotence of Christianity against creatures like vampires. *(VL 190)*

See also Eucharist, Religious Images.

Amadeo   The name on Marius's painting of Armand; it means "one who loves God." *(QD 175)*

See also *The Temptation of Amadeo*.

Amel   The spirit who fuses with Akasha to create the first vampire. Rice had read that *Amel* was an ancient Middle Eastern word for evil.

Known to the witches Mekare and Maharet, Amel appears to them several nights after their first communication from Egypt, warning them that they will need his power. He is jealous of their bodies and their ability to feel pleasure, and he brags that he can draw blood. As he longs for contact with the physical, he follows the twins to Akasha's court, where he performs tricks to enchant the queen. His antics undermine her beliefs, and she insists that the witches be punished. When Enkil sentences them to be raped by his steward, Khayman, Amel avenges them by menacing Khayman with poltergeistlike activity for six months. Some people, known as flesh eaters, construe Amel's attacks as a sign that they should return to the former cannibalistic practices that Akasha prohibits, and so when Enkil and Akasha attempt to communicate with Amel, the flesh eaters fatally stab the royal couple. *(QD 319–322, 338–343, 382–388)*

Amel then enters Akasha's body, seeking a place to fuse with her flesh. A cloud of blood droplets surrounds her, then disappears into her wounds, which magically heal as Amel settles into Akasha's heart and brain. Akasha then laps at Enkil's wounds, giving him her blood, and together they become deities demanding blood sacrifice. Their thirst is unquenchable because Amel is a spirit of gigantic proportions and requires much blood to sustain himself. Both Akasha and Enkil make other vampires until their intense thirst decreases. Amel spreads out into other vampires through the blood exchange, mentally and physically connecting them to one another. *(QD 400–409)*

Over the centuries, Akasha and Enkil no longer need blood to survive because the increasing numbers of other vampires have taken on the burden of feeding Amel. *(VL 437)*.

Memnoch identifies Amel as a soul from Sheol that had forgotten his human origins; as Amel watched people back on Earth, he had become envious enough of the flesh to try to possess it again. Amel was not the only such mutation. *(MD 247)*

See also Akasha, Blood, Sheol, Soul, Spirits, Vine.

Amon Ra   The sun god of the ancient Egyptians, formed from the union of Amon, the first god of Thebes, and the sun god, Ra.

When Enkil first becomes a vampire and is unable to endure the light, he assumes that Ra has turned against him. He then presents Osiris to the people as the god who conquered the demon and who is now the one to worship. *(QD 342, 389, 410)*

See also Enkil, Sun.

Amon Ra

Amsterdam   A city in Holland that, in the fifteenth and sixteenth centuries, gave sanctuary to people fleeing witchcraft persecutions. The presence everywhere of murky canal water symbolizes how Amsterdam embodies the meeting of the conscious mind with the unconscious. Lestat calls Amsterdam a vampire's city because it is full of late-night crowds and young people who never sleep.

The oldest Motherhouse of the Talamasca is located in Amsterdam. Lestat visits David Talbot there, where his concern for David deepens and their friendship acquires new dimensions. *(BT 30)* (See Vampire Atlas)

See also Motherhouse, Rembrandt van Rijn, Rijksmuseum, Vampire Cities.

Amulet   A vial filled with Armand's blood that Daniel wears to ward off the approach of other vampires, for they will then sense that Daniel is protected by one of the older, more powerful vampires. *(QD 102)*

See also Gold Locket.

Anabaptists   A German religious sect that became popular in the mid-seventeenth century. Its members made the act of baptism contingent upon a conscious confession of faith. This religion of the "inner light" caused peasant unrest and disturbed the established church. Both Catholics and Lutheran Protestants persecuted the Anabaptists, nearly annihilating the sect.

Memnoch mentions these martyrs to Lestat as an example of Christianity's violence. *(MD 287)*

See also Christianity.

"And now art Thou cursed"   What God said to Cain in Genesis 4:11 after he killed his brother. In Louis's guilt-ridden vision of Lestat's funeral in St. Louis Cathedral, Claudia quotes these words to Louis. *(IV 146)*

See also Bible, Cain and Abel.

Androgyny   The image of wholeness that involves opposites in complementary relationships, like male/female, good/evil, and pleasure/pain, although it is most typically used in connection with gender. The idea is that each half of a dualistic pair contains something of the other.

Rice views the androgynous being as the ideal: "It always has immediate intense emotional impact on me to see androgynous figures," she says. She wrote an article for *Vogue* (November 1983) on rock stars as romantic images of gender renunciation and sexual ambiguity. They represent, she claimed, the power, energy, and "wise innocence" of pregender childhood. Breaking down gender boundaries

does not destroy masculine and feminine distinctions, but ends gender tyranny and divisiveness. This issue has personal significance for Rice.

"I've always felt uncomfortable in the role of being a woman," she claims. "I feel like my intellect is masculine or androgynous. I think *all* of us are masculine and feminine. Perhaps in my writing I go to my secret side." Androgynous people, she believes, are better equipped to love more deeply and meet more of the increasingly complex demands of life.

Catholic traditions with which Rice was raised were replete with androgynous images. "I was always fascinated with the figures in church," she says, "those huge marble statues that look like both men and women combined. Most of the saints are androgynous, and most representations of Christ present him as androgynous. The stained glass windows contain very feminine-looking males, and males who weep over and over again."

As a result, the vampire figure in the *Chronicles* is highly androgynous. Males bond easily, and Lestat frequently weeps. Gabrielle abandons female garb and wears the clothing of young male victims. Attraction and affection are freely exchanged, regardless of the gender of giver and receiver, and the loss of traditional role boundaries and behaviors increases the erotic charge. Rice felt it thrilling to move through territory fraught with psychological and sexual risk, where new freedoms were discovered and exploited when resistance broke down. *(VL 171, QD 274)*

See also Clothing, Extraordinary Life, Relationships, Sensuality, Sex, Vampire Powers.

Angel   A symbol used throughout the *Chronicles* to refer to the vampires. Angels represent invisible forces, both good and bad (called demons or dark angels), and Western Christianity views the good ones as messengers of God. The word "angel" comes from *angiras*, the Sanskrit word for "divine spirit," and the Greek *angelos*, meaning "messenger." Most information about angels in Judeo-Christian tradition derives from the Bible, Apocrypha, Pseudepigrapha, and some theological writings. Angelology came into its own during the Middle Ages, when thousands of names of angels were compiled (often from combinations of the Hebrew alphabet). The angels named in the Old Testament originated in Babylonian mythology. As the intermediaries between God and humankind, angels are often depicted as winged, robed, and asexual, although their true essence is immaterial. Some lore holds that, after death, human beings may actually evolve into angels. There are many stories, even today, of angels disguising themselves as mortals to offer assistance or intervention. Their mission is to promote divine enlightenment and well-being.

Comparing vampires to angels emphasizes their spiritual qualities. For example, in IV, Louis lifts a finger toward heaven "as if he were an angel about to give the Word of the Lord." *(IV 25)* He makes the connection to angels himself when he speaks about his emotional detachment as similar to that of angels, and, in fact, he is mistaken for an angel when he visits Babette Freniere.

Other comparisons abound. In VL, Gabrielle bears the name of an archangel, yet she becomes a vampire. When Lestat kills men in Azim's temple, he views himself as an angel with an invisible sword. And Akasha calls him her angel. *(QD 294)*

Essentially, angelic imagery conveys the impression of an elevated spirituality that transcends the human condition. The paradoxical fusion of the monstrous vampire with the divine draws attention away from more bestial concepts of the vampire inspired by Bram Stoker's *Dracula*. Rice links the vampire to the highest order of spirituality. It is no coincidence that their white, luminous skin and incandescent eyes bear striking resemblance to descriptions of angels. "I always saw vampires as angels going in another direction," Rice admits, "as finely tuned imitations of human beings imbued with this evil spirit. They became for me refined and abstract rather than animalistic."

One of the most powerful uses of this imagery is in the painting of Armand done by Marius during the Renaissance. It depicts Armand surrounded by black-winged angels, a reversal of the typical "temptation" paintings of the period, for angels replace demons as the tempters. The black-winged angel is Marius, a vampire. *(QD 175)*

The imagery is further developed when Lestat talks about the human subjects of Rembrandt's paintings. He describes the love and purity in their faces as that of angels. David Talbot asks him if there are any vampires with such faces and Lestat grows upset. Vampires are immortal, with faces that could be mistaken for angels, yet none possess the glow of inner light depicted by Rembrandt, he realizes, whose paintings are spiritual visions of the best of the inner person that transcend physical appearances. *(BT 36)*

Lestat learns more about the nature of angels when he sees them firsthand. Many of the legends prove false as Memnoch, one of the original archangels, explains what it is like to be an angel. Memnoch appears to Lestat in several forms, one of which is that of a large human with diaphanous wings.

He explains that angels have "essential" bodies and can gather matter from various sources to create a functioning body. The form that Memnoch presents to Lestat is "the logical result of my essence drawing to it all the various materials it needs." *(MD 175)* God allows some angels, such as Michael and Gabriel, to appear in their glorified forms on Earth, but most of the time they move about in the form of mortals.

God created the angels in His image, giving them anthropo-

Angel

morphic shapes—a head and arms and legs. Since they were invisible and had no material form, they were aware of their limbs only when they were in motion. However, after God created matter, including human beings, angels came to understand their own forms in comparison. *(MD 176)*

Although the wonders of Heaven fully satisfy them, angels possess an innate curiosity, so they explore Earth. Some fall in love with water, some with mountains, and some with forests. These became the spirits that nature religions worshiped. As angels witnessed nature's evolution, their songs in heaven changed to include thanks to God for these new wonders.

When God created matter, the angels became aware of time, which made them conscious of failure and achievement. They also witnessed death and destruction and wondered what God had in mind. God gathered to Himself those who trusted Him by accepting His plan, despite their having questions about it, but frowned on those—like Memnoch—who rejected it. Since Memnoch was God's most clever angel and possibly the first He created, He tolerates Memnoch's rebellion to a point. However, when Memnoch mingles with humans, he goes too far by teaching and coupling with them. The "fallen angels" are those who follow Memnoch's lead, but their consequent contrition assures them a place in Heaven. They do not become demons, as biblical legend has it.

Memnoch describes how the angels are ranked in nine choirs, according to three triads: Cherubim, Seraphim, and Ophanim; Dominions, Virtues, and Powers; and Principalities, Archangels, and Angels. Although the Archangels are near the bottom of the hierarchy, they were in fact the first angels created, and they are God's special messengers. *(MD 175, 182)*

See also Angel of the Night, Archangels, Azazel, Cherubim, Fallen Angels, Gabriel, God, Heaven, Memnoch, Metatron, Michael, Nine Choirs, Ophanim, Raziel, Raphael, Religious Images, Rembrandt van Rijn, Remiel, Sariel, Seraphim, *The Temptation of Amadeo*, Uriel, Watcher, Zagzagel.

Angel of the Night   How Dora describes Lestat when he delivers Veronica's veil to her and confirms in her mind the miracle of Christianity. This imagery inverts his role as a vampire and affirms Rice's sense of vampires as angelic creatures. *(MD 348)*

See also Angel, Lestat de Lioncourt, Veronica's Veil.

Animal blood   What Louis survives on for a period of four years, although it does not really satisfy him the way human blood does. *(IV 32, 71, 74, 80)*

The film *Interview with the Vampire* emphasizes Louis's predilec-

tion for animal blood. He feasts on rats, poodles, and chickens, provoking Lestat to make jokes about it.

See also Aesthetic Choice, Blood, Killing, Louis de Pointe du Lac, Rat, Swoon, Thirst.

Antioch   A city in Turkey on the Orontes River where Marius first takes Akasha and Enkil for safekeeping when he carries them out of Egypt. At the time, it was a major Roman capital in Asia and rivaled Rome in its population and wealth. *(VL 462)*

See also Marius, Those Who Must Be Kept.

Apocalypse Now   A 1979 film by Francis Ford Coppola that Lestat watches in VL. Set during the Vietnam War, the story is a contemporary reworking of Joseph Conrad's *Heart of Darkness*. The protagonist is ordered by the army to annihilate a renegade officer, Kurtz, who leads a band of natives deep into the Cambodian jungles. His little kingdom is based on his own inner emptiness and nihilistic ideas, with the net result being savage and senseless violence. Kurtz is a self-justified godlike being, and his apparent lack of limitations has driven him into a moral abyss, where he thinks nothing of cutting off someone's head. Kurtz preaches befriending horror and mortal terror.

Lestat reacts negatively to Kurtz's perspective. He supports the beliefs of Western civilization that "pure evil has no real place." *(VL 10)* This means that *he* has no real place, except in art forms—such as vampire fiction—that repudiate evil.

Rice believes that the film is "exactly what I was trying to write about—what Marius told Lestat—that there's no easy solution in Western civilization; there's no easy accommodation of evil. Westerners never really give evil its due because we're always struggling to clean it up."

This is how Lestat, as a vampire, functions. He finds beauty in killing, although he also knows that it is evil. And despite his dark nature, he struggles to be good. He believes that if he can show mortals what he is by dramatizing his evil in rock music, he can turn his audience away from befriending evil as Kurtz suggests. *(VL 10)*

"There's no way that evil can be enthroned in a good way," Rice insists, "except as a symbol of something to be wiped out."

See also Evil, Lestat de Lioncourt, Rock Star.

Apocrypha   A collection of scripture-related books regarded as noncanonical due to uncertain authorship or fantastic content. The Roman Catholic canon includes some books rejected by Protestant groups but joins them in rejecting others. The word "apocrypha," which means "hidden," originally applied to writings from the first century A.D. that held "secret" teachings. Among the Apocrypha are

the Book of Tobit, the Wisdom of Solomon, and First and Second Maccabees. Although considered theologically spurious, they offer insight into early religious values and doctrines.

As part of her passion for religious doctrines, Dora studies the Apocrypha. *(MD 84)*

See also Bible, Flynn (Dora), Pseudepigrapha.

Appearance   After they have died as mortals, vampires retain their mortal features, but the change in their cellular makeup makes their skin and lips white, translucent, and reflective, and their fingernails gleam with a highly polished luster. After drinking blood, a vampire's skin and lips grow ruddy, and some of the more powerful vampires even withstand the pain of the sun to get a tan for a more human appearance. A vampire's hair grows thicker and fuller, yet stays the same length as it was at the time of mortal death. The skin also hardens, diminishing facial creases. The eyes take on a brilliant sheen, sometimes reflecting many colors, and fangs grow from the canine teeth. Often these vampires look like angels, beautiful and enticing—even innocent—because they were chosen to become vampires for their beauty. *(IV 3, VL 3, QD 2)*

Louis is the first vampire to be described. The reporter sees him as "utterly white and smooth, as if he were sculpted from bleached bone, and his face was as seemingly inanimate as a statue, except for two brilliant green eyes." *(IV 3)* He wears a black tailored coat and cape—the typical outfit of fictional vampires since Bram Stoker's nineteenth-century novel *Dracula.* Vampires can dress as they please, although some, like Louis, adopt what Lestat calls "vampire drag."

See also Clothing, Fingernails, Hair, Skin, Vampire, Vampire Eyes.

Archaeologist   In QD, a ninety-one-year-old archaeologist urges his daughter to contact his red-haired benefactor, who turns out to be the vampire Maharet, because he has had a significant dream. He had spent his life pursuing a link between cave drawings dating back to 4000 B.C. and drawings on stone tablets that depict the story of a pair of red-haired twins. Maharet financed his expeditions in South America, but he had found nothing more. He dies before he can tell his dream to Maharet, but he indicates in writing that someone is walking in the jungle. His dream is later revealed to have been about the movements of Maharet's twin, Mekare. *(QD 35–40)*

See also Dream of the Twins.

Archangels   The first fifty angels that God created, although biblical traditions name only Michael, Gabriel, Raphael, and Uriel; Mem-

noch adds himself to this list. The archangels are sometimes considered guardian angels. They are the most powerful of the angels and have the most personality and the most direct communication with God. Sometimes they fall into long periods of silence. Because they are more concerned about humankind, they pass back and forth between God and humanity more often than other angels. Memnoch claims, however, that the four principal archangels are never on earth at the same time; two always remain with God. According to lore, seven archangels are allowed next to God's throne. *(MD 206–209)*

See also Angel, Azazel, Gabriel, Memnoch, Metatron, Michael, Nine Choirs, Raphael, Raziel, Remiel, Sariel, Uriel, Zagzagel.

Aristotle   A philosopher from ancient Greece that Claudia reads, demonstrating to Louis that her mind has matured even though her body is still that of a child. Interestingly, Aristotle wrote about the concept of entelechy, through which he proposes that all things have their ends within themselves and will become more and more truly what they are. The oldest vampires believe in the inevitability of this process. *(IV 101)*

See also Claudia.

Armand   An auburn-haired, adolescent vampire made in the fifteenth century at the age of seventeen by Marius. He is a principal character in IV and VL, with a lesser part in QD. Originally, he had been intended as a central factor in the plot of QD, but Rice found that after developing him further, he was not evil enough.

Armand is first introduced when Louis encounters him in the streets of Paris. Armand has large brown eyes and the face of an angel. His manner is calm and unhurried, hypnotic to Louis in its centeredness and sense of agelessness. He is facile and detached, with a body at his command and eyes that seem to see and uphold only his own thoughts. Louis understands that Armand attempts to present the maximum truth, while simultaneously being deceptive. As leader of the coven that operates the Theater of the Vampires, he is an actor, appearing both innocent and cruel, simple and complex. *(IV 228)*

In the first draft of IV, there is no Theater of the Vampires and Armand is almost a different character altogether. He is a more innocent, angelic figure who had been made a vampire at the age of twenty-five rather than seventeen. He had grown up in Venice, the son of a guilder, and had lived with his vampire maker (who is not identified) for over a century. For Louis, Armand is the culmination of intense longing, and they travel the world in each other's company. At one point, Armand is even convinced by Louis's argument that what they do is evil, so he offers to die with Louis in the sun. Louis, however, cannot take such a step and comes to adopt Armand's austere ways.

They are still together at the end of the novel, and they ride off in a cab when Louis is finished with the boy reporter.

In this first draft, Armand's approach to vampirism is more highly developed. He shows Louis how to identify and mercifully kill Those Who Want to Die. Louis describes his encounter in a cemetery with a woman who has lost her mother and daughter and does not wish to remain alive. Armand is gentle with her and gives her what she wants—death.

The version of IV that was rewritten, then published, tells a different story. Armand, claiming to be, at four hundred years of age, the oldest living vampire, invites Louis to the Theater of the Vampires. (IV 240) Louis looks to him for wisdom and information about the supernatural, but Armand merely advises Louis to look to the power within himself for answers. He is drawn to Louis for he sees in Louis a vampire with passion who can connect him to the nineteenth century. (IV 288) Armand attempts to seduce Louis to become his companion. Louis resists, wanting to remain with Claudia, but Armand forces Louis to make Madeleine into a vampire to take care of Claudia. He then engineers Claudia's destruction, but in his obsession to have Louis for himself, destroys in Louis the very thing to which he is attracted—Louis's passion. They travel together without really connecting, and eventually Armand drifts away. For Louis, Armand has become a mirror of the only thing he can hope to be: an evil, cunning destroyer; for Armand, Louis has become a reflection of Armand's own inner emptiness. Louis believes that Armand has gone away to die, so he places Armand's coffin in his family crypt, then removes it and smashes it to pieces. (IV 341)

In VL, which is told by Lestat, who is describing earlier times, Armand is a scruffy, filthy creature of the night who practices satanic rituals beneath Les Innocents cemetery in Paris. He teaches a coven of vampires to practice secrecy and to live as demons. Armand does not actually believe the doctrines he teaches, but believes in what they are, because they provide a sense of identity and continuity. The little world he creates is shattered when Lestat and Gabrielle become vampires and walk boldly among mortals, even entering sacred places. Their behavior shows that his rituals are based on lies and it plants doubts in the minds of Armand's coven about following these rituals. (VL 199–218)

This enrages Armand, who leads his coven against Lestat and Gabrielle. It is too late, however; the damage is done. The coven will no longer trust and support Armand. Armand then takes his frustration out on his coven and destroys all but four vampires, who manage to escape. He then cleans himself up and presents himself in the full glory of his beauty, to try to lure Lestat to him in a different way.

To Lestat, Armand is like a "flash of heaven" in the pit of Hell

(VL 216). He seems to offer a promise of love and great intimacy—the state of grace Lestat seeks. However, Armand's allure is deceptive. He invites Lestat close, then bites him to suck into himself Lestat's power. They battle and Lestat wins, but out of compassion he takes Armand with him to his lair. When Armand recovers, he uses telepathic images to convey his story to Gabrielle and Lestat.

Armand was abducted as a boy in Russia by Tartars, who sold him to a brothel in Constantinople. Marius bought and apprenticed him in Venice, did a painting of him called *The Temptation of Amadeo*, then made him a vampire. To Marius, Armand was a wounded boy whose blend of sadness and simplicity was too great to resist. They understood each other as no one ever had before. Soon, however, a satanic coven of vampires invaded Marius's villa and threw Armand onto a burning pyre. They then relented, rescued him, and initiated him into the Dark Ways of the Roman coven. He became a missionary, perfecting the techniques of the kill to a degree that he considered spiritual, yet never himself making another vampire. To get victims, he conjured up visions that seduced those people who wished to die, so that they came unresisting to him. Rice described this technique more fully in "The Art of the Vampire at Its Peak in the Year 1876," which appeared in the January 1979 issue of *Playboy.*

Armand eventually took over the leadership of a coven in Paris, bringing the spiritual and carnal together in an inverted echo of Holy Communion; he considered himself a saint of evil and preserved these satanic rituals until Lestat's arrival brought his coven to an end. *(VL 290–306)*

Lestat describes Armand as a manipulative absorber, "the embodiment of thirst itself." *(VL 512)* Armand seems to Lestat to fall easily under the spell of an idea or person that represents to him a spiritual extreme; then, however, he wants to take control. He believes nothing, craves nothing, and exists in a void of deepening despair, though the burden of immortality seems never to have defeated him. Lestat believes that Armand has no substance; as such, Armand symbolizes the essence of vampirism on both a spiritual and physical level.

Armand begs to be allowed to accompany Lestat and Gabrielle, but they resist, believing he may be too treacherous in his dependency. Instead, they give him their tower lair for his own use and urge him to join with the surviving members of his former coven at the Theater of the Vampires.

Armand reluctantly accepts. He builds a mansion filled with books and lives there as a "gentleman," riding about Paris in a carriage and managing the theater. However, he dislikes what the vampires have become with their cheap theatrics. Nursing his bitterness, he later repays Lestat for these years of rejection by throwing him off the tower when Lestat seeks his assistance. *(VL 508)*

Over the years, while Armand manages the theater group, he keeps his eyes open for a kindred soul. Louis arrives, which is described in IV, and seems to Armand to be the perfect companion. However, their joy in each other's company is short-lived, and Armand then tries again with Lestat in New Orleans, but in vain. Not until Daniel arrives in New Orleans in the 1970s does Armand find the companion he wants. He falls completely in love with Daniel and uses him to connect with the mortal world. When Daniel's tormenting thirst for immortality overcomes him and he starts to die in an alcoholic stupor, Armand saves him with the vampire's kiss. *(QD 83–118)*

By the time Lestat writes BT, he is no longer sure where Armand is, because after recovering from the ordeal with Akasha, the surviving vampires went their separate ways. Raglan James, however, indicates that Armand has abandoned Night Island and vanished. *(BT 127)*

When Lestat needs to find David in New Orleans, he sees him through Armand's eyes, then meets them both in City Park. Armand has come to New Orleans because he is worried about Lestat. Despite their uneven history, Lestat admits to a strong affection for Armand. Lestat tells him about the Ordinary Man named Memnoch who claims to be the Devil and wants Lestat to accompany him to Heaven and Hell. Armand warns Lestat not to go. He is suspicious that Memnoch is making a moral issue of Lestat's involvement with the Devil's dispute with God. *(MD 140–148)*

Nevertheless, Lestat goes, and when he returns from his ordeal in Hell and describes what has happened, the story shakes Armand. He believes that Lestat has seen God. Armand begs to drink from Lestat to determine whether he has truly partaken of the blood of Christ, but Lestat refuses him. Then Lestat shows him Veronica's veil and claims that Christ himself entrusted it to him. Armand is shattered by this evidence. *(MD 330–334)*

These revelations bring Armand back full circle to his original religious fervor as part of Santino's vampire coven. He greatly needs to have a supreme spiritual experience. When Dora takes the veil to display it to the public, Armand decides to go die in the sun to confirm the miracle. He is completely enveloped by it, and, to Lestat's horror, destroys himself in a blaze of fire. His example draws other vampires, who likewise kill themselves in surrender to what they take to be the supreme religious truth. *(MD 335)*

Rice was disappointed that readers did not seem to respond to Armand in the way she had hoped. "I loved his story in VL," she says, "about how he was rescued by Marius, and how he loved Marius, and how the monsters [the satanic vampires] brainwashed him and took out all hope and joy, and how he became a slave to them. He believed he was the saint of evil. He believed that the only hope the Children of Darkness had was belief in this purpose. He was like Akasha in being

nihilistic, but he made a great emergence into the twentieth century. He'd been a horrible person in IV, but I think he's a good person with Daniel. I loved his affair with Daniel. That was the only real S&M in *Queen*. And his discoveries of the microwave and the telephone made *Queen* a rich kind of book. The section with Armand and Daniel involved a theme of exploration.

"If there was an inspiration for Armand, it might be in a movie called *The Tales of Hoffman*. I saw that in my childhood, and there was a companion to Hoffman who had beautiful red hair and was very angelic. The character was played by a woman, but as a child, I don't remember realizing that it was a woman. I remember the character as a transcendent person, and I thought it was Hoffman's guardian angel. Movies like that had a stunning influence on me. They were starbursts in a childhood like mine. The 1973 miniseries 'Frankenstein: The True Story' was also a seminal influence. I was inspired by the monster and Dr. Frankenstein going to the opera together. If there was any romantic, swooning influence for Armand, it probably came from that piece, from its ambience. I remember when I was writing about Armand, I kept seeing that image."

See also Armand's Coven, "Art of the Vampire at its Peak in the Year 1876," Dominance/Submission, *Interview with the Vampire*, Louis de Pointe du Lac, Molloy (Daniel), Our Oldest Friend, Roman Coven, The Spiritual, Theater of the Vampires, Those Who Want to Die, *The Vampire Lestat*, Veronica's Veil, Victim Psychology, Ways of Dying.

Armand's coven   A dozen vampires, both young and old, whom Armand leads in Paris below the cemetery of Les Innocents. He teaches them to abide by the Dark Rituals he learned three centuries earlier from Santino's coven. The coven members are barefoot and filthy, and dress in rags.

Lestat writes about this coven in VL, first noticing them as a "presence," one that seems to possess intelligence and to be aware of him. They only appear near cemeteries and they smell of death and decomposition. They keep their distance until they one day attack him and Gabrielle, who threaten their territory and practices. When the assault fails, they attempt to seduce Lestat telepathically by using his mortal friend Nicolas as bait. Lestat is mystified and enraged by such vampires, but being outnumbered, he and Gabrielle take refuge in Notre Dame Cathedral, where these creatures seem unable to follow. At this point, Armand reveals himself. He enters the church and overpowers Lestat, knocking him out to the square outside. Gabrielle urges Lestat to capitulate, and they do so. *(VL 116, 126, 184, 200)*

The coven then takes them to a domed room below the cemetery of Les Innocents where Gabrielle and Lestat discover that these vampires had been criminals as mortals, granted the Dark Gift only after

they had proven themselves worthy of evildoing. *(VL 210)* Armand had then taught them the satanic rituals, to give them the strength to endure the endless stretch of eternity. The coven members honor God's power, but see Satan as their leader. They shun light and Christian trappings of all kinds, and the purpose of their existence is to make mortals suffer. *(VL 213)*

Lestat tells them that they are wasting immortality, and that their doctrines and rituals are based on empty superstitions. They waver, and Armand resigns himself to the finish of all he has done. In rage and despair, he turns on the coven, destroying eight of them. The four survivors plead with Lestat for assistance. He tells them to perform pantomime and gives them the theater building that he owns, which then becomes the Theater of the Vampires. *(VL 245)*

Over a century later, when Louis arrives in Paris, he meets another group of vampires at the theater who also form a coven, with Armand as the leader. Although Armand claims he is not really a leader, they clearly look to him as the oldest and most intimidating vampire. *(IV 235)*

See also Armand, Innocents (Les), Theater of the Vampires.

Armstrong, Karen   See *A History of God*.

Art   Art is pervasive throughout the *Chronicles*, echoing a theme that the evolution of the soul is similar to the artistic process.

"Art accomplishes the creation of something orderly and meaningful out of the raw materials of an essentially random world," says Rice. "It is the human ability to make a small version of an ordered universe. Good art makes us see everything more clearly. It heightens, delights, and sends us home from its world with knowledge we didn't have before."

When Louis is transformed into a vampire, he does not lose his love of beauty; it is, in fact, enhanced, and he seeks the experience of it in poetry and paintings. When Armand invites him to go below the Theater of the Vampires, Louis enters a subterranean room filled with art. Most of it involves depictions of demons, hell, damnation, and torture as perceived by human artists. Through it, the vampires see that the human soul is more depraved than their own. This art contrasts sharply with the serene pastels that decorate the hotel rooms where Louis and Claudia reside. *(IV 250)*

While Louis contemplates this difference, he meets an artist who paints his portrait. Like the art, Louis is not alive, but he sees in the portrait his own capacity to imitate life. Louis kills the artist, but even the artist's blood cannot make him more human. *(IV 259)*

After Claudia is destroyed, Louis finds no purpose other than traveling around the world to study art and seek out transcendent

pleasure in beauty. It is the only desire he feels, and Armand compares Louis's overall indifference to the cold, inhuman forms of modern art. *(IV 339)*

In VL, Lestat insists that the theater is a form of art: it does good by inspiring profound emotions in its audience and by creating something out of nothing. Actors are akin to saints in this regard. After Lestat becomes a vampire, he gives the theater over to Armand's surviving coven and urges them to continue to make art with their supernatural powers. He tells Armand to join them, to use the power of illusion to make the theater as spiritual as Marius had made his paintings. *(VL 312)*

From Armand's story of his own origins Lestat had learned about the vampire Marius, who was a Venetian artist who did triptychs, frescoes, and portraits. A devil who painted angels, Marius used art to make meaning, fending off chaos rather than resigning himself to the void of eternity. One of his paintings, *The Temptation of Amadeo*, was saved and stored by the Talamasca. *(QD 175)*

Even rock music becomes an art form, as Lestat uses it for symbolic purposes. He creates a chemistry of the old and new as he sings about the vampire history.

"Rock music," says Rice, "is perhaps the only universally influential art form to rise from the proletariat. Rock stars embody the romantic concept of the artist; they can surprise and shock us."

The theme of vampires as rock stars reveals the depths that artistic illusion can achieve. In the *Chronicles* vampires onstage and in rock videos, as well as in novels, are pretending to be art, but in fact, they are real. Lestat's own "novel" about the revelation of this illusion is presented as art parading as reality.

Akasha is one of the few vampires who scorns art. She tells Lestat that art does not matter; it implies continuities that do not exist and merely caters to the human need for pattern and meaning. She encourages the women of Lynkonos to destroy museums; her spiritual coarseness and insensitivity prevent her from seeing any value in art. *(QD 368)*

Roger, Lestat's victim in MD, collects valuable religious art. In his collection, he has statues of saints and angels, a *Book of the Hours* believed lost in World War II, replicas of Veronica's veil, and most important, the illustrated religious manuscripts of the mystic Wynken de Wilde. Roger compares them to Bosch's *Garden of Earthly Delights*.

See also Bosch (Hieronymus), *Fall of the Rebel Angels*, Icon, Rock Music, Rock Star, Subterranean Room, *The Temptation of Amadeo*, *Triumph of Death*, Wilde (Wynken de).

Artist   One of Louis's victims, he has symbolic value for Louis, who is pondering the dilemma of being a vampire. The artist paints Louis's

portrait, and Louis observes that art is like a vampire in the way that it can imitate life but not be alive. Louis struggles with the artist over the portrait in the same way he tries to steal back his former mortality. Killing the artist and keeping the portrait shows how detached Louis truly is from his own human source. *(IV 258–261)*.

See also Art, Louis de Point du Lac, Victims.

"Art of the Vampire at Its Peak in the Year 1876, The" (Armand's Lesson)

A story Rice wrote for *Playboy* magazine (January 1979), which focuses on Armand, a master vampire, and his methods of seduction. The premise is based on the possibility that there were more tapes that the reporter possessed from his interview with Louis than were included in the book IV, and Armand's instructions to Louis are part of that material.

Each vampire has his or her own preference for selecting victims, Armand explains. Some vampires love the struggle, because for them it is the fulfillment of the human spirit. Armand, however, has no taste for such violence. He prefers a more sensual seduction, in which he allows his victims to find him through both their dreams and their desire for death. They are seeking an extraordinary love and when they see him, they know what he can be to them, because they understand the ecstasy of surrender. Armand uses their dreams about oblivion to connect with them and to call them to him. For Armand, the embrace then recalls a memory of his own brief mortal life. He can feel his desires through the victims, and they in turn find satisfaction in him.

Threaded throughout Armand's description is a repeated entreaty: "Do you love me?" It seems at first to originate with the victims, but in the end it is clear that Armand is the one making the plea. The extreme loneliness and intense need that he displays dissolve the facade that he has any more control than the victims.

Armand's tale was inspired by the original version of IV, where Armand teaches Louis the art of finding Those Who Want to Die. Since Louis prefers the struggle and does not respond to Armand's ways, Armand later teaches his method to Daniel. *(QD 198)*

See also Armand, Killing, Those Who Want to Die.

"A sleepless mind in his heart and an insatiable personality"

A poetry fragment that occurs to Lestat, although he cannot figure out where it came from. He believes it describes Memnoch. The Devil confirms this when he quotes the same line. He tells Lestat that it comes from an ancient Hebrew poem quoting the words of a Sibylline oracle as she described the Watchers. He feels the quote aptly applies to him. *(MD 24, 93, 188)*

See also Memnoch, Sibyl, Watcher.

"As sounding brass or a tinkling cymbal"   A poetic fragment from I Corinthians 13:1, it is part of the verse "Though I speak with the tongues of men and of angels, and have not charity, I am become as sounding brass, or a tinkling cymbal."

When talking with Roger, Lestat uses this phrase to describe himself, although it surprises him because he does not normally use biblical phrases to express himself. *(MD 50)*

Astral projection   The ability of the soul or mind to free itself from the body. While the body is anchored in one place, the soul can visit other places, which it sees with a detached vision.

Lestat and Akasha practice astral projection in QD. Through astral projection, Akasha experiences many cultures, eras, and perspectives. She sees through the eyes of vampires and mortals alike, and upon these sights she builds her visions for a new world. *(QD 260)*

When Lestat tests his new power in the palazzo on Lynkonos, he inadvertently projects himself out of his body. Things look hazy to him, even hallucinatory. He does not like the experience. The idea of being disconnected from the body, yet still earthbound as a spirit, terrifies him. *(QD 360, BT 137)*

In BT, Raglan James uses astral projection as the means by which to rise out of his body, push out someone else's soul, then occupy the other person's body. This is how he takes Lestat's body and how Lestat comes to inhabit a mortal body—one that James has stolen by this very method. As a mortal, Lestat no longer possesses the power to project himself astrally, and David Talbot must teach him this method so that he can retrieve his true body. *(BT 206, 307)*

See also Body Switching, Vampire Powers.

Astral tramps   Spirits that cause havoc in people's lives; usually called poltergeists. *(BT 73)*

See also Elementals.

Athens   The capital of modern Greece, it is the location of one of the vampire bars called Lamia.

In search of friendship, Khayman follows two young vampires here just as Akasha chooses this moment to annihilate them. *(QD 131)*

See also Khayman, Lamia, Vampire Bars.

Augustin   One of Lestat's older brothers and heir to the Auvergne properties, he is the voice of authority in the household. Augustin alienates Lestat by scoffing at him and by doubting that he has killed eight wolves. As a result, Lestat never again feels at home in the Auvergne. *(VL 29)*

See also Family.

Augustine   In the late fourth and early fifth centuries, he became one of the most influential thinkers in the Western Church. A prolific writer, he penned *Confessions*, a spiritual discussion of inner conflict, and *City of God*, a Christian philosophy of history.

Dora studies Augustine's writings. *(MD 84)*

See also Flynn (Dora).

Auto-da-fé   Literally "edict of faith," it is a term used during the sixteenth century to describe a public religious ceremony. It then evolved into a term for the official action of church authorities. The auto-da-fé consisted of a procession, condemnation, reconciliation, and, if appropriate, pardoning. Afterward, the guilty were punished. In this manner, Christians persecuted Jews. In Spain, Jews were given a choice between conversion or expulsion, and those who chose to remain became objects of suspicion by the Inquisition.

Memnoch mentions the auto-da-fé in Madrid to Lestat as evidence of how intolerant God's plan for humankind turned out to be. *(MD 287)*

See also Christianity.

Auvergne, The   An isolated region of France located in the Massif Central where Lestat's family's thousand-year-old castle stands; this is where Lestat, as a mortal, grew up, and where he destroyed a pack of wolves. Rice had modeled the castle on several she had seen in her research of the area. "I had in mind a very old castle with rounded towers which had survived the time when Richelieu made all the country nobles pull down their castles. It would have been fairly simple and rustic."

Noted for its precipitous rocks, eroded remnants of extinct volcanoes, and volcanic craters, the Auvergne is a land of hard living. It was said of the Auvergne that one could live no farther from Paris, which is a metaphor of Lestat's own despair of ever getting to that glorious city. *(VL 23)*

He revisits the Auvergne as a vampire with Akasha, who takes him there to remind him of his valor with the wolves. *(QD 254)* (See Vampire Atlas)

See also Castle, Lestat de Lioncourt.

Azazel   One of the chiefs, according to *Enoch I*, of the two hundred fallen angels who went to earth to have sex with mortal women. He taught men how to make weapons and develop language and women how to make themselves more beautiful with cosmetics. In rabbinic literature, Azazel is the scapegoat, and in *The Apocalypse of Abraham* he is called the lord of Hell. When God commanded the angels to worship Adam, Azazel refused. God therefore cast him from Heaven.

The description of Azazel parallels Memnoch's story about him-

The Auvergne

self as the one God cast from Heaven, and as the angel who taught humans how to civilize themselves. The latter may be a human myth devised to describe Memnoch's activities. *(MD 232)*

When Maharet binds Lestat with chains at St. Elizabeth's, he compares himself to Azazel. *(MD 349)*

See also Angel, Fallen Angel, Memnoch, Watcher.

Azim   One of the older vampires and the essence of vampire savagery, he resides in a secret temple in the Himalayas where he has ruled as a god for a thousand years. While no one ever returns alive after going to worship him, the stream of pilgrims remains continuous. Azim manages to maintain this by enticing mortals into the temple via Dionysian ceremonies, complete with dancing and drums. He consumes the mortals' blood while also allowing them to slash his skin and drink his. *(QD 63)*

When Pandora comes to him, he tells her that he hears Marius calling for help. He also has received the dream of the twins and wants to know its meaning. She cannot interpret it, so he grudgingly tells her where Marius is, then lures her into participating in his rituals. *(QD 67)*

Azim is one of the few vampires to survive Akasha's worldwide purge—but it is only temporary. She preserves him for a special purpose: to be her first martyr. Gorged with human blood, he is the ultimate symbol of the vampire evil. In front of human witnesses, she then ignites his blood and explodes his body. *(QD 288)*

See also Akasha's Plan, Nepal, Temple, Those Who Want to Die.

Aztec gods   The Aztecs settled in Mexico in the thirteenth cen-

Aztec sculpture of Goddess Coatlicue in Museum National, Mexico.

tury. They believed that all aspects of life were ordained by divine will, and they practiced ritual cannibalism and blood sacrifice (cutting out the heart) to provide nourishment to the sun and to life itself. Their principal deities included Omecihuatl and Ometecuhtli, the male/female creators, and Huitzilopochtli and Camaxtli.

Lestat views the Aztec gods as "greedy vampires" who exploit their power to convince mortals of their divinity and of the notion that the universe will continue to exist only if blood flows in constant sacrifice. (BT 27)

Baal A god of Carthage to whom people sacrificed their children by placing them on mechanical arms that tossed them into a fire. As Maharet touches her throat to make her a vampire, Jesse thinks of this image and feels the torment of dying souls. *(QD 240)*

Baal was a deity in one of the earliest creation myths who died, descended into a sterile underworld, and then regained his life. Memnoch mentions him when describing to Lestat how God's plan created bloodshed and suffering. The myth of Baal demonstrated to God the way humans worshiped death and suffering. Instead of creating a new myth, God, as Christ, became the fulfillment of the ancient myths of violence. *(MD 273)*

See also Christianity.

Babette Freniere See Freniere, Babette.

Baby Jenks A fourteen-year-old female vampire who rides a Harley-Davidson motorcycle, belongs to the Fang Gang, and dreams of the red-haired twins.

As a mortal, she was a prostitute and a heroin addict from Gun Barrel City, Texas. She is saved from a fatally botched abortion by a vampire named Killer, and through him she learns about the rock star Lestat. Before going with the other vampires to San Francisco to see Lestat's concert, she kills her mother and father, then goes to a coven house to find other "Dead Guys." There she meets her demise when Akasha, moving through the area and purging the world of vampires, burns her to ashes. As Baby Jenks dies, she sees a vision of a woman in white that reminds her of the Virgin Mary. The woman holds other vampires in a web, but Baby Jenks feels free and her spirit rises. Eventually she meets her mother in a great light of love.

As a character, Baby Jenks serves as a multifaceted device: the fact

that she receives the dream of the twins indicates how widespread the experience is among the vampires; her existence reveals that vampirism is not just for aristocrats; and her framing of the vampire experience in street language makes it accessible in a new way. *(QD 41–58)*

See also Borden (Lizzie), Fang Gang, Killer.

Baby-stealing vampire   According to Louis, this is one of Lestat's fledglings. Near the end of IV, Louis spots a vampire on St. Charles Avenue in New Orleans who steals a baby and takes it to a deteriorating house where Lestat resides. The vampire is Lestat's impatient assistant, who gets food for Lestat while Lestat remains in his house. The vampire eventually leaves Lestat in disgust and begs Louis to tell him the secrets of vampire existence.

Lestat claims that Louis made up the whole scene. In his own version of their story, told in VL, he remains alone in his house, without the strength to make other vampires. *(IV 327, VL 508)*

See also *Interview with the Vampire.*

Bach, Johann Sebastian   An eighteenth-century German composer, he is considered a genius of baroque music and is one of Lestat's favorites. Lestat listens to Bach's *Art of the Fugue* and *Goldberg Variations* on his Walkman as he rides around on his motorcycle. This shows how the old mixes with the new, how change and sameness commingle in the twentieth century. *(VL 6)*

Back Street Strangler   The name the press gives to a serial killer in Miami whom Lestat tracks down and eventually kills. He is one of several such murderers for whom Lestat has developed a predilection. *(BT 10)*

See also Serial Killer.

Bailey's   The Miami restaurant on Ocean Drive where Raglan James waits in David Talbot's body for Lestat. Rice chose the name to allude to the character George Bailey in the film *It's a Wonderful Life,* because the movie provides a thematic background for BT. *(BT 361)*

See also *It's a Wonderful Life.*

Bal Harbour, Florida   One of the stops made by the QE2, where Raglan James disembarks and makes a kill that makes headlines. *(BT 290)* (See Vampire Atlas)

See also *Queen Elizabeth 2.*

Baltimore Catechism   Written in 1884, it is an instructional book, in the form of questions and answers, of Roman Catholic teachings. The catechism is mentioned sarcastically in the declaration writ-

ten on the wall in the vampire bar Dracula's Daughter. There are no such specifics for vampires, although Lestat's autobiography presents the possibility for a vampire catechism, even a Bible. *(QD 11)*

See also Declaration.

Barbados   Located in the West Indies, it is the easternmost of the major islands in the Windward chain. The *QE2* is docked in Barbados when Lestat and David assault Raglan James in their attempt to retrieve Lestat's physical body. James is forced off the ship in David's body and David, in the young body Lestat had just inhabited, goes ashore to escape detection. David later returns to Barbados with a copy of *Faust*, as if to ponder how he regained his youth without selling his soul. Lestat encounters him here and makes him a vampire. *(BT 345, 378)* (See Vampire Atlas)

Barbara   The name of an imaginary fiancée that Lestat uses to shield his identity from being telepathically detected by Raglan James. *(BT 333)*

Baron Van Kindergarten   See Van Kindergarten, Baron.

Basilisk   A legendary reptile, reputedly hatched from the egg of a seven-year-old cock, that possessed fatal breath and a fatal glance. In some versions, the basilisk's look could turn people to stone. Lestat refers to it when he describes his fear that he will kill mortals just by looking at them. *(VL 133)*

Basilisk

Bat   A nocturnal flying mammal often associated with vampire legends. One order of bat sucks blood from animals. In nineteenth- and twentieth-century fiction, vampires were able to transform themselves into bats. However, the only reference to bats in the *Chronicles* is a metaphorical allusion inspired by the way Armand's coven hangs on the windows of Lestat's tower. *(VL 185)*

See also Superstitions.

Baudelaire, Charles   A nineteenth-century French poet quoted in the first draft of IV. Baudelaire's work was a precursor to the Symbolist movement. He joined romantic and classical imagery, and exhibited great sensitivity to his subjects, which included the morbid and macabre.

In unpublished material, Louis and Claudia are invited to a house on the Faubourg St.-Germain in Paris; the vampires who live there drink blood from a cauldron and recite "To the Reader," from Baudelaire's famous collection, *Les Fleurs du Mal* (The Flowers of Evil). The

poem contains dramatic images of Hell, the Devil, degradation, and death.

See also Poetry.

Bayou St. Jean (St. John)   The place near where Louis and Claudia toss Lestat's skeletal remains into the swamps. The swamps from those days have been filled in, and the road going through them is now a highway. *(IV 139)* (See Vampire Atlas)

See also Swamp.

Beauty   The criterion by which many mortals are selected to be vampires. There was even a rule in the satanic coven into which Armand was initiated that stated that vampires must be made from beautiful mortals to insult God, the creator of beauty. *(VL 301)*

Beauty is also the basis for the aesthetic principles that Lestat believes rule the Savage Garden. Beauty exists on its own terms, prior to any codes of ethics, justice, or order. Thus, the most despairing art could still be full of beauty, if only one does not ask of it too much perfect harmony or justice. *(VL 131)*

See also Rules, Savage Garden, Vampire.

Beauty and the Beast   A fairy tale about a young woman held prisoner in the castle of an enchanted beast. The beast needs her love, which will enable him to return to his former state—a handsome prince. However, his gruff manner only annoys her and he must learn a more refined way of winning her affection. Through his heroism, he finally does, and when she loves him, he achieves his former nobility.

In 1946, French director Jean Cocteau made a film of this fairy tale, retelling it in a suggestive, sensuous context. It is one of Louis's favorite films. *(BT 105)*

Lestat refers to himself as the beast and Dora as Beauty when he describes how he might live at St. Elizabeth's with her. He ends up with "the beast's castle" but loses Dora. *(MD 113, 123, 344)*

See also Flynn (Dora), Lestat de Lioncourt, St. Elizabeth's Orphanage.

Bela Lugosi   The vampire bar in Los Angeles named for the Hungarian actor who made the image of Count Dracula famous in the 1931 film *Dracula*. *(VL 528)*

See also Lugosi (Bela), Vampire Bars.

Beliefs   A consistent set of attitudes and values along with a corpus of knowledge that forms identity. Belief systems affect the vampire experience as much as they do the mortal, by restricting, enhancing, or guiding behavior.

Armand's coven illustrates the former, for Armand placed false and constricting superstitions and limitations on the powers of its members for over three centuries. Armand has no personal substance without some belief system; he desperately needs it to endure the void of eternity. His weakness is that he believes in the idea of having a system but does not really believe the doctrines he preaches. (VL 227)

Louis, too, illustrates how a belief system can impose limitations. He carries into immortality the need for something to replace his Catholic beliefs and, as a result, never allows himself to fully exercise his vampire powers. (IV 150, BT 104–105)

Lestat does just the opposite. He tells Gabrielle that his strength comes from believing in nothing. He expresses the positive form of nihilism, in which anything is possible. It frees, rather than crushes, the individual spirit—if the person involved can bear the multitude of choices available. (VL 354) However, in BT, Lestat claims he actually has two beliefs: that no one can refuse the Dark Gift, and that vampires want to be mortal again. Both of these beliefs are proven to be illusions. (BT 109)

See also Great Laws, Heretics, Nihilism.

Benjamin the Devil   The name given to Khayman by members of the Talamasca who spot him over the centuries. When Khayman sees David Talbot and Aaron Lightner at Lestat's concert, he telepathically sends them this name to identify himself. (QD 211, 221)

See also Khayman.

Beowulf   The hero figure from a poem of the same name, probably composed in the early eighth century. It tells of Beowulf's struggle with the monster Grendel and Grendel's mother, and of his victory in old age over a dragon. Daniel mentions Beowulf on the plane that takes him and Armand to San Francisco. (QD 108)

Bethlehem   In Israel, it is the town of Christ's birth. Akasha compares the village where Lestat had grown up in the Auvergne to Bethlehem because she thinks Lestat is to be her prince, who will help her to establish a new paradise on earth. (QD 259)

See also Akasha's Plan.

Betrayal   Deception, especially with the intent to harm. Vampires often use betrayal as a means of hindering or destroying the very intimacy they crave. Betrayal is at the heart of their conflicted existence, creating an uneasy tension between companions and within covens.

Lestat and Louis make Claudia, and she feels betrayed that they never told her about her origins. As a result, she tricks Lestat into drinking poison, then turns on him, betraying his trust. (IV 109, 137)

However, it is Armand who has developed betrayal into an art. He declares his love for Louis, but that love is merely possessiveness. Armand kills Claudia, although he acts as if he had nothing to do with it, then pays for his scheme when Louis betrays him by withdrawing from their relationship. *(IV 337)*

The most dramatic betrayal occurs when Akasha tells Lestat she loves him, but instead uses him merely to support and further her violent plan for mankind. She ends up threatening to destroy him when she believes that he has betrayed *her*. *(QD 364–377, 450)*

After visiting Heaven and Hell with Memnoch, Lestat believes that he may have been betrayed by either God or the Devil. He is horrified by the story that Memnoch has told him about how God is the source of human suffering, but when he receives a note from Memnoch thanking him for his participation, he realizes he may have been set up. Whether the note was actually from Memnoch or whether it meant what it implied is never clarified, yet the feeling of betrayal persists for Lestat. *(MD 350–353)*

See also Deception, Relationships.

Bible

The sacred scriptures comprising the Old Testament and New Testament. The vampires often use images or quotes from the Bible to convey an idea or sentiment.

See also Angel, Bethlehem, Cain and Abel, Christ, Devil, Eden, Esau, Genesis, "Giants in the Earth," God, Job, Jonah, Joseph, Judas, Saul, Witch of Endor.

Big-Game Hunt

What Lestat calls his hunt for serial killers. In doing so, he is drawing a direct parallel to David Talbot, who hunted big game in his youth. *(BT 10)*

See also Serial Killer, Tiger.

Bite

How vampires draw blood from their victims and how they make other vampires; also, how they receive greater abilities and intimacy from a more powerful vampire. In literature, a bite has two distinct meanings, both of which are relevant to the *Chronicles*. First, the teeth, which bite down, represent a fortress protecting the inner spirit; second, a bite indicates the imprint of the soul on the flesh.

Vampires leave two small holes where they suck blood—although Louis's first kill is more clumsy. His canine teeth are not yet developed and he has to tear the flesh. The crudity and roughness is a measure of his vampire soul at that moment: inexperienced and not quite ready for elegant precision. *(IV 29)*

The deception of the vampire's bite is that it is so small it seems harmless, almost insignificant, yet through it vampires can drain their victims of life. It also can infect mortals with madness, as when Louis bites Daniel. *(QD 83)*

See also Fangs, Rapture, Swoon, Transformation, Vampire, Vampire's Kiss.

Black   A color symbolic of night, shadow, the absence of color, death, and evil. Black is the color prized by the Parisian vampire coven. Its members dye their hair black and don black clothing, the better to "blend with the night," and one of them points out that black gives them a "funereal gleam." *(IV 246)* The coven believe that Claudia's blond curls and pastel dresses are conspicuous and out of place. In the first draft of IV, she then agrees to dress in black.

Louis attributes to Lestat the aesthetic principle that black is the best color for vampires, and demonstrates his own tendency to conform by wearing black until Claudia talks him out of it. He is again dressed in black when he tells his story to the boy reporter and when he reunites with Lestat, although he professes a revulsion for the conformity to black that he witnessed among the Parisian vampires. *(IV 100, VL 524)*

See also Clothing, Conformity, Hair.

Black Mask   A detective magazine in which Lestat reads about Dashiell Hammett's Sam Spade and learns English. *(VL 4)*

See also Sam Spade.

Black Sea   A body of water bounded by Turkey, Russia, Bulgaria, and Romania. Louis and Claudia cross it to reach Varna, Bulgaria. Its name comes from the fact that the heavy fog in that region makes the water appear dark. As Louis gazes into this murky water, he feels that his quest for Old World vampires is a movement into a similar sort of darkness. *(IV 169)* (See Vampire Atlas)

Blackwood, Sheridan   The alias Lestat uses to board the QE2 when in pursuit of Raglan James. It combines two names associated with supernatural literature: J. Sheridan le Fanu, the author of the vampire short story "Carmilla," and Algernon Blackwood, a darkly philosophical British writer from the nineteenth century. *(BT 299)*

See also Sheridan le Fanu (Joseph).

Blade Runner   A 1982 movie directed by Ridley Scott and starring Harrison Ford, Rutger Hauer, and Sean Young. In it Ford plays a futuristic Los Angeles cop whose assignment it is to track down fugitive androids.

Blade Runner is one of Armand's favorite movies. He loves how the rebel android played by Rutger Hauer kisses, then kills, his human maker. Armand sees in this the image of Lestat. Also, when Rice saw

Rutger Hauer in Blade
Runner

this film, she was immediately struck by how Rutger Hauer embodied the looks and iciness of Lestat. *(QD 95)*

See also Hauer (Rutger).

Blake, William   An English artist, poet, and mystic active during the late eighteenth and early nineteenth centuries. Rice once quoted from Blake's poem "Auguries of Innocence" to describe what the concept of light meant to vampires:

> God appears and God is Light
> To those Poor Souls who Dwell in Night
> But doth a Human Form display
> To Those who Dwell in Realms of day.

"That's the way I see these vampires," she says. "Light becomes a god to them, but they're denied the face of God. Light itself becomes their God."

William Blake's "The Good and Evil Angels Struggling for Possession of a Child"

Blake also wrote the poem "The Tyger," a line of which Lestat quotes ("Tyger, Tyger, burning bright") when he recalls his dream of a man-eater stalking David Talbot. Lestat sees the predatory beast as himself. *(BT 5)*

When Lestat examines Roger's religious relics and sees Memnoch's demonic form, which he takes to be a statue, he refers to Blake's drawings of supernatural creatures. He feels that Blake "had seen angels and devils and he'd gotten their proportions right." *(MD 37, 98, 164)*

See also Angel, Memnoch, Tiger.

Blanche de Wilde   See Wilde, Blanche de.

Bloch, Robert   See "Eyes of the Mummy."

Blond girl on stage   See Victims.

Blood   The substance that makes life possible, it provides a wide array of symbolic possibilities in the *Chronicles*. In ancient times, deities were thought to live in the blood and were invoked and appeased by blood offerings. Blood was believed to provide spiritual regeneration with the promise of immortality. Similar ideas infused Christianity and thus affected Christianized vampire tales and traditions. Creatures like vampires need blood to animate themselves.

The first mention of blood in the *Chronicles* occurs while Louis is still mortal. He is delirious, having been attacked by a vampire. The doctors bleed him to improve his health, foreshadowing how Lestat will bleed him to make him immortal. *(IV 11)*

The vampires' receiving immortality via blood is traced back to the spirit Amel. This spirit makes the first vampire by invading the body of the Egyptian queen Akasha through wounds she has received. Amel travels through her blood to her heart and, fusing with it as she is dying, reanimates her with his own immortal substance. When she gives his blood to others, she in turn makes them immortal. *(QD 401–403)*

The downside, however, is that the blood must be fed to keep the bodies alive, so vampires search for victims who can provide more blood. Without it, vampires grow weak and wither away, starving for eternity because they no longer have the strength to feed themselves. An interesting twist on this theme developed in the *Chronicles* is that the creation of fledgling vampires can help to alleviate the blood thirst for the older ones. The more the blood thirst is spread to others, the more it diminishes in the old ones, who drink blood simply to refresh themselves and heighten their powers. *(QD 120, 406)*

Although some of the vampires dislike the need to kill, they are

addicted to it because, along with being their sole means of survival, it is also the source of a vampire's greatest pleasure. "The blood is all things sensual that a creature could desire," says Lestat. *(QD 1)* Vampires crave the warmth and the swoon that accompanies drinking, something that animal blood simply does not provide. *(IV 73, VL 445)* Human blood alleviates the cold. *(IV 44)*

Since blood plays such a powerful role, it becomes a precious commodity; as such, some vampires use it as a gift of love. Lestat gives his blood to Louis and David because he loves them and wants them to join him. He expects Louis to give it to him when he needs it in BT, but Louis does not view the Dark Blood as a gift, so he refuses. Akasha allows only vampires she favors to drink from her, and she conveys her powers to Lestat by allowing him to drink from her. Armand gives his blood to Daniel to seal their bond and to protect him from other vampires. *(VL 497, QD 113, BT 409, 422)*

Since the blood flows through organs that create thought and contain soul, it enhances spiritual powers. The vampires feel and perceive with greater clarity and intensity. They can jump to great heights and attain great speed; they can also levitate and fly around the world. Mentally, they can read minds, confuse the thoughts of others, and communicate visions, either telepathically or through giving blood.

The blood also has the power to heal. When vampires are injured, they heal quickly, especially those who drink from one of the old ones. The Fang Gang heal the puncture wounds of their victims by placing drops of their own blood on the bite, effectively erasing all suspicion of vampire killings. *(QD 43)*

Yet that which can heal can also destroy. A unique property of the vampire's blood is its combustibility. Khayman discovers this when he grows angry at a trio of vampires fleeing him and one of them explodes. He tries to exert the same power on animals, but while he can kill them, they do not explode. Akasha is also aware of this power and utilizes it to destroy most of her progeny. *(QD 131, 202)*

One other feature attributed to a vampire's blood is its power to enslave. Those who drink it can become obsessed by it. Daniel is allowed a few precious drops of Armand's blood and thereafter nearly goes mad from his urgent need to be made immortal. Similarly, Lestat becomes addicted to Akasha's blood after he drinks from it. Whenever she gets near him, her blood is all he can think about; she uses his addiction to manipulate him to obey her. *(QD 76, 249)*

In the form of Christ, God offers Lestat a drink of his blood—the ultimate spiritual experience. Lestat accepts, driving his teeth into Christ's neck. In the process, he envisions a tunnel leading to an intense source of light. Afterward, Christ hands him the veil of Veronica, the woman whom He had cured of chronic menstrual bleeding and whose cloth bears an imprint of His face. Lestat grabs it and protects it throughout his ordeal in Hell, then returns to Manhattan and to Dora.

Having vowed never to take another human victim, he drinks from her menstrual blood—"blood that brought no pain, no sacrifice"—to replenish himself. *(MD 322)* He views her feminine issue as a symbol of her forgiveness, and a way to become part of her without hurting her. In this way, he gets nourished from a life-giving source and connects Dora to Veronica, through both of whom the miracle of the veil had great religious force. *(MD 116, 283, 322)*

Rice had learned about Veronica's story as she was writing the novel, and she instinctively saw the connection. To her, Lestat was merging back into the flesh after having been caught up in the cold abstraction of religion. The death-blood of Christianity's violence and sacrifice contrasted with the lifeblood of a woman's menses, as did the nonreproductive angels with the human species. The images were dramatic, but seemed right to her.

See also Addiction, Amel, Christ, Dark Blood, Flynn (Dora), Thirst, Vampire.

Blood of Christ A metaphor Lestat uses to convey how he sensed Louis felt about the Dark Gift; Louis took it gladly and with awe, as if it were the Blood of Christ. (BT, unpublished material)

Lestat also offers his blood to his fans as the Blood of Christ during his rock concert. *(QD 230)*

When Memnoch invites him to hear the story of God and creation, Lestat actually gains the opportunity to drink Christ's blood. Memnoch wants Lestat to be his lieutenant and help him stem the tide of evil that has emerged from the violence of Christianity, but Christ intervenes and invites Lestat to witness his passion. Lestat goes into Jerusalem to watch as Christ pulls His cross toward Calvary. Stopping in front of Lestat, He offers to let Lestat drink from him. Lestat is stunned, but accepts the opportunity. Drinking the blood, he experiences a warm, intense light and a tunnel leading directly to it from Earth. Then he is knocked away and he knows the agony of separation from God. *(MD 283–284)*

When he returns to New York, he is uncertain that he has really had this experience. Armand asks if he can drink from Lestat because he will know if the blood of Christ is in Lestat's veins, but Lestat refuses. *(MD 332–333)*

See also Christ, Eucharist.

Blood thirst See Thirst.

Blue The lead singer of a rock group that Roger had once managed in San Francisco. The group had planned to write songs based on the poems of Wynken de Wilde, but they never got around to it. Blue helped get Roger into dealing drugs, but then nearly got killed when he mismanaged a deal. Roger saved him by killing his assailants, thus

launching his own career as a killer. Afterward, Blue left the band. *(MD 66, 68–69)*

See also Ollie, Roger, Ted, Wilde (Wynken de).

Body   The physical structure of a person that organizes mental and spiritual identity. "The vampire is a great character to deal with," says Rice, "because he has a body that's still partially human."

When a human being is transformed into a vampire, the senses become more powerful and receptive, and although technically the body dies, it still exists. It can move, it can take nourishment, it can feel, but it is no longer vulnerable to sickness and decay the way a mortal body is. Vampires do not eat food, reproduce through genital sex, or eliminate waste. Thus, fluids no longer needed drain out as the body transforms. Passing fluids as the body dies is a metamorphic process that foreshadows other types of changes, for example, the gradual shedding of human emotions. Louis is the first to describe how transforming into a vampire affects his body. After he receives the blood, he experiences great delight. Then, in the midst of his euphoria, he experiences actual physical pain. His body tingles and itches until the process is finished. *(IV 21)*

Vampires also shed blood via sweat and tears. Although vampires become immortal within a day, the body's cells continue to change over centuries, becoming harder, thinner, stronger, and lighter as the vampires gain distance from their former humanity. It should not be forgotten that the vampire is an animated corpse. The fledglings notice this themselves when they encounter older vampires. Lestat experiences Akasha's skin as "icy" and difficult to penetrate, and Mael is shocked at the hardness of Khayman's skin. Conversely, Khayman realizes that the younger vampires are soft and nearly human, and knows he must move carefully so that his hard and powerful body does not crush them by its mere contact. *(QD 122)*

Although the body hardens with age, it also grows lighter and more flexible because the cells have changed into a new type of substance altogether. The first vampire was the result of the invasion of a spirit (Amel) into mortal flesh, which changed the blood chemistry to an immortal fluid. This blood then worked on other cells to convert the body; the process echoes the religious ceremony of the Eucharist and the belief in transubstantiation. In the ceremony, the flesh and blood of Christ is offered to God in sacrifice for the sins of humanity. Serving bread and wine to penitents allows them to consume the true flesh and blood of Christ, for the Holy Spirit has infused the physical substance and changed it. Flesh and spirit thereby become one. The spirit-empowered bodies of the vampires reveal them to be an inverse metaphor of this union with the divine. *(QD 404)*

Only when the body is destroyed by fire or the sun, or deprived

completely of blood, does the spiritual element let go, because there are no longer any cells to anchor it. The most dramatic incidence of this separation occurs when Akasha destroys Enkil: she deprives him of the spirit by taking all his blood, and his body becomes a hollow, transparent husk that disintegrates. *(QD 28)*

Their new body demands that the vampires experience an unremitting blood thirst. The body's cells need the blood to transform. Louis resists this craving, but Claudia urges him to "let the flesh instruct the mind" *(IV 122)*, meaning that he should put aside his books—pathways to the human spirit—and go out and be himself, a killer. The body's needs should take precedence because it gives substance to the vampire's will: the body can save itself from intruders while the vampire sleeps, as when Lestat's body wills itself to go beneath the sand when he loses consciousness in the desert sun, and it can surmount emotional resistance by urging reluctant vampires toward victims, as if it has a mind of its own. *(BT 48)*

Claudia is the exception to the notion that vampire bodies acquire great strength. Originally a six-year-old child, she will never change her form. Thus, often she is physically helpless. Her body is not as capable of achieving the greater powers that physically mature vampires experience; instead, it becomes a source of considerable grief and insecurity. In fact, she despises Louis and Lestat for giving her immortality in "this hopeless guise, this helpless form!" *(IV 264)* Claudia is a metaphor of the social pressures that trap many women in roles that hinder the full exercise of their female potential. She is aware, mature, and intelligent, yet treated as a child even by those who know better. "She's the person robbed of power," says Rice.

When Lestat switches bodies with Raglan James, he discovers what it is like to once again possess a mortal body. While he can go out into the sun, he is disturbed by the heaviness of limb, the demand of appetite and elimination processes, and the dimming of his senses. When he cuts himself, he does not heal. He feels the cold acutely. He gets ill, feels clumsy, and is faced with his own mortality within a very short time. The new body is intrusive; he wants his vampire body back. *(BT 167–239)*

The *Chronicles* echo the perennial mind/body problem of Western philosophy, which focuses on explaining in the context of natural law the interaction between two apparently opposite and incompatible substances: material body and immaterial soul. Rice, too, wants to honor the natural world despite the apparent deviation from the material universe of her supernatural theme. To her, the supernatural is explainable in terms of natural mechanics; to allow it any other form is to invite superstition, and with it, persecution. "When you don't listen to the flesh," she says, "you get into trouble. The body implies a wisdom and a virtue."

Rice develops her perspective by linking the morally superior qualities of the vampires to their bodies. Their cellular transformation is initiated by a spirit who can invade and fuse with mortal flesh only because he has a tiny physical core. The witch Mekare describes this aspect of the spirit, but Rice provides further explanation in her novel *The Witching Hour*, which is outside the *Chronicle* series. *(QD 308)*

In that book, another spirit, named Lasher, desires human form, so he pierces the chemical structure of the cells of a fetus and mutates them until they accept his own form of substance. He is made up of a giant colony of microscopic cells that can feed off energy in the air. It becomes clear that spirits are not invisible; it's just that their material component is too tiny to be seen with the naked eye. Thus, they are not supernatural, but merely capable of performing what appear to be supernatural feats, like passing through denser matter, because their cells are small enough to do so.

The vampires, then, being made by the same type of spirit as Lasher, are the result of a natural process—the act of a physical entity that is given the name "spirit" because of its apparent difference in substance. Vampires are "supernatural" beings only in that they participate in a form of existence not yet explained by science, yet potentially accessible to scientific method. Their spirit is not really supernatural. Nevertheless, the physicality of their bodies empowered by an equally natural process does not diminish the symbolic value of spirit-infused bodies as a union with the divine, or change the metaphor of transformation as a psychological process of empowerment and renewal.

Lestat learns from Memnoch that angel bodies differ from mortal and vampire bodies. Angels possess "essential" bodies that are invisible and immaterial. Prior to God's creation of matter, they had been aware of their limbs only via movement. Once they learned about matter, however, the angels were able to gather to themselves the materials needed to take form—albeit a form that does not match their angelic bodies for magnificence.

Thus, in early times, Memnoch had created a physical body for himself (he preferred to be a male) to learn about the mortal experience. He soon learns firsthand about fear, suffering, and lust. God disapproves, and when they argue over God's plan for humankind, Memnoch's physical form becomes his penance. He must wander the earth as a man until God allows him back into Heaven. Later, God also condemns him to take the form of a Pan-like beast of the earth. *(MD 220, 292)*

See also Androgyny, Angel, Blood, Body Switching, Cannibalism, Memnoch, Sex, Skin, Soul, Spirits, Substance, Transformation, Transubstantiation.

Body and Soul A 1947 Robert Rossen film, it is the story of an

amateur boxer who sells himself, both body and soul, to get a shot at the boxing title. As he accepts evil people into his life, his girlfriend tells him he reminds her of the "tyger" in Blake's poem. She uses the reference to describe his beauty, although she leaves him when he yields to corrupt influences. In the end, he decides to retain his integrity no matter what the price.

Body and Soul is one of Rice's favorite films, and she used the same title as a working title for BT. "I felt the book was indeed about body and soul," Rice explains, because Lestat sold himself—at least his body—to Raglan James, provoking him to think about the relationship of body and soul. Rice also acknowledges the influence of Blake's poem in that film by having Lestat quote it when he views himself as the tiger who threatens David. *(BT 337)*

See also Tiger.

Body switching

Body switching One of the central themes of BT, it is engaged in when Lestat is offered the opportunity to become mortal. Raglan James proves to him that body switching is possible. James initially entices Lestat with fictional pieces written by H. P. Lovecraft and Robert Bloch describing such a process. Lestat then agrees to the exchange because he wants to see the sun. *(BT 26, 83, 91)*

James explains that the soul has two parts. One part, the residual soul, stays in the body and keeps it minimally alive during the switching process, while the other projects itself out. The residual soul craves union with the higher soul and readily receives it (or any other higher soul) back into the body. In a power struggle between two higher souls, however, the residual soul will recognize and choose its own part over any invading soul.

As James and Lestat start the body-switching process, Lestat feels disoriented, as if he is floating in a dream. He experiences the sense of being forced out through the top of his head. Floating to the ceiling, he can see two bodies and he aims his concentration on the one James has provided for him. James had instructed him to resist fear or the need for explanation, and to use his imagination to visualize connecting with the cells of the new body. Lestat does all this, then finds himself within the other body, looking at what was formerly his own. *(BT 156–165)*

The new body feels dense and constricting. Not only is it mortal, but it is also taller than Lestat was, with a heavier build. Lestat retains his speech patterns, but speaks with a lower timbre. As he looks through its eyes to anchor himself inside, the residual soul begins to bond itself with his brain.

James ends up absconding with Lestat's body, and David Talbot has to teach Lestat how to make the switch back. David explains to him how to knock another soul loose from its body. Such a process demands extreme concentration, but it is aided by the body cells that

know their own true soul and strive to keep or reattain it. *(BT 307–310)*

See also James (Raglan), Soul.

Body Thief   The name David Talbot and Lestat give to Raglan James when he completes a body switch with Lestat and runs off with his body. *(BT 280, 300)* It is also how James refers to himself *(BT 120)*, and part of the title of Rice's fourth book in the *Chronicles.*

See also James (Raglan).

Boethius   A Roman philosopher famous for *On the Consolations of Philosophy*; Claudia reads him as she grows older. *(IV 101)*

See also Claudia.

Book of Enoch   Also known as *Enoch I* or the *Ethiopic Enoch*, it is an ancient book naming scores of angels. Attributed to the biblical patriarch Enoch, it is considered one of the noncanonical books of Old Testament lore. The Enoch literature reportedly comprised some 366 books, although if they ever existed, most have been lost. In the *Book of Enoch*, "Enoch" claims to have been transported to Heaven (also reported in Genesis 5:24). There, by some accounts, he became the archangel Metatron and encountered all manner of angels. He claims to understand their functions and to be able to foresee the future. *(MD 232, 235)*

In the *Book of Enoch*, angels are described as Watchers, and Memnoch details how they witnessed the creation of the Earth and humankind. *(MD 182)*

See also Angel, Metatron, Pseudepigrapha, Watcher.

Book of the Hours   Illuminated books of prayers, psalms, or devotions to be recited at canonical hours. These books were made during the Middle Ages, and they became a contributing source for the modern Catholic Liturgy of the Hours.

Roger mentions a *Book of the Hours* among Old Captain's collection, in the context of his discovery of Wynken de Wilde's illuminated books. David Talbot later recognizes such a work among Roger's treasures—a *Book of the Hours* believed to have been lost in Berlin in the Second World War. *(MD 60, 100)*

Rice treasures such manuscripts and takes every opportunity to study them in museums or other archives.

See also Wilde (Wynken de).

Borden, Lizzie   A woman from Fall River, Massachusetts, who in 1892 was accused, then later acquitted, of killing her father and stepmother with an ax.

Baby Jenks's father alludes to this notorious figure as Baby Jenks raises an ax to split open his skull after she has killed her mother. *(QD 52)*

See also Baby Jenks.

Boredom

Boredom The bane of immortals, who remain the same through centuries of change. Boredom kills the spirit just as effectively as sunlight or fire destroys the body.

Louis and Claudia first hear about this form of disintegration from the vampires in Paris. "Boredom is death!" one of them declares, and goes so far as to call it a cardinal crime. Armand points out that few vampires possess the stamina, flexibility, and imagination required to face inevitable change. "This immortality," he says, "becomes a penitential sentence in a madhouse of figures and forms that are hopelessly unintelligible and without value." *(IV 285)* Most vampires despair and wither away from boredom and from lack of meaning.

Armand resists boredom by seeking ways to link himself with the present era, choosing Louis to show him the nineteenth century. When Louis eventually fails to sustain the passion Armand requires, Armand confesses that boredom has finally defeated him and that he is dying. Yet Armand does not die, returning in QD more vital than ever, for he is linked to the pace and progress of the twentieth century through Daniel.

Although Armand comes the closest of any of the principal vampires in the *Chronicles* to succumbing to boredom, Magnus actually seems to do so. After making Lestat his heir, he throws himself into a fire to end his existence. While Magnus never pinpoints boredom as his motivation, a cell full of dead victims who all look alike indicates that he experienced monotony during his final days. *(IV 248, VL 107)*

See also Change, Endurance, Suicide.

Born to Darkness

Born to Darkness A phrase Lestat uses to refer to the process of being transformed into a vampire. *(VL 303, BT 1)*

See also Dark Gift, Transformation.

Bosch, Hieronymus

Bosch, Hieronymus A Flemish painter of the late fifteenth century, Bosch was known as a moralizer and a prophet of doom. He translated the rich imagery of medieval mystics into colorful, almost hallucinatory, visual fantasies. Bosch was interested in human nature, with an emphasis on evil, sin, and the Devil, and divided the world into sinners and saints. His depiction of monsters and other weird creatures is a precursor of modern-day surrealism.

Louis describes reproductions of Bosch's work that he sees on the walls in a room beneath the Theater of the Vampires. He mentions

Hieronymus Bosch, Death and the Miser

Hieronymus Bosch, "The Garden of Earthly Delights," which Roger compares to the style of Wynken de Wilde's artwork

none by title, although in the first draft of IV, in a different setting, he recognizes *Death and the Miser* in the vampires' house on the Faubourg St.-Germain. *(IV 230)*

Bosch also painted the famous *Garden of Earthly Delights*, to which Roger compares the sensual paradise of Wynken de Wilde's illuminated manuscripts. *(MD 61)*

See also Art, *Death and the Miser, Garden of Earthly Delights,* Subterranean Room, Wilde (Wynken de).

Bosnia-Herzegovina   One of the republics of the former alliance of Yugoslavia, located between the Sava and the Adriatic, it has been a frequent site of ethnic and religious warfare. Citing unresolved issues from the two World Wars, fundamentalist Moslems, backed by Catholic Croatians, struggle against both secular and religious minorities for control of the Bosnian state.

Memnoch cites the violence in this country as evidence in the twentieth century of God's bloody plan for humankind. *(MD 288)*

See also Christianity, God.

"Botticelli angel"   A phrase based on the work of fifteenth-century Italian artist Sandro Botticelli, which is used to describe the innocent beauty of Claudia and Armand. *(IV 136, 233)*

See also Armand, Claudia.

Boulevard du Temple   Once called the boulevard du Crime, it

Botticelli, Madonna and Child with Angel

is one of the grand boulevards of Paris, where street performers reigned. Actors lured audiences from the streets into their theaters, which specialized in melodrama or farce.

In VL, Lestat finds employment as an actor on this boulevard, at Renaud's House of Thesbians. Renaud's eventually becomes the Theater of the Vampires, which is quite successful until Louis burns it down. *(IV 313, VL 65)*

When Lestat visits Paris a century later in BT, he walks down the boulevard du Temple. The Theater of the Vampires is gone, although he notes other theaters of its vintage still standing. *(BT 85)* (See Vampire Atlas)

See also Theater of the Vampires.

Boy reporter, The   See Molloy, Daniel.

Brain   The residence of the human spirit, according to the beliefs of the tribe to which the twins Maharet and Mekare belong.

Although Rice seems to emphasize the heart as the organ to which Amel fuses to create vampires, she later decided it was both the heart and brain. "The Egyptians thought that the heart was the seat of intelligence," she says, "but they were wrong. It's an open question, but I'd say it [the fusion] was in the brain." *(QD 323)*

See also Heart.

Brand, Ethan   See Hawthorne, Nathaniel.

Brat prince   How Marius refers to Lestat when he is disgusted over Lestat's irresponsible antics that acknowledge his favored position with Queen Akasha. *(QD 14)*

See also Lestat de Lioncourt, Prince.

Brazil   See Rio de Janeiro.

Brethren of the Common Life   A mystical fraternity of the late Middle Ages, begun in 1374 by a group of women who wanted to live an exemplary Christian life. Later, a community of men with the same vision developed. The Brethren held goods and money in common and believed that anyone could know God; mediation via priests was unnecessary. Thomas à Kempis articulated their practices in his book *Imitation of Christ*.

Roger had aspired to be a saint and to form a religious community based on the Brethren of the Common Life, albeit with modern sexual values. He went to San Francisco with this goal in mind, but subsequent events changed his plans. *(MD 58)*

See also Religion, Roger.

Brueghel, Pieter (the Elder) Influenced by Bosch, this sixteenth-century Flemish painter explored the relationship between humanity and nature in vivid metaphorical fantasies.

Louis sees his paintings *Triumph of Death* and *Fall of the Rebel Angels* in the underground rooms of the Theater of the Vampires. *(IV 229)*

See also Art, *Fall of the Rebel Angels*, Subterranean Room, *Triumph of Death.*

Bulgaria The first country of Eastern Europe that Louis and Claudia explore in their search for Old World vampires. They disembark at the port of Varna. *(IV 197)* (See Vampire Atlas)

See also Eastern Europe.

Bull The form of the god worshiped by Maharet's people, although Maharet and Mekare do not share those beliefs. *(QD 312)*

Burden How some of the vampires view immortality.

Louis describes the horror of his endless vampire existence, and thereafter resolves to make no more vampires after Madeleine. Armand reveals a similar attitude when he tells Daniel that he would not even punish someone he despised with the Dark Gift. Claudia, too, finds it a burden, primarily because, as a child, she is unable to develop her powers. *(IV 289, QD 86)*

Some of the vampires decide to rid themselves of their immortal burden. Magnus and Nicolas jump into the fire and destroy themselves, and Lestat attempts to fly into the sun after a period of self-doubt and moral torment (although he later acknowledges that his true motive was pride). *(BT 42–44)*

See also Boredom, Despair, Immortality.

Caesar, Julius The Roman ruler who, sixty years before Christ, helped to make Rome the center of a mighty and vast empire that stretched across Europe.

Marius refers to Caesar's accounts for his understanding of the Druids, because Caesar had written the earliest descriptions on record of how the Druids sacrificed criminals to vegetation gods. *(VL 402)*

See also Roman Empire.

Café Centaur The restaurant in St. George, Grenada, where David Talbot and Lestat meet Jake before they board the QE2. *(BT 304, 315)*

See also Jake.

Café de la Paix The Parisian restaurant in the Grand Hotel, where Lestat sits and watches mortal activities while he ponders what Paris means to him. *(BT 89) (See Vampire Atlas)*

See also Grand Hotel.

Café du Monde A French Quarter restaurant at 800 Decatur Street in New Orleans, famous for serving beignets and café au lait. Here Lestat ponders his situation after Marius and Louis reject him for becoming mortal. *(BT 273) (See Vampire Atlas)*

See also French Quarter.

Cain and Abel In the Bible, Cain, the son of Adam and Eve, deliberately murders his brother, Abel. Louis alludes to this story after he has killed Lestat, feeling that he is responsible for the deaths of both his mortal brother and his immortal brother, Lestat. He also envisions Claudia cursing him, just as God cursed Cain. *(IV 146)*

Lestat also uses Cain as a metaphor of vampires, who forever

seek the blood of their mortal brothers. *(BT 234)* He calls himself Cain. *(MD 240)*

See also "And Now Art Thou Cursed."

Cain, James M.   Author of *The Postman Always Rings Twice.* At the beginning of BT, Lestat quotes the first line from Cain's novel, "They threw me off the hay wagon at noon," as he ponders beginning the fourth *Vampire Chronicle. (BT 2)*

Cairo   Capital of Egypt and one of the destinations for Lestat and Gabrielle on the Devil's Road, where they discover that the vampires of Cairo are revenants that haunt the Egyptian tombs. In Cairo, Lestat's estrangement with Gabrielle reaches the breaking point. *(VL 341–351)* (See Vampire Atlas)

See also Egypt, Revenant.

Calamity   What the northern European vampires call the event that resulted in all of them being either burned or destroyed at the same time. The superstitious ones believe it was the sun god's revenge.

Marius discovers the origin of the calamity in Alexandria, where he is told about Akasha and Enkil, the vampire progenitors. Whatever happens to them happens to the entire race; thus, when Akasha and Enkil had been placed in the sun, all the vampires had been adversely affected. *(VL 416, 434)*

See also Druid Vampire, Sun, Those Who Must Be Kept.

Café du Monde, New Orleans

57

Candle

Camus, Albert A twentieth-century French existential philosopher and novelist, most famous for his concept of the absurd: a meaningless universe that contains creatures who search for meaning.

Gretchen cites him as an author who wrestled with the question of God's existence in the face of human suffering. *(BT 248)*

Candle A religious symbol indicating the light of faith; also, a metaphor of the regenerative death of the sun (at sunset). In religious ceremonies, extinguishing a candle alludes to the desertion of Christ's disciples, or a loss of spiritual faith.

"I have many memories associated with candles," says Rice. "A huge Mass in an open stadium where thousands of us held small lighted candles; a little vigil light burning before a statue on an altar made by my mother; pictures of Christmas trees decked with candles. I love candles and the light they give. I like for them to be pure and white, like 'blessed candles.' The play of shadows and light fascinates me. Sometimes I write by the light of a candelabra so that I can experience what Louis and Lestat would have experienced with their human vision before they became vampires.

"Candles will forever remind me of church. The smell of wax was always present, mingled with incense, and connected in my mind to the entire realm of magnificent murals, stained glass, and the firm belief in a spiritual world. In every Catholic church, a sanctuary light burns, which means the Blessed Sacrament—the Body and Blood of Christ— is in the church."

The vampires frequently refer to candles, and often when the candles are lighted or extinguished, it has meaning. For example, the candles in the hotel where Louis and Lestat are staying had burned down to almost nothing on the night they bring Claudia there to give her the Dark Gift. The candles indicate that her human life is to be extinguished in exchange for a vampire spirituality connected to darkness. *(IV 90)*

Claudia and Lestat, both of whom practice their vampire nature to the fullest, always light lots of candles upon arising, whereas Louis, who shrinks from his blood thirst, prefers the dim light of one candle.

On the night that Claudia demands to know how she was made a vampire, Louis stands before a mirror and lights a candle; he is about to illuminate her origins to her. *(IV 113)*

Armand's coven shuns all light. After the coven is disbanded, however, Armand goes to Nicolas's house in Paris and lights every candle in the place while he sits and reads all the books. The candles burn brightly as images of enlightenment. Auras from the candles surround Armand as he claims he can be Lestat's teacher, but Lestat rejects him, knowing that his light is false. *(VL 246)*

In BT, Lestat lights a candle in St. Louis Cathedral and wonders at the miracle of a candle, which can increase the light in the universe

by the lighting of many others. It is a metaphor of creating life. When Lestat finally resigns himself to the fact that he likes being a vampire, he lights a candle in memory of his former selves: the boy who killed the wolves and went off to Paris, the young man he was as a mortal, the vampire who thought he could do good by being evil, and the vampire who made Claudia. "It [lighting the candle] was for all those beings, and for the devil who stood here now, because he loved candles, and he loved the making of light from light." *(BT 409–410)*

Lestat also uses a candle to illuminate himself to Gretchen in the South American hospital where she works. He shows her what he is, hoping she will go with him; however, through the candle she sees the truth and turns from him, throwing herself into total faith in God. Lestat sees the vision of Claudia—his conscience—by the light of this candle, and he symbolically blows the candle out. *(BT 116–117, 269, 352, 409)*

See also Light.

Candomble   A sect of the Macumba cult, this Brazilian-based spiritist religion mixes African religion, European culture, Brazilian spiritualism, and Roman Catholicism. Its practitioners, led by mediums in a trance, participate in animal sacrifice and ritual dances. They do so in an attempt to host the spirits in their bodies and to acquire the attributes of deities.

David Talbot tells Lestat that his lover's mother was a Candomble priestess who cursed him by making the evil spirits attack him—a parallel to how the spirit Amel attacked Khayman, Akasha, and Enkil. David apprenticed himself for a year to the very priestess who had cursed him so that he could become a Candomble priest. *(BT 65–67)*

See also Shaman, Talbot (David).

"Cannibal"   A poem by Stan Rice that introduces Part 3 of QD, where Lestat describes his adventures with Akasha. It is about self-blindness and self-destruction.

"It's like a prayer," Stan Rice explains. "I know I'm in trouble; I'm destroying myself. There's a part of me that's eating another part. I feel like I'm possessed by something that has crawled into me, like a demon." *(QD 247)*

See also Poetry, Rice (Stan).

Cannibalism   The eating of human flesh. The form of cannibalism described in QD is actually known as omophagia, which is the practice of cannibalism as a symbolic means of preserving life by transforming physical substance into spiritual. It holds that the eating of meat is sacred, akin to eating the flesh of gods. Through this meat, celebrants can absorb the deity's essence.

The tribe of the twins practices this form of cannibalism. They honor dead relatives by cooking and consuming the flesh. Mekare and Maharet prepare for such a feast when their mother, a powerful witch, dies. They are about to consume the brain and the heart—the most sacred parts—when Akasha's soldiers interrupt them and force them to go to Kemet (Egypt). There they discover that their practices go against the emphasis on eating grains brought into Egypt by the new queen.

Prior to Akasha's arrival, the people of Kemet had also practiced

Caravaggio, Amor Vincitore, Lestat's vision of Armand

cannibalism. However, they not only consumed their ancestors, but also ate their enemies simply because they liked the taste of flesh. Akasha instituted new laws that forced the people to give up this practice. Some people, however, resented the queen's edict and attempted to assassinate the royal pair, who instead became vampires and continued to rule Kemet as gods.

Although Akasha's soldiers had interrupted the twins' funeral feast, they complete it symbolically six thousand years later when they are able to eat the brain and heart of Akasha, their vampire mother. *(QD 312–313, 322–323, 456)*

See also Body, Dream of the Twins, Funeral Feast, Substance, Twins, Witches.

Capital crime   The only act among vampires that means death to the perpetrator, according to the coven at the Theater of the Vampires, is the killing of their own kind. Armand tells Louis this is because it is exciting to kill another vampire and must thus be forbidden to all, save those who are designated to carry out the death sentence. *(IV 258)* Eventually, Claudia is destroyed for attempting to kill Lestat. *(IV 249, 306)* This development is a change from the story in the first draft of IV, wherein Armand tells Louis it does not matter that they killed their vampire maker; there are no consequences.

See also Claudia, Great Laws, Rules, Trial.

Caravaggio, Michelangelo Merisi da   A revolutionary Italian painter of the late sixteenth and early seventeenth centuries who used strong realism to make religious ideas both tangible and meaningful.

Lestat thinks of Caravaggio's work when he sees Armand, the boy devil who possesses the face of an angel. *(VL 86, 200, 202)*

See also Armand.

Carlos   A Brazilian man who had been David Talbot's lover in David's younger days. Carlos's mother was the Candomble priestess to whom David Talbot apprenticed himself. *(BT 64)*

See also Candomble, Rio de Janeiro, Talbot (David).

Carmel Valley   A place near Monterey, California, where Lestat and his rock band have a secret hideout. They stay in a deluxe ranch house with such tight security that neither fans nor vampires can find them. Here the group first hears their music on the radio, and it is where Lestat's reunion with Louis takes place. Lestat also takes Gabrielle and Louis here after the rock concert on the night he is abducted by Akasha. *(VL 519, 524, 546, QD 242–245)* (See Vampire Atlas)

See also The Vampire Lestat.

Carmilla   The vampire bar in New York that is named after the famous vampire short story by Sheridan le Fanu. *(VL 528)*
See also "Carmilla," Vampire Bars.

"Carmilla"   A short story written in 1872 by Sheridan le Fanu about a female vampire, Carmilla, who comes into the care of a family and seduces their daughter. As the girl wastes away, a doctor warns the family that Carmilla is a vampire. They open the tomb where she sleeps, perceive that she is a long-dead countess, and destroy her by driving a stake through her heart, then beheading and burning her. This story deals quite openly with the sexuality of the vampire, and Bram Stoker admits that this tale influenced his novel, *Dracula*.
See also Vampire Tales.

Carpathians   A mountain system of Central and Eastern Europe that runs nine hundred miles in a half-circle formation through Czechoslovakia, Poland, the Ukraine, and Romania.
Louis and Claudia travel through these mountains in their search for other vampires. The region is a fertile ground for superstition, for peasants here use garlic and crucifixes to ward off vampires; this provides Louis and Claudia with important clues that vampires exist. When they finally encounter the Old World vampires, however, they are disappointed to find that they are "mindless, animated" corpses dressed in rags. *(IV 197)* (See Vampire Atlas)
See also Eastern Europe, Old World Vampires, Transylvania.

Castle   The home in which Lestat grew up in the Auvergne region of France. Castles often symbolize a defense of spiritual powers.

An ancient castle in the Auvergne

Lestat's family castle has stood firm for over a thousand years, but it is deteriorating, hinting at a power that once existed but exists no longer. Lestat cannot live here; he wants to escape the castle and make his life more substantial. *(VL 23)*

See also The Auvergne.

Cathars   A medieval Christian sect of Manichaean origin whose members believed that good and evil were represented in spirit and matter and who affirmed suicide by self-starvation as a means of liberating the soul from the body's prison. The established Christian church considered them heretics. In religious wars, the French Dominicans slaughtered one sect of Cathars, the Albigenses.

Memnoch mentions this religious bloodbath to Lestat as evidence of God's "glorious plan" gone awry. *(MD 287)*

See also Christianity, God.

Catholicism   See Beliefs, Eucharist, Christianity, Religion, Religious Images.

Celeste   One of the oldest female vampires in Armand's coven at the time Louis arrives in Paris. One of the actors in the Theater of the Vampires, Celeste expresses great contempt for anything human. Like the others in the coven, she wears black and has black hair. She exhibits a vicious streak and is jealous of Claudia's youth and beauty. *(IV 244, 303)*

See also Armand's Coven, Theater of the Vampires.

Cemeteries   See Lafayette Cemetery, Innocents (Les), Montmartre Cemetery, St. Louis Cemetery, Trinity Church, Wall Street.

Central Europe   See Eastern Europe.

Central Market   The marketplace on the Left Bank in Paris next to the cemetery of Les Innocents, where Lestat finds letter writers so he can communicate with his mother. *(VL 63)*

See also Paris.

Central Park   A large park of 843 acres in Upper Manhattan situated between Fifth Avenue and Central Park West and Fifty-ninth and One hundred and tenth streets, it divides the Upper East and West sides.

Lestat and David sit at the edge of Central Park together watching the spectacle of believers line up to see Veronica's veil effect miracles in St. Patrick's Cathedral. *(MD 336)* (See Vampire Atlas)

See also Manhattan, St. Patrick's Cathedral.

Chambre Ardente   A special tribunal for the 1679 trial of the renowned French witch Katherine La Voison and her associates; it occurred at the height of the French witchcraft persecutions, and thirty-six people were sentenced to death. Nicolas mentions this case when he hints about Lestat's strange new powers. *(VL 144)*

See also La Voison (Katherine).

Change   One of the principal nemeses of the vampires. Those who cannot cope with the changes in the world over the centuries usually wither away and die from boredom or fear. "Everything around the vampires changes," says Rice, "until they find themselves in a world of confusing forms. Everything they value in life is gone, so they may find that immortal life is not what they want."

Armand is struck by the quick rate of change present in the twentieth century. It is a horror to him, a metaphor of the chaos he fears in which meaning and memory are lost or distorted. He sees loneliness at work in the mortal world in the way that people seem to be growing increasingly distant and detached from one another. *(IV 285, QD 90)*

See also Boredom, Endurance.

Chaos   Lack of order, clarity, or meaning. Louis views the vampire's existence as chaos when he begins to realize that there may be no God and no Devil, and thus no structure in which clearly to define himself. Although greater creativity is more likely to occur in chaos than in a state of rigid structure, it can also be overwhelming; Louis feels paralyzed by his growing awareness of an eternity without identity or purpose. *(IV 341)*

To Lestat, chaos is the meaninglessness of routine, of continual sameness—the way his life was in the Auvergne. Becoming a vampire provides for Lestat the adventure he craves. *(VL 55)*

It is Armand, however, who best articulates his dread of chaos. He tells Daniel that he fears the possibility of chaos after death: "Imagine drifting half in and out of consciousness . . . straining forever for the lost clarity of the living. . . ." *(QD 88–89)*

See also Dark Moment, Death, Nihilism.

Charing Cross Station   A location in London where Lestat looks for a cutthroat to have as "dinner," but instead kills an old beggar woman and other derelicts. His actions impress upon him that he kills without regard to his victim's guilt or innocence. *(BT 56–57)*

See also London.

Cherubim   One of the highest orders of angels, they are the guardian spirits of Eden and the Tree of Life, as well as the entrance to

Heaven. As God's charioteers, bearing his throne, they render Him unceasing praise. In some theologies, cherubim are interchangeable with the archangels.

When they tour Heaven, Memnoch mentions these angels to Lestat. *(MD 207)*

See also Angel, Nine Choirs.

Child of the West How Marius and Lestat view themselves in their affinity with Western ideas, which stress the repulsiveness of evil and the value of human life. *(VL 464, 467).*

Children How vampires often refer to their offspring. *(VL 248)*

See also Fledglings.

Children of Darkness Another name for vampires, it was coined by Santino's coven but is used more widely. Sometimes it means that vampires are children of the Devil; at other times, it merely means that they are creatures of the night. *(VL 298)*

See also Roman Coven, Santino.

Children of Darkness, The One of Lestat's twelve rock music videos depicting the rituals and history of the vampires. *(VL 520)*

See also Music Videos, Rock Music, Rock Star.

Children of the Millennia Ancient vampires who had survived for thousands of years and become legend. Some of these old ones include Mael, Pandora, and Marius. They are considered outlaws by those vampires who follow the ways of the Roman coven. *(VL 302)*

See also Mael, Marius, Pandora.

Choice The manifestation of free will that confronts vampires with the necessity of taking charge of their existence, especially when faced with moral imperatives of right and wrong. Two or more vampires in debate often represent the complexities involved in having eternity in which to ponder their options, and in having powers that allow them to do more than they could as mortals.

Louis is disturbed about having chosen to be a vampire; he feels qualms about what he needs to do to survive, yet the promise of rapture motivates him as strongly. Lestat (as Louis presents him) seems more sociopathic because he experiences no guilt. The two vampires clash time and again in moral debate. *(IV 84)*

Lestat is offered the chance to become mortal again and when he acts on it, he is faced with a choice: to remain mortal and do good works or to return to his vampire form. Although he has believed for two centuries that he is an unwilling vampire, he chooses to go back to

his evil ways, thus dispelling the illusion he holds about himself and his desire to be mortal. *(BT 120–130)*

The most difficult choice is faced by the assemblage of vampires who survive Akasha's attack: they can destroy her and die themselves, or allow her to rampage unchecked through the mortal world. What they view as the proper moral choice involves their own annihilation— and that is what they choose to do. *(QD 427–453)*

See also Destiny, Free Will.

Christ   The image of Christ is an expression of the potential for cosmic connectedness, rebirth and salvation, the defeat of death, and the achievement of perfect goodness.

Louis compares Lestat to Christ, and himself to a disciple, when he ponders what would have been required to motivate him to follow Christ: "Dress well, to begin with. And have a luxurious head of pampered yellow hair." *(IV 278)* It shows the shallowness of Louis's religious beliefs as a mortal and how easily he is lured by appearances.

Lestat also views Christ as one form of the dying and resurrected god that appears in many cultures—as another Dionysus or Osiris. Lestat adopts this image for himself during his rock concert, when he compares himself to Christ. The bloody rivulets of sweat down his face are reminiscent of the crown of thorns, and both his overwhelming authority and the predictions of his downfall make him seem like such a god. To join with Lestat was to live forever, and he offers his body and his blood up in Christlike fashion for destruction and symbolic resurrection. *(QD 230)*

Lestat discovers more about Christ from Memnoch's story. Memnoch claims that it was he himself who challenged God to take human form, and for that he was sentenced to roam the earth. After many years, he returned to Palestine and encountered God in the desert. To his surprise, God was in the body of the man Jesus. It annoyed Memnoch that, in this form, God still possessed the knowledge that He was God. Thus, He could not really suffer as a man suffers. *(MD 268–271)*

Memnoch believes that God, as Christ, decided to die a sacrificial death to imitate the many myths of the vegetation gods and to sanctify the centuries of human agony. In the process, He needlessly created a religion based on blood. Such an enterprise was not really true to His nature, and He could have instead given meaning to human existence via the glory of love and creation. In His own way, God found a place for suffering—what Memnoch views as the flaw of His creation—and used the worst human superstitions to convey that meaning. After dying on the cross, Christ then went into Sheol, the storehouse of souls, to reveal His wounds and take the souls to Heaven. *(MD 298)*

God as Christ invites Lestat to witness the crucifixion. He knows that Lestat must make up his mind about Memnoch's desire for Lestat's service, and God wants Lestat to see Christ's passion for himself. In agony, Lestat watches Christ bear the cross on the way to Calvary. He sees Veronica step forth and offer her veil, then witnesses the miracle of God imprinting His human image onto the cloth. Christ invites Lestat to drink His blood and, when Lestat does so, gives him the veil. *(MD 283–285)*

See also Blood of Christ, Christianity, Dionysus, God, Memnoch, *Memnoch the Devil*, Religious Images, Suffering, Veronica's Veil.

Christ

Christianity   The practice of beliefs and doctrines surrounding the figure of Jesus Christ. The rise of the Christian religion during the reign of the Roman Empire put to rest the worship of Roman and Greek gods. Such gods, along with the vegetation gods of previous cultures, were demonized; thus, vampires who took blood sacrifices as the pagan gods had done were also viewed as demons.

In the *Chronicles*, Santino's Roman coven adopt the Christian mythography and pervert themselves into followers of Satan in order to give value to evil, but Lestat is born to darkness at a time when the practice of Christianity is losing its hold and, as a vampire for a new age, dismisses the superstitions of the satanic covens. He shows their belief system to be empty and worthless. *(VL 297–301)*

When Memnoch invites Lestat to take a closer look at God's plan for humankind, Lestat learns how diverse are the views of God and the Devil. God views Christianity as a glorious plan: His sacrifice in the body of a mortal provided redemption for human souls that would otherwise have been eternally lost in Sheol. Memnoch disagrees with God's means of redemption. He believes that Christianity was formed from the most brutal human superstitions and that God's bloody sacrifice was revolting, unnecessary, and unproductive. Redemption could have been achieved through love. Even better, God's entire creation could have been gloriously free of death and suffering.

God insists that it is all part of the energy exchange of nature, but Memnoch takes the view that humans are not entirely part of nature and should be treated as creatures that partake in divinity. God could have offered them something more attuned to his glory and truth. To Memnoch, Christianity has been one long history of blood and slaughter, based on a filthy death, in the name of Christ. *(MD 288)*

See also Christ, Evil, Goodness, Human Evolution, Memnoch, Nature, Redemption, Roman Coven, Soul, Suffering.

Christine   Lestat's lawyer in New Orleans who helps to set up his career as a rock star. *(VL 7, 519)*

See also Agents.

Cimetière des Innocents   See Innocents (Les).

Cinderella   A fairy tale about a woman in poverty and servitude who is granted the opportunity to go to the prince's ball. The prince falls in love with her beauty, but she must leave before the magical garments she is wearing disappear. Eventually the prince locates her and the two live happily ever after.

Lestat describes Armand as Cinderella when he first sees Armand cleaned up at the ball in the Palais Royal. *(VL 275)*

See also Armand.

City Park   A fifteen-hundred-acre recreational area in New Orleans, it includes an art museum, lagoons, a golf course, and a botanical garden.

Lestat meets Armand and David here to tell them about his encounter with Memnoch. Armand is suspicious, David intrigued. *(MD 140–148)* (See Vampire Atlas)

See also New Orleans.

Clarence Oddbody   See Oddbody, Clarence.

Claridge's   A luxury hotel in London that Lestat favors; he is assaulted there by Raglan James, who is attempting to steal Lestat's body. *(BT 81)*

See also London.

Claridge's, London

Claudia   The five-year-old child made into a vampire in 1794. (In the first draft of IV, Rice described Claudia as three or four years old.) Louis first comes across the blonde, blue-eyed child as he roams New Orleans asking himself whether he is damned. Since he wants to die, he has denied himself the sustenance of blood; when he sees the child crying beside the corpse of her plague-infested mother, Louis feels so trapped in his self-condemnation that he drinks from this child, who is his very first human victim in four years. When Lestat sees what Louis has done, he ridicules him. *(IV 73–75)*

The next night, Lestat locates Claudia at a children's hospital, brings her to the hotel, and urges Louis to drink. Louis drains her nearly to the point of death, but Lestat rescues her and makes her a vampire child so that he can keep Louis with him. That she is made into a vampire on a bed involves significant sexual imagery: she is losing her innocence through an act that involves penetration, domination, and blood. *(IV 89–95)*

Lestat declares that Claudia is now their daughter, and Louis is so taken with their creation that he remains with her for another sixty-five years. He protects her from Lestat's veiled threats and eventually becomes dependent on her as his companion.

Claudia seeks blood with the demanding hunger of a child, and while she learns refinement from Louis, her killing style more closely resembles Lestat's. She learns to play with her victims, and she develops a taste for families, taking them one at a time. She particularly likes to feed on mothers and daughters. *(IV 101)*

Lestat and Louis treat Claudia like a doll, despite the fact that her mind matures into that of an intelligent, assertive, and seductive woman. She reads Boethius, Aristotle, and sophisticated poetry, and can play Mozart by ear, yet still they dress her, comb her hair, and buy her pretty things. Claudia is resentful that her developing maturity is not acknowledged. *(IV 102, 106)*

"I saw Claudia as a woman in a child's body," says Rice. "There are women who are eternally called girls—cute, sweet, adorable, pinchable, and soft—when in fact they have a strong mind that's very threatening. And there are beautiful men who feel that way, too."

Eventually Claudia discovers that she was once a mortal child and comes to hate her two "fathers" for making her while she was in such a helpless form. Finding out that Lestat was responsible, she poisons him, then dumps him in the swamps outside New Orleans. When he returns, Claudia and Louis flee, boarding a ship bound for Eastern Europe. *(IV 109, 137)*

When it becomes clear that Eastern Europe holds no answers to their vampire existence, Claudia plots a course for Paris. There she senses Louis's emotional infidelity as he grows attached to Armand, one of the vampires they encounter there. Claudia demands that

Louis make Madeleine the doll maker into a vampire to be a mother-protector for her. Madeleine, Claudia, and Louis live together for a brief time until the vampires in Paris grab them and take them to the Theater of the Vampires for trial. Lestat has arrived, and his accusations against Claudia result in Claudia and Madeleine being locked into an airshaft and burned to death when the sun rises. *(IV 306)*

Rice based Claudia's appearance on her own daughter Michele, who died at the age of five from leukemia. Claudia even shares Michele's birthday, September 21. *(QD 183)* However, despite the intense tone of suffering and guilt evident in Louis's telling of the story, Rice insists that she had not been aware that she had included her feelings about Michele's tragic death. "I never consciously thought about it when I was writing the book," she says. "I wasn't conscious of the connection. I knew that I was using the physical beauty of Michele as the model, but Claudia was a fictional character in her own right. The character, the voice, and the things Claudia say have *nothing* to do with my daughter—but there's no question that this is the symbolic working out of a terrible grief. What else can it possibly be?"

In the first version of IV, Claudia eventually goes off with three vampire brothers whom she meets in Paris. She does not die. As such, it was as if Rice had attempted to give her daughter a form of immortality. Rice, however, experienced psychological problems that cleared up only after she had rewritten the ending—by killing off Claudia and taking Louis through an experience of intense grieving. This version was much more cathartic for Rice.

In BT, Lestat is haunted by an image of Claudia after he loses Akasha. More cynical, he is prone to despair over what he is, and she appears to him as his conscience. Would he do it again, she asks; would he make her, a child, a vampire? She is present throughout BT as Lestat ponders the pressing question of his own evil nature. He is confronted with his self-deceptions and finally says good-bye to Claudia as a moral force when he accepts what he is and knows that he would do it all again. *(BT 208, 410, 433)*

See also Capital Crime, Doll, *Interview with the Vampire,* Madeleine, *The Tale of the Body Thief,* Trial.

Claustrophobia   An extreme dread of confined spaces.

Louis suffers from this phobia, and when Lestat insists that they share a single coffin, Louis is appalled. He faces a greater ordeal, however, when Armand's coven nails him inside a coffin to starve him to death. The sides seem to close in on him, and he must mentally discipline himself to keep from going mad. *(IV 24, 76)*

See also Louis de Pointe du Lac.

Climate   See Darkness, Snow, Weather.

Cloaking   The ability to block the mind from being scanned; it is a skill shared by both vampires and humans. Some mortals do it naturally, but others, like Raglan James and members of the Talamasca, deliberately practice it for their own purposes.

Since all vampires are telepathically connected, those vampires hiding from others must cloak their thoughts. Lestat, Louis, and Gabrielle all hide in this manner before Lestat's concert, making it impossible for the other vampires to locate and destroy them. *(QD 18)*

As a mortal, Lestat must relearn this skill in order to get close enough to Raglan James to regain his vampire body. *(BT 306)*

See also Reading Minds, Telepathic Powers, Vampire Powers.

Clothing   The clothing the vampires wear often dates them to a given era and culture, and can offer clues to their personalities. "If a vampire leaves out details like clothes, the story doesn't make sense," says Lestat. *(MD 325)*

Louis, the first vampire described, is dressed in the traditional garb of aristocratic vampires of nineteenth-century fiction: a tailored black coat, a black silk tie over a white shirt, and a black cape. At one point Claudia talks him into giving up black for more dandified clothing, but Louis eventually returns to it. *(IV 3, 100)* When Lestat visits him in BT, Louis is still wearing old-fashioned clothing—"loose shirts with gathered sleeves and long cuffs . . . a rider's jacket." *(BT 104)* Preferring simplicity and ease to luxury, Louis wears his clothes until they wear out.

Lestat, on the other hand, loves style and excess. As a vampire, he shows a predilection for velvet, no matter what the dictates of current fashion. Even as a mortal, he had dressed flamboyantly, wearing a red velvet cape lined with the fur of the wolves he had killed. While Louis claims in IV that Lestat believes black to be the best color for vampires, Lestat frequently dresses himself in colors other than black. As soon as he becomes a vampire, he dons a suit of red velvet embroidered with rubies and pearls, and has luxurious clothing made in every color to wear to the opera and theater. *(VL 100–101, 123)* Nevertheless, in BT, he describes what he had worn for a long time: a black cape, white gloves, and a walking stick, as if on his way to the opera. But as Lestat moves into the twentieth century, he adopts new fashions, displaying a preference for silk, velvet, and leather. He also wears gloves to hide his gleaming fingernails and sunglasses to hide his piercing vampire eyes.

Claudia wears pastel ribbons over puff-sleeved white dresses, tiny bonnets, and lace gloves. Louis and Lestat outfit her in the latest children's fashions, making her look like a doll. Her yellow dress presents a sharp contrast to the black garb worn by the vampires in Paris; they view her pretty clothes with suspicion, claiming that such

clothing is tasteless and inappropriate for what they as vampires are. *(IV 100, 246)*

Armand displays the most variety in his choice of clothing, either taking outfits from his victims or deliberately buying something new. He often wears a piece of apparel and immediately discards it thereafter. Initially, when a coven leader, he had gone barefoot and in rags of filthy black velvet, believing that vampires were dead things that should not be mistaken as mortals. But when his coven under Les Innocents is disbanded, he chooses to dress splendidly in lace and silk outfits. *(VL 275, QD 94)*

Marius seems always to be dressed in red velvet, wearing different cuts to fit into different periods of time. Yet he dresses in gray wool when he goes to meet with Maharet, to reflect his somber mood of despair. *(VL 362, QD 264)*

The clothes in which Memnoch appears to Lestat as the Ordinary Man are part of the impression he wants to give of being inconspicuous. Lestat recalls that his clothes were black and somewhat dusty, "not noticeable." *(MD 96)*

Lestat discovers that in Heaven and Hell, his clothing changes according to Memnoch's will. In ancient Palestine, for example, he finds himself wearing the robes of the natives. After escaping Hell and reaching Manhattan, Lestat is once again wearing the tattered Brooks Brothers suit that he originally had worn when he left. Dora confiscates it and proclaims his clothing to be religious relics, worn by the Angel of the Night who brought her Veronica's veil from the hands of Christ. She gives these clothes to the Vatican officials as Lestat bemoans how he has unintentionally infused new blood into a destructive religion. *(MD 341)*

See also Appearance, Black, Ordinary Man, Religious Relics/ Artifacts.

Coffins   The traditional sleeping place of vampires and central to all vampire literature, it serves as a forceful reminder that vampires are the living dead. Because coffins fully enclose their contents, the external appearance hints that there are great secrets within. The coffin does serve as a womblike receptacle, for it offers protection, but it can also be a trap and thus is an ambiguous symbol of both strength and vulnerability.

In many cultures, coffins are viewed as a sort of chrysalis, a place of mystery and transition. The dead are sealed inside as a caterpillar in a cocoon, and are expected to transform into spirit and move on. Alchemists referred to coffins as the "philosophical egg," meaning a vessel of transmutation. Vampires reverse the symbol by making a transition to eternal substance.

In past vampire literature, coffins were central to the vampire's existence, and the vampire had to return to it before daybreak. In films like *Son of Dracula*, burning the vampire's coffin just before he returned meant his doom. However, when IV was written, Rice did not think coffins were necessary, although they did serve the purpose of keeping out the light, which *was* necessary. She viewed Lestat's insistence on using coffins as a superstition; the need to use a coffin was mere artifice: "They could sleep any place where they were not hit by the sun. In a sense, using a coffin is also metaphorical. Vampires sleep in coffins because they're dead."

Rice admits that she had not clearly developed her vampires' motivations for resorting to coffins, and so by the second book in the *Chronicles* she modified this tradition by having vampires sleep in the earth (Gabrielle), in sealed chambers (Akasha and Enkil), or in abandoned temples (Lestat). It was only the stronger vampires like Gabrielle who realized that they did not need coffins. Lestat, however, simply

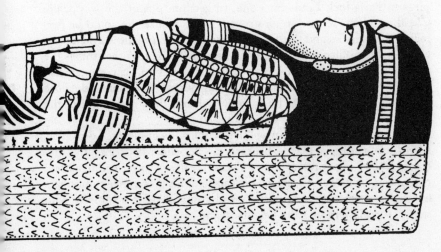

Coffin

preferred the romance of rising from the grave and continued to use a coffin for several centuries. In BT, he recalls how he had once polished his coffin to a nice luster, as if it were a treasure.

Not all of the vampires appreciated the fact that a coffin was their resting place. Louis, in particular, shows a claustrophobic distaste for the experience of being enclosed into a human-shaped box. When Lestat makes Louis a vampire, he realizes too late that he has provided no coffin, and finally he makes Louis sleep on top of him in *his* coffin. The image of two vampires enclosed face to face is humorous and even sensual, while at the same time it is loathsome. Louis is disgusted by the intimate experience with Lestat, "handsome and intriguing though he [Lestat] was." *(IV 24)*

Yet even as coffins provide beds, they retain their ties to death. The vampire child Claudia sleeps with Louis in his coffin until she decides she wants a coffin of her own. She makes Louis go with her to select one that will fit her tiny body. Louis cannot tolerate the idea of a child's coffin, and this scene evinces both a parent's agony over losing a child and despair over the cosmic injustice that coffins should ever be necessary for children. For Claudia, however, the coffin seems to provide a source for meditation on the mystery of death. Rather than sleep in it, she sits and watches it by the hour. *(IV 103–104)*

In a hotel room in New Orleans, Lestat brings in whores to tease before he kills them. As one of the women is dying, Lestat places her in his satin-lined coffin and pushes her down when she attempts to rise. It is a hideous scene of sadistic pleasure. The coffin, a means of security for vampires, is a place where no mortal wants to be. *(IV 84–86)*

When Lestat places Gabrielle in a sarcophagus the first night she is made a vampire, her trancelike sleep appears so similar to death that Lestat bites his tongue to allow his blood to drop on her lips and briefly revive her. *(VL 174)*

In one of the most momentous scenes involving coffins, the vampires in Paris lock Louis into one, to get him out of the way while Claudia and Madeleine are destroyed. Louis realizes he could be permanently nailed in and this terrifies him. His entrapment is a metaphor of his vulnerability, passivity, and suffering. He knows that this is the way a vampire is starved, and he reacts violently to his confinement. His experience is the same as that of being buried alive, but made more dramatic by the fact that he is immortal and thus must endure the agony for so much longer. *(IV 299–301)*

Even where vampires place their coffins is significant. Louis likes to go into a solitary place—beneath the floorboards or into the oratory—while Lestat prefers higher places. He uses a tower room, a hotel room, and an attic as his special retreats, and his preference symbolizes his higher forms of consciousness and control. He is a vampire who strives for mastery and the heights of the gods.

In MD, Lestat describes how David Talbot keeps his coffin disguised inside a chest in a bedroom at the Royal Street town house. *(MD 108)*

Central to the vampire mythology Rice developed is the Egyptian legend of Osiris, in which a coffin plays a significant role. Osiris was a beloved vegetation god, tricked into getting inside an elaborately decorated (and thus enticing) coffer that had been made to fit his body. He was sealed inside, then set adrift. Eventually, his coffer was absorbed by a tree, the trunk of which was used as a roof pillar for the house of a king. Finally anchored, the body of Osiris was then rescued by his sister Isis. His coffer was thus both a trap and a means of protection— just as it is for the vampires.

Related to this legend, the coffin is also used by Egyptian followers of Osiris as a reminder of mortality. Khayman recalls how, during a prebattle feast, he had passed a tiny coffin to King Enkil, who passed it to Queen Akasha, before the slaughter that resulted in a chain of events that turned them all into vampires. The symbol of death became a symbol of life, albeit life dependent on death. *(QD 219)*

See also Death Sleep, Lair, Magnus's Lair, Vampire.

Coleridge, Samuel Taylor A nineteenth-century English poet best known for "The Rime of the Ancient Mariner." Louis is reading this poem the night Claudia urges him to put up his books and "let the flesh instruct the mind." *(IV 154)* Louis's books represent his attempt to attune himself to the mind rather than to his blood-hungry body— yet "The Rime of the Ancient Mariner" seems to depict a vampirelike creature. Louis reads some lines from Section 3 of the poem, where a female figure named Death-in-Life claims the souls of the sailors. *(IV 154)*

See also Poetry.

Comédie-Française A government-sanctioned theater at the time that Lestat lives in Paris during the reign of Napoleon III. The actors and actresses used both the Théâtre Français and the Théâtre de L'Odéon for their performances, and usually presented serious classics of the seventeenth century, including works by Molière, Racine, and Voltaire. Ostensibly this theatrical group existed to instruct, enlighten, and encourage musings on the ideas of civilization.

As a mortal, Lestat aspired to be one of the actors on this stage. *(VL 64)* (See Vampire Atlas)

See also Lestat de Lioncourt, Paris.

Commedia dell'arte See Commedia Italia.

Commedia Italia A type of theater performed throughout the

seventeenth and eighteenth centuries by troupes of itinerant Italian actors. These actors relied on improvisation and a deep and consistent knowledge of the characters and basic story line. Common character types that they depicted included the clown, the lover, and the old man, and most of the plots dealt with love affairs in a boisterous, comic manner.

When one such company comes through the Auvergne, it inspires Lestat to run away and join the troupe. Lestat performs with them for only one night before his brothers find him and forcibly take him back home. However, the experience motivates him to go to Paris to become an actor when he acquires the means. *(VL 33–34)*

See also Lestat de Lioncourt.

"Commotion Strange"   Part of line 531 in Book Eight of John Milton's *Paradise Lost*. Adam is describing to the angel Raphael the strange passion he felt upon seeing his mate, Eve. He was weak against her charms.

Lestat sees these words written on the door frame of Dora's room at St. Elizabeth's. *(MD 123)*

Rice wrote the same words on the door frame of her own office, and when she started a newsletter for readers, she named it *Commotion Strange*.

"I read Milton's *Paradise Lost* while writing the book [MD]," Rice acknowledged. "I read it, dipping in and rushing, inspired, to the computer. I am happy to discover how eccentric and lush and sensuous it is. It's a great find for me. [But] I didn't by any means really cover it. I have yet to really read Milton. I am enthralled with him. This is a great treat that lies in store for me."

Community   A unified body of individuals who share common interests and a common location. Some of the vampires described in the *Chronicles* join together in covens, and the rules that they abide by mark them as members of a particular community. For example, the coven that kidnaps Armand insists that their members worship Satan and abide by a set of guidelines and prohibitions. These Dark Ways remain consistent across several centuries, paralleling the experience of eternity and helping the vampires to endure it.

In VL, when Lestat encounters Armand's first coven, he tells them that their superstitious beliefs are foolish and unnecessarily limiting, and his words dissolve several centuries of ritualized habits. Armand then destroys most of the coven, but when four surviving members seek out Lestat's protection, Lestat gives them Renaud's theater building, where they form a new sense of community, the Theater of the Vampires. Although they invite Lestat to join, he de-

clines. Group identity is not attractive to him, for he cannot abide by anyone's rules but his own (and, at times, not even by those). *(VL 244)*

Generally, a vampire community does not welcome other vampires; they may kill them first, especially if the newcomers are flawed. The community is also a metaphor for killing the individual spirit. When Louis meets the coven that Armand commands at the theater, he finds that they all dress in black and dye their hair black as part of the community identity. He is disturbed by the impression that they are all made of the same material, and their pettiness and lack of imagination disappoint him: they have made of immortality a conformist's club. *(IV 244, 248)*

Despite the shortcomings of a community, some vampires desire such a company to diminish their loneliness. Louis feels a great gap between himself and Lestat; that is why he seeks out other vampires with whom he is sure he will have more in common. He believes others may possess a better sense of their powers and be willing to teach him more than Lestat has. *(IV 81)*

Claudia in particular had wanted communion with her "own kind," a hint to Louis that she is closer to her vampire nature than he is and that she tires of his near-human companionship. Yet when she meets Armand's coven, she does not like these vampires and wants to start a coven of her own with Madeleine (although in the first draft of IV, she fits in nicely with the coven). *(IV 250, 263)*

The theme of community and individuality has personal significance for Rice. As a child, she felt different from other children. "I wanted desperately to fit in," she said, "and I was very upset by being an outcast in school." Nevertheless, she was also an individual and detested the emphasis on gender roles and preferential treatment for boys. Her ambivalence comes through in the vampires' own conflicting desire for community and dislike of its typical conditions.

See also Armand's Coven, Conformity, Coven, Theater of the Vampires.

Company of Wolves, The   A 1985 film by Neil Jordan that Louis watches repeatedly. It parodies the fairy tale of Little Red Riding Hood, creating a metaphor of the sexual anxieties of young girls approaching puberty. The wolves in the film are meant to represent the men girls face and somewhat fear when they approach their sexual thresholds. *(BT 105)*

Conformity   Actions that are consistent with some specified standard of authority.

The first evidence Lestat encounters of conformity is through the story Armand tells him about Santino's Roman coven. Their practices were rife with rules that regulated the members' behavior. To be ac-

cepted by the coven, rather than be labeled a heretic and destroyed, required the strict following of rules. Armand keeps the Great Laws to the letter, leading his own coven in Paris for two centuries with these rules. *(VL 300–304)*

The vampires who form a coven in the Theater of the Vampires also prize conformity, for it gives them a sense of identity and community. To be accepted and approved in their society, they dress in black and even dye their hair black, giving Louis the feeling that they were all "statues from the same chisel." *(IV 246)* That Louis and Claudia look different immediately puts them under suspicion and is one of the motivations for killing Claudia. *(IV 248)*

In the first version of IV, Claudia agrees to dress in black, but she will only dye her hair white.

Although the vampires who survive Akasha's rampage are some of the very heretics that the above-mentioned covens attacked, they nevertheless attempt to develop their own rules of behavior; Lestat resists this. *(QD 468)*

See also Black, Community, Coven, Great Laws, Rules, Theater of the Vampires.

Conscience   See Moral Dilemma.

Conscious death   What the vampires in the theater claim to represent: knowledge of one's own death. They let their victims know when the moment is at hand. It is better, they claim, than random death, which strikes any time, any place. *(IV 224)*

See also Theater of the Vampires.

Conspirators   Also called flesh eaters, they were people in ancient Egypt under Akasha's and Enkil's reign who were deprived of their practice of eating the flesh of their dead relatives, and who plotted against the royal couple in an effort to restore their former practices. Their assassination attempt starts a chain of events that results in Akasha becoming the first vampire. *(VL 439, QD 385–388)*

See also Cannibalism.

Constantinople   An ancient city, once the capital of the Byzantine Empire, it fell to the Turks in 1453. It remained the Turkish capital until 1923.

When Memnoch gives Lestat a tour of the bloody history of Christianity, Lestat finds himself in Constantinople during the Fourth Crusade, in the Hagia Sophia. He is horrified by what he sees of the violence and destruction. *(MD 286–287)*

See also Christianity, Fourth Crusade, Hagia Sophia.

Construction company   One of Louis's business operations in the Faubourg Marigny in New Orleans. He leaves it to Lestat when he makes plans to depart with Claudia. *(IV 120)*

Continual awareness   A concept that Marius describes to Lestat, it captures his longing for an eternal preservation of values and identity. Since Marius fears chaos and ultimate meaninglessness, and since he cannot tolerate the possibility that even the simplest memories might be lost, he wants to believe that there is an omniscient force in the universe that keeps track of everything. He longs for something that possesses extended awareness, to give meaning and structure to life and death. As a vampire, he sees himself as the embodiment of this concept when he tracks human progress across a millennium. *(VL 398)*

This concept is significant for Rice. The idea that she might die and be forgotten, or that she may never find out why certain events happened, signifies an unacceptable degree of chaos in the universe. Such darkness and disorder do not make sense to her.

"I have always found the idea of a continual awareness to be seductive," says Rice. "It was an idea I had as a child that I took for granted. I saw it then as a sense of God and Christ at the final judgment, that there would be a moment when everyone gathered together and the truth of every single moment would be told. All suffering, pain, and confusion would be redeemed in a moment of great illumination and understanding. But I'm afraid that there really is no continual awareness, that there is no one who knows everything that's happened."

The vampire figure offers a source of awareness that extends beyond a mortal life span. In Rice's short story "The Master of Rampling Gate," the mortal character Julie sees through a vampire's eyes the lost towns of past years, of people now dead and forgotten. The immortal vampire is a being who knows of these people; his memory preserves them from having meaningless, obscure deaths.

The sense of a continual awareness increases with each of the *Chronicles.* Louis sees that Lestat offers the possibility of a greater life span, but it is Armand who represents to him the meaning of several centuries of awareness. Armand is four hundred years old and claims to be the oldest vampire in existence. But after Lestat hears Armand's story, he seeks out Marius, Armand's maker, who has lived for a thousand years. Marius tells Lestat about the vampire progenitors who still exist and who were made thousands of years earlier. For Marius, it is Akasha and Enkil who embody the continual awareness to the greatest degree. When Enkil is destroyed, Marius mourns the memories that go with him. *(QD 29)*

By QD, Lestat has learned of several vampires who trace their existence back as far as Akasha; one of them, Maharet, has kept track

of her human lineage through the mortal child she birthed. She possesses extensive documents that trace what she calls the Great Family back across both time and continents. Since she has survived and remained conscious across the millennia, she offers the truest sense of continual awareness of any of the vampires. (QD 267)

Parallel to the vampires is the Talamasca, the organization that documents paranormal activities. In existence since A.D. 758, they have observed and kept records of vampires, witches, ghosts, and anything else that hints at the realm of the occult. The Talamasca represents a more limited, yet clearly focused dimension of continual awareness. (QD 163)

Akasha turns the concept of continual awareness on its head when she exploits her awareness of over six thousand years to devise a plan of great violence. Her use of this concept, although she does not recognize it as such, is the opposite of what Marius thought the knowledge should be used for. He wants to witness and care about human evolution; Akasha uses it to aid her in intervening and changing human existence. (QD 292)

See also Akasha's Plan, God, Maharet, Marius, "Master of Rampling Gate."

Corona's Bar   A long-standing bar on Magazine Street in the Irish Channel of New Orleans, it is now called Tia Corona's. This is the setting that Dora describes when she relates to Lestat the story of her uncle Mickey's eye. In Corona's, a bookie's thugs had beaten her uncle up, kicked out his eye, and then stepped on it so it could not be saved. (MD 153)

See also Eyes, Uncle Mickey.

Corona's Bar in New Orleans

*A manor house in the
Cotswolds*

Cotswolds   A region of hills in England, lying northeast of Bath, where David Talbot's ancestral home is located.

Lestat comes here to heal himself after his suicidal exposure to the desert sun. *(BT 39)*

See also Talbot (David).

Coven   What vampires form when they desire community. It is composed of three or more powerful vampires who agree to share a territory and not kill one another. Covens are actually rare in the history of the vampires, and they often involve battles over conformity or for supremacy. Vampires, Marius says, are solitary and distrustful, preferring to hunt alone in their own territory and to guard their privacy. They may have one or two companions to assuage loneliness, but usually not more than that. *(VL 478)*

"Vampires don't really like others of their kind," Lestat claims, "though their need for immortal companions is desperate." *(BT 2)* As Louis says, "We could not bear to live alone." *(IV 117)*

The coven in Les Innocents is defined by the satanic rules that Armand had brought with him from the Roman coven. After Lestat shows the emptiness of their superstitions, the coven breaks up and reforms as the Theater of the Vampires. They then attract vampires from all over Europe, but they use strict standards to maintain their theatrical integrity. The original coven evolves over a century into the Parisian coven that Louis and Claudia meet. *(VL 328)*

In QD, vampires meet in coven houses all over the world. These houses are places of refuge and safety, marking a line between the vampire "establishment" and the rogues. The houses, however, are destroyed when Akasha rises from her trance. *(QD 55)*

The Cow Palace, San Francisco

After Akasha's demise, the remaining vampires attempt at first to come together and set up rules of conduct, but they fail to form a coven and eventually move off in their own directions. *(QD 468)*

See also Armand's Coven, Community, Conformity, Roman Coven, Theater of the Vampires, Vampire, The Vampire Connection.

Coven Houses   See Coven, The Vampire Connection.

Cow Palace   The arena on Geneva Avenue near San Francisco where Lestat schedules his rock group's debut. The Cow Palace seats just over fourteen thousand and reminds Lestat of the Roman Colosseum. The three-hour concert involves focused, contained energy that borders on worship but threatens to erupt into chaos. The mass excitement of the frenzied crowd exhilarates Lestat; it reminds him of a Dionysian ceremony in which the god—himself—risks being torn apart. *(VL 533, QD 197–231)* (See Vampire Atlas)

See also Dionysus, Halloween, Rock Concert.

Cremation   See Fire, Ways of Dying.

Cross-dressing   See Androgyny, Clothing, Gabrielle.

Crucifix   A representation of Christ on the cross, it is one of the traditional devices used in superstitious areas to ward off vampires. The peasants of Eastern Europe invest their crucifixes with the power

Crucifix

of God, and so they believe themselves to be protected when they hold one.

Louis explains to the boy reporter that crucifixes actually have no such power. In fact, he himself likes to look at them. *(IV 22)* He realizes, however, that if a crucifix hangs over a house, it may signal that the local peasants believe that a vampire resides nearby. Louis and Claudia rely on this possibility as they track down Old World vampires. When they find out from an innkeeper about one such creature, they accept a protective crucifix from her so that they will not evoke suspicion about themselves. *(IV 172, 185)*

In the chapel of St. Elizabeth's Orphanage, Lestat stares at a large crucifix as he meditates on the bloody but mystical nature of Christianity. This same crucifix was removed from St. Elizabeth's and now hangs in Rice's home. *(MD 114)*

See also Religious Images, Superstitions.

Curaçao   One of the southernmost Caribbean stops of the *QE2*, it is next to Aruba and above Venezuela. Raglan James gets off here to make a kill. *(BT 291)* (See Vampire Atlas)

See also *Queen Elizabeth 2.*

Curse   Mekare utters a curse on Akasha when Akasha imprisons her and her sister. Before her tongue is cut out, she cries, "Let the spirits witness: for theirs is the knowledge of the future. . . . You are the Queen of the Damned, that's what you are! Evil is your only

destiny. But at your greatest hour, it is I who will defeat you." *(QD 135)*

Khayman gives Mekare the power to fulfill this prophecy by making her a vampire. When Akasha rises six thousand years later, Mekare rises at the same time, locates Akasha, and destroys her. *(QD 454)*

See also Mekare.

Dance of les Innocents, The One of the twelve rock music videos recorded by Lestat and his band. It shows scenes of the Old Ways that Armand's coven practiced. *(VL 528)*

See also Music Videos, Rock Music, Rock Star.

Daniel (slave) The slave who replaces Louis's murdered overseer on Pointe du Lac. He becomes suspicious of Louis's and Lestat's strange nocturnal behavior, especially when he sees Lestat's teeth; Louis eventually kills him by stabbing him with a knife. (In the first draft of IV, Louis kills him by drinking his blood.) The slave's death is the beginning of the end for the vampires' tenure on the plantation. *(IV 52)*

See also Pointe du Lac, Slavery.

Daniel Molloy See Molloy, Daniel.

Dark Blessings What some of the rituals that were performed by Armand's satanic coven are called. *(VL 303)*

Dark Blood Vampire jargon referring to their own blood through which mortals can be transformed into vampires. This power is a result of the spiritual infusion of Amel, who initially transformed the blood of a mortal being, Akasha, into immortal substance. *(VL 304, BT 26, 419)*

See also Amel, Blood.

Dark Court The term Lestat uses to refer to members of the vampire realm. *(BT 286)*

See also Vampire.

Dark Gift The power to become immortal that is transmitted

through the vampire blood. It is conferred through what vampires call the Dark Trick.

According to the rules of Santino's coven, the Dark Gift was to be given only to beautiful mortals, as an insult to God. Although most of the vampires in the *Chronicles* do indeed select beautiful victims, they are motivated by love rather than any rule. Magnus alone is old and ugly, but that is because he had stolen the Dark Gift and had never been targeted for immortality. *(VL 301, 351)*

See also Beauty, Dark Trick, Great Laws, Immortality, Rules.

"Darkling, I listen"   A phrase from John Keats's poem "Ode to a Nightingale."

Lestat discovers these words scrawled on the door frame of Dora's bedroom at St. Elizabeth's. *(MD 123)*

The same phrase has been written in black felt pen on the door of Rice's office. It is one of her favorite lines and has long inspired her dark imagination.

See also Keats (John).

Dark Moment   The sensation of dread that can accompany the loss of support that occurs when one doubts the existence of absolute values; it is the stark recognition of unbuffered chaos.

Louis first reveals his pervasive anxiety as a dark moment when he is still a mortal, grieving over his brother's sudden death. After he becomes a vampire he undertakes a long search for a luminous moment that will dispel his cosmic confusion. He feels trapped in an eternity of damnation. For a while he uses the beauty of creation to fend off his encroaching despair, but his search ends in an even darker moment when Armand, the oldest vampire he has ever encountered, denies any knowledge of God. "It was as I'd always feared," Louis says, "and it was as lonely, it was as totally without hope." *(IV 240)* For him, there is no meaning, there is nothing to know. He has only his companion Claudia, although even with her the world seems fragile and insubstantial, as if "a fault in the earth were about to open up." *(IV 105)* When she is put to death, his passion for art and beauty dies. *(IV 321)*

Claudia, too, experiences a dark moment—"something worse than fear"—as a result of years of acquiring knowledge and maturity. *(IV 112)* One day she realizes that she was once a mortal child. She has a coffin made to the proportions of her tiny body and stares at it for hours in a meditative trance. Eventually her anger against Louis and Lestat for trapping her vampire nature in such a helpless form explodes. Louis is unable to check her rage. For her, the dark moment means finding out a terrible truth that she cannot change.

As with Louis, the dark moment for Lestat begins when he is a mortal; his friend Nicolas calls it the "malady of mortality." *(VL 55)*

In a discussion with Nicolas, Lestat is suddenly seized by a pervasive sense of dread. Contrary to what they call "the Golden Moment," when meaning crystallizes and the world seems lucid, the dark moment confronts Lestat with nothingness and the inevitable frailty and corrosion of things around him. It is a painful epiphany that colors his later perceptions: "The world looked different forever after." *(VL 59)* He recognized that there would be no righting of wrongs, no time when everything would be explained. For Lestat, everything was and would always remain in the limbo of ultimate chaos.

Rice based this scene on her own experience. She had smoked some marijuana when she was twenty-six and had suddenly realized that everyone, including herself, was going to die. "I realized that we might not even know, when we died, what this [world] was all about— which is exactly Lestat's experience. I was a basket case for six months. I could hardly function. I never again felt the same about life or death."

After his ordeal with Memnoch, Lestat's boyhood fear that there may be nothing after death becomes an even greater terror. Now he believes that there may in fact be *something* and that it may be more horrible than nothingness or chaos: it may be God himself. *(MD 308)*

In QD, Marius moves into black despair when Akasha rises, mocks him for his two thousand years of idealistic servitude, and then chooses Lestat as her prince. She traps Marius in ice, where he stays for ten days pondering what has happened. He becomes bitter and indifferent. Life seems senseless to him, and consciousness—or his continual awareness—a joke. His illusion that he was wise has disintegrated, and he expresses hatred and anger over his humiliation. Only when he sees Armand do his feelings lift; Armand reminds him of love. Later Marius speaks out in chorus with Maharet against Akasha. *(QD 266)*

Akasha's life represents darkness personified. Maharet describes her as a woman who fears her own inner nihilism and thus forces beliefs on others. "For always in her there was a dark place full of despair. And a great driving force to make meaning because there was none." *(QD 330)* She uses a belief structure to comfort herself and she wants the world to conform to it. There *must* be meaning, and it *must* originate with her. When Lestat and the other vampires resist her, she experiences another dark moment of loneliness and isolation that makes her vulnerable to her own doom. *(QD 452)*

See also Chaos, Darkness, God, Golden Moment.

Dark Monarch Gabrielle believes, after seeing vampires around the world, that they are ripe for a Dark Monarch to lead them toward true evil. The Dark Monarch would be a Nietzschean "overman" who would present a new vision and new values based on true vampire powers rather than superstitions. It is Gabrielle's hope that such a

being would wreak havoc on the mortal world, creating such chaos that whole civilizations would be destroyed and nature—the Savage Garden—would take over. Man would be reduced to the nakedness from whence he came.

Lestat is appalled by Gabrielle's statements; he claims that he will stand against any such attempt on the part of a vampire. Yet he betrays his own prediction when Akasha rises up in the manner described by Gabrielle, ready to destroy civilization by slaughtering most of the men. Lestat initially follows her, and it is only with great effort and the strength of other vampires that he can resist her allure. *(VL 334–345)*

See also Akasha.

Darkness The realm of vampires in legend and folklore.

Vampires live in the dark because they cannot bear the direct rays of the sun, a symbol of God. Thus, vampires are associated with death and evil.

Darkness implies the mystery of the unknown. In many creation stories, darkness precedes the creation of light and the differentiation of matter, corresponding to chaos or undeveloped potential. However, once light is introduced as a contrast, darkness takes on regressive and frightening connotations. As a realm deemed inferior to light for its lack of clarity, it is often associated with baser instincts.

Darkness then becomes the realm of shadow; in psychodynamic terms, the shadow is the repository of things feared, undeveloped, or disowned in the human psyche. The shadow is in conflict with acknowledged cultural values and is thus avoided and unacknowledged by individuals and societies who consider themselves enlightened and civilized. As a consequence, the shadow and all its corresponding fears are pushed into deeper recesses of the psyche. But the stronger and more pervasive the repression, the more energy and vitality the shadow attains. It becomes a vicious circle, for the more energy the shadow possesses, the more the shadow batters at the mind's psychological defenses; the more it batters, the stronger those defenses become, and the more frightening the shadow appears. The most common manifestation of this power struggle is that of a monster that wants to devour, maim, or kill that which is hiding behind defenses.

The vampire, then, is a monster of the shadows. It lives in darkness and performs its bloody deeds in secret, ensuring that the realm of night retains its threatening connotations. When the psyche sets up rituals to deal with or destroy such monsters, it invests certain devices with power; traditionally, vampires are warded off by garlic and crucifixes, and destroyed by beheading or stakes through the heart. However, these devices fail to work for Rice's vampires because the boundary between humanity and vampires is more diffuse, and the defenses less secure. Rice's vampires are more human than monster,

more "us" than "evil other." Inevitably, they find within their experiences sources of light, making them complex rather than stereotypical monster images.

Anyone who ventures near the darkness and sees it for what it is—a place of potential creativity rather than merely evil—may discover that it contains something of value. For while vampires kill, they also offer immortality, power, and sensual rapture. Louis and Lestat are much more than the one-dimensional vampires of legend. Their humanity and search for meaning in the supernatural realm of darkness offer a new perspective on, and appreciation for, the very human condition that casts them into the shadow. What has once been seen as evil, says psychologist William James, may be what opens our eyes to the deepest levels of truth.

One of the "authors of darkness" to influence Rice was Nathaniel Hawthorne. "I was very influenced by the short story 'Young Goodman Brown,' " she affirms, "and also 'The Minister's Veil.' I loved the way he treated darkness, and the mood, the ambience and the richness of his language. I loved the way he described Goodman Brown's innocence and how his [Brown's] attitudes were changed: the darkness was the Sabbat in the forest and the capacity for sin that he saw in the facades around him. Hawthorne's stories were very macabre and bizarre. I felt a kinship with him and Edgar Allan Poe; they were both American writers that I connected with."

See also Vampire.

Dark Powers   The name Santino's Satan-worshiping coven gives to vampire abilities. This group insisted that vampires use their powers only in the service of Satan. *(VL 301)*

See also Vampire Powers.

Dark Rituals   See Dark Blessings, Dark Ways.

Dark Trick   The act of transforming a mortal into an immortal by draining the mortal of blood and feeding him or her the blood of a vampire. The victim was to be drained nearly to the point of death so that the immortal spirit could fuse with the heart.

The Dark Trick results in a veil of silence between the vampires and their children, destroying the intimacy that the vampires were trying to capture by creating a companion. Lestat discovers this with Gabrielle, who grows colder; with Nicolas and Claudia, whose love for him turns to hate; and with Louis, with whom he cannot fully connect. He has more hope that such grief will not occur with David, who shares many of his interests and concerns. *(VL 301, 351, BT 418, 422)*

See also Dark Gift, Making a Vampire, Transformation.

Dark Vows   Part of the rituals of Santino's coven that Armand takes over and practices in his Parisian coven. *(VL 301)*

Dark Ways   The name Armand gives to the rituals, incantations, and prayers practiced in Santino's coven. *(VL 303)*

David Copperfield   See Dickens, Charles.

David Talbot   See Talbot, David.

da Vinci, Leonardo   See Leonardo da Vinci.

Davis   One of the leaders of the Fang Gang, he is a black vampire whose skin glows with a golden sheen. He steals jewelry from his victims and loves to dance to Lestat's music, until Akasha destroys him. *(QD 42, 44)*
  See also Fang Gang.

Dead, The   A 1987 film by John Huston based on a short story by James Joyce. The central scene involves a traditional family Christmas dinner where the assorted guests discuss mundane subjects and attend politely to the display of mediocre talents. Only one man sees beneath the commonplace chatter to the deep but unexpressed feelings of loneliness and passion in all their hearts.
  Louis watches this film. A quote from the story, read at the end of the film, captures the vampire's ambivalence about mortality: "Better to pass boldly into the other world in the full glory of some passion than fade and wither dismally with age." *(BT 105)*

Dead blood   Slang that the Fang Gang uses to refer to vampire blood. *(QD 43)*
  See also Fang Gang.

Dead guy   Slang that the Fang Gang uses to refer to a vampire. *(QD 44)*
  See also Fang Gang.

Death   The extinction of vital functions, death is a pervasive theme in the *Chronicles*. Although vampires survive their own physical deaths as mortals, they never escape death itself, nor the threat of annihilation. "What fascinates me," says Rice, "is how a person faces the fact that we're all going to die; I'm interested in how the exceptional person, like a vampire, copes with that."
  Vampires are the living dead. Through immortalized blood, they experience their own death without losing consciousness. The physical

body sheds fluid it no longer needs and acquires new powers. For a mortal to become a vampire, he or she must be drained of blood nearly to the point of death or the powerful blood that makes the transformation possible cannot take hold. Once the body dies, the vampire experiences a sense of invincibility and can survive many things that would have killed him or her as a mortal; the fact of death then loses some of its impact. "What does it mean to die," Louis asks, "when you can live until the end of the world?" *(IV 142)*

Yet while vampires are free of the inevitability of death, they can still be plagued by mortal dread, for they can be destroyed by fire or sun. Many of the vampires express their fear of death in this sense; for example, Armand cannot bring his existence to an end because he cannot face the possibility of what death may portend: eternal chaos. *(QD 88)*

Lestat is plagued by an urge to end it all. In BT, he decides to fly directly into the sun because it seems the surest way to destroy himself. It doesn't work and he is left to ponder, with David Talbot, the meaning of what he did. Lestat tells David that he believes death may be awful, for it may not reveal any secrets and there is no more chance to know anything. And when Lestat regains mortal form, he becomes obsessed, to the point of near paralysis, with all the ways that he can die. *(BT 44, 257)*

Despite possessing personal fears about death, the vampires do not hesitate to bring death to mortals; not only is it necessary to their survival, but they find it irresistible. Vampires kill so they can drink into themselves the essence of life. While some, like Louis, feel guilty about taking human life, the swoon that accompanies the act is so exhilarating that it far outweighs the moral issues.

After Lestat's visit to Hell, in which he realizes that he may one day have to face all of his victims, he vows never to take another human life. Having seen how it may come back to haunt him (as Roger's ghost did, but with more horrifying results), he decides to turn away from his thirst and try to do without. *(MD 348)*

See also Addiction, Chaos, Human Evolution, Killing, Soul, Swoon.

Death and the Miser   A painting by Hieronymus Bosch that depicts a dying man. In the first draft of IV, Louis sees this painting in the coven house in the Faubourg St.-Germain.

See also Bosch (Hieronymus).

Death in Venice   A 1971 film by Luchino Visconti based on Thomas Mann's story about Gustave von Aschenbach, an older man who visits Venice and becomes enamored of a beautiful boy. His desire contrasts strongly with his intellect, for it raises the question of

whether beauty resides in the person looking at a beautiful object or in the object itself.

Lestat refers to this film when he quotes an actor who says that evil is necessary for the existence of genius. Lestat disagrees with this thought, for he does not believe evil needs to exist for any purpose. *(VL 18)*

See also Evil.

Death Sleep   The daytime trance that vampires go into when the sun rises. It is a form of sleep so heavy that the vampires actually appear to be dead; should a mortal venture too close when a vampire is in this state, the vampire's body will protect itself by reaching out and strangling the intruder. *(QD 96, 251, BT 53, 322)*

See also Body, Coffins.

Deception   Double-dealing or subterfuge. Many of the vampires practice deception and betrayal as a means of both manipulation and self-protection. They even exploit their deceptively angelic appearance to attract mortals, whom they intend to kill. *(BT 62)*

Armand is the essence of this form of deception. Chosen to be a vampire for his innocent beauty, and made a vampire as an adolescent, he seems too sweet and boyish to be truly dangerous—yet, he is one of the most ruthless of the vampires. It is appropriate that he manages the Theater of the Vampires, which plays on the deception that killing victims onstage seems merely an actor's illusion. Armand attempts to deceive both Lestat and Louis into a relationship with him, but his schemes backfire, leaving him alone. His worst act of deception is to make Louis believe he had nothing to do with Claudia's death, when in fact he is the one who made it happen, so that he could have Louis as his own. *(IV 337)* Armand also claims that he is not like Marius because he lives honestly, whereas Marius had lived among mortals by deception, pretending not to be a vampire. *(VL 309)*

The fourth *Vampire Chronicle*, BT, takes on deception as a central theme. Raglan James is a thief and con artist, and he deceives Lestat about what he is up to. He convinces Lestat that he will switch bodies with him for a period of only thirty-six hours, and will then return to claim his twenty million dollars. Instead, he makes the switch permanent and absconds with the money. Most of what he says to Lestat is a lie, but his actions are a metaphor of how Lestat lies to himself about his own inner goodness. James further tricks Lestat by meeting him in David Talbot's body and asking for the Dark Gift. He uses imagery to try to convince Lestat that he is David, but Lestat manages to see through the deception at the last minute. *(BT 206, 361–368)*

Although Rice frequently depicts deception as a way to achieve a goal, she also views it as a psychological defense. Vampires are loners, and they guard themselves against trusting one another too much and achieving deep intimacy. Once again, Armand is a master at this form of engagement. He often appears to other vampires to offer a special type of close companionship, when in fact what he wants is to drain the other vampires dry, both physically and psychologically. Louis is victimized by Armand's false vision, but Lestat recognizes it and resists.

Lestat thinks he may have been deceived by the Devil. He had agreed to accompany Memnoch to Heaven and Hell as a potential lieutenant. Memnoch had allowed him to see God and had told him the story of creation, implicating God as the true source of evil in the world. Lestat had also been invited to see things from God's perspective, and he had acquired the icon, Veronica's veil, as physical evidence of his encounter with Christ. Once he escaped from the Devil's clutches, however, he realized that the veil proves nothing. It could be part of a deception devised by either the Devil or God, and he has no idea whether he has played his part or defied some plan. Either option could have played into the scheme of either party, and the Devil could be a liar altogether.

Lestat gives the veil to Dora, a televangelist, who uses it against his wishes to bring new life to Christianity. Lestat then receives a note from Memnoch thanking him for a job performed perfectly. Yet even this message could be part of the deception. It may not even be from Memnoch. Lestat believes his experience with the Devil was real, but he also knows it could be interpreted in several ways and he could as easily have been the dupe of the forces of good as of evil. (MD 334–335, 350)

See also Betrayal, James (Raglan), Memnoch, Relationships.

Declaration   A lengthy message written in felt-tip pen on the back wall of Dracula's Daughter, the vampire bar in San Francisco.

When Lestat publishes his autobiography and releases his rock albums and music videos, he angers vampires all over the world because he is breaking rules and telling secrets to which no mortal should be privy. Some vampires like his music, but others gather at bars and coven houses to plot against him. They write up a declaration calling for vampires everywhere to take a stand against Lestat.

The declaration mentions IV and VL, summarizing their contents and ridiculing much of Lestat's story about the vampire mythos. It urges all vampires to destroy Louis, Gabrielle, Armand, and Lestat, along with any other vampires who show Lestat loyalty. Copies of the declaration are sent to every meeting place on the Vampire Connection, urging vampires who see it to attend Lestat's debut rock concert in San Francisco so that they can join together and cut him to pieces. (QD 11–14)

See also Baltimore Catechism, Rock Concert.

de Lenfent, Nicolas   See Nicolas de Lenfent.

de Lioncourt, Lestat   See Lestat de Lioncourt.

Demons   Creatures of the dark that symbolically embody the human tendency to diabolize people of different cultures or beliefs. Their monstrous forms mirror the human fear of inadequacy and the need to dominate and control such a fear. A demon is usually the husk of an old god of past seasons. For example, patriarchal religions treated as demons people of older religions who believed that their souls originated with their mothers.

Demons are credited with the ability to cause every possible disaster. In Christianity, demons are the henchmen of Satan, who directs them to inflict great harm on believers. Such demons can possess bodies and need to be exorcised by priests. Vampires are thought to be a form of demon, and the vampires occasionally employ this word to describe themselves.

However, the use of *demon* in the *Chronicles* is generally metaphorical. In Lestat's song, "The Age of Innocence," he names the new demons of the twentieth century: pain, hunger, and war. These are the true evils of a self-centered culture. There is no necessity anymore to frame demons in supernatural belief systems, for suffering is the essence of evil. *(VL 541)*

Memnoch's explanation of demons is that they are souls from Sheol, not fallen angels, who have no more memory of having once been human. Now, intrigued with mortals, they try to possess mortal bodies and wreak havoc in the lives of humans. Amel is one such demon. *(MD 247)*

See also Amel, Devil, Evil, Fallen Angels, Sheol, Soul.

Denis   A mortal boy Armand offers to Louis and Claudia when they first meet at the Theater of the Vampires. Denis is Armand's whore, trading his own blood for Armand's attention and protection. The boy is eager for the bite, and he is kept in a locked bed until Armand eventually kills him. *(IV 231)*

In the first version of IV, this boy was a woman.
See also Armand.

de Pointe du Lac, Louis   See Louis de Pointe du Lac.

Descartes, René   A seventeenth-century French philosopher whose argument for making a distinction between mind and body established the school of thought known as dualism. Part of his explorations included an argument for the existence of God, known as

the Ontological Argument. In short, he stated that God is perfect; perfection implies existence; therefore, God exists. He also argued that imperfect and finite human minds cannot by themselves conceive of the idea of an infinite, perfect entity. Thus, since humans have such an idea, an infinite, perfect being must have been its origin.

When Lestat starts to ponder the logic of God, Memnoch compares him to Descartes. *(MD 135)*

See also God.

Desert   A negative landscape where the sun's heat is most intense, and a place of divine revelation. In myth and literature, the sun represents a divine presence, or Truth, and while those who venture into the desert's intense sun do risk overexposure, they may also gain purification and clarity of insight.

Little grows in the desert, so spiritual distraction is minimized. To walk full force into the face of God indicates a bold willingness to confront the dangerous unknown, to increase self-awareness, and to awaken to the realm of the spirit. The desert may also signify inner emptiness, and it is an ambiguous symbol of both life and death. It is a place of silence and waiting, of vulnerability and temptation (i.e., Christ in the wilderness). Only the most hardy forms of life can grow in the barren desert soil.

The Elder places Akasha and Enkil in the desert sun when he tires of watching their immobile, unyielding forms. Although vampire lore dictates that no vampire can endure the sun's rays, the ancient blood is so powerful that Akasha and Enkil are preserved, although much of their progeny is annihilated. *(QD 435)*

Scene from the Gobi Desert.

Remembering this story, Lestat decides in BT to expose himself to the desert sun. It is an act of despair, like Faust's desire to "follow the setting sun" when life seems empty. It is also an act of hubris: Lestat will either end his existence or prove how strong and immortal his power truly is. He selects the Gobi Desert, which is five hundred thousand square miles of sand in southern Mongolia, where the sun-baked soil should be too hard to allow him to dig himself into the sand when the sun rises. It is also a graveyard, filled with fossils of dinosaurs, so it seems to Lestat an extremely appropriate place to destroy himself. When the sun rises, Lestat flies full force toward it; the experience is agonizing. Eventually, Lestat begins to lose consciousness and falls to the earth. He lies in the sun a full day, but his body buries itself by the time the sun rises again. He survives with bronzed skin, tortured nearly beyond endurance, yet obviously immortal.

This confrontation with his nemesis in the desert transforms Lestat: he gains greater self-knowledge and an intense thirst for life. (BT 46–51) (See Vampire Atlas)

See also Immortality, Lestat de Lioncourt, Suicide, Sun.

Despair   A pervasive sense of hopelessness that often evolves into madness or boredom, it can affect a vampire who faces eternity without an inner sense of strength and adaptability. As such, when one vampire injects it into the thoughts of another, it can function as a mental weapon.

Throughout the telling of IV, Louis is in a constant state of despair. He despairs over Paul's death and over his decision to become a vampire who must kill to survive. He agonizes over the lack of clarity in the universe and his loss of faith. He is despondent over his lack of deep intimacy with Lestat, his loss of Claudia, and his inability to do anything more with his immortality than just live from one day to the next. When Armand tells him that many vampires die of boredom, Louis faces the possibility of his own eventual demise. (IV 340)

However, it is Armand who most clearly embodies despair. He craves nothing, takes no pleasure in his power, and possesses no belief structure, but merely believes in its utility. Every moment for him is a void of nothingness broken only by the kill. Armand's despair deprives him of substance and makes him a slave to everything that claims him. He has to be dominated, and his agony arises from the absence of being enchanted by something. Lestat feels that Armand has to suffer through his emptiness to discover what truly motivates him. Armand has to learn to understand the world in which he lives, to connect with the age and find a way to keep his need from drowning him. (VL 227–229)

Armand's coven uses despair to attempt to manipulate Lestat, who finds himself acting out of character when he sinks into a state of

hopeless gloom. Seeking the reason, he realizes that the coven members are playing tricks on him; he is too strong for them, however, and their power to control him dissipates. *(VL 200)* Yet Lestat does succumb to despair when he acquires the body of a mortal man. After Raglan James absconds with his vampire body, Lestat seeks Louis's help, but Louis refuses. Marius also rejects him and Lestat cannot conceive of how he will get his body back. He feels abandoned, alone, and vulnerable in his mortal state. *(BT 273–274)*

See also Dark Moment.

Destiny   The feeling of entrapment by fate, that no matter what choices are made, they will yield the same results in the end.

Although Lestat feels that his will shapes his life and that free choice is a factor in how things turn out, he is confronted several times with the possibility that he is just a pawn in a game larger than he can conceive, and that things will turn out as they are meant to be. Not even immortality can conquer destiny. For example, when he hears that Armand has cut off Nicolas's hands in an attempt to keep Nicolas under control, Lestat recalls that Nicki's father had threatened to break his hands for the same reason. Lestat sees in this pattern a mirror of Gabrielle, whose mortal coldness and distance only increases with her vampire experience. He feels a need to subvert destiny, in order to triumph as a hero. *(VL 355)*

On the other hand, the notion of destiny strongly motivates Akasha. She cannot believe that the spirit Amel entered her on a whim, and that becoming a vampire was a mere accident. Instead, she claims that she was meant to be immortal. Similarly, she believes her vision for the human race is meant to be, and she proceeds to kill those who do not fit into her plan. Destiny, however, turns against her after Mekare utters a prophetic curse: that she, Mekare, will rise against Akasha and bring her down in her hour of greatest triumph. The vampires debate whether such a prophecy can be fulfilled if there really is no destiny, for if not, they have to do something themselves to stop Akasha. However, Khayman, who had made Mekare a vampire so that she would possess the power to fulfill her curse, claims that the power of prophecy is the power of the will, and indeed Mekare does arrive at the opportune moment to accomplish her goal. *(QD 400, 411, 454)*

Destiny is still an issue for Lestat in BT. When he gets pneumonia while in a mortal body, he thinks the Body Thief may have come along just when he was despairing of existence and given him a way to die—as if their meeting had been ordained by a higher power. He struggles against this notion but is faced with yet one more apparently fateful meeting: the nun Gretchen offers him the opportunity for achieving another one of his aspirations—redemption. Her leave of absence from the mission coincides almost too well with his "leave of absence" from

vampirism. Lestat, however, resists the feeling that this is his destiny because it would deprive him of the power to choose his life. *(BT 207, 230, 250)*

See also Accident, Akasha's Plan, Choice.

Detachment
An aloof indifference, this trait must be cultivated by vampires in order for them to survive by killing; retaining a concern for human beings hinders their ability to take lives without guilt. *(IV 62)*

Louis struggles to achieve this distant stance, for while he swoons over drinking blood, it makes him conscience-stricken and even angry that he must do such a thing to survive. By the end of IV, however, he achieves a state of detachment, much to Armand's despair. *(IV 340)*

Gabrielle more perfectly exhibits this characteristic ambivalence, although initially she resists detachment for Lestat's sake, until she tires of his concern for mortals. After ten years, Gabrielle drifts off into nature, a metaphor of supreme detachment and a reflection of where her vampire nature is taking her: far from the civilized world of mortals. *(VL 348)*

The vampires who survive Akasha's global annihilation struggle with achieving this ambivalence. Their vampire nature draws them toward detachment, but the part of them that remembers their former humanity connects them enough to it to stand against Akasha and risk their own annihilation. Thus, detachment becomes a barometer of whether vampires are moving away from or toward the human pole of their dichotomized existence. *(QD 435–452)*

See also Vampire, Vampire Nature.

de Valois
See Valois, de.

Devil
The symbol in Western civilization for radical evil. The name is derived from the Sanskrit *Devi*, meaning "goddess," and the entity was often depicted with female breasts. The Devil is said to be the force behind actions of violence and cruelty, and responsible for most of the world's suffering and the imperfection of creation. He also personifies the weakness of one's will ("The Devil made me do it").

The Devil is clever, intelligent, powerful, and deceptive, the "father of lies." He made his first appearance in Babylonian and Zoroastrian mythology. Viewed for centuries as a genuine entity, he is now recognized in psychology as a manifestation of the human impulse toward violence and corruption.

The Devil is often presented as a devourer of souls (e.g., the image in Dante's *Inferno*). He finds a vulnerable individual and possesses that person, depriving him or her of power, humanity, and life. The Devil represents human intelligence gone awry, fear of the ultimate exercise

of freedom, and the destruction of the integrity of the self. Once worshiped as the dark side of God, he is still considered in some belief systems to be integrally connected to God—as the flip side of order and light.

"I don't really think there's a devil or an abstract concept of evil," says Rice. "I think most evil comes from a lack of imagination, the inability to empathize with others, [and] objectifying people and subjecting them to ideas."

The idea of the Devil is a concern primarily for Louis. Early in IV, a priest tells Louis that his brother Paul's religious visions were the result of demonic possession, and that the Devil is rampant in France. It was the Devil, insists the priest, who killed Paul. Louis is enraged to hear this, and once he becomes a vampire he feels that he is now a child of the Devil, eternally damned. *(IV 11)*

Babette believes Louis to be from the Devil when he seeks her assistance after the burning of Pointe du Lac. At first, she had thought him an angel because he had come with advice that had helped her to manage her plantation, but soon she associates him with rumors of evil. It is Louis's first realization that he knows nothing of the Devil or its existence. The implications rock him: if he is not the Devil's own, then who and what is he? *(IV 66–68)*

He seeks in vain for the answer to his question in Eastern Europe, then believes he may find it among the Parisian vampires, whose domicile is covered with macabre and garish paintings of torture, demons, and death. When he puts to them the question of the existence of God and the Devil, Armand tells him that neither exist; Louis has difficulty accepting this. He has believed for so long that he is damned that Armand's greater awareness cannot easily persuade him otherwise. *(IV 236–240)*

In Armand's chambers, Louis sees a painting of the Devil, as depicted in medieval times, with horns and hooves. Louis asks whether vampirism comes from the Devil and Armand tells him that it is just a picture. When Louis persists in his belief, Armand turns Louis's own logic against him: If God exists, then God made the Devil. If God made the Devil, and vampires are children of the Devil, then they are children of God. Louis is stunned, not just by the revelation but by what it portends: that his evil is his own responsibility. No longer can he use the Devil as a convenient scapegoat to structure the mode of his existence. *(IV 234–235)*

A century earlier, Armand's first coven, in the tradition of Santino's Roman coven, sees the Devil as their leader and the members pledge to him their souls. "In Satan, all is understood and all is known." *(VL 303)* He is their lord and master, and they fear his wrath if they do not punish the heretics Lestat and Gabrielle.

Philosophically, the Devil is also a metaphor invoked by the

vampires when they speak of human foibles. Louis remarks that people who cease to believe in God still believe in the Devil, because evil is more evident, while Gabrielle points out that people use the word "satanic" to describe behaviors that threaten the established order. *(VL 334)*

Lestat tells Louis that he would like to meet the Devil. Saying so is an arrogant display of Lestat's power, because Lestat now feels that he is stronger than any such entity. "I am the Devil," he claims. *(IV 37)* He retains this view of himself throughout the *Chronicles*, also saying, "Am I not the Devil in you all!" *(QD 230)* Little does he know he will eventually meet the Devil in the flesh.

A devil from The Last Judgement *by Michelangelo*

The question of the Devil is raised again in BT, by Talamasca scholar David Talbot. When David grows dissatisfied with his life at the age of seventy-four, he reads *Faust* and scribbles drawings of the Devil on napkins in a tavern. Later he tells Lestat that he has a theory about the Devil, based on a vision he once had in a Paris café. He saw two beings from another realm in conversation and realized they were God and the Devil. As a result, he thinks the Devil is an entity who can learn and who can grow tired of the role God requires of him. He only became the Devil because he warned God that making humanity was a serious mistake, that allowing cell division to run wild was a bad idea. David thinks the Devil may actually be redeemable because he can change his mind and his ways, and that there may be in fact more than one Devil, as each creature that takes the role may eventually decide that he can no longer do the job. *(BT 40, 70)*

"That's very much on my mind," says Rice about David's vision, "the idea that the Devil learns and changes. How do they get him to keep the job? That's what this book is all about. It's about Lestat learning and changing, and not really wanting to be the Devil."

Lestat actually meets the Devil, first in the form of a stalker that seems to be a huge, winged creature and then as an ordinary man. The Devil calls himself Memnoch. Requesting that Lestat refrain from using such names as Lucifer, Marduk, Satan, or Mephistopheles, Memnoch insists that he is not evil. In fact, he claims that his purpose is to resist what he considers to be the evil inherent in God's plan for humankind. He wants Lestat to accompany him to Heaven and Hell so that Lestat can understand that serving him, the Devil, is actually in the interest of goodness.

Lestat agrees to go but feels uneasy when certain things Memnoch says about Roger fail to add up. Lestat is aware of the Devil's reputation as the Father of Lies and feels caught in the dilemma of possibly being duped but not knowing for sure. What he sees and hears of Memnoch's story amazes him and gains his sympathy. However, after visiting Hell and realizing what a loathsome place it is, he opts out and flees from Memnoch's grasp. Nevertheless, when Lestat delivers the religious icon, Veronica's veil, to Dora and unintentionally helps to infuse new life into Christianity, Memnoch sends him a note thanking him for a job perfectly accomplished. In the end, Lestat is unsure what really happened. It could all have been a lie devised by either God or the Devil, or it may all be true. He has no idea what to make of it, but he believes that these two supernatural forces are somehow in on it together, and he fears for his own safety. *(MD 20, 96–97, 115, 129–140, 162–320, 350)*

See also Deception, Demons, Evil, Father of Lies, God, Hell, Lestat de Lioncourt, Memnoch, *Memnoch the Devil*, Mephistopheles, Visions.

Devil's Road   How Lestat refers to the vampire's journey from being a mortal to becoming a vampire, and his name for the ten-year quest he undertakes with Gabrielle to know more about his vampire existence and to find Marius. He first heard of the term from the queen vampire in Armand's coven.

Lestat and Gabrielle explore countries all over the world, from Europe to Asia, so they can discover what the vampires in each place are like. *(VL 218, 289, 306, 323)*

See also Quest.

de Wilde, Wynken   See Wilde, Wynken de.

Diana   A nature deity, moon goddess, and virgin huntress in Roman and Greek mythology, she is also called Artemis or Selene. Diana was the patron goddess of women. The cult of Diana flourished among fifth- and sixth-century pagans, which gave Christians reason to view her throughout the Middle Ages as the leader of witch covens.

The mystic Wynken de Wilde and his female cult were accused of practicing the rites of Diana. *(MD 80)*

See also Wilde (Wynken de).

Diane   One of the five women with whom Wynken de Wilde had religious orgies. They met in the garden at de Wilde castle until Wynken's brother killed him. *(MD 84)*

See also Wilde (Wynken de).

Diary   Jesse finds a secret compartment in Claudia's room in the New Orleans town house. Inside is a doll, a rosary, and a diary. The diary is Claudia's birthday gift from Louis and the first entry is dated September 21, 1836—the anniversary of the day she was born as a vampire. In these entries, Claudia expresses her frustration with her two "fathers." In her own mind, she is a grown woman but they do not seem to realize or admit it. The diary also contains other entries, but Jesse is too disoriented to read them; the Talamasca later tell her that they revealed nothing further. *(QD 183–185, 188)*

Dickens, Charles   Louis is reading a biography of Dickens, the nineteenth-century writer, when Lestat visits him in BT. *(BT 105)*

Dickens was a pervasive influence on Rice: "My teacher, my mentor, my guardian angel, my love, my god is Dickens," she asserts. Dickens concentrated on such themes as the inner struggle between being a hero and being a villain, and the complexity of good and evil.

"The clearest theme to me is the theme of *David Copperfield* and *Great Expectations*," Rice explains. "We are in a world without parents and we have to discover who our true brothers and sisters are. How do we define our values as orphans in a storm? And as the values that

provided the scaffolding of, say, medieval literature collapse, how does the wanderer find new values? How do we become our own parents? It's a theme in IV, when Louis stops looking to Lestat as the total authority and accepts the fact that he himself knows as much as anybody else. Lestat is my hero because he does not make that mistake. He wants to hear what the old ones have to say, but he never really thinks they're Mom and Pop. He's too smart for that."

When Lestat visits Armand nearly a century after he had left him in Paris, he thinks Armand possesses the essence of such characters in Dickens's novel, as David Copperfield and Steerforth. *(VL 503)* He also paraphrases a quote from *David Copperfield* as a theme for QD: "I don't know whether I'm the hero or the victim of this tale." *(QD 6–7)* As in Dickens's novels, the dichotomies of good/evil and hero/victim are interconnected concepts.

Lestat also quotes from Dickens's *A Tale of Two Cities* when he searches for an opening line for BT. *(BT 2)*

Diogenes   A disillusioned Greek philosopher who, in the fourth century, is reputed to have walked around with a lantern during the daytime looking for an honest man. Raglan James presents himself to Lestat as the person whom Diogenes had wanted to find. *(BT 137)*

See also James (Raglan).

Dionysus   A figure from Greek mythology that Rice uses to link vampire history with ancient legends. Dionysian worship is one of the oldest Greek mystery religions, dating from Crete circa 3000 B.C.

The story of Dionysus is similar to that of the Egyptian god Osiris, who is more clearly related to the vampire origins. Both were vegetation gods who were violently torn apart, and both rose from the dead. Their transformation from human to immortal bears strong parallel to that of the vampires.

Like the vampires, Dionysus was half mortal, and he appealed to the Greek love of mystery, uninhibited excess, desire, and savagery—the urge to become a god, if only for a moment. He represents the abandonment of repression and inhibition, which can then lead to chaos and self-annihilation. However, such death also means rebirth. Dionysus plays out the unconscious urge toward extremes that can provide a religious awakening and a deeper connection with life. Standing in contrast to sober Reason, Dionysus represents transcendence through sensuality and abandon. After his resurrection, he presided over ceremonies filled with wild dancing—orgiastic rituals that liberated instinct and emotion. *(VL 407)*

The philosopher Nietzsche utilized the dynamic of Dionysus as a symbol of the chaos needed to shake up the existing moral order of nineteenth-century Europe. In the wake of the resulting nihilism, Nietzsche believed, an "overman"—a person of great moral courage and

Dionysus

integrity—would arise and create a more enlightened morality. Although Rice did not read Nietzsche, Lestat identifies himself with Dionysus and portrays himself in Nietzschean fashion as a vampire for a new age. The energy and excess evident in Lestat's rock star performance echo that of the ancient orgies, and his lyrics resemble Nietzsche's vision. Lestat's association with Dionysus is most explicit in his memory of being cut into pieces by Claudia, then resurrected by his immortal blood; as his blood began to flow again, his thoughts traveled back to the "dimly envisioned groves of mythical lands where the old Dionysian god of the wood had felt again and again his flesh torn, his blood spilled." It was a "stunning repetition of the same old theme. And the god dies. And the god rises." *(VL 501–502)*

Since Dionysus is also the patron god of the theater, Lestat notes his symbolic connection to the Theater of the Vampires. *(VL 330)*

Memnoch mentions Dionysus as one of the gods of death, dismemberment, and regeneration that inspired human imagination. He believes that God based his idea for Christianity partly on this violent and bloody superstition. *(MD 298)*

See also Christianity, Lestat de Lioncourt, Osiris, Vegetation Gods.

Dismemberment   The act of cutting off limbs from a body or tearing a body into pieces. Armand tells Louis that this is one of the ways a vampire can die, but no vampire in the *Chronicles* ever does die in this manner. Magnus contradicts Armand's belief, when he claims that to truly be annihilated vampires not only must be burned but must also have their ashes scattered. *(IV 292, VL 96)*

Dis Pater   Taken from Julius Caesar's writings about the Keltoi of Gaul, this is the Roman name for the "god of the night."

Marius refers to this god when he listens to a Druid talk about his people's religious practices. *(VL 402)*

See also Druids.

Divisadero Street   The San Francisco street where the boy reporter interviews Louis. It cuts across San Francisco, terminating in the Castro District, a gay neighborhood. Locations have great significance for Rice, and Divisadero Street evolves in its meaning as the *Chronicles* develop.

Rice had visited a small radio station on Divisadero when she was lengthening a short story called "Interview With the Vampire." She had noted on it the tragic contrast of tall, narrow Victorian houses sitting in the midst of contemporary squalor and gloom; bars with flashing neon signs contrasted sharply with deteriorating gingerbread lace. "What was working for me as a writer," she said, "was an intuitive sense of the utter gloom, this deep urban Gothic that used to be captured years ago in comic books.'' She wanted to set her story in an old Victorian building with dingy, sparsely furnished rooms, to emphasize how the vampire telling his supernatural tale was out of place in the twentieth century; like the house, he, too, was a relic left over from bygone times. A house set so near the street would also provide modern textures to the background, such as car headlights and traffic noise, thus retaining the contrast as Louis spoke. When Rice went back to write her story, her memory of a specific house with a stained glass window permeated the first scene. Louis remains in this house during the whole story, then returns to it after IV is published. (IV 2–3, 23, 67, 346)

In VL, Lestat rides up and down Divisadero Street in his black Porsche searching for Louis among the ruined Victorian houses. Writing this scene gave Rice a feeling for the way the street cut across San Francisco in a metaphorical joining of diverse neighborhoods—rich

House on Divisadero Street where Interview with the Vampire *takes place*

and poor, gay and straight, white, yellow, and black. That Louis, a vampire who had left behind political and economic concerns, was situated on this street gave the story an interesting juxtaposition between background and character. *(VL 520, 525)*

By the time QD was written, Rice realized how significant it was that Divisadero Street terminated in the Castro District, where Rice placed the vampire bar Dracula's Daughter. "That's why I put Louis there again," she explains about his return. Rice's vampires had been embraced by gay culture, and as outsiders who often meet in bars in the Castro, they give strong expression to the experience of existing on the fringes of life and of transcending the limitations of gender categories. *(QD 18, 85, 114)*

Note: The house in which Louis told his story as he looked through the window to Divisadero can be seen a few blocks from Haight Street. (See Vampire Atlas)

See also *Interview with the Vampire*, Louis de Pointe du Lac, Molloy (Daniel), Reunions, San Francisco.

Dixie Gates   What Lestat nicknamed the twin river bridges that cross the Mississippi River from New Orleans; the official name for them is the Crescent City Connection. *(BT 113)* (See Vampire Atlas)

See also New Orleans.

Dogs   See Mastiff, Mojo.

Doll   The image of youth and perfection that Rice sets against the imperfections of humanity, or the former mortal life of the vampires.

"Dixie Gates," New Orleans

Two of Anne Rice's many dolls

"I think dolls are beautiful," says Rice. "They combine innocence and beauty with a sinister quality." Her emphasis on dolls in several of the *Chronicles* underlines a theme of how art—in this instance, the craft of doll making—is sometimes treated as if it is superior to life.

Louis and Lestat both think of Claudia, with her tiny body and beautiful features, as a doll. They dress her in pretty dresses and comb out her curls. She has been cut loose from her human mother—a metaphor of the loss of her own humanity—yet is preserved in her childhood, being a vampire who has a white, porcelainlike, and, over-all, doll-like appearance. In line with Rice's own appraisal of dolls, Claudia combines the sinister quality of her vampire nature with child-ish, innocent features. *(IV 100, 103)*

Louis and Lestat give her dolls to play with, even when it is clear that her mind has matured to the point of being a woman. They want her to remain as childlike as she looks, so they can take care of her and, by doing so, give meaning to their own lives. By the time she is nearing forty, she counts over thirty such dolls from Lestat, and his treatment

of her angers her. *(QD 183–184)* Claudia wants recognition for the woman she is, but Lestat and Louis continue to treat her as a child. She burns or crushes her dolls, believing this to be the appropriate gesture toward lifeless things that so strongly resemble her. "The doll expects it," she claims, and her destructive act foreshadows what eventually happens to her. *(QD 184)*

In Paris, Claudia brings a doll to the hotel room and tells Louis about a doll maker named Madeleine who has lost a child and who consequently makes the same doll over and over in an effort to replace her missing daughter and quell her grief. Claudia gets Madeleine to make for her a lady doll, the form to which she aspires. But then Claudia crushes the doll, expressing her frustration over her sense of helpless entrapment. *(IV 201, 208)*

Later Claudia asks Louis to make Madeleine into a vampire, so that Madeleine can become a "lady" doll of sorts. In this way they would be preserved together in vampirism as a never-dying mother and daughter pair. It is clear that Claudia has become a substitute for Madeleine's dolls, which initially were a substitute for Madeleine's lost child. When Madeleine becomes a vampire, she burns her doll shop; she is letting go of her dolls now that she has Claudia. *(IV 266, 269)*

Developing the idea of a doll as a representation of art, Rice opens the second section of BT with a poem by W. B. Yeats entitled "The Dolls." Through this poem, Yeats expressed the notion that when perfectly crafted dolls are juxtaposed against filthy, crying babies, the dolls seem the superior product. Lestat lives out this theme as he continues to think of Claudia as a perfect little doll, captured immutably in her childhood glory when he makes her a vampire. In his visions of her, she resists being viewed as a doll, and her dialogues with him represent his ambivalence between being a vampire and wanting to be a mortal. His uncertainty over which of the two is superior ends when he realizes how much he dislikes being human; this experience also resolves his indecision about David Talbot. He wants Claudia to be an eternal doll and he would make her into one again, despite her protests; similarly, he would make David a vampire, and not let him remain a fragile mortal.

See also Art, Claudia, "The Dolls," Yeats (William Butler).

Doll maker   See Madeleine.

"The Dolls"   A poem by William Butler Yeats that introduces Part 2 of BT. It develops the image of dolls that protest the noise and imperfection a human child displays in their presence. The doll maker's wife also rejects the same child, claiming its birth "was an

accident." The wife desires to duplicate the perfection that her husband achieves with his craft, as if she believes that the art of doll making is superior to giving birth. Children are noisy and messy; dolls, however, possess no such annoyances or imperfections. (BT 394)

See also Art, Doll, Poetry, *The Tale of the Body Thief*, Yeats (William Butler).

Dominance/Submission
The primitive desire to achieve intimacy through violation, which is enacted through erotic rituals of sadomasochism. These rituals often involve going to sexual extremes to achieve a temporary transcendent state.

Vampires dominate victims, exciting them by requiring the process of surrender. Yet the victims also dominate by satisfying the vampire's need for blood; in return, the vampire is surrendering to the power of the thirst. As such, the dynamics of dominance and submission in the *Chronicles* involve ambiguity and reversal: no definite locus of control resides in a particular party. The dominant can become the submissive, the submissive the dominant, and the symbiotic bond they form prevents them from being either wholly the victim or wholly the victor.

Rice developed her own take on the psychology of this relationship, with an emphasis on masochists. No one, she believed, is a pure type; each is a mixture of both, although some people may be more inclined toward one pole than the other. For example, masochists, she explains, "want to be passive; they want to be ordered about. They want to be in the focus of that intense devotion and attention and control. And of course, they want to control all of that."

Rice utilizes this dynamic throughout the *Chronicles* to explore and exploit the psychological tension of such relationships: "Vampire literature has always said that what matters is a deep desire to be dominated, a response to that domination, and a terror of the one who will fulfill that desire."

Blending power over others with fear of them intensifies erotic excitement. This ironic mix enhances and complements Rice's emphasis on breaking down gender roles through androgynous behavior. For example, Lestat is excited as he watches Haitian women forcing men to their knees. Those who traditionally have been weak are now strong, mirroring what Akasha is doing to him but also foreshadowing Lestat's eventual success over her. The turmoil Lestat feels from watching the Haitians simultaneously energizes and paralyzes him, and his restrained energy heats up the scene. (QD 375)

The dominance/submission theme is also reflected through the image of slavery, which occurs when Lestat explains to Louis that the reason one vampire makes another is to acquire a slave. One domi-

nates, the other submits. Louis reacts against the image, although his passive nature makes him a perfect submissive. He searches for a way to be dominant in his relationship with Lestat, so he withholds money as a way to keep some form of control. *(IV 60, 84, 120)*

A similar dynamic occurs between Louis and Claudia, and Louis and Armand. Each exhibits weaknesses and strengths that contribute to feeling insecure about the balance of power. The resulting ambiguity, in turn, increases the passion of the relationships. Armand especially wants to be dependent on someone else, to be dominated, and he sets out to force other vampires into that role. And when the submissive personality desires to make the conditions just right for surrender, those that surrender become dominant. *(VL 311)*

In Armand's story, "The Art of the Vampire at Its Peak in the Year 1876," the victims also become the masters. Both vampire and victim long for each other, both surrender, both are slaves, and yet both control.

See also "The Art of the Vampire at Its Peak in the Year 1876," Erotic, Flagellation, Intimacy, Molloy (Daniel), Victim Psychology, Villa of the Mysteries.

Dominican Republic   A country in the Caribbean occupying the eastern two-thirds of the island of Hispaniola.

Raglan James visits this island while he is in Lestat's vampire body. *(BT 281)* (See Vampire Atlas)

Dora Flynn   See Flynn, Dora.

Dostoevsky, Fyodor   A nineteenth-century existential Russian writer famous for such novels as *Crime and Punishment* and *The Brothers Karamazov*.

Gretchen cites him as an author who asked difficult questions about the existence of God in the face of suffering. In a conversation between the characters Ivan and Alyosha in *The Brothers Karamazov*, Ivan claims that God's plan for redemption is not worth the suffering of even one child. *(BT 248)*

Dracula   Bram Stoker's 1897 novel about a vampire that influenced twentieth-century vampire images. Lestat mentions this book when he refers to vampire tales of the nineteenth century that gave Louis and him a place in society.

In the novel, Count Dracula is a hypnotic figure of overpowering evil who travels from his castle in Transylvania to London in search of fresh blood. He is detected by Dr. Van Helsing who, with a troupe of vampire hunters, follows the Count back to his castle. They destroy him by driving a stake through his heart.

From the film Dracula,
1931

It was through the depiction of Count Dracula that the vampire gained such famous and universal traits as being immortal, aristocratic, corrupt, unholy, seductive, and ruthless.

See also Lugosi (Bela), Vampire, Vampire Tales.

Dracula's Daughter   The vampire bar in San Francisco mentioned in VL and described in QD. It is a cabaret on Castro Street, divided between mortals in the front room, who dance to Lestat's tunes, and vampires in the back room, who decorate their area with images of death. Marius visits this bar and reads the declaration against Lestat in the back room. *(VL 528, QD 11)*

The bar's name is based on the 1936 film *Dracula's Daughter*,

From the film Dracula's Daughter

which starred Gloria Holden. Rice had seen it as a child, and the sensual qualities of the film had deeply influenced her. "The best seduction scene is in that film," she says. "It's beautiful and delicate. I loved the tragic figure of Dracula's daughter as the regretful creature who didn't want to kill but was driven to it." (See Vampire Atlas)

See also Holden (Gloria), Vampire, Vampire Bars.

Dream of Family

What Lestat calls one of his significant visions in VL. After he hears that his mortal family was murdered by peasants during the French Revolution, he dreams about them, resurrecting them as white-skinned vampires embracing one another in the ruins of their castle. Lestat's Dark Gift has even given his father back his vision. The dream is indicative of Lestat's need for connection, his desire to be a hero, and his ties to his former mortality. It also shows vampirism as a symbol of health, restoration, resurrection, and vision. *(VL 531)*

The scene was, for Rice, a personal favorite because she felt that she had penetrated into a deep layer of Lestat's soul. It is one place in this novel, she says, where her language gets close to intimacy and vision.

See also Family, Lestat de Lioncourt.

Dream of the Twins

When Lestat awakens Akasha, he sets into motion an ancient drama of retribution that spawns a vision in the mind of one of the oldest vampires, Mekare, of what had happened to her and her twin sister, Maharet. Vampires worldwide receive the vision as a series of fragmented dreams, as do select mortals. Some see

only part of the twins' ordeal; others see more. Nothing is clear as to why the dreams recur, why vampires everywhere receive them, or what they are about. All that the recipients seem to know is that the dream is connected to Lestat and his rock concert. (QD 109)

The dream involves the story of Maharet and Mekare, peaceful, life-enhancing witches who lived in ancient Palestine. It details the ceremonies of cannibalism that they celebrated at the time, the twins' rape, mutilation, and punishment, and Maharet's resulting pregnancy. Although in the dream the twins speak in an ancient unknown language, it is fully comprehensible to the dream recipients.

This dream touches Louis and Gabrielle only lightly, sends Santino into a horrid trance, and endlessly recurs for Marius during his ten-day imprisonment. Pandora fails to receive it at all. The dream comes to Lestat after he participates in a slaughter with Akasha. It seems important, but then fades in his mind, echoing what is happening with his moral sensibilities. After the second slaughter, he sees the dreams through Mekare's eyes (although he does not realize to whom the eyes belong); this has the effect of dispelling Lestat's unequivocal acceptance of Akasha's delusions of peace and prosperity. Soon Lestat's sense of right and wrong reasserts itself, and he rebels against Akasha. (QD 30, 35, 40, 42, 67, 74, 137, 304)

Finally, it becomes clear that the dream is being sent from Mekare. The fragmented images indicate that her own mind is damaged, yet she moves with great purpose toward the place where the vampires are discussing ways to stop Akasha. At one point, Marius sees through the eyes of Mekare and he experiences her as a powerful, unstoppable momentum. Jesse's dream connection gives Mekare the sense of direction she needs. When Mekare shows up and kills Akasha, the vampires all understand the meaning of the dreams. (QD 241, 454)

"That whole part of the book felt like a dream," says Rice of her writing experience. "To write it was the most heightened wonderful experience: to do those two twins and the funeral feast and the whole way it happened—it was the biggest dare I've ever tried to pull off in a book. To have everyone see the funeral feast and understand what the message of the dream was—that they could continue if the heart and the brain were consumed—was so complex, there were times when I thought I couldn't pull it off. All those characters were trying to deal with that total awareness of Maharet's that goes all the way back to those prehistoric people. When I think about it, QD has more meaning in it than anything I've written, [for it's] about the truth being in substance and what that sacred ritual of cannibalism meant."

See also Maharet, Mekare, Legend of the Twins, Twins, Witches.

Dreams   Thoughts or images that occur during sleep, dreams can

reveal parts of the self that have not been expressed, making the dreamer confront feelings of loss, repression, or fear.

Louis tells the boy reporter that vampires experience dreams, and with their vampires' heightened sense of imagery, such dreams can be vivid and haunting. As a vampire, Louis experiences dreams that are longer and more twisted than any he had as a mortal. He lies in his coffin for hours ruminating about his dreams, seeing a great wasteland that chills him: "It was as if all figures walked and talked on the desolate home of my damned soul." *(IV 77)* On the ship going to Eastern Europe, Louis dreams of his aging sister putting white roses on his grave in complete ignorance of what he has become. *(IV 169)*

In BT, Lestat dreams about a man-eating tiger pursuing David Talbot. The tiger seems threatening, but all it does is snatch the gold chain from David's neck before David kills it. Lestat wonders if the tiger might be him endangering David. What Lestat fails to see is that it represents a man-eater, Raglan James, who is stalking *him*. *(BT 5–6)*

Lestat also dreams of his mortal boyhood before he killed the wolves, and of Claudia, which pressures him with the question of whether he would make her a vampire if he had the opportunity to do it over again. The latter is a dream that brings Lestat's self-deception to the surface; he wants to think of himself as regretting that act, of wanting to do good, but he comes to realize that he enjoys his vampire life and that he would make Claudia again. Thus, Lestat *is* the tiger. His dreams help him to confront what he really is and that he has chosen his evil path. *(BT 5–6)*

Jesse, too, has dreams that symbolically indicate how the vampire is a creation of the subconscious. Although Maharet has attempted to black out Jesse's memories of the Sonoma compound, the images that Jesse had seen return years later in her dreams. When she reads IV and investigates the New Orleans town house, her dreams about vampires increase, for the book reminds her of the summer at Sonoma. Eventually she remembers everything from Sonoma, including finding Maharet and Mael in their deathlike daytime slumber. *(QD 178)*

The tribe of the twins relied on dreams for vision. They drank potions to induce trances so that they could travel through their dreams into the past, to speak with ancestors and walk ancient streets. They also sought truth from the subconscious images that arose in dreams. It thus makes sense that after six thousand years, Mekare would use a dream to give herself the necessary motivation and direction to fulfill her curse against Akasha. *(QD 454)*

See also Dream of the Twins, Hallucinations, Tiger, Visions.

Drinkers of the Blood A name the early Egyptians used for vampires. The Druids also referred to the vampire they kept imprisoned as their god by this name.

The Drinkers of the Blood often took advantage of mortals by demanding blood sacrifices, which the mortals provided. Some vampires sanctified the process by using as sacrifices only human evildoers, while others were ruthless in their quest for blood, initiating and glorifying random death. These latter vampires became gods of the Orient; they had no concern for life and made the deliberate onset of death guilt-free. They even wore skulls and garments dyed in human blood.

As Egyptian religion changed over the centuries and became more conscious of the value of life, the gluttony of bloodlust lost its power over mortals, although the Drinkers of the Blood became respected symbols of life in the afterworld. *(VL 442–443, 459)*

See also Druid Vampire.

Drinking blood See Bite, Blood, Swoon, Thirst, Vampire's Kiss.

Dr. Polidori The vampire bar in London named after Dr. John Polidori, author of *The Vampyre*, the first substantial vampire tale in the English language. Polidori served as Lord Byron's doctor and admitted that his story was influenced by Byron's ideas about vampires. *(VL 528)*

See also *The Vampyre*.

Druids The ancient priesthood of the Keltoi (Celts), who worshiped oak trees. The priests were also the judges and lawmakers. The Druidic religion involved human sacrifice and the worship of many gods to promote the fertility of the earth; adherents also believed that the immortal soul left the body at death and entered a new one.

Druidic ceremonies were illegal under the dominion of the Roman Empire, but Marius discovers secret Druid cults that practice their religion deep in the northern forests. While he is still a mortal he is abducted by a Druid who claims that one of their gods sent him to Marius. Another Druid priest, Mael (who later becomes a vampire), teaches Marius songs, poetry, beliefs, and laws, all in preparation for Marius to become a vampire—a new god for the Druids. *(VL 399–425)*

See also Druid Vampire, Feast of Samhain, Mael, Marius.

Druid vampire A vampire kept in an oak tree to preside over the harvest. The Druids refer to him by many names, including the God of the Grove, the Lover of the Mother, the Drinker of the Blood, the White One, the God of the Night, and the God of the Oak. They starve him each month as a symbol of death, then feed him blood sacrifices to ensure the fertility of the land and to sanctify the forests. This vampire is badly burned when Akasha and Enkil are placed in the sun, and the Druids must seek another god. They bring back the mortal

Druids burning human sacrifices

Marius. The Druid vampire makes Marius, exchanging blood with him several times to ensure his strength, then urges him to go to Egypt to discover why he and other vampires he has heard about have been so badly injured. He wants to accompany Marius, but the Druids get to him first and toss him into the fire, where he is destroyed. *(VL 416–423)*

See also Calamity, Druids, Marius, Oak.

"Duet on Iberville Street"   A poem by Stan Rice that opens *Memnoch the Devil*. It is about the ruthless brutality of God's creation, despite its beauty. Memnoch's story follows the same theme.

See also Memnoch, *Memnoch the Devil*, Poetry, Rice (Stan).

Dürer, Albrecht   A German painter and engraver active in the late fifteenth century known for combining Gothic art with the forms

and ideas of the Italian Renaissance. He was preoccupied with themes of salvation and the torment of Christ, and he believed in the power of cosmic forces. Dürer is one of the artists Louis mentions as he walks through the lavishly illustrated passage to the room beneath the Theater of the Vampires. *(IV 230)*

See also Subterranean Room.

Albrecht Dürer, The Four Horsemen of the Apocalypse

Earthbound A term Lestat uses for Vampire. *(MD 121)*
See also Substance, Vampire.

Eastern Europe The area where Louis and Claudia seek out other vampires who might be able to explain to them the meaning of their existence or provide better companionship for them than did Lestat. Louis refers to these creatures as Old World vampires in light of the fact that much of the superstition and legend regarding vampires comes from this part of the globe. Claudia has read the vampire stories and legends available, and insists that Eastern Europe is the most obvious starting point for their quest. *(IV 150)*

Despite his desire for answers, Louis views this venture with bitterness. He believes he is engaging himself more firmly with darkness and moving away from the mortal world that he still treasures. The entire quest poses a psychological risk for him. *(IV 168)*

He and Claudia arrive at the port of Varna, then travel by carriage, à la Jonathan Harker in *Dracula*. They observe a dark, barren countryside filled with disturbing ruins. The countryside itself is a symbol of the aspect of vampire existence they will encounter here: stagnant and desolate. As they listen for rumors of vampires, they remain incognito, knowing that as outsiders they provoke suspicion and could easily become a source for rumor themselves. Louis is aware that more secrecy is needed in this region than had been the case in New Orleans, because here the people actually believe in vampires. *(IV 171–172)*

Eventually, Louis and Claudia discover a small village in Transylvania under siege by a vampire. Louis finds the vampire's lair, but discovering that the vampire has no mind and can tell them nothing, kills it and moves on. He and Claudia find the situation to be the same in every country in Eastern Europe that they visit; throughout Transyl-

vania, Bulgaria, and Hungary, all they find are a handful of creatures who hold "no secrets, no truths, only despair." *(IV 197)* (See Vampire Atlas)

See also Old World Vampires, Quest, Transylvania.

Eden The garden God created as an earthly paradise for humanity; the locale for a life of innocence and grace. According to the Bible, it was the place where human beings first heard the voice of God and sampled fruit from a tree that gave them knowledge of good and evil. Eating the fruit made them akin to God, and thus they were cast out. The only way back to Eden was through redemption, by means of a savior who ensured acceptance into Heaven.

Armand viewed his coven housed under Les Innocents as Eden; he extends this metaphor when he claims that Lestat drove them out with a flaming sword as God had done with Adam and Eve. *(VL 507)*

Akasha refers to herself as a creator of the "new Eden," promising a new beginning and a paradise based on peace. She intends to achieve it by eliminating ninety-nine percent of the world's population of men and becoming a goddess for women—the only ones who can realize the dream. *(QD 334)*

Eden as portrayed in Paradise *by Peter Paul Rubens and Jan Brueghel the Elder.*

After Lestat visits Heaven with Memnoch, they walk together in a perfect garden that Memnoch claims was the original state of the world. The word "paradise" is actually a memory of this place. Such beauty will only come again after the second Ice Age. *(MD 178)*

See also Akasha's Plan, Armand's Coven, Ice Age.

Egypt   An Arab nation in the northeast corner of Africa. Most of the country is covered by dry, windswept deserts, although the fertile valleys of the Nile River bisect the arid landscape. One of the early birthplaces of civilization, Egypt has a history that dates back more than five thousand years. Rice is enamored of Egyptian history and culture: "When I was a little kid, I absolutely loved the books I got from the library on Egypt. I was in love with the pyramids, the pharaohs, Egyptian art—the whole idea of the country." Her fascination made her link the vampires' origins with that country.

Egypt is one of Louis's destinations when he leaves Paris. He wants to see the pyramids and their treasures, and look with his vampire eyes into unopened graves. IV was written before Rice had visited Egypt, so she merely sends Louis there and does not actually detail his experience. *(IV 325)* She eventually went there herself and presented many of her impressions in *The Mummy.*

For nearly four thousand years—until Alexander the Great arrived in 332 B.C.—there was little change in Egyptian language, art, religion, or law. "There was," says Marius, "a sense of something beginning there." *(VL 453)* It was a seemingly timeless land, and Enkil and Akasha, the forebears of the vampires from Egypt's earliest period, become symbols of both beginnings and eternity.

In VL, Lestat views Egypt as a place in love with death, and he makes it a destination for Gabrielle and himself on the Devil's Road. Gabrielle loves the mountains and ruins of Egypt. The unchanging landscape and the huge statues make it seem like a land full of ancient gods and mysteries. *(VL 348)*

Marius is sent to Egypt by the Druid's vampire god to discover the cause of the "calamity"—why vampires everywhere have been burned. He goes to Alexandria, where a vampire tells him the story of Akasha and Enkil, who are then over four thousand years old. Marius sees these ancient forebears as the symbols of Egypt itself, and thus of timelessness. However, he is about to change their location by taking them out of Egypt, just when Egypt itself is changing. *(VL 426)* (See Vampire Atlas)

See also Akasha, Kemet, Saqqâra, Those Who Must Be Kept.

Elder, The   An early Egyptian vampire who is the reluctant guardian of the oldest vampires, Enkil and Akasha.

In VL, Marius recounts how he was sent into Egypt to discover why vampires everywhere had been burned. There he meets with the black-skinned Elder, who has been silent since the calamity, but who informs Marius that the vampire race originated with Enkil and Akasha; it is their preservation or destruction that determines the fate of the entire vampire race.

The story, the Elder said, had become a dubious legend that begged to be tested; someone had placed Akasha and Enkil in the sun deliberately. It soon becomes clear to Marius that the Elder himself had done the deed. Shortly thereafter, Akasha seeks Marius's assistance to take her and Enkil out of Egypt. The Elder becomes enraged and tries to kill Marius, but he is himself killed by Akasha. His death is a metaphor for the end of an era. *(VL 430–444, 453–456)*

See also Calamity, Those Who Must Be Kept.

Elders   An anonymous group of men who run the Talamasca and to whom David Talbot reports. There is no direct communication with them, and their formation and management style remain a mystery. They forbid direct contact with Lestat, but David ignores them, for Lestat is his friend. He thinks they have a medieval sense of things, with their archaic rules and directives. The Elders appear more prominently in Rice's novel *Lasher*, where their directives are intercepted by a corrupt faction. Accordingly, the Elders issue orders for a bogus excommunication and for kidnapping Lasher. When this corruption is discovered and eliminated, the Elders assure the Order that steps will be taken to prevent any such activity in the future. It becomes clear that they operate via the Motherhouse in Amsterdam, but their motives and origins remain elusive. *(BT 77–78)*

See also Talamasca, Talbot (David).

Eleanor   One of the five women with whom Wynken de Wilde held religious orgies in the garden of de Wilde castle. She was a cousin and confidante to Blanche de Wilde, the wife of Wynken's brother. Roger possesses Eleanor's letters to Blanche, and Blanche's to her, which describes their activities. Eleanor may also have made crude copies of Wynken's illuminated manuscripts. *(MD 84, 85)*

See also Roger, Wilde (Blanche de), Wilde (Wynken de).

Electronic Map   See Great Family.

"Elegy"   A poem by Stan Rice that introduces the section of QD about the Legend of the Twins. "It's an elegy to the victims of the sixties," said Stan Rice, "the people who wanted to go all the way and who went too far and literally died. As the poet, I'm trying to find a

way to go on singing songs in the midst of what I've seen of failed idealism. We couldn't survive if everything were totally tragic all the time." *(QD 35)*

See also Poetry, Rice (Stan).

Elementals   A term the Talamasca uses for pesky spirits, what David Talbot calls "trickster spirits" or "astral tramps." When Lestat first enters St. Elizabeth's Orphanage, he listens for evidence of elementals. He senses faint emanations of personalities but no real spiritual turbulence. Memnoch then appears and speaks to him, and it seems to Lestat that the elementals cannot hear Memnoch the way he can. The second time he enters St. Elizabeth's to meet Dora, he hears and feels nothing. *(MD 18, 111)*

Louis believes elementals are certainly present: "They're small, but I feel them." *(MD 346)* When he mentions this, Lestat listens and vaguely hears children singing songs, speaking in rapid whispers, and reciting the times tables. He thinks he hears their feet on the stairs and later he sees children swinging in the courtyard, a scene from former days when the place was an orphanage. *(MD 353)*

St. Elizabeth's is reported to be haunted. During its renovation, one of the workers fell from a scaffolding when he saw the face of a child at the window. A former administrator of the residential treatment program once housed at St. Elizabeth's reports that a security officer called her one night. It seems that the reliable officer had spotted a very solid pair of tennis shoes, *sans* legs, running through the foyer. Other stories involve noises from "Lestat's attic," attributed to a man whom they called Job who had once had his rooms up there. Some of the staff refused to go near that attic. In later years, when the girls heard about the once traditional practice of laying out deceased nuns in the community room for viewing, they made up stories about ghosts and skeletons discovered at St. Elizabeth's.

A team of clairvoyants recently reported impressions of a dark-haired man in "Lestat's attic," and the ghosts of several children in various places in the building.

See also Astral Tramps, Ghosts, Haunted Houses, St. Elizabeth's Orphanage.

Eleni   A dark-eyed female vampire in Armand's first coven who catches Lestat's eye, and who is one of only four survivors of Armand's wrath against his coven. Eleni begs Lestat to help protect them from Armand, and she becomes one of the founding members of the Theater of the Vampires, writing letters to Lestat to keep him informed about the theater group. *(VL 212, 243, 328)*

See also Armand's Coven, Theater of the Vampires.

Eliade, Mircea   A prominent contemporary scholar of comparative religions.

Lestat mentions Eliade as an author he reads. He also spots several volumes of Eliade's histories of religion among Roger's treasures in a house in Manhattan. Rice has used much of Eliade's work in her own studies. *(BT 101, MD 32)*

Elohim   A Hebrew word for God that Lestat uses, inversely, to refer to the vampire realm. *(BT 274)*

Emily   A victim of a vampire in Eastern Europe. Her tragic death is the first clue that Louis and Claudia find that indicates the presence of a vampire.

Louis and Claudia listen to the story about how a vampire had drawn Emily outside the previous night, leaving her drained of blood. The innkeeper had then laid her out in a room in the inn, which is where Louis and Claudia first see her. *(IV 175)*

See also Morgan, Old World Vampires.

Enchanted sleep   What Louis calls the death of his victims. *(IV 55)*

Endurance   The ability to continue in the same state by adapting to change.

One issue among vampires involves identifying which of them is truly immortal; in other words, which vampires can and do hold the secret of endurance through century after century. Vampires who fail to find a way to endure may succumb to despair or boredom. *(IV 248, 285)* Those who do find the strength to endure discover different ways to motivate and inspire themselves. Lestat latches onto risk and optimism to keep himself interested and active. Marius lasts because he wants to see what becomes of the human race. *(VL 467)* Gabrielle chooses detachment from the mortal world and allows her absorption with the unchanging images of nature to stimulate her. *(VL 348)* Louis, the most human of the vampires, seems resigned to a state of acceptance. *(BT 104–105)* Maharet finds purpose in watching over the Great Family, a line of human descendants with whom she interacts as a generous and eccentric aunt. *(QD 426)* Akasha and Enkil maintain themselves by falling into a comatose state of awareness. *(QD 417)* Armand searches for someone—mortal or vampire—who can connect him to a defined age. *(IV 288)*

See also Boredom, Change, Immortality.

Endymion   A story told by the third-century poet Theocritus

about a young shepherd whose great beauty seduced Selene, the moon, to come and lie beside him. At Selene's request, Zeus grants Endymion a wish. Desiring perpetual youth, he requests eternal sleep. Night after night the moon visits and covers him with kisses, although this unrequited passion brings Selene great pain.

Lestat refers to Endymion when he describes the way Louis moons over his lost mortal nature. He is as helpless as the moon goddess, who wishes for Endymion's love in vain. *(IV 83)*

See also Louis de Pointe du Lac.

Enkil An ancient Egyptian king who reigns before language was written and who is the first vampire made by Akasha.

Enkil marries Akasha, and together they turn their people away from the practice of cannibalism and toward a worship of Osiris and the cultivation of grains. He has a vision of all things united in good, of channeling all forces to the same divine course. *(QD 314)*

However, when Akasha brings the twin witches Mekare and Maharet to their court, she invites disaster. A spirit named Amel besieges them, and Enkil, along with Akasha, attempts to harness the spirit's power for good. In the process, he and Akasha are struck down by their own people, who dislike their new decrees, and Amel enters Akasha, making her a vampire. In turn, Akasha passes vampirism on to Enkil. Together they become deities. *(VL 438)*

The vampires believe that Enkil houses the vampire spirit and that to destroy Enkil would be to destroy the entire vampire race. He and Akasha initially are trapped by rogue vampires for their blood, which is the most powerful because it is closest to the immortal source—the spirit Amel. Eventually Enkil and Akasha break free but become as living statues, motionless and silent. The Elder, an Egyptian vampire, stands guard over them for centuries, placing them in the sun when he tires of his task. Marius delivers the couple, known as Those Who Must Be Kept, from the Elder and keeps them in shrines that he builds around the world. *(VL 438, 448)*

In one such shrine, Marius reveals the king and queen to Lestat. Lestat succeeds in waking Akasha from her trance, but Enkil also awakens and moves to protect her. Lestat believes that Enkil actually imprisons her in the trancelike state. *(VL 386, 487)*

Marius keeps Enkil and Akasha safe for nearly two thousand years, until 1985, when he finds Enkil's transparent corpse, bloodless and deteriorating. This makes it clear that Akasha is really the one who keeps the vampires alive, and that when she had no more need of Enkil, she destroyed him. *(QD 29)*

See also Amel, Akasha, Osiris, Shrine, Those Who Must Be Kept.

Entombed vampires Starving vampires enclosed in a room below the cemetery of Les Innocents who scream for blood, release, and forgiveness. They are weak vampires who are unable to break out of their coffins, and thus, according to Armand, have not proved themselves worthy of the Dark Gift. *(VL 211, 224)*

Louis hears vampires screaming in the same manner when he goes below the Theater of the Vampires; it is possible that they may be the very same creatures that Lestat heard a century earlier. *(IV 302)*

See also Starvation, Theater of the Vampires.

Erasmus, Desiderius An early-sixteenth-century Dutch Renaissance scholar and Christian humanist, he published the first Greek version of the New Testament. Opposed to religious fanaticism, he attacked Luther's theology.

Dora reads this famous theologian as part of her religious studies. *(MD 81)*

See also Flynn (Dora).

Erebus According to Greek mythology, a place of darkness through which souls pass on their way to Hades. Lestat uses the word to refer to the vampire realm. *(IV 133)*

Eric A three-thousand-year-old vampire who accompanies Santino to the Sonoma compound when Jesse is there. Eric is one of the vampires who survives Akasha's worldwide vampire slaughter. Since he was made by Maharet, it is the strength of her blood that protects him from Akasha's destructive intent. Near the age of thirty when he became a vampire, he has brown eyes, wears handmade clothing, and exhibits androgynous grace. *(QD 155)*

See also Gathering of Immortals, Maharet.

Eric Sampson See Sampson, Eric.

Erotic That which strongly arouses sexual desire. The relationship of vampire to victim, and vampire to vampire, is inevitably erotic because of what the vampire is and what the vampire desires.

"The vampire is an inherently erotic image," Rice claims. "I suspect that it [the vampire] is an echo of the old lusty gods. For thousands of years religion included passionate, sensuous gods and goddesses, but we don't have them now. They're gone from our traditions, but the vampire image lingers in our imagination—this mythical creature that seduces you, puts his arms around you, kisses your throat, then kills you while you're in a state of great rapture. It's very sensuous."

Much of the sense of eroticism in the *Chronicles* arises from the

fine detailing of the vampiric experience, which is told with great delicacy, intense focus, and deep appreciation for the sensual, such as when Louis describes how Lestat's lips on his throat actually made the hair rise all over his body *(IV 18)*, or when Lestat tells the story of Gabrielle's transformation: "I drove my teeth into her, feeling her stiffen and gasp, and I felt my mouth grow wide to catch the hot flood when it came." *(VL 157)*

In IV, the encounter where Armand offers the mortal boy Denis to Louis has teasing sexual overtones, providing the buildup and frustration often associated with erotic literature. Louis drinks from Denis, rocking with him and feeling his erection, yet there is no climax for either party. *(IV 231)*

Later, Louis and Armand confess their mutual love, and touch each other in the intimacy of a quiet place, where their discovery of one another flowers. It is a description of the experience of first love, intensified because those involved are vampires, who feel more deeply than mortals and whose powers enhance their receptivity toward one another. *(IV 230)*

In VL, describing earlier times, Armand makes a pass at Lestat at the Palais Royal, when he strikes the pose of a beautiful and alluring male prostitute. Lestat is overcome: "We were the sum of our desires." *(VL 275)* Armand gently draws Lestat after him and, just as Lestat makes himself vulnerable, Armand attacks with a bite that is akin to rape: "He was draining me!" *(VL 276)* Lestat loses the sexual attraction he feels for Armand, although Armand continues to intrigue him.

When Lestat first sees Akasha, he is as frightened as he is intrigued. She is utterly beautiful, yet he wants to flee her presence: she is the powerful seductive vampire and he the epitome of an enticed victim. When he is actually alone with her, he uses a violin to wake her from her trance. She comes toward him and urges him to drink from her, sweeping him into a swoon greater than any he has ever known. The swoon increases in power and erotic sensation when she locks her teeth into his neck at the same time, creating a "shimmering circuit" of her blood passing into him and then back into her. The embrace rises to an orgastic moment—but Enkil interrupts and tears Lestat away from her. *(VL 487)*

See also Dominance/Submission, Intimacy, Relationships, Sensuality, Sex, Vampire.

Esau   A biblical reference to the son of Isaac. Esau was cheated out of his father's blessing and his birthright by his crafty brother, Jacob, who pretended to be Esau at their father's deathbed.

Louis feels that he is participating in a similar type of fraud when he pretends to be Lestat for Lestat's dying father, although Louis is really only carrying on the pretense to be kind to the old man; he is not attempting to cheat Lestat out of anything. *(IV 55)*

Estelle   A female vampire in Armand's second Parisian coven who is one of the actors in the Theater of the Vampires. Estelle informs Claudia that the capital crime among the vampires is boredom. *(IV 244)*

See also Theater of the Vampires.

Estrangement   The development of animosity or indifference where formerly there had been love; estrangement seems to be an inevitable development in the relationship between vampires and their children. This fate is foreshadowed in the fact that vampires cannot hear their children's thoughts, although they can hear what other vampires are thinking. "The Dark Trick never brings love, you see," Armand warns Lestat. "It brings only the silence." *(VL 249)*

Estrangement first occurs between Lestat and Claudia. Claudia grows to hate him so much that she attacks him, and afterward, Louis ends up feeling estranged from Claudia. He cannot accept how vicious she was with Lestat, and he does not want to sleep with her or speak to her. She eventually wins him back, but he is still uneasy around her. *(IV 140–141)*

Gabrielle's estrangement from Lestat is caused by her cold and distant personality, and in the way her values contrast with his. She prefers to wander all night communing with nature, while Lestat would rather spend his time reading or talking with mortals. She finally drifts away from him, leaving him depressed and lonely. *(VL 354)*

Although alienation seems to be a vampire's lot, Louis and Lestat work to overcome that which has grown between them; they realize that they care deeply for each other and desire to be reunited despite their past hurts. *(VL 526)*

See also Intimacy, Relationships, Veil of Silence.

Eucharist   The Holy Communion, the most important of the seven sacramental ceremonies originated by the Roman Catholic Church. It involves the conjunction of spirit and flesh, also known as transubstantiation. Bread and wine are used to symbolize the flesh and blood of Christ the Savior. In the rite they are thought to change into real flesh and blood, enabling believers to be made one with the transcendent God. Through the blood, penitents are washed clean of sin and infused with the power of the Holy Spirit.

The Eucharist figures both physically and conceptually in *The Vampire Chronicles*. Vampires mirror this sacrament, for the spiritual power of Amel works on their blood, "not only to animate the tissue, but to convert it slowly into something else." *(QD 128)* This connection with such a profound religious ritual adds spiritual depth to the vampire image, and when the vampires refer to the Eucharist, it is often a metaphor of some facet of themselves.

Louis had been a devout Catholic when he was mortal, but his vampire nature gives him a different perspective on the sacraments. He visits St. Louis Cathedral in New Orleans, where he has a vision of himself trampling the sacred wafers, or symbolically crushing his faith. He even goes to confession and ends up, in an act of revolt and despair, killing the priest on the steps to the Communion rail. *(IV 145)*

Lestat acts as a priest for his mother Gabrielle on her mortal deathbed in VL. Gabrielle has refused the official church priest for her Last Rites and chooses Lestat as a priest-substitute. He takes her life and gives her immortality through his blood, which symbolizes the Viaticum, or the last Communion before death. Although no actual Communion is administered, the parallel is clear. *(VL 157)*

Similarly, as Armand makes Daniel a vampire, Daniel imagines Armand as a priest offering his blood as the Holy Communion wine. "Drink, Daniel," Armand tells him. Then Daniel envisions the red-haired twins offering their mother's brain and heart, which are symbolic of Christ's body, to be devoured. *(QD 114)*

Vampires simultaneously mimic and pervert all kinds of Catholic rituals. The Eucharist is evident in the very nature of the vampire, since the race originated with the penetration of a spirit, Amel, into the flesh of the Egyptian queen Akasha. This event is similar to the infusion of the power of the Holy Spirit into the bodies of mortal worshipers. Just as Christ was both man and God, so also do the vampires mix the human and the supernatural. Blood is central to the essence of the vampire, as it is to Catholics, and the vampire acts as a priest, dispensing the possibility of transcendence and rebirth into immortality. The victim senses transformative possibilities, which makes the vampire as seductive as the Church's equivalent promises.

See also Priest, Religious Images, Transubstantiation.

Eugénie   One of only four vampires from Armand's first Parisian coven who survive Armand's attempts to destroy them, and who goes to Lestat for help. She becomes one of the founding members of the Theater of the Vampires. *(VL 246)*

See also Armand's Coven, Theater of the Vampires.

Eve   The first woman, she was created by God to be Adam's mate in Eden.

After Akasha dies, Lestat refers to Maharet as the "Eve" of the vampires, the new "Mother of Us All." *(MD 347)*

See also Akasha, Maharet.

Evil   Something that causes suffering, calamity, or wanton destruction.

Rice views evil as being concrete and as what we do to others:

"Evil happens when we hurt each other. It's frequently connected with viewing people as symbolic—as objects." She detests religions or other philosophical systems that inspire maiming or killing of people in the name of an idea. Yet rarely is evil present in purified form; that's what makes it difficult to detect.

"To understand evil," says Rice, "you have to understand all its motives." She does not wish to glorify it or to urge her readers to sympathize with it. In fact, of BT, she says, "Its evil is that Lestat is evil and that he triumphs *again*. Life is filled with those bargains [e.g., in BT, body switching] with the Devil."

Some of the vampires, particularly Louis, struggle with the concepts of good and evil. Louis believes that as a vampire and a killer, he is of the Devil and is therefore evil. For him, being evil is a dark and empty existence, a "great perilous gulf." *(IV 236)* He resists both Lestat's notion that evil is merely a point of view and Armand's claim that there are gradations to evil. He insists that there really is no consolation in either of these points of view, although he can find no evidence within his supernatural condition for a clearly defined absolute evil. *(IV 319)*

Eventually Louis realizes that the root of his evil is his passivity, that he allows things to happen that he knows to be wrong, like the making of Claudia and Madeleine. He is spinning the very web that makes him a victim. Because Louis shrinks from acting as an evil creature, Claudia feels that she suffers for it, and it makes their vampire experience less than it could be. "Your evil is that you cannot be evil," she tells him. *(IV 263)* Nevertheless, he continues to view himself as damned, and the crowning evil, he believes, is that he and Armand can love each other even when there is nothing in either of them but evil.

Although Lestat eventually agrees with Louis that vampires are evil and thus unredeemable, he resists Louis's despair and is able to view the problem of his evil more philosophically. Lestat believes that just as forms of goodness change over the ages, so do forms of evil. He views Armand's satanic practices as being passé, belonging to a defunct Christian age that gave that form of evil meaning. "I am the vampire for these times," Lestat announces to Armand's coven. *(VL 228)* By that he means that he represents a new form of evil that is more in line with the secular beliefs of the age: he is the monster who looks and dresses like a mortal and who mingles freely among mortals rather than hiding out in cemeteries.

Lestat realizes that pure evil has no place in the twentieth century, that it cannot be exonerated or befriended. This fact makes him and all other vampires irrelevant, except as an art form that repudiates evil. Hence he becomes a rock star to do just that. Lestat wants to believe that he can create a purpose for himself by showing mortals how evil vampires are through his music. Humans can then eradicate the evil in

their midst. By BT, however, Lestat realizes that he is fooling himself by believing that he can redeem himself by using his evil for good. He *is* a vampire; he *is* evil; and he has freely chosen it. *(BT 70, 418)*

Armand honors evil in his Parisian coven; he views himself as a "saint of evil." *(VL 312)* He cannot be mediocre, petty evil, as he imagines Lestat is suggesting when Lestat urges him to join the theater group. Gabrielle tells him to make the theater *uncommon* evil, to shape it with his vision and use his vampire sensuality to join the carnal and the spiritual. Armand decides to try to do so and a century later, when Louis arrives, Armand has achieved his goal. The performances, while evil, are also spiritual, and the paintings the vampires collected to decorate their lair are great works of macabre, tormented art. *(IV 217–230)*

When the Devil comes to Lestat, he claims that his name is Memnoch, and that he despises evil, and that it is God who is responsible for all human suffering. Memnoch requests Lestat's assistance in stemming the tide of evil before it destroys the world. He believes that suffering and death are the worst flaws of God's creation, and he desires to change the direction of its evolution. Although God claims that the magnificence of suffering is its capacity to bring humans close to Him and to provide a path to redemption, Memnoch dismisses this imperfect reasoning. He cannot believe that suffering is necessary for goodness and feels it is simply evil. *(MD 138–139)*

Lestat is nearly convinced by Memnoch's story, but when his refusal to assist Memnoch unintentionally contributes to increasing human faith in Christianity, Memnoch tells him he performed his role perfectly. Lestat is confused over whether the Devil—the Father of Lies—actually duped him into contributing to evil or whether everything he had heard was true and all evil emanates from God. It is an issue he cannot resolve. *(MD 353)*

See also Devil, Faust, God, Goodness, Human Evolution, Memnoch, Redemption, Rock Star, Suffering.

Evildoers   People who seek to harm others, they are the type of victim that both Marius and Lestat prefer. *(VL 424)*

See also Roger, Serial Killer.

Evil Eye   What the Fang Gang calls the ability to look at mortals and get them to behave in a certain manner. *(QD 48)*

See also Fang Gang.

Extraordinary life   Developing exceptional qualities by enhancing or adding to existing abilities.

The vampires themselves provide a metaphor of enhancement and extension because they are, as Lestat puts it, the nonpareils of their

species. They have an extreme body awareness because they are anchored to substance in a way that powerfully binds spirit to matter, and they are capable of profound sensations and activities. They use their bodies in ways available only to some humans—most notably mystics—and many see this freedom from their former limitations as liberating. *(IV 20–21)*

Vampires embody and enact a wide variety of areas of nonutilized human potential. Having once been human, they realize how limited that experience was. In part, vampire abilities derive from the change in cellular structure that had taken place with the infusion of the spirit Amel, but a psychological component also affects the expression or exhibition of these vampire powers: each vampire can choose to live fully or can willfully block his or her full range of potential. Lestat is an example of the former; Louis, the latter.

The following vampire powers are each an enhancement of human abilities:

1. Heightened perception—the ability to see the environment in a fine detail that escapes most humans and to hear sounds beyond the range of the human ear. Vampires feel pleasure and pain acutely, and are much more physically sensitive than they had been as humans. *(IV 20)*

2. Hyperdimensional consciousness—transcending limitations in awareness and gaining clarification on natural processes and the cycle of life and death. Lestat calls this the ability to see as if from a god's point of view. *(IV 82)*

3. Lightning speed—the ability to move so fast that, to mortals, vampires seem to disappear. However, vampires themselves perceive their own movements as slow. *(IV 25)*

4. Clairvoyance—the ability to read minds and intrude on the thought processes of others. *(VL 284)*

5. Androgynous power—the state of transcending socially imposed gender role limitations. As such, vampires have access to greater energy resources made available through the broader range of experiences that accompany transgender activities. *(VL 171)*

6. Unitive mind—the knowledge that something greater than the individual connects the species. For vampires, this connection comes from the spirit Amel, and some vampires understand that to surrender to this force is to achieve greater strength and a wider range of abilities. Vampires use this network or web to send along warnings, visions, dreams, and inquiries to other vampires. *(QD 110)*

7. Greater concentration—the full participation in the experience of a vampire.

Thus, vampires illustrate a new paradigm of what it can mean to be human. If humans were to fully achieve their powers, they could move freely into life, accepting it with all its ambiguity and unforesee-

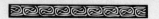

able possibilities, and thus enhancing their possibility for greater creativity. Just as the cells of a vampire regenerate into a new structure, so can the life of a human who seeks to transcend ordinary limitations.

There is a dark side to consider, however, before embarking on this path. Individuals who have experienced heightened consciousness or who have broken through to new abilities or achievements previously considered impossible claim that the experience can stimulate destructive energy. Egocentrism, addiction, despair, and even psychosis can result. Nicolas presents a portrait of being overwhelmed by his vampire powers to the point of madness. (VL 342)

See also Androgyny, One Powerful Mind, Reading Minds, Senses, Telepathic Powers, Vampire Powers.

Eyes   Many descriptions of characters throughout the *Chronicles* center on the color, luminosity, or impact of their eyes.

Louis thinks that the experience of looking into his brother's blue eyes is similar to standing alone on a windswept beach at the edge of the world. When Paul is dead, Louis wants to open Paul's eyes because to him they represent life. (IV 9)

Louis himself is described as having brilliant green eyes that look like flames lighting up a skull. Vampirism has given his eyes a luminescent glow that contrasts sharply with the dead whiteness of his skin; his eyes attract mortal victims. (IV 3)

Lestat describes his gray eyes as having the ability to absorb colors and thus to become blue or violet. Gray is the color of ambiguity—neither black nor white, but a mix of both. Lestat himself is the essence of ambiguity, for he strives to be both good and bad, vampire and human, saint and devil. When he wants to mingle with mortals, he often wears sunglasses to shield mortals from his penetrating stare and to prevent suspicion about the unusual quality of his eyes. (VL 3, BT 12, 54)

Mekare and Maharet believe that because the eyes are connected directly to the brain, the seat of consciousness, eyes take on special significance. They symbolize vision and perception. When the twins' mother dies, they prepare her eyes with her brain to be consumed in a ritual celebration, and Mekare, who has greater spiritual vision, is chosen to receive the eyes and brain into herself. (QD 323)

Akasha's soldiers pluck out Maharet's eyes to punish her for the "evil" she has envisioned against Enkil and Akasha, the king and queen of Kemet. Khayman gives them to her afterward and she consumes them. Hereafter she must then rely for sight on the eyes she takes from her victims, which fail to last for very long. (QD 411)

When Memnoch wants to give Lestat proof that, as the Devil, he possesses secret knowledge, he tells Lestat to ask Dora about her uncle Mickey's eye. When Lestat does so, Dora relates the story of how her uncle Mickey had a falling-out with a bookie, who then had him beaten up in a bar. Thugs tore out his eye and stepped on it, and relatives ever after claimed that it could have been saved if only they had not crushed it. Lestat finds the story interesting, not realizing that it foreshadows what is about to happen to him. *(MD 138, 152–153)*

When Lestat attempts to flee from Hell, Memnoch reaches to grab him but instead tears out his left eye. The souls in Hell shout at each other to step on it. Lestat escapes, fearing he has lost his eye for good, in a way similar to Dora's Uncle Mickey. But Maharet—the vampire whose eyes had been torn from her—returns the eye to Lestat, along with a message from Memnoch thanking him. The impression is that the Devil had set Lestat up. He puts the eye back into its socket, and it instantly heals. His vision grows stronger with his increasing realization of the possibility that he has seen the terrible reality of God's plan for the world. *(MD 320, 349–350)*

See also Appearance, Corona's Bar, Hell, Lestat de Lioncourt, Maharet, Uncle Mickey, Vampire Eyes.

"Eyes of the Mummy"

"Eyes of the Mummy" Robert Bloch's contemporary short story about a man who accompanies an archaeologist to Egypt to explore a recently discovered tomb. Purportedly the mummy inside is that of a priest who worshiped Sebek, a dual god of light and dark who demanded blood sacrifices.

As the narrator and the archaeologist open the mummy's box, they observe that the eyes have been replaced by strangely luminous yellow stones. The stones turn out to have absorbed the will and intelligence of the dead priest, whose only thought was to eventually achieve resurrection. The narrator is hypnotized by these stones and his soul is switched with the one that resides within the mummy. He finds himself locked inside the mummy's rotting body, while the soul of the priest walks away in his vibrant body.

Lestat receives this story from Raglan James in London. It is one of several fictional pieces about body switching that James uses to impart to Lestat his intentions of exchanging bodies with him. *(BT 83)*

See also Body Switching, James (Raglan)

Fallen Angels   The angels that rebelled against God and were cast to earth. The Book of Revelation indicates that fully one third of the angels fell with Lucifer. Some lore holds that they became demons.

Memnoch tells Lestat that while some of the angels followed his example in cohabiting with mortals, they repented sincerely enough for God to accept them back into His presence. There actually are no fallen angels, although angels do roam the earth in human form. When God condemns Memnoch to wander among humans, Memnoch requests these angels for his assistants. God refuses, telling him he must recruit assistants from among the souls in Sheol. *(MD 238, 293–294)*

See also Angel, Demon, Memnoch, Sheol, Watcher.

Fall of the [Rebel] Angels   The name of a painting by Pieter Brueghel the Elder that Louis sees in the subterranean ballroom below the Theater of the Vampires. It depicts the damned being driven from Heaven into a chaos of monsters. *(IV 229)*

See also Art, Brueghel (Pieter), Subterranean Room.

Family   A group of individuals who share common ancestry or who live together in familial relationship under one roof. Family exists literally and metaphorically to shelter and/or enable creative potential. It is also the arena for the potential conflict that can arise between conformity and individuation. While often demanding certain sacrifices, a family can provide support, identity, and a sense of personal continuity.

Both Louis and Lestat describe their mortal families: Louis has a mother, brother, and sister, while Lestat has a mother, father, and several brothers. Louis watches his family age and die (except for Paul, who dies young). Lestat saves his mother, Gabrielle, by making her a vampire (although Lestat's mother in the first draft of IV died young),

Fall of the Rebel
Angels, *Pieter Brueghel
the Elder*

and he joins his blind, aging father over in New Orleans after becoming
a vampire. Eventually Lestat asks Louis to kill his father, because he
cannot.

Lestat expresses more of a need for family than Louis. As a
vampire, he likes to feed on one member of a family after another.
Louis views this behavior as a supreme act of contempt against life, but
the fact that Lestat gives his mother the Dark Gift to keep her with him
and that he remains with his father—a grumpy old man—until his
father's death indicates his powerful desire for family bonds. *(IV 44,
VL 157)*

Louis and Lestat live together as loosely allied outsiders until
they make the child Claudia into a vampire. They then form a new
family unit, with two fathers and a child, although Louis functions as
more of a mother. (In one script Rice wrote years ago for a possible film
treatment of IV, she makes Louis into a woman). Together the three
vampires present the picture of a dysfunctional family bound together
by love and hate. *(IV 117)* Lestat had made Claudia to keep Louis with

135

him in the same way that some couples desperately have children to form a bond as all their other marital ties are breaking down. In such families, the stress might end up destroying the child. This becomes the case with Claudia, who eventually reaches the point at which she can stand it no more and attempts to kill Lestat. *(IV 95)* Her actions eventually bring about her own destruction.

Despite Claudia's rage against Louis and Lestat for making her a vampire, she does adopt traits from them, just as a human child might from his or her own parents. Evident in her is Louis's understanding of economics and love of books; from Lestat, she seems to have received a passion for spending money and the ability to kill without compunction.

Despite being part of this family unit, Claudia exhibits an overwhelming longing for a true mother, as Lestat points out about her blood thirst: "Claudia has a taste for families." *(IV 131)* When she kills

Vampire fangs

a mother and daughter who had been loyal servants, her message is clear: Lestat and Louis have taken her from her mother and she is looking to find that bond again. *(IV 106–107)*

When Claudia becomes aware that she was once a mortal child, she becomes angry and rebellious, like a teenager trying to upset the status quo. Claudia tells Louis they must leave Lestat, and the declaration shakes him out of his self-imposed habituation to Lestat. Claudia takes it into her own hands to destroy the family unit, and Louis passively acquiesces. *(IV 125)*

In Paris, what remains of their family is threatened again. Louis feels an attraction to Armand, but faced with the possibility of leaving Claudia, he cannot abandon her; she is his child. However, Claudia finds a substitute for him in Madeleine, a full-grown woman who has lost a child her age and who can be a surrogate mother to her. *(IV 258–265)*

See also Claudia, Dream of Family, Madeleine, Relationships.

Fang Gang   The vampire coven made of motorcycle riders named Killer, Davis, Tim, Russ, and Baby Jenks. They listen to Lestat's music as they dance in graveyards, and are on their way to San Francisco to support Lestat when they are annihilated by Akasha. *(QD 42–49)*

See also Baby Jenks, Davis, Killer.

Fangs   Vampires grow tiny sharp teeth which they use to open the veins of their victims and drink their blood. Louis's fangs develop slowly, so he must tear open the throat of his first victim. *(IV 29)* Lestat thinks fangs send a "primal message of alarm" *(BT 57)* through mortals, who react as if an animal is attacking them, and the tiger's fangs in his dream show how the tiger symbolizes him. *(BT 55)*

See also Bite, Tiger, Vampire's Kiss.

Farm   The image Louis has of where Lestat came from, because he heard Lestat's father reminiscing about his "little farm." (Actually, Lestat was raised on a large estate in France.) *(IV 36)*

Father Kevin   The Jesuit priest and Latin scholar who helps Roger translate Wynken de Wilde's books in a covert exchange for Roger's physical, semierotic proximity. Father Kevin discovers that Wynken was a heretic in love with his brother's wife. He urges Roger to sell the books to pay for a college education. Later he sends Roger a more complete history of this mystic. *(MD 63, 64, 66)*

See also Roger, Wilde (Wynken de).

Father of Lies   The name Claudia uses for Lestat when she is angry that he hides from her the truth about her origins. It is another

name for the Devil. *(IV 133)* Lestat refers to the Devil's dishonesty as well, feeling that Memnoch may have duped him. *(MD 136)*

See also Devil.

Faubourg St.-Germain　An elegant, aristocratic section of Paris in the seventh arrondissement where, in the first version of IV, Armand and his vampire coven live in an old mansion. The Faubourg St.-Germain lies in the Left Bank of the Seine, across from the Tuileries and east of the Invalides. It is known for its stately private residences, many of which have become government buildings. (See Vampire Atlas)

See also *Interview with the Vampire*, Paris.

Faubourg St.-Marie　The name for the uptown area of the Garden District in New Orleans at the time Louis was a mortal. *(IV 326)*

Faust　The protagonist of the classic seventeenth-century story told by Wolfgang von Goethe as a two-part poem. Heinrich Faust is weary of life and longs to experience a moment of existence so intense and so satisfying that it would inspire a hunger in him for immortality. To achieve this, he makes a pact with the Devil and sells his soul.

Influenced as a child by Gounod's opera *Faust*, Rice read the poem as she prepared to write BT. About BT, she said: "It has to do with the extent to which we all sell our souls to the Devil. There's this bottom line of ruthlessness in every person where you decide what you have to do to make life exciting enough. That's what the whole book is about to me."

What she appreciated in Goethe's version was the fact that Faust follows the Devil yet still manages to defeat evil and find redemption. He lets loose his true human desires but is not banished by God, as was the case in older versions of the story. This echoes Rice's own rejection of doctrinal religious judgments that vilify the darker aspects of human experience. Lestat refers to *Faust* repeatedly in the fourth *Vampire Chronicle*, providing a subtle but forceful theme: the human potential for self-improvement, even if it results in misguided actions, is to be honored and celebrated rather than condemned.

In Goethe's story, Faust is a burned-out scholar who seeks to go beyond human limitations in order to discover the most intense dimensions of knowledge and experience. His previous efforts have been in vain, and he is contemplating suicide as an answer to his inner emptiness. He seeks wholeness, for so far his truncated life has been limited to the intellectual sphere. He longs for renewal but does not know where to get it.

As with many such archetypal situations, Faust must die in order

to receive a new life. He must travel through the shadows, represented by the appearance of Mephistopheles, who is the spirit of negation. Mephistopheles is Faust's dark side, the part of himself that he has repressed in his single-minded pursuit of the scholarly world. He must acknowledge this part of himself if he is to achieve transcendence. He seeks a way to believe in himself, but he can only do that by merging who he is with who he has pretended he is not.

Longing for knowledge of absolute truth, Faust turns to the supernatural—a book of magic. He relies on Mephistopheles to guide him, experiencing love, seduction (and corruption of the innocent Gretchen), accomplishment, status, and excess. None of these states, however, are lasting. Faust eventually dies in disillusionment, but Mephistopheles does not get to claim his soul. Instead, Faust is admitted to Heaven because of the integrity of his striving for truth and his desire to believe in something higher than himself.

In BT, Lestat and David Talbot each mirror the Faust story. Both buy copies of the book from the same shop in Amsterdam, and both are plagued with many of the same questions. The most immediate issue they face is whether one must sacrifice one's soul to achieve youth or immortality. A secondary theme involves the duality of the human soul, for which the vampire is a metaphor. *(BT 32)*

For both David and Lestat, the essense of life is striving for union with ultimate truth, although they approach this puzzle from different perspectives. David pursues this through mystic experiences, through dangerous situations, and through attainment of detailed knowledge of life's darkest secrets—the occult. For David, Lestat becomes a sort of Mephistopheles, tempting him to choose immortality as a vampire (although David denies that this is the case). *(BT 60)*

Lestat chooses a life of excess that takes him as close as possible to the utmost extent of his supernatural powers; he exposes himself to situations that challenge and stretch his powers. Like Faust, his adventures are larger than life, giving the two of them a kinship as tragic heroes who strive to triumph to the greatest degree their limitations allow. Unlike Faust, however, Lestat is not redeemed.

David takes his copy of *Faust* to Barbados after his ordeal with Raglan James. He now has acquired the body of a physically fit and beautiful twenty-six-year-old man and realizes he has achieved youth without selling his soul. He acquires immortality in the same way—without selling his soul—when Lestat makes him a vampire against his wishes. David later admits that he wanted immortality but, unlike Faust, could not in good conscience give in to his desires. So he is not Faust, although he now has the span of eternity to pursue the great questions. Lestat, too, is not Faust because, given the choice, he preferred a life of evil in which redemption is not possible. In fact, he *is* Mephistopheles, for he claimed David's soul. *(BT 410, 418)*

See also Goethe, Gretchen, Immortality, Lestat de Lioncourt, Mephistopheles, Talbot (David).

Fearful symmetry   A reference to the poem "The Tyger" by William Blake. David Talbot uses the term, as Blake did, to describe God's creation. *(BT 67)*

See also Blake (William).

Feast of All Saints   The Catholic Holy Day that follows Halloween, it occurs on November 1. It is a celebration of life, redemption, and immortality, wherein relatives of the deceased often go to cemeteries to whitewash the tombs and provide fresh flowers.

Claudia mentions this tradition when carrying a bouquet of white chrysanthemums. Ironically, she herself is the image of both death and immortality, for she is one of the living dead. *(IV 108)*

Feast of Samhain   A ceremony in which Druids sacrifice a great number of criminals, imprisoning them in giant wicker edifices that look like a female and a male—the Great Mother and her lover. The purpose of this sacrifice is to ensure the fertility of the crops. The ceremony takes place on November 1, the same day as the Feast of All Saints.

In VL, the Druids intend to transform Marius in this ceremony into their new god. They want Marius to restore the magic that was lost with the crippling of their old god, who has been mysteriously burned. *(VL 407)*

See also Druids, Marius.

Félix   A tall male vampire who is part of Armand's coven. He is one of only four who survive Armand's attempts to destroy the coven and he begs for Lestat's help. He is also a founding member of the Theater of the Vampires.

Lestat sees Félix's death through Akasha's eyes, for she burned Félix along with the other vampires she destroyed. *(VL 246, QD 250)*

Fever   The passengers aboard the *Mariana* suffer from a mysterious "fever," and some of them die. It involves a sore throat and weakness, and sometimes small wounds on their throats or bodies. This is actually Louis and Claudia at work, who wish to feed themselves blood without arousing too much suspicion. *(IV 163)*

See also *Mariana*.

Financial concerns   What the vampires do over the centuries for financial support. Louis owns a construction company, and he and Lestat both invest in property; Lestat makes money on his music and

books; and Armand pursues a wide variety of ways to make himself a millionaire.

See also Agents, Armand, Christine, Lestat's Houses, Materialism, Real Estate, Roget (Pierre).

Fingernails   They reveal the presence of a vampire because after the transformation, a vampire's fingernails look like glass. Some of the vampires wear gloves to hide them. *(VL 3, QD 151)*

See also Appearance, Vampire.

Fire   A form of energy associated with life, vitality, regeneration, spirituality, transcendence, and change. The medieval alchemists retained the notion from the ancient philosopher Heraclitus that fire is at the center of creation, being the primary agent of transmutation. All things derive from fire and eventually return to it. Without it, survival is difficult, although fire paradoxically possesses the power to destroy. Fire also shares qualities of the sun and, as such, partakes in the concept of divinity. Many cultures view fire as a means of purifying and/or annihilating forces of evil. Thus, fire is traditionally used against vampires, to burn their coffins or their remains after driving a stake through their hearts.

David Talbot tells Jesse that "vampires are endlessly associated with fires. . . . It is the one weapon they can use effectively against one another." *(QD 176)* Although vampires can be destroyed by fire, they often utilize fire for their own means, to destroy something or someone else.

The first fire mentioned occurs when Louis burns down Pointe du Lac to distract the slaves and allow him and Lestat to escape. The house becomes a funeral pyre for Lestat's dead father. The next night, Babette throws a lantern on Louis and he is stunned by the action, unable to save himself, until Lestat puts out the fire. Only later does Louis realize the danger he was in. *(IV 57, 70)*

Louis burns down his next residence as well. He and Claudia plan their trip to Eastern Europe, but when Lestat, whom they believe to be dead, turns up, a struggle ensues. Louis uses fire as a weapon and the town house goes up in flames. Louis and Claudia escape, erroneously believing that Lestat has perished. Many years later, Louis finds the town house restored, just as Lestat himself is restored. *(IV 158, 327)* Lestat gets his revenge over a century later when he burns down Louis's small hideaway. *(BT 270)*

Louis also helps Madeleine incinerate her doll shop. For her, fire is a means of destroying all traces of her mortal past; the fire allows her to let go of her grief over her daughter's death. As they watch the shop burn, Claudia says, "Fire purifies." But Louis rebuts, "Fire merely destroys." *(IV 279)* Their statements represent their different perspec-

tives: hers is active, his passive and filled with regret. Nevertheless, burning the plantation, the town house, and the doll shop all prefigure what Louis will do in his one act of purification: burning the Theater of the Vampires.

Lestat witnesses the destructive effects of fire when Magnus, his maker, jumps into the flames and destroys himself. *(VL 96)* Later Lestat hears that his friend Nicolas has done the same. This reminds him of his childhood fear of fire, which had been caused by the story of how the villagers had once burned witches at the stake. *(VL 343)*

Armand had seen his own maker, Marius, burned by fire and had mistakenly believed him to be destroyed. *(VL 297)* He also destroys part of his first Parisian coven by forcing them into the fire after Lestat has destroyed their belief structure. *(VL 243)*

Ironically, however, fire can originate within the vampires, as the most powerful ones demonstrate. Akasha generates fire simply by willing it when she burns down coven houses. She also incinerates other vampires via their combustible blood. *(QD 55, 131, 250)* Despite how threatening fire can be, there is a kind of kinship between fire and vampires: both feed on other lives to survive and both offer the double-edged gift of life and death. Attracted to fire, vampires often warm themselves with it, despite its destructive potential. Thus, it functions as a threat as well as a source of power, and both qualifies and enhances the vampire existence.

See also Madeleine, Magnus, Marius, Nicolas de Lenfent, Theater of the Vampires, Town House, Ways of Dying.

First Brood   The original group of vampires, made in ancient times. Akasha, an Egyptian queen, and her husband, Enkil, are the first two vampires. They make Khayman, who gives the Dark Gift to Mekare, who then passes it to Maharet. At first their powers are weak, and the blood thirst drives them to kill humans to survive. However, as vampirism spreads across continents and through centuries, the powers of this brood increase as their cells change and harden into an immortal substance. All survive to the twentieth century, when Akasha rises up, kills Enkil, and threatens Maharet and Khayman. Mekare then kills Akasha. *(QD 399–415, 417)*

See also Akasha, Enkil, Khayman, Maharet, Mekare.

First death   What Marius calls going into the ground when a vampire despairs of existence. It is a form of hibernation and starvation that prepares vampires for rising again into life; it imitates the cycles of life that allow them to endure. The first death is the time to make peace with all things, to descend to an inner stillness, and to dream the dreams of gods.

Marius, who awakens Lestat from this trance, is surprised that

Lestat experienced the first death before he had lived out a full lifetime. Few vampires come to such despair so quickly. *(VL 377)*

See also Underground.

First kill   The first time a vampire takes a mortal victim, draining him or her of blood. Both Louis and Lestat describe their first kill experiences in the *Chronicles*.

For Louis, the experience is a nightmare. He is completely unprepared. Lestat takes him to an encampment of runaway slaves and tells him to take one. He cannot do it, so Lestat captures the man and insists that Louis drink his blood. Louis's fangs are not yet developed, so he must chew the neck to get to the vein. He gluts himself and drinks to the point of the heart stopping, then feels shaken and sick. After drinking with his heightened vampire senses and killing a human being, Louis finds that his view of everything has changed. He develops more respect for life than he ever had as a mortal. *(IV 29)*

Lestat's first kill is Magnus's coachman, who calls Magnus his master. Lestat takes him quickly, fascinated by the stages of his death. As a result of his first kill, Lestat feels more powerful and his vision becomes sharper. *(VL 111)*

See also Killing, Victims.

Flagellation   The act of punishing or exciting by whipping. Daniel and Armand look together at a mural in the Villa of the Mysteries in

Flagellation scene in Villa of the Mysteries, Pompeii

Pompeii of a ritual flagellation. From the mural it is clear that whipping heightens erotic sensation in S&M practices. The mural serves as a metaphor of Armand's treatment of Daniel, in which Armand controls Daniel through the seductive tools of dominance and submission. *(QD 92)*

See also Dominance/Submission, Villa of the Mysteries.

Flaminia   The character that Lestat woos when he gets a part as Lelio in a play in Renaud's theater. *(VL 67)*

See also Lelio, Renaud's House of Thesbians.

Fledglings   What young vampires are called, but the term is relative since a one-hundred-year-old vampire would view as a fledgling a vampire recently made, while the six-thousand-year-old Khayman would view a vampire a century or two old as a fledgling.

Marius urges Lestat not to make fledglings before they have had a sufficient taste of mortal life. He also offers several other pieces of advice: fledglings should be kept as a family, not a coven, and only so many should be made in a century because succeeding "children" are going to be weaker. Also, fledglings should be chosen in love, so that the vampire who makes them can endure their company. *(VL 469)*

See also Children, Making a Vampire.

Flesh eaters   See Conspirators.

Flight   One of the powers vampires acquire as they age and move closer to what they are meant to be. Flying represents moral power, growth, imagination, and transcendence. Since the essence of a vampire is spiritual, vampires can move with a light step and eventually jump higher than mortals, levitate themselves, and fly across continents. It is a frightening and humbling experience for some, and requires lots of energy and a great force of will.

Akasha, Khayman, Pandora, Santino, and Marius all fly in QD, and Akasha teaches the skill to Lestat. *(QD 286)* He is frightened at first, but he utilizes it with glee when he transports Louis to London. *(QD 481)* He also employs it to fly into the sun when he decides to end his existence in BT, and in a scene later cut, he takes David through the air to Istanbul. *(BT 47)* Although it is one of his greatest powers, Lestat feels helpless in flight and experiences despair; he thinks that perhaps this power is related to a celestial realm and is final proof that vampires are not human. "We fear perhaps we will one night leave the earth and never touch it again." *(BT 232)*

See also Vampire Powers.

Flowers   Because of their fleeting bloom, they are transitory symbols of beauty and life. Their rounded shape is representative of the soul. Flowers often are present on occasions of death, such as funerals and death processions, and this is especially true of white flowers, which symbolize life after death.

In IV, wisteria covers the oratory where Louis sleeps in his coffin, and honeysuckle vines tangle themselves over the unused kitchen where Louis finds two of Claudia's victims, a mother and child. The night Louis makes Madeleine, he notices on the balcony a carpet of flower petals, in which Madeleine later bathes herself. *(IV 107, 273)*

Claudia collects flowers, as if seeking her lost innocence and acknowledging how fleeting her mortal life was. She pulls apart lavender while contemplating what Louis and Lestat did to her in making her a vampire, and she often puts petals in her hair. Rice creates a juxtaposition between the way Claudia collects flowers and kills, for Claudia collects lives more indifferently. Although Louis has tried to teach her about the beauty of life, Claudia treasures the beauty of flowers more than that of any mortal. *(IV 108, 206)*

Lestat remarks on the parallel for Claudia between flowers and mortals when she brings in a bouquet of white chrysanthemums—which to Claudia symbolize death—right after she has killed a mother and child. She also puts white chrysanthemums in a vase the night she kills Lestat, and laces some of them on the sheet in which she wraps his body. There is clearly a link among flowers, death, and life for Claudia. *(IV 130)*

In QD, as Daniel is about to become a vampire, he recalls that there is an ancient language in which the same word is used for both flowers and blood. Wisteria blossoms stroke his face as he makes the transformation, symbolizing that he is now a part of the living dead. *(QD 114)*

Wisteria

Flynn, Dora (Theodora)   Roger's only child, she preaches on television about nourishing the soul through religion. She sings and dances on her program and possesses intelligence, imagination, and charisma. Tall, with short, black hair and black eyes, Dora is obsessed with the moral state of the world. At the age of twenty-five, she boldly lives alone at St. Elizabeth's Orphanage and hopes to make a spectacular impact one day through religion that will change the world for the good. *(MD 11–13)*

Although Roger had hated Dora's mother, Terry, he had loved the daughter he had had with her. When Dora was six, Roger killed Terry and raised Dora himself, eventually sending her to Harvard, where she studied religion. Roger wanted her to share in his own spiritual beliefs, but she had other plans. Although Roger takes pains to prevent Dora from knowing about his drug dealing and racketeering, she discovers it and subsequently rejects his gifts. *(MD 72–82)*

Dora believes that, to revive Christianity, the world needs a new

revelation. In her opinion, prohibitions against sex from earlier times to the present are what destroyed it. She is looking for "the angel to come" who will provide a miracle that will inspire profound belief. *(MD 89)* "I have put a question to the supernatural," she says. "I have asked it to give me a vision." *(MD 158)*

After Lestat kills Roger, he goes to New Orleans, to Dora's home at St. Elizabeth's. Roger's ghost has urged him here in the hope that he can protect her. She encounters Lestat and realizes he is not human, but she shows no fear. She is hoping for a miracle, so she remains open to any type of messenger. When Lestat confesses that he is a vampire, she views him as a sign of confirmation. *(MD 110–128)*

Lestat transports Dora to Manhattan to show her Roger's relics, which are stored in the Olympic Tower. He tells her about his encounter with Memnoch, who claims to be the Devil, and she encourages him to go with Memnoch to see Heaven and Hell. *(MD 149–162)*

While Lestat is gone, Roger's death is discovered, along with his connection to Dora. Her televangelism show is canceled, and she remains in seclusion in Manhattan. Lestat returns and drinks from her menstrual blood, connecting with her in a way that nourishes him but does not harm her. She allows it, unafraid. She wants to sleep in his arms. *(MD 324)* He shows her Veronica's veil, astonishing her. Dora claims that God used Memnoch and Lestat for His own ends: to retrieve the veil and bring it to the twentieth century. Roger's death made all this possible. Grabbing the veil, Dora takes it to St. Patrick's Cathedral. *(MD 334–336)*

She declares it to be an authentic miracle, brought to her by an Angel of the Night. In short order, her news is televised around the world. People flock to Manhattan to witness the miracle, echoing the religious pilgrimages of former times when such icons were revered. Since Dora now has what she wanted, she deeds St. Elizabeth's to Lestat, along with all of Roger's treasures. Cutting all ties with her former life, she becomes the official guardian of the veil. Lestat is unhappy that he has lost her and distressed that bringing back the veil infused new blood into a religion he considers savage and destructive. *(MD 337–340)*

See also Blood, Christianity, Flynn (Terry), Lestat de Lioncourt, Olympic Tower, Religion, Roger, St. Elizabeth's Orphanage, St. Patrick's Cathedral, Veronica's Veil.

Flynn, Roger   The alias Roger uses to marry Terry. It prevents the marriage from being legally binding, but it gives Dora a name that will connect her to him. *(MD 101)*

See also Roger.

Flynn, Terry   Dora's mother, whom Roger married under a false

name. Five foot seven, with bleached blond hair, she had been a practical nurse for Roger's mother. On a visit to his mother, Roger had gotten Terry pregnant. To get the child, he married her. He offered her $200,000 to turn the baby over to him, but Terry kept Dora instead.

When Dora was only six, Terry decided to leave the state with her new boyfriend, Jake, taking Dora with them, so Roger killed them both. Terry was his fifth victim. He dumped their corpses in the swamps near the old forts on the Rigules River. *(MD 38–40, 72–78)*

On the very day Terry "disappeared," Dora had wished her mother dead. Believing there was some connection, she refrained for years from asking her father where her mother was. When he told her Terry had passed away, she did not press the matter. *(MD 78–125)*

Lestat sees Terry with Roger in Hell. Since she was one of his victims, she is bound to him there until they can both learn to accept and forgive. *(MD 313–314)*

See also Flynn (Dora), Hell, Jake, Metairie, Roger.

Fontainebleau   A town outside Paris where one of the royal palaces is located.

Louis goes to Fontainebleau to get away from Paris the night he sets fire to the theater. *(IV 311)* (See Vampire Atlas)

Fool of the Gods   A phrase used to describe the goodness, simplicity, and purity of Khayman's heart. *(QD 130)*

See also Khayman.

Forbidden acts   When Lestat becomes a vampire, he engages in several behaviors that, unbeknownst to him, are forbidden to vampires by the codes of the satanic covens. The Parisian coven in VL declares him to be an outlaw because he conducted business among mortals, sought the comforts of the hearth, attended mortal entertainments, entered churches, made another vampire without community consent and ritual, held property, flaunted his powers to mortals, and used the Dark Gift for mortal vanities. *(VL 226)*

Later, when Lestat publishes his autobiography and records his rock music, he is also engaging in forbidden acts, for he has revealed his name and the history of the vampires to the mortal world. *(VL 528, QD 11–12)* He also tells his name to Dora Flynn. *(MD 127)*

Marius, too, is declared a heretic because he mingled with mortals and used his powers for mortal vanities like art, of which the vampire covens do not approve. *(VL 296)*

The vampire who commits the most strictly forbidden act is Claudia. She has turned against Lestat, her vampire maker, in an attempt to kill him. In IV, this act is declared a capital offense by mem-

bers of the Paris coven, and they destroy Claudia in punishment. *(IV 249)*

Akasha, too, destroys vampires, committing the "capital crime" throughout the world. However, since she is the vampire through whom all other vampires are made possible, she sees herself as a deity who is above the laws. The vampires who survive her onslaught do not agree. Although they seem to have no qualms about her destruction of vampires, they do resist her plan to destroy mortals in mass numbers. Their plan to stop her is a moral imperative on their parts, and not a vampire law. When they destroy her, it is an effort to prevent further destruction rather than to punish Akasha for the breaking of laws.

See also Capital Crime, Great Laws, Names, Rules, Trial.

Forgiveness An unresolved issue between Lestat and his father keeps the father alive in the hope and need for his son's absolution. Irritated by the old man's plea, Lestat wants Louis to kill him, but Louis's compassion for the man urges him to demand that Lestat give his father what he asks for and forgive him for whatever wrongs he may have perpetrated. Although Lestat reluctantly does forgive his father, his voice is strained with annoyance. *(IV 55)*

Lestat is also faced with the task of forgiving Louis in BT because if he does not, he may destroy Louis. They sit together in a church as Lestat contemplates the fact that Louis denied him help when he needed it, and so he retaliated by burning down Louis's house. Lestat then shows his forgiveness by inviting Louis to live with him again. *(BT 402–406)*

After Memnoch explains the workings of God's creation and the plight of human souls to Lestat, he takes Lestat to Hell to see where souls remain until they are ready to be in God's presence. What prevents them from entering Heaven is the issue of forgiveness: they must learn to accept the suffering they have both received and inflicted. Perpetrators and victims are bound together in Hell until they let go of the suffering that joins them.

Memnoch learns about this principle in Sheol when God sends him to find ten souls worthy of Heaven. He encounters many enlightened souls who have come to terms with God's creation: "We accept that our lives have been wondrous experiences, and worth the pain and the suffering . . . and we have forgiven Him for not ever explaining it all to us, for not justifying it, not punishing the bad or rewarding the good." *(MD 254)*

See also Heaven, Hell, Redemption, Sheol, Soul, Suffering.

"Four Days in Another City" A poem by Stan Rice on the relationship between substance and perception that introduces Part 1 of QD—the assembling of the central characters.

"There's always a tug of war between what's there and what you think is there," Stan Rice explains. Substance keeps check on flights of imagination, threatens imaginative freedom, yet also provides the key source of inspiration. *(QD 33)*

See also Poetry, Rice (Stan).

Four Seasons   A hotel in Georgetown in the District of Columbia that overlooks the Potomac River.

Lestat reserves a room there when he first switches bodies with Raglan James. After he succumbs to pneumonia, Gretchen goes to the hotel to retrieve Lestat's money and clothing. *(BT 201)*

See also Georgetown.

Four Seasons Hotel, Georgetown

Fourth Crusade   The fourth in a series of military expeditions organized to recover the Holy Land from the Moslems. The First Crusade started in 1095. In the name of Christianity, it precipitated a great deal of pillage and slaughter for several centuries. One of the most horrendous episodes was the Fourth Crusade, launched by Innocent III in 1202. When he was unable to raise enough funds for the passage from Venice of ten thousand crusaders, the Venetians persuaded him to divert the Crusade from Palestine to Zara and then Constantinople. They were seeking monetary gain and redress of grievances. Thus, the Crusaders turned on their fellow Christians in the Byzantine Empire. They sacked Constantinople in 1204, destroying many irreplaceable books and relics and slaughtering the citizens. This Crusade weakened Byzantium, leaving it vulnerable to Islam.

Lestat finds himself with Memnoch in the midst of the violence of the Fourth Crusade because Memnoch wants to show him what a bloody, destructive religion Christianity became. (MD 286–288)

See also Christianity, Constantinople, Hagia Sophia.

Fragonard, Jean-Honoré   An eighteenth-century French artist to whom Lestat refers when speaking philosophically about the relationships among art, beauty, and savagery. (VL 131)

France   The country from which both Louis and Lestat originated. Louis emigrates to New Orleans from France, having received a land grant on which he establishes two indigo plantations. He still loves France and follows its political affairs, and feels that Europe shaped him both intellectually and emotionally. France draws him in a mysterious way, and eventually he returns there after he has become a vampire, seeking spiritual enlightenment. When he gains no real answers and loses his beloved Claudia, he leaves France to travel the world, eventually returning to America. (IV 4–5, 149, 204)

Lestat grew up in the French countryside as an aristocrat, all the while longing to make his home in Paris. He lives in Paris for only a short time before he is made a vampire. Shortly afterward he leaves France, and although he returns several times, he never makes it his home. Unlike Louis, Lestat never loses his appreciation for Paris. He is attracted by how lively and adaptable Parisians seem to be over the centuries. His penchant for New Orleans is his way of residing in America while retaining a French sensibility, since New Orleans was first settled by the French. (VL 23, BT 84) (See Vampire Atlas)

See also The Auvergne, Fontainebleau, Paris.

Franciscans   An order of priests and nuns who profess observance of the Rule of St. Francis of Assisi.

Dora wants the Franciscans to take custody of Veronica's veil. *(MD 339)*

See also Veronica's Veil.

Frankenstein   The name of Mary Wollstonecraft Shelley's nineteenth-century novel and of her fictional doctor, who creates an artificial man who becomes a monster. The monster itself came to be known as Frankenstein.

Lestat refers to himself as Frankenstein's monster when he takes on the body of a mortal in BT. His arms feel too long, his body too dense, and his hands unconnected. He feels disproportional, just as the monster was. *(BT 222)*

Free people of color   Black people in New Orleans who were allowed a limited number of rights, including practicing trades and educating their children. This put them on a level above slaves but one still not equal to that of whites. In a metaphoric way, these people echo the vampire, for both exist in a limbo. Rice writes about the free people of color at length in *The Feast of All Saints.*

Louis and Lestat use free people of color as their servants in their town house in New Orleans. *(IV 39)*

Free will   The struggle of the vampires against the limitations of their condition is a metaphor of free will, of being able to choose one's destiny rather than giving in to the dictates of conditioning or genetics. Without free will, the issues of morality would make little sense, and the *Chronicles* are inherently about moral heroes resisting their own inner evil.

Free will is an issue for Lestat when he muses over the possibility that people are doomed to some form of destiny. He does not relish being a pawn in the hands of some unknown force, and he insists that he is responsible for his choices. *(VL 344)*

"We have to continue to believe in free will," says Rice, "whether there's evidence for it or not. We must operate as if we are the moral beings of the universe."

See also Choice, Destiny, Moral Dilemma.

French Guiana   A South American country where Gretchen works in a mission hospital. She invites Lestat, when he is in a mortal body, to go there with her to do work that could save his soul. But he decides that he would rather attempt to regain his vampire form. After he succeeds, Lestat visits Gretchen in the mission to put into her hands the decision about joining him and becoming a vampire herself, but she is shocked and repulsed by him. *(BT 239, 347)*

See also Gretchen, Mission of St. Margaret Mary.

French Quarter   Also known as the Vieux Carré, it is the oldest part of the city of New Orleans. First settled by the French, it followed the plan of a late medieval town, with streets forming a grid around a large public square. The French Quarter extends from Jackson Square to Rampart Street and from Canal to Esplanade. Several events from *The Vampire Chronicles* occur in or around the French Quarter.

Lestat, Louis, and Claudia live in a town house on the Rue Royale. It burns in a fire, but Lestat and Louis later reclaim it. Lestat also keeps a penthouse apartment on Dumaine and Decatur, near the French Market. He visits his dog, Mojo, there. *(IV 100, BT 100, 273)*

Near Jackson Square, Claudia plots Lestat's destruction and Lestat meets Raglan James. They discuss James's proposal in the Café du Monde. *(IV 123, BT 118)*

Dora Flynn tapes her televangelism program in a French Quarter studio on Chartres Street, and it is here that Lestat grabs her and transports her to Manhattan. *(MD 12, 149)*

Lestat first sees Roger in a French Quarter bar. *(MD 13)* (See Vampire Atlas)

See also Café du Monde, Jackson Square, New Orleans, Penthouse Apartment, Spanish Hotel, Town House.

French Revolution   On July 14, 1789, peasants stormed the Bastille and overran the French aristocracy. Lestat and Gabrielle are out of the country at the time. Lestat receives word that his brothers and their families were slain in the revolt and that his father has fled to New Orleans. *(VL 340–341, 350)*

Freniere   The name of the family who owns the sugar plantation near Pointe du Lac, it is also the name of the plantation. Two of the Frenieres play significant roles in IV.

THE FRENIERE BOY   The only son and head of the family, Freniere is a young man Lestat targets to become his victim. The loss of Freniere's life means the potential loss of the family livelihood, since social propriety at the time dictated that women could not run plantations. Indifferent to these concerns, Lestat takes the boy anyway, which greatly upsets Louis. In VL, Lestat tells his side of the story; he claims that the Freniere boy deserved to die because he was a card cheat and wanton killer who was about to gamble away the plantation. *(IV 43–46, VL 499)*

BABETTE FRENIERE   Of the five Freniere girls, Babette is the most practical and intelligent. Louis falls in love with her strength, so he appears to her as an angel to guide her in the successful management of the plantation after her brother's death. When Louis is in need of assistance the night he burns down Pointe du Lac (it is nearly dawn and he can think of no other place to go), he turns to her. She helps him

but then sees him for what he is and demands that he leave. Louis is saddened by her loathing, because it mirrors his own. His tender feelings for Babette reveal to him the truth about immortality: those he loves will always die. When Lestat tries to kill her, Louis prevents it. *(IV 43–48, 57–71)*

To Louis's great regret, he later hears rumors that Babette died both young and insane, wandering toward the ruins of Pointe du Lac in search of the Devil. He recognizes that he and Lestat are responsible for this tragedy. *(IV 131)*

See also Insanity, Mortals.

"Frog Prince, The"   A children's fairy tale about a prince turned into a frog who must get a princess to take him as her companion or, in some versions of the story, kiss him. Only then will the prince's original form be restored.

Lestat refers to this fairy tale when he describes how he wants a mortal lover to understand and desire him with a spiritual love; this will give him back some sense of his mortality, just as the princess did when she finally made the frog human again. *(VL 337–338)*

See also Lestat de Lioncourt.

Funeral feast   When the mother of the twin witches, Maharet and Mekare, dies after she senses that evil lies ahead for them, the twins prepare her body for their tribal ritual. They remove her brain, eyes, and heart, then roast their mother in preparation for a noontime feast—the sacred moment of greatest illumination. (Because she was a witch, only her daughters are allowed to eat her.) Mekare takes the eyes and brain, Maharet the heart. As they are about to partake of the food, Enkil's soldiers interrupt the feast, upset the body, kill the villagers, and take the twins prisoner. This scene shows up in the Dream of the Twins that many of the vampires receive once Akasha rises from her comatose trance. *(QD 322–323)*

See also Cannibalism, Dream of the Twins, Legend of the Twins, Maharet, Mekare, Miriam.

Gabriel One of the archangels ("Hero of God"), he is Heaven's treasurer and one of God's primary messengers on Earth. Gabriel is the angel that told Mary she would be the mother of Christ, and Moslems believe he dictated the Koran to Mohammed. At the end of time, Gabriel will blow the final trumpet for the Final Judgment.

Gabriel accompanies Memnoch to question God about the things they observe during the creation of Earth and humanity. *(MD 205)*

See also Angel, Archangels.

Gabrielle Lestat's mortal mother and first vampire companion. She is named for an archangel and a messenger of God, who announced the birth of Christ and will also announce the Day of Judgment.

Gabrielle is a marquise, the wife of a blind and indigent lord in the Auvergne. Originally from Naples, she has eight children, but only three—all sons—survive to adulthood. Blond, with cobalt blue eyes, she keeps mostly to herself, reading books. She does not like to be touched or to communicate with words. She never voices ordinary thoughts and, when she does talk, can be blunt to the point of cruelty. She hates to be called "Mother" and exhibits no sense of humor. Her dream is to detach herself from her family and take lovers of all kinds to her bed. She wants to be purely herself, belonging to no one. *(VL 30–36)*

There is a bond between Gabrielle and Lestat, her youngest son, because they are alike in their hatred of castle life and their family's attitudes. They are two parts of the same soul, and Gabrielle tells Lestat that he is the male part of her, the organ she does not possess. She intervenes for Lestat when she can and uses her own gold and jewels to obtain things for him, like a pair of mastiffs, a riding horse, and a trip to Paris. *(VL 38–40, 60–62)*

154

Gabrielle has consumption, a fatal disease, and urges Lestat to leave for Paris before she dies. After he becomes a vampire, Gabrielle comes to Paris and Lestat visits her. Gabrielle realizes that he is "not alive," and when he offers existence as a vampire to her, she takes it without hesitation. Their union as they engage in the transformation is highly erotic. *(VL 157–158)*

"She was the best person around for Lestat," says Rice. "It took a great act of maturity for him to realize that this was the person he wanted, even though she was his mother. He treated her as an equal."

As a vampire, Gabrielle quickly discards her mortal ways and female garb; she wants to be free of all female entrapments. Instead, she dresses as a young man and chooses for herself the sarcophagus of a man, rather than one carved for a woman. She tries to cut her hair and when it grows back to its natural longer length, is greatly upset. *(VL 171, 180)*

Gabrielle is obsessed with finding truth and beauty in nature. Her curiosity leads her away from mortals, in much the same way she had been withdrawn from people in her mortal life. She wants to unite with that which never changes: the mountains, the jungles, the deserts. Soon she learns to sleep in the earth and abandons the use of coffins. She quickly acquires her own strength and no longer needs Lestat to be her "male part." She is completely androgynous, bold, tenacious, and practical. She embodies a sense of freedom that Lestat cannot grasp: the freedom from gender, social roles, familial expectations, and the demands of relationships. Despite Lestat's aspirations for their relationship, a strange mental silence falls between them; this is a metaphor of their destined estrangement. *(VL 178, 253, 331)*

Ganymede

Gabrielle claims that she would be happy if nature totally overran the world of men. In this desire, she prefigures Akasha. In fact, Gabrielle even predicts that some dark monarch may arise and attempt to sow chaos in the mortal world. She tries—and fails—to get Lestat to go with her to the jungles of Africa, to live in her world, with her vision. His continuing attachment to mortals irritates her, so she leaves him. *(VL 334–335, 347)*

The character shows up again near the end of VL; she is the limousine driver who takes Lestat away from his chaotic rock concert to a retreat in Carmel Valley. Their reunion is happy but short-lived, for Akasha abducts him that same night. Gabrielle then joins with other vampires in planning a stand against the vampire queen that could be potentially fatal for them all. *(VL 543, QD 276, 439)*

See also Androgyny, Gathering of Immortals, Nature, *The Queen of the Damned*, Relationships, Reunions, *The Vampire Lestat.*

Ganymede   A mythical young man of Phrygia who was so beautiful that Zeus, the king of the gods, took Ganymede into his service. The

name of this boy is used to denote any physically beautiful youth, and Daniel refers to Armand as a Ganymede. *(QD 82)*

See also Armand.

Garden District   An area in New Orleans that features antebellum Italianate and Greek Revival mansions. While Rice was growing up, she used to walk through the district, staring at the houses and imagining herself owning one some day. In 1989 she bought one of the Garden District mansions on First Street.

Lestat owns two houses in this district, and both are falling into ruin. The Garden District is also the setting in WH and *Lasher* for an investigation by the Talamasca. *(VL 5)* (See Vampire Atlas)

See also New Orleans.

Garden of Earthly Delights   A three-paneled triptych that Hieronymus Bosch painted around 1500. It is a panoramic scene in a gardenlike setting of densely compacted groups of people engaged in various sensual activities. The feeling is one of pandemonium.

Roger compares the tiny illustrations from Wynken de Wilde's prayer books with this painting. *(MD 61)*

See also Art, Bosch (Hieronymus), Wilde (Wynken de).

Garden of Waiting   The splendid setting in front of the giant Gates of Heaven, it is flooded with a benign, penetrating light. The colors are sharp and pure. Here Lestat sees individuals of varying degrees of distinctness greeting, embracing, and communing with one another. Souls come to this place during near-death experiences and are told it is not their moment and sent back to their earthly bodies. *(MD 163, 295–296)*

See also Heaven.

Garlic

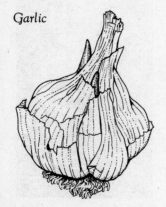

Garlic   The peasants of Eastern Europe used garlic in an attempt to ward off vampires. They attributed to it the power to cure illness and protect against evil spirits. Its origin as a vampire repellent is traced back to the Moslems' dislike of garlic, which they believed sprang up in Satan's footprints as he walked out of the Garden of Eden, combined with the Christian superstition that Moslem corpses were especially prone to becoming vampires.

The presence of garlic hanging over the door of an inn indicates to Louis and Claudia that the peasants think there are vampires nearby, but since using garlic is only a superstition, Louis and Claudia are not adversely affected by its presence. *(IV 172)*

See also Superstitions.

Gateway to innocence   Akasha's phrase for what she thinks she is, as the creator of a new world order. *(QD 369)*

See also Akasha's Plan.

Gathering of Immortals, The   In QD, after Akasha has destroyed most of the vampires around the world, the surviving vampires gather together to ponder their next move. "Marius had never laid eyes on such an assemblage—a gathering of immortals of all ages from the newborn to the most ancient; and each endowed with immeasurable powers and weaknesses. . . . Marius doubted that such a 'coven' had ever come together before." *(QD 278)* There are twelve of them: Santino, Pandora, Eric, Daniel, Armand, Louis, Gabrielle, Maharet, Mael, Marius, Khayman, and Jesse. They hypothesize that some of them were spared because Lestat might want to see them again, and others for Akasha's purposes. Also, as the oldest immortals, Maharet and Khayman were immune to Akasha's attack, and because Eric was made with Maharet's blood, he was immune as well. They are all that remains, says Maharet, in terms of destiny and decision.

The vampires gather together at Maharet's Sonoma compound in a mountaintop room of glass walls. They follow TV news reports of Akasha's rampages and debate how to stop her—they know that to destroy her means their deaths, since she is their life source. *(QD 264–285, 306–352, 378–390, 399–432)*

For two nights they listen to Maharet tell the story of the vampire origins. Then Akasha arrives, confronting them with the decision of joining her or dying. They attempt to talk her out of her plan but she deflects their reasoning with her own. As they talk, one other immortal, Mekare, is moving toward the gathering. She rushes in and throws Akasha against a glass wall, severing her head. The vampire race is saved when Maharet feeds Akasha's brain and heart to Mekare, giving her the organs with which Amel had fused to make the vampires. *(QD 435–456)*

The immortals recover, then go to Armand's Night Island off the coast of Florida. Eventually, they wander off, going their separate ways, while Lestat writes about them in QD. *(QD 461–473)* (See Vampire Atlas)

See also Akasha, Akasha's Plan, Maharet, Mekare, Night Island, Sonoma Compound.

Gaul   What Marius calls the place where the Druids live. Known to the Romans as Gallia, it included parts of Germany, Switzerland, the Netherlands, France, and Belgium. The Gauls are known as the Celts, who were eventually Romanized and Christianized. *(VL 400)*

Gehenna   The Jewish version of Hell, it was named after a fiery

157

garbage pit in Jerusalem's Valley of Hinnon, where the bodies of animals and criminals were tossed into fires that burned perpetually. During earlier times, human sacrifices to Moloch may also have been practiced in this pit. The concept of Gehenna as a place of torment derived from Sheol, the original resting place of deceased souls. At first, all souls were thought to go to Sheol, but eventually there seemed a need for a separate place for bad souls. Corrupt Jewish souls and all Gentiles were relegated to Gehenna. For the Jewish souls, however, the punishment was only temporary.

God describes Gehenna to Memnoch as a place of fire and eternal torment, using this image to threaten him. *(MD 236)*

See also Hell, Sheol, Soul.

Genesis   The first book of the Bible, it contains the story of creation.

Lestat mentions the opening phrase of Genesis, "In the beginning," when he is mulling over first lines in BT *(BT 2)*. David Talbot thinks that the answer to the secrets of the universe lie in this book. Since it mentions that God created man in His own image, David thinks that humans are thus meant to be creative forces. *(BT 68–69)*

See also Bible, "Giants in the Earth," God, Talbot (David).

Gentleman Death   The name Louis gives to Armand when Armand appears in a black cape and silk tie. Lestat refers to himself by this name in VL, when he shows Armand's ragged Parisian coven how they can dress better and walk about town with mortals. His image is a precursor of nineteenth-century tales of aristocratic vampires who mingle undetected with mortals. *(IV 280, VL 229)*

See also Vampire Tales.

Georgetown   The area of Washington, D.C., where Raglan James has a redbrick town house. Lestat meets James there to switch bodies. It is also the place where Lestat acquires his dog, Mojo, and meets Gretchen. *(BT 150)* (See Vampire Atlas)

See also Four Seasons, Gretchen, James (Raglan), Mojo.

"Get Thee behind me, Satan!"   In Mark 8:33, the words Christ spoke to Peter when Peter resisted the idea that Christ would soon suffer many things. Christ was rebuking him for turning his mind away from God's divine plan.

Babette quotes this phrase to Louis, to let him know that she now believes he is the Devil and wants him gone from her presence. *(IV 66)*

Ghosts   Although the *Chronicles* are primarily about vampires, Rice mentions other supernatural entities, including apparitions or ghosts.

Ghosts are spiritual entities but are differentiated from the spirits that Maharet describes in her story about vampirism, for ghosts once had physical bodies. Spirits like Amel have only had spiritual substance.

"I think ghosts probably exist," says Rice, "although I've never actually seen one. My feeling is that there's a great deal to be discovered about telepathy and the occult, and it revolves around energy."

The ghost of Louis's brother Paul is said to appear on the gallery where he fell to his death. *(IV 10)* Louis's appearance to Babette Freniere is thought to be that of an apparition. *(IV 46)* Lestat, too, is described as a ghost when he is seen killing one of his victims near a haunted house on Nyades Road near Melpomene. *(IV 111)* Later in IV, when Armand takes Louis up a tower in Paris, Armand informs Louis that the inhabitants of the house believe him to be a ghost and therefore will not disturb them as they talk. Louis is spooked by the idea of being perceived in this manner. *(IV 281)*

While they are on the Devil's Road, Lestat and Gabrielle study haunted houses to see what they can learn about other supernatural entities. They do see apparitions and hear strange voices but learn nothing that mortals have not already surmised. *(VL 166, 169)*

Ghosts play a larger role in QD, especially in the section that describes Jesse. Jesse has an extraordinary ability to perceive the spirit world. She can see the dim outline of buildings that no longer exist, like the Stanford White mansion, and she sees souls of the dead even in crowds. When they seem to become aware of her, she panics. However, when the spirit of her dead mother, Miriam, appears to her, Jesse feels comforted. Miriam's ghost continues to materialize, especially when Jesse is in danger. *(QD 148–150, 162, 171, 229)*

Maharet tells Jesse that spirits of all types are attracted to people with her coloring (red hair, pale skin, and green eyes); she also points out that ghosts like to waste people's time and can be vindictive. In fact, understanding them makes no difference to the larger scheme of things in the world. Basically, they are insignificant, although their existence may inspire the creation of harmful religions. As a result, Maharet feels that those who study spirits, like the Talamasca, cannot accomplish great things. Jesse, however, wonders if ghosts are people who cannot accept death, and describes their presence as a "dim and chaotic afterglow before the ultimate darkness." *(QD 169)*

Jesse also sees the ghost of Claudia, which interests the Talamasca for it is a new sort of paranormal phenomenon—the ghost of a vampire. Claudia appears to Jesse several times after Jesse discovers Claudia's diary in New Orleans. At first, she thinks the spirit is menacing, and she grows very ill. But afterward she believes that the spirit's appearance was significant in some manner, although Jesse is never able to ascertain what it meant. When Louis hears of this apparition, he goes to New Orleans to search for Claudia. *(QD 187)*

159

While Lestat is haunted by Claudia, she appears to him as a projection of his own troubled conscience rather than as an actual apparition. "Real hauntings," Lestat believes, "have nothing to do with ghosts finally; they have to do with the menace of memory." *(QD 478)*

Memnoch explains the phenomenon of ghosts as the tenacity of individuality to maintain its form and perpetuate itself. Self-consciousness and awareness of death created individuality, and individuality craved continuity. Having no other focus in Sheol, some souls desired to reach back into the world of their descendants to try to help them. *(MD 210)* "Some souls knew they were ghosts when they came to mortals. Others thought they were alive and the whole world had turned against them. Others simply drifted, seeing and hearing the sounds of other living beings but remote from this as if in a stupor or dream." *(MD 215)*

After Lestat kills Roger, Roger appears to him as a ghost in a bar in Lower Manhattan. He has no scent, but seems fully realized, appearing as he did before he had died (although he wears a different coat). Contrary to what ghost lore suggests, the bartender can see Roger, and Roger is able to drink. He is also aware of what Lestat is and that Lestat has killed him. He desires to tell his story so that Lestat will protect his daughter from his enemies. *(MD 48–50)*

See also Astral Tramps, Elementals, Haunted Houses, Roger, Sheol, Soul, Spirits.

"Giants in the Earth"

A phrase from Genesis 6:4 that refers to the mutant offspring that resulted when some of the angels defiled their holiness and coupled with mortal women.

Memnoch explains to Lestat that when he taught the skills of civilization to early human tribes in Palestine, they originally viewed him with suspicion and condemnation. Lies were told that fallen angels created giants by fornicating with human women when, in fact, no such offspring existed. *(MD 233)*

See also Angel, Fallen Angels, Genesis.

Girdle book

Sixth-century manuals, such as a prayer book, carried in a leather satchel called a *polaire*, that could be attached to a girdle or carried by hand.

Roger describes some of Wynken de Wilde's books as girdle books. *(MD 60)*

See also Wilde (Wynken de).

Gobi Desert

See Desert.

Goblet

A symbol of the human heart in Romanesque times; a container wrapped around a mystic center; a ritual instrument for

Goblet

feeding blood to the gods. A blood-filled goblet or chalice indicates resurrection; a smashed goblet, a vow that cannot be erased.

Lestat uses a goblet to drink a rat's blood, sipping it with elegance, as if he is drinking wine. Then he smashes the goblet in the fireplace; this act is a metaphor of his disdain for human life. *(IV 32)*

God   A being believed to have supernatural attributes and powers, the source of ultimate reality. God images in most cultures are represented as light or the sun. Although the vampires are creatures of the night, the idea of God, either as a deity who can potentially damn them or as a nonexistent and thus empty concept, is a focal point for them.

As a mortal, Louis was a Catholic, although when he first hears about what it is like to be a vampire, he recognizes that his true gods were actually food, drink, and the security that arises from conformity. When he becomes a vampire, he sets out to find out what God means in the context of his former religious beliefs: Is he, as a vampire, damned? Or is there no God, and thus no absolute meaning in the universe to condemn him? The positive confirmation of either question would be abhorrent to him, yet he persists in his quest for answers. *(IV 13, 16)*

When Louis encounters Armand, he asks what Armand, as the oldest vampire he has ever met, knows of God. Armand claims to know nothing, which depresses Louis. If he and the other vampires are the only existing creatures with supernatural powers and higher consciousness, yet have no knowledge of a supreme deity, then *they* bear the burden of making meaning; *they* are the gods, deciding ethical questions and creating definitions for good and evil. To him, then, taking life would be evil, because life is all anyone has. *(IV 236–238)*

What Louis is describing is Nietzsche's concept of the "overman"—a person of moral courage who can face ultimate nihilism and use it to create new values rather than succumb to despair. Louis understands the position but cannot achieve it; he is a victim of nihilism, not a moral hero, and thus fails to possess the requisite self-esteem. Yet despite not knowing how to now define evil in the absence of an Absolute Power, he continues to think of himself as evil.

He speaks about Satan, which puzzles Armand, for if Satan is the source of evil, and if God as the Creator also created Satan, then all evil ultimately derives from God; vampires would be, as the children of Satan, the children of God. Louis cannot accept Armand's logic. *(IV 236)*

Lestat, on the other hand, wastes little time on this issue. Although he cries out to God to help him when Magnus abducts him, he comes from a Catholic family of little religious fervor. He is not so sure that he even believes in the being to whom he so desperately prays. After he becomes a vampire, it soon becomes evident to him that no

God exists; this fact is further clarified for Lestat when religious icons fail to have any adverse effect on his vampire body. Yet unlike Louis, Lestat is ready to take on the consequent rush of religious nihilism and to make the most of his new status as a vampire. Once he realizes that good and evil are neither absolute nor originating with a source external to himself, he decides what he himself thinks it means to be good while still being evil. *(VL 101)*

That Lestat possesses godlike qualities is suggested by the halo that Louis sees around Lestat's head during an argument Lestat is having with Claudia. Lestat has indicated that he is a giver of immortal life, but Claudia resists his self-elevated status; her frustration is similar to that of mortals from whom a supreme deity withholds knowledge. Claudia decides that Lestat, in fact, knows nothing, but she is mistaken for, like a god, he actually knows a great deal more than he is telling. *(IV 121)*

Lestat compares himself with God several times. As a vampire, he acts as the divine hand of God whenever he takes a life, and his vampire eyes allow him to see the whole of the person's life from a godlike vantage point. He claims that no creature is as nearly like God as the vampire, because vampires, too, are free of the limitations of mortal conscience and can make whatever meaning they please. "God kills," Lestat says, "and so shall we." *(IV 89)*

Marius, a vampire who was mortal during the time of polytheistic Rome, also seeks a godlike presence in the universe in the form of a "continual awareness." He wants to believe that there is some omniscient thing that cares about everyone. In a scene in BT that was later cut, Marius looks for this being through his high-powered telescope. *(VL 398)*

David Talbot tells Lestat that he believes that God is not spirit but body, a creative force who also made humanity into a creative force. God holds the secret of cell division, and gave rise to the division of cells that made life and humanity possible. All physical cells possess part of God's spirit, thus sanctifying the flesh. In fact, the "Big Bang" happened when God's cells divided.

David's God is not perfect and not necessarily brilliant; He can make mistakes. In David's view, God is good, but His creative process cannot be construed as perfect. David's description matches that of Maharet talking about Amel. It is also how Lasher is depicted in WH. David tells Lestat that his theory comes from a vision he had of God and the Devil in a café in Paris. *(BT 68–69)*

Lestat admits that he thinks God exists, as does some form of the Devil. He believes that God plays games of uncertainty to see who will continue to uphold their religious faith. There are no clear answers to the secrets of the universe and never will be. Therefore, Lestat looks to the physical world for his truth. *(BT 78)*

There are many parallels between the vampires and the way God is described in Christianity. Christ presents the connection between Himself (God) and His believers as a vine to its branches. The same metaphor fits the relationship of the vampires to Akasha, via the spirit of Amel. And Lestat offers his body and blood to his mortal audience with words from the Eucharist. *(QD 230)*

Lestat believes that God is not really dead to the twentieth-century mind; "It's that everybody hates Him." *(MD 161)* To his astonishment, he actually gets the opportunity to meet God. The Devil, Memnoch, comes to him and asks for his assistance. Lestat agrees to accompany him to see Heaven and Hell and to learn about the Devil's function in God's creation. They enter Heaven together, and Lestat sees a tall, dark-haired man in the midst of a great light, leaning over a balustrade. When this man turns, Lestat sees that he has brown eyes and a flawless, dark golden face. It strikes him at once that he is looking at God. As light floods forth from the man's intense gaze, it becomes clear that He is suffering. He says to Lestat, "You would never be my adversary . . . not you!" *(MD 169)* The statement disturbs Lestat, but Memnoch takes him away before he can respond.

Memnoch claims to know nothing of God's origin or nature; for created beings, there is no way to comprehend it. Indeed, he believes God is trying to find this out for Himself by watching His creation evolve. For Him the world is an experiment to determine if Beings like Himself evolve from matter: God wants to see what it would have been like if He had once been matter. Through longing for it, He had created matter from His own imagination. Thus, He is exploring its ramifications for Himself as God. *(MD 176–177)*

Memnoch thinks that God does not realize the consequences of His actions. He has the power to put evolution in motion, but essentially He is an observer, and it is possible that His design is flawed from lack of foresight. The key to God's nature, Memnoch says, seems to lie within the concept of energy: when energy transformed into matter, it became an interdependent circular exchange independent of God. *(MD 177)*

The angels all had witnessed the unfolding of creation; in the first stages, they sang songs of awe and praise for the beauty of color and the harmony of nature, but the eventual emergence of decay, death, and suffering confused them. There followed a Great Discussion, but God reassured them with love and gave them a feeling of security. Memnoch alone continued to challenge Him. God suggested that Memnoch go observe human beings more closely, and to do so, Memnoch became flesh. When he participated in the human community, thereby corrupting his angelic nature, God barred him from Heaven. *(MD 180–197)*

Eventually, God recalled Memnoch, who made a case for allow-

ing human souls into Heaven. God sent him to Sheol to find ten worthy souls; he returned with millions. God accepted them all. Memnoch then challenged Him to become flesh Himself and experience His creation from a mortal perspective. For this impertinence, God sentenced Memnoch to wander the Earth, but God eventually took up the challenge. He planted His own seed in a virgin girl, was born, and grew up to become a man. Memnoch encountered Him during His prolonged fast in the Palestinian desert. *(MD 203–268)*

God told Memnoch that His mission is to teach humans the "awareness of Creation and the Understanding of its deliberate unfolding; an appreciation of its beauty and laws which makes possible an acceptance of suffering and seeming injustice and all forms of pain." *(MD 269)* God Himself had to learn this, and He explained that He plans to die on the cross to give suffering meaning and redeem it.

Memnoch resisted this idea. He could not believe that God would base his glory on the worst human superstitions and on a dirty, bloody death. Such a path to redemption seemed unnecessary and would only perpetuate suffering in the name of religion. In fact, Memnoch felt God's suffering had little real merit because while in mortal form He still possessed the knowledge that He was God; thus He did not really suffer the same horror and anxieties a mortal does when facing death and the unknown. God ignored Memnoch's complaints, leaving Memnoch to wonder again about the possible imperfection of God's foresight and wisdom. *(MD 273)*

As Memnoch relates this conversation to Lestat, Lestat sees the figure of God in the body of Christ, watching them. Christ invites Lestat to witness the Passion and Crucifixion for himself before he makes up his mind about Memnoch's proposal. So Lestat joins the people watching Christ carry his cross. He sees the crown of thorns piercing His skin. A woman named Veronica steps forth and offers her veil. Christ wipes his face with it. To Lestat's astonishment, Christ's face is imprinted on the veil. Christ invites Lestat to drink from Him, so he does. He experiences an overwhelming sense of light and sees a tunnel connecting Earth to the source of this light. Christ gives him Veronica's veil and he runs away with it, unable to watch God die on the cross. *(MD 280–285)*

Lestat then learns that God went into Sheol, showed the souls there His wounds, and took them to Heaven. He gave Sheol to Memnoch for unrepentant or unbelieving souls who came later and damned Memnoch to spend at least one third of his existence on Earth and one third in Hell. He was allowed to enter Heaven only by God's leave. Memnoch was now part of the cycle of God's plan. Memnoch responded by telling God that He was majestic, creative, and imperfect. He tells Lestat that he believes God to be an uncaring divinity who willingly receives souls worthy of Heaven but who cruelly dismisses all

others as irrelevant and expendable. Thus, His sacred scheme is flawed. *(MD 291–294)*

Lestat does not know what to think of Memnoch's tale, but his firsthand experience of the violent history of Christianity lends credibility to Memnoch's description. Lestat feels disappointed that the God he has experienced as the source of a rich, penetrating light could have been the creator of such a terrible, wasteful religion. Yet he cannot assist Memnoch in turning back the tide of evil because he is uncertain about Memnoch's version of things and too horrified by what he witnesses in the loathsome pit of Hell. Nevertheless, Lestat does contribute unintentionally to Christianity (and perhaps to the Devil's actual plan) when he brings Veronica's veil to the twentieth century. The miraculous icon infuses new blood into a religion that has become mediocre and strengthens its role in the lives of believers. Yet it is not clear to Lestat whether this actually serves God or the Devil or possibly both. *(MD 335–336, 349)*

See also Angel, Blood of Christ, Christ, Christianity, Continual Awareness, Eucharist, Evil, Goodness, Heaven, Hell, Human Evolution, Jerusalem, Lestat de Lioncourt, Memnoch, *Memnoch the Devil,* Religion, Religious Images, Sheol, Soul, Suffering, Superstitions, Thirteen Revelations of Physical Evolution, Veronica's Veil.

Goddess   How Akasha refers to herself when she sets out to create a "new Eden" on earth by subjecting mortals to her will. *(QD 366–372)* Lestat also tells Gabrielle that, as a vampire, she is now a goddess. *(VL 182)*

See also Akasha, Gods, Great Mother, Queen of Heaven.

God of the Grove   See Druid Vampire.

Gods   Incarnations of deity or supernatural power.

Rice often describes the vampires as gods, thus inverting the notion of evil as base. Since vampires have entered a metaphysical realm, and since they acquire no knowledge about, or proof of, the existence of God, they imagine that they themselves are gods. Vampires through the ages have adopted this status, demanding, like Azim, blood sacrifices from their mortal worshipers. Several vampires in the *Chronicles* refer to themselves as dark gods. *(QD 67, BT 1)*

Akasha devises a plan through which she will redefine the concepts of good and evil: she will be a goddess and her vampire followers will be gods. As a goddess, she is her own justification for whatever action she takes. *(QD 338, 358, 438)*

See also Akasha, Angels, Dionysus, God, Goddess, Great Mother, Inversion, Osiris, Tammuz of Sumer, Tiamat, Vegetation Gods.

Godwin, Matthew and Maria   The couple who adopt Jesse when her mother is killed in a car accident. *(QD 146)*

See also Jesse.

Goethe, Johann Wolfgang von   Author of the eighteenth-century German literary classic *Faust*, a work on human nature and the human spirit. Goethe was hailed as a leader of the Romantic movement for his intense assertion of freedom and imagination, and for validating the experience and emotions of the individual. Lestat echoes the same sentiments, mostly in his actions, and sums it up with the statement: "Sheer will had shaped my experience more than any other human characteristic." *(VL 497)*

In a short dedication to *Faust*, Goethe describes his state of mind as he prepares to work on the manuscript. He sees vague, shadowy forms—ghosts that have haunted him which are now making themselves more forceful to him, as if they have an independent existence. The spiritual world and the real world vie for his attention, simultaneously showing that he cannot escape his past and giving him artistic direction. As he readies himself to write, he is preparing for an encounter with his subconscious, just as Faust is with Mephistopheles. The drama is initiated by his inner being; it is a struggle between two aspects of his soul.

Similarly, Lestat offers a short discussion prior to the action in BT, where he describes several haunting dreams. The image of Claudia forces him to ponder the evil in his own nature, and, like Goethe, he accepts that any action—even one that might bring regret—is better than passivity or nonaction. True freedom is the freedom to err as part of striving for truth in life, and action is redemption. *(BT 5–6)*

See also Faust, Mephistopheles, *The Tale of the Body Thief*.

Golden Moment   During a moment of supreme drunkenness, Lestat and Nicolas christen the Golden Moment as the time at which everything in their conversation makes sense and disappointments have little weight. The Golden Moment starts to disperse when one or the other can no longer follow the conversation, and is lost altogether when Nicolas tells Lestat that they are brothers in sin. For Lestat, their initial bond is lost. *(VL 51)*

After seeing Heaven, Lestat recalls this moment of bliss. He believes he could have forgiven everything, tolerated anything at that time. Had he died during the Golden Moment, he might have entered Heaven. *(MD 307)*

See also Forgiveness, Heaven, Nicolas de Lenfent.

Gold locket   A piece of jewelry that preserves miniature paintings.

Both Claudia and Madeleine's deceased child are depicted in these tiny frames. The Talamasca eventually come into possession of the locket with Claudia's portrait. Lestat discovers this fact from Raglan James, who had seen it in the Talamasca's collection. David Talbot gives the locket back to Lestat, who throws it into the ocean; he wants to be haunted no more by Claudia's indictments. With it go his guilt and yearning for redemption, and he then makes David a vampire. However, David rescues the locket and gives it back to Lestat in a symbolic gesture. *(BT 130, 149, 419, 435)*

A gold locket also protects the vial of vampire blood that Armand gives to Daniel to wear as protection from other vampires. Armand's initial is engraved on the locket, along with mutilated and dead human figures. Daniel thinks the design horrid but nonetheless wears the locket until the night Armand makes him a vampire. *(QD 102)*

See also Amulet.

Gold pocket watch   When Daniel discovers a gold pocket watch with Lestat's name on it in a crumbling house in New Orleans, he decides that the house must have belonged to Lestat. *(QD 84)*

Golem   In Hebrew folklore, an artificial man constructed from mud or clotted blood and endowed with life but lacking a soul. Daniel compares Khayman to this image. *(QD 229)*

See also Khayman.

Goodness   A concept generally thought to be the opposite of evil, but shown in the *Chronicles* as being more complex and elusive than religious doctrines admit. Because the vampires believe there are no absolute standards for moral concepts, they play with the notion of goodness to create paradoxes and to find a way to view some of their behavior as "good."

"Being good always seemed to interest me," says Rice. "I loved the Catholic saints for their excessiveness, for going out on a limb, for their willingness to fight everybody, and for the misjudgment they endured."

Louis equates self-esteem with goodness and, suffering from low self-esteem, believes himself to be evil; he also thinks that evil behavior comes more easily to most people than performing good deeds. *(IV 12)* One cannot love goodness, Louis claims, when one does what one knows to be evil: "you can only have . . . the chasing of phantom goodness in its human form." *(IV 340)* Although Louis is obsessed with his own evil, he does one thing that he claims to be good: he kills other vampires when he burns down the Theater of the Vampires. He views this as his one truly moral act: "And they are the only deaths I

have caused in my long life which are both exquisite and good." *(IV 315)*

Lestat is more obsessed with goodness than Louis. As a boy, he wanted to enter a religious order because to him it seemed to possess the possibility of goodness. He would kneel on the marble floor with his arms outstretched and offer to be a martyr if only God would make him good. *(VL 131)* When he later becomes a stage actor, he sees himself doing good by making something out of nothing and provoking emotions in others. After he becomes a vampire, he realizes that he is evil, but he still wants to try to do good, and by killing evildoers he can use his powers to make the lives of others better. *(QD 262)* In BT, for example, he stalks and kills serial killers. Lestat's brief career as a rock star was likewise meant to accomplish some good by urging mortals to dispense with superstition: "I thought that as a symbol of evil I'd do some good." *(BT 221)*

Gabrielle thinks Lestat's desire to be good contradicts being a vampire. When she points out that he is so good at being what he is, he plays with the ambiguity inherent in the word "good," claiming he does not know how to be bad at anything, including being bad at being bad. He equivocates, changing a discussion about morality into a discussion about skill, then shrugs it off with: "So much for our understanding of the word 'good.' " *(VL 336)* Such slippery semantics foreshadow Lestat's claim to Armand that forms of goodness change and that he is a vampire for a new age. *(VL 227)*

Lestat also struggles with the concepts of good and evil with Gretchen and David Talbot. To Gretchen, Lestat offers up a confession of his life, to persuade her that he wants to do good. Gretchen believes that goodness does not depend on the logic of Christianity, yet since goodness is all that truly matters, this is why she rejects Lestat when he comes to her as a vampire. *(BT 221–222)*

In the end, Lestat realizes that all his attempts to be good fail to neutralize or outweigh what he is and what he does as a vampire. Given the chance, he knows that he would make Claudia and Gabrielle into vampires again, and send them off to kill. Vampires are evil, and he has deliberately made the choice to be one; this means that he will never be good again. *(BT 418)*

When Akasha wants to draft Lestat into her vision, she takes him first to the Auvergne, to remind him of his boyhood urge to be good. She claims that he can achieve his goal with her; he can be more than a saint, he can be a god. She will redeem him if he acts according to her plan. Lestat resists, sensing that the concept of goodness has at least a tradition to respect, if not an objective validity. What Akasha wants to do seems clearly wrong to Lestat, and he stands with other vampires against her and her kind of evil. *(QD 262)*

David Talbot, too, seems to be searching for answers as he reads both the Bible and *Faust*. He wants to understand the structure of a universe that includes both God and the Devil, although he does not concern himself as intensely with questions of goodness as does Lestat. David's ruminations seem to be more metaphysical than ethical in origin. *(BT 40)*

Memnoch the Devil exploits Lestat's urge to be good by making a moral issue of his request that Lestat accompany him to Heaven and Hell: "There's no point if I cannot count upon your willing intent to see the truth, your willing desire to turn your life from aimlessness and meaninglessness into a crucial battle for the fate of the world." *(MD 136)* He wants Lestat to listen to his side of things and learn about the true nature of his resistance to God. Insisting that he himself is not evil, Memnoch claims that he needs help in stemming the tide of evil that threatens to destroy the world. "My ways are the right ways," he says, "and the ways of God are bloody and wasteful and exceedingly dangerous." *(MD 136)*

Lestat feels compelled to accompany the Devil. He likes Memnoch and believes there is some possibility that he is speaking the truth. Ironically, assisting the Devil may offer Lestat an opportunity for redeeming past deeds. However, after visiting Heaven, meeting God, listening to Memnoch's account, and seeing what Hell is like, Lestat withdraws. He is not certain that what he has experienced is real or that siding with either God or the Devil is in the interest of goodness. For all he knows, the Devil may be a liar. In fact, although Memnoch had agreed to allow Lestat to talk with God for as long as he desired, that promise had been broken. *(MD 136, 169)* Lestat grows further confused when he receives a note from Memnoch that implies that Memnoch had been deceiving him all along; he was merely a dupe in Memnoch's plan. Neither the issue of truth nor goodness is clarified for Lestat from what should have been the ultimate opportunity for moral resolution. *(MD 350)*

See also Bible, Evil, Faust, God, Memnoch, Moral Dilemma, Redemption, Saint.

"Good night, sweet prince"   A quote from Shakespeare's *Hamlet*, said by Horatio to Hamlet as Hamlet lay dying from poison.

Lestat uses this line when he kills a man who has done him a favor. It shows his proclivity for Shakespeare and his ability to make classically ambiguous statements fit his own framework. *(IV 71)*

See also *Hamlet*, Shakespeare.

Gorgon   In Greek mythology, any of the three "grim ones," sisters with claws for hands and snakes in place of hair whose eyes turned

Francisco Goya, from Los Caprichos

people to stone. Medusa was the only one who could die, and it was the hero Perseus who beheaded her.

Lestat thinks of this powerful image when he looks at the imprint of Christ's staring face on Veronica's veil. *(MD 333)*

See also Christ, Veronica's Veil.

Goya, Francisco An eighteenth-century Spanish artist famous

for a series of etchings called *Los Caprichos*, depicting people acting out their strongest passions. These nightmarish paintings, done while Goya was in ill health, are filled with violence and dark colors and accentuate human frailties and vices. His work is replicated on the walls of the room beneath the Theater of the Vampires. His art also decorates the house in the Faubourg St.-Germain that was described in the first draft of IV. *(IV 230)*

See also Art, *Interview with the Vampire*, Subterranean Room.

Grand Anse Beach   See Grenada.

Grand Bay Hotel   A luxury hotel in Miami in Coconut Grove.

David Talbot brings Lestat here after Lestat has dealt a fatal blow to Raglan James, whose soul was residing in David's body. *(BT 371)*

Grand Canal   The location of Marius's villa, it is the busiest canal in Venice.

Grand Canal, Venice

It was in this house that Marius did a painting of Armand as a mortal boy, entitled *The Temptation of Amadeo*, and it is here that Marius made Armand into a vampire. Santino's satanic coven of vampires burned down the villa, although the Talamasca was able to salvage various items from the resulting ruins, including the painting of Armand. *(VL 293–297, QD 174–175)*

See also Marius, Venice.

Grand Hotel   A hotel in Paris, and one of the largest in Europe when Louis and Claudia arrive. Located on the boulevard des Capucines, it served as a model for the Hôtel Saint-Gabriel, where Louis and Claudia take rooms. *(IV 205, BT 89)* (See Vampire Atlas)

See also Hôtel Saint-Gabriel.

Grand Sabbat   The name of one of Lestat's rock music videos in which he depicts vampiric activities. Although the content of the video is not specifically described, it probably depicts Lestat's experiences with the Sabbat of the Roman coven, since this is the only vampire Sabbat he mentioned encountering. *(VL 537)*

See also Music Videos, Rock Music, Rock Star.

Great Family   The term Maharet uses to describe the vast matrilineal lineage of her descendants, traced through centuries and across continents. To disguise the fact that she never dies, she invents a fictional branch of her family and a fictional series of women, all named Maharet, who take on the task of keeping the extensive records of the family members. Maharet preserves these records in books and parchment rolls at her Sonoma compound; for her, it is a way of watching over her mortal progeny, and by using her deceptions, she herself is accepted into the family as a member throughout its generations. *(QD 147)*

To Maharet, the Great Family is a metaphor for families everywhere and, thus, of the human family itself, or "the thread we cling to in the labyrinth which is life." *(QD 141)* That different branches of the family reside in different countries and embrace many ethnic groups mirrors the idea of the Great Family as being representative of all humankind. The Great Family's lineage parallels the biblical listing of generations—although here the emphasis is on the female side—and the Talamasca's study of witch families, also traced through the female line. *(QD 428)*

To Jesse, an orphan, these family connections make a protective womb of love for her. All her relatives believe in the family and take pains to extend hospitality to all those of their blood. Maharet denies

Jesse access to the actual records, but she does show Jesse the family tree she has drawn on a world map, which traces the family for hundreds of generations to every country. The map, which stretches across the walls of a room, is covered with thousands of lights and the tree's ink-drawn lines bear countless names. The spectacle is made more amazing in light of the fact that vast numbers of male descendants are not represented at all. *(QD 159, 427)*

When the vampires come to the compound and are shown this electrically lighted tree, Maharet explains its significance: "The family taught me the rhythms and passions of each new age; the family took me into alien lands where perhaps I would never have ventured alone; the family took me into realms of art which might have intimidated me; the family was my guide through time and space. My teacher, my book of life. The family was all things." *(QD 426)*

As a result of Maharet's loving concern for and "continual awareness" of her lineage, she reminds the other vampires of their human roots and of their responsibility to protect humanity from Akasha's destructive plan.

"The idea of the Great Family," says Rice, "was born from the idea of what it would be like if we *could* trace our roots back that far. It's completely horrible that most families disappear into chaos within a few generations. I guess it's part of our mortality. The little gem that inspired this tree came from H. Rider Haggard's novel *She*. A man at the beginning of the novel says his family dates back to ancient times. I also had read a book on European families which basically said that there was no family in Europe today that could trace itself back to the Dark Ages. I thought it would be wonderful if you really knew your family all the way back, and everyone kept in touch!"

See also Continual Awareness, Maharet, Jesse.

Great Laws/Great Commandments

The five rules devised in Santino's satanic coven into which Armand is inducted after he is taken from Marius. These laws are the "condition of existence among the Undead." *(VL 302)* They stipulate that each coven must have a leader, who alone performs the Dark Trick; mortals who receive the Dark Gift must be beautiful and never crippled; old vampires are not allowed to work the Dark Trick; only the coven leader is allowed to destroy another vampire and must destroy outcasts and vampires not properly made; and vampires must keep their names and history secret from mortals.

Vampires who do not observe these rules are considered to be rogues and outcasts. *(VL 301–303)*

See also Armand's Coven, Beauty, Heretics, Names, Rogues, Rules.

Great Mother/Mother Goddess　The symbol of earth and fertility; the one who gives birth to all. Known under many names in other cultures—Diana of Ephesus, Cybele, Demeter, and Isis—she represents wholeness and integration. The Great Mother is present in all things but is without form; she is the earth that swallows the remains. The bloody rituals of the Druids capture this negative aspect of her. More generically, the Great Mother symbolizes the process of fertility, creativity, and regeneration. The mother in primitive culture was viewed as the supreme creative deity. Worship of this Goddess acknowledged the spiritual empowerment of the feminine, and many early cultures believed that the human soul was passed to the child from the mother. *(VL 409)*

When Akasha arises and attempts to force upon humankind a "new Eden" of her own design, she presents herself as the Great Mother. She exhibits her power in primitive places where women are exploited and victimized by men. When she kills most of the men, she suggests that she is the Virgin Mary, a savior to the women. Many mortal women worship her, viewing her evil as redemptive, beautiful, and holy. *(QD 305, 376, 379)*

Yet it is Maharet who more truly represents the Great Mother archetype. She has never lost consciousness of her mortal descendants through the centuries and caringly watches over them. Her family keeps her going, and she is much more connected than Akasha with the process of regeneration. Maharet presents the positive side of the Great Mother, while Akasha is the one who demands sacrifices. *(QD 426)*

See also Akasha, Eve, Goddess, Inanna, Isis.

Greece　One of the destinations on the Devil's Road that Lestat and Gabrielle take. The vampires they encounter there initially attack them, but flee from their prayers of protection, which they say to drive them away. *(VL 324)* (See Vampire Atlas)

See also Devil's Road.

"Greek Fragments"　A poem by Stan Rice that introduces Part 4 of QD, which entails the confrontation between Akasha and the other vampires. The poem is about nature's barbaric beauty. *(QD 433)*

See also Poetry, Rice (Stan).

Gregor, Lestan　One of Lestat's aliases, which he uses for legal purposes. With this name he transfers twenty million dollars to the account of Raglan James; the sum is meant as a bribe to get James to return Lestat's body after the allotted time. James fails to return the body and uses Lestat's alias to acquire the money via computer after it reverts back to Lestat's account. *(BT 139, 206)*

Lestan is an old French name that Rice had intended to use when she was first naming characters in IV. She discovered later that she had recalled it inaccurately as Lestat; this mistake was especially ironic since she had given to Lestat many of the physical attributes of her husband Stan (as in Le*Stan*). Using this name, then, as a pseudonym for Lestat seemed a perfect way of retrieving the correct French name.

The second part of the name, Gregor, may have its origins in a story that Rice has read several times, Kafka's *Metamorphosis*. In that story, a man wakes up to find that he has become a large beetle-type insect overnight. Since the alias is used for a transformation, and since Rice has associated vampiric activity with insects in earlier novels, an unconscious influence may have been at work here.

Grenada   An island in the West Indies where Lestat and David Talbot prepare for a confrontation with Raglan James in which they hope to steal back Lestat's body. They stay in Grenada in a hotel on Grand Anse Beach. *(BT 301–302)* (See Vampire Atlas)

Greenwich Village   An area of Lower Manhattan located between Fourteenth and Houston streets and the Hudson and East rivers, it is known for its brownstones, offbeat shops, and artistic community.

Lestat deposits the last pieces of Roger's remains—his chest, arms, and legs—in a warehouse trash heap in the Village. Not long afterward, he meets Roger's ghost in a Village bar. *(MD 44, 47)* (See Vampire Atlas)

See also Manhattan, Roger.

Gretchen   The nun who nurses Lestat back to health while he is in the body of a mortal man. Named after a character in Goethe's *Faust*, she also shares with that character the religious name, Sister Marguerite. *(BT 212)*

Forty years old, and large-boned with hazel eyes, Gretchen lives in a small cottage in Georgetown but has spent her life in foreign missions in Venezuela and Peru, nursing the sick and caring for children. She had given up a promising piano career earlier in her life to become a nun because the music had made her too self-centered. However, she believes that trying to know God is pointless, for that which is real is suffering. She wants a life of all-consuming and heroic work, like the saints she admired as a child, and she believes in self-sacrifice to decrease the world's misery. Gretchen also admits that as a child she had prayed for the miracle of the stigmata, which is reserved for people of great faith. *(BT 240–246)*

When Lestat has pneumonia, Gretchen sees something special in him and takes him from the hospital to her home. He admits to her that

he is actually a vampire seeking to return to his own body, which has been stolen. She listens sympathetically but does not take his story literally. *(BT 249)*

Gretchen has her own agenda when it comes to Lestat. She confesses that she is seeking a man to lift her "curse of chastity." To her, virginity seems cowardly, so losing it has become an obsession. This wavering in her truth is similar to the way Faust, under the influence of Mephistopheles, swayed the Gretchen of that tale. Lestat and Gretchen make love. She is neither swept away by it nor ashamed of doing it, but the act relieves her obsession. *(BT 235, 238)*

Gretchen then tells Lestat that she must return to the mission. She invites him to join her, offering him an alternative to going after and recovering his vampire body. *(BT 250)* This way he can save lives, not destroy them, and thereby redeem himself. However, Lestat says he will come to her when he is himself again. He will then offer to her what he has—immortality.

After he recaptures his vampire form, he visits her in French Guiana. Similarly, Faust had visited his own Gretchen, imprisoned for murdering their illegitimate child, to urge her to escape and join him. This Gretchen saw him as the Devil, rejected him, and turned to God—in the same way that Lestat's Gretchen rejects him.

Gretchen also seems to lose her reason and blood springs from her hands and feet—a sign of intense unwavering faith in a supernatural entity. Like Mephistopheles with Faust, and Faust with Gretchen, Lestat has inspired, contrary to his actual intent, spiritual transcendence in a mortal. *(BT 349–355, 357)*

Lestat later hears that Gretchen has become a saint. She has not spoken since his visit to her, and her stigmata has become a spectacle for believers. He thinks of her with regret, believing she has lost her mind, and this makes him somewhat cautious in his dealings with Dora. To his chagrin, Dora, too, interprets his existence religiously and becomes fanatical, albeit in a more functional manner than Gretchen. To Lestat, belief in God and madness are the same. *(MD 102, 134, 146)*

See also Faust, Insanity, Redemption, Sex, Stigmata, *The Tale of the Body Thief.*

Grim Reaper A death figure to which Louis compares himself when he confesses his murders as a vampire to a priest. He then kills the priest, turning his words into a prophecy as well as a description. *(IV 148)*

See also Death.

Guardian Angel See Archangels.

Grim Reaper

Guilt   See Redemption.

Gulliver   A fictional character in Jonathan Swift's book *Gulliver's Travels* who encounters in his adventures people both smaller and larger than he.

Louis feels like Gulliver in the land of the Lilliputians—the little people—as he watches Madeleine craft a miniature world for Claudia that gives her the illusion that she is adult in size. He wonders if he will one day be an unwelcome giant in Claudia's world—and he is. *(IV 277)*

See also Louis de Pointe du Lac.

Haggard, H. Rider An English novelist and the author of *She* and *King Solomon's Mines*, Haggard is one of the writers from whom Lestat claims to have learned the English language. His novels also influenced the idea of the Great Family. *(VL 4)*

See also Great Family.

Hagia Sophia A church in Istanbul considered the most famous example of Byzantine architecture. Its name means "Holy Wisdom," and it was built as a Christian cathedral between A.D. 532 and 537.

In the first draft of BT, in a scene later cut, David Talbot confides to Lestat that he longs to revisit the Hagia Sophia. When Lestat transports him there through the air, David is clearly shaken but still wants to see the church before they return to Venice.

After grabbing Veronica's veil from Christ, Lestat flees. The scene shifts and he finds himself with Memnoch in the Hagia Sophia during the bloody slaughter of the Fourth Crusade. He is appalled by the human misery all around him and the loss of so many treasures. *(MD 286–287)*

See also Christianity, Constantinople, Fourth Crusade.

Hair Hair receives significant attention in *The Vampire Chronicles*. It is used as a symbol of self-expression, fashion, health, immortality, beauty, strength, and vulnerability.

In world mythology, hair represents spiritualized energy and power, as with Samson, who lost his strength when his hair was cut. Head hair indicates a higher force than does body hair, and a full head of hair represents a will to succeed, fertility, and the burgeoning of primitive forces. Locks of hair are often used to ward off evil spirits or to transmit curses. Golden hair is associated with awareness and immortality, and dark hair with unconscious motivations. Some cultures

Inside the Hagia Sophia Basilica

treat hair as the lodging place of the gods or the soul. Rice herself uses male hair as a symbol of armor and animal power; for females, hair represents protection and freedom. And for both sexes, hair is a means of making a person irresistibly attractive.

Hair color is especially important in the *Chronicles*. Dark hair indicates to Rice a person who lives a life of secrecy, while blond expresses sunlight. Gray connotes aging, offering both the blessing of wisdom and the curse of mortality, and red the power of primitive forces. In fact, in the Osirian myth, redheads were sacrificed to the gods to ensure the success of the corn crops. Black hair is also significant.

Since the Gothic image of the vampire is that of a black-haired creature, the vampires in the Theater of the Vampires all dye their hair black to conform to that image. *(IV 246)*

Hair color, however, can have its disadvantages. Magnus is attracted to blondes and it is partly the reason he snatches Lestat from life to turn him into a vampire. And the young woman killed on stage in IV had been warned that her beautiful blond hair might attract someone who would kill her just for her hair. *(IV 222, VL 107)*

Another feature of hair is its texture. Mortals who become vampires experience an increase in the thickness and glossiness of their hair, which emphasizes their increased vitality and strength. When Marius is prepared by the Druids to become their new god, a vampire, his hair grows thick and full, and they prevent him from cutting it. *(VL 408)*

Lestat refers continually to his hair, describing it as thick and long with a high luster and possessing vitality. Its beauty attracts Louis into choosing vampirism: "What would Christ need have done," Louis muses, "to make me follow him like Matthew or Peter? Dress well, to begin with. And have a luxurious head of pampered yellow hair." *(IV 278)* In fact, Lestat's hair is referred to as a blaze of light and a reflection of the sun—an ironic symbol for a vampire who must shun the sun to survive.

A detail that Rice added to the vampire experience is that, when mortals transform into vampires, their hair will always remain the length it had been when they were first made. Thus, vampires are tied into the fashion of an era. If they try to cut their hair, it immediately grows back. (Lestat notices the same thing with his finger- and toenails, which grow back if he files them.) *(VL 124)* Gabrielle is extremely frustrated when she cuts her hair to shed the trappings of femininity, because it grows right back overnight. She fears that if she cut it every night, she would soon fill the tower; hers is the image of trapped Rapunzel. The vampire's inability to be rid of hair by cutting it is also an image of immortality: it is persistent, even when the vampire tires of it. *(VL 174)*

Armand manages to view this fact more humorously by making a film of himself in his coffin. He "sat before the slow-moving film for hours, watching his own hair, cut at sunrise, slowly growing against the satin as he lay motionless with closed eyes." *(QD 96)*

See also Appearance, Black, Rapunzel, Vampire.

Haiti   The Caribbean island where Lestat and Akasha go following the slaughter they perpetrated on Lynkonos. Overcome with shame at his participation, Lestat resists Akasha here, even though the island of Haiti has been the scene of male violence for over four hundred years.

Lestat ironically refers to Haiti as the "Garden of God," for revolution, aggression, slavery, and bloodbaths have turned this virtual paradise into a land of mud and poverty. It is in Haiti that Lestat begs Akasha to bring him to the other surviving vampires who are currently in California. *(QD 391, 395)* (See Vampire Atlas)

See also Akasha's Plan, Saint-Domingue.

Halloween   October 31 is traditionally designated as a night when evil spirits roam the earth before the dawning of Hallowmas, or All Saints' Day. It is also the eve of the Celtic (Druid) festival of Samhain, on which Marius was made a vampire.

Lestat schedules the debut of his rock group in San Francisco on Halloween night. *(QD 195)*

See also Cow Palace, Feast of All Saints, Feast of Samhain, Rock Concert.

Hallucinations   The perception of objects with no reality, it arises from a disorder of the nervous system or an altered state of consciousness. Since vampires move into an altered state of heightened perception after the transformation, they are more prone than they were as mortals to perceptual illusions. Carlos Castenada's novel *The Teachings of Don Juan: A Yaqui Way of Knowledge* influenced how Rice developed this aspect of the vampire experience; through altered states of consciousness and hallucinogenic experiences, the fictional narrator of that book changed his entire understanding of reality.

Louis and Lestat both describe the way their senses were heightened after becoming vampires. Louis feels as if he were seeing shapes and colors for the first time, and his heartbeat sounds like a loud drum. Lestat is caught up in a whirl of colors and sounds that create for him both confusion and euphoria. It seems to him as if time were standing still. *(IV 20, VL 82, 88–89)*

In BT, Lestat also experiences auditory and visual hallucinations. When he is at the brink of death—when he exposes himself to the sun, and when he is a mortal dying of pneumonia—he sees and hears Claudia addressing him. His hallucinations of the vampire child arise from his conscience and lead him to question the motives behind his past behavior. *(BT 48, 208, 212–215)*

See also Dreams, Hallucinogen, Visions.

Hallucinogen   A substance that alters the senses and allows access to other levels of the subconscious. The vampires' "magical blood" works as a hallucinogen for initiates. As mortals transform into vampires, they are aware of the sensory world in a whole new way. It causes temporary disequilibrium and an infatuation with even the simplest

elements of their experience. Louis's description is the most vivid and complete in this regard. *(IV 20–21)* Lestat laughs and Louis hears each distinct sound running into the next until they overlap. Lestat seems not merely white but radiant and full of life; Louis stares at Lestat's buttons, enthralled, then spends an hour looking at the moon on the flagstones. The night sounds are like women whispering to him. *(IV 20–21)*

Other vampires add to this description of the transformation by seeing full-blown images of things that once had happened to their maker and hearing disembodied voices.

See also Transformation, Visions.

Hamilton, Jason   The alias Raglan James uses to book passage on the *QE2* ocean liner. *(BT 298)*

See also James (Raglan).

Hamlet   A Shakespearean play about a tormented Danish prince who broods over his father's death, then feigns madness. Hamlet is paralyzed by his inability to act on his inner moral imperative that demands he avenge his father's murder.

Lestat quotes from this play when he kills the man who has arranged for his hotel room in IV. "Good night, sweet prince," he says, echoing what was said to Hamlet when he lay dying. The quote reinforces Lestat's notion that he is the hand of fate, just as Hamlet was. *(IV 71)*

Louis, however, is the character that actually has many of Hamlet's brooding, passive qualities. "Louis, my first hero, is in some ways like Hamlet," says Rice. "Louis is the most tragic character in the book. He says yes to becoming a vampire and then suffers terrible regret."

See also Shakespeare.

Hammett, Dashiell   See Sam Spade.

Happy Hour   A theater in New Orleans where Lestat goes when he is healing from his many wounds after the fiasco in Paris. There he watches the newly invented black-and-white silent films, and the image of the sun in them frightens him. The films are to him a metaphor of the monotony and gray tones of the early twentieth century. *(VL 509)*

Harley-Davidson   The brand of motorcycle that Lestat drives around New Orleans in VL. Baby Jenks also rides a Harley, although she is only fourteen years old. The fact that she possesses a vampire's strength gives her the power to handle such a large bike. *(VL 6, QD 41)*

See also Baby Jenks, Lestat de Lioncourt.

Harley-Davidson

Harpy A carrion-eating creature of Greek myth whose name meant "plucker." Harpies were symbols of the death goddess and emblems of victory.

   Daniel describes Armand as a harpy because of the way Armand pursues him. *(QD 83)*

Hassler Hotel Lestat's favorite hotel in Rome. It is located at the top of the Spanish Steps. *(BT 128)*

Haunted houses Buildings reputed to be inhabited by ghosts which Lestat and Gabrielle explore together when they are on the Devil's Road. While they do see apparitions, flying objects, and possessed children, they learn nothing through their supernatural perception except that which mortals already know. This mutual interest, however, keeps them together for a time, blunting their growing estrangement. *(VL 333)*

   See also Elementals, Ghosts, St. Elizabeth's Orphanage.

Harpy

183

Hauer, Rutger   A contemporary actor mentioned by both Armand and Lestat.

Lestat mentions him as a character he likes to watch, and Armand tells Daniel that Rutger Hauer's role as an android in *Blade Runner* is a good representation of Lestat's character.

Rice has said that she wants Hauer to play Lestat if a film of *The Vampire Chronicles* is made. By the time the novels came to the screen, however, Hauer was not in the running. *(QD 95, BT 337)*

See also *Blade Runner*.

Hawthorne, Nathaniel A nineteenth-century American Gothic writer who believed himself cursed by an ancestor's participation in the Salem witch trials. Rice read his works for their sense of atmosphere. She appreciated how he seemed to feel horror in a deeply religious manner. "I read plenty of Hawthorne and James while preparing to plunge into *Memnoch*," she said. "I wanted to read stories about good and evil, God and the Devil. I reread 'Young Goodman Brown' at this time, and other material. I continue to be deeply inspired by Hawthorne and to feel some link with him." Among Hawthorne's best-known works are *The Scarlet Letter* and *The House of the Seven Gables*.

David Talbot mentions Hawthorne to Lestat because he identifies with one of Hawthorne's characters, Ethan Brand, from the 1851 short story of the same name. Brand searches obsessively for the unpardonable sin and loses his humanity in the process: he becomes a cold observer, looking upon other people merely as subjects for his experiment, puppets for his study. As a result, his moral nature loses pace with his intellect. As Brand explains it, the unpardonable sin is "the sin of an intellect that triumphed over the sense of brotherhood with man and reverence for God, and sacrificed everything to its own mighty claims." This imbalance turns Brand into a fiend and, feeling damned, he destroys himself in a fire.

David believes that this same process happens with vampires, and he, too, feels distanced from his humanity. "That's our damnation. . . . Our moral improvement has reached its finish, and our intellect grows by leaps and bounds." *(MD 107)*

Similarly, Memnoch describes God as an unfeeling experimenter with the souls of humanity. But if Memnoch's final note to Lestat has any legitimacy, he himself seems to be doing the same thing with Lestat.

The concern David expresses foreshadows Lestat's involvement with these two supernatural beings, neither one of whom seems clearly innocent of the unpardonable sin. In this way, vampires are aligned with both God and the Devil, and all are indicted together.

See also God, Lestat de Lioncourt, Memnoch, Moral Dilemma, Talbot (David), Vampire.

Heart A focal point of the human body, regarded in Egyptian mythology as a symbol of eternity and the essential center of the universe. In many cultures, it is also considered the seat of intelligence, with connections between the heart and the sun (enlightenment) showing up in ancient records. Maharet says that, in her beliefs, the heart is the seat of conscience. It is no wonder, then, that the vampires consider the beating heart as an essential part of the experience of drinking blood.

When Louis receives Lestat's blood for his transformation into a vampire, he hears a "dull roar" as he drinks, which becomes a sound like two drums pounding out a steady rhythm. He realizes that the drums are his heart in unison with Lestat's, and the sound intensifies as he makes the change. This experience is repeated whenever he takes a victim, most notably when he drinks from the mortal child Claudia. Her heart is tenacious, "refusing to die," and pulls on his with increasing speed. Before he reaches the climax, however, he is interrupted, and Claudia survives to eventually become a vampire. *(IV 19, 75)*

It is the taking of a life, which is related to the beating heart, that makes the experience ecstatic. Louis sees each death as a celebration of the lost life. His heart beats in perfect accord with that of his victim's, signifying fusion—an intense, intimate union unlike any ever experienced by mortals. When Louis drains his first victim to the point where the heart stops beating, he feels dizzy and weightless. Lestat chides him for this, claiming that vampires are vulnerable at that moment to being sucked into death along with their victims. Drinking to the point of death is especially overwhelming for new vampires because the blood rushes too quickly into their own and makes them ill. *(IV 30, VL 165)*

In an interview shortly after IV was published, Rice identified the source of inspiration for this idea as a passage from Keats's poem "Ode to a Nightingale":

> Now more than ever seems it rich to die
> To cease upon the midnight with no pain,
> While thou art pouring forth thy soul abroad
> In such an ecstasy!

"I would like to think," Rice explains, "that it would be like that to drink after the victim died—to just glide out of existence, to go out with the tide. It would be like being seduced by death."

Thus, that which draws vampires to the most intensely satisfying aspects of their existence is also the most dangerous. The moment just before a mortal's heart stops is orgasmic for vampires, yet it can also threaten annihilation. They are no longer drinking life, but death. In VL, however, Lestat explains that this experience is threatening only to weak vampires; he likes to, and can, swallow the death whole. He

learned to do this on his second victim, a highwayman who assaulted him. Not only does Lestat survive drinking the death, but he feels more powerful and ecstatic, and thus makes it a regular practice. *(VL 118)*

Moments of intimacy between the vampires typically involve the heart. They feel or hear the other's heart pounding as they get closer to one another. When a starving and despair-filled Lestat goes underground the first time, he hears the pounding of a heart coming toward him. It belongs to Marius, who is coming to rescue him. *(VL 360)*

According to Lestat in VL, the power of a vampire seems to reside in the heart. When Lestat encounters Marius, he hears a low pulse like a heartbeat, and he believes that Marius's power emanates with this rhythmic beat. And according to vampire legend, Akasha claims that the spirit Amel entered her and fused with her heart. *(QD 404)* Centuries earlier, Maharet had pierced Akasha's heart with a knife and, upon feeling faint, realized that Akasha's heart did indeed house the spirit that keeps the vampire race alive. *(QD 418)* When Akasha rises in the twentieth century from her comatose state, Maharet leads the resistance against her, despite the fact that blocking Akasha's actions threatens all vampires with annihilation. However, after Mekare kills Akasha, Maharet then feeds Mekare Akasha's brain and heart, preserving the vampires by finding a new body in which to house the spirit. *(QD 456)*

Later there is some speculation among the vampires whether Akasha's heart had really been functional at all; it may be the brain in which the spirit resides. *(QD 465)*

See also Akasha, Amel, Blood, Brain, Swoon.

Heaven   The realm of God and the angels, often depicted as a place of nearly unbearable beauty, light, and harmony. In many artistic or theological depictions, sharp colors, laughter, and music are often central elements of Heaven. Being in God's presence is presumably an unending experience of total ecstasy, and such joy and satisfaction are thought to be the rewards of a life that God honors.

Memnoch takes Lestat to Heaven. He stands in the Garden of Waiting before the heavenly gates, awed by the brilliant colors and overwhelming light. Memnoch tells him that the laughter he hears is the sound of pure joy. Inside, multitudes of interconnected beings engaged in all forms of encounter surround him. He feels a balance between disorder and order and sees flowers, sculptures, trees, flowing water, and highly ornate buildings. "This was very simply the densest, the most intense, the busiest, and the most profoundly magnificent place I'd ever beheld," he says. *(MD 164)* He laughs and cries, convulsing over the beauty. As Memnoch leads him past the most amazing sights, he spots books containing the answers to every question ever raised. Lestat tries to read them, but Memnoch explains that as soon

as he leaves Heaven, he will forget everything he has learned from such books. Indeed, all he recalls later are a few scientific terms. In Heaven, Lestat experiences a sense of supreme safety and satisfaction; all sadness seems transformed to harmony. *(MD 163–170)*

After discussing angels, Memnoch takes Lestat straight to God, Who insists that Lestat would never be His adversary. Lestat is shaken by this confrontation, but Memnoch whisks him away to a paradisial garden to describe the events of creation. Lestat learns that Heaven itself had expanded with the burgeoning of matter into all its forms, as the angels sang praises to celebrate the wonderous event and Earth became their focus. *(MD 191–195)*

As Memnoch's lieutenant, Lestat would have ready access to Heaven; he would be able to enter God's presence whenever he liked, although first he must die and deliver his soul over to the Devil. Memnoch describes his own experience of Heaven and how he had learned about the way humans participate in it: he had taken on human form, had sex, and realized that orgasm was a brief moment of heavenly ecstasy. *(MD 224, 234–235)* When he had returned to Heaven to persuade God to allow mortal souls into Heaven, God had sent him to Sheol to find ten that were worthy.

Since God had given Memnoch no criteria with which to judge their worthiness, Memnoch had formed his own. He had decided, from his observations of Sheol, that souls would be worthy of Heaven if they understood life and death in the simplest terms; appreciated the beauty of creation and accepted its cycles of life and death as part of that beauty; were ready to believe in Heaven; and were tranquil, forgiving, and without resentment toward God or man. Such souls already looked as radiant as angels. They were intensely visible and more substantial than other souls in Sheol. Memnoch had found millions of such souls and had taken them into God's presence. They were amazed and delighted and immediately started to sing with the angels. God had accepted them all into Heaven. *(MD 248–258)*

The souls from Sheol had brought with them the power to project their imaginations and thus had helped create the environment that Lestat witnesses. They transformed the geography of Heaven. "These souls took the invisible fabric of Heaven . . . and in a twinkling surrounded us all with wondrous constructions representing their curiosity, their concepts of beauty and their desires!" *(MD 257)*

However, Memnoch had pressed his luck with God when he had insisted that all human souls should have a chance to enter Heaven. He had challenged God to see for Himself what it is like to be a mortal, and for that, God had cast him from Heaven. Eventually, though, God had accepted Memnoch's challenge and had become a man, dying for the redemption of souls who will believe in Him and His sacrifice. He had entered Sheol to show His wounds to the souls there and had taken

Luca Signorelli, "Angels Guiding the Elect into Paradise"

them to Heaven with Him. Others are allowed in as they understand and accept His plan. Those that do not are relegated to Hell to be purged and purified before being allowed into Heaven. In short, every soul can make it to Heaven eventually, but some may take a longer, more arduous route. *(MD 301–302)*

"My concept of Heaven," said Rice, "is the result of immense research into personal accounts of Heaven by those who have had near-death experiences, as recounted in the books of Kenneth Ring, Raymond Moody, Dr. Melvin Morse, Betty Eadie, and numerous scholarly works on the question. I also used my imagination, of course. You might say it is an original conception influenced by other conceptions. You can find similar descriptions of Heaven throughout history,

but my vision of it tends to correspond more directly with the contemporary near-death research."

See also Angel, Christ, Christianity, Garden of Waiting, God, Hell, Lestat de Lioncourt, Memnoch, *Memnoch the Devil*, Religion, Sheol, Soul, Suffering, Thirteen Revelations of Physical Evolution.

Hell   The place of eternal torment of impenitent souls that cannot enter Heaven; it represents a physical and spiritual separation from God for those souls that He, in His purity and goodness, cannot abide. Hell comes from an Anglo-Saxon word that means "concealed" and suggests a place hidden in the heated center of the Earth. In early Sumerian accounts, a Land of the Dead was first mentioned four thousand years ago, and the concept of a place for punishing bad people after death has become universal. Typical depictions of what one endures in Hell are based on the worst tortures that humans can imagine and usually involve extreme heat or cold.

Enoch II located Hell originally in the northern regions of the third Heaven before God eventually moved it to the underworld. Satan and his legions were thought to reside in the fiery regions (or regions of ice, depending on the account) to inflict the requisite torment. Christian versions of Hell evolved from the Judaic notions of Sheol and Gehenna. Sheol was a joyless place where all souls, good or bad, went after death. In later lore, however, Sheol was distinguished from Gehenna, which became the place where bad souls were temporarily punished and Gentile souls earned ever-lasting torment. While some cultures view their forms of Hell as a purgatory, Christians insist theirs is one of eternal damnation. Dante's *Inferno* is one of the most detailed accounts in literature of the degrees of torment endured in Satan's kingdom.

Louis thinks that he is in Hell; he feels responsible for his brother's death and, as a vampire, is the source of even more death. He continually torments himself over the question of whether or not he is damned. He, along with Lestat, is amazed that vampires are capable of love for mortals and for one another. They both had believed—as Claudia points out—that creatures in Hell would know only hate. From this they discover that evil does not eradicate love. *(IV 134, 286, 319)*

Throughout BT, Lestat thinks he is doomed to Hell; at one point, he even imagines hell as a hospital filled with sick children. This image is an indictment of his rescue of Claudia by making her a vampire, for this event is the one that most dogs his conscience. *(BT 210)*

Lestat thinks that vampires may suffer worse torment in Hell than damned mortals do. *(MD 20)* When Memnoch approaches him, he gets the opportunity to see Hell for himself. But first Memnoch tells Lestat the story of creation and of his on-again/off-again relationship with God. Due to Memnoch's adversarial role on behalf of human

souls, God had assigned Hell, formerly Sheol, to Memnoch for educating those souls not yet fit for Heaven. He had condemned Memnoch to spend at least one third of his existence in Hell among these wretched entities. Memnoch tells Lestat that Hell far exceeds Heaven in its numbers of souls, then asks what Lestat imagines Hell to be. Lestat thinks that it must be a place of madness, where "all your demons come and get you just as fast as you can think them up." *(MD 23)*

As Lestat discovers, no one is beyond redemption, no one condemned eternally. Memnoch describes Hell as closer in concept to Purgatory than to Christian images of endless torment. It is where people can realize what they have done to others and can forgive themselves, each other, and God. The lesson of Hell is love. "Hell is where I straighten things out that He has made wrong," says Memnoch. ". . . where I teach men and women that they can be better than He is." *(MD 306)*

Anxious but intrigued, Lestat enters this educational inferno with Memnoch. He sees a landscape of hills, chasms, and plains without end, covered with the wandering, wailing dead. They are bathed in a hellish light, and all around them are replications of earthly horrors. They have projected images of the other souls that torment them, creating their own Hell, just as souls in Heaven project a delightful landscape around themselves. (This raises the question of whether the Hell Lestat sees is actually his own projection since, before they entered, Memnoch had asked him to describe his concept of Hell.) Lestat sees images of torture reminiscent of Dante's vision, then gets a glimpse of Roger and Terry, Dora's parents. He realizes that souls in Hell meet their victims. It is a place where people "face every detail of it [their reprehensible deed] . . . so that they would *never, never* do the same thing again; a place where souls are reformed, literally, by knowledge of what they'd done wrong." *(MD 304)* Souls see the consequences of their harmful action with a full comprehension of how little they knew of their mistake when performing the deed.

It is not long before Lestat discovers what Hell means for him. One of the Helpful Dead—souls trying to assist others in their spiritual evolution—shows Lestat a door behind which his own victims wait. Horrified, Lestat flees. Memnoch grabs for him, ripping out his left eye, while the Helpful Dead try to stop his flight, but he manages to escape. No matter what Memnoch has told him, he cannot bring himself to be part of Memnoch's scheme. *(MD 292, 300–320)*

"The idea of Hell as Purgatory," said Rice, "is based on the first-person accounts of near-death experiences, in which they speak about how they saw everything they had done in their lives and how they had wronged others, and how bad the others had felt, and yet this experience had not been a cruel one. They had judged themselves.

Hieronymus Bosch,
"Hell," right panel of
"The Garden of Earthly
Delights"

"The concept that we have to forgive God is not original with me. It is perhaps most eloquently stated recently by Rabbi Kushner in his book *When Bad Things Happen to Good People*. My book emphasizes strictly the author's fiction, but it was influenced somewhat by Rabbi Kushner's notions, and by other notions that God is not perfect, which I had already begun to explore before writing *The Tale of the Body Thief*."

See also Demons, Devil, Gehenna, God, Helpful Dead, Lestat de Lioncourt, Memnoch, *Memnoch the Devil*, Redemption, Sheol, Soul, Suffering, Victims.

Helpful Dead   In Hell, the souls who try to help other souls toward greater enlightenment. They are the well-formed ghosts from all ages and nations. When Lestat enters Hell, they recognize him and announce that he has come. They also try to prevent him from leaving. When he loses his eye, they want to crush it so it cannot be salvaged. *(MD 309, 319–320)*

See also Hell, Sheol, Soul.

Heretics   Vampires who submit to no higher authority and/or no coven master; also called rogue vampires. The Children of the Millennia, including Mael, Pandora, Ramses, and Marius, are considered heretics and, thus, outlaws to be destroyed. Parallel to the authority invested in the Roman Catholic Church, it is the Roman coven that decides which vampires are heretics and which are not. *(VL 302)*

See also Children of the Millennia, Outlaws, Rogues, Roman Coven.

Hero   One who shows great courage, daring, and initiative. A hero is often larger than life and demonstrates self-realization, power over the odds, an intensity of experience, the ability to keep balance amid conflicting forces, a desire for an extraordinary life, and the ability to face pain and fear. This list adequately describes Lestat, Rice's ultimate hero.

Facing constant risk in order to have the most intense experiences, Lestat presses forth in one adventure after another. He goes on a hero's journey when he seeks Marius. For ten years he travels Europe and Asia in a sincere effort to locate this legendary vampire, who, for all he knows, might annihilate him on the spot. Yet he is willing to take the gamble if it means finding a teacher who can assist him in further developing his powers. When Marius finally makes himself known, he welcomes Lestat as if Lestat is indeed a hero. *(VL 372)*

Lestat frequently throws caution to the wind, sometimes endangering himself and others, but always triumphing. He awakens Akasha, then stands against her; he flies into the sun; and he switches bodies

with a mortal, all to keep himself at the edge, where the excitement and intensity of experience most often occur. "Heroes seek adventure," he claims, "but the adventure itself does not swallow them whole." *(BT 88)*

Lestat equates heroics with adventure until he meets the nun Gretchen. To his surprise, Gretchen also proves to be heroic. She possesses the same motivations as he does for having intense experiences, but she goes about achieving them in less dramatic ways. Heroism is not always about adventure; it is about the inner person. Gretchen has put herself at risk in the name of a higher quality of experience, and Lestat acknowledges that her actions and desires greatly expand his concept of heroism. *(BT 240)*

All of the vampires who stand up to Akasha are heroic. They risk their very existence for the sake of the moral good; that is true heroism. *(QD 281–282)*

See also Lestat de Lioncourt, Quest.

Hildegard of Bingen   A twelfth-century German saint, visionary, and healer, she advocated the full participation of women in the spiritual life. Believing the spiritual realm to be as tangible as the physical, Hildegard tried to teach her nuns the heavenly music that she claimed to hear.

She is one of the mystics that Dora reads. *(MD 82)*
See also Flynn (Dora), Religion.

History of God, A   A 1993 account by Karen Armstrong of the history of monotheism. She explains, from ancient creation myths to the present, how the concept of God has evolved under the influences of Judaism, Christianity, and Islam. Philosophy, mysticism, skepticism, doctrinal conflicts, and theories from the Enlightenment are all fully explored.

Lestat notices this book among Roger's collection. *(MD 32)*

Rice was deeply influenced by this book, which she considers brilliant. "It had a very strong impact on me," she admitted. "I loved the scholarship of it, and it taught me a lot. I keep it near my desk. I'll be studying that book for years."

See also Christianity, God, Moslems, Roger.

Hitler, Adolf   Although he is not specifically named in the *Chronicles*, Akasha alludes to this German dictator during her confrontation with the other vampires. She calls him a madman who was responsible for making the twentieth century one of the bloodiest in human history. *(QD 441)*

Holden, Gloria   An actress mentioned in QD who played the part

of a vampire in the 1936 film *Dracula's Daughter*. Khayman sees posters of her, along with Bela Lugosi, who played Dracula, on the walls of the Greek tavern Lamia. *Dracula's Daughter* was one of Rice's favorite films when she was a child and had a strong influence on her own development of the vampire. *(QD 131)*

See also Dracula's Daughter, Vampire.

Holy Communion   See Eucharist.

Holy Faces, Secret Places   A book about iconography that Shroud of Turin expert Ian Wilson wrote. It is a history and survey of the legends and places associated with the "holy faces" of Christ—His visage imprinted on cloth. Wilson thoroughly covers the phenomenon of Veronica's veil and the "Holy Face of Edessa," including the work of artists who perpetuated the myths, as well as those of other icons like the Shroud of Turin. Wilson discusses the problems of faking icons during the Middle Ages but tries to make a convincing case for the reality of the original Veronica's Veil and Shroud. In the end, he cannot make a definitive claim. The icons remain, as they always were, matters of faith.

Rice used this book for research, and she wrote in its pages, "The Veronica, my passion! Symbol of my art?"

When Dora reveals Veronica's veil to the public and inspires believers everywhere, *Holy Faces, Secret Places* is one of the books that becomes available in stores. *(MD 338)*

See also Icon, Religion, Shroud of Turin, *Veronica and Her Cloth*, Veronica's Veil.

Hong Kong   An Asian port, it is one of the places where Lestat sees Raglan James. Lestat views Hong Kong as a place of greed and hunger. *(BT 26, 107)*

In the first draft of BT, in a scene later cut, Lestat awakens in Hong Kong with his senses befuddled. He discovers that Marius had asked Khayman to bring him there so that Marius could scold him. They argue about their relationship, and it becomes clear that Lestat no longer feels any obligations to Marius.

See also Vampire Cities.

Horse   See White Stallion.

Hôtel Saint-Gabriel   The hotel where Louis and Claudia stay when they arrive in Paris after traveling through Eastern Europe. Ironically, the name refers to the archangel Gabriel. Although the name is fictional, the hotel is based on the Grand Hotel, located on the boulevard des Capucines and thought to be one of the largest hotels in

Europe. Designed specifically for wealthy travelers, the Grand Hotel was considered a novelty for Paris.

Louis and Claudia take one of the finest suites in the hotel, for Claudia points out that a bustling hotel provides the perfect cover for their clandestine activities. There they acquire freedom and luxury along with the illusion that they are not really vampires. They keep their rooms as mortals might, with books and flowers and playing cards set out, and they sleep in beds. They remain at this hotel until Armand's coven abducts them. *(IV 205)*

Louis returns to the hotel after Claudia's death, but ultimately decides to just leave their belongings in the room. *(IV 320)* (See Vampire Atlas)

See also Grand Hotel.

Huayna Picchu   A mountainous area in the Andes in Peru where an archaeologist discovers a set of carvings featuring the Legend of the Twins. These carvings are similar in style to—but not the same as— some cave writings found across the world on Mount Carmel, indi-

Machu Picchu Ponui

cating that perhaps another person had drawn them. *(QD 37)* (See Vampire Atlas)

See also Archaeologist, Legend of the Twins.

Human evolution

Changes over the centuries that indicate moral progress for the human race. Some of the vampires care about this progress, while others are either indifferent or fail to see it.

Marius is deeply concerned with what it means to be human. He views himself as a continual awareness, and he wants to witness how the human race will evolve. He describes how one religious system replaces another throughout history and how, with each change, the value of human life increases. With the demise of Christianity, Marius surmises that something more powerful than a new religious system may evolve. He holds that past superstitions involving deities and demons are now passé. And as demons pass out of practical myth and superstition fades, vampires, too, lose their value. *(VL 382, 398)*

Maharet takes up the same theme in QD when she confronts Akasha with the evil of Akasha's abstract scheme. Human beings, says Maharet, no longer build religions on the antics of spirits, and this is a positive step. Akasha believes the opposite is true: religion will never lose its hold, and those who believe it are limited in their understanding of the world as a whole. *(QD 423)*

Akasha's view of human evolution is that nothing has changed, although human violence has increased over the centuries. Increased technology has resulted in mass destruction. Marius protests that she sees too little, for the twentieth century has experienced the expansion of vision and the capacity to care. There is a greater collective outcry against the horrors that take place, and a desire to put an end to injustice. Technology—rather than doing evil—has spread throughout the world the dream of all humans coming together as one great family. It has also increased the quality and quantity of food, shelter, and health care. Marius insists that the human soul is evolving toward perfection; humans are better at learning how to love and forgive. They resist viewing things as miraculous, and their use of reason for ethical truths has removed the oppression of superstition and created an atmosphere of greater tolerance. *(QD 440–446)*

When Memnoch shows Lestat the Thirteen Revelations of Physical Evolution, Lestat learns about the way humans originally evolved from matter. The development of the human spirit was the Twelfth Revelation, and it caused the angels consternation. Since human form looked like their own and human spirit was unlike anything else in nature, some of them wondered if God intended to replace them with another type of creature.

Memnoch studies humans further, disturbed over the way God has included death and suffering as part of human experience. He

debates with God over the issue of whether humans are merely part of nature. Memnoch believes the human spirit, so like that of angels, makes humans something between nature and divinity, and thus they ought not to be subject to the energy exchange that necessitates death. He makes it possible for souls to have access to Heaven, although God still insists that humans are part of nature. *(MD 198–206)*

See also Akasha's Plan, Continual Awareness, God, Heaven, Hell, Nature, Sheol, Soul, Suffering.

Human guards   Mortals that the vampires at the Theater of the Vampires use as ushers during performances. These guards are absent when Louis burns the theater. He later learns that Armand, in anticipation of his act, had dismissed them. *(IV 217, 318)*

See also Theater of the Vampires.

Humanity   The state of being human that influences the way vampires view themselves.

Despite his need to kill, Louis tries to retain his sensitivity to the moral issues he respected when he was human. His sense of humanity accounts for his deep sense of guilt and his drive to find something good in his existence. He remains the most human of the vampires in the *Chronicles*, partly because he avoids developing total detachment and retains his deep moral sensitivity. *(IV 81–85, BT 105)*

To Louis, Claudia represents a vampire who has no humanity because she has no memories to link her to her former human nature. She kills totally without compunction. Her only link to humanity might be her experience of a deep-seated, albeit unconscious, pain with regard to the mother she does not remember. She is drawn to families, especially mothers and daughters, yet cannot bring herself to kill a woman whom Louis believes resembles her dead mother. *(IV 98, 104, 118)*

Louis also allows himself to be pulled toward mortal trappings that allow him to forget that he is no longer human. He reads poetry, appreciates art, lives in luxury (in IV), and mingles with crowds of mortals in the streets and in places of entertainment. He believes, however, that his last vestige of humanity dies when he makes Madeleine for Claudia. *(IV 290)* He knows it to be wrong and fights the impulse, yet he eventually gives in; her potential for selecting victims multiplies the evil that he is. Claudia agrees with him that this act of making Madeleine evens the score between them, for Louis had taken her humanity from her when he allowed her to be made a vampire. *(IV 274)* After he loses Claudia, Louis sinks into an indifference that mirrors his changeless state. He detaches himself from humanity, the source of endless change, and goes on with life in such a static manner that even Armand grows bored with him and drifts away. *(IV 325)*

Armand fails to exhibit much humanity because he was made a vampire when he was seventeen and, like Claudia, possesses little memory of what being human was like. As such, he exhibits the vampire quality of detachment to such a degree that he seems inhuman to Louis and Lestat. *(IV 228, VL 200–202, QD 89)*

Lestat lives two centuries as a vampire who believes he wants to be human again until he meets Raglan James and gets his wish. Upon becoming mortal he realizes that he does not like the experience. Given the opportunity to retrieve his former body and become a vampire again, he jumps at the chance and in doing so rejects his desire to be human. After becoming a vampire for the second time, he no longer resists the impulse to do evil and makes David Talbot a vampire—a killer as evil as himself. *(VL 476, BT 418–422)*

See also Claudia, Detachment, Lestat de Lioncourt, Louis de Pointe du Lac.

Humbert Humbert   See Nabokov, Vladimir.

Hungary   One of the countries of Eastern Europe through which Louis and Claudia travel in IV on their quest to find Old World vampires. *(IV 197)* (See Vampire Atlas)

See also Eastern Europe.

Hunger   See Thirst.

Hunter   What David Talbot was in his youth, and what Lestat is as a vampire. Both of them are the hunted as well. Lestat hunts David, just as the tiger did in Lestat's dream, and Raglan James hunts Lestat. *(BT 12, 61)*

See also Lestat de Lioncourt, Talbot (David), Tiger.

Hybrids   A vampire who is neither human nor vampire and who can exist in neither realm. Early attempts to steal blood from Akasha and Enkil resulted in such creatures; they did not endure for very long. They were not near enough to the point of death when they were made, so the blood did not take hold. Many ultimately perished in horrible ways. *(VL 442, 471)*

After Louis and Claudia experience the mindless, corpselike Old World vampires in Eastern Europe, Claudia asks Louis if it is possible that he has made hybrids by accident, leaving behind a trail of creatures like those they saw. He cannot abide even the thought that this could be true. *(IV 200)*

See also Revenant.

Hypnosis   See Spell-bind.

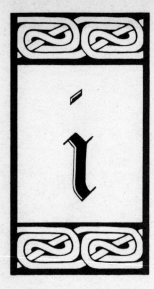

Iago   The jealous villain in Shakespeare's *Othello*, he is responsible for Othello's death.

When Louis disapproves of Lestat's plan to meet with Raglan James about switching bodies, Lestat protests that he does not plan cunning scenarios like Iago. He is merely curious and adventurous. *(BT 111)*

Lestat claims that he prefers victims who possess the mentality of Iago, the sophisticated murderer. For this reason, he stalks and kills Roger. *(MD 12)*

See also *Othello*, Roger, Shakespeare.

Icarus   The son of Daedalus, who with his father donned a pair of artificial wax-and-feather wings to escape the labyrinth of Minos. Icarus flies too close to the sun, however, and, when the wax melts off the wings, falls to his death.

Lestat refers to Icarus when he worries he might not successfully fly without Akasha's strength. He wants to take Louis with him to London, but it would be his first attempt to use the power of flight since Akasha's demise. He decides to go ahead and succeeds in lifting Louis high into the air. They cross the Atlantic Ocean and arrive in London. *(QD 481)*

See also Flight.

Ice Age   A period of extensive glaciation during the Earth's history, it is believed to have resulted from years of buildup when summers were too cool to melt a previous winter's ice. The end of Europe's last Ice Age is estimated around the year 6740 B.C.

When Memnoch tells Lestat the story of creation, he takes him to a paradisial time before the Second Ice Age. *(MD 178, 183)*

Daedalus and Icarus

Icon   An object that bears an image of divinity not made of human hands, it is imprinted by God Himself. "A revelation in material form" is how Rice describes it. *(MD 100)* Examples of icons are the Shroud of Turin and Veronica's veil. Some such images have been reputed to transfer themselves onto other objects when touched, and some are said to possess the power to heal.

Roger is ever in search of these kinds of icons. He wants Dora to have one upon which to found her religion, although she rejects all

gifts from him. He actually possesses several valuable relics, such as thirteenth-century replicas of Veronica's veil. *(MD 100)*

When Christ invites Lestat to watch Him go to His Crucifixion, Lestat actually witnesses the making of an icon. A woman named Veronica steps forth and offers her veil for Christ to wipe His face. When He does so, an image of His facial features appears on the cloth. Christ hands it to Lestat, and he keeps it safe from harm. Eventually, he delivers it to Dora, who displays it to the public, believing that the death of her father made it possible for her to possess the real thing. The resulting media blitz and pilgrimage to see the veil infuses Christianity with new purpose. *(MD 284–285, 333–343)*

See also Christ, *Holy Faces, Secret Places,* Religious Relics/Artifacts, Shroud of Turin, Vera-icon, *Veronica and Her Cloth,* Veronica's Veil.

Ile de la Cité   The old heart of Paris that contains many medieval residences. Notre Dame Cathedral stands here. Nicolas and Lestat take rooms here when they first arrive in Paris. *(VL 63)* (See Vampire Atlas)

See also Paris.

Ile St.-Louis   A small island in the Seine upstream from the Ile de la Cité; this is where Nicolas resides after Lestat becomes a vampire and sends him money to buy a fine house. *(VL 127)*

Lestat visits this house one night in search of Nicolas's violin and encounters Armand there, pulling books off the shelves and reading them one after another. *(VL 248)* (See Vampire Atlas)

See also Paris.

Illusions   A misleading or deceptive image, either as a hallucination or a conceptual misperception. The heart of the vampires' existence is to use illusion to seduce victims and each other.

Vampires strive to create an illusion of romance and beauty; this then hides the reality of their evil. This is most clearly portrayed in the Theater of the Vampires, which perpetuates a double illusion. The vampires pretend to be actors who are merely pretending to be vampires so that they can kill on stage and make their audience believe that the victim's death is an illusion. *(IV 218–227)*

In QD, Akasha walks in the bodies of selected mortals and immortals to experience the rawness of life, then realizes that all she has seen through them is illusory. She is actually a motionless, purposeless thing sitting still upon a throne. The resentment builds in her until she rises in response to Lestat's rock music and employs him to help her achieve her world plan. Akasha then suffers under another illusion— that she is creating a new paradise on earth when, in actuality, she is destroying much of humankind and her own race. *(QD 260)*

Lestat also participates in illusions. He believes that although he is evil as a vampire, he can do good. He gets his first hint at this self-deception when Akasha tells him that she is the logical consequence of such thinking: she is striving to accomplish the very same goal, but it is one in which Lestat cannot see any good. *(QD 359)* After Akasha's demise, Lestat confronts this reality again—that as a vampire he cannot really accomplish good—when he kills innocent people rather than evildoers. *(BT 22–23)*

Lestat possesses other illusions that are shattered. In BT, he claims that he has lived by two beliefs: that no one can resist the Dark Gift, and that vampires wish to be mortal again. David Talbot's refusal shows the former belief to be false, and Raglan James helps Lestat to see that the latter belief is untrue as well, after they switch bodies. *(BT 45, 109)*

Memnoch the Devil may have drawn Lestat into an illusion when he showed Lestat Heaven and Hell. Lestat believes the experience was real, but he is not certain. *(MD 331, 353)*

See also Deception, Self-deception, Theater of the Vampires.

Immortality The condition of not being susceptible to death, or the feeling that a moment stretches endlessly in all directions; it also may involve the sense that all things seem possible and that there is all the time in the world to do them. Immortality is usually reserved for godlike beings and differentiates them from mortals, who have a limited span of years.

Louis, who never fully relinquished his mortal existence, views immortality as an endless series of lonely nights once he is spurned by Babette. His attitude shows that immortality can be a trap that seems immutable. *(IV 77)*

Armand tells Louis that most vampires fail to possess the stamina necessary for appreciating their immortality and living fully through the centuries because they are limited by their human psychological baggage. Many cannot endure the changes that inevitably sweep one century into another and have no idea how to find or create anchors for themselves, as Armand has done with rituals, companions, and religious structures. Immortality then becomes a prison sentence "in a madhouse of figures and forms that are hopelessly unintelligible and without value." *(IV 285)* Some vampires then deliberately end their lives (via fire or the sun), or bury themselves deep in the ground where they try to escape their immortal existence.

Marius describes immortality as the living out of one lifetime after another, plunging into the stream over and over. As he retains a keen interest in human progress through the centuries, he is thus able to view immortality in stages rather than as one long, monotonous existence. *(VL 469)*

As a mortal, Daniel is obsessed with becoming immortal. This desire starts when he first hears Louis's story and believes it to be a grand adventure, and it grows when Louis bites him and gives him a taste of the swoon experienced by victims. He then encounters Armand, who eventually gives Daniel a small, teasing dose of his immortal blood; this fuels Daniel's obsession even more. Daniel then becomes an alcoholic to try to numb his unquenched desire, until Armand finally makes him a vampire. *(QD 83, 89, 99)*

Another form of immortality is explored in BT. Raglan James, a mortal, can take possession of other people's bodies; he is thus able to leave his own aged, diseased body for that of a twenty-six-year-old, physically fit mechanic. If he continues on this path, then he could conceivably live for an indefinite period of time. *(BT 110)*

See also Boredom, Endurance, Insanity, Vampire Powers.

Immortals   In VL, Marius tells Lestat about the existence of other immortal creatures that are not vampires. These creatures are able to walk in daylight and do not drink blood. They are very old and perpetuate the image that they are powerful and wealthy men. Marius names one, Ramses the Damned in Egypt, and recalls that Pandora thought there was also a woman. Her theory was that these creatures are vampires who have ceased to drink, but Marius believes that vampires who have been destroyed in fires may return in other forms. Pandora herself thinks she had been a vampire who perished when Akasha and Enkil were placed in the sun. *(VL 474)*

See also Ramses the Damned.

Impressionists   Nineteenth-century artists who utilized vaguely defined patterns of light and color to depict a distinct way of seeing the world.

Louis and Claudia purchase Impressionist paintings for their hotel room in Paris, although Louis is disturbed by the intense colors and the way these paintings seem to depict his own hazy delirium. This soft artistic effect contrasts sharply with the harsh, violent art collected and replicated by the vampires at the Theater of the Vampires. *(IV 206)*

See also Art, Monet (Claude).

Inanna   The fertility goddess that Akasha worships before she marries Enkil and comes to Kemet. Also known as Ishtar and the Queen of Heaven, she, with Anu, was one of the two principal deities of Uruk. *(QD 314)*

See also Goddess.

Incest   Symbolically, a union of analogous matter that, psychologically, represents a desire for union with one's own essence. Incestuous

relations are practiced by the vampires, who make the mortals they desire as lovers into their own children. Lestat also makes his mortal mother into his vampire child and lover. *(VL 158)*

See also Erotic, Intimacy, Relationships, Sex, Vampire.

Indigo   A dark blue dye obtained from plants. Louis cultivates indigo on his plantations in New Orleans. As a color, indigo represents movement toward spirituality. *(IV 4)*

See also Pointe du Lac.

Individuality   See Conformity.

Infant Death   Lestat's nickname for Claudia as he watches her go after derelicts in cemeteries. He also calls her Sister Death and Merciful Death. *(IV 105)*

See also Claudia.

Innocence   Freedom from guilt or sin. Vampires value innocence in one another, although their appearance of innocence is often merely an illusion that is created by their beautiful faces.

Armand and Claudia both possess youthful faces that give vampires who meet them the impression that they are angelic and innocent. In fact, Claudia is capable of great violence and Armand relies strongly on deception. He tells Louis that he is evil, with "infinite gradations" and without guilt. *(IV 289)* With vampires, appearances are often not what they seem, and Louis believes that no vampire is truly capable of innocence.

In VL, Marius takes a different position. He views Lestat as an essentially innocent creature, first because Lestat is free of religious influence, and second because he wants purpose and love and does not clutter his life with self-defeating beliefs. Although Lestat questions things, he does not seek a dishonest system of self-justification, nor does he exhibit the false grief of sin and superstition. He has no need for illusion because he respects what he sees right in front of him. He may be a vampire who commits evil acts, but within the vampire world there is room for an attitude of innocence. (Subsequent events indicate that Lestat may be more complicated than Marius realizes.) *(VL 380–381)*

See also Angels, Armand, Beauty, Claudia, Lestat de Lioncourt.

Innocents, Les   The Parisian cemetery once located north of the place de Grève. Known as Cimetière des Innocents, it opened in the twelfth century and soon became Paris's main burial ground. It acquired its name when the Church of the Holy Innocents was raised next to it, although the church itself did not endure. The cemetery measured only about 130 yards by 65 yards, which necessitated the

Les Innocents, a former cemetery in Paris

dead being buried nearly 30 feet down. About two million corpses were eventually interred there, and it was only after 1780, when two thousand of these corpses broke through the wall of an adjoining building, that the city finally closed Les Innocents. In fact, for many years, the cemetery had stood side by side with the central market. Sellers and buyers both had to contend with the stench of decaying corpses.

As a mortal, Lestat goes to this nearby marketplace to have an Italian letter writer compose letters for his mother. There he describes the atmosphere of death the cemetery exudes, "with its old vaults and stinking open graves." *(VL 63)*

Later as a vampire, he finds the stench even more intolerable, and he is extremely surprised to find that the vampires living in a catacomb below the cemetery endure the noxious smell all the time. When he and Gabrielle are captured by this coven and taken below Les Innocents, they pass by skulls and rotting corpses as they are led into a domed chamber. Lestat even hears vampires sealed deep in the walls wailing for blood and begging for release. *(VL 228)*

When Lestat informs Armand that the cemetery is about to be moved from central Paris to another location, it startles the entire coven. This dramatic change foreshadows an equally definitive change in the vampires' manner of existence; Lestat's prediction is as much about the demise of their place of residence as it is about their manner of vampirism, which is passé. Lestat is becoming a new form of vampire for a new age. While they haunt cemeteries, he walks freely among mortals. They cling to superstitious rituals, dress in tattered black rags,

and avoid churches, while Lestat adopts flamboyant clothing, disdains religion, and proves that religious icons and sanctuaries have no power over him. *(VL 228, MD 125)* (See Vampire Atlas)

See also Armand's Coven, Entombed Vampires, Paris.

Insanity   What happens to vampires and mortals alike when they tangle with the realm of immortality. Where boundaries break down and maximum freedom seems possible, insanity can result for those who cannot face up to the resultant chaos and abyss. As Marlow said in Joseph Conrad's *Heart of Darkness*, the specter of limitlessness for those who are not gods is madness.

As several vampires point out, there is no way to predict what kind of vampires mortals will become. They may become titans or they may become imbeciles; there is no means of controlling the outcome. *(VL 470–471)* A vampire who makes several fledglings takes definite risks, since succeeding fledglings will be weaker, physically and/or mentally. Lestat discovers this to be true when he makes Nicolas so close on the heels of making Gabrielle. Already unstable as a mortal, Nicolas, when he becomes exposed to vampirism, finds his outlook is even darker. He behaves so erratically among mortals—making careless kills, ineptly trying to make other vampires, and saying shocking things—that it threatens the coven's safety. When the plays he writes take on increasingly darker themes, Armand finally locks him up and removes his hands. Nicolas decides to go into the fire and destroy himself rather than endure immortality in the mad intensity of his mind. *(VL 342–343)*

Madeleine's crazed obsessions intensify as a vampire. She had been living in unreality for so long with her dolls that she has no way of coming out. Vampirism only intensifies her unreal world and gives her a way to maintain it. *(IV 276–278)*

Other vampires indicate that, with their heightened sense of perception, they hear so many voices of souls, both living and dead, that insanity threatens unless they learn to shut the voices out. The oldest vampires are most vulnerable to this torment. *(QD 124)*

Daniel feels he is going insane as a result of his contact with vampires. He fears them, but he fears death even more and he wants what the vampires have: immortality. Daniel's dilemma is the human struggle of finding a balance between a finite nature and the desire to break past the limits. Emphasizing either at the expense of the other brings stagnancy or psychosis. *(QD 83)* Armand knows this and tells Daniel: "You will go mad in time from this knowledge. That's what always happens." *(QD 86)* Initially Armand refrains from killing Daniel and instead pursues him around the world, watching and studying him. Daniel feels and seems on the verge of madness several times, until Armand finally gives him a drink of his powerful blood and makes him a vampire. *(QD 112–114)*

Lestat believes he has unintentionally caused a woman he loved to go insane. In the body of a mortal man, he had made love to a nun named Gretchen. Although he had confessed to being a vampire, she had not really believed him, so he had told her that when he retrieved his true body, he would show her. When he did, she was so stunned that she immediately fell into prayer and began to bleed from her hands and feet. Although she never spoke again, she was viewed as a saint and became the focus of pilgrimage. Lestat believes that as a result of this contact with him, Gretchen simply went mad and her insanity manifested according to her religious beliefs. *(BT 357, MD 134)*

See also Freniere (Babette), Gretchen, Immortality, Madeleine, Nicolas de Lenfent.

Insect

Insects   Regarded in folklore as mystically powerful creatures filled with magical secrets. Louis views insects as an image of insignificance and disgust, and uses this image several times to describe himself and Lestat. When the vampires are watching the camp of runaway slaves, Louis feels as if he and Lestat are no more conspicuous than insects, and when he is drinking blood from his first kill, Lestat's attempts to hurry him are nothing more to him than the buzz of an insect. Plus, Lestat's musician friend dismisses a bite mark on his neck as an insect bite. *(IV 27, 28, 152)*

The insect theme was inspired by a short story Rice had read in the fifties in a collection of science fiction stories. The story opens with a discussion about how insects can camouflage themselves to look like leaves and other things. The narrator then describes a pale, mysterious man in a dark coat and hat who turns out to be a giant insect, and who has laid eggs that hatch. The eggs' contents fly out into the world as more little insect-men, and the narrator worries until he sees what had appeared to be a chimney turn into insects and fly out after the little men, as if they are predators who will ensure a balance of nature. Rice was inspired by the idea of something sinister behind a facade, and the implication was that this kind of camouflage occurs everywhere.

"That has always been part of my image of the vampire," says Rice, of the tall, dark man in the story. "I'm fascinated by the idea of the thing that looks human but really isn't. Of course, I thought of this idea in connection with my vampires, and I have never forgotten it."

Lestat views Magnus as moving about in an inhuman way that borders on that of an insect. When Lestat becomes a vampire, he realizes that he is no longer repulsed by insects but, in fact, has something in common with them. "I was of the dark ilk," he says, "that makes others cringe." *(VL 99)* When he encounters Armand reading books with a strange, intent expression, he describes Armand as an insect that is chewing. *(VL 247)*

Daniel also sees Armand at one point in their complex relation-

ship as a "great insect," a "monstrous evil predator who had devoured a million human lives." *(QD 92)* Enkil's corpse sounds to Marius like the scraping of an insect when it falls over, and the vampires who follow Lestat, Gabrielle, and Louis in their van after Lestat's rock concert are described as insects. *(QD 29, VL 544)*

Insects are also like vampires in that both represent forces of entropy, taking energy out of the universe and contributing to its disintegration. Insects devour wood, flesh, and other substances; vampires devour lives. Since some form of organization tends to retard the forces of entropy, the vampires search for meaning to give structure to their lives, in an attempt to deny this insectlike aspect of themselves.

See also Vampire, *The Vampire Chronicles.*

Interview with the Vampire The title and story of the first *Vampire Chronicle.* IV details Louis's confession of his vampire experience to a boy reporter looking for interesting tales. The "interview" is set in a sparsely furnished room in a house on Divisadero Street in San Francisco; it unfolds as a moral quest on the part of a "monster" who is searching for integrity and redemption. "This book," says Rice, "is about stepping out of life so you can better see life."

IV began as a short story that Rice wrote in the late sixties. "I wrote about vampires on a whim," she explains. "I was just sitting at the typewriter wondering what it would be like if a vampire told you the truth about what it was like to *be* a vampire. I wanted to know what it really feels like. I wanted to see through the vampire's eyes and ask the questions I thought were inevitable for a vampire, who once had been human, to ask. What do you feel when you drink blood? Is it erotic? Is it glorious? Is it spiritual? I followed my imagination and my instinct."

The subject of vampires had interested Rice since childhood; stories and films about vampires had always grabbed her attention. In particular, she had enjoyed a story—Richard Matheson's "Dress of White Silk"—told from the point of view of a child vampire, and the film *Dracula's Daughter,* which depicted vampires as both tragic and sensual. Her own short story tried to capture a vampire's perspective.

"It was about thirty pages long," says Rice. "The vampire makes it plain that the room is not his room, but just a room. The tone was light, a little ironic, and intentionally witty. The vampire was not Louis, really, but an Oscar Wilde type of character. He talked very casually, very breezily, of the whole thing; he was very satisfied with himself and his immortality. At the conclusion of the interview, the vampire makes it plain to the boy that he, the vampire, will wait for the return of the room's occupant, implying that he will feed on the occupant. The boy then hurries away."

Rice rewrote the short story several times and by the last version,

she had added a few elements. She finished it in August of 1973, one year after her five-year-old daughter Michele had died of leukemia. For the first ten pages, it bears similarities to the novel that Rice would eventually write, but then it veers off and describes quite a different set of circumstances.

The vampire (never named) meets the boy reporter in a San Francisco bar called the Pink Baby on Chestnut and Union streets. The boy wants interesting interviews to broadcast on an FM radio station, so they go to a room together to converse. The vampire himself owns a house (with a houseboy) and a suite of hotel rooms, but despite this he takes the boy to someone else's place which has ominous overtones. The vampire's attitude is less that of a depressed angst-ridden soul than of someone who has decided to make the best of his condition. He claims he likes being immortal; it makes him laugh. He did not fight against becoming a vampire, as he did in the novel, and he has some adventurous personality traits later attributed to Lestat.

He explains that the mysterious death of his obsessive, saintlike brother drove him out of France with his mother and sister. He then bought a large Louisiana plantation and three town houses in New Orleans. The guilt and grief over his brother's death is glossed over, although the vampire's carelessness during his mourning made him vulnerable to attack.

Lestat is the vampire who makes him, but there is little description of Lestat other than the fact that he owned his own plantation, had slaves, was a theatrical prankster, did not exploit his powers for all they were worth, and was viewed by the narrator as a bore. Lestat took the narrator to the plantation where Lestat's blind brother, an old man, lived, and transformed him (described quickly without the perceptual detail of the swoon and the experience of acquiring "vampire eyes"). Lestat told the narrator all about the world the night he made him a vampire, and they lived together on the plantation for a while until Lestat went to Europe. The vampire never saw him again.

The vampire lived off swamp animals for a time, learning things from the various types of animals. One of his favorite experiences was sucking the blood from a panther in a zoo. Eventually he took human victims, and he describes his first memorable victim as a female poet who had known Keats. On the plantation, he lived off slaves, sometimes not killing them; one survived to become a local lunatic. Eventually the plantation went to ruin. By 1863, to avoid watching the South lose the war, the vampire decided to return to France.

When he finally came back to Louisiana, he met his own niece. Wanting to take care of her and disliking her good-for-nothing husband, he killed him.

He then discovered that Lestat's plantation had been restored by a family from Brooklyn who had invented a fake history for the house. The vampire decided to kill them all, and just as he began, other men

came from Brooklyn. They were gangsters and they shot at the vampire, but it had no effect. As he killed them, one man asked him to become his partner in getting rich. The vampire could be his hitman and in return he would offer the vampire protection. The vampire refused so the gangster asked to be made into what he was. This enraged and disgusted the vampire. He would have nothing to do with a man who had watched his friends and family die yet thought only of his own fortune. The vampire killed him.

He tells the reporter that he now lives in San Francisco, frequenting bars and telling people he is a vampire. They take him home and become his victims. If he declines to kill them, he makes sure they cannot remember that he has fed on them. It is easy to find victims this way, he maintains, because no one really believes him. He plans to tell the boy a few more details, but the tape runs out. The vampire says that the owner of the room is about to return and he wants to wait there for him, so the boy leaves to go play his tapes back at the radio station. (Note: To see the short story on which *Interview with the Vampire* is based, please see pages 553–572.)

Rice began to write again late in 1973. At this point, the short story evolved into a work of length and introduced an element of deep grief. When Rice began to describe Louis's feelings about his brother's death, she found that the fiction provided her with a means of touching old griefs of her own. The vampire's life then grew and acquired rich psychological dimensions that removed him from the flat caricature of genre fiction. His perspective and profound appreciation for mortal life transformed a cliché "monster story" into a complex and engaging tale. Louis became a sympathetic, even a moral, hero of sorts, rather than a creature simply to be shunned and destroyed.

Louis was the mouthpiece for many of Rice's own yearnings, questions, and fears. "I was Louis when I wrote it," she acknowledges. The theme of Louis's story—a fruitless quest for redemption through empty religious concepts—held great personal significance for her. When she finished with the writing, she found she had experienced a cathartic release that moved her away from her own passivity and helplessness.

"In any sort of contemporary novel I had worked on, I had not been able to touch the reality of growing up in New Orleans, the loss of my mother, and the loss of my daughter. Suddenly, in the guise of Louis, I was able to touch painful realities. Through Louis's eyes, everything became accessible."

What is the story of Louis? He is first made a vampire in 1791 in the wake of grief over his brother's death, and he experiences the magic of the transformation with wonder and great guilt. For four years, he lives with Lestat, his maker, but becomes disillusioned with Lestat's crude ways. Louis decides to venture out on his own and confronts Lestat with his intention to leave. At this point, Lestat creates a child vampire, Claudia, to keep Louis there with him. Louis falls in love with Claudia, and the three of them live together for sixty-five years until Claudia, in a rage over being made a vampire when she was only a child, decides to kill Lestat and set out with Louis for Europe to seek out other vampires. Lestat does not die, however, and Claudia and Louis end up leaving him behind in a burning town house as they flee to their ship. Although Louis dislikes Lestat, he feels guilty over their treatment of him and is frightened of Lestat's possible retaliation.

Louis and Claudia go first to Eastern Europe, which holds only horror for them, as they discover that the vampires there are merely animated, mindless corpses. They then go to Paris, where they find vampires more like themselves. The oldest vampire there, at the age of four hundred years, is Armand. Louis falls in love with him, and Claudia, fearing abandonment, pressures Louis to create Madeleine for her. Louis debates with himself over whether he should go with Armand or remain with his two fledglings, but soon Madeleine and Claudia are destroyed due to Lestat's untimely arrival. Lestat knows these Parisian vampires and he claims that Claudia has committed what they consider to be a capital offense: attempting to kill her maker. The coven members quickly dispense their form of justice and Louis retaliates by burning down their lair, the Theater of the Vampires. He then falls into a state of gloomy indifference.

Years later, Louis sees Lestat again but dismisses him, and does the same with Armand and his pleas to get involved again with life. Louis winds up alone in San Francisco, where he tells his story to the reporter.

The first draft of IV was somewhat different from the version that was eventually published. The boy reporter guesses Louis's age to be around thirty-five rather than twenty-one, and much of Louis's story remains the same—with the exception of his discovery that Lestat wrote poetry as a boy—until he and Claudia arrive in Eastern Europe.

Although Louis and Claudia made plans to go directly to Paris, they stay only two days, for Claudia's reading of vampire lore urges them toward the superstitious lands of Hungary and beyond. The description of their travels is brief, but the vampiric discoveries are the same as in the published version: mindless, animated corpses. Louis realizes that this is what Lestat became after he was resurrected from the swamp, and Lestat is never heard from again in this version.

They return to Paris, take a flat on the boulevard du Temple, frequent art galleries, and attend parties and balls. Soon they see a lone vampire on the banks of the Seine, then a pair walking, and another in a theater. These vampires flee from them, so Louis and Claudia make themselves more conspicuous in the hope of inviting the vampires to approach them.

One night they return to their rooms to find one female and nine

The first edition jacket

male vampires, all dressed in black. These vampires are rather inscrutable, but they invite Louis and Claudia to a house on the Faubourg St.-Germain. The house is a musty old mansion that is staffed by elderly human servants who hope to be made vampires one day. Inside, Louis and Claudia see paintings similar to those described in the subterranean room in the Theater of the Vampires. They are met by Armand, who invites them to a ball, where he ladles animal blood from an ornate cauldron into crystal goblets.

About twenty vampires enter the room and form an oval. They recite from Baudelaire's poem "Les Fleurs du Mal," which offers images of hell, degradation, and death. Louis believes that the vampires must be connected to Satan in some fashion, which gives him some small comfort: he is about to uncover answers to his pressing theological questions.

Two servants then bring in a blond girl, and the scene is a repeat of that in the Theater of the Vampires. She begs for her life, but succumbs to the death they offer, and is passed around. Louis drinks from her, although he is horrified at the orgy of feasting. Armand then takes Louis to a bedroom where another mortal woman is sleeping, and Louis crawls in with her and drinks from her as she sleeps.

Louis then engages with Armand in a theological discussion similar to that in the published version of IV. It becomes clear to Louis that Armand has no knowledge of God or Satan, for Armand describes himself as merely part of the natural rhythms of life and death.

Later Louis observes the coven's ceremonies and mannerisms: they prize conformity, abhor wasted opportunities, and delight in provoking one another with elaborate dares and challenges. Also, the making of a new vampire is for them a communal act, involving a democratic process. Louis remains aloof and detached from this coven. He does not like what he sees of their rigid rules. But Claudia quickly exchanges her lavender dresses for black and allows her hair to be dyed white so that she fits in with the coven. She also befriends three brothers who teach her how to torment priests.

When the other vampires learn that Claudia killed Lestat, they decide that his death was just, and there are no punitive consequences; Claudia does not die in this version of the story. However, she does leave Louis for vampires who seem to her to be more her own kind.

Left on his own, Louis wanders around Paris alone. One night Armand catches up with him and asks why Louis has shunned him. Louis insists he is completely taken with Armand but does not feel kinship with the rest of the coven. Armand leaves them for Louis. He tells Louis how he was made a vampire in Venice at the age of twenty-five and how he lived with his vampire maker/lover for over a century. They leave Paris together and travel the world.

Louis convinces Armand that what they do is evil, and Armand

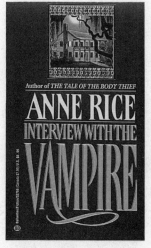

The mass market edition cover

agrees to go into the sun with Louis and destroy himself if that is what Louis wants. However, Louis does not really desire this, and he eventually gives in to pressure from Armand to go to New Orleans. There he learns how to use the cemeteries to find Armand's favorite victims: those who want to die. One poignant scene describes a mother one year after the death of her daughter. She has also lost her mother and cannot conceive of continuing with life without these two. Time has given her no reprieve, and she suspects that life is just not worth it. It is the expression of Rice's own despair at the time (1973).

Louis admires Armand's ability to draw close to such victims, but he prefers those who struggle to hang on to life. He then also informs the boy reporter that New Orleans was the place of his greatest suffering as a vampire, for it was where he met his mortal love. As tantalizing as this piece of information is, the tale ends here, and the identity of this character is not made known. The boy realizes that dawn is approaching and backs out of the room, hoping Louis will not notice.

By the time he reaches his car, Louis is there, angry that the boy had kept him talking simply to keep his mortal body safe, and he wants the tapes back. Armand arrives and tells Louis that the boy will do with the tapes what Louis wants done: he will make them public. Louis and Armand get into a cab together, while the boy goes to the radio station to listen to what he has recorded.

"The ending wasn't right," says Rice of this version. "It just didn't reach its cathartic pitch. In fact, it didn't really have an ending, so I went back and rewrote it, and then it had a horrendously different ending."

By the time Rice revised her manuscript, she was ready to let go of her daughter, and the second and final ending evolved in which Claudia is killed in the Theater of the Vampires. Louis, whom Rice considered the spokesperson of her feelings at the time, goes through an evolutionary process as well.

"There's a real change in tone in the published novel," Rice points out. "The Louis who opens it is not the same Louis by the middle. I remember wondering if that was a problem, and then I realized that the tone at the beginning tied in perfectly with the tone at the end. This was an accident, but it worked out: the cynical, cold person had warmed up and then grown cold again."

The end of Louis's confession, however, is not the end of the story. When the boy reporter publishes *Interview with the Vampire*, his action spawns the second *Chronicle*, *The Vampire Lestat*. Lestat hears about *Interview* from a rock band, reads it, and decides to tell his own story, correcting Louis's "lies" in the process. He talks about how Louis was too passive and burdened by guilt to really understand and experience his vampire powers. As a result, he had resented Lestat for

making him a vampire, and his resentment created a misperception of Lestat. *(VL 498–499)*

The third *Chronicle*, *The Queen of the Damned*, includes two other characters who are also affected by reading *Interview*, Daniel and Jesse. Daniel is the boy reporter who published the first *Chronicle* and who is haunted enough by it to seek out a vampire who might grant him immortal life. He comes to the attention of the Talamasca, who wonder at his motives for publishing it, and who use the book to guide their investigations into the Theater of the Vampires. They assign Jesse to go to New Orleans to document other physical evidence mentioned in the "novel." Jesse reads *Interview* and is disturbed by the way it makes vampires attractive. She sets out to show the Talamasca that the story is false. Instead, however, she finds incontrovertible proof of the existence of the vampires. *(QD 172–188)*

Vampires enraged by the public revelation of vampire secrets try to find Louis to destroy him. He remains in the house on Divisadero Street, which he believes is an unlikely spot for them to look. *(VL 525)*

Khayman reads *Interview* and summarizes its central theme as "Behold, the void." *(QD 204)*

In November 1994, after many false starts over the course of eighteen years, *Interview with the Vampire* finally made it to the big screen. In a swirl of controversy over the casting of Tom Cruise as Lestat, the film had first weekend earnings of nearly $40 million, proving it a hit. Although Rice had been skeptical, even apprehensive, about the film's casting and production, she was deeply moved and tremendously pleased when she saw the finished product: "I was knocked out by it. I completely forgot that I had written it. I was swept up." She took out a two-page ad in *Variety* to let fans know her position, and a month after the film was released, she wrote an eight-page supplement to express her views fully.

"The look of *Interview with the Vampire* for me was perfect," she wrote. "The art direction, costumes, lighting, cinematography, and craft of the film were sumptuous and thrillingly successful for me. I was grateful for the uncompromising lushness of the film, for its magnificent interiors and brutal exteriors, for its relentless attention to detail throughout in creating an immense and tantalizing and utterly convincing world. . . . It caught the dimness, the filth, the fragile, handmade luxury and ornate aspirations of the eighteenth and nineteenth centuries; it caught the mud on the hem of the garment.

"Brad Pitt immediately infused the despairing Louis with understandable feeling. . . . He got what guilt is all about, a guilt sometimes that is unattached to any one death or loss. He captured the despair of someone who has fallen from grace, lost his faith, seen what he cannot abide." Some of her favorite moments involving Pitt included when Louis said "no" to Lestat's suggestion to make Claudia a vampire, his

last scene with Claudia, and his discovery of her ashes in the airshaft—
"one of the most painful and exquisite moments in a film that I have
ever watched. Magnificent."

For Tom Cruise, her praise was effusive. "From the moment he
appeared [on the screen], Tom was Lestat for me. He has the immense
physical and moral presence; he was defiant and yet never without
conscience; he was beautiful beyond description yet compelled to do
cruel things. The sheer beauty of Tom was dazzling, but the polish of
his acting, his flawless plunge into the Lestat persona, his ability to
speak rather boldly poetic lines, and speak them with seeming ease and
conviction, were exhilarating and uplifting. The guy is great." Her
favorite moments involving Cruise included his attack on Louis, his
frustration with Louis's inability to fully realize his vampire nature, his
confusion after Claudia rejects his doll, and his horseback ride through
the fires as he looks back at the suspicious slaves. "That [Lestat] was
and is my hero . . . Lestat just won't be afraid of anybody. He won't
stand for it."

Kirsten Dunst as Claudia reached deeply into Rice's heart. She
felt the young actress was flawless and shocking. "The actor showed
incredible cunning, and yet a child's tragic vulnerability and heart-
rending capacity to be disappointed. . . . That none of her gestures,
words, or acts were prurient was a major achievement." Rice especially
loved the transformation scene, the scene in which Claudia realizes she
will never grow up, and Claudia's final scene with Louis. "I feel a
special love for her," said Rice, "because the role was so much beyond
the imagination. She did a beautiful job of it."

When Rice watched the film for the first time in the theater, she
broke down afterward. "I was shaking more violently than I ever had
in my life. It was a hysterical reaction. My body just gave out." So
much had been at stake over the years, and the film had reminded her
of many of the dark moments she had suffered when writing the novel
and of difficult questions that remained unanswered. Yet she was
thrilled beyond belief to see the novel finally made into film and she
praised David Geffen's courageous vision: "David Geffen is my hero
for getting this film made."

Although there were some digressions in Neil Jordan's script—
his vampires were less elegant and more brutal than Rice had envisioned, and he had ignored essential aspects like blood tears and the
full experience of the swoon—Rice felt that, overall, the film had been
quite faithful to the book. She even appreciated the new ending. She
was glad to have Lestat back, to see him pull the tattered lace out from
under his sleeves. "All that worked for me. It was enough in keeping
with the ending of my script and the book for me to be happy, for me
to see the possibilities of a sequel."

To her mind, the novel and film together emphasized many im-

portant human questions: "How far we will go not to be alone; how much we will sacrifice morally in order to attain our definition of magnificence, greatness, or independence; the nature of dependency and love. The film isn't talking about mere survival. It's talking about the possibility of grand achievement as well as endurance—it's talking about reaching for the sublime.

"I think they did something larger with this film than they even know. They got the larger questions we all face, that we don't know if there's a God. It was all the feelings I had back in Berkeley writing the novel. I started with pain and just went deeper into it."

It is Rice's belief that "fantasy and horror can speak to the ordinary and the most eccentric; fantasy and horror can embody and reflect the most common and most dreaded pain we all share. . . . The ambition and potential of these genres is limitless."

The film begins in San Francisco with the boy reporter (Christian Slater, who replaced the deceased River Phoenix). Brad Pitt as Louis begins to tell his tale, shifting the scene to a seedy, eighteenth-century New Orleans. Lestat (Tom Cruise) makes Louis a vampire, and director Jordan's script emphasized Louis's early predilection for animal blood. He sucks on poodles, rats, and chickens before he finally gives in to his blood thirst. A few of the scenes involving female victims were bloodier than Rice had written them, earning the film an R rating.

Louis drinks from Claudia, portrayed as a girl a few years older than the Claudia in the novel, but still effective as a child. Lestat makes her a vampire, and she moves into her new life with blood-chilling ardor. Several scenes involving Claudia's vampire education provide comic relief, another contribution of the film. However, as Claudia begins to realize that she will always remain a child, she grows angry. Finally she attacks Lestat for making her a vampire—much less brutally than in the novel—and after he returns from the swamps, she and Louis flee the burning town house and head to Europe.

In Paris, they encounter Antonio Banderas as Armand—much older than the seventeen-year-old boy vampire of the book, and with long black hair, but effective as the masterly and evil leader of the Theater of the Vampires. Stephen Rea plays the cruel and suspicious Santiago. The performance of these vampires on stage is more harsh and less elegant toward the female victim than Rice had intended, but it is in keeping with the way the vampires treat the newcomers, Louis and Claudia. The film remains true to the novel from this point, although with less detail and less philosophical dialogue, until Claudia and Madeleine die in the airshaft. Contrary to the novel, Lestat is nowhere to be found. Louis burns down the theater, rejects Armand, and returns to New Orleans. In a decrepit mansion, he finds a pathetically weakened Lestat. Eventually he wanders to San Francisco, where he tells his story.

The boy reporter is stunned that Louis cannot see what a magnificent existence he has. Louis threatens him, then leaves. The reporter gets into his car and drives across the bridge. Lestat sits up in the backseat, pushes him to the passenger side, and takes over the wheel. He takes a drink, feels "better already," and dismisses Louis's eternal whining. The sequel is set up, to the tune of "Sympathy for the Devil," as he offers the reporter "the choice I never had."

The producer, David Geffen, was pleased with the way the film turned out. Ever since a friend had brought the novel to his attention, he had wanted to turn it into a film. "I read it when it first came out. I got completely engrossed in the characters, and I thought it was a lot of fun. After I read it, I thought what a great movie it would make. I called to find out who owned the movie rights and found out they were owned by John Travolta at Paramount. So I forgot about it. Periodically it would come up, and since no movie was made, I'd check on it. I subsequently learned that it had been sold to Lorimar. When Warner bought Lorimar, I called the people at Warner Brothers and said, 'I love this project. Let me have it,' and so they gave it to me.

"The one thing I had said to Anne Rice from the beginning was that I was going to make a high-quality film of this and I wouldn't allow it to be made as an exploitation film. Unless I could do that, I wouldn't make the movie. I wanted it to be as compelling as *The Godfather*. By the way, I don't know that we succeeded at that. *The Godfather* is a pretty compelling movie, but we tried to model that experience, in the sense that it was epic, that it took place over long periods of time, that it was a first-class, high-quality film. Great sets, great actors. In that sense, I tried to model it after *The Godfather*.

"Anne told me that I was the only person who was willing to make the book [into a film] with Claudia being a child, without changing the essence of what the characters were. I was not afraid of it. You know, people were saying, 'These people are pederasts.' That stuff never occurred to me. I never got caught up in the things that troubled most people.

"I had a lot of input into the final movie in many ways—into the casting, into the choices, into the budget. I was very happy with the job that Neil did, with the job that everybody did, and frankly, I was very happy with the job that I did."

About his controversial casting of Tom Cruise, Geffen said, "He's a very good actor and he was completely taken with the script and completely willing to go on the ride that we were going to send him on. Contrary to all the rumors, he didn't try to change anything. It was a big risk for him, and I admire his willingness to take that risk. He's a very talented actor. He's a big star, and he made the movie better.

"I'm very happy with the film. It was a really good movie. I think it was the most difficult of the books to do, and now that we've done

it, it will be easier to do the next one. We're going to do *The Vampire Lestat* as the next movie and take it from there. It will be more of an adventure, and of course you now know the characters so you don't have to establish them."

Tom Cruise found the role of Lestat to be quite challenging. He had already read *The Vampire Lestat* and had thought it exotic. When he read the script for *Interview with the Vampire*, he was eager to be involved. "To have a chance to make a movie like that was great. People I talk with go on about how evil he was, but I personally don't think that Lestat is truly an evil character. You can't approach him that way. You approach him from the point of view of understanding him. Having read *The Vampire Lestat* first, I knew more about Lestat's past. But just taking *Interview with the Vampire* as a movie and a book all on its own, there are about four or five sentences in the whole book that really tell about the depth of Lestat's isolation and his compassion and love. For example, when he's holding Claudia's dress after she dies, he's devastated. There had to be love there in the first place. Why else would he weep when he's holding her dress? And how else can this child get Lestat to drink the blood from those two dead boys? He trusted her. That's the only way I could have played that scene. If he didn't trust her and he hated her, there was no way. He would be too suspicious of her. It's love that really brought him down."

Cruise felt that Lestat was deeply disappointed in Louis. "Lestat said, 'In the old world, Louis, they called it the Dark Gift, and I gave it to you.' You see, Lestat feels this is a gift he has given, and he has chosen Louis, and he's frustrated with his own miscalculation. Everyone understands giving someone a gift and having it be unappreciated—especially when you think you've given them the ultimate gift. And Lestat tested Louis. He said, 'Do you still want death or have you tasted it enough?' So he was very frustrated with that. I wanted people to understand him the way that I understood him. Not make him a linear kind of guy, because he's not that way in the book—the complexity is there. And the wonderful thing is that it's hidden from Louis's point of view, but even Louis himself, in telling his story about how bad Lestat is, makes the mistake of explaining how wonderful this guy was.

"Lestat certainly is special to me. I take a lot of time developing characters and fleshing them out and exploring them. But certainly for me, Lestat was a very special experience. It was an incredibly exotic movie and the role was like nothing that I had played before. You know, Anne Rice talked about his [Lestat's] wit and his humor, and that was what I really wanted him to have. But Louis didn't see it.

"One of my favorite scenes in the book was the scene with the two prostitutes. It's a horrific scene, but I went back and discussed it with Neil Jordan and said, 'Look, I want more of *Othello* in it.' I

paraphrased more of *Othello* when he [Lestat] was killing this girl, because he's an actor and it was a performance for Louis. It was really built on the frustration of him wanting Louis to just be what he was. It was a seduction of these women and it was a seduction of Louis— kind of the last effort to have him realize how wonderful this gift is that he has given him.

"Lestat is an adventurer. He's the only vampire in New Orleans. He's the only one that left the Old World. Here's a guy that travels out among people and goes to the opera and studies music. I mean, he was a fascinating character. Hence the frustration with Louis. So I always saw him in that way. I mean, in the scene with the prostitutes, he's angry. He's frustrated. He's hurt. He would have been extreme in that scene. With this role, the fun was playing the humor and exploring the depth and trying to make Lestat come alive and be what I envisioned him to be. I gave it everything I had and I was very pleased with it."

See also Claudia, Divisadero Street, Eastern Europe, Lestat de Lioncourt, Louis de Pointe du Lac, Molloy (Daniel), New Orleans, Paris, Theater of the Vampires, Vampire, *The Vampire Chronicles*.

"In the beginning"   The first line from the Book of Genesis that Lestat muses over when he is seeking an appropriate opening line for BT. *(BT 2)*

See also Bible, Genesis.

Intimacy   A close association or familiarity. Although vampires are essentially loners, they have access to great familiarity with one another through telepathy. They also strive for one or two intimate companions to ease some of the monotony and isolation that can accompany immortality. However, in the very act of trying to achieve intimacy, they often destroy its possibility.

Armand seeks intimacy with Lestat because he views Lestat as a powerful vampire and wants some of that power. He links his mind to Lestat's and shows Lestat the story of his life. This mental bond nearly overwhelms Lestat with its raw contact, and he resists Armand because he does not desire this form of intimacy with Armand; he did not invite it.

The irony is that, although Lestat would like to have this form of contact with some other vampire, he cannot achieve it with those he chooses; one of the greatest hindrances to achieving intimacy is the fact that no vampire can be aware of the inner world of any vampire he or she makes. A vampire may target a mortal for the Dark Gift because the vampire desperately wants that mortal's eternal companionship, but instead they are suddenly cut off from each other by a veil of silence. As Armand tells Lestat, "The Dark Trick never brings love, you see, it brings only the silence." *(VL 249)* Often the fledglings grow independent and resentful of their maker as well, so the avenue that would seem to yield the greatest intimacy is blocked, as if loneliness is meant to be the vampire's lot.

Lestat describes how this estrangement happened with Gabrielle, his mortal mother and first vampire child. At first, they are glad to have each other's company, but an uneasiness invades their relationship and increases as they develop values that bring them into conflict with each other. Lestat loves Gabrielle desperately and fears being alone, yet he wants to find the vampire Marius; Gabrielle desires to forget Marius and go into the African jungles. Lestat loves mortals; Gabrielle despises them. Both want the other to see the world their way, and both fail. Although they attempt, over a period of ten years, to postpone their inevitable separation, they drift apart spiritually until finally each goes his or her own way. *(VL 352–353)*

For a while, as Lestat feels this estrangement growing, he turns to mortals, playing a game of falling in love. He imagines deep intimacy with some supremely spiritual person who will understand what he is and accept him. He would then "pass into" this mortal lover and become flesh and blood again. *(VL 337)* He knows that he needs someone as strong as himself, who can respond to the "size of his soul," so Lestat seeks out Marius, who responds warmly to him but who sends him away for his own good. *(VL 468–471)* Finally, two centuries later, Lestat encounters the mortal who seems to be his equal, who understands and accepts him: David Talbot. They flirt with an unequal friendship and even go on an adventure together, but finally Lestat gives in to an evil urge and makes David a vampire, bringing down the veil of silence once more. *(QD 485, BT 45, 418–422)*

Due to this inability to communicate telepathically with their children, vampires who desire closeness often rely on the simple gesture of touching one another. Because there are no gender issues, male vampires bond as easily with other males as they do with females, and vice versa. Their heightened senses make them more aware of the erotic qualities of touch, and they embrace one another freely.

Even more sensual is the type of embrace only a vampire can experience. Vampires can bond by biting each other and sucking the blood. They can touch another's life through the beating heart, and there is nothing more powerful. Louis calls mortal sex a pale shadow of the intimacy and orgasmic experience of drinking blood, and when vampires give to each other their own blood, they achieve a union between body and spirit. It is a closeness unlike anything humans experience. Lestat describes this bonding with Gabrielle in detail in VL, then with Akasha in QD.

When he makes Gabrielle into a vampire, he finds the experience highly sexual. His teeth penetrate as if he is having intercourse and they

experience a mutual swoon. *(VL 158)* Later, as he places her in her sarcophagus, he lets a drop of blood fall on her lips. She lifts her head to kiss him and he slips his tongue into her mouth to let the hot blood flow between them. *(VL 175)* Although as vampires they no longer can claim a familial relationship, Lestat still calls her Mother and with the increased intimacy between them, this seems somewhat incestuous.

This ultimate form of intimacy happens for Lestat with Akasha, when she allows him to bite into her neck to suck her powerful blood. She then bites him at the same time in a different spot to create a wildly sensual "shimmering circuit" of taking back the blood she gives him. *(VL 486)* In the throes of the swoon, nothing else exists. The experience builds toward an orgastic state that has the potential of overwhelming Lestat until it is interrupted by Enkil tearing him away from Akasha.

Armand achieves a semblance of this form of intimacy with a mortal, Daniel. They love one another but remain in separate worlds. Armand washes and dries Daniel in an erotic display of affection, and even allows Daniel to drink his blood in limited amounts. When Daniel is finally made a vampire, they lose a powerful dimension of their intimacy. Although they now have a similar nature, many of their differences disappear, and with that goes the dynamic that had compelled them to be together. *(QD 92, 97)*

See also Estrangement, Relationships, Sex, Veil of Silence.

Inversion   The metamorphosis of one idea, object, experience, or concept into its opposite. For example, life is assured by the death of something else, and evil can turn into good. Inversion represents the dynamic of existence, the movement of thesis to antithesis that keeps life fluid and changing. As a literary device, inversion provides tension and a way to grasp the elusive quality of complex concepts and relationships.

Inversion captures paradoxical or contradictory psychological experiences that often defy clear and accurate expression in language. Presented as a pair of contrasts, each part of the pair is shown to contain its opposite, inducing conflict and potential change in the relationship. Alchemists who worked with this concept believed that the closer any phenomenon came to the focal point of inversion—the point of contradiction—the more intense the conflict; the more intense the conflict, the more possibility there was for creating something unique out of the contrasting pair, as happens when a male and female create a child.

The most obvious inversion in the *Chronicles* is the notion of the vampires as angels or gods. Rather than presenting them as demons from Hell and thus purely evil, Rice views them as "angels going in another direction," and as vegetation gods dethroned by Christianity.

That is, vampires were once deities who then became demons. Religious allusions throughout the *Chronicles* emphasize this theme. For example, when Mael touches Khayman's hand to ascertain its hardness, Khayman remembers the story of the disciple Thomas who had to touch Christ to believe the miracle of resurrection. *(QD 212)* Louis first appears as an angel to Babette, although she later sees him as a devil when she has a new frame of reference. *(IV 58, 66)*

As demons, some of the vampires in the *Chronicles* seek to use their evil to achieve a facade of good. It makes sense, then, that they often speak in polarities: "Your evil is that you cannot be evil." *(IV 263)* "The measure of my hatred is that love. They are the same!" *(IV 264)* Or, "Tell me how bad I am. It makes me feel so good!" *(QD 491)*

One vampire, Akasha, decides to exercise inversion as a form of power, using it both to destroy and re-create. She wants a world dominated by women, so she plans to annihilate ninety-nine percent of all mortal men. She wants to be a goddess and to create a "new Eden," so she strives to change the concept of the vampire as a creature of evil. She desires to establish peace through violence, and she tries to create meaning from nihilism. Her plan calls for first draining moral concepts of meaning so that good and evil become equivalent as empty concepts, making them interchangeable. *(QD 212)* Once they are reversed, Akasha redefines the concepts and the meaning of each becomes that which had been its opposite: the vampire is god; myth is reality; murder is benevolent rather than malevolent. Akasha expects to create her new world by inverting moral concepts, but she does not succeed. In the end, inversion is merely a conceptual abstraction rather than a practical reality, and in actual practice Akasha's blueprint collapses.

The fourth *Vampire Chronicle* is an inversion of the Capra film *It's a Wonderful Life*. In that story, George Bailey considers suicide when his options seem to run out and his life is full of despair. But Clarence Oddbody, an angel, then reveals to him how meaningful his life really is by showing him what would have happened if he had never existed. By the end of the film, George proclaims in joy, "I want to live!" Lestat, too, comes to the point of suicide in BT and then gets the opportunity to see what life as a mortal is like—what would happen if he were not a vampire. He rejects the experience and wants to go back to his vampire existence. He wants to live, but as a vampire, not as a mortal. Thus, he inverts the message of Capra's movie.

Relationships among the vampires throughout the *Chronicles* are also inverted. The most obvious are those that exhibit the sadomasochistic bond between the seducer and the seduced. Vampires are as much a slave to their victims as their victims are to them; both exercise some degree of control, but both also surrender to the other.

Another example of inversion is the relationship between Lestat and his serial killers: here the hunter becomes the hunted. Lestat in

turn becomes the hunted when Raglan James seeks him. Then James takes his turn as Lestat seeks him out. Such relationships exhibit the malleability of identity.

See also Akasha's Plan, Dominance/Submission, *It's a Wonderful Life*, Paradox.

Investors   See Agents, Christine, Financial Concerns, Roget (Pierre).

Invisibility   The ability to disappear, rendered possible by magical herbs that Armand had once described to his second Parisian coven. The coven eventually mocks him for perpetuating this myth, yet Armand's use of the theater to present vampires as actors making a "pretend" kill that is, in fact, real serves the same purpose: the vampires are essentially invisible to the mortal audience as true vampires. *(IV 247)*

Irrelevance   The state of having no purpose.

Marius tells Lestat that as humanity progresses and leaves behind religious constructs to guide their beliefs and behavior, vampires as either gods or demons become irrelevant in the course of human events. They have no purpose. Lestat resists this notion and decides to create a purpose for himself. He becomes a rock star singing songs about vampires and demons to make himself relevant as symbolic evil, which may inspire mortals to destroy him and other vampires. *(VL 10, 446)*

Akasha, too, suffers from a distaste for irrelevance, so she creates for herself a divine and glorious plan of a new Eden on earth. She will kill most of the men and give the earth to women. With Lestat by her side, she will make the old myths real and thus make a place and purpose for herself as the goddess who will rule over all. She can thus justify her existence. *(QD 289, 292, 299, 303)*

See also Akasha, Lestat de Lioncourt.

Isaiah   A major Jewish prophet of the Old Testament, he is credited with foretelling the events of Christ's life. When God transported him to Heaven, Isaiah reportedly envisioned the virgin birth of Christ and the Final Judgment. Isaiah's response to God's call for a prophet to preach to His rebellious people was "I am here, Lord." (Isaiah 6:8)

Lestat is reminded of Isaiah when Maharet says, "I am here, Lestat." *(MD 347)*

Isis   As the sister and wife of the ancient Egyptian king Osiris, she went in search of his body and brought him back to life. He was then dismembered, so she pieced him back together. Once the principal

The goddess Isis

goddess of Egypt, Isis was a fertility goddess associated with mystery cults who worshipped the moon.

Akasha identifies herself with Isis when she and Enkil are made vampires and reign in Egypt as deities. The association with a moon goddess is appropriate for a vampire, a creature of the night. *(VL 433, QD 416)*

See also Akasha, Egypt, Osiris.

Istanbul   The largest city in Turkey and, as Constantinople, the capital of the Byzantine and Ottoman empires.

Lestat and Gabrielle visit this city on their trip on the Devil's Road. Here they find vampires who live in houses and dress in the flowing robes of mortals. *(VL 324)*

See also Constantinople, Devil's Road.

Italian Commedia   See Commedia Italia.

Italy   The country in which Gabrielle grew up (in the city of Naples), and where Gabrielle and Lestat visit on their Devil's Road journey. They settle in Italy for a while, and Gabrielle sometimes departs from Lestat for long stretches of time. Italy is also the location of the Roman coven and of Marius's Venetian studio. *(VL 37, 293, 325)*

See also Devil's Road, Gabrielle, Roman Coven, Venice.

It's a Wonderful Life   A 1946 film by Frank Capra, starring Jimmy Stewart, Donna Reed, and Lionel Barrymore.

George Bailey wants to see the world but is anchored to his small hometown by the death of his father. He must take over his father's building-and-loan company to save the town from the hands of the greedy Henry F. Potter. When George's uncle loses several thousand dollars of bank funds, George feels he has no options left to him but to take his life by jumping from a bridge. Just as he is about to take the plunge, he hears a cry for help and rescues a man floundering in the water. That man is Clarence Oddbody, an angel who must earn his wings by keeping George alive. Clarence shows George how different the town would be if George had never been born, and George realizes how much he has aided nearly every citizen in the town. He decides he wants to live, and his good deeds are repaid when the townspeople save him from debt.

Lestat refers surreptitiously to this movie when he chooses the name Clarence Oddbody for the passport he gives to the body thief, Raglan James. He also uses the alias Lionel Potter. Lestat is about to reenter the realm of mortality, to live as a human again. However, his mortal experience ends up disappointing him and he decides he does not want to live. The theme of BT thus inverts that of the movie, for Lestat chooses a reunion with his vampire powers and is unable to see anything wonderful in being a mortal. Unlike George Bailey, he does not choose life as a mortal.

"This novel," says Rice, "is an inverse of *It's a Wonderful Life.* Lestat says, 'I would make Claudia again, I don't want to be human, I want to be a vampire.' "

Other parallels to the movie include names of restaurants (Bailey's and Martini's); Lestat's suicide attempt; Lestat's rescue from fatal illness by a nun (who is an angel of mercy); and Lestat's visions about whether he would do things the same were he to live his life over (e.g., making Claudia). As with Bailey, things surely would have been different if Lestat had never existed. However, the world would have progressed in a more positive direction, with fewer deaths resulting from him and his vampire "children." *(BT 161, 178, 356)*

See also Bailey's, Inversion, Martini's, Oddbody (Clarence), Potter (Lionel), *The Tale of the Body Thief*.

"It is finished"   The last words Christ spoke on the cross, quoted in John 19:30.

Armand echoes these words when he realizes that Lestat's arrival has irreparably disrupted his coven. *(VL 222)* He also repeats this phrase following Claudia's trial and consequent death, after which he believes he will both acquire Louis as a companion and punish Lestat with the same act. Armand has come full circle, and his words this time mark his triumph rather than his defeat. *(VL 507)*

See also Christ, Religious Images.

"It was the best of times and the worst of times."
A paraphrase of the first line of Charles Dickens's *A Tale of Two Cities*, which Lestat questions when pondering opening lines of BT. *(BT 2)*

See also Dickens (Charles).

J The conjectured author of the oldest continuous narrative strand in the Bible, which runs through Genesis, Exodus, and Numbers. "J" might have written one of three documents that seem to have been blended together to create the book of Genesis, which originated in the first century of the Davidic monarchy. Yale critic Harold Bloom proposed that "J" was in fact an educated woman.

When he witnesses the evolution of humankind, Memnoch wonders whether it would be appropriate to quote J. *(MD 195)*

See also Bible, Genesis.

"Jack and the Beanstalk" A fairy tale about a boy who acquires magic beans that give him access to a giant's lair.

Jackson Square, New Orleans

Lestat refers to himself as the giant who will get the human as he approaches Nicolas to make him a vampire, and does so again two centuries later when he dreams about attacking David Talbot. *(VL 235, BT 6)*

Jackson Square   The square in front of St. Louis Cathedral near the French Quarter in New Orleans. Here Claudia makes the decision to kill Lestat; it is also where Raglan James meets with Lestat to discuss body switching. *(IV 123, BT 118)* (See Vampire Atlas)

See also New Orleans.

Jake (BT)   A member of the Talamasca located in Mexico who assists Lestat and David with booking cabins and smuggling guns aboard the *QE2*. He also acquires information on "Jason Hamilton," the alias Raglan James uses. *(BT 304)*

See also Talamasca.

Jake (MD)   The bankrupt engineer with whom Terry Flynn had decided to move to Florida, provoking Roger to kill her. Along with her, Roger also shot and killed Jake, dumping both bodies in the swamps. Jake was Roger's sixth victim. *(MD 38, 76–77)*

See also Flynn (Terry), Roger.

James Bond   A fictional spy and adventurer created by Ian Fleming in his popular novels of the 1950s and 1960s.

Lestat refers to himself as the James Bond of vampires, for he, like the film and novel character, is also a man of action who gravitates toward risk and usually wins. *(BT 4)*

See also Hero.

James, M. R.   A British scholar who wrote ghost stories in the early part of the twentieth century, he devised images specifically intended to frighten the rational mind. His tales greatly influenced Rice, most notably "Count Magnus," which inspired the character of Magnus.

See also James (Raglan), Magnus.

James, Raglan   A vampire hunter with a unique agenda, he first appears in BT. His name, according to Rice, is "a bit of a nod at the horror writer M. R. James."

Born in India, raised in London, and educated at Oxford, James is a sixty-seven-year-old man currently inhabiting the body of a twenty-six-year-old. A computer genius, thief, con man, and psychic, he is adept at taking possession of other people's bodies; he knocks their souls out of their bodies, replacing them with his own. His original

physical body had been dying of cancer, so he worked in a British hospital until the perfect specimen came along: a healthy, vigorous, and attractive man whose mind was easy to manipulate. James chose to reside in this tall, athletic, brown-haired, youthful body not only to escape his own illness, but to offer to Lestat the type of mortal body Lestat would want to inhabit. James cannot manage this new physical body very easily, and his movements are often awkward; his clumsiness is partly what convinces Lestat that body switching can be done.

James initially attracts Lestat's attention when he shows up in various places around the world Lestat has traveled to, thus proving he can successfully track the elusive vampire. Lestat sees him in Miami, Paris, London, Venice, and Hong Kong. James attempts to forcibly knock Lestat out of his body several times, but, failing in these attempts, gives Lestat several fictional pieces about body switching to provoke his interest. James is also able to block Lestat's scanning so that Lestat cannot determine what James is up to until they meet face to face at a designated spot in New Orleans. There James claims he wishes to temporarily switch bodies with Lestat, so that Lestat can experience once again what it is like to be mortal and James can discover what it is like to suck blood and take another person's life—the ultimate theft. *(BT 119–136)*

David Talbot warns Lestat against undergoing the switch, informing him that James is clever, dangerous, and had been thrown out of the Talamasca for theft and unethical behavior. Lestat decides to switch bodies anyway, and immediately thereafter James runs off with Lestat's body, desirous of keeping it forever. James then murders Lestat's New York agent and not content with merely the theft of Lestat's body, attempts to access Lestat's files to take from him his wealth. He manages to obtain twenty million dollars by learning one of Lestat's aliases but fails to crack the rest of Lestat's codes. However, James then begins to kill in a pattern that gives his location away to David and Lestat: from reports of excessive murders in New York, Florida, the Dominican Republic, and Curaçao, it becomes apparent that James is traveling on the ocean liner *QE2*. Interestingly enough, James had once been a crew member along with his father, but had been fired, amidst scandal and disgrace, for theft. It may have been defiance that prompted James, under the alias Jason Hamilton, to book one of the *QE2*'s most elaborate staterooms—the Queen Victoria Suite—and parade about as a rich man. The deaths of several elderly women aboard the ship provide the final proof to Lestat and David of his whereabouts. James's clumsiness, coupled with his need for attention, is his downfall, and Lestat and David manage to successfully track him down and knock him out of Lestat's body.

Yet as the struggle occurs, James manages to knock David's soul out of its body, leaving David to take over the body of the young

mechanic. Lestat gets away from the stateroom with his own body intact, but unaware of the switch that James had forced upon David.

James, realizing that Lestat has been desirous for a long time of David becoming his companion, later presents himself to Lestat in David Talbot's body and requests the Dark Gift. When Lestat willingly starts to suck his blood, James attempts to continue tricking Lestat into believing that he is David. Yet his mind cannot uphold the false images, and when Lestat realizes who he is, he hurls him in a fury against a wall. James then dies in a hospital in David's body. *(BT 360–367)*

See also Body Switching, Mechanic, Mephistopheles, *Queen Elizabeth 2*, Soul, *The Tale of the Body Thief*, Theft.

James, William   A turn-of-the-century American philosopher and psychologist, he was best known for his philosophy of pragmatism. He also wrote *The Varieties of Religious Experience* (1902) in which he took seriously reports of mystical experiences.

As part of her religious studies, Dora reads William James. *(MD 81)*

See also Flynn (Dora), Religion.

Janis Joplin and Big Brother and the Holding Company
A San Francisco–based rock group in the sixties, they were considered one of the groups to emulate. *Cheap Thrills*, their second album, released in 1968, sold over a million copies. Janis Joplin was known for her off-color language, for her intensely erotic performances, and for downing Southern Comfort on stage. Prone to drug addiction, Joplin died from an overdose in 1970.

The rock group that Roger manages aspires to the sort of fame that Joplin's group had gained. *(MD 68)* Roger's ghost also refers to Janis Joplin when, in a bar in Greenwich Village, he orders Southern Comfort. Lestat acknowledges that he, too, had loved this singer. *(MD 51)*

See also Roger, Southern Comfort.

Jeannette   One of the actresses at Renaud's theater in Paris whom Lestat favored when he was a mortal. *(VL 133)*

See also Renaud's House of Thesbians.

Jefferson Memorial   A monument in East Potomac Park in Washington, D.C. Erected in 1943, it contains a statue of Thomas Jefferson along with quotations from the most famous of Jefferson's writings.

Lestat visits this edifice in Washington, D.C., as a mortal man. He feels connected to the sentiments expressed, although he does not refer specifically to any particular quotation. "I deliberately kept this

Jefferson Memorial,
Washington, D.C.

vague," says Rice. "I felt the scene—this mythical heroic figure dipping into something as specific, yet sacred, as the Jefferson Memorial—was difficult to pull off and I wanted to keep my use of it on a subtle, yet grand, scale. To quote directly would have trivialized the experience and made the entire fabric of the novel less convincing. I often do this in my books. I avoid being specific for fear of limiting the evocative and resonant power of certain places, countries, or buildings. The authenticity of the scene depends upon my having been true to my feelings when I stood in the Jefferson Memorial myself and read the words engraved on the wall. From my otherworldly, out-of-time perspective, the writings seemed miraculously brilliant."

The themes that bind Jefferson's excerpts in his memorial include freedom of mind, freedom of the individual, and the need for education. *(BT 198)*

See also Washington, D.C.

Jerusalem   The seat of the Israeli government, it is a city sacred to Jews, Moslems, and Christians alike for the religious events that occurred there. Founded during the second millennium B.C., Jerusalem

was chosen by King David as the Hebrew capital. With Solomon's temple, it became a spiritual center. When Rome took over and destroyed the temple, Jerusalem became a pagan city. Then it became Christian, fell to the Moslems, and became the focal point for the Crusades. Its subsequent history has been one of war and division between Jews and Moslems.

Jerusalem was the scene of events that occurred during Christ's last days. He was sentenced to die here, beaten, humiliated, and forced to carry His cross to the spot where He was then crucified. Three days later, He opened the tomb in which He had been buried to show that He had risen from the dead.

Memnoch takes Lestat near Jerusalem to describe his wanderings and his encounter with God in the desert. As they talk, Lestat sees God in the form of Christ, who invites him to witness His final days in the city. Lestat joins the throngs in Jerusalem who watch Christ pull the cross along the road to Calvary. Lestat witnesses the making of Veronica's veil, drinks Christ's blood, and flees with the veil. (*MD 267, 281–285*)

See also Christ, Christianity, God, Lestat de Lioncourt, Memnoch, Palestine, Veronica's Veil.

Jesse   Maharet's mortal descendant, who plays a significant part in QD.

With long, curly red hair and green eyes, Jesse is only one in a long line of women in her family who possess these features and who inherit the ability to contact the supernatural. She was born prematurely when her teenage mother was killed in a car accident, and as the only surviving member of her family, Jesse was placed by Maharet with relatives, the Godwins. As she grows, she is tutored and supported through letters from her "Aunt Maharet," who also arranges visits for her with other members of her family throughout the world. (*QD 145–148*)

Jesse is psychic and sees phantom buildings and ghosts. It disturbs her that the ghosts seem aware of her, too, but Maharet reassures her that the ghosts cannot hurt her. However, one spirit appears that Jesse cannot forget: the ghost of Miriam, her deceased mother. Miriam appears when Jesse seems to be in danger, as if striving to protect her. (*QD 148–151, 240*)

When Jesse is studying archaeology in college, she finally meets Maharet in person, who eventually invites her to visit the Sonoma compound where Maharet lives. Jesse goes for two weeks and meets Mael. She also learns about the records that Maharet has kept that trace their family lineage back thousands of years, and Jesse wants to become, along with Maharet, a caretaker of these records. She notices that Maharet and Mael keep strange hours, have peculiar habits, and

seem almost nonhuman at times. Mael feels protective of Jesse and attempts to make her a vampire so that she can escape her mortal vulnerability, but Maharet intervenes and sends Jesse away. *(QD 151–160)*

Aaron Lightner of the Talamasca soon contacts Jesse to work for them exploring paranormal activity, and she accepts, hoping to lose her own personal mystery, associated with Maharet, in a "wilderness" of mysteries. With the Talamasca, Jesse finds a new family until the day they ask her to investigate a house in New Orleans formerly inhabited by vampires. It is the beginning of the end of her relationship with the organization. *(QD 162–172)*

Initially, Jesse is skeptical about the existence of vampires. She had been shown vampire artifacts in the Talamasca's underground vaults, but she goes to New Orleans still skeptical. *(QD 172–177)* In the town house that Louis and Lestat once owned, however, Jesse discovers proof of a fire and sees the mural commissioned by Lestat and described by Louis in IV. In a secret compartment she finds a doll and Claudia's diary. The more she discovers, the more she suspects that her aunt Maharet is a vampire. However, the more work she does, the more disoriented she gets, to the point of endangering herself, and the Talamasca pull her off the assignment. *(QD 179–187)*

When VL is published, Jesse reads it and is convinced that Lestat is her link to enlightenment about Maharet. If he is truly the vampire he says he is in his lyrics, and if he looks and feels like Maharet, then Maharet must be a vampire. She quits the Talamasca to attend Lestat's rock concert. *(QD 190–193)*

At the concert, Jesse reaches the stage and is embraced by Lestat, who mysteriously seems to know her; she tastes his blood-sweat and feels how hard his body is, but she is then grabbed away from him and thrown across a room by another vampire. Her back broken, she lies there dying. However, she knows now what Maharet is, for Maharet's skin was like Lestat's. *(QD 222–225)*

When Maharet arrives to offer the Dark Gift to save her life, Jesse recalls the serenity she had experienced tasting Lestat's blood and she readily receives Maharet's Gift. Although Miriam beckons to her, Jesse ignores her and Miriam disappears. Jesse feels anchored to substance in a way she has never before experienced, understanding that truth lies in the flesh. *(QD 240–241)*

Jesse becomes one of the thirteen vampires who stand with Maharet against Akasha, and once the conflict is resolved, she goes off with Maharet. *(QD 462)*

After David becomes a vampire, he joins Jesse on occasion. *(MD 7–8)*

See also Gathering of Immortals, Ghosts, Maharet, Reeves (Miriam), Sonoma Compound, Talamasca, Transformation.

Joan of Arc The Maid of Orleans was a fifteenth-century French peasant girl who claimed to hear the voices of saints urging her to save France from the English. The French dauphin, Charles VII, put her in charge of his army, which she led to victory. However, the English captured her, tried her for heresy and sorcery, then burned her at the stake. She was later canonized as a saint.

David Talbot discusses God and Satan by addressing Job's situation. God never really knew what Job would do, David claims. Since it was an experiment, it proves that God is not omniscient and thus not necessarily perfect in all that He does. *(BT 73)*

Lestat compares Dora to Joan of Arc, considering them a species set apart from ordinary humans: "She knows something about God and the Devil that I don't know." *(MD 146)*

See also Flynn (Dora), Saint.

Job A figure from the Old Testament, he is an upright, God-fearing man possessing both wealth and a family who loves him. Satan tells God that Job is good and true to God only because he has lived a successful life that has been relatively free of suffering. God allows Satan to inflict suffering on Job to test Job's faith. In the face of adversity, Job shows himself to be a truly righteous man. Although he questions God at times, he remains steadfast in his faith and devotion. Eventually, God restores Job's happiness and prosperity to him.

David Talbot discusses God and Satan by addressing Job's situation. God never really knew what Job would do, David claims. Since it was an experiment, it proves that God is not omniscient and thus not necessarily perfect in all that He does. *(BT 73)*

To make sense of what Memnoch tells him, Lestat tries to recall Satan's role and actions in the account of Job. Memnoch's description of his relationship to God and Heaven contrasts with many popular accounts but does seem consistent with the Book of Job. *(MD 170)*

See also Devil, God, Memnoch.

Jonah A Jewish prophet mentioned in the Bible whom God punished for disobedience when Jonah was too frightened to preach to the sinners of Nineveh. He boarded a ship to hide from God, but God caused a great storm that frightened the sailors; when Jonah admitted his plight to them, the sailors threw him overboard to save themselves. Jonah was then swallowed by a whale and for three days lived inside the whale's stomach until the creature spit him out.

As Daniel travels with Armand in Armand's private plane, he views it as a technological reinvention of the whale's belly; they, too, are being carried inside to their destination. *(QD 107)*

Joseph In the Bible, the favorite son of Jacob who was sold into slavery by his envious brothers. Despite these circumstances, Joseph manages to achieve a high profile with the king of Egypt, where he is a slave, and he receives a favored position. He saves the country from famine and forgives his brothers, eventually reuniting with his father.

Lestat's dying father refers to Lestat as Joseph, indicating that he views Lestat as the gentlest of his sons, but Lestat later claims that this was merely a deathbed plea for forgiveness. *(IV 56)*

Journey   See Devil's Road, Quest.

Judas   The betrayer of Christ, who sold Christ out for thirty pieces of silver, then hung himself because he believed he was damned.

Louis compares himself to Judas because he, too, chose a path of damnation—becoming a vampire—for betraying a spiritual vision, in this case, that of his brother Paul. *(IV 72)*

Akasha also uses this metaphor when she confronts Lestat. She tells him that he has been part of her resurrection and he can either join with her or become a mere instrument of her plans—as Judas was for Christ, destroyed when his usefulness was past. *(QD 299)*

Julian of Norwich, Dame   An English mystic in the late fourteenth and early fifteenth centuries. She wrote a book called *The Sixteen Revelations of Divine Love* from visions she had experienced in 1373 during a prolonged illness. She claimed that Christ had revealed to her his great love for all people. Dame Julian depicted the Trinity as residing within the human soul, rather than as an external phenomenon, and claimed that sin was a necessary part of human experience.

As part of her religious studies, Dora reads the writings of Dame Julian. *(MD 82)*

See also Flynn (Dora), Religion.

Juliet of the Spirits   A 1965 Italian film by Federico Fellini about a bourgeois housewife plagued by self-doubt. She is introduced to the spirit world in a seance, which moves her to search for the core of herself.

Eric brings a videotape of this film to the Sonoma compound, and Jesse is especially moved by it. *(QD 156)*

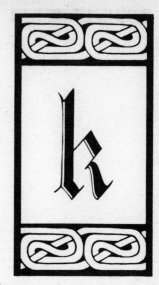

Ka A wandering being in Egyptian legend who sends out visions. In the story of Osiris, Ka is a ghost-soul who assists in conceiving Horus, Osiris's son, after Osiris is dead. Ancient Egyptians believed that each person was born with a higher soul, Ba, and a lower soul, Ka. Since the lower soul required nourishment, Egyptian pyramid keepers would leave food out for it.

Khayman compares himself to this figure, as if he, as a vampire, is actually his own lower soul still requiring nourishment. *(QD 124, 130, 237)*

See also Khayman, Soul.

Kant, Immanuel An eighteenth-century German philosopher, Kant was the founder of Transcendental Idealism. His most famous work is *The Critique of Pure Reason*, in which he claimed that human knowledge via the senses was limited and described the way the mind processed information—through mental categories such as space, time, and causality. He believed that ultimate reality was intellectually inaccessible, but insisted that moral imperatives implied the existence of God.

When Lestat tries to contemplate God logically, Memnoch compares him to Kant. *(MD 135)*

See also God, Lestat de Lioncourt.

Katherine La Voison See La Voison, Katherine.

Keats, John A nineteenth-century English Romantic poet engaged in the quest for the ideal and the transcendent. His work appeals strongly to the senses.

Lestat claims that Keats's poem "Ode on a Grecian Urn" inspired him when he purchases a Greek vase for his New Orleans town house. The ode focuses on an inanimate object that has survived for several centuries as the image of the way art seems to preserve beauty and happiness forever. This is in sharp contrast to the brevity of happiness in a human's life. The poem eventually expresses sadness at the failure of this illusion. *(BT 396)*

Rice also claims that Keats's "Ode to a Nightingale" inspired her description of how a vampire can die if he continues to drink after the victim is already dead. This poem emphasizes the antithesis of numbness and acute happiness, both of which result from the bird's sweet song. Rice also quotes from this poem in her vampire short story, "The Master of Rampling Gate." As the vampire kisses Julie's neck, Julie recalls several lines that describe both ecstasy and a sense of power.

"The Art of the Vampire at Its Peak in the Year 1876," the vampire story in *Playboy*, also refers to lines from "Ode to a Nightin-

Grecian urn

gale," and Lestat sees the line "Darkling, I listen" scrawled in St. Elizabeth's. *(MD 123)*

See also Heart, Poetry.

Keltoi   Another name for the Celts, a race of people in Northern Europe, who date back to 700 B.C. They are known as the Gauls to Marius, who first mentions them. The Keltoi were tall, fair-haired warriors who rode naked against Julius Caesar, frightening his troops with their fierce demeanor. Caesar eventually conquered them in 55 B.C., but Keltic cultures were preserved in Ireland, Scotland, and England.

Their priests were Druids, who practiced human sacrifice in elaborate ceremonies to appease the gods and goddesses of the harvest. Every five years they burned condemned criminals and animals associated with sorcery as sacrifices to the fertility gods. Marius sees the giant wicker structures that house the victims as he is being prepared to become a vampire and a new Druid deity. *(VL 412)*

Marius's mother had been a Keltic slave of the Roman who had fathered him. *(VL 397)*

See also Druids, Druid Vampire, Feast of Samhain, Marius.

Kemet   During the reign of Akasha and Enkil, the name for an area of ancient Egypt. The word refers to the black soil of the Nile Valley. *(QD 319)*

See also Egypt.

Keyholes   In legend and fiction, vampires were believed to have the ability to change into mist and glide through keyholes. The boy reporter asks Louis about this legend and Louis denies possessing this ability, although he wishes he had it. *(IV 22)*

See also Steam, Superstitions.

Khayman   One of the First Brood, he is the third vampire in existence. In mortal life, he is the steward for King Enkil and Queen Akasha. When the royal couple want to prove the spiritual impotence of the red-haired twins, they order Khayman to rape the two women. He reluctantly obeys, inadvertently fathering a child with Maharet. As a result of this act, the spirit Amel torments Khaymen until Akasha and Enkil step in to try to persuade the spirit to serve them. *(QD 327, 343–344, 382–383)*

After Enkil and Akasha become vampires, Maharet tells Akasha that the blood thirst will diminish if more blood drinkers are made, so Akasha gives the Dark Gift to Khayman, against his will. In a rage at this betrayal, he makes Mekare a vampire so that she can gain the power she needs to go against Akasha and fulfill her prophecy of Akasha's doom. *(QD 412–414)*

Khayman lets the twins out of their prison cell and leaves with them. The twins are caught by Akasha's soldiers in Saqqâra, but Khayman escapes. He continues to make other vampires in order to incite rebellion against the king and queen. His treason results in the vampire wars that entrap Akasha and Enkil. *(QD 414–416)*

Khayman survives into the twentieth century. His flesh is hard and no longer vulnerable to the sun. Although he is powerful, he does not like wanton brutality and he is lonely. He no longer experiences the blood thirst, but he enjoys the refreshment and clarity it provides. He now has the power to kill mortals telepathically. After he kills, he breaks open his victim's bones to suck out the marrow, but will not take blood from any mortal who has made a friendly gesture toward him.

Khayman is otherwise gentle, optimistic, and friendly, inviting mortals to his rooms and entertaining them with poetry and music. He lives by various guises in many different places, and when he stops having fun or feels pain, he fades out and forgets who he has been. His is a simple soul. When he is first introduced in QD, he does not remember much about himself except his name. Attempts to think back to his origins are painful, and so he avoids doing so. When he sees Akasha, however, he remembers how he became a vampire and what crimes he had perpetrated in her name. He is immune to her attack and follows her to San Francisco to attend Lestat's rock concert. *(QD 119–135)*

Since Khayman has been studied by the Talamasca under the name Benjamin the Devil, he recognizes David Talbot and Aaron Lightner at Lestat's concert. He tells them who he is and warns them to leave because there might be danger for them there. *(QD 221)*

He sees Mael and Armand, to whom he is strongly attracted, although Armand offers no friendly gestures in return. Khayman advises Mael to shield his thoughts from Akasha, and accompanies Louis and Gabrielle to Maharet's house for the gathering of immortals. Here he indicates several times that he believes in Mekare's prophecy of Akasha's doom, and he awaits Mekare's coming as he takes a stand against his former queen. *(QD 430)*

See also Benjamin the Devil, First Brood, The Gathering of Immortals, *The Queen of the Damned*, Saqqâra.

Kill, The

How vampires sometimes refer to their victims. It provides a way of thinking of human beings as objects, so that the idea of living at the expense of someone's death seems less hideous. *(VL 530)*

Louis explains in the first draft of IV that it is instinctual for vampires to leave the kill immediately so as to escape before decomposition begins to set in.

See also First Kill, Killing, Swoon, Thirst, Victims.

Killer   One of the leaders of the Fang Gang in QD. He makes Baby Jenks a vampire when she is in danger of dying and teaches her the vampire mythology as they listen to Lestat's music. Akasha destroys him when he is on his way to Lestat's concert in San Francisco. *(QD 42–50)*

See also Baby Jenks, Fang Gang.

Killing   What vampires do to survive.

Louis describes the experience of killing a mortal for blood to the boy reporter. "Killing is no ordinary act," he insists. *(IV 28)* It is not just about glutting himself. To him it means reexperiencing and celebrating the loss of his own life that occurred when he sucked blood from Lestat. Killing grants the ultimate satisfaction. Through the victim's blood, he is aware that the person's precious life is slowly draining out of the body, and it satisfies all his longings in a way that they never were when he only drank blood from animals. "I knew peace only when I killed," Louis insists. *(IV 87)* The blood of the kill also alleviates the cold and gives vampires a more human appearance by flushing their skin with color. *(IV 89, 287)*

Louis believes that Lestat does not fully appreciate the kill. Lestat is clumsy and quick, glutting himself with a vulgarity that defies the kind of exquisite sensitivity Louis believes is needed for the greatest enjoyment of the experience. Lestat, however, insists that Louis simply did not understand his actions. Although there are times when a quick kill is necessary, he describes his own approach to killing as often being highly sensual and erotic. It gives him the feeling of being like a god. *(IV 31, 81–83)*

Akasha shows Lestat what killing can be like at its most extreme when she dubs herself a goddess and leads Lestat into killing people en masse as part of her plan for world peace. He experiences great pleasure when he destroys one mortal after another, watching them explode from his mere thought that they should do so. The license he feels in those moments to kill wantonly is rather intoxicating. However, in quieter moments, Lestat knows that such all-out murder is morally wrong, and he puts an end to his participation. *(QD 292–295, 396)*

Another spiritual approach to killing is the one Armand takes. He believes there are already mortals who wish to die and those are the ones who should be sought; he gives them what they crave and believes that makes him something of a saint. *(VL 303)*

The vampires' participation in the cycle of life and death is characteristic of all living things. "We're always in the process of destroying in order to survive," says Rice. "The vampire is just doing what we all have to do. The tragic thing is that he *creates* nothing in the process."

See also Addiction, Blood, First Kill, Vampire Nature, Victims.

Killing a vampire   Although vampires are immortal in terms of immunity to disease and many other mortal threats, they can be destroyed. First and foremost, they exist by virtue of a spirit that inhabits Akasha and, as such, whatever happens to her happens also to all of them. If she is destroyed and no other host body is found to replace her, then the vampire race perishes. However, until Lestat reveals this secret through his autobiography, few vampires are aware of this danger to themselves. (Mekare later becomes the host.)

Although vampire lore dictates that vampires can be killed by stakes through the heart, decapitation, exposure to the sun, and cremation, the *Chronicles* accept only two ways, apart from the loss of Akasha, their vital source: exposure to the sun and cremation, with only cremation and the subsequent scattering of the ashes being a sure thing. "One must aim for total obliteration," says Lestat. *(BT 3)* Claudia, Armand, and Mael are destroyed by the sun, and Magnus and Nicolas are cremated when they jump into fire.

Yet some vampires seem immune to the sun. Akasha, Enkil, Maharet, and Lestat are all bronzed by the experience but not destroyed. However, young vampires connected spiritually to Akasha disintegrate or turn black when she is put into the sun. *(VL 433–434, BT 46–48, 54)*

See also Akasha, Amel, Armand, Claudia, Fire, Mael, Magnus, Nicolas de Lenfent, Superstitions, Sun, Ways of Dying.

Kindergarten, Baron Van   See Van Kindergarten, Baron.

Kingdom of Heaven   What Akasha calls the paradise she expects to create on earth with her plan of female domination and male annihilation. It alludes to Christ's words in Matthew 5:3 to believers about their just rewards. *(QD 393)*

See also Akasha's Plan, Heaven.

Kiss   See Vampire's Kiss.

Knowledge   The condition of apprehending truth that motivates vampires throughout the *Chronicles* to pursue answers to their questions about immortality and the supernatural. For some, it is a burden, as if getting their questions answered will confront them with uncomfortable truths; for others, gaining knowledge is a source of freedom, energy, and wisdom.

Louis views knowledge as a means of expanding his life and developing his mind. It allows him to take solace from his vampire nature. He urges Babette to learn what she can in order to make her existence better than it would otherwise be, and his advice to her

provides the reason why he himself goes on a quest to know more about himself. *(IV 48, 58, 81)*

It is Louis's need for knowledge and his uncertainty that Lestat has told him everything he needs to know to survive as a vampire that bonds him to Lestat, despite his hatred. Lestat plays on this fear by telling Louis he does not know everything yet and should not strike out on his own. Only when Louis believes that Lestat has nothing more to reveal to him does he finally order Lestat to be gone. (Lestat, however, then uses Claudia to keep Louis with him.) *(IV 33, 81–84)*

When Claudia's mind matures, she presses for answers about how she became a vampire and what it means. The search for truth obsesses her, and Louis senses that she is driven by some dark fear to know. He warns her that the wiser route is not to ask because there may be no real answers. When Claudia discovers how she was made, she hates Louis and Lestat for making her when she was so young. *(IV 109, 112, 117)*

Lestat, too, is plagued by the need for knowledge. Orphaned by his maker, he must survive and learn about his vampire nature as best he can. When he hears tales about Marius, he goes in search of him. After ten years, Marius comes to him and takes him to the secret sanctuary of Those Who Must Be Kept. There he informs Lestat that the acquisition of further knowledge may change him, for to ask is to "open the door to the whirlwind." *(VL 380)* He must apply his own meaning to any knowledge he gains, for otherwise it could leave him bereft. Lestat's openness to whatever the unknown brings attracts Marius enough to tell Lestat his story.

The vampire who seems to have the most unusual obsession with knowledge is Armand. He seeks someone who will tie him to an era and help him to understand it. He wants Louis to do this for him in the nineteenth century because Louis's despair is the despair of the age. *(IV 288)* When Louis fails to respond, Armand thinks he may die from his inability to bridge the gap between himself and the changing world. He comes upon Daniel, the boy reporter to whom Louis told his story, and makes him a reluctant channel for his own questing. Armand follows Daniel around the world asking questions about what Daniel is doing and why. *(QD 87–98)* When Daniel asks about Armand's experience with former centuries, Armand reveals his learning disability: he cannot synthesize knowledge in a way that he can understand it well enough to graduate from one perception to another. He deals only with the most immediate reality and cannot recall his past well enough to describe it. *(QD 90)*

Memnoch's promise to show Lestat supernatural truths seems to hold the possibility of Lestat finally getting all the answers he seeks. In Heaven, Lestat sees books in which everything is explained, but when he tries to remember what he is reading, Memnoch tells him that he

will forget it all as soon as he leaves, and he does. Even after he experiences Heaven and Hell and speaks to God Himself, Lestat finds that his quest for ultimate knowledge falls short of certainty. As Maharet tells him, it is the age-old dilemma: ambiguity hinders a definitive interpretation. Lestat reluctantly affirms this: "What if every particle of it was a lie! What if Memnoch wasn't the Devil, and God wasn't God, and the whole thing was some hideous hoax worked on us by monsters who are no better than we are!" *(MD 342)*

See also Heaven, Memnoch, Quest.

Kwaidan   A 1964 Japanese film by Masaki Kobayashi that uses sensual ghost stories to present the Japanese concern with mythology, legend, and the spirit world. Its primary themes are those of love, tragedy, and betrayal.

Eric brings a videotape of *Kwaidan* to the Sonoma compound for entertainment. *(QD 156)*

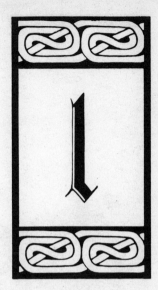

Lair   What the vampires call the place where they sleep by day; often it is where they place their coffins (when they use one). For example, Louis's first lair is the unused oratory on his plantation, Magnus's lair is in a deteriorating tower, and one of Lestat's lairs is the attic of his New Orleans town house. *(IV 34, VL 99–109, BT 398)*

See also Coffins, Lestat's Houses, Magnus's Lair.

Lafayette Cemetery   A cemetery in the Garden District of New Orleans where Lestat had hid some gold and jewels before he went underground in 1929. He also uses a vault in this cemetery to hide the key to his penthouse apartment, and sometimes it is where he sleeps. *(VL 5, BT 257)* (See Vampire Atlas)

Lagniappe   A word used in New Orleans that means "a little extra."

Lestat describes Memnoch's "gift" to him as lagniappe: Memnoch had told Lestat to mention "Uncle Mickey's eye" to Dora. When he does, Dora confirms that Memnoch knows things that few people know, adding to his credibility that he is indeed the Devil. *(MD 152)*

See also Uncle Mickey.

Lamia   The vampire bar in Paris; the name derives from the Greek word for "devouring monster." According to Greek legend, Lamia was a beautiful mortal who bore Zeus several children. In a rage, Zeus's wife, Hera, killed all of Lamia's offspring. Lamia then became identified with a serpentlike goddess who, deeply grieved, wandered the earth attempting to kill and devour as many children as possible. In other cultures, lamias were viewed as female demons or vampires who seduced young men. *(VL 528)*

Lamia is also the name of a tavern in Athens, where posters of

Lamia, a female vampire

actors portraying vampires decorate the walls. It is a gathering place for young vampires. Khayman is about to enter this tavern when Akasha destroys it with the vampires inside. *(QD 131)*

See also Vampire Bars.

Larry   A tall, blond member of the band Satan's Night Out, who helps Lestat to become a famous rock star. *(VL 13)*

See also Satan's Night Out.

Lasher   The incubus spirit in *The Witching Hour* and *Lasher*.

Originally, Rice had planned to use the character of Lasher in QD. He was going to come to Armand and together they were going to solve the problem of stopping Akasha's evil plan. However, Lasher's character developed beyond the scope of that novel and required not only a novel of his own, but also a sequel. The descriptions of Lasher in WH greatly expand the cosmology of spirits Rice initially developed for the evil spirit Amel; they provide a more specific description of the genetic structure of spiritual substance. Although the witch Mekare recognizes that spirits have a physical core, it is Rowan, the neurosurgeon in WH, who links this physical core to DNA structures. *(WH 886)*

An incubus, Lasher haunts a house where witches live and excites them sexually. He requires their attention to give himself substance. Like a vampire, he offers the lure of immortality through surrender, and represents the human potential for destruction at its most seductive. Echoing Amel, who entered a mortal and made the first vampire, Lasher craves mortal form. Because Lasher's cells possess a physical core, it is possible for him to mutate into flesh, and he manipulates the family of witches through multiple generations until his goal is achieved. *(WH 932–933)*

See also Amel, Spirits, *The Witching Hour.*

On facing page: Lafayette Cemetery, New Orleans

Latin Quarter   A section of Paris on the Left Bank of the Seine, near the Sorbonne.

Here Louis experiences his first encounter with vampires other than Lestat who might be able to offer him the answers and the community he seeks. The vampire who appears to him here is Santiago. This is also where Louis first sees Armand. *(IV 211)* (See Vampire Atlas)

See also Santiago.

Laudanum   An opium-based pain medication that could be purchased in the 1800s without a doctor's prescription. Claudia uses laudanum mixed with absinthe to weaken Lestat before she stabs him. *(IV 137)*

See also Absinthe, Claudia, Lestat de Lioncourt.

Laurent (VL)   A sixteen-year-old male vampire in Armand's satanic coven who strongly supported burning Lestat and Gabrielle for heresy. He becomes one of the four vampires who survive Armand's destruction of the coven, seek Lestat's protection, and develop the original performances of the Theater of the Vampires. Two centuries later, Lestat recognizes through Akasha's visions that Laurent is one of her victims, burned to death before the rock concert. *(VL 220, 246, QD 250)*

See also Armand's Coven, Theater of the Vampires.

Laurent (QD)   A vampire that Baby Jenks meets near the incinerated coven house in St. Louis. Young with silvery hair, he tells Baby Jenks that coven houses all over the world are being destroyed, although no vampire knows how or by what force. Laurent is burned to death as he attempts to flee the scene with Baby Jenks on her motorcycle. *(QD 54–56)*

See also Baby Jenks.

La Voison, Katherine   One of the ringleaders involved in the most sensational criminal case in seventeenth-century France. Also known as Katherine Deshayes, she confessed under torture to telling fortunes, dispensing love charms and poisons, and organizing Black masses for commoners and nobility alike. She also confessed to killing over twenty-five hundred children for her rituals. King Louis XIV's mistress was alleged to have been one of her clients.

Nicolas tells Lestat about this case, then refers to it later when he suspects Lestat of being in league with the Devil. *(VL 125, 144)*

See also *Chambre Ardente.*

LeClair, Madame   The woman who sponsored the recital of the

musician befriended by Lestat. Lestat also occasionally visits her home to amuse himself at her gatherings. *(IV 128)*

See also Musician Vampire.

Left Bank   An area of Paris that borders the Seine, it comprises the fifth and sixth arrondissements.

David Talbot has a vision of God and the Devil conversing in a Left Bank café. *(BT 73)* (See Vampire Atlas)

See also God, Talbot (David), Visions.

Legacy of Magnus, The   One of Lestat's rock videos, which reveals the vampire history to mortals. This specific video details the story of how Lestat became a vampire and what happened to Magnus, his maker. *(VL 520)*

See also Music Videos, Rock Music, Rock Star.

Legend of the Twins, The   The events involving Maharet, Mekare, and Akasha, when Akasha broke up a funeral feast the twins had prepared for their deceased mother, forced the twin witches to come to her land, punished them for being witches, and became a vampire after Mekare instructed the spirit Amel to avenge them. Maharet and Mekare became vampires as well and were then separated, but not before Mekare uttered a prophecy that she would be the agent of Akasha's destruction at some distant hour.

Egyptian soldiers who witnessed the affair first told the tale and, later on, scribes wrote down the stories. Miriam, Maharet's daughter, also orally told of the events to succeeding generations of her family. *(QD 416–417)*

Throughout the centuries Maharet searches in vain to locate her twin. She carves their story into caves on Mount Carmel in Palestine, depicting how she and her sister made rain, mourned their mother, came before Akasha, were punished, and were then separated. Thousands of years later, an archaeologist discovers similar cave drawings in a cave in Peru, on a six-thousand-year-old vase in Berlin, on an Egyptian papyrus, and on two clay tablets found in England. The words *The Legend of the Twins* are written in the ancient Sumer language on the papyrus and the vase.

Maharet funds the archaeologist's expeditions to South America, since she is certain that her lost sister is responsible for the cave drawings there. Nothing more, however, turns up, except for an image in one of the archaeologist's dreams of a woman walking in a jungle. *(QD 35–40)*

The vampires themselves become acquainted with the legend through the broken dreams they receive. It turns out that the lost twin,

Mekare, has risen from a comatose state in response to Akasha's awakening and is projecting the dreams telepathically to vampires and psychics around the world as she moves toward her meeting with Akasha. *(QD 271)*

See also Dream of the Twins, Maharet, Mekare.

Lelio   A name associated with solar power, strength of will, and a clear, penetrating light. The mortal Lestat uses it onstage when he plays a young lover. He first takes the part of Lelio with a wandering troupe of Italian actors, then acquires the same role later on in Paris. As Lelio, he anticipates what he himself will become: he makes himself up in white-face makeup with reddened lips. Thus, he looks just as he will when he is a vampire. *(VL 33, 67)*

See also Commedia Italia, Lestat de Lioncourt, Renaud's House of Thesbians.

Lenfent, Nicolas de   See Nicolas de Lenfent.

Leonardo da Vinci   The most versatile artistic and scientific genius of the sixteenth-century Renaissance, Leonardo is most famous for his inventions and for the celebrated painting *Mona Lisa*.

Lestat compares Armand with the way Leonardo depicted saints, because he appears radiant and full of wisdom and goodness, rather than evil. *(VL 316)*

See also Armand.

Les Innocents   See Innocents, Les.

Lestan Gregor   See Gregor, Lestan.

Lestat de Lioncourt   The vampire who made Louis into a vampire and therefore was responsible for the telling of *The Vampire Chronicles*. He is the narrator of VL, QD, BT, and MD, but makes his entrance in IV.

When Louis becomes a vampire in IV, he claims that a blond, blue-eyed, angel-faced vampire who quoted Shakespeare—Lestat—seduced him. However, Lestat loses this air of innocence and enchantment when Louis notes that Lestat seemed quite nonchalant, even wasteful, about the act of killing. Louis goes on to present Lestat as a thoughtless, vulgar, self-centered being who covets Louis's plantation and who whines whenever things fail to go his way. *(IV 13, 25–34)* Lestat even makes a child vampire, Claudia, whom he intends to use to control Louis (although in BT, Lestat almost redeems himself by confessing that his motives for that act were to acquire a friend, pupil, muse, and daughter). Louis and Claudia eventually attempt to rid themselves of their maker by cutting him to pieces and tossing him into a swamp, but Lestat survives and returns for revenge. They manage to escape Lestat's clutches when he is trapped in a burning town house. *(IV 95–160)*

In the first draft of IV, Lestat's involvement with Louis ends here. Louis leaves him in the burning town house, concluding that what he left behind was not really Lestat but an animated corpse much like the creatures he later sees in Eastern Europe. To his mind, Lestat is dead. Another dimension of Lestat added in this early version is that Lestat had been a poet as a boy; it was his poetry, full of dreams and longings, that endeared Louis to him. When Louis tries to get Lestat to talk about his poetry, Lestat curtly dismisses it, as if he views it as merely an idealistic boy's worthless fancies.

In the published version of IV, Lestat reenters the lives of Louis and Claudia in Paris, where he incites the coven at the Theater of the Vampires to destroy Claudia. (In VL, Lestat claims to have only been guilty of not defending her.) Louis does not mention Lestat again until he encounters him years later in New Orleans, when Lestat is too weak to kill for himself and seems to be slowly dying from his inability to adapt to change. Despite Lestat's pleas for Louis to remain there with him, Louis leaves and is not really sure what happened to Lestat. *(IV 297–306, 329–335)*

However, Lestat was never laid to rest in Rice's mind. Following the publication of IV and across the years, Lestat began to take full shape as a character. "Lestat formed in the corner of my eye as I was writing *Interview*," Rice explains, "and then he took on great strength. He developed this amazing coherence." Rice wrote six other novels before she returned to the vampire novels; two of them, *Exit to Eden* and *Beauty's Release*, helped her find Lestat's voice. "When I went back to the vampire Lestat, I was loosened up by that writing to make Lestat the infinite, warm-blooded man. As a writer I put myself into Lestat much more deeply than I had put myself into Louis because I was dealing with aggression in Lestat, and dealing with my own repressions. Lestat was my male hero who could do what I couldn't. I wanted to get out of the mind-set of the passive grieving person [which Rice was feeling while writing IV, due to the loss of her daughter]. Lestat really became part of me." In fact, Lestat became the male that Rice herself secretly wanted to be.

VL picks up after the publication of IV. Lestat had weakened to the point of going into the ground in a trancelike state from 1929 until 1984. Barely aware of the changing world, he is awakened by the sound of rock music being played down the street. He rises and feeds on animals until he is ready to face the world again. He visits the rock group down the street, they hand him a paperback copy of IV, and Lestat reads it and decides to write his own story. In Lestat's mind,

Louis, whom Lestat describes as the "sum of his flaws," has misperceived their whole relationship because of his dependent, resentful perspective. Lestat wants to set the record straight, and he begins his story by showing how he jumps right into things. *(VL 13, 498)*

"Lestat is the man of action," says Rice, "the person who cannot be paralyzed with guilt the way Louis was. It fascinated me to do a portrait of a different kind of personality, of someone who had never had a teacher [a mentor who could teach him how to be a vampire] and who had never really bemoaned the lack of one. I wanted to get into the head and heart of someone who would not give up, no matter what."

In VL, Lestat tells about his life as a mortal in France, where he was the seventh son of an indigent marquis, and one of only three sons who survived. His character is formed from the conflicting demands of being aristocratic but poor. At the age of twelve, he decides he wants to pursue life in a monastery because he loves the rituals, orderliness, and sense of being good. His father forbids it and takes Lestat's books away. Lestat later attempts to run away with a wandering theater group, but is once again thwarted. *(VL 23, 30–35)*

Responsive to change and resistant to monotony, Lestat goes out to hunt a pack of wolves and nearly dies trying to fight off these eight hunger-maddened animals. As a result of his bravery, Nicolas, the son of a local merchant, befriends him. *(VL 23–28, 42–63)* Together, Lestat and Nicolas go to Paris, where they eventually become part of a theater group. There, a vampire, Magnus, targets Lestat to become his heir. Lestat resists but is overpowered. The same night Lestat becomes a vampire, Magnus destroys himself, leaving Lestat to learn all by himself what it means to be a vampire. Lestat's sense of adventure and curiosity propels him into his new form of existence. He is twenty years old. (Lestat gives his age as twenty-one when he fought the wolves, so this is a contradiction in the text.) *(VL 63–96)*

Eventually Lestat makes his dying mother, Gabrielle, a vampire, along with Nicolas. *(VL 158, 238)* In the process he encounters Armand and his coven, which then strive to bring Lestat's new existence to an end. They have existed for centuries according to a system of rules and rituals, and Lestat's "unvampirelike" behavior, according to their ideas, threatens their manner of existence. Much to Armand's grief, Lestat instead empowers the coven to break free of their long tradition of religious superstition. Armand then wants to join with Lestat and Gabrielle, telling them his story in an attempt to gain their sympathy, but they leave him behind in Paris. Lestat decides to seek out Armand's maker, Marius, in a quest to find a deeper understanding of what it means to be a vampire. *(VL 209–233, 282, 318)*

The search takes ten years, and Lestat eventually despairs of achieving any success, going into the ground to experience "the first

death." *(VL 323–363)* Marius then arrives and resuscitates him, taking him to an island where he tells Lestat the tale of the origins of the vampire race and shows him the vampire Father and Mother, Enkil and Akasha. *(VL 367–466)* Lestat brashly wakes the Mother, Akasha, and drinks of her blood until Enkil tears him away from her; nevertheless, this brief nourishment empowers Lestat to sustain a near-fatal attack years later from his fledglings, Louis and Claudia. Marius sends Lestat away for his own good, and Lestat arrives in New Orleans to be with his aging mortal father. *(VL 486, 492, 493)*

When Lestat encounters Louis there, he senses in him an echo of Nicolas: an intense, self-destructive, and cynical nature, one filled with despair. *(VL 497)* Louis's beauty, refinement, and "staggering dependence" seduce Lestat, and he makes Louis into a vampire. Louis's anger and resentment strain their relationship until Lestat makes Claudia, both to see what would happen when the Dark Gift was given to a child and to keep Louis with him. He also performs the act in an attempt to feel like God, for he is creating another being in his own image. He enjoys the little "family" he has created, but Louis and Claudia view him with fear and mistrust. After an uneasy bond that lasts sixty-five years, Lestat's two fledglings decide to seek their freedom and rise up against him. *(VL 498–501, IV 112–137)*

After the attack, Lestat is considerably weakened and his injuries only increase when he seeks out Armand to help him. Nursing nearly a century's worth of bitterness for having had his life (i.e., his coven) dismantled and for having been rejected, Armand pushes Lestat off a tower. He also uses Lestat to help destroy Claudia so that Armand can have Louis for himself. *(VL 505–508)* Lestat finally takes refuge in a house in New Orleans, where he lives off the blood of animals. (Lestat claims here that the scene Louis describes in IV, of him groveling and pleading with Louis not to leave him, never took place; and both go on to allude to this fabrication in BT.) In 1929, Lestat goes into the ground for the second time to allow his battered body to heal. *(VL 508–513, BT 108)*

Lestat lives according to his own whim and in brash defiance of social propriety and rules of conduct. "My strength, my will, my refusal to give up," he claims, "those are the only components of my heart and soul which I can truly identify." *(BT 252)* Yes, Lestat courts disaster and tragedy, such as the time he decides to fly straight into the sun *(BT 47)*, but he also gains rewards from his excesses and the risks he takes. For example, although he is told not to reveal what he knows of other vampires, he deliberately tells all about his race in his autobiography. "I want to affect things," he exclaims, "to make something happen!" *(VL 522)* The vampire establishment does rise against him, but Akasha chooses to favor and protect him.

As a vampire, Lestat wants to use his evil image to do good. His

goal is eventually to redeem himself, and so he chooses to feed on those mortals who commit the most evil against their own kind: serial killers. "Lestat," says Rice, "is the bloodthirsty, wolf-killing, violent person who aspires to be something infinitely good and can't be." Lestat also becomes a rock star, partly because he wants to spread vampire lore through his songs in order to inspire mortals to eradicate vampires, and partly because he loves to play to an audience: "I could feel the attention as if it were an embrace." *(VL 67)* He equates actors and musicians with saints, so the medium of rock music seems to him to be the perfect way to do good with his evil nature. *(VL 520, 531)*

Yet his music brings the Mother, Akasha, out into the open, and she abducts him to make him her partner in killing off most of the world's population of men so that she can reign over women as the vampire goddess. *(QD 299)* Lestat resists, but in the process becomes more aware of what he is: a vampire. Akasha teaches him the true strength of his powers and he moves toward the more godlike aspects of being a vampire. He can fly through the air, move or burn things telepathically, survive the sun, and exercise other vampiric powers to their greatest degree. Although he craves blood more than ever, he discovers he is actually free of requiring blood for his survival. *(QD 466, BT 2, 10)*

On the heels of his experience with Akasha, Lestat befriends the mortal David Talbot of the Talamasca. He lures David toward vampirism even as he is lured toward becoming human. *(BT 31)* Lestat's two firm beliefs—both of which are proven to be illusions in BT—are that no mortal can refuse the Dark Gift (but David does) and that vampires want to be mortal again. *(BT 109)* Lestat meets Raglan James, who offers to temporarily switch bodies with him so that Lestat can experience once more what it is like to be human. Lestat agrees but upon making the switch and becoming mortal soon realizes he prefers being a vampire. Raglan James, however, has other ideas; he has taken Lestat's body permanently, which requires Lestat to forcibly steal his body back. This adventure dispels all of Lestat's illusions about being redeemed. Of his own free will, he has chosen to be reborn to darkness and he also furthers his notion of himself as an evil creature by forcing David into accepting the Dark Gift. *(BT 165–167, 206, 340, 417–422)*

Lestat dictates his next book, *Memnoch the Devil*, to David Talbot, who records it for him. He begins with an episode of being stalked while he himself is stalking a notorious killer named Roger. Sensing something different about his stalker, Lestat believes the Devil is after his soul. He discusses the possibility with David, who wonders whether there is some connection between Lestat's targeted victim and this creature that so frightens him. Lestat is unsure, so he kills Roger to find out. To his astonishment, Roger then appears to him as a ghost. *(MD 4–39)*

Roger tells Lestat the story of how he acquired wealth via criminal activities and how he used it to collect valuable religious artifacts from around the world. He wants to give something to his daughter, Dora, a televangelist, to help ground her religion on something solid and miraculous. Among his possessions are twelve books by a mystic named Wynken de Wilde, who had devised a spiritual path that involved great sensuality. Roger wants Lestat to keep these books safe and also to appear to Dora as proof of the supernatural. Lestat is unsure about the latter, but he agrees to do what he can for Dora. (MD 48–92)

He meets Dora in New Orleans at her home, St. Elizabeth's, a former orphanage. Although she realizes he is not human, she shows no fear. He tells her he wants to help her, but the presence of his stalker, whom he now knows is most definitely interested in his soul, causes him to flee. (MD 110–128)

The stalker turns out to be the Devil, although he calls himself Memnoch. He tells Lestat that he is not evil and that, in fact, he desires to reverse the tide of evil in the world. For that, he needs help from someone as strong as Lestat. He invites Lestat to come with him to meet God and to see Heaven and Hell. Afterward, he can make his decision whether or not to become the Devil's lieutenant. (MD 129–140)

Lestat consults with Armand, David, and Dora. Although Armand is suspicious and David reserved, Dora approves, so Lestat goes off with Memnoch to Heaven. He is amazed by what he sees there and completely overcome with a sense of beauty, joy, and supreme satisfaction. He meets God, who insists that Lestat would never be His adversary. These words frighten Lestat, but Memnoch insists that he listen to the whole story of creation. (MD 140–170)

Memnoch tells Lestat about the nature of the angels and the stages of creation. The key point he wants to emphasize is that by making destruction, death, and suffering part of the energy exchange of nature, God Himself included evil in His plan. Human beings, God insisted, are part of nature and thus part of the cycle. Memnoch claims to disagree with this, believing that the human spirit places humans somewhere between nature and divinity. He pleads with God to allow the souls of deceased humans into Heaven, but God allows only those He feels are worthy. At Memnoch's urging, however, God temporarily became a man to experience for Himself a human's perspective. Contrary to Memnoch's wishes, He offered Himself as a sacrifice for the purpose of redeeming more souls. Memnoch thinks this scheme only resulted in more tyranny, suffering, and evil among humans. (MD 171–172)

God invites Lestat to witness His passion. Lestat lines up with the crowd, who watch Christ carry the cross to His execution. He sees

Veronica offer her veil and watches as Christ's face miraculously imprints itself on the material. Christ invites Lestat to drink his blood. As Lestat does so, he experiences a powerful sense of light and divinity, followed by an excruciating feeling of separation. For safekeeping, Christ then gives him the veil. Lestat flees with it, but Memnoch takes him on a journey straight into the bloody history of Christianity. Lestat keeps the veil out of harm's way, particularly during the Fourth Crusade. (MD 280–290)

For Lestat's benefit, Memnoch replicates the discussion he had with God over the Devil's function on Earth in which it was decided that Memnoch's activities would contribute to purifying and illuminating souls in preparation for redemption. Memnoch then takes Lestat to Hell to show him where souls are purged; however, they suffer extreme torment in the process. When Lestat sees how these souls are plagued by their victims, he realizes his own victims are awaiting him. Fleeing from Hell, he refuses to serve either God or the Devil. Memnoch tries to grab him and hold him fast, but instead ends up ripping out his left eye. Lestat escapes to Manhattan, where he had left Dora, feeling that none of them will ever truly be safe again. To gain sustenance without harming her, Lestat drinks from her menstrual blood, linking her to Veronica, the woman whom Christ had healed of a chronic flow of blood. Lestat vows never to take another human victim. (MD 291–324)

David and Armand are with Dora, so Lestat tells them all at once what he has been through. He shows them the veil. Against Lestat's wishes, Dora takes it and displays it to the public as a miracle of Christianity. The media creates an event of it and people flock to Manhattan. To Lester's horror, Armand destroys himself in the sun to affirm the veil's authenticity and the truth of God's existence, and other vampires soon follow suit. Lestat realizes that he has inadvertently given new life to a destructive religion. The spectacle drives him back to New Orleans; Dora has given him St. Elizabeth's and all of Roger's relics, so he goes there. Louis is waiting for him there, and Maharet arrives with a message from Memnoch. (MD 329–350)

She gives Lestat back his eye, then binds him in chains as she tells him what Memnoch has to say. Memnoch congratulates Lestat on a job well done. Shocked and outraged, Lestat cannot bear to believe that he might have been a pawn in the Devil's game. When Maharet deems it safe, she unchains him and leaves. Lestat wanders the city, unable to feel any sense of certainty or security. What he had witnessed may have been the ultimate truth, a pack of lies and hallucinations, or part truth, part fiction. He does not know the meaning of his story, but he believes it happened just as he told it: "This is *all* I know." (MD 353) He ends the book by saying that he will pass now from fiction to legend. Upon finishing the novel, Rice felt that Lestat had indeed walked out of her

life "and into any legend that luck would allow. As I completed the last page, I knew Lestat was leaving. We both knew that what we had done together in the five books was finished."

Given the opportunity, Lestat is the vampire Rice would be: "He is my hero." She views him as a side of herself that she has not developed, cherishing his "strength, penchant for action, lack of regret, lack of paralysis, ability to win over and over again, and his refusal to lose." Although she thought that *Memnoch the Devil* might be her last novel with Lestat, he remains an insistent voice for her and may yet show up again.

See also Akasha, Armand, The Auvergne, Blood, Blood of Christ, Body Switching, Christ, Christianity, Claudia, Dark Moment, Deception, Desert, Dream of Family, Flynn (Dora), Forgiveness, Fourth Crusade, Gabrielle, God, Golden Moment, Goodness, Gretchen, Hagia Sophia, Heaven, Hell, Hero, *Interview with the Vampire*, James (Raglan), Lestat's Brothers, Lestat's Father, Lestat's Houses, Louis de Pointe du Lac, Manhattan, Marius, Memnoch, *Memnoch the Devil*, Moral Dilemma, Nicolas de Lenfent, Olympic Tower, Paris, Penthouse Apartment, *Queen Elizabeth 2*, *The Queen of the Damned*, Quest, Rock Concert, Rock Star, Roger, St. Elizabeth's Orphanage, Serial Killer, Talbot (David), *The Tale of the Body Thief*, Theater of the Vampires, Tiger, Town House, Vampire, Vampire Nature, Vampire Powers, *The Vampire Lestat*, Veronica's Veil, Victims, Wolves.

Lestat's brothers   As the seventh son, Lestat had six brothers, but only two of them survived to adulthood. Lestat briefly mentions them in his account of his mortal life, naming only one of them—Augustin—but he feels unconnected with their concerns. They ridicule him and seem to only just tolerate him. Both brothers are killed with their families during the French Revolution and thereafter Lestat dreams that he has made them all into vampires, thus saving them from their deaths. *(VL 23, 29, 350–351)*

See also Dream of Family, Family.

Lestat's father   Lestat describes his father as a distant man who exhibits little concern for his youngest son, and whose blindness leaves him bitterly dependent. He is an indigent marquis, owning a thousand-year-old family castle in the Auvergne region of France. Out of stubborn family pride, he denies Lestat the opportunity to better himself by entering the priesthood and takes away his son's books; eventually Lestat runs away. Ten years after he becomes a vampire, Lestat hears that many of his family members have been killed during the French Revolution, so he goes to his father, who has escaped to New Orleans. *(VL 29, 31, 350)*

There Lestat takes care of the old man at Louis's plantation—

although Louis indicates that Lestat is not pleased by this responsibility. *(IV 36)* When the old man is dying, Lestat asks Louis to kill him. He wants to be finished with his father but cannot do the act himself. The father asks for Lestat's forgiveness for burning the books he had as a boy, and Louis presses Lestat to grant it. He does so, begrudgingly. Then Louis himself makes the fatal wound that bleeds the old man to death, and they burn down Pointe du Lac with the old man's corpse inside. (Louis's rather brutal depiction of Lestat's apparent callousness toward his father can be traced, according to Lestat, to Louis's own bitterness against Lestat.) *(IV 52–56)*

The father's blindness is a metaphor of the way potential victims are blind to the dangers of vampires. Lestat's father believes that his son is taking care of him when, in fact, it is all pretense (at least, according to Louis); Lestat cannot wait to be rid of him.

See also Dream of Family, Family, Forgiveness, Pointe du Lac.

Lestat's houses   Lestat owns several properties in New Orleans. In VL, he mentions a dozen mansions, and his favorite is the one he occupies to recover from injuries he sustained from Claudia and Armand. *(VL 508)* Louis claims in IV that he had seen Lestat in this house and had believed that Lestat was dying; Lestat insists that the scene Louis describes never took place. *(IV 328, BT 108)*

Lestat's house in the Garden District, New Orleans

In either case, the fictional location of the house is a deteriorating mansion in the Garden District on Prytania Street, one block away from the Lafayette Cemetery. *(VL 5)* Louis claims it is filled with corpses of animals from which Lestat has drunk blood, and books piled to the ceilings. Lestat seems afraid to leave the house, a metaphor of how he has distanced himself from life and is trapped in his deteriorating soul. The house itself was inspired by a house Rice had seen on Philip and Carondelet streets, although she "moved" it in her novels to Prytania.

In BT, Lestat restores and moves into the New Orleans town house he had shared with Louis and Claudia. This is the place Jesse explores in QD, which allowed her to document the events of IV.

After his ordeal with Memnoch, Lestat acquires the largest property he has ever owned: a former Catholic orphanage called St. Elizabeth's. Located on Napoleon Street in New Orleans, it is a massive building with four towers. Dora Flynn had lived here but later deeded it to Lestat. He calls it his "beast's castle." Having lost Dora to her religion, he decides to set up Roger's treasures in this building and call it his own. *(MD 340, 344)*

See also Real Estate, St. Elizabeth's Orphanage, Town House.

Light   A form of energy associated with spirituality, knowledge, and superiority, it symbolizes the manifestation of virtue, grace, and intellect. In superstitious folklore, vampires shun the light, but in the *Chronicles* Rice dismisses this myth, and varying degrees of intensity of light indicate aspects of a vampire's personality.

In IV, Louis shows the boy reporter what he looks like in a harsh light. Ready to fully reveal himself psychologically as well, he is not the least bit uncomfortable in the light, although he does use shadows and dim lighting throughout the story to conceal his vampiric appearance. He claims to look less supernatural in candlelight, which is somewhat ironic, since mortals look *more* supernatural by candlelight. Thus, for vampires, dim lighting provides a cloak of deception. With Babette, to whom Louis desires to appear as a voice of wisdom, he uses the play of light off his smooth, reflective face to make her think he is an angel. When she later sees him more closely by the light of a lantern, though, she comes to believe he is from the Devil. *(IV 47, 65)*

Claudia and Lestat prefer an abundance of light. When they rise in the evening, they light candles and lamps all over the house, contrasting with the single candle that Louis chooses. Their individual preferences indicate how comfortable they are with their vampire nature. Lestat also believes that light is a metaphor of grace and often remains as long as he can in the growing light of dawn before he surrenders to darkness. *(IV 164, BT 345)*

In VL, Armand shows his own relationship to light through his

story about Marius, the artist. Marius teaches Armand that as a vampire with heightened senses, he will see light as no mortal sees it: as endless illumination. *(VL 294–295)* This ability plays into the theme that vampires possess godlike qualities. However, when Santino's coven burns Marius (last seen as a torch of light), Armand descends into a world of darkness for three centuries—and for three centuries he develops a dark, nihilistic despair. *(VL 297–305)* He replaces what Marius had taught him with Santino's Dark Ways. Even in Paris, the City of Light, Armand lives in darkness below a cemetery and teaches other vampires to do the same. These rituals give meaning to his otherwise empty existence. After Lestat comes and represents, with his blond hair, the ability to go into the lighted arena of mortals, Armand finally emerges. *(VL 305)*

See also Candles, Darkness.

Lightner, Aaron   A member of the Talamasca who invites Jesse into the order and who accompanies David to San Francisco to attend Lestat's rock concert. A dignified British gentleman with white hair, he can move objects by telepathy (this is his "calling card"). *(QD 162)* He arrives in Miami when Lestat reports to the Talamasca that David Talbot is dying. *(BT 388)* Eventually, Lightner learns that David is still alive in another body and visits David in Barbados. *(BT 414)* Lightner is present in QD and BT, but plays a much stronger role in *The Witching Hour* and *Lasher* through his investigation of Lasher and the Mayfair witch family. He dies in *Taltos.*

Lestat mentions Talbot's disgust with the Talamasca over Lightner's death. David has not told Lestat the details, but Lightner was killed by a corrupt faction in the Order who wanted him out of the way as they planned to acquire the Taltos. Further details of this event can be found in Rice's trilogy, *Lives of the Mayfair Witches. (MD 101)*

See also Talbot (David), Talamasca.

Lilia   Named after the lily, she is the "daughter of men" whom Memnoch encounters when he takes on human form. Upon seeing her, he feels sexually aroused. She knows he is a divine creature and invites him to have sex with her; Memnoch does so and comes to realize that this is the human experience of Heaven. To prove that she has made love with a god, Lilia brings Memnoch to her tribe. He realizes that she has been cast out, but in his company she is received again. When she finally dies, Lilia is venerated as the wife of God.

For his part in having sex with Lilia, Memnoch is cast out of God's presence. Other angels who had observed Memnoch's pleasures and had done likewise were nearly banned from Heaven along with him, but their contrition saved them. *(MD 223–229, 235)*

See also Fallen Angels, Memnoch, Sex.

Lioncourt   Lestat's family name, it symbolizes the power of the sun gods and indicates that Lestat is a natural lord and master. The Talamasca use this surname to trace Lestat's landholdings through two centuries. *(VL 66, QD 177)*

See also Lestat de Lioncourt.

Lioncourt, Lestat de   See Lestat de Lioncourt.

Lionel Potter   See Potter, Lionel.

Little drink   The term the vampires use to describe the ability to drink blood from a mortal without taking a life. Not all vampires can do it because it requires restraint to take only a little of the precious liquid.

Armand takes the "little drink" from Denis in IV and Daniel in QD; Marius does it in QD with the girl in the music store. Louis, however, is never quite able to achieve this ability because he is so caught up in the swoon that his victims inevitably die. *(IV 233, QD 22, 93, BT 104)*

Lestat is also guilty of this response at times. In BT, he intends to take only a "little drink" from the old woman who had been the near victim of a serial killer, but is unable to hold back and kills her instead. His failure plagues his conscience, and Lestat begins to perceive that it is not true that he kills only evildoers. *(BT 22)*

See also Addiction, Blood, Swoon.

"Little Red Riding Hood"   A children's story about a girl who walks through the woods to her grandmother's house, only to discover that there is a wolf disguised in her grandmother's bedclothes waiting to eat her.

Lestat refers to the face of the wolf from this story when he looks at his dog, Mojo. *(BT 152)*

See also *The Company of Wolves.*

Living specimen   Some vampires believe that if mortals in the twentieth century ever caught a vampire, he would become a living specimen for scientific study.

Louis worries that Lestat risks this possibility because he reveals too much to the mortal world about vampires, and once scientists examine the preternatural skin and become convinced that the folklore about the existence of vampires is real, mortals may then attempt to destroy the vampire race. *(VL 530)*

Lestat dismisses Louis's concerns, citing that mortals require more than mere physical evidence to change the way they typically interpret their world: the supernatural is not acceptable to modern

minds attuned to secular beliefs. However, the idea of being a specimen on display secretly thrills Lestat. He would love to be examined, and indeed the challenge of risking capture and escaping thereafter is tempting to him. "It could be such fun," he says. *(QD 5)* He reiterates this excitement to David Talbot, thus showing how alluring both intimacy and the dynamic of dominance and submission are to him. *(BT 72)*

See also Dominance/Submission, Talamasca.

Lolita   See Nabokov, Vladimir.

London   The location of one of the Talamasca motherhouses and where Lestat hunts after he survives his exposure to the sun. Raglan James tracks him down and gives him the Robert Bloch story here. *(BT 83)* (See Vampire Atlas)

See also Charing Cross Station, Claridge's, Motherhouse.

Lord Ruthven   The vampire bar in New York, named for the vampire in the first vampire story in the English language, *The Vampyre,* by Dr. John Polidori. *(VL 528)*

See also Dr. Polidori, *The Vampyre,* Vampire Bars.

Lost souls   When Daniel drinks Armand's blood, he describes the sounds that he hears as the cries of lost souls. Lestat mentions something similar when he drinks from Marius, as does Akasha, who experiences the greatest sensitivity to these voices. *(VL 91, QD 114, 259–260)*

See also Voices.

Louis de Pointe du Lac   The first vampire to tell his story to a mortal. The protagonist of IV, Louis describes to a young reporter what it has been and is like to be a vampire. After nearly two centuries, he is weary of his existence. Rice originally intended his tone to sound like that of Oscar Wilde. "He was supposed to be a sort of George Sanders–type of character, world-weary and comical." However, Louis's voice changed when Rice transferred her perspective from that of being the reporter to seeing the experience through the eyes of Louis himself.

Louis is twenty-five years old when he becomes a vampire in 1791. A plantation owner in New Orleans, he owns seven other pieces of Louisiana property. He had made himself vulnerable to the vampire Lestat while he was deep in grief over his brother's death. Louis felt responsible for this death because his brother had taken a fatal fall after Louis had refused his request to sell the plantation and use the money for religious work. *(IV 4–8)*

Lestat had then spotted Louis and had fallen in love with his air of despair. Although Louis had been unable to accept the possible sainthood of his brother, he sees Lestat as an angel and suddenly knows "totally the meaning of possibility." *(IV 13)* Lestat offered him immortality and Louis took it, although at first he had begged merely to be killed. *(IV 16, 19–20)*

When he is transformed, Louis is amazed at the vividness of the world around him and at the love he feels for everything. Yet he is horrified by the necessity of killing mortals for survival. Louis is a dark-haired man of the shadows who prefers contemplation and reading to action and adventure. He does not look willingly into mirrors because there he sees what he cannot control. An intellectual, Louis thinks through the consequences of his behavior rather than acting on whim, as Lestat often does. He is impelled to search for answers to the ultimate questions of life, and is especially concerned to discover whether God exists, and if so, if that makes him a child of the Devil.

Although Louis soon despises Lestat and mourns his decision to become a vampire, he finds a new purpose when he helps Lestat to make Claudia, a five-year-old child, into a vampire. *(IV 95)* She comes to mean everything to him, and he attempts to keep her a child, despite the evidence that inside her tiny body she has matured into a woman. He accompanies Claudia to Europe and when she is destroyed, his world changes dramatically. Louis clings to Claudia's memory and resists the approach of another vampire, Armand, who is strongly attracted to him and who manipulated Claudia's destruction in order to gain Louis's exclusive companionship. By the end of his story, Louis seems cynical; he is unable to appreciate what a gift he has in immortality. *(IV 335–341)*

Lestat's perspective on Louis is that he is the most human of all the immortals, the least godlike. *(BT 105)* Louis was never able to surrender to his vampire identity, and, as a result, his memories are erroneous, the "sum of his flaws." *(VL 499)* He does not kill only evildoers—as Lestat does—because he is too passive to make any such judgments. In fact, he causes more innocent blood to be shed than many of the other vampires because he simply kills almost any person he runs into. *(QD 443)*

Resentful and dependent, Louis is never quite able to rise above his human needs and is limited by his fears. He experiences claustrophobia, fear of being alone, fear of heights, and fear of his own passion and freedom. He cannot move into an indefinable immortality and spends much of his vampire existence looking for security, even if it means he must see himself as a child of the Devil and thus eternally damned.

When he is later reunited with Lestat in VL, after Lestat has told his own side of the story, they are as lovers rejoined. Nevertheless, Louis never quite gets over his horror at being a vampire and when Lestat comes to him in a mortal form in BT and asks for his help in

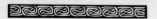

becoming a vampire again, Louis refuses. He will not willingly pass on the Dark Gift to anyone ever again. *(BT 268)*

Louis is also one of the surviving vampires in QD; Akasha spared him because Lestat loves him. He moves through the novel passively, noticed by the others but saying little, although he does brave Akasha's anger by pointing out that she has no right to intervene in the human world. She responds that he is actually the most predatory of all the immortals. *(QD 443)*

After Akasha's demise, Louis goes in search of Claudia. *(QD 475)* He follows Jesse's lead that Claudia's ghost has appeared in New Orleans and he makes his permanent home there, living in a shack behind a large but empty Victorian house. There he reads by candlelight and is seemingly unaware of all the broken windows. Lestat angrily torches this shack after Louis refuses to help him become a vampire again. *(BT 270)* Once Lestat gets his body back, however, he confronts Louis, then upon forgiving him invites Louis to live with him again in the refurbished town house. Louis accepts. *(BT 258, 405, 429)*

Louis is a passive character whom Rice used to express her feelings of loss and grief upon the death of her five-year-old daughter. At times he displays a heroic impulse, as when he decides to leave Lestat and find out for himself what it means to be a vampire, but he eventually succumbs again to his weakness—passivity—when Lestat makes Claudia. Rice eventually grew to dislike him. "At the time, I loved him. I don't now. I don't have a great deal of sympathy for a person who's that dependent and that vengeful toward people who won't fulfill his needs." Rice longed for a character of true heroic strength. Thus, Lestat replaced Louis in the remaining *Chronicles* as the protagonist.

However, as a character, Louis remained important to Rice. In MD, Lestat mentions that Louis has been with Armand in Paris. This is a breakthrough for Louis because he had been avoiding Paris due to the pain it had caused him from Claudia's death there. However, when Lestat goes to New Orleans after his ordeal with Memnoch, Louis is waiting for him.

David and Armand had shipped Roger's religious treasures to St. Elizabeth's, Lestat's new home, and Louis had set them up and dusted them. "It seemed the right thing to do," he said. *(MD 345)* He tells Lestat that he is inclined to believe in the authenticity of Veronica's veil, but he makes no real commitment to a religion that has long plagued him with guilt. To prepare Lestat to hear Memnoch's message, Louis helps Maharet chain him. Yet he begs Maharet not to nail Lestat into the windowless, bricked-up room (probably due to the recollection of his own claustrophobic experience when Armand's coven had nailed him into a coffin).

While Lestat recovers from his shock and horror, Louis takes

Wynken de Wilde's books back to the town house to read them. He appreciates the skillful artistry and invites Lestat to join him one day soon in looking through them. *(MD 108, 345, 350, 351–352)*

See also Armand, Claudia, Claustrophobia, Coffins, Eastern Europe, Enchanted Sleep, Fire, The Gathering of Immortals, Immortality, *Interview with the Vampire*, Lestat de Lioncourt, Louis's Mother, Louis's Sister, Love, Madeleine, *Memnoch the Devil*, Molloy (Daniel), New Orleans, Paris, Paul, Pointe du Lac, *The Queen of the Damned*, Quest, Redemption, Relationships, Reunions, Santiago, Slavery, *The Tale of the Body Thief*, Theater of the Vampires, Town House, Uptown, Vampire, *The Vampire Lestat*, Vampire Nature.

Louisiana   Where Louis has an indigo plantation called Pointe du Lac. He views his mortal life there as both primitive and luxurious; it is a metaphor for what he is to experience in his life as a vampire, which demands the primitive brutality of blood lust coupled with a heightening of the senses. *(IV 4)*

See also New Orleans, Pointe du Lac.

Louis's brother   See Paul.

Louis's mother   A minor character in IV. Louis lives with his mother, sister, and brother, Paul, until Paul dies. Louis then moves his mother and sister to New Orleans. His mother suspects that he has something to do with Paul's death and even says as much to the police. She dies after he has become a vampire and, because he cannot appear in the daytime, he finds an excuse not to attend her funeral. *(IV 48)*

Louis's sister   Louis has one sister and, after he becomes a vampire, he sometimes still sees her at night. His new appreciation for life prompts him to urge her to marry rather than to waste away on their plantation. It is she who first confronts him with the tragedy of immortality: as a vampire, he does not age but must watch as his sister grows old and eventually dies, leaving him behind. *(IV 5, 12, 37–38, 48, 168–169)*

Claudia remembers Louis's sister and uses this knowledge to clue her into the fact that Louis was once mortal and so, possibly, was she. *(IV 109)*

Louis's sister's husband   A minor character who helps Louis to invest money after Louis becomes a vampire. *(IV 48)*

Louvre   A museum in a former palace in Paris that houses one of

Louvre, Paris

the world's largest and most important art collections. It was built in the thirteenth century as a fortress and was opened to the public as a museum in 1793. As one of the greatest collections of art in the world, the Louvre represents the collective unconscious of humanity; artists on exhibit there have attempted to capture universal symbols and images that come from within the depths of the human psyche.

Louis enters the Louvre to find transcendent pleasure after he has burned the Theater of the Vampires and is mourning Claudia's death. He looks at art, which had once meant for him the "promise of a deeper understanding of the human heart" *(IV 321)*, to try to obliterate his pain. Now, however, the paintings are dead to him because his own human spirit, which he once had treasured, has lost any meaning for him. *(IV 317, 320–321)*

"In a sense," says Rice, "the book finally had to end with his being on the threshold of the Louvre and saying, 'My experience with human life and feeling is over, and this is the beginning of my life with art.' " (See Vampire Atlas)

See also Art, Louis de Pointe du Lac.

Love   A warm attachment or devotion that vampires crave almost as much as they crave blood. They love life more than they did as mortals and may fall in love with their victims. Many of the vampires also love one another, and often their bonds involve the types of petty conflicts characteristic of the love experienced by mortals, but at other times the experience transcends its human limitations and becomes more like the unconditional *agape* love of the gods.

As Louis describes to the boy reporter what it is like to be a vampire, the boy asks him if it is like being in love. Louis acknowledges

the accuracy of this observation, which means to him to take things gently and delicately rather than to rush headlong into the experience. *(IV 31)* He marvels at everything around him, as if infatuated with his own sensory experience, but his excitement eventually dissolves into an oppressive feeling of being trapped in an evil existence.

Lestat, too, expresses love for his new existence as a vampire, but his way of expressing this love differs from Louis's. An adventurer, he goes to extremes and takes great risks so that he can expand his relationship with life itself. However, doing this on his own becomes lonely, so he seeks a companion. *(VL 121)*

His first fledgling is Gabrielle, his own mother. There was no one to whom he felt closer and, when she is dying, he can think of no more loving act than to bring her into immortality with him. He offers the Dark Gift, and she accepts it.

As a mortal, Lestat had developed an intimate relationship with his friend Nicolas. After Lestat becomes a vampire, he hesitates to approach Nicolas, afraid he might be incapable of feeling affection. This turns out not to be the case, although when they embrace, Lestat's warm feelings become the bloodlust of a vampire for a victim. It occurs to him that the height of the vampire experience would be to drink the blood from those with whom he is most intimate, so he selflessly tells his lawyer to urge Nicolas to get out of Paris. *(VL 133–134, 143)* However, Nicolas is abducted by Armand's coven and when Lestat saves him from them, Nicolas demands the Dark Gift and Lestat reluctantly gives in. He hopes that their bond will survive, but once Nicolas is a vampire, Lestat no longer feels affection for him. He attempts several times, in vain, to revive the old feelings, but it becomes clear that Nicolas hates him, and he finally leaves Nicolas behind at the Theater of the Vampires. *(VL 266–267)*

Over a decade later, Lestat makes Louis into a vampire because he is enchanted by him. *(VL 497)* Yet they develop a problematic relationship because Louis is not Lestat's equal in vampiric skill and demands of him greater sensitivity and more profound mentoring than Lestat is willing or able to give. But when they eventually reunite at Lestat's rock concert, the love between them has evidently developed and grown. *(VL 524)* They remain in contact as Lestat travels the world, and Lestat even eventually forgives Louis for turning on him and denying him what he most needs to survive—life as a vampire. By the end of the fourth *Chronicle*, Louis and Lestat appear to have a more intimate bond than ever, although Louis believes it is the crowning evil that vampires, who deserve nothing short of destruction, can love each other. *(BT 405, 430)*

Throughout two centuries, Lestat craves a companion who could really be his equal. He loves Louis but cannot get Louis to fully partici-

pate in his vampire nature. Lestat has played games with other mortals in search of the kind of person he wants, and finally he finds the perfect candidate in David Talbot. David, however, declines to become a vampire. Lestat carries on an affectionate friendship with David that deepens into love when David stands by him on several occasions. Lestat worries that David, at the age of seventy-four, will die soon and deprive Lestat of his company. Finally, Lestat makes him a vampire; however, when David disappears, Lestat fears that he has lost David's love forever. Lestat returns to New Orleans and discovers David waiting for him so they can go together to the carnival in Rio. It seems to be the beginning of a friendship deeper than any Lestat has previously known. *(BT 430–435)*

Louis, too, searches for love and has a short-lived affair with Armand. Louis desires a sense of completion with a vampire who can make his life better, and his love for Armand springs from the fact that Armand appears to be the teacher for him that Lestat never was. In return, Armand admits that he loves and wants Louis more than anything else in the world. He goes so far as to manipulate circumstances to bring Louis even closer to him, but the end result is Claudia's death, which Louis cannot tolerate. Louis loses his attraction to Armand and eventually they drift apart. *(IV 284, 338)*

Armand is especially desperate for what he calls love, although Lestat and Louis both believe that what he really desires is to draw out the life force of others by demanding that they dominate him; he wants to be a slave to some greater power or person, but he also wants to control how the relationship evolves. Lestat immediately recognizes this no-win paradox and rejects Armand's plea to be allowed to accompany Lestat. Armand had actually experienced an ecstatic love once with Marius, but there had been little time to cultivate that relationship because Santino's coven had driven Marius away and forced Armand into their practices. *(VL 292)* As a result, Armand does not possess the skills for loving deeply and sacrificially. In fact, he has learned best how to manipulate, and although both Lestat and Louis are immensely attracted to him, they both resist for they realize that he cannot participate in a truly loving bond. He is too dependent and too prone to using deception to control. *(VL 311)*

Armand does not give up, however. After pursuing Daniel around the world for four years to learn from him about the modern world, Armand falls in love with him. Daniel finds Armand simultaneously ghastly and beautiful; he loves Armand the way people love evil, "because it thrills them." *(QD 92)* They become "secret lovers," and Armand has a "little drink" from Daniel, then allows Daniel to drink his blood from time to time. Although Armand is still prone to developing a relationship based on manipulation, Daniel wants immor-

tality so much that he willingly participates; they take turns being dominant and submissive, which satisfies Armand. After ten years, Daniel's desire for immortality becomes so obsessive that he wastes away. Armand needs and loves him too much to let him go, and finally makes him a vampire so that they can be companions for endless years. (QD 114–115) Eventually, Lestat and Armand acknowledge their mutual fondness as well. (MD 141)

Vampires also feel love for their victims, possibly even stronger love than that which they feel for one another. Lestat is surprised when the old queen vampire in Armand's coven tells him that love is the enemy of a vampire who dwells among mortals. "He grows irresistibly to love mortals," she says (VL 230), and as a result such vampires cannot bear to take life. Lestat challenges this notion, insisting that love is the very essence of the Dark Gift and the bond between victim and vampire can be even more satisfying—short-lived as it is—than bonds between vampires. "Drinking up their life, their death, I love them," Lestat claims about his own victims. (VL 231) No relationship reaches the heights of that experience. (IV 289)

"The act of killing," says Rice, "is the only act in which vampires get complete satisfaction, so it takes on tremendous power. They fall in love with the victims and feed off the very essence of the victims' lives."

See also Dominance/Submission, Erotic, Intimacy, Relationships, Reunions, Sex.

Lovecraft, H. P.   An author of supernatural fiction who was extremely popular in the 1930s. His short story "The Thing on the Doorstep" is the first communication that Raglan James uses to get Lestat's attention. (BT 26)

See also "The Thing on the Doorstep."

Luchina   An actress in Renaud's theater group that Lestat especially favored. (VL 133)

See also Renaud's House of Thesbians.

Lucifer   The name of an angel often equated with Satan, or the demon of sinful pride. In some lore, he fell from Heaven in a blaze of fire.

When Mael goes to immolate himself on the steps of St. Patrick's Cathedral, Lestat compares him to Lucifer: "to fall like Lucifer in a blaze." (MD 337)

Memnoch claims to be the Devil but dislikes being called Lucifer or any other of the names commonly associated with Satan. (MD 135)

See also Devil, Mael, Memnoch.

Bela Lugosi as Dracula,
1931

Lugosi, Bela   A Hungarian actor who took the role of Count Dracula in the 1931 film *Dracula*. Rice named one of the vampire bars after him. *(VL 528)*

See also *Dracula*, Vampire Bars.

Lynkonos   A fictional Mediterranean island off the tip of Greece where Akasha takes Lestat and continues her rampage. There Lestat argues with Akasha over her actions and plan. Lestat claims that she should not subject all people to her will, especially when it entails murdering nearly half the world's population. Akasha, however, discounts his objections. *(QD 353, 379)* (See Vampire Atlas)

See also Akasha's Plan.

Macbeth A tragic play by Shakespeare about a man whose ambitions provoke him to doing murder and are eventually responsible for destroying him. It is one of Lestat's favorite plays. *(IV 129)*

Initially Rice had included another reference from *Macbeth*. Louis mentions Birnam Wood as a metaphor about how he feels when the slaves are drawing threateningly close to his plantation house; he is referring to the scene in which Malcolm's soldiers camouflage themselves with tree branches to conceal their actual numbers as they approach Macbeth's castle to attack it. But the copy editor suggested removing this line from the manuscript because it seemed to lack context. Rice later regretted cutting it, since the quote was consistent with the influence on Louis of Lestat.

See also Shakespeare, "Tomorrow and Tomorrow and Tomorrow . . ."

Madame LeClair See LeClair, Madame.

Madeleine A doll maker in Paris whom Claudia targets to make a vampire. She has dark red hair and violet eyes.

Madeleine has lost a child near the age Claudia was when she was made immortal; in Madeleine's obsessive grief, she makes china dolls endlessly, all in the image of her deceased daughter. Claudia requests from her a "lady doll"—the form to which she aspires and which will also serve as a mother figure for her—and Madeleine gladly creates it. Madeleine loves both Claudia's doll-like appearance and domineering manner. She sees Claudia as a child who cannot die, and she wants to let go of her grief and grab onto that source of strength.

Claudia bites Madeleine but is not powerful enough to make her into a vampire, so she demands that Louis finish it. He resists, but Claudia insists that she needs a protector since she knows that Louis

will eventually desert her for Armand. Realizing Claudia's pain, Louis gives in, although unbeknownst to him it is Armand who empowers him to succeed in the act.

When Madeleine becomes a vampire, she fashions miniature furniture for Claudia, then burns down her doll shop as a symbolic gesture; she now has the child she needs in Claudia, who will remain a perfect little doll for eternity.

Angry that Madeleine was made, Armand's coven abducts her one night along with Louis and Claudia. She is locked in an airshaft with Claudia, where the sun comes in and kills both of them. They die wrapped in each other's arms. *(IV 261–279, 293–306)*

Madeleine is the representation of Louis's internal struggle over choosing between Claudia and Armand: Claudia ties him to his humanity, while Armand draws him toward his vampire nature. Louis wants to avoid dealing with this choice, and his assessment of Madeleine—that she lives in a dream world and possesses little self-awareness—is therefore as much about him as it is about her.

"I saw her [Madeleine] as a shallow, vain character," says Rice. "I think the things Louis says about her are true."

See also Claudia, Dolls, Fire, Insanity.

Madness   See Insanity.

Mael   A tall, blond, blue-eyed Druid priest with a hawk nose who teaches Marius the customs, laws, and poetry of the Druids so that he can become an appropriate god for them. Mael also explains to Marius what will happen to him when he is transformed into a vampire. *(VL 405–423)* After Marius flees the Druids, Mael drinks from a vampire himself and goes through the transformation. He soon loses his belief in his Druidic religion and becomes one of the wandering rogue vampires. *(VL 463)*

Later he visits Marius in Venice and sees Armand, the mortal boy whom Marius intends to turn into a vampire. *(QD 265)*

Mael shows up more prominently in QD, in the company of Maharet. He is protective of Jesse, who he knows to be descended from Maharet; he fears the fragility of her mortality and believes she should be made a vampire. One night he even attempts to bite Jesse, but Maharet intervenes and sends Jesse away. Mael appears to Jesse once in London, as if he is looking after her from afar, but avoids her when she approaches him. He goes to Lestat's rock concert to watch over her and there encounters Khayman, who frightens him. Khayman advises him to cloak his thoughts of Maharet and Jesse or he will expose their presence to Akasha. Mael's love for Jesse weakens him because it distracts him from protecting himself from Akasha's vengeance. *(QD 152–159)*

Of Mael, Khayman decides that he is a quarrelsome, angry vampire whose mind does not make sophisticated distinctions, and that he both fears and loves Maharet. *(QD 206–216)*

When Jesse's neck is broken at the concert, Mael goes to the hospital and gives her his healing blood. He wants to make her a vampire himself, but Maharet arrives to initiate and perform the transformation. *(QD 239)*

Mael is also one of the vampires who survives Akasha's attack and joins with Maharet to stand against her. *(QD 276)*

When Dora displays Veronica's veil as evidence of God's miraculous manifestation as Christ, Mael arrives in Manhattan to see it for himself. To affirm this miracle, Armand had already destroyed himself in the sun on the first day it was displayed. Mael does likewise. On the steps of St. Patrick's Cathedral, in front of the media, he lets the sun take him. Lestat dismisses this as the act of a priest who cannot let go of his need for such beliefs. *(MD 339)*

See also Druids, The Gathering of Immortals, Jesse, Marius, St. Patrick's Cathedral, Silver Bracelet, Sun, Veronica's Veil, Ways of Dying.

Magical Forest   A mural Lestat commissions for Claudia's room in the New Orleans town house. Running across all four walls, it depicts fruit trees, streams, and unicorns against a vermilion, moonlit sky. *(IV 100)*

Jesse later uses this mural as evidence that vampires had once lived in this town house. When she sees a castle in the mural with a door, she realizes it camouflages a real door, and she opens it. She finds some of Claudia's former possessions concealed behind it. *(QD 181)*

See also Town House.

Magnus   The maker of Lestat, he has survived for over three centuries. He symbolizes the darkness that exists beneath the Parisian facades of frivolity. Rice's inspiration for this character came from the short story "Count Magnus" by M. R. James.

"What I liked," says Rice, "was the name and the general mood of the story." According to the tale, Count Magnus is a sixteenth-century Swedish aristocrat. "Phenomenally ugly," he is both powerful and cruel, and the general populace fears him. Interested in alchemy and the secret of eternal life, he makes a "black pilgrimage" to the city of Chorazin—where, reputedly, the Antichrist was born—and returns home with a mysterious stranger. After the count's death there are sightings of two figures: a tall man in a dark cloak, and a short figure wearing a black hood. A gruesome murder on the count's land suggests that Magnus has risen from the dead, possibly with his companion's assistance. The tall figure (Magnus) appears to possess the power to

hypnotize people and to move objects at will. He also pursues people relentlessly, appearing wherever they are and making it clear that he is slowly closing in on them, as if he intends to kill them.

In VL, Rice's Magnus is first described as a deeply lined, smiling white face in the audience at Renaud's House of Thesbians where Lestat is performing. Lestat feels a sense of foreboding, a feeling of being watched—of something closing in—and he connects this feeling with the strange, white face. He also believes that the man behind the face knows that he has killed eight wolves. One night he awakens to see the man from the audience standing in his room. The man says, "Wolf-killer," as he abducts Lestat and carries him through the air to a distant tower. Lestat struggles when he realizes his abductor is a vampire, but loses consciousness in a sweep of rapture when he is bitten. (VL 70, 71, 73)

Lestat later awakens in a stone house outside Paris, where he sees his abductor uncloaked for the first time. Magnus is old with silver and black hair, spidery limbs, and surprisingly soft skin. He wears ragged clothing from another century, and his only teeth are fangs. He repeatedly bites Lestat and, during these attacks, Lestat experiences a vision of Magnus as a mortal.

When human, Magnus had been an alchemist who had trapped a vampire and stolen from him his blood and with it the immortal gift. Whether the vampire was near the point of death (as Marius later indicates is necessary for this theft to occur) is not clear from Lestat's vision. Lestat sees Magnus as a dark Prometheus, the Greek titan of legend who stole fire from the gods and gave it to humankind. (VL 79–96)

The fact that Magnus is an alchemist is also significant. Representative of spiritual illumination, the process of alchemy strives to make gold from ordinary materials. It combines substances that represent latent inner forces, passion, innocence, and transmutation. The stages of alchemy involve dissolving that which is inferior and purifying it, joining forces of opposition, and suffering through the tension of these conjoined opposites. As these opposites are bound together, they invert weakness into strength, which is the very image of the vampire joining life and death to turn mortal weakness into immortal power. Rice takes this blending of opposites a step further for she develops androgynous qualities in her vampires, thus transcending gender, and she shows how good and evil are both present in that which had been depicted in literature and folklore as an unambiguously evil creature.

Magnus tempts Lestat to ask for the gift of immortality—similar to the way Satan tempted Christ—offering it up as the Blood of Christ, an inverted metaphor of divine immortality. At first, Lestat resists, but eventually he succumbs. As Lestat is Magnus's only "child," it means

he receives the full power of three centuries of vampiric strength. *(VL 219)* Magnus reveals that he chose Lestat because of the courage and stamina he displayed while fighting the pack of wolves on his father's land, and that he will now inherit Magnus's tower and all the treasures collected and stored within it. Magnus then lights a fire, dances around it, extracts a promise from the reluctant and terrified Lestat to scatter his ashes, and jumps in to destroy himself. As promised, Lestat tosses Magnus's ashes into the wind. *(VL 96)*

It is not ever clear why Magnus chose to destroy himself. The old queen of Armand's coven later suggests that Magnus suffered from an affliction common to the old ones: he could no longer bear to take human life or cause suffering, and only death would ease his pain. Whatever the reason, Lestat at the time is horrified, for he realizes that he is alone with his new experience. *(VL 218–219)*

He eventually recovers his wits and explores Magnus's tower. There he discovers four empty stone sarcophagi, fine clothing, and a chest of treasures. He also comes upon a shocking scene: a prison cell filled with corpses of blond men, all of whom look like him. He realizes that he barely escaped their fate. *(VL 99–109)*

In his discussion with Lestat about Hell, Memnoch mentions Magnus. Since the issue of getting through Hell into Heaven centers on forgiveness between victims and perpetrators, he asks Lestat what it would take for him to forgive Magnus. Lestat believes that he has already forgiven him. *(MD 301)*

See also Alchemy, Coffins, Fire, Forgiveness, James (M. R.), Lestat de Lioncourt, Magnus's Lair, Transformation, Vampire, Wolves.

Magnus's lair   Magnus lives in a dilapidated stone house with a tower a few miles outside Paris. The decaying condition of his residence reflects his deteriorating state of mind.

Lestat awakens in the tower and is made a vampire. Magnus takes him down a winding stair to a low-ceilinged room with a hidden passage, then lights a bonfire and jumps in to his death. After recovering from his shock, Lestat crawls through the passage and finds Magnus's abandoned sarcophagus, along with a chest full of gold, silver, and jewels. He also finds a suit of fine red velvet, which he puts on. On the floor just below ground level, he discovers another room with a fireplace and three empty sarcophagi—a hint that there are, or once were, other vampires living there. The floor below is filled with corpses in various stages of decay. Outside the house is a stable with a coach and four black mares. *(VL 99–109)*

See also Coffins, Magnus, Tower.

Maharet   One of the red-haired twins, she is one of the First Brood of vampires and makes her first appearance in the *Chronicles* as Jesse's

"aunt." In fact, throughout Jesse's family lineage there has always been a woman named Maharet who kept the records—and it turns out that it was the same Maharet, who pretended through the centuries to be many different women to disguise her vampirism. Maharet invites Jesse to her home in California, the Sonoma compound, and there shows her the interconnections of the Great Family. *(QD 150–159)*

As Jesse later discovers, Maharet is actually a vampire who was one of the first generation of vampires made when Akasha was transformed. Her body is so ancient it is as hard as stone, yet it can still breathe. Maharet did not choose to be a vampire, but as one she utilizes her power to maintain a loving, nurturing consciousness of the human family that has descended from her only child—a mortal—whom Khayman fathered.

Maharet gathers together the vampires who survive Akasha's mass destruction and tells them the full story of the origins of the vampire race. The tale goes as follows: She and her twin sister, Mekare, once had been witches in a Palestinian tribal culture during the reign of the Egyptian king Enkil and his queen, Akasha. Their powers allowed them to attract spirits and make rain, and when their supernatural abilities attracted Akasha's attention, she forced them to come to her court so she could find out their secret. *(QD 306–342)*

Akasha punished them for being witches and subjected them to public rape by the court steward, Khayman. They were then freed. From her rape, Maharet had a baby, Miriam. Later on she and her sister were brought back to Egypt to witness how one of their spirits, Amel, had transformed Akasha and Enkil, who now reigned over their people during the night hours. *(QD 343–348)* When Mekare and Maharet explained to Akasha the truth about her new existence—that she was now an immortal vampire—Akasha imprisoned them, sentenced them to die, and had Maharet's eyes poked out. As Maharet lay in prison awaiting her execution, Khayman made her sister Mekare a vampire, who then passed the Dark Gift on to Maharet. But when the twins attempted to flee, they were caught. Reluctant to endanger the spirit which now occupied the twins as well as herself, Akasha decided that the best course of action to take was to separate them from one another. Taken to the eastern shore of Egypt, Maharet was sealed inside a stone coffin and set adrift. She remained in the floating coffin for ten days and nights until the coffin sank and the water that seeped through opened its lid. Maharet spent the next few millennia in search of Mekare, borrowing the eyes of her human victims so that she could see. Yet she never found anyone with knowledge of her lost sister. *(QD 384–390, 399–425)*

Maharet avoided Akasha until three millennia had passed, then went to view for herself how the king and queen had become living statues. A thousand years later, she located Akasha in Antioch in

Marius's shrine. By plunging a dagger in Akasha's heart, she was able to ascertain the truth of her suspicion: that Akasha contained the life force of the vampires and must thus be protected. *(QD 417)*

During the gathering of the immortals after Akasha has risen, Maharet lets Marius know that she is the one true immortal; it is she who has endured, fully aware and self-conscious, through six millennia without resorting to the relief of madness, silent trances, or going into the ground. She, not Akasha, is the true embodiment of Marius's notion of "continual awareness," for she keeps herself interested in life by interacting with her descendants. The character of Maharet is feminine and vulnerable, yet at the same time she exhibits a "savage simplicity" with her blunt and direct statements. Maharet relies on reason to guide and motivate her actions, rather than on insight from spirits. *(QD 267–269, 323, 426)*

After David becomes a vampire, Maharet spends time with him looking through her treasures and documents. David has the most scholarly mind of all the vampires, and this gives him the deepest appreciation for these historical records. The connection between these two gives Lestat a way, via Maharet, to send David the message that he needs him. *(MD 6, 8)*

Lestat ends up going to Heaven and Hell with Memnoch, who claims to be the Devil. Afterward, Maharet comes to Lestat at St. Elizabeth's in New Orleans. When Lestat sees her, he believes she means to tell him to do as she has done: to take a human eye to replace his missing one. He refuses, but in fact she has come to give his missing eye back to him. It comes with a note from Memnoch that Lestat has performed well for him, implying that he was a dupe in the Devil's scheme.

As Maharet delivers this message, she binds Lestat in chains. She feels that because Lestat could do much damage as a result of his misery over this message, they must either chain or destroy him. While he is still in shock, she nails him into a windowless, bricked-up room. During Lestat's recovery, David records his tale. When he has trouble getting things right, Maharet assists him by reading Lestat's mind. Finally, she feels she can safely free Lestat. She unchains him and leaves. *(MD 347–351)*

"It was a very important challenge," says Rice, "to take people who were supposed to be thousands of years old and imbue them with wisdom, yet try to imagine their shortcomings. The challenge with Maharet was particularly heavy. I wanted this really wise person, yet also someone who had flaws that came from the time in which she was made a vampire."

See also Continual Awareness, Dream of the Twins, Eve, Eyes, The Gathering of Immortals, Great Family, Jesse, Khayman, Legend of

the Twins, Mekare, Miriam, Moral Dilemma, St. Elizabeth's Orphanage, Talbot (David), Twins, Witches.

Maimonides, Moses   A twelfth-century Spanish-Jewish physician, theologian, and philosopher, he attempted to reconcile biblical and rabbinic doctrines with Aristotle's ideas. His best-known work is *Guide of the Perplexed*.

As part of her religious studies, Dora reads Maimonides. *(MD 84)*

See also Flynn (Dora).

Making a vampire   Selecting a mortal and making him or her into a vampire is a complex and involved process. Some covens have explicit rules that oversee the way the transformation is brought about. These requirements ensure that no fledgling will possess more strength than any member of the coven, and that none of the chosen are ugly.

Lestat hears about these rules from Armand, but he views them as mere superstition. However, he listens when Marius urges him to be wise about the process: Lestat should make a vampire companion only out of love, and he should be sure that the mortal has experienced an adequate number of years of mortal life, so that he or she can make an informed choice. *(VL 301, 470–477, QD 89)*

Making a vampire involves draining the chosen mortal to the point of death—just before the mortal's heart stops—so that the powerful vampire blood can take hold and fuse with the heart. *(IV 18–20, VL 441)* The process is risky because the vampire thirsts for the human heart and might drink until the heart stops and the mortal dies. Plus, anything less than taking the blood until the heart nearly stops would result in "hybrids," which are more monster than human, or a vampire that is too weak to survive. *(VL 471)* The vampire then gives his (or her) blood to the mortal, depleting himself until he is greatly exhausted. As the mortal sucks blood from the vampire, the vampire feels intense pain around and about his heart.

"I could see it [the pain of losing blood] as if it were molten metal," says Lestat when making Gabrielle, "coursing through my vessels, branching through every sinew and limb." *(VL 158)* He then feels numb, and wants to stop the process, but he forces himself to go on. He grows dizzy and weak, until he automatically thrusts Gabrielle away when his body knows it is time.

When Lestat makes Nicolas, he experiences a vision of a bird flying over an endless ocean. He feels that all he has ever loved has fled into an unbearable darkness. As Nicolas takes Lestat's blood in return, a veil of silence arises between them. All vampires experience this veil with their chosen companions, for in their search for intimacy, they destroy it. *(VL 239)*

No vampire can predict what qualities the new immortal will possess. Nicolas becomes grimly intense to the point of madness; so does Madeleine. Claudia fights against being a woman trapped in a child's body. The vampires of Eastern Europe are nothing more than unthinking, animated corpses. And the "children" often abandon their vampire makers in resentment and the urge for independence.

See also Intimacy, Relationships, Transformation, Vampire, Veil of Silence, Voices.

Malarial chill   The excuse Louis uses after he becomes a vampire to explain why he does not show up at daytime functions, such as his sister's wedding and his mother's funeral. *(IV 48)*

See also Pretense.

Mandylion   A term meaning "mantle," it usually refers to the Holy Face of Edessa, an image of Christ imprinted on a piece of cloth. Some sources claim it as the original Veronica's veil, while others believe it is a facial impression that Christ sent to an Edessa citizen in failing health. As it was a revered relic, the Christian church kept it in Constantinople, where it may have been lost during the Fourth Crusade's destruction of relics. *(MD 99)*

See also Icon, Veronica's Veil.

Manhattan   One of the five boroughs that comprise New York City, this twenty-two-square-mile island is the city's financial, commercial, and cultural center. Several Manhattan locations are featured in MD, and two of the vampire bars are situated here. *(VL 529)*

Lestat keeps a room in Manhattan's Stanhope Hotel for his use. As he tracks a victim named Roger, he winds up in Manhattan on a regular basis since Roger lives on the Upper East Side, near Madison Avenue. Lestat watches Roger meet with his daughter, Dora, in a hotel across from St. Patrick's Cathedral, and when he finally kills Roger, he cuts him into pieces and hides them around the city. Lestat wanders around Lower Manhattan, near Wall Street, then goes to the Village. In a bar there, he encounters Roger's ghost. After they talk together, Lestat rents rooms in the Olympic Tower across from St. Patrick's Cathedral to store Roger's religious relics. *(MD 5–9)*

Lestat brings Dora here to see the artifacts and to tell her that he has been invited by the Devil to meet God and to see Heaven and Hell. She encourages him to go, and when he returns, he goes straight to Dora in the Olympic Tower to show her that Christ has given him the famous icon, Veronica's veil. Dora takes it over to St. Patrick's Cathedral. The sight of it stirs up religious fervor and attracts pilgrims from everywhere to Manhattan. On the steps of the cathedral, Armand and

Mael allow the sun to burn them, while Lestat and David watch the spectacle of pilgrims from a vantage point in Central Park. *(MD 150, 321, 336)*

All these events occur in the winter, against a backdrop of cold and snow that Rice views as symbolic of penitential suffering. Although situating the action in Manhattan reflects her own love of the city, its climate while she was writing the novel in 1994—one of the worst winters in history—was perfect for what she wanted to accomplish with the story. *(MD 324)* (See Vampire Atlas)

See also Central Park, Flynn (Dora), Greenwich Village, Lestat de Lioncourt, *Memnoch the Devil*, Olympic Tower, Religious Relics/ Artifacts, Roger, St. Patrick's Cathedral, Snow, Stanhope Hotel, Upper East Side, Vampire Bars, Veronica's Veil, Wall Street.

Marcion   A second-century Christian philosopher, he taught that the God revealed in Christ was a distinct entity from the wrathful Creator God of the Old Testament. According to him, the Creator God was the lesser of the two.

As part of her religious studies, Dora reads Marcion's writings. *(MD 84)*

See also Flynn (Dora).

Mardi Gras   The annual two-week costumed celebration of Fat Tuesday, the feast day prior to the beginning of the religious serious-ness of Lent. New Orleans observes Mardi Gras with numerous street parades and large-scale balls. On Shrove Tuesday, the crowning of Rex, the King of Mardi Gras, brings it all to an end. Although Mardi Gras officially started in 1857 with the Comus procession, it was not until 1870 that the Rex parade commenced.

Roger mentions the events of Mardi Gras in the background during his breakthrough work with Father Kevin on Wynken de Wilde's books. During the Proteus parade—dedicated to the shape-changing god of chaos—they discovered the secret sexuality embedded in the illustrated psalms. These parallel events emphasize the human potential for frenzy and ecstasy and the way such madness can be ritualized. *(MD 63)*

See also Father Kevin, New Orleans, Roger, Wilde (Wynken de).

Mariana   The French ship that carries Louis and Claudia across the ocean to Eastern Europe. On board, the two vampires have a lavish stateroom. Passengers die mysteriously—of a "fever," the mortals think—and the vampires make it to Bulgaria without incident. *(IV 162)*

See also Fever.

Marie Antoinette A queen of France who was beheaded during the French Revolution.

Lestat claims he saw her in Paris when he first went there to become an actor. *(VL 63)* Claudia has a deck of cards with Marie Antoinette's picture on them. *(IV 164)*

Marionettes Puppets moved by strings.

The vampires who start up the Theater of the Vampires act like marionettes during their initial performances. They imitate the mechanical actions, reinforcing the theme that they are like dolls, or a nonhuman form imitating human life. *(VL 261–262)*

See also Mummers, Theater of the Vampires.

Marius A vampire who represents the figure of the wise teacher.

"I'm always fascinated with the idea of the older, wiser teacher," says Rice. "It captured my imagination in *The Teachings of Don Juan*— that an older, more experienced mystic or adept would teach one [an apprentice] how to use such powers."

Lestat first hears of Marius when Armand explains how he became a vampire. When Armand first knew him in the fifteenth century, Marius had been a Venetian nobleman and artist. He chose to work among mortals, have mortal apprentices, and make religious art. It was Marius who bought Armand from a brothel and fell in love with him. He then painted *The Temptation of Amadeo* in an attempt to capture on canvas Armand's qualities forever, and he made Armand so that he could join with another kindred soul. Marius desired their bond to be permanent, but their happiness became short-lived when, only six months later, Santino's coven put a torch to Marius and captured Armand. Marius managed to escape to his secret shrine in the mountains of northern Italy, where he healed himself by drinking the healing blood of Those Who Must Be Kept. He did not see Armand again until 1985 in Sonoma, although he had been aware that Armand was suffering through three centuries of loneliness. *(VL 292–300)*

"I don't remember the first moment Marius sprang into my mind," says Rice. "Maybe it was when Lestat said he wanted to know whether immortals had been made in Roman times, when it was more enlightened and sophisticated than the Dark Ages. So Marius evolved as a character who really had the wisdom of that ancient world—the cleverness, the wit, the perspective on the world that I feel a sophisticated Roman should have had. He may have even evolved from the force of Armand's image. I might have written Armand's story before I knew who Marius really was."

After hearing about Marius from Armand, Lestat decides Marius could teach him a lot about the best way of living as an immortal. He sets out to find him, for ten years leaving messages all across Europe until Marius—won over by Lestat's persistence and innocence—finally

comes to him. Marius then takes Lestat to his sanctuary on a Greek island. *(VL 310, 323, 338, 360–363)*

With blue eyes and white-blond hair, Marius wears red velvet, no matter what the era. His face astonishes Lestat: "What one of us could have such a face? What did we know of patience, of seeming goodness, of compassion?" *(VL 361)* Marius seems to depict a pure image of human love. Gentle, vital, and noble, he emanates a godlike power, although he is more human than any vampire Lestat has ever encountered. Marius does have the ability to perform supernatural feats like levitation and mental telepathy, but he prefers to do things the human way. To him, human gestures are more elegant and require less energy. "There is wisdom in the flesh," he claims. *(VL 379)* His goal is not to transcend human emotions but, rather, to refine and understand them. He also seems connected to everything around him—thus being the antithesis of Armand, who is connected to nothing. Marius shows Lestat Those Who Must Be Kept—Akasha and Enkil, the original vampires—then tells his own story. *(VL 378, 385–396)*

The bastard child of a Keltic woman and a wealthy Roman, he was a citizen of the Roman Gallic city of Massilia during the time of the Roman Empire. Never bored or defeated by life, he always felt a sense of invincibility and wonder. An important life theme for him was the idea of the existence of a continual awareness because Marius desired that nothing spiritual ever be lost. A scholar, he was, at the age of forty, at work on a history of the world when a Druid abducted him. Because he was an extraordinary human being, the Druids wanted him to become their new god and thus replace the God of the Grove, a burned and crippled vampire who no longer inspired their ceremonies.

The Druid priest, Mael, forced Marius to learn the Druid language and customs. On the night of their great Feast of Samhain, the Druids took Marius to the giant oak tree where they had imprisoned their other god. Inside it, the vampire god taught him the lessons of the vampires and urged him to go to Egypt, to find out why vampires in other places—and himself as well—had been burned or destroyed. After being made a vampire, Marius broke free of the Druids and pursued this new course.

In Alexandria, Marius encountered other burned vampires. One of them took him to the Elder—a vampire who told Marius about Akasha and Enkil, the vampire progenitors. Marius learned that he, like other vampires, is vitally connected to them, and that if they suffered harm, he and all other vampires would experience similar damage. Since they had been placed in the sun, as a consequence vampires everywhere had been burned or destroyed. The recognition that whatever happens to them happens to him upsets him, although it affirmed Marius's desire for the existence of a continual awareness.

That same night, Akasha asked Marius to take her and Enkil out of Egypt before the Elder—the one who had deliberately placed them

in the sun—destroyed them. Marius took them as requested, traveling with them around Europe until he settled on an island fortress in the Aegean, where he built a shrine for them and where he now sits with Lestat. *(VL 396–466)*

Marius feels he is truly immortal, that he is the perfect guardian for Akasha and Enkil, and that he is now the "continual awareness." He is in love with humanity's progress, although he realizes that human evolution away from belief in gods and superstitions has made him, as a vampire, obsolete. No purpose is left for him. *(VL 466–467)*

After Marius tells his story, he sends Lestat away to live on his own, for the equivalent of one mortal lifetime. He tells Lestat not to look to history to give himself meaning because the dilemma of how to live one's life is always a personal one. However, Marius vows that he will be available if Lestat ever needs his help, and extracts from Lestat the promise never to tell anyone about him or his whereabouts. *(VL 468–470)*

They do not meet again until the twentieth century, when Lestat becomes a rock star and reveals the whole vampire history in his songs. By that time, Marius has moved his immortal charges to a northern wasteland where he plays Lestat's music videos for them. In response, Akasha rises and destroys the shrine, trapping Marius in ice for ten days. Marius sends out signals of danger to the other vampires. His child and lover, Pandora, urges Santino to help dig Marius out, and while Marius survives, the experience has humiliated and spiritually bruised him. *(QD 17–31, 68, 264)*

Marius joins those vampires who stand against Akasha and Lestat and their rampage of destruction, and uses his own belief in the need for human evolution to attempt to reason with Akasha. After her demise, he urges Lestat not to write about it, but Lestat ignores his advice. The surviving coven drifts apart, and Lestat believes that Marius has gone into Asia. *(QD 264–275, 437–444)*

He appears again in BT only as an angry presence at Lestat's antics; he turns his back on Lestat in front of Louis's burning shack as if he is finally finished with him. *(BT 272)*

In a segment that was included in the first draft, then condensed to a few lines, Marius uses Khayman to bring Lestat to Hong Kong. There he scolds Lestat for making himself conspicuous to the mortal world. At this time Marius is still the scholar, reading newspapers and books in many languages, and looking through a high-powered telescope in search of the continual awareness about which he dreams. *(BT 4–5)*

See also Art, Continual Awareness, Druid Vampire, The Gathering of Immortals, Grand Canal, Lestat de Lioncourt, Massilia, *The Queen of the Damned*, Shrines, Teacher, *The Temptation of Amadeo*, Those Who Must Be Kept, *The Vampire Lestat*, Venice.

Martini's   The café in Georgetown where Lestat tastes his first meal as a mortal after switching bodies with Raglan James. He dislikes the experience. He also meets a waitress there and has sex with her. The name of this café is based on a restaurant in the film *It's a Wonderful Life*. Rice used the characters and places from this film to emphasize Lestat's distaste for mortal life. *(BT 178)*

See also *It's a Wonderful Life*, Waitress.

Mass   See Eucharist.

Massilia   The oldest and second largest city in France, now known as Marseille. Established in 600 B.C., the city grew rich on trade, for it linked the Mediterranean with northern Europe. Massilia fell to Caesar in 49 B.C. and, in 1481, became part of the kingdom of France.

Massilia is the city where Marius was born and where the Druid abducts him and brings him north, to be made a vampire. (It is not clear if this Druid is Mael, for although Mael claims to have been in Massilia, Marius does not seem to know him until they meet in the Druid grove.) *(VL 396)* (See Vampire Atlas)

See also Marius.

"Master of Rampling Gate, The"   A 1984 short story Rice wrote for *Redbook* that expanded her sense of the vampire.

The story opens inauspiciously with the date; it is the spring of 1888 and the year of Jack the Ripper. Told in the first person by a young woman writer/poet named Julie, it describes a visit she and her brother, Richard, made to their family's four-hundred-year-old estate in the village of Rampling, England. Their father had decreed on his deathbed that its manor house must be torn down, but they cannot abide the thought.

At one point in the story, Julie flashes back to a time when she was six years old. She remembers seeing the striking face of a dark-haired man on a train; he represented to her the ideal of masculine beauty. Yet her father had reacted negatively to the sight of this man, describing him as an "unspeakable horror," and the memory of this stays with Julie.

At their estate, Rampling Gate, Julie and Richard spend serene days by the gardens and the lakes, becoming more convinced each day that they should not destroy the house. One night, however, Julie awakens, and feeling a sense of emptiness and need, wonders what the house is doing to her soul. Rising from her bed, she discovers a man sitting in a chair reading her typed manuscripts. To her surprise, he is the beautiful man she saw years ago on the train. When he calls her by name, she screams in fright and the man leaves. Richard awakens and Julie tells Richard about the man, but he does not believe her.

The following night, she sees the man again. This time she confronts him but his gentle manner soon seduces her. He kisses her on the throat, revealing himself to be a vampire. She swoons, and is surprised that he seems so loving.

The vampire tells her he is the master of Rampling Gate, and the reason Julie's father had wanted the house demolished. He gives her visions of how he became a vampire—he took the Dark Gift to save himself from the plague—and of how the two of them might have been together in past eras. The vampire asks Julie to help him embrace modern life and makes her a vampire to be his eternal companion. Julie takes over Rampling Gate from her brother in a clever move that saves it from destruction. Then together she and her vampire lover go to London to hunt, presumably setting off the crime spree attributed in history to Red Jack.

Rice's original version of this story had a twist that *Redbook* cut, but was then restored when Innovative Corporation made it into a graphic novel. There is a blind housekeeper who is aware of the vampire, and her long tenure at the mansion is a metaphor of endurance that parallels the vampire's existence. When Richard finds ominous diary entries his dying uncle wrote describing the presence in the house of a demon, he mentions tearing the house down, and the housekeeper warns him not to do it.

Master/slave   See Dominance/Submission, Slavery.

Mastiff   The breed of dog that Lestat owns while he lives as a mortal in France on his father's estate. After his father forbade him from entering the priesthood, Lestat receives from his mother two puppies, and he founds a large kennel on them. Years later, when he goes out to hunt a pack of wolves, he takes along his two favorite dogs; both mastiffs are slain, and Lestat finds their loss heartbreaking. *(VL 24, 32–33)*

Two centuries later, when he dreams in BT of his mortal days, the image of lying in bed with these dogs repeatedly haunts him. The dogs represent some of his best memories as a mortal, and it is those memories that entice him to switch bodies with Raglan James. *(BT 8)*

See also Dreams, Lestat de Lioncourt.

Materialism   A metaphor of prosperity in any form. The Talamasca attributes this trait to the vampires, for they have collected "vampire refuse"—what vampires leave behind—over several centuries. Many vampires steal from their victims and/or induce mortals to sign over to them property deeds. *(QD 174)*

Louis affirms this materialistic tendency when he describes Lestat's profligate spending, lavish tastes, and apparent need for status.

Mastiff

Louis himself deplores such a lifestyle, although as a mortal he had enjoyed this luxury. He is appalled to discover that Claudia also shares Lestat's desire to have the best. She insists on expensive rooms in Paris, a continuous supply of fresh flowers, and the best carriages for traveling. *(IV 35, 170, 205)*

By the time Lestat writes BT, he has a fortune in money and property so vast that he can afford to lose twenty million dollars to Raglan James without extensively worrying about it. *(BT 294)*

Of all the vampires, however, Armand seems to be the most materialistic. In IV, he lives rather spartanly in a cell with only a desk and books, and he tells Louis that vampires really need very little. However, by QD, Armand buys everything that appeals to him, including an island off the coast of Florida. When he feels he has become attuned to the spirit of modern times through Daniel, he decides to become a millionaire. He discovers lost treasures and stolen art to raise his income, and when he has enough money, he buys every kind of technological invention that fascinates him, along with yachts, planes, expensive cars, fine clothing, and art. He also builds a luxurious villa, restaurants, and hotels on his island to make it into a tourist attraction. *(QD 98–99)*

That vampires amass fortunes echoes the fact that their transformation into immortals has magnified the qualities of their existence. If

they choose to develop their full potential, they are perceptually, and sometimes spiritually, enriched, as well as materially.

See also Financial Concerns, Night Island, Real Estate.

Matisse, Henri   A twentieth-century French painter, illustrator, and sculptor, Matisse developed a radical approach to using bold, inventive colors to create luxurious decorative pieces.

Louis acquires one of Matisse's paintings for the town house on Royal Street. *(MD 108)*

See also Town House.

Mechanic   A twenty-six-year-old man who murdered his family during a hallucinogenic trip on acid. When he comes into the hospital where Raglan James works, James forcibly switches bodies with him, then kills his own aging, diseased body and flees the hospital.

James presents his new, brown-haired, six-foot-two, physically fit and handsome body to Lestat, knowing that this body will attract Lestat and possibly might make Lestat willing to switch bodies with him and experience life in the mechanic's mortal form.

James is correct in his assumption. Lestat is pleased with the look of the mechanic's body and does decide to make the switch. Once inside it, however, Lestat is not pleased. The body feels dense and heavy, and is vulnerable to disease, hunger, and death. Lestat eventually rids himself of it, although David Talbot inherits it to spend eternity in it. *(BT 142, 206, 376–381)*

See also Body Switching, James (Raglan), Talbot (David).

Media   Channels of communication, usually by publication or broadcast, that Louis and Lestat both utilize to get their stories out to the mortal world.

Louis "confesses" what it is like to be a vampire to a curious boy reporter. The reporter then publishes the story as a novel, under the pseudonym Anne Rice. When Lestat reads the book, he decides to tell his own story. But not only does he write his autobiography, he also records what he knows about vampirism in rock videos, thus using the media to reach audiences worldwide. His book and videos create quite a stir, with many of the vampires plotting to destroy him at his debut concert in San Francisco. *(VL 520, 521, QD 11–14)*

The media are also responsible for bringing Akasha's atrocities to the attention of the vampires. Although she is able to shield her mind and whereabouts from the vampires, they find they can track her through television news reports about incidents of mass hysteria, death, and claims of seeing the Virgin Mary. The media, however, work to downplay the presence of the supernatural. Newscasters explain these deaths as possibly due to contaminants in water or food,

and attribute the events of the rock concert to mass hysteria and special effects. Thus, the media work to guard human assumptions about reality. (VL 3–16, QD 379, 468)

It is through news reports about "vampire killings" that Lestat ascertains the location of Raglan James. The pattern allows him to find that James is on a luxury liner, the QE2. (BT 280, 290–293)

See also Interview with the Vampire, The Queen of the Damned, Rock Concert, The Vampire Lestat.

Meister Eckhart   A late-thirteenth- and early-fourteenth-century German Dominican mystic and philosopher, he was one of the fore-runners of Protestantism. He believed that reason could not form an adequate conception of God because God was far richer than the human mind. Knowing God required a purely mystical experience: God is Nothing, and we must become as nothing to be joined with Him.

Meister Eckhart influenced Wynken de Wilde's writings. (MD 58)

See also Religion, Wilde (Wynken de).

Mekare   One of the red-haired twins who haunt the dreams of vampires in QD. The first born of the twins, she is the more powerful, brazen, and outspoken of the two. She can see the physical core of the spirits and control the spirits better than her sister, Maharet. As a visionary, she is planning to eat the eyes and brain of their dead mother in a cannibalistic ceremony until soldiers interrupt the funeral feast and force her and Maharet to Akasha's court. (QD 306–311) Mekare then takes the lead in answering Akasha's questions about the nature of their sorcery, and in threatening the queen. As punishment for not providing clear answers about the supernatural realm, Enkil and Aka-sha command their court steward, Khayman, to rape Mekare and her sister. When they are brought to court for a second time and see that Akasha has become a vampire who desires to be a goddess, Mekare foretells that she herself will be the instrument of Akasha's downfall. In retaliation, Akasha has Mekare's tongue cut out. When Khayman makes her a vampire, she in turn gives the Dark Gift to Maharet. The twins are then forcibly separated, and Mekare is set adrift on Egypt's western shore. For centuries to come Maharet searches for her sister but never finds her; cave drawings in Peru indicate that she exists, but is possibly insane. (QD 321–348, 382–417)

The images of what had happened to the twins appear in QD in dreams to vampires and selected mortals the world over. Mekare is their source, and their confused and sporadic nature reinforces the idea that Mekare has no conscious understanding of what she is doing, but, rather, is spurred by a memory. The dreams start when Akasha awak-

ens and begins her slaughter. *(QD 31, 35, 43, 67, 74, 137, 251)*

Some recipients of the dreams have the chance to see through Mekare's eyes and note that she seems to be an unstoppable force moving with great momentum. She is covered with mud, as if she is the earth saving itself from the destructive plundering religious ideas have justified for centuries. *(QD 284)*

Akasha's erratic movements make Mekare's progress equally unpredictable, and so Maharet continues to have difficulty in locating her. Khayman believes Mekare is moving to fulfill her prophecy, and she does indeed show up at the compound at the opportune moment, pushing Akasha into a glass wall that severs her head. Thinking quickly, Maharet saves Akasha's brain and heart by giving them to Mekare to consume; thus, the mad Mekare becomes the new Queen of the Damned. Mekare is then taken to a secret place so that the new life-spirit of the vampires is protected. *(QD 453, 462–463)*

See also Cannibalism, Curse, Dream of the Twins, Funeral Feast, Legend of the Twins, Maharet, Queen of the Damned, *The Queen of the Damned*, Twins, Witches.

Melmoth, Sebastian   An alias Lestat uses in BT to book a hotel room in London, it is based on Oscar Wilde's use of the name after the disgrace he suffered over his homosexuality in the 1890s. Wilde had combined the name of Saint Sebastian, who was wounded by arrows, with that of a wandering spirit from a nineteenth-century Gothic romance by Charles Robert Maturin, *Melmoth the Wanderer*. The theme of this novel involved the notion of never-ending life; the ghostly character of Melmoth has been damned for failing to accept his human limitations and wanders the earth tempting people to sell their souls to the Devil. *(BT 81)*

Members of the Drapers' Guild, The (The Syndics)
One of Rembrandt's most famous paintings, it depicts a group of men whose wise faces seem to possess great secrets.

Lestat and David Talbot study this painting together in the Rijksmuseum in Amsterdam, discussing the angelic quality of the mortals depicted in it. This discussion prompts Lestat to write David a letter about his theories on Rembrandt's work. *(BT 33)*

See also Rembrandt van Rijn.

Memnoch   The being who approaches Lestat in the guise of the Ordinary Man. He claims to be the Devil, but he hates to be referred to as Azaziel, Sammael, Beelzebub, Lucifer, Marduk, Mephistopheles, or Satan. Rice made up his name, saying she based it on the thirteenth letter of the Jewish alphabet. *(MD 135, 206)*

Lestat first becomes aware of Memnoch in Rio, then again in New

Orleans, when he feels he is being stalked by something that is not human, and hears odd snatches of conversation that disorient him; he feels he is being discussed by two beings. An odd phrase passes through his mind: "A sleepless mind in his heart and an insatiable personality"—the words of the Sibylline Oracle from an ancient Hebrew poem describing the Watcher angels. (MD 24, 188) Lestat feels the phrase is somehow connected to his stalker. He fears that this stalker is the Devil coming for his soul, particularly when he sees a dark, terrifying, winged creature. (MD 17, 22) He encounters this form again in the home of Roger, one of his intended victims: Lestat sees what he takes to be a black granite statue of a fallen angel with goat legs and feet. The statue seems to move, which scares him. (MD 31–32, 39)

In a Manhattan hotel room, Memnoch finally makes his presence known to Lestat, appearing just before Lestat loses consciousness with the rising sun. Lestat remembers him as having Anglo-Saxon features with no distinct nationality, "a routine flavor of American." (MD 96) Wearing black, he was about six feet tall, with ash blond hair and an alert, agreeable face. (MD 96)

Memnoch approaches Lestat again in New Orleans, at St. Elizabeth's and at the town house. He wants to make Lestat an offer but seems uncertain of the proper timing. Although he can take many forms commonly associated with the Devil, he claims to prefer the form of the Ordinary Man because it does not attract attention. (MD 115). "The Devilish body is a penance. The Ordinary Man is a subterfuge." (MD 175) To prove his claim, he turns into the goat-footed, armored, monstrous being that had frightened Lestat in Roger's house. When Lestat tries to fight him, Memnoch tells him that he is as strong as the fallen angels. (MD 131)

Memnoch has been waiting centuries for such a creature as Lestat; he loves his inquisitiveness and his willingness to accept the consequences of the answers he receives. Insisting that he is not evil—that he actually *detests* evil—Memnoch predicts that unless he can stop it, evil will destroy the world. He is tired of his job—just as David Talbot had overheard him say in Paris—and he needs Lestat's help. He proposes to take Lestat to Heaven and Hell, to allow him to speak with God and to see for himself the real source of evil. (MD 116–117, 129–139)

Lestat decides to go with Memnoch. They arrive at a place where thousands of souls surround them. Darkness drains from Memnoch's form, his profile becomes bright and translucent, and his body feels "pliant and warm and alive." (MD 163) In this Garden of Waiting before Heaven's gates, Memnoch resembles the angels that William Blake depicted. He tells Lestat that if he chooses to become the Devil's lieutenant, he will be able to enter Heaven and Hell at will. (MD 164–165)

Memnoch takes Lestat into Heaven, where they encounter God.

Although Lestat is overwhelmed by all the grandeur and by God's familiarity with him, Memnoch sets out to persuade him of the true reality underlying God's seeming omniscience and wisdom. He tells Lestat the story of creation via the Thirteen Revelations of Physical Evolution and implies that God Himself does not really understand what He has set in motion; He learns as it unfolds and seems to have made some decisions that only increased suffering and death in the world. Memnoch had resisted God on this issue, which set him apart from the other angels, who either accepted God's wisdom or were too afraid to question it. For every incremental increase in suffering and fear within the human race, Memnoch had challenged God. "There is no angel more powerful or clever than I am," he claims, "and there never was." *(MD 207)* When God insisted that Memnoch study humanity more closely, Memnoch adopted human form and went to Earth.

For practical purposes, he chose the body of a man and suddenly knew what he had never known as an angel: the experience of gender. His maleness felt powerful, and this was reinforced by the shield of his angelic essence. His experience made him believe that humans were not just part of nature and its cycles but in fact participated to some degree in divinity. Soon he encountered a woman named Lilia and had sex with her. It was, to him, the single glimpse of Heaven that humans have in an otherwise miserable existence. *(MD 220–226)*

God chastised him for his participation in humankind and for polluting himself with sexual intercourse and cast him from Heaven. Unsure whether he was still immortal, Memnoch knew the fear of death. Yet he still loved God. As an offering of his finest skills, Memnoch decided to help civilize the human tribes. He taught them symbols, numbers, and metal-crafting and expanded their knowledge of language. Memnoch believed he improved the quality of their lives, although scriptures later castigated him, blaming him for the demise of civilization into war and harlotry. *(MD 226–234)*

God then brought Memnoch to Heaven and threatened him with eternity in Gehenna. He showed him other angels who saw him have sex with mortal women and followed his example. Memnoch made a case to God for allowing human souls into Heaven. The violence to be found among them, he claimed, does not equal the viciousness of nature, and the family is an unprecedented creation; love separates humans from all other species. The souls thirst for the Light of spirit. *(MD 234–242)*

God sent him to Sheol to find ten souls he deemed worthy. Memnoch formed his own criteria for evaluating them; it was based on understanding and appreciating God's Creation. It was not long before he found millions who had evolved to such a degree that he felt he

could present them to God. He took them to Heaven, and God accepted them all. Their songs of joy and their imaginations enriched the
geography and music of Heaven. *(MD 244–260)*

God now wanted Memnoch to leave things alone, but Memnoch
insisted that there were many more souls that, to be worthy, merely
needed further illumination. He challenged God to go to Earth Himself, become a man, and see what His plan was like from the other side.
Memnoch considered it morally reprehensible not to offer all souls the
opportunity for salvation. For this impertinence, God once again cast
him from Heaven. He wandered the Earth and eventually encountered
God as Christ in the desert. Yet he was still disappointed because in
this form God still knew that He was God and thus could not fully
appreciate the mortal experience. God described to him His plan to
suffer and die to redeem the lost souls, but Memnoch challenged the
validity and necessity of it. Such an image, he claimed, was based on
the worst human superstitions rather than on God's true glory and
love. God insisted that it was Memnoch who could not fully comprehend the glory of it. *(MD 260–280)*

While Memnoch tells Lestat this story, Christ observes them
from a distance. He invites Lestat to come to Jerusalem and witness His
passion before making up his mind about Memnoch's plea. After
Lestat witnesses Christ's suffering for himself, sees the miracle of
Veronica's veil, drinks Christ's blood, and then flees, Memnoch takes
him on a jarring tour of some of the bloody events of Christianity. He
wants to impress upon Lestat how God's plan, founded on death and
sacrifice, inspired even more of the same. And yet many souls still did
not get into Heaven. He shows Lestat how God gave him what had been
Sheol and named him His adversary until the day Sheol, now Hell, was
empty. He had damned Memnoch to spend at least one third of his
existence on Earth and one third in Hell. "On the Earth, let them see
you as the demon! The Beast God—the God of the dance and the drink
and the feast and the flesh and all the things *you* love enough to
challenge *Me.*" *(MD 292)*

Memnoch's angelic wings had darkened, and he had grown horns
like the god Pan, turning into the human conception of evil, the pure
absence of color. He now runs Hell in a manner that educates souls to
get into Heaven. God had insisted He still loved Memnoch, but now
Memnoch is part of the cycle; all his activities will assist in the larger
picture of God's greater glory. *(MD 289–294)*

Memnoch claims his personal agenda is to tear down the edifices
built to honor the suffering and sacrifice of Christianity. He wants to
destroy God's lies and dethrone Him as a being worthy of human
worship. God did no favors for the human race, and His plan is flawed.
Memnoch, however, has also stressed that his "endeavors are not

unreconcilable to Heaven, surely, or I would not be allowed to do what I do." *(MD 217)* After hearing all this, Lestat is confused over whether assisting Memnoch would be serving God or the Devil or both.

Memnoch questions Lestat about his concept of Hell, then takes him to see what the souls suffer there. Horrified by the images of torment before him, Lestat flees, refusing to assist either God or Memnoch. Memnoch grabs him, ripping out his left eye and yelling for the souls to stop him, but Lestat escapes. *(MD 320)*

He is not free of Memnoch, however. He delivers Veronica's veil from Christ's hands into Dora's and comes to realize that by doing so he has unwittingly assisted the cause of Christianity. He then goes to New Orleans, where Maharet appears and returns to him the eye he lost. She then binds him in chains and reads him a note written in blood, ink, and soot: "To My Prince, My Thanks to you for a job perfectly done. with love, Memnoch the Devil." *(MD 350)* Lestat cannot believe he has been a pawn in the Devil's game with God. He realizes that what Memnoch showed him could all be lies, but there is no way to be certain. The experience diminishes his sense of well-being and security. No matter how he looks at it, he can give it no definitive interpretation.

Rice felt great sympathy for much of Memnoch's perspective. "Memnoch's view of suffering coincides perfectly with my own," she affirms. "And his perception of the family and sexual love coincide perfectly with my perceptions."

See also Angel, "A sleepless mind in his heart and an insatiable personality," Christ, Christianity, Deception, Devil, Eyes, Fallen Angel, Gehenna, God, Heaven, Hell, Human Evolution, Lestat de Lioncourt, Lilia, *Memnoch the Devil*, Nature, Pan, Sex, Sheol, Soul, Suffering, Thirteen Revelations of Physical Evolution, Uncle Mickey.

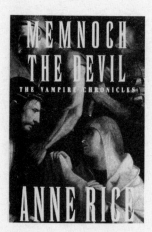

The first edition jacket

Memnoch the Devil   The fifth novel in the series *The Vampire Chronicles*. Although Lestat continues to use the pseudonym Anne Rice, he tells the story in the first person, dictating it in chains "to my friend and my scribe," David Talbot (with Maharet's assistance). *(MD 4)* Originally this novel had featured a nearly unredeemable man like Roger who was visited by ghosts. It's title was *A Dark and Secret Grace*, but Rice could not make it work. She had also called it *Of Heaven and Hell*, then changed it to *Memnoch the Devil*.

As Lestat opens the story, it is clear he is afraid. He is being stalked, and he thinks his pursuer is something more terrible than any mortal vampire hunter. He meets David in Manhattan to describe his experience, which had begun in Rio nearly a year earlier. This same creature had stalked him in New Orleans, and he believes it may be the Devil finally coming to claim his soul. He overhears fragments of strange conversations that seem to link his stalker to the vision David

once had in Paris of God and the Devil. Lestat thinks that God and the Devil are discussing him.

At the same time, Lestat himself is stalking a drug dealer and assassin named Roger. Vaguely, he wonders if there is some connection. Aware that Roger has a beautiful daughter, Dora, who is a sincere televangelist, Lestat decides to kill Roger in a way that will cause the least harm to Dora.

David believes that Lestat's stalker has some connection with Lestat's intended victim and perhaps is following Lestat because he/it does not want Lestat to kill him. Lestat decides to kill Roger and see. He goes to Roger's house and takes him, then, to protect Dora, cuts his body into pieces and hides the parts around the city. All the while, his stalker is nearby, aware of what he is doing. In a bar, Roger's ghost appears to tell Lestat his life story. As a boy, Roger had discovered the illuminated books of a religious mystic named Wynken de Wilde. He had responded to the way Wynken wove together the joys of the flesh and the idea of union with God. Roger had wanted to found a cult on his ideas, so he had set out to collect all of the mystic's books. Along the way, he had become a drug dealer and killer, acquiring the money to collect all manner of valuable religious art. He wanted to give Dora some relic on which she could ground her religion and raise funds, but because his wealth was tainted, she had rejected his money and his relics.

Roger begs Lestat to save the religious artifacts he has spent his life collecting, as he wants Dora to have them. He also wants Lestat to look after Dora. Then his ghost fades and gets taken by a huge winged figure that resembles Lestat's stalker. Lestat is so amazed, and so in love with both Roger and Dora, that he stores the relics in the Olympic Tower, then goes to New Orleans to tell Dora her father is dead. Roger had believed that Lestat's appearance to her would give her what she craves—evidence of the supernatural world—and would help her view his death as a way to cleanse her inheritance from the crimes that had built it.

Dora lives alone in St. Elizabeth's Orphanage, and this is where Lestat goes. He encounters the man he believes to be the Devil, who wants to discuss his soul but who will wait for a better moment. Dora arrives, and Lestat explains what he is and what he has done to her father. She is unafraid, wanting only to know how he might fit into her plan to produce some spectacular vision to affirm her religious truth. Lestat is confused about what he should do. The man approaches again, scaring him, so he leaves and returns to his town house. But there he soon realizes his stalker is once again upon him.

He calls himself Memnoch, and he does indeed claim to be the Devil. To prove it, he takes the form of a large, black, goat-legged creature with armor and wings. Lestat gets into a fight with him, and

Memnoch declares that Lestat is just the creature he has been waiting for centuries to address. Memnoch affirms David's vision and insists that he is not evil. In fact, he needs Lestat's help to turn back the tide of evil in the world. To do this, he wants to take Lestat to Heaven to speak to God and to Hell to see how he can best serve the truth.

Lestat consults Armand and David to see what they think of the Devil's offer. Armand is suspicious; David is interested but noncommittal. Lestat decides to ask Dora's advice, but first transports her to Manhattan to see Roger's relics. Dora encourages Lestat to accompany Memnoch, so Lestat meets him near St. Patrick's Cathedral.

Memnoch adopts an angelic form—slightly larger than human with diaphanous wings—to tell his story. He first takes Lestat to Heaven, as promised, and the light, perfection, and glory of the place overwhelm Lestat. The interconnectedness among the beings he encounters astonish his sensibilities. He wants to sing with them, longing for what they have. Memnoch takes him to a balustrade, from which he realizes he will be able to comprehend the entire history of the Earth, and he sees a man who seems to be the source of the light radiating through Heaven. It is God.

To Lestat's amazement, God turns to him and insists that Lestat could never be His adversary. Memnoch snatches Lestat away, taking him to an earthly paradise a few thousand years before his time. There he divulges the Thirteen Revelations of Physical Evolution, laying out the stages of God's creation of the world. The angels had all witnessed it, and some had been concerned about the creation of human beings: they looked like angels but were divided into the male and female sides. Memnoch had led the way in questioning God's wisdom, but God had instructed him to study humankind first. Memnoch did so and disliked the suffering he saw; he tried to persuade other angels to join him in questioning it, but they left him to stand on his own.

Memnoch then adopted human form and experienced the joys of sex. For this, God banned him from Heaven. He returned to Earth to teach the human tribes skills for improving their lot. Over the course of three months, he coupled with many women, but God disapproved of his activities and recalled him to Heaven. Memnoch made a case on behalf of humans, citing their spirituality and questioning why death and suffering were part of God's plan for them. God explained that humans are part of the energy exchange of nature, but Memnoch insisted that they are not part of nature. God then sent him to Sheol, the realm of the souls of deceased humans, to see if there were ten souls there worthy of Heaven.

Memnoch returned with millions, which God accepted into Heaven. Memnoch, however, wanted God to open Heaven up to all human souls, not just those who were spiritually evolved enough to be worthy. He challenged God to adopt human form Himself and see

what He has made. God rejected the idea and cast him from Heaven. For a long time, Memnoch wandered the earth. Finally, he went back to Palestine, where he heard about a man who emanated divine presence, then wandered into the desert and encountered God in the form of a man. God claimed that, as a man, He had learned to love human souls; as a result, He would offer, via His death on the cross, holiness, glory, and redemption to humanity. Memnoch was appalled that God based His plan on the worst human superstitions. He even questioned the merit of God's suffering as a human, in view of the fact that all along He had known He was God and would be able to escape back to Heaven.

Before Memnoch finishes his story, God invites Lestat to witness for himself Christ's passion rather than base his decision merely on Memnoch's interpretation. Lestat watches Christ pull His cross along the road. Christ invites Lestat to drink His blood, and when he does so, he experiences a tremendous sense of light. Veronica steps out and offers her veil to Christ. When Christ wipes His brow, His face miraculously imprints itself on the cloth. Christ then gives Lestat the veil. Overwhelmed, Lestat flees with the icon.

Memnoch then takes him in a whirlwind to the Fourth Crusade and describes other events during the bloody history of Christianity. Lestat witnesses the debate between God and Memnoch about Memnoch's function in God's plan, then goes with Memnoch to Hell. Horrified to discover that people are tormented there by their victims, he realizes that behind a door, his own victims await him. They are all in Hell because they have not learned that the way to Heaven is through forgiveness and acceptance. Lestat refuses to be Memnoch's lieutenant; he cannot abide the thought of participating in such a horrifying place nor is he sure of the truth anymore. He flees, but Memnoch grabs him, ripping out his left eye. Lestat escapes and returns to Dora in Manhattan, where David and Armand have joined her. He feels as if no one is safe nor ever will be again.

Lestat tells his story and, when asked, shows them all the veil. Dora grabs it and takes it to St. Patrick's Cathedral as evidence of a religious miracle. Armand surrenders to its implications; he goes out to die in the sun, bursting into flame as confirmation. Other vampires come and do the same, including Mael. As the media picks up these events, people flock to see the veil and to experience its power. Lestat is appalled that he has unintentionally perpetuated this destructive, bloody religion. Dora cuts all ties to her former life to become the Keeper of the Veil. She gives Lestat all of Roger's relics and St. Elizabeth, her home in New Orleans, where the relics have been sent.

Lestat and David go there and discover that Louis has arranged all the icons. Maharet arrives and gives Lestat back his eye, then binds him in chains as she delivers a message from Memnoch: Lestat has served the Devil perfectly, a job well done. He reacts angrily, believing this to be a lie, but Maharet reminds him that it is the age-old dilemma: he cannot be certain one way or the other. As Lestat recovers from this horrifying revelation, David writes down the whole story. Eventually, Maharet unchains Lestat. Unsure what it all means, he wanders around New Orleans and says he will now pass from fiction to legend.

Rice says this novel will end the vampire series for some time to come. "It was a deeply disturbing book to write," she says, "which feels wonderful. It has much blasphemy, but then you have to love God greatly and deeply in order to be a true blasphemer, I think. I loved writing it; it felt like dancing—instinctive, athletic, not calculated or analyzed or rational, or even sequential. I've spoken in my dramatic images and must stand by them and take the consequences."

See also Angel, Armand, Blood, Blood of Christ, Christ, Christianity, Deception, Eden, Evil, Eyes, Fallen Angel, Flynn (Dora), Forgiveness, Fourth Crusade, Ghost, God, Heaven, Hell, Human Evolution, Icon, Jerusalem, Knowledge, Lestat de Lioncourt, Louis de Point de Lac, Mael, Maharet, Manhattan, Memnoch, Nature, Palestine, Religion, Religious Relics/Artifacts, Roger, St. Elizabeth's Orphanage, Sheol, Soul, Suffering, Talbot (David), Thirteen Revelations

The abandoned Mercedes car dealership in New Orleans where Lestat saw his reflection before he receded from Rice's imagination

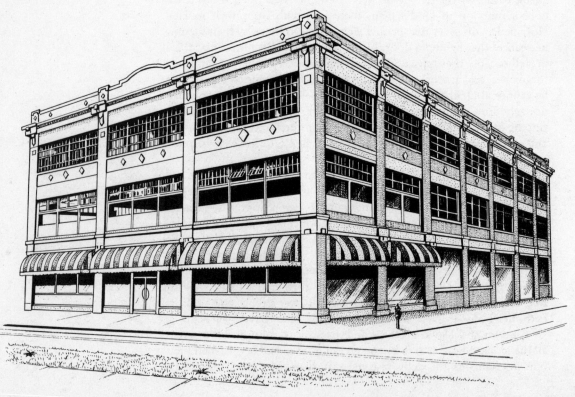

of Physical Evolution, Uncle Mickey, *The Vampire Chronicles*, Veronica's Veil, Wilde (Wynken de).

Mephistopheles   The name for the Devil that an unknown Renaissance humanist invented in 1587 for the Faust legend; he put together several Greek words that translated into the phrase, "not a lover of light." Mephistopheles is one of the seven chief devils from medieval demonology, and represents the negative, infernal aspects of the psyche. Goethe adopted this name for the Devil in his version of the Faust story, and Lestat mentions his own possible connection with this symbol of evil in BT.

Mephistopheles is a suave, ironic, and detached character that transcends the simplistic Christian devil. He debates with God about the way reason has debased humanity and makes a wager with God over Faust's soul, for Mephistopheles knows Faust is in a transitional state and is thus vulnerable to temptation. When he appears to Faust, inviting him to give up his soul in exchange for satisfying his most intense yearnings, Faust capitulates.

As it is with Lestat, Mephistopheles is both clever and foolish, and embodies the tension between self-centeredness and openmindedness, darkness and enlightenment. He is God's opponent as well as God's instrument, indicating the absence of a clear duality between good and evil. Even as he goads Faust into corrupting the innocent Gretchen, he sets into motion events that result ultimately in her, and Faust's own, salvation.

Mephistopheles is never quite what he seems, and his nature is never completely clarified in *Faust*. He is a figure who promotes negation, and yet temptations that result in spiritual decline and self-disintegration can become a significant threshold to inner growth. Mephistopheles is thus Faust's shadow side—his denied vitality and creativity, and his Dionysian link with intensity. Through accepting Mephistopheles's offer, Faust is forced to confront the chaos of life from which his academic pursuits had shielded him.

The dynamic between Faust and Mephistopheles is similar to the one that exists between David Talbot and Lestat. David is like the character of Faust: he, too, seeks to penetrate the secrets of the universe. The Talamasca takes a passive stance toward uncovering these secrets, and David is becoming restless—as Faust did—with their lack of activity just at the time that Lestat is pressuring him to become immortal. Lestat represents all that David has repressed—action, vitality, power—but David resists the Dark Gift, viewing it as a slide into moral corruption. Lestat continues to tempt him, as Mephistopheles did with Faust, by offering him a life that he has never known. Also, the wager between Faust and Mephistopheles was signed in blood—just as it would be between Lestat and David should David agree to

become a vampire. And like Faust, David, too, would then be forced to recognize his own inner darkness.

David clearly struggles with the desire to give in and experience his dark side, just as Faust did. When he reads about Faust's dilemma, he ponders its implications in his own life. Immortality as a vampire offers the possibility of salvation from death even as it seems to offer nothing but moral corruption. However, it is clear in *Faust* that disintegration of the self is necessary for rebirth into something greater, and like Faust, David is both frightened of such a change yet powerfully tempted by it.

Lestat recognizes that he is a Mephistopheles figure to David, but he questions that the symbol is truly evil. In opposition, David tells him that Lestat is not like Mephistopheles, and even if he is, David would not be willing to sell his soul. So Lestat gives up trying to seduce David and makes him a vampire against his will (unlike what Mephistopheles did with Faust). Because he did not actually choose vampirism, David feels that he has not lost his soul like Faust did. Nevertheless, he is glad to be immortal: he gets what he wants without having to make a pact with the Devil. *(BT 60, 381, 418)*

In some ways, Raglan James is the true Mephistopheles. He approaches Lestat, just as Mephistopheles did with Faust, at a time when Lestat is in despair and ruminating about going into the sun. James tempts him, for through James Lestat can become the mortal he longs to be, and so Lestat sells himself—his body—to experience the human perspective once again. As with Faust, the experience fails to satisfy Lestat, but he cannot easily back out of the deal. In the end, he triumphs, as Faust did, having had what he wanted and still not relinquishing his vampire soul. *(BT 406)*

See also Devil, Faust, Goethe (Johann Wolfgang von), Immortality, James (Raglan), Talbot (David).

Mesopotamia   A fertile region in southwestern Asia between the Tigris and Euphrates rivers, it was the location of one of the earliest human civilizations. Written history began with the Sumerians around 5000 B.C., although settlements date to much earlier times. Tradition locates the Garden of Eden in Mesopotamia.

Memnoch says that at the time he first went to Sheol, Mesopotamia existed. *(MD 246)*

See also Eden.

Metairie   A suburb of New Orleans.

Terry took Dora to Metairie to raise her. She moved into a small tract house, and Roger eventually killed her there before she could take Dora away from him. *(MD 77–78)*

See also Flynn (Terry), New Orleans, Roger.

Metatron An archangel whose name means "closest to the Throne." He is one of the tallest angels, has seventy-two names, and is the scribe of Heaven and the patron angel of Israel. In his earthly incarnation, he was thought to have been the biblical patriarch Enoch. The Cabbala names him as the angel who led the children of Israel through the wilderness. When invoked, he appears as a pillar of fire.

When Memnoch takes Lestat to Heaven, Lestat mentions this angel. *(MD 206)*

See also Archangels.

Miami A bustling city on the eastern coast of Florida. Lestat calls Miami a vampire's city, for it is a happy hunting ground of the Devil. Its "winterless winters" are a metaphor of the vampire's life within death. Miami is clean, thriving, and full of intense motion and speed. Its atmosphere is drowsy but relentless, with a "menace beneath the shining surface" of desperation, greed, risk, danger, and high energy. *(QD 461, BT 9)*

Lestat first mentions Miami in QD, when he explains where he and the other vampires had gone after Akasha's demise. He calls it the "parody of both heaven and hell," just as the vampire is. *(QD 466)*

Off the coast of adjacent Miami Beach's South Beach, just beyond Fisher Island, lies Armand's Night Island. Armand and Lestat both hunt Miami's teeming metropolis for a while, although Armand eventually leaves it to Lestat, whose favorite victims are dope lords, pimps, and killers.

Lestat's adventures in BT begin in Miami. There he kills a local serial killer in his attempt to do some good with his vampire nature— but then kills an innocent elderly woman as well. As he stands on the beach pondering the darkness of his soul, he encounters Raglan James. James gives him the first of a series of stories about body switching that eventually lure Lestat in performing a risky experiment. This particular story is by H. P. Lovecraft. *(BT 10–27)*

Lestat goes to Miami again after his ordeal with the Body Thief, for he receives a message that David Talbot is waiting there for him. They meet in Bailey's restaurant, where David asks to be made a vampire. Lestat is shocked but willing. However, when Lestat discovers in the process that "David" is really Raglan James in David's body, he kills him in a fury. The real David arrives in the body of the mechanic and takes Lestat to the Grand Bay Hotel. Here Lestat perceives that he has lost David to his newfound youth, and he departs from Miami. *(BT 392)* (See Vampire Atlas)

See also Park Central Hotel, South Beach, Vampire Cities.

Michael One of the archangels, he cast Satan from Heaven and drove the demons into Hell. His name means "one who is like God."

As one of the most powerful angels, he is God's chief soldier and defender of the righteous. He conducts newly dead souls into the afterlife and, in the Final Judgment, weighs their deeds.

David compares Michael's mythical task of physically slaughtering the First Born of Israel's captors to the need for him and Lestat, as supernatural beings, physically to wrap and transport Roger's treasures to a new location. *(MD 103)*

Memnoch describes Michael as one of the calmest, most reasonable of the angels. Michael joins Memnoch in exploring God's creation of the material world. No matter how things may appear, he trusts God. When Memnoch complains about God's plan, Michael points out that the souls have only begun their evolution. Memnoch still fails to understand and accept, so Michael returns to Heaven. When Memnoch takes human form and explores creation from that vantage point, including the experience of sex, God sends Michael and Raphael to bring him back to Heaven. *(MD 197, 217, 235)*

See also Archangels.

Michelangelo　A sixteenth-century Florentine painter, architect, poet, and sculptor, he is one of the major figures of the Italian Renaissance. He spent his life depicting human beauty, nobility, and spirituality. Among his works are the Pietà, the statue of David, and the painting of the story of God and man that covers the ceiling of the Sistine Chapel.

When Lestat wants to describe the power and beauty of angels sculpted by human beings, he refers to the work of Michelangelo. *(MD 199)*

Mickey, Uncle　See Uncle Mickey.

Miriam (the mother of the twins)　A powerful witch during tribal times in Palestine, who teaches her daughters how to work with the good spirits and ignore the evil spirits. When Egyptian emissaries arrive with an invitation for her daughters to come to the Egyptian court, she senses evil. She calls on the spirits and even consults an evil one, Amel, who confirms her fears. After Amel pricks her skin to show her that spirits can indeed interact with flesh, Miriam sickens and dies. Her daughters prepare her body to consume in a funeral feast, but they are interrupted when Egyptian soldiers arrive to take them away by force. Maharet later names her baby daughter after her mother. (See next entry.) *(QD 310–323)*

Miriam (the daughter of Maharet)　After Khayman rapes Maharet, she becomes pregnant. She has a daughter, Miriam, whom she turns over to a woman from her tribe when Enkil's soldiers insist that she

return with them to the king's court. She does so fearing that she will never see her daughter again. *(QD 345)*

Miriam is the start of a long line of Maharet's mortal descendants that stretch across centuries and continents; Maharet names these descendants of hers the Great Family. *(QD 427)*

See also Great Family.

Miriam (the mother of Jesse)   See Reeves, Miriam.

Mirrors   Since Bram Stoker's *Dracula*, vampire lore suggests that vampires are unable to see their reflections in mirrors. Since mirrors traditionally represent the soul, this deficiency symbolizes the absence of a soul; using a mirror thus became a sure way to detect the presence of a vampire.

Rice felt that her characters, despite their supernatural status, should have no more proof of the existence of God than do mortals. "If Louis failed to see himself in a mirror," she says, "he would know that some force was at work." But Rice wanted her vampires to "possess supernatural powers without explanation" and to exist as what they logically were: beings outside humanity, but still part of it and still governed by the same physical laws. Since vampires take up physical space and represent eternal substance, they naturally would see themselves in mirrors.

Louis is the first to describe his experience of seeing his vampire image. He is amazed, because he had expected that, as a vampire, he would be unable to do so. It means to him that perhaps he does have a soul and there are no supernatural processes at work. But when he catches the image of himself sucking blood from a rat, he comes to wish that he could not see himself. *(IV 37, 196)*

Lestat is horrified when he first picks up a mirror in Magnus's tower and perceives the image of a replica of himself. "I became frantic to discover *myself* in it." *(VL 103)* It is clear that he has lost some of his humanity and the mirror seems to mock that. Gradually, however, viewing what he has become fills Lestat with an eagerness to know all about his new existence. *(VL 104)*

On a later occasion, after he has been on a killing spree with Akasha, he looks at himself naked in a full-length mirror and thinks back to his original experience. "I was just as afraid right now," he claims. *(QD 357)* Examining his white skin, he grows more aware of what becoming a vampire can mean. There seems to be something beyond the mere reflection in the mirror, and the scene hints at the larger theme of self-deception.

Lestat next gets a jolt when he sees the image of a mortal man as he looks into a mirror. He has just switched bodies with Raglan James and is not used to the idea that he is now a brown-haired, six-foot-two

human being. The expression on his face is fearful, foreshadowing what his experience as a mortal will be like. *(BT 170)*

More symbolically, a mirror represents the concept of doubles, and Rice often uses pairs of characters to mirror each other. For example, Louis sees himself mirrored in the hypocrisy of the priests. The effect makes him more self-aware and more appreciative of what his vampire experience offers him. By the end of IV, however, after Louis loses his passion, Armand sees in Louis a reflection of his own emptiness and despair; unfortunately, neither of them is able to utilize this insight for psychological growth.

Louis also mirrors Nicolas because he, too, possesses the same grim intensity and capacity to suffer, and this attracts Lestat to him. Lestat makes both men vampires because he wants mortals that he loves to join him as immortal companions. Louis and Nicolas represent Lestat's darker side—a part of himself that he wants to avoid. Yet his attraction to mortals who possess these traits shows that he cannot really escape his own.

The mortal who mirrors Lestat is David Talbot: both look for adventure, initially refused the Dark Gift, possess great moral strength, and willingly take risks. Because David is so similar to Lestat in these ways, he makes a more suitable companion for him than either Louis or Nicolas.

See also Inversion, Symmetry, Twins, Vampire.

Mission of St. Margaret Mary A mission in French Guiana, where Gretchen works in a hospital. When she takes a temporary leave of absence from it and goes to Georgetown, she meets Lestat in the body of a mortal man.

It is after Lestat makes a successful switch with Raglan James and regains his own immortal body that he goes to the mission and shows himself in his true form to Gretchen. He is hoping that she might choose immortality and come with him, but she is repulsed and tells him to leave her. *(BT 241, 349)*

See also Gretchen.

Mohammed The seventh-century visionary prophet who founded Islam.

To indicate the extent of his daughter Dora's religious ambition, Roger compares her to Mohammed. Her grand goals set her apart from most other contemporary religious leaders. *(MD 88)*

See also Flynn (Dora), Religion.

Mojo A German shepherd that befriends Lestat in Georgetown just before Lestat switches bodies with Raglan James. The word *Mojo* is a good charm in voodoo, used for protection.

Mojo with Anne Rice

Mojo exhibits no instinctive aversion to Lestat as a vampire and even stays with Lestat after Lestat is made mortal. He becomes Lestat's dog, and the attachment Lestat feels for him reminds Lestat of how he felt about his mastiffs in France.

Although Lestat himself claims that Mojo has no real function in the book, the dog does symbolize loyalty and reinforces a central theme—the ability to see beyond appearances.

Lestat makes several references to how the dog's demonic appearance hides a warm and tender soul; this is a reverse metaphor for the character of Lestat himself. He wishes he looked like the Devil and was full of goodness, rather than looking like an angel yet being full of evil. Mojo gives to Lestat the sense of something good and meaningful in the world. When Lestat must depart to find the Body Thief, he temporarily leaves Mojo with a woman who lives in one of his New Orleans buildings. *(BT 152–156, 276, 350)*

Lestat pays a visit to Mojo when he arrives in New Orleans in MD. He thinks the Devil is stalking him, and being with Mojo makes him feel safe. *(MD 109)*

Molloy, Daniel   The reporter from a San Francisco radio station

who records Louis's confession about being a vampire and publishes it under the pseudonym Anne Rice, as *Interview with the Vampire*. Tall and slender, with violet eyes and a beautiful face, Daniel is about twenty (or twenty-two) years old when he meets Louis, for he is thirty-two at the time of Lestat's rock concert. (There is some discrepancy in the text concerning Daniel's age. He may have been thirty or thirty-two.)

As Louis tells his tale, Daniel listens nervously, then chides Louis for not seeing what a wonderful gift it is to be a vampire. Louis bites him and leaves him in the room unconscious, but when Daniel wakes, he listens to his tapes for clues about Lestat's location, then heads to New Orleans. Louis's bite has left him with obsessive dreams of immortality. *(IV 345)*

Daniel finds Lestat's house and plays the recordings of Louis's voice until he sees Armand, who imprisons him, then lets him go so that he, Armand, can learn about the late twentieth century through him. Although Daniel wants to be made a vampire, he runs from Armand, but Armand always finds him. Eventually they become companions, talking philosophy together and attending parties. After four years, they meet at the Villa of the Mysteries in Pompeii where Armand bites Daniel, then offers him his vampire blood, thus marking Daniel as his lover. Armand gives Daniel a small vial of his blood to wear as protection from other vampires, who would sense from it Armand's power and not harm Daniel.

Yet Daniel continues to hunger for immortality. Armand's persistent refusal is a source of conflict, and finally Daniel leaves. In Chicago, he succumbs to drunkenness and becomes a mortal recipient of the dream of the twins. He sends out a message telepathically to Armand to come for him. He has read the newly published VL and wants to go to Lestat's concert. Armand appears, takes him on a plane bound for San Francisco, and realizes that Daniel is wasting away and will soon die. He cannot bear to lose him, so he makes him a vampire; Daniel is his only child. *(QD 73–118)*

The ten-year relationship between Armand and Daniel is the epitome of the fluctuations of dominance and submission. Each struggles for both surrender and control. Armand likes to be dominated and wants a teacher, although he is in fact a powerful vampire who can torment and even kill Daniel at will. When Daniel feels strong, he walks away from the relationship, but inevitably he disintegrates and surrenders to Armand, who is always ready to come and get him. They play a game, for each has something the other wants. Daniel describes himself as a mortal slave, the "devil's minion," but Armand is as much a slave to him. When it becomes clear that Daniel is dying, Armand cannot face existence without him and, against his better judgment, gives in to Daniel's demand and makes him a vampire.

Rice was delighted with the erotic anguish she had created between them. "That part of QD is transparently sadomasochistic in theme. Armand dominates Daniel entirely: tormenting him, choosing his clothes, showering him with wealth. The culminating scene in the Villa of the Mysteries expresses this, for when Armand finally yields and makes Daniel a vampire, he gives up his masterful position. He gives in to what Daniel wants. The S&M relationship shifts. It is while in the state of surrender that Armand performs the Dark Trick.

"The future of this rearranged relationship is unknown. In urging Daniel to his first kill, Armand is once again controlling, dominating, being harsh with him. All this can be explored in future books. It seems that Armand somehow always dominates, even when yielding."

See also Armand, Dominance/Submission, *Interview with the Vampire*, Villa of the Mysteries.

Monastery   The place in an Eastern European village where Louis and Claudia find a zombielike vampire. It is a deteriorating building in a barren countryside and has been the lair of vampires for several generations. Having vampires inhabit this building is a statement on the emptiness and impotence of religion. Vampires can invade religious consciousness because good is never entirely pure but contains something of its opposite within itself.

The deteriorating monastery symbolizes a soul that utilizes ignorant habits and static beliefs that inhibit growth and self-awareness. *(IV 185–190)*

See also Carpathians, Eastern Europe, Old World Vampires, Religion.

Monet, Claude   A French Impressionist artist whose paintings Louis collects. Lestat respects art, so he saves these paintings when he burns down Louis's cottage. *(BT 270)*

See also Impressionists.

Monster   How vampires are commonly regarded. Monsters are fantasy creatures formed from those characteristics that an individual or society views with fear or intolerance.

Louis is expressing his own self-hatred when he admits that he feels monstrous. He has a distorted sense of self as the result of not being able to be fully human or fully vampire. He lives between two realms, a monster in both but unable to give up either. *(IV 73, 80–84)*

Memnoch tells Lestat that other mutations exist between spirit and human, like that of Amel and Akasha, which produced the vampire race. He does not reveal what they are but says they exist "twixt the visible and invisible." *(MD 247)*

See also Darkness, Vampire.

A street in Montmartre

Montmartre   A northern part of Paris in the eighteenth arrondissement, known since the turn of the century for its artistic community.

    Louis accompanies an artist to the artist's studio in Montmartre. He then sits for his portrait and kills the artist once the drawing is complete. *(IV 259)* (See Vampire Atlas)

    See also Artist, Victims.

Montmartre cemetery   Louis takes refuge in this cemetery in Montmartre after Claudia has died, digging himself into a used coffin and there indulging his grief. He emerges a changed man, ready to take

action for the first time in his existence. He briefly considers placing Claudia's and Madeleine's things in coffins and burying them in this cemetery, but ultimately decides against it. *(IV 310, 320)*

Lestat, too, goes to the Montmartre cemetery; it saves him from the fire Louis later sets at the theater that kills all the vampires housed there. *(IV 325)* (See Vampire Atlas)

Moral dilemma A conflict resulting from wanting to do what is morally right or good, while acting contrary to that desire. In order to survive, vampires must kill, yet this necessity plagues many of them because they consider killing morally wrong and do not want to be evil.

In an attempt to avoid killing humans, Louis lives for four years on the blood of animals. Animal blood, however, provides only vague satisfaction, and Louis only knows true peace when he kills mortals. He hates the act but he is also addicted to it, and he finally resigns himself to being a creature that chooses to do evil. His one way of not fully succumbing to it is that, after Madeleine, he refuses to make other vampires. *(IV 71–72, 85, 87, BT 268)*

Lestat wrestles with the same dilemma. As a mortal, he had been obsessed with being good. Becoming a vampire puts him strongly at odds with this desire. He goes on a quest to find Marius, whom he believes understands how to carve out of his vampire existence some sense of goodness. Although Marius strives to redeem his vampirism by creating beauty, he does protect the source of vampirism itself—Akasha. Lestat decides to search for a way to make his evil good, so he becomes a rock star, using his lyrics to show the mortal world how evil vampirism really is. *(VL 10)* He also practices vampirism as a vigilante, targeting the scum of society; his favorite victim is the serial killer. Yet at times he succumbs to blind, overwhelming compulsion and kills innocent people as well. By the end of BT, he knows he is evil as a vampire; he has been offered an opportunity to abandon his nature and redeem himself, but he decides to remain a vampire. *(BT 10–22, 409–410)*

Akasha resolves her moral dilemma by devising her own system of morality, one that opposes the traditional values of good and evil. Unfortunately, her "new Eden" involves the elimination of ninety-nine percent of the male mortal population. On the surface her logic makes sense: to stop violence, get rid of its primary perpetrators. However, to Lestat, correcting violence with more violence seems abhorrent and contradictory: "She was absolutely right and absolutely wrong." *(QD 367)* What he cannot stand is "the chaos, the total loss of all moral equilibrium" her slaughters create. *(QD 364)* The other vampires stand with him against Akasha, telling her that humankind has the right to establish its own codes of morality, and that, in fact,

the essence of humanity is its ceaseless struggle over good and evil. Akasha is not convinced by these arguments, and the only way to eradicate her destructive powers is to destroy her.

This raises another moral dilemma for the vampires: to destroy Akasha risks annihilating their race. However, they feel morally responsible to stop Akasha's rampage and decide to put themselves in jeopardy. Fortunately, when Mekare pushes Akasha against a glass wall, which beheads her, Maharet saves the vital organs and gives them to Mekare to consume, thus preserving the vampires. Yet they still must face the fact that, while they did something good by destroying Akasha, they are all still evil, for they are vampires who kill mortals. (QD 435–452)

David Talbot compares himself to Nathaniel Hawthorne's Ethan Brand, whose moral development fell far behind his intellectual development. As a vampire, David believes the same thing has happened to him. Vampires lose their humanity because, with their need to kill, their moral development stops, while their intellect continues to grow. (MD 107)

Lestat is faced with the decision of helping the Devil resist God. Memnoch presents Lestat's alternatives in a moral light: either help him or evil will eventually destroy the world. Armand is suspicious that the Devil's bargain has this moral edge. He thinks the Devil is using Lestat's conscience to trap him. In the end, Lestat is not sure what has happened, but he cannot join the Devil. Whether or not his decision is the morally correct thing to do is never resolved. (MD 136, 145)

See also Aesthetic Choice, Akasha's Plan, Evil, Goodness, Hawthorne (Nathaniel), Lestat de Lioncourt, Memnoch, Redemption, Talbot (David), Vampire Nature.

Morgan   The Englishman in IV who first witnesses a ritual for locating vampires in Eastern Europe, then loses his wife to a vampire. Louis and Claudia meet him at a small Transylvanian inn where he is mourning his wife. He had been on his honeymoon, painting quaint scenes for a book. One day he had watched the peasants use a white horse to locate an underground vampire, whom they dug up, beheaded, and burned. Morgan's wife, Emily, was found dead the next day—supposedly from the bite of a vampire—and Morgan is now trying to protect her body from suffering the same fate. He begs Louis, as a civilized man, to assist him against the peasants. (IV 174)

Louis, however, is unable to stop the innkeeper and her companions from enforcing their rituals, but he does seek out the vampire who killed Emily. He and Claudia locate him in the ruins of a monastery, where they see him carrying a victim. After they disable him, they discover that the victim, still alive, is Morgan. He is glad to see Louis,

but Claudia knows they need blood so she bites Morgan and leaves him dying, yet alive enough for Louis. Louis, though, is unable to drink from Morgan because he had known the man. *(IV 193)*

See also Eastern Europe, Emily, Superstitions.

Mortal   What Lestat claims he wants to be until he once again experiences what life as a human being is really like.

In BT, Raglan James offers to switch bodies with Lestat so that Lestat can be mortal again for a short time. Lestat accepts, but once the switch is made, he immediately realizes what a burden a mortal body can be. In his new form he is plagued by appetite, disease, the need to eliminate waste, and the fear of death. To him, his new body is a "weak, flopping, sloshy, repulsive collection of nerves and ganglia" *(BT 287)*, and he loses his telepathic abilities. His vision is blurred, he feels unsteady on his feet, his skin is more porous, and his other senses are limited. He is disgusted by his bodily functions and nauseated by the smell of food; also, to him genital sex seems surprisingly quick and lonely. "What the hell was mortality?" he asks rhetorically. "Shitting, pissing, eating, and then the same cycle all over again!" *(BT 217–218)* His thinking processes are occasionally impaired, and pleasures he had imagined fail to occur. He feels uncharacteristically timid and no longer sees the beauty of life as he did when a vampire. In fact, he feels like Frankenstein's monster.

Because he is not used to protecting himself from exposure, he gets pneumonia and nearly dies. Only the sunrise, and later Gretchen's attention, dispel his disappointment at becoming mortal again, yet neither provides enough reason for wanting to remain mortal. He desperately desires his old body back.

When he seeks Louis's help, Louis resists. He claims that, as a mortal, Lestat has found a way out of vampirism; he can thus redeem himself and should remain a mortal. Lestat acknowledges the opportunity, but his experience as a mortal has taught him that he actually prefers being a vampire, even if it means he will never find redemption. *(BT 165, 194, 267–268)*

See also Body Switching, James (Raglan).

Mortal nature   See Humanity.

Mortals   Characters who play both major and minor roles in *The Vampire Chronicles*. The vampires depend on some mortals—agents— to help them make business transactions, and they feed off mortals for their survival. They claim to love mortals and long to be mortal again,

yet mostly they treat mortals as a means to their ends. Some vampires also must watch and endure as the members of their mortal families die.

The first thing all vampires must face is that, while mortals may be physically weaker than vampires, they can pose great danger. If mortals were ever convinced that vampires truly exist, they could hunt vampires by day and take advantage of the sleeping state to destroy them. *(VL 475, 479)* Nevertheless, vampires still remain strongly attracted to mortals.

Both Maharet and Marius love mortals in the larger sense of being deeply concerned for humanity's progress. Marius views himself as a "continual awareness" that watches over what happens in the mortal world for over a thousand years. And Maharet traces her mortal descendants through a massive genealogical family tree that she calls the Great Family. *(VL 467, QD 425–427)*

Some individual mortals are so compelling that the vampires want to bring them into vampirism to be immortal lovers and companions. Marius falls in love with Armand, who in turn gives the Dark Gift to Daniel. Lestat transforms Louis, Claudia, Gabrielle, Nicolas, and David, although usually he ends up disappointed.

Louis, however, does not feel that making a mortal into a vampire is morally acceptable. Instead, he suffers the loneliness that is a vampire's lot when he attaches himself, his feelings unrequited, to a mortal. Louis alludes to such a person when he tells his story to the boy reporter. *(IV 4, 60)* He mentions a love foreshadowed in his feelings for Babette and someone to whom he has told his entire story before. Although he does not clarify this relationship, it is more clearly spelled out in the first draft of IV. In that version, Louis tells the reporter that his return to New Orleans resulted in the greatest suffering of his vampire existence, for there he met his mortal lover. He does not elaborate on this relationship, however, because the boy reporter runs from the room, afraid he might become Louis's victim.

The most intense relationship between a vampire and a mortal is that between Lestat and David Talbot. David is a member of the Talamasca, an organization that studies paranormal phenomena such as vampires; thus, he understands what Lestat is, but is nevertheless attracted to him. He even goes so far as to claim that Lestat is his only friend. *(BT 45)* Lestat is equally attracted to David and wants him to become a vampire, particularly because David is old and might die at any time. Yet it is David's very resistance that makes him attractive to Lestat; he is a highly moral individual who will not willingly become a killer. Finally, Lestat can no longer endure not having David as his companion and makes him a vampire. *(BT 420–422)*

Lestat falls in love with another mortal, Roger. He loves Roger's

sophisticated criminal mind, so he kills him. Roger returns as a ghost. When he tells Lestat his story, Lestat loves him all the more and agrees to protect Roger's daughter, Dora. Lestat also loves her, for her uniqueness and passion. He wants to drink from her, but when he finally does so, he takes only her menstrual blood so as not to harm her. After his visit to Heaven and Hell, Lestat had vowed never again to take a mortal life. (MD 9, 322)

See also Agents, Armand, Continual Awareness, Flynn (Dora), Great Family, Lestat de Lioncourt, Louis de Pointe du Lac, Maharet, Marius, Molloy (Daniel), Roger, Talbot (David), Victims.

Moslems   Believers in the religion of Islam, which is based on the teachings of Mohammed and preserved in the Koran and the Sunna.

Memnoch mentions Moslems as another group that became entangled in the violent struggles of Christianity. They had taken advantage of the weakening of Constantinople during the Fourth Crusade, and they are also involved in the bloodshed of Bosnia-Herzegovina. *(MD 288)*

See also Bosnia-Herzegovina, Christianity, Constantinople, Fourth Crusade, Mohammed.

Mother Goddess   See Great Mother.

Motherhouse   The central headquarters and residence of the Talamasca in major cities around the world. The first Motherhouse was in Amsterdam, where Lestat meets David as he walks along the Singel gracht. *(BT 31)*

"In Amsterdam," says Rice, "I saw many beautiful three-story step gable houses along the canals. I pictured the Motherhouse as including several of these—say, three or four houses connected to make one grand building."

Jesse describes the London Motherhouse as a four-story edifice with lead-mullioned windows. Surrounded by ancient oaks and stately in appearance, it has Elizabethan furnishings and a warm atmosphere. Huge libraries and reading rooms occupy one floor, while another houses living quarters for its members. The Motherhouse is like a womb, for the Talamasca takes care of its members' needs until the day they die. Aaron Lightner, David Talbot, and Jesse all reside in this London Motherhouse. Below the house are cellars in which the organization stores items left behind by vampires, or "vampire refuse." Jesse sees Marius's painting of Armand in these underground vaults. *(QD 164)*

Jesse also lives in the Motherhouse in Delhi, India, for four years, where she documents cases of reincarnation. *(QD 189)*

*The Motherhouse,
Amsterdam*

One more Motherhouse is described in WH: it is the place near New Orleans where Aaron Lightner takes Michael to read the Talamasca files on the Mayfair witches.

See also Amsterdam, Jesse, London, Talamasca.

Mount Carmel A mountain in Palestine in northwest Israel, near where Jericho had been in the Dead Sea depression below Jerusalem. It stands nearly 1,800 feet above sea level.

The archaeologist in QD finds the first cave drawings of the red-haired twins on Mount Carmel. Appearing to be about six thousand years old, they were carved, then colored in with natural pigments. The scenes include the twins in a rain dance, kneeling at the altar of their dead mother, being imprisoned, escaping from Akasha, and being separated from one another. Maharet drew these paintings in her search for her lost sister. *(QD 38, 312)*

The twins had actually grown up in the caves on Mount Carmel, while their tribe had lived on the valley floor. *(QD 311)* (See Vampire Atlas)

See also Maharet, Mekare, Palestine, Witches.

Mountaintop room   See Sonoma Compound.

Mozart, Wolfgang Amadeus   An eighteenth-century classical composer with whom Nicolas studied the violin and whose music Lestat and Claudia frequently play on the harpsichord. When Jesse is investigating the New Orleans town house, she hears someone playing Mozart skillfully, but too quickly, on the piano. The mystery of who was playing is never solved; as Jesse imagines she sees Claudia's ghost, she may have hallucinated the sound or experienced a ghostly phenomenon. *(IV 101, VL 45, 50, QD 181)*

See also Nicolas de Lenfent, Violin.

Mummers   Parisian boulevard actors who paint their faces white, mime, and do acrobatics. Lestat suggests that the four vampires who survived Armand's disbanded coven become mummers. It would be a perfect disguise with which to mingle with mortals and learn about them. The vampires agree to try it, and their performance is so successful that it soon evolves into the Theater of the Vampires. *(VL 245)*

See also Marionettes, Theater of the Vampires.

Mummies   Practiced for over four thousand years in Egypt, mummification consisted of preserving and wrapping corpses so that the spirits of the dead would fare better in the next world. *Mummy* comes from the Arabic *Mumiya*, which was the word for bitumin, a substance mistakenly thought to turn the bodies black. The practice of mummification consisted of removing the internal organs (except for the heart and kidneys), filling the body cavity with unguent-soaked linen or sawdust, drying the outer body, anointing the corpse with oil, and wrapping it in linen bandages. The entire process took seventy days.

When Marius takes Akasha and Enkil out of Egypt to save them from the Elder, he wraps them up as mummies and places them in gold-plated mummy cases, both to protect them during the journey and to prevent mortals from accidentally seeing them. This situation is especially ironic as it had been Akasha and Enkil who had originally instituted the practice of wrapping bodies in linens. They did so to stop the cannibalism of corpses in their country. *(VL 452, QD 315)*

See also Those Who Must Be Kept.

Mummy

Mummy, The   A novel Rice wrote about Ramses the Damned, an ancient Egyptian king. In it, Rice describes the dilemmas of immortality from a different angle, since Ramses can mingle with mortals in the daylight and is immune to destruction of any kind. He is made immortal through a secret elixir and actually needs the sun for it to work its power. The story describes his adventures in England and Egypt during the Edwardian period and includes his reunion with Cleopatra.

See also Immortals, Ramses the Damned.

Music   Music influences the vampires' world in a variety of ways, tying them to their former humanity.

As a mortal, Nicolas played the violin. He continued to do so as a vampire, because his music had expressed his inner darkness and despair. Unfortunately, because he is a vampire, these feelings now became magnified.

Lestat sings from operas he has attended and plays the piano. He befriends a mortal musician and brings his dark, haunting compositions home to play. Although Louis feels that Lestat has no real passion for music *(IV 129–131)*, it is Lestat's musical prowess that makes a dramatic impact on the world, both for mortals and for vampires. Lestat becomes a successful rock star, documenting in song the names, history, and practices of vampires. *(VL 3)* As a result, he awakens Akasha; his voice outshouts the din of voices that drowned her in overstimulation and kept her silent for countless centuries. *(QD 259–260)*

In *Lasher*, Rice develops a connection between spirits and music. According to her description, music enthralls and distracts the spirits. Through its patterns music delivers to them a form of organization for which they long. Thus, it was most likely the spirit of Amel existing in Akasha that responded so strongly to Lestat's rhythms and melodies.

See also Music Videos, Rock Concert, Rock Music, Violin.

Musician Vampire   A young man who lives on the rue Dumaine in New Orleans and becomes a mortal companion for Lestat. Musicians are commonly used in literature to represent fascination with death, and this musician writes dark, haunting compositions that Lestat frequently brings home to play on the piano.

Lestat's association with this musician lasts longer than with any other mortal that Louis has witnessed, making him wonder if Lestat is setting the mortal up for a grand betrayal or something else entirely. Lestat does hint about killing the musician but instead merely preys on victims who look like him. When Lestat declares that he has found someone who would make a better vampire than Louis or Claudia, the two of them fear that he is referring to the musician.

Before Lestat has the chance to either kill the musician or bring him into vampirism, however, Claudia attacks Lestat, stabbing him until he loses blood and seems a mere corpse. She and Louis then toss his remains into a swamp. The musician looks for Lestat, and returns later in the story as a vampire, whom Lestat made after surviving the brutal attack. Lestat and the musician together attack Louis and Claudia, who flee the burning town house and board their ship. What happens to the musician at this point is not clear; he may have died in the fire. *(IV 128–132, 151–152, 157–159)*

See also Lestat de Lioncourt.

Music videos   Lestat records twelve songs that he releases on a rock album in 1985 and uses the finest available directors to make them into music videos. Actors in these videos enact such scenes from Lestat's autobiography as the rituals Armand's coven practiced, the playing of a violin for Akasha and Enkil in their shrine, the making of Gabrielle, Mael's abduction of Marius, and the existence of Pandora and Ramses. The titles of these videos are *The Legacy of Magnus, The Children of Darkness, The Grand Sabbat, Requiem for the Marquise* (which is Khayman's favorite), *Age of Innocence, The Dance of Les Innocents,* and *Those Who Must Be Kept.* Some of the songs are hymn-like and melancholic; others are excellent dance tunes. *(VL 520, 528, 540, QD 48, 120)*

See also Rock Concert, Rock Music, Rock Star.

"Mystery opposes theology"   A phrase that Lestat sees written on the door frame of Dora's bedroom at St. Elizabeth's. It refers to the mystical belief that religious experience is known inwardly rather than revealed in explicit doctrines. *(MD 123)*

Roger believes that Dora has not quite caught on to this principle. She tries to mix the two, but "it wasn't working with the proper fire or magic." *(MD 123)*

"If memory serves me right," Rice explains, "this was my own statement, a synthesis of what I had come to understand of my own readings in religion and religious history. I had come to see that mysticism lies at the opposite side of the codification of theologians. The division had never been terribly clear to me before. I might have been quoting someone else, but I believe it was my thinking. It's written on my wall somewhere."

Myth   See Dionysus, Osiris, Vegetation Gods.

Nabokov, Vladimir A twentieth-century Russian writer who specialized in themes of deception and artistic duplicity. His most famous novel, *Lolita,* was about Frenchman Humbert Humbert, whose erotic obsession with the twelve-year-old Lolita results in him marrying her mother just to be near her and murdering his rival for her affections.

Nabokov's highly visual prose in *Lolita* inspired Rice's early writings. She was fascinated with what she viewed as Humbert's extreme devotion to the girl, and her own child character Claudia exhibits an adult sensuality similar to Lolita's.

In BT, when Lestat is quoting opening lines from literature, he mentions Humbert Humbert's declaration: "You can always count on a murderer for a fancy prose style." *(BT 2)*

See also Claudia.

Names Naming involves the process of creation and, symbolically, bestows a soul and/or destiny on someone. The ancient Egyptians believed that names reflected the soul and possessed great power. For example, Maharet's people refrained from writing their names down so that they would not be vulnerable to their enemies; they believed that the knowledge of someone's name provides a way to turn the spirits against that person. *(QD 311)* Ironically enough, however, Maharet writes down the names of her mortal descendants, an activity that culminates in her creation in the Sonoma compound of the electronic mapping of the Great Family. *(QD 424–427)*

One of the rules of Santino's coven is that vampires are never to tell a mortal their name, nor the name of any other vampire, and allow that mortal to live. *(VL 302)* Confiding such a secret is an act of supreme intimacy, as well as a threat to the vampire's existence, and

Armand warns Daniel—who knows from Louis Armand's name—that it is unusual for a mortal to survive with that knowledge. This links the vampire nature to that of God, whose name is also kept from mortals or known only through symbols. *(QD 86)* The vampires thus use aliases for many of their legal transactions, although some of them tend to keep a single alias across the centuries, which assists the Talamasca in tracking them. *(QD 177)*

Louis first tells his name to Morgan, the Englishman he meets in Eastern Europe, and because of the intimate nature of the act, he is later unable to make Morgan his victim. *(IV 176)* Louis also reveals his name to the boy reporter and allows his story to be published so that, potentially, millions of mortals will know his name (although, in all fairness, the story *is* presented as fiction).

Lestat also disregards this rule, for he publishes an autobiography, makes videos and albums, and stages a concert; in all these instances he reveals the names of himself and other vampires. *(VL 13, 520)*

Without hesitation, Lestat tells Dora, a mortal, his name and what he is. Yet he has no intention of harming or killing her. Instead, he hopes she might somehow benefit from knowing. *(MD 127)*

See also Great Family, Great Laws, Rules.

Naples   The city in southern Italy where Gabrielle grew up. *(VL 37)*
See also Gabrielle.

Napoleon Avenue   The street in Uptown New Orleans where St. Elizabeth's Orphanage is located. *(MD 110)*
See also St. Elizabeth's Orphanage.

Nature   Gabrielle is intrigued with nature more than humanity, and gravitates toward it for its timeless beauty and aesthetic principles.

Shortly after Gabrielle becomes a vampire, she goes out into the woods, preferring to dig herself into the ground rather than sleep in the coffin in Magnus's tower. As she and Lestat travel the Devil's Road throughout Europe and Asia, Gabrielle wanders away for increasingly longer periods of time to commune with the wilderness. She wants to explore why beauty exists and why nature has such strong symbolic power for mortals. Gabrielle is intrigued with Lestat's notion of the Savage Garden, and expresses her vision that one day nature will rule the earth again. She wants Lestat to explore the jungles of Africa with her, but as he is too much in love with human beings and civilization, eventually Gabrielle leaves him and goes off on her own. After Akasha's death, however, Lestat wanders off alone through the redwoods, feeling unified with nature. *(VL 178, 253, 288, 334, 348, QD 464)*

Lestat sees in nature a reflection of his ideas about the savagery and deceptiveness of vampires: "We're beautiful like the diamond-backed snake . . . yet we're merciless killers." *(BT 62)* From nature he derives his notions about the Savage Garden, which operates strictly by aesthetic principles.

Akasha uses nature to justify her plan for world domination. She claims that bees and ants exemplify species that limit the males to only the few needed to reproduce. Males are otherwise an aberration. *(QD 368)*

Nature becomes central to the debate between Memnoch and God. After he experiences what it is like to be mortal, Memnoch believes that God is wrong when He says that humans are merely part of the energy exchange of nature that involves suffering and death. Memnoch claims that the human spirit places man somewhere between nature and divinity. Family, love, and the thirst for the spiritual set humans apart from all other natural species. As such, they deserve a place in Heaven. Even when God agrees to allow them in, He continues to disagree with Memnoch on this point. *(MD 205–206, 219, 244–247, 261–262, 300–301)*

See also Akasha's Plan, Beauty, Gabrielle, God, Human Evolution, Savage Garden, Thirteen Revelations of Physical Evolution.

Near-death experience

Near-death experience The experience of people who have been declared dead but then revived. Some claim to have risen out of their bodies; others describe going through a dark tunnel in the company of other people toward a brilliant white light. Rice was impressed with the medical literature on the subject and had several of her vampires undergo this experience.

When Baby Jenks's mother dies, something unusual happens to her. Her thoughts seem to expand, as if she is connecting to something larger than herself, and she now knows all about good and evil, love and God. This allows her to forgive her daughter and move on toward great beauty. Later Baby Jenks has the same type of experience when Akasha destroys her. She feels her soul float up and look down upon the scene of her death. Thousands of other souls linger around her as she slowly moves through a dark tunnel toward a light, where her mother greets with love the daughter who had murdered her. *(QD 51–52, 57)*

At the moment she died as a mortal, Akasha also experienced leaving her body. First, she saw herself on the floor, covered in blood. Then she had been drawn through a tunnel where there was no more suffering, until she was pulled back into her body, where her pain came alive again. *(QD 401)*

The Himalayas, Nepal

When Akasha dies again as a vampire, Lestat wonders if she saw what Baby Jenks had seen. *(QD 466)*

Rice based her concept of Heaven in MD on reports from near-death experiences.

See also Baby Jenks, Heaven.

Nepal   A kingdom in south central Asia, north of India. Nine-tenths of it is covered by the Himalaya mountain range. This is where Azim has his temple and where Akasha begins her rampage against the men of the world. (QD 59, 289) (See Vampire Atlas)

See also Akasha's Plan, Azim, Temple.

New Orleans   The city in Louisiana mentioned in each of the *Chronicles*, it is a location for much of the action. Because of its multicultural milieu, New Orleans is both a metaphor of, and the perfect

319

setting for, vampires. Louis views New Orleans as a "dream held intact . . . by a tenacious, though unconscious, collective will." *(IV 205)* A unique city of frivolity, superstition, contradiction, and sensuality, it serves as a magnet to vampires, who feel at home here.

Founded in 1699 with a cross staked on a bend along the Mississippi River, New Orleans was officially settled by a Canadian-born Frenchman in 1718. It is unique among American cities in its cultural history and population.

The first residents of the city were misfits from French prisons, along with whores and "casket girls"—women the Ursuline nuns brought over, who carried their belongings in caskets. Then came aristocrats, merchants, and farmers, followed by Acadians from Nova Scotia, who made up the population called Cajun. When King Louis XIV gave the city to Spain in 1762, Spanish bred with French, and the descendants became known as Creoles. The city went back under France's rule in 1800, then came into American hands three years later. Americans settled the Garden District, and Irish and German immigrants began to pour in, along with people from the Caribbean, some of whom were slaves and some of whom were free people of color.

For much of its history, New Orleans had a reputation as a city of open vice; it was easy to access gambling, "bawdy houses," and numerous saloons. The spirit of the city was lively and colorful, and, despite the strong presence of the Catholic church, crime was rampant. The citizens were, paradoxically, fun-loving yet repentant, imparting an atmosphere of ambiguity and contradiction. They loved stability and tradition as well as change, took both religion and corruption in stride, and honored their dead in high style.

New Orleans is home to Rice. She was born and raised there, until she was forced to move at the age of fifteen with her family to Texas. She went on from there to San Francisco, but after twenty-seven years, she returned to her native city.

"It was very important for me to come back to New Orleans," she says. "I wanted to be around the colors and textures, the shapes and smells, that I had experienced as a child. I felt homeless in California."

Lestat is the very first vampire to enter this city. He views it as the most forsaken outpost of the Savage Garden, a reflection of his own primitive nature. *(VL 494)* He goes there to join his blind, aging father after the French Revolution has wiped out the rest of their family. "As time passed," he says, "I came to love it [New Orleans] more than any spot on the globe." *(VL 493)* He appreciates its smells, colors, even its dampness. The lawlessness of such a place, he feels, diminishes his suffering as a vampire and increases his pleasure. Here he is not an outsider, but "the dim magnification of every human soul." *(VL 494)*

Lestat meets Louis in New Orleans and half of Louis's story is set here. Prior to becoming a vampire, Louis lives south of the city on a plantation. He remains on this plantation as a vampire, until its slaves drive him away. He then moves to the oldest outpost of the city, the French Quarter, where he lives with Lestat for sixty-five years. Louis then leaves New Orleans with Claudia to seek out other vampires, but returns to his hometown after Claudia's death. In IV, Louis describes New Orleans as a "magical and magnificent" place in which a vampire, "richly dressed and gracefully walking through the pools of light of one gas lamp after another might attract no more notice in the evening than hundreds of other exotic creatures." *(IV 40)* While Louis does live in San Francisco for a while, after the rock concert and the confrontation with Akasha he settles again in New Orleans, in a shack behind one of the Victorian mansions in the Uptown area. *(BT 104)*

Armand, too, comes to New Orleans in the company of Louis, and it is where the two of them end their intimate association. *(IV 325)* Armand grows bored and even feels he may be dying, but ultimately he claims New Orleans as his exclusive hunting ground for most of the twentieth century, killing any young vampires who venture too near. *(VL 529)* Eventually he connects with Daniel, who has come to New Orleans in search of Lestat's house. *(QD 83–85)*

After the publication of VL, Jesse arrives in the city to investigate for the Talamasca the vampires' properties. To her psychically attuned mind the city seems to possess a haunted and sinister quality. *(QD 177)*

Dora Flynn lives in New Orleans, in St. Elizabeth's Orphanage on Napoleon Street. Her home is based on the former Catholic orphanage that Rice bought and is currently renovating. Lestat comes here to show himself to Dora. He also returns here when, after his ordeal with the Devil and his delivery of Veronica's veil, Dora relinquishes the building to him. *(MD 11, 108, 340)*

Dora grew up in Metairie, a suburb of New Orleans, despite her father's wish that she live in the heart of New Orleans, where the houses have more character. Roger himself had grown up in an old house on St. Charles Avenue, near the Garden District. *(MD 59, 77)*

After stalking Lestat for nearly a year, Memnoch meets Lestat in his town house on Royal Street. He claims that he needs Lestat, who then goes to City Park at the end of Esplanade Avenue to discuss the situation with Armand and David. *(MD 140)*

The city also houses one of the vampire bars. (See Vampire Atlas)

See also City Park, Dixie Gates, Free People of Color, French Quarter, Garden District, Jackson Square, Metairie, Pointe du Lac, Roger, Roger's Mother, St. Elizabeth's Orphanage, Spanish Hotel, Town House, Uptown.

New York   See Manhattan.

Nicolas de Lenfent
The merchant's son, also known as Nicki, who befriends Lestat after Lestat kills the wolves. He invites Lestat to tell him about the battle, and the resulting dialogue forms a bond between the two young men. *(VL 41)*

Lestat expresses his curiosity about Nicolas's schooling in Paris, and they quickly develop grand ideas of running off together to that city. Both of them feel that they fail to fit in with others' expectations, and as outsiders they share a secret loneliness. Nicolas wants to be a violinist, having studied with Mozart, and Lestat wants to be an actor. Although their friendship grows, they soon discover that their opposing philosophies start to alienate them from each other. Nicolas is full of cynicism and dark despair, while Lestat firmly believes in goodness. His moral light often overwhelms Nicolas (although Lestat is unaware of this until after he makes Nicolas a vampire). *(VL 44–62)*

Lestat's mother gives them money to go to Paris, and they both find work in a small theater. *(VL 65)* After Magnus abducts Lestat and makes him a vampire, Lestat avoids Nicolas but sends him gifts, including a Stradivarius violin, while revealing nothing of what has happened to him. *(VL 119)* Lestat does visit the theater one night and Nicki embraces him, but Lestat hungers for his blood and must push him away. Once Nicolas sees Lestat survive a bullet, he is sure Lestat knows sorcery and is holding something back from him. He grows bitter about the deception and goes about drunk in the streets. *(VL 129)*

But Armand's coven knows what Nicolas means to Lestat and uses him to lure Lestat to them. *(VL 211)* Lestat rescues Nicolas, who then begs for the Dark Gift. Gabrielle warns Lestat not to do the transformation, but Lestat does it anyway. This new level of intimacy only serves to distance Nicolas and Lestat further, and makes Nicolas more despondent and cynical. *(VL 235)* It gets to the point that Lestat can no longer stand his former friend, and he brings Nicki his violin in the hope that playing it will restore their bond. However, Nicolas plays an intense and chaotic music that reflects his state of mind. He then confesses that he had wanted both himself and Lestat to come to ruin in Paris; he hates Lestat's exuberance and ability to triumph in the face of adversity. *(VL 264–267)*

Rice did not like Nicolas as a character, although she created the love between him and Lestat. "I meant him to be someone enormously attractive to Lestat, but Lestat couldn't save him. His view was too dark. When he was made a vampire, the darkness in him just erupted. So much of his life was based on rebelling against authoritarian principles and crazy bourgeois delusions that he just didn't have strength. Once he had maximum possibility and maximum nihilism, he couldn't handle it. Lestat was infinitely bigger and stronger, and tried to protect him, but Nicki was doomed."

Nicolas goes on to write plays for the coven who run the Theater of the Vampires. He views the Dark Gift as confirmation of pure evil. As a vampire, he is sloppy, scandalous, and difficult to control. He tries to make other vampires, so Armand, his caretaker, must restrain him. Eventually Armand imprisons him and cuts off his hands to keep him from playing his violin. Nicolas goes into the fire to destroy himself, requesting that Eleni send his Stradivarius on to Lestat. (VL 328, 340, 342–343)

When Lestat sees Louis years later, he recognizes in him the echo of Nicolas—grim, intense, and filled with despair. This is partly the reason he falls in love with Louis, and partly the reason he later despairs of their relationship; Louis is as dark and melancholy as Nicolas had been. (VL 497–498)

See also Destiny, Fire, Lestat de Lioncourt, Music, Nihilism, Our Violinist, Theater of the Vampires, Violin.

Night   See Darkness.

Night Island   The island that Armand and Daniel own off the coast of Miami. It is meant to be near Fisher Island, which can be viewed from South Point on South Beach.

Armand creates a tourist attraction there with shops, theaters, and restaurants that are open only from dusk until dawn. Armand and Daniel have a villa on this island, which they modeled on the Villa of the Mysteries in Pompeii. Armand slips through its secret doorways to mingle with mortals as they browse in the shops. (QD 100)

After Akasha's demise, the surviving vampires temporarily congregate on Night Island. Lestat then describes the villa in more detail: its white rooms are framed in gray velvet curtains and filled with priceless art and oriental rugs. The villa becomes a temporary coven house, a point of anchoring for the vampires, and a sanctuary. (QD 461)

See also Materialism, Miami.

Nihilism   The denial or absence of values, particularly the belief that there are no absolute standards for deciding what is right or wrong.

The vampires grapple with this concept and some, like Louis, are overwhelmed by despair at the possibility that a moral reality has no foundation. He wants to find a frame of reference through which he can find purpose for himself; if there are no absolute values, then he himself must be the source of moral judgment, and that, for him, is too great a burden to bear. (IV 238–241)

In contrast, Lestat courageously faces the task of making his own

meaning. Once he realizes that religion is empty and that he cannot find a sense of purpose or direction from either history or mentors, he embarks on the path that is most pleasing to him. When he ultimately chooses vampirism, he knows he has resolved, once and for all, the fact that he will never be redeemed for his acts. *(VL 354, BT 410)*

The characters who most clearly embody the concept of nihilism are Nicolas, Armand, and Akasha. Nicolas destroys himself to avoid living through a dark and meaningless eternity; Armand buries himself for centuries in superstitious ritual; and Akasha forms a vision in which her values are absolute for everyone else. *(VL 300–305, 343, QD 300)*

See also Armand, Akasha, Moral Dilemma, Nicolas de Lenfent.

Nine Choirs The ranks of the angels that make up the *bene ha elohim.* They are grouped according to three triads: Seraphim, Cherubim, and Ophanim (or Thrones), which are closest to God's glory and are often His messengers; Dominions, Virtues, and Powers, which keep the laws of the universe working, give orders, and work miracles; and Principalities, Archangels, and Angels, who guard nations and individuals and deliver messages.

Although Archangels appear to rank near the bottom, Memnoch claims they are in fact the closest to God and the most powerful of the angels. He also points out that the second triad is more docile and not as clever as the first. *(MD 207–208)*

See also Angel, Archangels, Cherubim, Ophanim, Seraphim.

Nineteenth century This era is significant for its famous vampire tales, and much of the action in IV takes place at this time. Louis and Lestat even fashion themselves like the kind of vampires depicted in the fiction of this century: they, too, are aristocratic, aloof, elegant, and merciless. Of this time period, Lestat writes in VL, "Maybe we had found the perfect moment in history, the perfect balance between the monstrous and the human." *(VL 500)*

The vampires also mirror the spirit of this age in their abandonment of religious values: Louis's loss of faith accurately reflected the belief in nihilism that became popular during the nineteenth century. *(IV 288)*

See also Nihilism, Vampire Tales, Zeitgeist.

Notre Dame Cathedral Situated on the Ile de la Cité in the center of Paris, this Gothic structure was built in the twelfth century. The name is a reference to "Our Lady," the Virgin Mary.

Lestat spends the night in this famous Parisian cathedral after his

Notre Dame Cathedral, Paris

crazed performance at Renaud's, where he fed on a beggar woman and her child and got his first taste of "innocent" blood. He found their blood to be richer and warmer than that of murderers and thieves. *(VL 142)*

Notre Dame is also a scene of confrontation. Armand's coven chases Lestat and Gabrielle to the place de Grève, which is in front of

325

the cathedral. When Lestat and Gabrielle enter the church, only Armand follows them inside; he does so surreptitiously, for he does not want his coven to realize that entering a religious institution is a possibility for vampires. It would call into question the rituals he established over the past three centuries. *(VL 197)* (See Vampire Atlas)

See also Armand's Coven, Paris.

Nyades Road ghost   See Ghosts.

Oak A sacred tree in some religions, the oak stands for strength and long life. Legends claim that, of all trees, the oak attracts lightning—a symbol of God—more than any other. Trees in general represent sturdiness, longevity, and immortality, for they join the Earth with Heaven.

The Druids worshiped the oak tree, imprisoning within it the vampire they view as their God of the Grove. He is kept there, starving from one feast to another, in order to sanctify the forest and imitate the cycles of death and rebirth. *(VL 413)*

The London Motherhouse, a symbol of longevity, is surrounded by a "great park of ancient oaks." *(BT 28)*

See also Druids, Druid Vampire, Motherhouse.

Oak

Obsession   Several mortals become obsessed with the vampires, who appear to them to possess power over death and the ability to enhance their mortal existence with unlimited possibilities.

Louis is obsessed with Lestat and so he agrees to become a vampire. He has been living in the darkness of grief, and Lestat appears to him a wondrous means of escape. Louis is enchanted by Lestat and wants to be what Lestat is. *(IV 13)*

In VL, Nicolas is obsessed with getting the power of the Dark Gift. Against his better judgment, Lestat finally gives it to him. But Nicki's intensity soon drives him insane. He plays his violin like a mad musician for the Theater of the Vampires, and when he cannot endure the endless nihilism any longer, commits suicide. *(VL 262–265, 343)*

Daniel's obsession with Armand is the most detailed and drawn out. After Daniel hears Louis's confession, he searches for Lestat to try to gain immortality for himself. Instead he encounters Armand, who uses him to discover the wonders of the late twentieth century. They form a type of S&M bond, then a friendship that grows into love. When Armand will not give him what he wants—immortality—Daniel eventually descends into a destructive alcoholism, a metaphor of his obsession, until Armand gives in. *(QD 83, 88)*

See also Addiction, Dominance/Submission, Immortality, Insanity, Slavery.

Occult   Secretive or supernatural agencies. Claudia seeks knowledge of the occult when she searches for answers about her vampire nature. She reads books on the occult, particularly about witches and vampires, then urges Louis to go with her to Eastern Europe. From her reading, this seems the most logical place to begin their quest for other vampires. *(IV 111)*

David Talbot also searches the occult for metaphysical truths. *(BT 59–70)*

See also Candomble, Shaman.

Ocean Drive   The street in Miami Beach that Lestat describes as his Champs-Élysées (in Paris) and Via Veneto (in Rome) because of its ceaseless activity and parade of beautiful bodies. While there, he stays at the Park Central, an art deco hotel. *(BT 11)*

See also Park Central Hotel.

Oddbody, Clarence   The name Lestat uses to make up a passport for Raglan James who had requested one as part of their body-switching deal.

Clarence Oddbody was the name of the angel in the classic movie *It's a Wonderful Life.* Clarence helped George Bailey, the character Jimmy Stewart played, to see that life was good and worth living.

As Lestat is about to reenter mortality, he is thinking of Jimmy Stewart, who shouts at the end of the movie, "I want to live!" However, before long Lestat's adventure has soured, thus inverting the symbolism. Lestat recognizes that he does not want to live as a mortal, but as a vampire.

"At the time, Lestat thought [by getting a mortal body] he was getting another chance," Rice explains. "He chose that name for that reason. He hoped for redemption, but he doesn't get redeemed." *(BT 162)*

See also Inversion, *It's a Wonderful Life.*

Clarence Oddbody and George Bailey in It's a Wonderful Life

"Offering, The"   A poem by Stan Rice that opens *Memnoch the Devil* and describes human suffering as an offering to whatever force may prevent random pain. This poem refers to Rice's experience of witnessing the chronic illness of his own father.

See also *Memnoch the Devil*, Poetry, Rice (Stan), Suffering.

"Of Heaven"   A poem Stan Rice wrote that introduces the section in QD about Daniel and Armand; it alludes to a creature similar to Armand. *(QD 73)*

See also Poetry, Rice (Stan).

Old age   See Aging.

Old Captain   One of the boarders in Roger's mother's boarding house on St. Charles Avenue in New Orleans. He was a smuggler and a collector, and he ran an antique shop. He introduced Roger to the art of medieval manuscripts, including the books of Wynken de Wilde, then later gave him Wynken's books. Old Captain lusted after the young boy, trying to engage him in a sexual tryst, but Roger kept his distance. The old man continued to love him but refrained from touching him. Because Roger shared the Old Captain's passion for Wynken de Wilde's writings, he continued to spend time in his company. The man passed away during Roger's senior year in high school. *(MD 36, 38, 55–63)*

See also Roger, Wilde (Wynken de).

Old World vampires   In IV, Louis and Claudia search in Eastern Europe for what they call Old World vampires: creatures of their own kind, but ones who have lived for a long time and might possess greater knowledge of what it means to be a vampire. The search fills Louis with bitterness, because he knows he is moving closer to the world of darkness and away from the mortal world that he still prizes. His primary concern is to discover why such suffering as his is allowed to exist, and how it can be ended. He wonders if these other vampires will really have any truths: "What can the damned really say to the damned?" *(IV 168)* Nevertheless, he cannot end his existence without trying to find out.

As Louis and Claudia travel, they hear rumors of the existence of these vampires. At one village, they encounter a man who has witnessed such rituals and whose wife is the victim of a vampire. Louis and Claudia seek out this vampire and find him in the barren ruins of a monastery. The vampire clearly is not Louis's equal: he lacks the heightened vampire vision, perception, and strength, and his clothing is as rotted and decaying as the state of his mind. *(IV 190)*

He and Louis clash, each struggling for dominance, and when Louis grabs the other vampire's head, he realizes it is nothing but a skull: "I was battling a mindless, animated corpse." *(IV 192)*

Claudia assists Louis by dropping rocks on the vampire's head. When they break his skull, this creature of the Old World is dead; he does not have the endurance of true immortality. Louis and Claudia travel through more of Eastern Europe, but their encounters with vampires there are always the same; they yield "no secrets, no truths, only despair." *(IV 197)* Louis ends up wondering if Lestat is the only vampire besides him and Claudia to possess consciousness and intelligence. *(IV 197)*

The condition of these vampires raises questions in Louis's and Claudia's minds: perhaps the vampires went mad from being sealed into a grave, or, worse yet, perhaps they were the result of a few precious drops of vampire blood being inadvertently left in their veins. *(IV 198)*

In the first draft of IV, the part of their journey that takes place in Eastern Europe is described only briefly. But the monsters are in the same type of decay, and Louis associates what they are with what Lestat has become upon his resurrection from the swamp. Louis believes that Lestat is now either dead or only a mindless corpse.

The Old World vampires symbolize what vampires have become in fiction since Bram Stoker published *Dracula* in 1897. Many contemporary authors present vampires as monsters who kill without compunction and, for decades, films have depicted the same image. In contrast, Rice's vampires suffer guilt and loneliness because they experience strong connections to their former humanity. They thus offer a psychologically richer portrait of the vampire experience.

See also Eastern Europe, Revenant, Transylvania.

Ollie One of the members of the rock band that Roger managed in San Francisco. When a drug deal went bad, forcing Roger to leave, the band split up. *(MD 70)*

See also Blue, Roger, Ted.

Olympic Tower A modern office and apartment building on Fifth Avenue and West Fifty-first Street in midtown Manhattan, located across from St. Patrick's Cathedral.

David Talbot rents rooms here—which are level with the spires of the cathedral—so that Lestat can safely store Roger's religious artifacts. The room has a glass wall overlooking the cathedral. *(MD 27)*

To see the relics and to tell her about his meeting with the Devil, Lestat brings Dora Flynn here. She urges him to accompany Memnoch. Lestat does so, then returns to the Olympic Tower to recover.

Olympic Tower, near St. Patrick's

Dora is still there, along with Armand and David. As he watches the snow falling through the glass wall, Lestat tells them his story. *(MD 27, 95, 150–163)*

Rice based her description of this condo on her own visit to the Olympic Tower. She had looked at the cathedral through the glass wall, albeit from a much higher vantage point. (See Vampire Atlas)

See also Flynn (Dora), Lestat de Lioncourt, Manhattan, Religious Relics/Artifacts, Talbot (David).

One Powerful Mind   This concept derives from the idea that the vampires are all spiritually connected to one another through Amel's fusion with Akasha, the first vampire. When the vampires begin to receive the dream about the twins, Armand describes his theory about the phenomenon to Daniel: he thinks that either a powerful vampire mind is picking up images from another such mind and passing those images along to others, or that a single central mind is telegraphing the images to many. Either way, one vampire has the ability to unify his mind with other vampires to such an extent that he or she can see through the other vampires' eyes. Through this one mind—whether it is Akasha's or some other vampire's—thoughts travel along the threads of the weblike network that connects all vampires. That vampires worldwide can hear Marius's warning of danger substantiates Armand's theory. *(QD 110)*

Akasha shows Lestat proof of this notion when she tells him how she has traveled astrally, experiencing things from the viewpoints of others. Also, when she gives to Lestat Baby Jenks's vision of light after Baby Jenks was destroyed, Lestat sees the vision as if he were Baby Jenks. *(QD 249–250)*

See Baby Jenks, Telepathic Powers, Vampire Powers, Vine.

Ophanim   One of the nine ranks of angels that Memnoch describes to Lestat, part of the first triad. Memnoch says they are the least articulate or eloquent of the three and may remain silent for eons. When Memnoch introduced human society to the wheel, he based its round shape on the Ophanim, whose name literally means "wheel." *(MD 200, 207, 233)*

See Angel, Nine Choirs.

Oratory   A private chapel meant for prayer and meditation.

In IV, the mortal Louis builds an oratory for his devout brother, Paul. Surrounded by rose trees, it has a flagstone floor, a prie-dieu, and an altar. As a result of the hours he spends in the oratory, Paul has religious visions. He neglects to eat and even allows the oratory to deteriorate as he stands in the pose of the crucified Christ receiving "instructions." He tells Louis that St. Dominic and the Virgin Mary have come and urged him to sell the plantation and use the money for God's work. Louis dismisses these visions and Paul, in a rage, goes out to the gallery and falls down a stairway to his death. *(IV 5–6)*

When Louis becomes a vampire, he inverts the spiritual purpose of the oratory by moving his coffin into it and transforming it into a vampire's crypt. This act represents not only the death of his brother but the demise of Louis's own faith. As the years pass, the oratory falls into physical ruin, although Louis continues to sleep in it. It is partly

his emergence from the oratory night after night that alerts the slaves to his vampire nature. *(IV 34, 50)*

See also Coffins, Paul, Visions.

Ordinary Man   See Memnoch.

Orphans   What Claudia calls those vampires left behind by their makers who are still struggling to survive and make sense of what they are. She is referring specifically to the vampire revenants of Eastern Europe, but she is also speaking about her own trauma of being made a vampire as a child. *(IV 200)*

See also Claudia, Hybrids, Old World Vampires, Revenant.

Orpheus   The son of Apollo and Calliope, he was a master musi-

Hermes, Eurydice, and Orpheus

cian and lyre player in Greek mythology. His music was so inspiring that animals, trees, and stones followed him, and rivers stopped flowing to listen. When his wife, Eurydice, was killed, Orpheus wanted to bring her back from Hades, the underworld. The King of the Dead consented, with one condition: Orpheus must not look back as he leads her out of Hades. Yet when Orpheus emerged into the light, he was unable to resist looking back—and Eurydice fell back into Hades, never able to join the world of the living again.

Lestat refers to himself as Orpheus when, after fleeing from Armand's coven, he glances back. He uses the same metaphor when he leads the person he thinks is David Talbot to a place where they can discuss David's becoming a vampire. This time, however, he doesn't dare give a backward glance. *(VL 233, BT 365)*

Osiris   One of the chief gods of ancient Egypt, he forms a trinity with his sister/wife, Isis, and his son, Horus. He was a corn god and a fertility god.

Originally, Osiris was a wise king who spread civilized ways throughout Egypt. He turned his people away from cannibalism and toward the practice of eating grains. But his brother Set (also called Typhon) murdered him by tricking him into a coffin, which he then sealed. The coffin was put into the Nile, where it floated away. Isis eventually recovered the corpse, but Set discovered the body and cut it into fourteen pieces.

Isis regained all the pieces except the genitals and wrapped them in fine linen wrappings. Thus, Osiris became the first mummy. Isis used her magical arts to bring Osiris back to life as the King of the Dead and Lord of the Underworld, and the ancient Egyptians saw in him the power of resurrection and life after death. As part of their ritual worship, they would then sacrifice red-haired men on the harvest field, burning them and scattering their ashes. These celebrants believed that Osiris drank the redheads' blood in the name of the great goddess, the Earth. Members of his cult kept the celebrations secret, so that evil priests could not steal from them the secret of immortality. The cult also protected Osiris from the sun god Ra, who might be able to destroy the god of the underworld with the sun's burning rays. *(VL 433)*

Osiris's connection to the vampires comes through Enkil and Akasha, who worship both Isis and Osiris. They credit Osiris with saving them from the demon Amel, and with giving them the divine attributes of immortality and spiritual visions. In his name, they condemn Maharet and Mekare, and Enkil later takes on the identity of Osiris. *(VL 443, QD 416)*

What Lestat finds fascinating about the story of Osiris is how it parallels the legend of Dionysus, and how both prefigure the crucifix-

The god Osiris

ion and resurrection of Christ. As a vampire, he sees himself reflected in each of these mythological figures. *(VL 330, 501)*

Memnoch mentions Osiris as one of the death-and-dismemberment gods that humans created, based on their pessimistic, violent superstitions. *(MD 298)*

Rice decided upon this connection with Osiris when she read Sir James Frazer's *The Golden Bough.* She was astonished at the similarities between vampires and the vegetation gods, including the fact that, as with Osiris, for vampires, the genitals are no longer functional. "I was swept up," she says, "with how the Osirian myth seemed to have to do with vampires—with Osiris becoming the king of the night and coming back from the dead, and how they [the ancient Egyptians] would sacrifice blood at their festivals. Once I got on the trail of the vampire being a sort of vegetation god, I took it back to the earliest vegetation god we know of, which is Osiris. It was a natural progression."

See also Akasha, Christianity, Dionysus, Egypt, Enkil, Isis, Vegetation Gods.

Othello   A Shakespearean play about the Moor Othello, who kills his wife after the villainous Iago tricks him into believing she has been unfaithful. As he goes to smother her, he says, "Put out the light, and then put out the light."

Lestat quotes this line in IV as he bites a whore who, in trying to escape him, upsets a table and extinguishes a candle. *(IV 79)*

See also Iago, Shakespeare.

Our conversation   The way the mortal Lestat refers to his long discussions with Nicolas; he means that they understand one another and take great pleasure in confiding their fears and dreams to each other. From out of their conversations grow both the Golden Moment and the Dark Moment. *(VL 50–51)*

See also Dark Moment, Golden Moment, Nicolas de Lenfent.

Our Oldest Friend   The name Eleni uses in her letters to Lestat to refer to Armand. She does this so as not to reveal Armand's true name should mortals inadvertently find and read her letters. Vampire law prohibits revealing a vampire's name to mortals. *(VL 328)*

See also Armand, Names, Rules.

Our Violinist   The name Eleni uses in her letters to Lestat to refer to Nicolas. She does this so as not to reveal Nicolas's true name, should a mortal inadvertently find and read her letters. Vampire law prohibits revealing a vampire's name to mortals. *(VL 328)*

See also Names, Nicolas de Lenfent, Rules.

Outcasts   There are rules that guide the vampire communities (or covens), which say that those who conform are accepted and those who do not are outcast.

Armand's coven views Magnus as an outcast, since he lives in defiance of the Dark Ways. Any fledglings he made would thus also be outcasts. This makes Lestat doubly an outcast, rejected not only for his freedom from the Dark Rituals, but for his association with Magnus. The same power of association applies to Gabrielle. However, Lestat and Gabrielle crush the coven's attempt to disempower them. *(VL 166, 210, 217–220)*

A century later, Armand again declares Lestat an outcast after he has requested help in bringing Claudia to justice—simply because Armand, nursing a grudge against Lestat, has waited that long to gain power over Lestat and now has his chance because Lestat is so weak. After Louis burns down the Theater of the Vampires with the vampires inside, the vampire community at large views both Louis and Armand as outcasts for their part in destroying the theater. *(IV 304, VL 525)*

Marius is also an outcast from the vampire community because he chooses to be an artist with mortal apprentices, and also because he seeks beauty and light while the nearby coven is practicing principles of darkness. *(VL 296)*

See also Covens, Heretics, Outsiders, Rogue Vampires, Rules.

Outsiders   Those who exist on the fringes of a community, either because they feel too different to fit in or because they are deliberately shunned.

The vampires embody the psychology of the outsider. They had been human once but are no longer (although many retain ties to their former mortality). Outsiders, as Louis says, are "secret infidels." They suffer loneliness and need to believe in themselves in order to survive the greater rejection of society. However, vampires additionally feel as if they no longer deserve the kind of love they expected as mortals. *(IV 65)*

"I believe that when you write from the point of view of an outsider," says Rice, "you can best describe natural life. They [vampires] are in the midst of everything, yet are completely cut off, so they're able to see things that human beings aren't able to see. I see the vampires as outsiders, people outside life who can speak about it like Mephistopheles could speak about it to Faust. They are able to perceive what the inside is better than those who are actually there."

Part of the agony of the outsider, according to Rice, is "the longing to have choices." They would like to be able to fit in or not, as they please, but are definitely held apart. They are shut out from ordinary life, alienated, and exist in a state of social limbo; when there

is no choice, that which is inaccessible becomes highly desirable. Lestat confirms this when he tells Akasha that human life has become a romantic ideal to vampires (just as vampire life is to mortals). *(VL 451)* He believes he wants to experience mortal life again—although when he gets the opportunity, he realizes he has made human life better than it actually is, and no longer does he want it. *(BT 269)*

As outsiders who are shunned from one community, vampires seek another form of community: one among themselves. Yet even these communities, which operate within the rules of conformity, create yet another category of outsiders: outcasts or heretics.

See also Community, Coven, Heretics, Outcasts, Rogue Vampires.

Overseer   See First Kill, Victims.

Palais Royal The principal location in Paris of the royal balls during the eighteenth century. Located in rue St.-Honoré, it was once the residence of Cardinal Richelieu.

As Lestat grows used to mingling with mortals, he decides to attend a ball to see if he can pass undetected. He encounters no difficulties, and is even quite appealing to the ladies. At one of these balls, he encounters Armand, who poses seductively, as if waiting for him. Lestat feels a strong attraction to him and they embrace. Armand then

Palais Royal, Paris

339

attempts to bite him, to suck from Lestat his power. The two struggle, but Lestat triumphs. *(VL 273–278)* (See Vampire Atlas)

See also Armand, Paris.

Palestine   Known in the Old Testament as Canaan, it is a region on the eastern shore of the Mediterranean and is bordered by the Dead Sea. Used as a continental bridge between Africa and Asia, Palestine was traveled extensively by early tribes. Jews considered Palestine the Promised Land, Christians revere it as the birthplace of Christ, and Moslems view it as a destination for pilgrimage.

The tribe of the twins had lived in the Palestinian wilderness, near Mount Carmel, during the time when Jericho still stood. *(QD 311)*

It was in the valley of Palestine that Memnoch first became flesh. He met Lilia, had sex, and mingled with the human tribes. During the time of Christ, he shows Lestat the wilderness, where he had first seen God in the form of a man. While they are there, God invites Lestat to witness Christ's crucifixion. *(MD 222, 266, 279–280)* (See Vampire Atlas)

See also Christ, Human Evolution, Jerusalem, Lilia, Memnoch, Mount Carmel, Twins.

Pan   In Greek mythology, the lascivious god of flocks. He is represented as a man with goat legs and horns. His symbol is the phallus. Greeks invoked him during fertility rituals.

God decides that, in imitation of Pan, Memnoch will sprout horns during his earthly manifestation. *(MD 292)*

See also Devil, Memnoch.

Pandora   In Greek mythology, Vulcan fashioned Pandora, the "all-giver," from clay in the image of Aphrodite, although ostensibly each of the gods and goddesses participated in her creation. Zeus offered her as a gift to Epimetheus, the brother of Prometheus. Having stolen fire from the gods to give to humankind, Prometheus knew the gods were angered at him and warned his brother not to accept the gift; Epimetheus took Pandora anyway. Jupiter gave Pandora a sealed earthenware jar to take with her and endowed her with an insatiable curiosity. He then instructed her never to open the container, but, of course, she did, thereby letting out all manner of diseases and evil and bringing the Golden Age to an end. She closed the jar just in time to seal Hope inside. From then on, sickness and death separated humans from the gods, and humanity's only salvation was hope.

Pandora's tragic act is akin to that of the vampires, who take the Dark Gift and only perceive its evil when it is too late. This is especially true of the vampire named Pandora.

Marius falls in love with the tall, brown-haired Greek courtesan when she is a mortal. She knows exactly what he is and seduces him into making her a vampire; she claims she once had been a vampire, destroyed when the Mother and Father were placed in the sun, then reincarnated into mortal form.

Marius does not know whether her account of herself is accurate, but he makes her into his vampire companion at the shrine of Akasha and Enkil, allowing Pandora to drink from Akasha and receive the powerful blood. They live together for two hundred years, singing hymns and bringing flowers to the Mother and Father, but arguments eventually divide them. Marius sees her once more in Dresden, then loses her until she rescues him from the ice under which Akasha has buried him. *(VL 463–474, QD 237)*

Pandora is a dark, despairing immortal. Although she had wanted immortality initially, she is soon unhappy with her choice. Lestat thinks she was damaged in some crucial way even before the confrontation with Akasha. She had failed to receive the dream of the twins as the other vampires did, only learning of it and Marius's subsequent dilemma from Azim. *(QD 59–72, 462)*

Although Pandora is one of the vampires who confronts Akasha, she remains distant during the scene, staring out the window. Apparently indifferent to her fate, she only rouses herself enough to say that Akasha is attempting to validate deplorable methods of bloodshed, and her ideas bring moral dialogue to an end. *(QD 446)*

Even after Akasha dies, Pandora remains detached, immersing herself in videos and barely noticing Marius's solicitous attention. There is no sense of recovery in her, as there is with the others. She departs early from Night Island, still despairing. *(QD 462)*

See also Gathering of Immortals, Marius, Reincarnation.

"Pange Lingua" A processional hymn sung in the Catholic church on Holy Thursday to honor the Eucharist. "Pange Lingua" is the phrase that starts off the hymn; it means "Sing my tongue."

"I heard this hymn many times as a child," says Rice, "sung in a glorious solo soprano. I remember hearing it at a convent when I was twelve and particularly loving it."

Louis hears the hymn in St. Louis Cathedral and it sets off a series of nightmarish visions of a sinister procession: Lestat's funeral. *(IV 144)*

Paradox Something with seemingly contradictory qualities or phases. Rice utilizes paradox as a literary device to complicate the psychological undertones of her novels. The use of paradox balances

and acknowledges such opposing impulses as: the measure of love is hate (Claudia); power comes from surrender (Akasha); vampires can be angels (Louis, Lestat); one can be good at being bad and can use evil to do good (Lestat); evil can result from not being evil (Louis); substance makes the spiritual possible (Maharet); feeling nothing increases the intensity of feeling (Louis); the taking of life increases the appreciation for life (Louis); loners can actually crave community (Louis); and a body shrinks in self-protection while expanding in power (Jesse). The paradoxes in the *Chronicles* are numerous.

Akasha is one of the more perfect examples of paradox. Lestat describes her as soft and yielding while at the same time she has skin that is hard. While her powerful blood, when fed to Lestat, improves and perfects him, the perfection that it offers is also a form of destruction: becoming more of a vampire makes Lestat less of a human. Akasha fights aggressively, in a masculine style, yet does it in the name of women. She wants to use violence to achieve peace and paradise. *(QD 372, 376)*

Akasha is both right and wrong; her logic makes sense, but her ethics do not. In fact, even her ability to do what she wants to do depends on paradoxes: that evil can be made good, that a vampire can be a god, and that darkness can mean enlightenment. Akasha transforms concepts by endowing them with her own meaning, which, paradoxically, is created out of her own inner sense of meaninglessness. *(QD 367)*

However, Akasha cannot make her paradoxical actions work for her because in practice the moral framework is difficult to dissolve. Opposites have their own meaning, and those meanings do conflict. So while paradox works stylistically for Rice, it is the source of Akasha's vulnerability. *(QD 372)*

See also Akasha's Plan, Symmetry.

Paris Traditionally called the City of Light, it is the largest city in France. Paris is considered a major cultural center of Europe, and the vampires find it a city of enlightenment. It is a central place in IV and VL for sophisticated vampire debates. In these early novels, Paris seems to be the capital of the vampire world.

Paris is like the vampires in many ways as it, too, has a reputation for being volatile, reclusive, intense, impulsive, changeable, intellectual, arrogant, passionate, and animated. Architecturally, it is a strange conjunction of the old and the new, blending disparate elements into a fascinating whole.

The vampires love Paris for its sophistication and elegance. It is the city that Lestat and Nicolas run away to as young mortal men *(VL 63)*, and the place where Lestat is made a vampire. *(VL 90)* Louis claims he felt the closest to being happy in that city, for there he was able to forget temporarily that he is damned. He sees it as an exotic and sophisticated place, indestructible, explosive, and enchanted. *(IV 204)*

Louis and Claudia seek out their own kind there during the reign of Napoleon III, encountering a coven that has formed a theater. (In the first draft of IV, this coven lived in a mansion in the Faubourg St.-Germain.) The leader is Armand, who, at the age of four hundred, claims to be the oldest vampire in existence. When he turns Louis's quest for answers into a search for inner power, Louis loses his religion altogether and falls in love with Armand. *(IV 278)*

In the first draft of VL, Claudia joins forces with three young vampires who are brothers, but in the published version, she loses her life in Paris, having come under suspicion by the jealous coven. Her search was not for enlightenment but for a sense of who she is as a woman; in Paris she finds a "mother" but ends up having no opportunity to develop their relationship. *(IV 306)*

Lestat gets his start as an actor in Paris, bringing him to the attention of a vampire, Magnus. After Lestat is made a vampire, he gives his mother the Dark Gift, then meets Armand. He leaves the city in search of vampires who know more than Armand's ignorant coven, yet returns to Paris over and over again to further his growth. He is attracted to the rich materialism of Paris—it echoes his own preferences—and he also loves the energy of its people. After Claudia's death, Lestat avoids Paris, but returns finally in BT.

He then sees the city as a place of innovation and wanders around, ruminating on his experiences here. He has also come to see if Raglan James can track him here, which James is able to do. In Paris, Lestat receives another communique about switching bodies and calls David to discuss the matter. *(BT 85–88)*

It is in Paris that David Talbot had seen a vision of God and the Devil in a café, arguing about metaphysical questions. From that experience, David has formed his theory of the two entities that he later describes to Lestat. *(BT 74)* (See Vampire Atlas)

See also Armand's Coven, Innocents (Les), Montmartre, Notre Dame Cathedral, Ritz, Theater of the Vampires, Visions.

Park Central Hotel

An art deco hotel, painted lavender, pastel blue, and mint, and located on Ocean Drive in Miami Beach's South Beach. The Park Central mixes luxury with casual style, and its rooms recapture the atmosphere of the thirties.

Lestat stays in this hotel when he hunts the serial killer that haunts the back streets of South Beach. *(BT 11)*

Returning to Miami after his fiasco with the Body Thief, he meets up with David Talbot and they return to his rooms in the Park Central.

Park Central Hotel, South Beach, Miami

David has asked him for the Dark Gift, but when Lestat begins to drink David's blood, he realizes that Raglan James is occupying David's body. Lestat throws the man against a wall, and realizes too late that he has now killed David's body. *(BT 365)*

See also Miami, Ocean Drive, South Beach.

Parker   A twelve-year-old hitchhiker who becomes Baby Jenks's first victim. *(QD 44)*

See also Baby Jenks.

Passion Play   How Lestat refers to his annihilation of a serial killer. It is a religious reference to a type of play that is composed of scenes related to the passions of Christ during his final days. *(BT 11)*

Past   All of the vampires must learn how to deal with their past, for

otherwise it becomes a burden that depletes immortality of its value. Many of the vampires focus on their mortal past.

Louis never quite comes to terms with his past. He had become a vampire because of grief and a desire to be damned. *(IV 16)* He remains the most human of the vampires because he forever regrets his decision to join Lestat, living his life like an adult bemoaning a lost childhood. *(IV 81–82)*

Madeleine, on the other hand, immediately burns down her doll shop to release herself from her past and get on with her new existence. She is completely done with mourning. *(IV 220, 279)*

Armand clings to the power of human tradition when he involves himself so thoroughly with satanic beliefs for three centuries. It is his way of not freeing himself from the past. He does not believe in what the rituals prescribe, but he requires a belief structure. *(VL 301–305)*

Marius believes that history cannot save anyone, that immediate existential problems must be solved individually by the person who is facing them. Although Marius, too, uses ritual for continuity, he does change with the times, utilizing the available technology for protecting and enhancing his shrines. *(VL 465)*

Lestat does not look back after he becomes a vampire, except when he is struggling over the problem of his evilness. In BT, he dreams about his past mortal life and feels haunted by his previous decisions. The dreams seem to paralyze him at times, and he considers ending his existence. He eventually lets go of the past—symbolically casting Claudia's locket into the ocean—and no longer looks to his former mortality for answers. He realizes he wants to be a vampire, for he did not take the opportunity for freedom and redemption when it was available. *(BT 5–6, 208–210, 418, 420)*

See also Dreams, Humanity.

Paul   Louis's younger brother, mentioned briefly in IV, who dies before Louis becomes a vampire. Although his age is not mentioned, Paul was fifteen in the first draft of IV. His religious aspirations create a rift between himself and Louis; his zeal embarrasses Louis. He claims to have had a vision of St. Dominic and the Virgin Mary, who told him to use the money from selling the family plantation to do God's work. Louis refuses to abide by the vision's instructions and Paul walks away, falling down the stairs to his death. Louis's overwhelming grief over the loss of Paul and the subsequent guilt he suffers because of that refusal make him vulnerable to Lestat's invitation to become a vampire. *(IV 4–9)*

After becoming a vampire, Louis continues to dream of his brother. On the night he first realizes that the Devil may not exist— four years after he has become a vampire—he has a vision of Paul frantically trying to tell him something that he cannot hear. Later he

"sees" Paul in St. Louis Cathedral, where his vision of Paul's corpse transforms into the corpse of Lestat. *(IV 77, 146)*

See also Oratory, Visions.

Peace A feeling of security and satisfaction that the vampires achieve only when they kill mortals and drink their blood.

Louis is restless and unhappy in IV because he is resisting what his vampire nature compels him to do. For years, he torments himself over the morality of killing and believes that he is damned. Lestat informs him that peace will only come when he can kill night after night without regret. Louis acknowledges this: "I knew peace only when I killed." *(IV 87)* His struggle is a metaphor of what Aristotle called entelechy, which is a Greek word meaning "having its end within itself." Aristotle believed that each organism has a specific function and only when it develops in harmony with that function can happiness and inner peace result. Since Louis fails to surrender to his vampirism, he cannot find peace. *(IV 82–83)*

See also Killing, Swoon, Vampire Nature.

Peasants The people of Eastern Europe in the mid-1800s who still believe in vampires and who still practice the rituals for repelling and destroying vampires.

Louis and Claudia encounter these peasants on their trip through the countryside of Eastern Europe. They listen for rumors of vampires (while taking pains not to draw attention to themselves as potential victims for these superstitious folk). In one town they discover that a vampire does indeed exist in the area. Louis asks about the vampire's suspected location, pretending to be a vampire hunter who will free the peasants of their scourge. He finds the vampire and, discovering that it is a mindless corpse, destroys it. After reassuring the peasants about the vampire's death, he and Claudia leave, knowing they will find no answers in such a superstitious place, and that, by remaining, they would only be putting themselves at risk. *(IV 171–185)*

See also Eastern Europe, Superstitions, White Stallion.

Penny dreadful A nineteenth-century form of fiction, usually dealing with violence or crime, that cost only a penny. The first vampire tale, *Varney the Vampire,* was a penny dreadful.

Posters of vampires from penny dreadfuls hang in the Theater of the Vampires. *(IV 217)*

See also Vampire Tales, *Varney the Vampire.*

Penthouse apartment In BT, where Lestat lives on Decatur and Dumaine streets in the French Quarter of New Orleans, before he

refurbishes the old Royal Street town house. It is the top floor of a four-story building with a view of the Mississippi River. Lestat keeps his computer equipment there, which he uses for writing, monitoring his accounts, and tracking serial killers. He puts up a heavy iron gate in the courtyard, uses heavy locks on the doors, and puts bars on the windows to guard the penthouse against penetration by mortals. But this turns out to be to his disadvantage: after he switches bodies with Raglan James, he realizes his decreased strength will hinder him from getting inside. Fortunately, he finds that David Talbot has broken in with more sophisticated methods than mere brute strength, and is inside, waiting for him. *(BT 100, 273, 276)* (See Vampire Atlas)

See also New Orleans.

People of the Book   All people whose religion is based on the One God, but allowing for deviations in their prophets and prophecies. This would include Jews, Moslems, and Christians. *(MD 288)*

See also Christianity, God, Moslems.

Perception   See Senses, Vampire Eyes.

Phallus   The male sexual member, it is a symbol of the perpetuation of life and active power.

Lestat tells the story of Osiris, the Egyptian vegetation god whose brother dismembers him. All his body pieces were then found except for the phallus, which Lestat thinks is appropriate. The legend of Osiris is connected to the vampires as a dying mortal who became a god and who received blood sacrifice from worshipers. He has no phallus, and similarly, vampires need no phallus, since their sexual contact is made by sucking blood. *(QD 357)*

See also Osiris, Sex, Vegetation Gods.

Phantom of the Opera   Andrew Lloyd Webber's musical based on Gaston Leroux's novel of the same name about a man with a physically deformed face who takes refuge from the world in one of the deepest cellars of the Paris Opéra; he soon gains the reputation of being a ghost. Using his talent for music, he lures a beautiful singer named Christina into his lair. From her father's stories, she believes the Phantom to be the Angel of Music, who can take her talent to new heights, but when she unmasks him, she realizes he offers her nothing. Christina then leaves with her lover.

While talking with David in the Manhattan hotel as he watches Roger and Dora, Lestat hears a piano tune from this musical that foreshadows his own seduction by an underworld figure, as well as his eventual deformity. *(MD 20)*

Picasso, Pablo   A twentieth-century artist drawn to exhibit tension and conflict in his work. He used bizarre and fragmented dream-like images to arouse his viewers, although in his "classical period," his paintings of Grecian scenes were more realistic.

Lestat compares Gretchen to Picasso's painting of Grecian women, who were physically heavy-set. (BT 228)

See also Gretchen.

Pied Piper (of Hamelin)   In German legend, the Pied Piper was a traveling magician who, in 1284, offered to eliminate the rats from the town of Hamelin for a fee. Dressed in a multicolored coat, he played his pipe and lured the rats to the river, where they all drowned. When the town's burghers refused to pay him, he lured away all the children of the town with his pipe, and they were never seen again.

In the first draft of IV, Armand is compared to this figure as he calls to himself victims to whom he refers as "those who want to die." He uses visions, just as the Pied Piper used music, to make himself too alluring to resist.

Lestat also refers to himself as the Pied Piper when, weakened and needing sustenance to recover, he calls rats to come to him in his New Orleans mansion. (VL 509)

See also Those Who Want to Die.

Pierrot   A standard comic character from old French pantomime, he usually has a white face and wears loose white clothing. He is the French version of Pedrolino, a servant in the Italian commedia who wears white clothing and a floppy hat. Both are childlike figures of incurable stupidity.

Khayman compares himself to Pierrot when women smile at him. (QD 134)

See also Khayman.

Piraeus   A port in Greece where the ship carrying Louis and Claudia stops on its way over to Eastern Europe. (IV 168)

See also Eastern Europe, Quest.

Place de Grève   The square in Paris in front of the Cathedral of Notre Dame. During Lestat's mortal era, punishments are meted out to criminals here, and Lestat often catches glimpses of a hanging. This is also the place where Armand's satanic coven confronts and overpowers Lestat and Gabrielle. (VL 65, 205)

See also Armand's Coven, Notre Dame Cathedral, Paris.

The constellation Pleiades

Pleiades   A star constellation which is part of the larger constellation of Taurus. In Greek myth, Orion pursued the seven daughters of Atlas and Pleinone, so they were transformed into doves and placed among the stars, just beyond his reach.

Maharet calls the Pleiades constellation "the seven sisters," and she believed all blessings issue from it; generations of her family considered these stars to be sacred. *(QD 310)*

Daniel looks up at this star formation just before he is made a vampire, yet he is not truly seeing it because it is only a vision that Armand has created. Yet its creation is significant, because by choosing a constellation that enraptured the twins, Armand is revealing how closely the vampires are connected to each other. *(QD 113)*

See also Stars.

Pneumonia   The illness Lestat develops when he temporarily becomes a mortal in BT. After walking in a blizzard, oblivious to the effects of exposure, he succumbs to the disease. He is taken to a hospital, where he nearly dies. Through his illness, he discovers how vulnerable mortals really are and meets Gretchen. During his ordeal, he hallucinates about Claudia and begs to be saved from death. Gretchen eventually takes him to her home to heal. *(BT 194)*

See also Gretchen.

"Poem on Crawling into Bed: Bitterness" A poem by Stan Rice that introduces Parts 4 and 5 of QD—respectively, the confrontation between the vampires and Akasha, and the vampires' subsequent recovery in Miami. This poem focuses on the past and mentions that some forms of grief become art.

Lestat turns his grief over losing Akasha into literature when he writes down his adventures. *(QD 433, 459)*

See also Poetry, Rice (Stan).

Poetry A powerful use of language that conveys feelings and images. Rice mentions and uses poetry throughout the *Chronicles* to frame the vampires' stories.

"When I was little," says Rice, "my mother used to read poetry all the time, and she said she read it to us [Rice and her sisters] just to give us a sense of rhythm."

The first poem mentioned in the *Chronicles* is in IV—it is written by Samuel Taylor Coleridge, and Rice uses it to refer to Claudia *(IV 154)*—but it is not until QD that Rice uses poetry extensively. In QD, each section is framed by Stan Rice's poems.

"Originally I was looking for one poem to put at the front of QD," Rice explains, "but I was finding all this stuff that dealt with the same themes that I was dealing with. It was almost like I'd written each chapter to go with his [Stan's] poems, but that was not true at all. His poems were written years before [my writing of QD]. I was knocked out by the fact that we seemed obsessed with the same themes and the same images." Both shared a belief in substance and the idea that careful observation leads to the truth.

"I've been influenced a great deal by Stan," Rice admits. "I can remember specific conversations we've had about language and writing. I think a lot of Stan's rhythms and ways of doing things are deeply ingrained in my writing."

Rice does use work from other poets as well. Besides Coleridge, she was influenced by John Keats. Although she does not specifically quote him, she does admit to using in her work the sense of swooning that she perceived in his "Ode to a Nightingale." She also quoted from this poem in her two short stories, "The Master of Rampling Gate" and the vampire story in *Playboy*.

Interestingly, the first draft of IV utilizes poetry to advance the story. Just as Louis is growing more frustrated and resentful of Lestat, he discovers that Lestat wrote poetry as a boy. Lestat's father still has one of Lestat's poems in his possession—one that Lestat's illiterate mother had managed to keep even though Lestat's father was burning all his son's poems—and Louis reads it when they take refuge at Babette's. It was written in 1754, and although it is not sophisticated, it conveys the importance and fragility of dreams. In it Lestat expresses his fear that circumstances will consume his life. The poem (which is not quoted) gives Louis a new perspective on Lestat, and the hope that there may be a way to forge a bond between the two of them. If Lestat can write poems of such feeling, then he must have a glimmer of sensitivity within his vampire soul. But Lestat dismisses the poem and Louis despairs of any real friendship between them.

Later in this first version of IV, Louis and Claudia are invited to a vampire ball at Armand's mansion. They watch as the vampires stand around and recite a macabre poem by Charles Baudelaire. The words give Louis the impression that these vampires are acknowledging the Devil as their master, but Armand tells him that no one there believes in the Devil; their use of the poem was simply an aesthetic choice because they thought the poetic images beautiful or sublime.

In BT, Rice also uses a line from a poem by William Blake and two poems by William Butler Yeats to convey images and themes.

Rice then returns to her husband's poetry, including three poems that strongly relate to the themes she develops in MD. All three come at the beginning to introduce and foreshadow events in the novel.

See also Baudelaire (Charles), Blake (William), Coleridge (Samuel Taylor), Keats (John), Rice (Stan), Webster (John), Yeats (William Butler), and specific poems by name.

Pointe du Lac

Louis's indigo plantation, where he is made into a vampire, and where he lives with Lestat in the early part of their relationship. A French name, it means "point of the lake." In the first draft of IV, it was called Font du Lac. Rice viewed plantations as unapproachable paradises, embodying whole worlds unto themselves.

She based the plantation house itself on the West Indies–style house of that era. "I meant it to be primitive," says Rice, "with porches all around." It also had a raised floor and wooden posts for a simple, rustic look.

French and Spanish settlers built these self-sufficient communities along the Mississippi River on large tracts of swampy land for the purpose of raising crops like indigo, cotton, and sugar cane. These first houses were small and made of mud, Spanish moss, and cypress. The builders' increasing affluence meant larger houses, and some of these homes were viewed as small palaces. They had large rooms with high ceilings, massive pillars, broad galleries, and magnificent central hallways with tall staircases. Since farmers acquired the most wealth when they had slave labor, most of the magnificent ones that survive today are from the antebellum period.

Rice's acquaintance with plantations came from her exposure as a child to such mansions as Pitot House at 1440 Moss Street, and

Madame John's Legacy at 632 Dumaine Street in the French Quarter of New Orleans. The former was built in 1799 and the latter in 1726; both were West Indian "raised cottages" with above-ground basements. Rice also became acquainted with legends about plantations in books like *Louisiana Plantation Houses* and *Ghosts Along the Mississippi*. She was most impressed, however, by Harnett Kane's *Plantation Parade*, which detailed stories about the families who owned the plantations, and by George Washington Cable's description in his short story "Jean-ah Poquelin."

According to the story, Jean Poquelin owns a plantation in the swamps; it is somewhat hidden but conspicuous enough to engage the attention of his neighbors. He travels with his half-brother, a studious, book-loving recluse like Louis, on a two-year expedition, but only Jean returns. The house then becomes a source for superstitious rumors. Some of the townspeople spy a white figure on the grounds that exudes an odor of death—perhaps the dead brother's ghost! At the end of the story it is revealed that the missing brother actually lives at the house,

Pitot House, New Orleans, model for Pointe du Lac

but his brother has attempted to protect him from inquiring eyes because he is a leper.

"Cable described the house," says Rice, "and it was swimming in my mind when I wrote my novel."

In IV, Louis's family receives a land grant for their plantation and they settle there into a life of primitive luxury, surrounded by slaves. They furnish the house with velvet drapes, imported rosewood furniture, and expensive ornaments. These luxurious furnishings soon become a point of contention between Louis and his brother, Paul. *(IV 4–5)*

Paul is a religious devotee and he informs Louis that, in visions, St. Dominic and the Blessed Virgin have instructed him to sell off the plantation and use the money for God's work. The resulting argument inadvertently results in Paul's death. Deep in grief, Louis leases the plantation to an agency. *(IV 10)* His despair makes him vulnerable to the vampire Lestat, whom he believes wants Pointe du Lac. (Lestat later denies this in his own story.) Lestat and Louis live together at the plantation with Lestat's blind, aging father until the slaves become suspicious and force action. Lestat has been using the plantation as a front to lure weary travelers, who become his victims. *(IV 21, 35)* Since vampires do not belong in paradise, both physically and metaphorically, Louis and Lestat are forced out. Louis then burns down Pointe du Lac, symbolic of how he is cutting himself off from his human traditions and his religion. Louis feigns his own death in this fire so that he no longer has to pretend to be mortal for his surviving family. *(IV 32–57)*

See also Fire, Indigo, Louis de Pointe du Lac, New Orleans, Paul, Slavery.

Pointe du Lac, Louis de   See Louis de Pointe du Lac.

Pompeii   A town on the eastern coast of Italy that was buried under ash and lava when Mount Vesuvius erupted in the first century A.D.

Here Marius builds one of his many sanctuaries for Those Who Must Be Kept, but he abandons it and takes the occupants to another place when archaeologists come to dig up Pompeii. It is also the place where Daniel and Armand, inside the Villa of the Mysteries, become lovers. Years later Armand makes this villa the setting of the vision he creates for Daniel during Daniel's transformation. *(VL 476, QD 91, 112)*

See also Shrine, Villa of the Mysteries.

Porsche   Lestat's car of choice in VL when he becomes a rock star.

Lestat's Porsche

He drives a black Porsche around Carmel Valley and down Divisadero Street. Louis then spots him and comes to him. *(VL 519, 520)*

Raglan James informs Lestat that he will have a red Porsche to use during his stint as a mortal; this, as it turns out, is a lie. *(BT 162)*

Potter, Lionel   One of the aliases Lestat uses in France when he makes business transactions. Through it Rice is blending two names: *Lionel* Barrymore, the actor who played Henry *Potter*, the villain of the film *It's a Wonderful Life*. Potter is a banker who threatens to devour the life of the community. *(BT 200)*

See also *It's a Wonderful Life.*

Power   See Extraordinary Life, Flight, Reading Minds, Telepathic Powers, Vampire Powers.

Predators   How Lestat describes vampires. He compares them to wolves and tigers in their capacity for viciousness and detachment. He views himself as a man-eating tiger that threatens David Talbot. *(IV 83, BT 5–6)*

See also Tiger, Wolves.

Presence, The   See Armand's Coven.

Pretense   When vampires come in contact with mortals whom they do not intend to kill right away or at all, they must devise some form of pretense in order to prevent discovery of their vampire nature.

Thus, Louis and Lestat pretend to eat dinner night after night when with Lestat's father, rattling their knives and forks to aid this

deception. This pretense fails to make an impact, however, since the slaves realize that Louis and Lestat eat no food, and also see Lestat's coffin in the bedroom. The slaves eventually force the vampires to flee Pointe du Lac. *(IV 48–49)*

Lestat also pretends to eat and drink with those victims whom he wants to seduce gradually. Early in his vampire life he learned that he could easily pass for a mortal if he drank enough blood to soften his skin, modulated his voice, and kept his movements restrained. Initially, he wanted to enter into the fabric of life and carry on relationships with mortals, but that way of life became impossible when he realized he would probably kill them eventually. *(IV 337)*

Louis devises what he thinks is a clever pretense with Babette, a mortal woman whom he loves. He wants to assist her with her plantation, so he appears to her as an angel giving divine instruction. This disguise falls apart, however, when Babette finally sees him for what he is—a devil. *(IV 47)*

Claudia lures victims to her by pretending to be a lost little girl who needs help. She then plays with them before she kills them. *(IV 101)*

Maharet takes great pains to fool Jesse when she invites Jesse to spend two weeks with her at her Sonoma compound. She pretends to be Jesse's aunt, a mortal world traveler. Jesse, however, is aware that there is something different about Maharet and her companions, and after she reads IV and VL, suspects they are vampires. *(QD 152–160)*

The most elaborate pretense vampires carry out is enacted at the Theater of the Vampires in Paris. The vampires put on plays in which they pretend to be actors pretending to be vampires; this allows them to kill onstage with abandon, because they know the audience will believe the killing to be merely a performance. *(IV 217)*

See also Deception, Illusion, Malaria, Theater of the Vampires.

Priest   A person who is authorized to perform the sacred rites of a religion, especially as a mediating agent between humankind and God. As it is the highest supernatural being they know, the vampires often put themselves into the roles of priests, speaking words from the Catholic religion to emphasize the association.

The vampires act as priests when they offer their own blood to a mortal for the purpose of making him or her into a vampire. For example, Magnus tells Lestat, "This is my Body. This is my Blood." He tempts Lestat to take the "wine"—his vampire blood—which will give him life everlasting. Lestat resists but eventually succumbs. Then, two centuries later, he, too, implies that he is a priest and/or Christ when he sings, "This is my Body. This is my Blood." *(VL 89–90, QD 230)*

Armand is described as a priest when he makes Daniel. During

the transformation, he says, "Drink," as does a priest who pours wine—which is, during Holy Communion, symbolically the blood of Christ. The promise of Communion is union with the divine, which is what Daniel receives when he sheds his mortality for immortality. And Louis plays the role of a priest when he listens to the confession of a dying whore that Lestat has brought to the Spanish hotel. *(IV 86, QD 114)*

For Louis, taking the role of a priest is significant in view of the fact that he has lost his Catholic faith. After Paul's death, a priest hears the story of Paul's visions and denounces them as the Devil's work. Louis is astonished by the priest's reaction, and becomes even more cynical about religion. He drives the priest from his room, foreshadowing what he is about to do with God in his life. He metaphorically puts an end to his own superstitious religion by killing a priest in St. Louis Cathedral. *(IV 11, 149)*

See also Eucharist, Religion, Religious Images.

Prince   The title Akasha confers on Lestat when she wants him to be her companion and assist her in carrying out her plan. In many legends, princes are often heroes who possess the virtue of intuition. Lestat displays this quality, for he realizes that Akasha's plan for the human race is wrong and eventually rejects her vision.

See also Akasha's Plan, Brat Prince, Lestat de Lioncourt.

Procreation   Vampires cannot procreate as humans do, through genital sex. The phallus is the one part of a vampire that is not enhanced by the Dark Gift; instead, it becomes impotent. Vampires achieve sexuality, and procreation, only through the drinking of blood. To make a child or a fledgling, the vampire drains the chosen mortal to the point of death; this human blood travels through the vampire's system and alchemizes into a new substance powerful enough to fuse with mortal cells and transform them into an immortal substance. The vampire then allows the mortal to drink this blood from him and become a vampire. *(IV 19–20, VL 90–92)*

See also Children, Fledglings, Phallus, Sex, Transformation, Vampire.

Prometheus   Son of a Titan in Greek mythology, he stole fire from the gods and gave it to humans. The king of the gods, Zeus, punished Prometheus by chaining him to a rock, where an eagle fed daily on his liver until Hercules rescued him. Prometheus represents the spark of divinity in humans and the end of ignorance. As such, he became a symbol of freedom to the Romantic artists and poets.

Lestat perceives Magnus as a dark Prometheus when he envisions

Prometheus Carrying
Fire *by Jan Cossiers*

Magnus stealing the powerful blood from a vampire. Louis also describes Lestat this way, and Marius uses the same metaphor to convey to Armand his vampire nature. *(VL 89, 295)*

See also Magnus.

Prytania Street   The location in New Orleans of Lestat's crumbling house, Louis claims to see him here (Lestat later disputes this). It is where Lestat goes underground, and where Daniel, the boy reporter, seeks him out and finds Armand instead. *(VL 5, QD 83)*

See also Lestat's Houses.

Pseudepigrapha   Writing that is falsely attributed to an author, especially in reference to biblical figures or subjects. Such writings make up some of the apocalyptic literature. For example, the *Book of Enoch* and the Sibylline Oracles are considered Pseudepigrapha.

In her religious studies, Dora Flynn reads the Pseudepigrapha. *(MD 84)*

See also Apocrypha, *Book of Enoch*, Flynn (Dora), Sibyl, Watcher.

Punchinello and Harlequin   Clownish figures from the Italian commedia dell'arte, they were white-faced, mute acrobats.

Lestat describes himself and Tough Cookie as these characters when they improvise a highly erotic dance on stage during their San Francisco rock concert. *(VL 538)*

See also Rock Concert.

Purgatory   An intermediate state between Heaven and Hell, experienced after death for expiatory purification. According to Roman Catholic doctrine, there are two dimensions of sin: that which upsets God's design and that which alienates believers from God. The Almighty can pardon the latter but not the former, and sinners must purge their sins by temporarily living in a state of purgatory. In Purgatory, they experience varying degrees of penitential suffering until they satisfy the Divine's sense of justice.

Louis uses this as a metaphor to describe to Lestat his experience of being a vampire. *(BT 111)*

See also Hell, Humanity, Religion.

"Put out the light, and then put out the light"   A quotation from Shakespeare's play *Othello* in reference to a murder. Othello, erroneously convinced that his wife has been unfaithful, speaks this line as he is about to smother her.

Lestat uses the line on a whore he intends to kill after she has knocked over a candle and extinguished it. *(IV 79)*

See also *Othello*, Shakespeare.

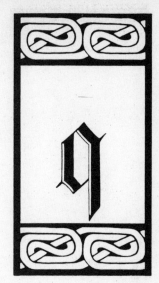

Queen Elizabeth 2 (QE2)   The fastest cruise ship in the world and the flagship of the Cunard line. On board are thirteen stories of restaurants, movie theaters, spas, pools, sports facilities, classrooms, a casino, and an international shopping promenade. The *QE2* makes both transatlantic crossings and Caribbean cruises.

     By tracing Raglan James's patterns of killings while he is inhabiting Lestat's body, Lestat and David are able to track James to the *QE2*. Lestat also remembers that James had mentioned wanting first-class passage on this ship when the Talamasca had banned him from the order, and David recalls that James had once been fired from the crew for theft. They then form a plan to retrieve Lestat's body. *(BT 295)*

     With the help of the Talamasca, they book three cabins under aliases and smuggle guns and a trunk aboard. When Lestat boards the *QE2*, he is simultaneously dazzled and repulsed by all the glitzy plastic and chrome. They locate James's stateroom (the Queen Victoria Suite),

The QE2

wait for the opportune time, then force the body switch. Once back in his own body, Lestat rushes to a deck on the fifth level, where he barricades himself in a small cabin. The next night, after discovering that David and Raglan James are gone from the ship, he disembarks. *(BT 315–319)*

Much of the material about this ship and the experience of being on board came from Rice's own Caribbean cruise. "I was in a welter of excitement during the whole cruise," she says, "taking down notes for the novel and seeing the scenes. I was Lestat on that ship; I wasn't Anne." (See Vampire Atlas)

See also *The Tale of the Body Thief.*

Queen of Heaven   A name by which Akasha refers to herself in QD, it is possibly derived from the goddess Inanna, whom Akasha once worshiped and who also had this title. Akasha believes she can re-create a worldly paradise by killing off the majority of mortal men and bringing about a reign of women, all of whom will worship her as their goddess. *(QD 297, 300)*

See also Akasha.

Queen of the Damned   The name by which Mekare refers to Akasha after Akasha announces how she intends to punish Mekare and her twin sister for speaking the truth about Akasha's evil destiny. Ironically, after Mekare destroys Akasha and consumes Akasha's heart and brain—thus ingesting the vampire spirit—she becomes the new Queen of the Damned. *(QD 411, 457)*

See also Akasha, Mekare.

The first edition jacket

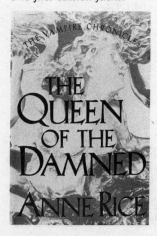

Queen of the Damned, The   The third vampire *Chronicle,* told by Lestat as a sequel to VL. Lestat writes QD as part of his recovery after Akasha's death. Much of the story comes from plumbing the memories of the other vampires as they ride from the Sonoma compound to Miami. Marius does not want him to write the story, Jesse asks him to change the names (which he ignores), and Maharet urges him to get the Legend of the Twins right. Lestat himself calls the novel a "chronicle of seduction and pain." *(QD 463)*

The idea for the theme of this novel came to Rice on a plane: "I was watching one of the *Star Wars* movies. I think Luke Skywalker was fighting with Darth Vader, and Vadar was saying, 'Give in to the dark force inside you.' It was horribly cliché. That's when it came to me what *Queen of the Damned* ought to be. Essentially, the queen should have an extremely good idea, but it should still be evil. The real evil in the world is always a complex and seductive thing that sounds brilliant."

Switching styles from VL, Lestat in QD weaves together the events and activities of a number of characters, both vampires and mortals, in order to build up to his abduction by Akasha. In QD, he introduces Khayman of the First Brood, Jesse, Maharet, Daniel, Pandora, Azim, and Mael. He also covers the story of Baby Jenks as representative of what happened to ordinary, otherwise nameless vampires when Akasha went about destroying the Children of Darkness.

Akasha wants Lestat to join with her as she slaughters mortal men in order to bring about her plan for world peace. They debate the pros and cons of her plan as Lestat twice participates in the blood fest. Although Lestat is strongly attracted to Akasha, he feels increasingly alienated from her bloody vision. (QD 260–263, 391–398)

Meanwhile, the vampires who survived or were spared Akasha's worldwide purge of her own progeny meet together with a vampire who is as old as Akasha: Maharet. This vampire is one of a pair of twins who, as mortals, were witches, and it was one of the spirits that the twins knew, Amel, who entered the body of Akasha and made her a vampire. Akasha in turn made her husband, Enkil, and her steward, Khayman, into vampires, and Khayman then gave the Dark Gift to Maharet's sister, Mekare, because she had foretold that she herself would be the agent of the queen's downfall. Mekare gave the Gift to her sister, who is now insisting on the need for the surviving vampires to stand against Akasha to protect the human race. The other vampires know this would mean their demise: because of the powerful blood, whatever happens to Akasha happens to them. But ethics and morality inspire them to stand together and resist the queen. (QD 399–431)

Eventually, Akasha comes with Lestat to the Sonoma compound where these vampires are meeting. A philosophical confrontation between Akasha and the other vampires ensues, and then Mekare arrives. She has traversed continents to fulfill her promise of bringing down Akasha. Mekare shoves Akasha against a glass wall, which shatters and slices off Akasha's head. Thinking quickly, Maharet has Mekare eat Akasha's heart and brain, thus destroying Akasha, aborting Akasha's plan, and preserving the vampire race. (QD 435–456)

"*The Queen of the Damned* was the first book I wrote exactly the way I wanted to write it," says Rice. "All the other novels involved a compromise that had to do with my abilities. I wasn't skilled enough to do what I wanted. With *Queen*, the [storytelling] process started, and I thought, no, I can't pull that off. And then I thought, I'm going to do it, those two twins, the whole thing. I'm going to do everything it takes to tell the story. It was the first totally realized vision that I had ever created, and it was a very pleasant experience. It was scary, because it's much safer to compromise—to say, I can't pull *that* off."

See also Akasha, Akasha's Plan, Gathering of Immortals, Lestat de Lioncourt, Maharet, Mekare, Moral Dilemma, *Vampire Chronicles*.

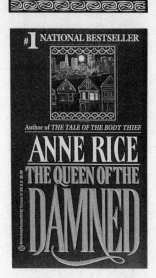

The mass market edition cover

Queen's wreath

Queen vampire In VL, Lestat refers to an older female vampire in Armand's coven as the "queen vampire," although there was never any real indication of this sort of leadership. This vampire does accompany Armand as if they rule together, but she also taunts Armand and seems to stand apart from the rest of the coven. Her babbling exhibits a degree of lunacy and she makes reference to several predictions, which seem fulfilled upon Lestat's arrival. She accepts and encourages Lestat and Gabrielle when no one else does, and claims to have known Magnus. When Armand tries to destroy the coven, the old queen throws herself into the fire to "join Magnus." *(VL 216–233, 243)*

See also Armand's Coven, Innocents (Les).

Queen's wreath A delicate evergreen vine with clusters of purplish blue, star-shaped flowers, it is one of Lestat's favorite flowers. Lestat says that a good rule of thumb is to live only where the climate can support such a flower. *(BT 302)*

See also Flowers.

Quest A journey made to attain knowledge or wisdom. It represents the soul leaving its center to go after a possibly unattainable ideal. Those who embark on a quest typically confront challenges and surmount hurdles that involve risk. The adventure itself signals inner development, and reaching the goal indicates an initiation into eternal mysteries. The rewards that come from successfully accomplishing a quest also include self-integration, balance, wisdom, and spiritual health.

Louis and Claudia set out on a quest to find other vampires who can tell them about themselves and give purpose to their existence. On the ship, Louis realizes that his quest is for darkness, and not those concerns typical to mortals. "The myths of men are not your myths," he tells himself. "Men's treasures are not yours." *(IV 168)*

The quest takes him and Claudia to Central and Eastern Europe, where they discover that the vampires there are mindless creatures who offer nothing but horror. They then journey to Paris—the City of Light—and encounter Armand's coven. *(IV 170–196)* Armand, too, has no answers of the kind Louis seeks, but he does urge Louis to look to the power within himself to make meaning. On one level, then, Louis's quest ends in his experiencing frustrated, nihilistic despair—no answers, no God, no Devil, no definition from an external source, and no true sense of his own power. However, on another, Louis does attain a form of wisdom—the idea of relying on his own inner strength—that could empower him were he only to reach for it. *(IV 235–242)*

In VL, Lestat also goes on a quest. He tries to find Marius, an ancient vampire who may possess vital secrets about vampire existence. Lestat travels from one country to another, leaving messages in each place for Marius. Not only does this journey test Lestat's persistence, but it puts him in real danger, for Marius has killed other vampires who have sought him. Ultimately, Lestat despairs and goes into the earth, a form of psychological death for vampires. Marius, as he is intrigued with Lestat, comes to him and brings him to the island sanctuary where he keeps the vampire progenitors, Enkil and Akasha. Marius treats Lestat as a hero who has made an arduous journey and rewards him by bringing him into the inner circle of select vampires who know about the vampire origins. Marius even tells Lestat about his own quest to find the vampire Mother and Father, thus showing a heroic kinship with Lestat. *(VL 232–480)*

Yet those who seek do not always find what they hoped for, nor are they always spiritually prepared to acknowledge the results of their quest. Lestat is clearly not ready to be brought into the dark secrets on an equal status with Marius. He risks his life through the brash act of waking Akasha from her trance, and Marius sends him away, instructing him to live out the equivalent of a full human life; Lestat needs to gain more wisdom from life before taking on the greater burden and greater reward of vampire enlightenment. *(VL 468)* Lestat ignores Marius's advice, breaking all the vampire rules and nearly bringing the world to ruin by waking Akasha for a second time, before he realizes he must temper his tendency to act on whim. *(QD 4–5)*

The ultimate quest involves Lestat's journey with Memnoch the Devil to Heaven and Hell. Memnoch claims that he needs Lestat's assistance to help turn back the tide of evil in the world, which he attributes to God. He offers to show Lestat Heaven and let him talk to God. Lestat agrees. In Heaven, Lestat is overcome by what he sees and awed by God Himself, but after considering Memnoch's perspective, experiencing Christianity's violence, and realizing Hell's horrors, he cannot bring himself to be part of either God's or Memnoch's plan for humankind.

Whether or not God or the Devil is the true source of evil, both are too overwhelming for Lestat to endure. What he experiences seems entirely real to him, but he realizes that even though he wants to believe Memnoch, he cannot be sure of anything. Memnoch could have shown him a false conception of things, as evidenced by the note he sent (if he did indeed send it) thanking Lestat for performing well. Lestat's quest took him into unearthly realms, at least in his imagination, but provided no real answers. He cannot judge whether the Devil duped him or whether God might have prevented Memnoch from proving anything definitely. *(MD 350)*

See also Devil's Road, Eastern Europe, God, Heaven, Hell, Hero, Lestat de Lioncourt, Marius, Memnoch, Teacher.

Ra See Amon Ra.

Radio A device that receives and transmits impulses or signals by means of electromagnetic waves. Maharet uses this metaphor to describe how vampires are attuned to Amel's energy. *(QD 422)*
See also Amel.

Raglan James See James, Raglan.

Ramses the Damned One of the Children of the Millennia. Marius indicates that Ramses has been called a vampire but is in fact an immortal man who is unconnected to the vampire race. Ramses can walk in the daylight and does not drink blood. While Marius speculates that he may have once been a vampire who died in fire and was reincarnated into another form, Ramses's full story is told in Rice's novel *The Mummy*, and goes as follows:

Ramses is an aging Egyptian king who is informed by a Hittite priestess about an elixir that grants immortality. He drinks the white liquid, which is made from common natural ingredients. Immediately his gray hair returns to its original brown, his dark eyes become blue, and he is once again in his body as it was in the prime of his life. The elixir saturates all of his cells, changing their chemical structure and ever renewing them. While Ramses experiences physical hungers that are never quenched, he has no real need for food or water, since nothing can kill him. He becomes a world traveler and an adviser to the Egyptian rulers until he tires of life.

He then hibernates as a mummy until Cleopatra, with whom he eventually falls in love, revives him. He buries himself again after her suicide and nothing disturbs him until the year 1914, when he is three thousand years old. It is the time of Edwardian England, and archaeologist Lawrence Stratford has discovered Ramses's resting place.

Stratford inadvertently lets in the sun when he uncovers Ramses. The sunlight activates the immortal elixir, and Ramses rises. He comes to love Stratford's daughter, Julie, and together they explore Egypt, where Ramses discovers Cleopatra's mummy and brings it back to life. The tale is left unfinished, for a sequel may follow.

Rice originally decided to include Ramses in the *Vampire Chronicles*, because she was possibly going to have him join the vampires at Maharet's Sonoma compound. She thought better of it, however, and decided that he should have his own story. *(VL 302)*

See also Immortals, *The Mummy*.

Rangoon   The capital city of Burma in southeast Asia, it lies on the banks of the Rangoon River.

Jesse meets Maharet and Eric in Rangoon after Mekare is taken to a secret place to guard the new source of vampire existence. *(QD 463)* (See Vampire Atlas)

Raphael   One of the chief archangels, Raphael specializes in nurturing creativity and protecting spiritual pilgrims. He also watches over the young and innocent. In *Paradise Lost*, Raphael told Adam angels had sex by merging their bodies, for the finer matter of the angel body can take the form of either gender. *Enoch I* describes Raphael as a guide in Sheol.

Raphael is one of the angels enthralled with the unfolding of God's creation; he notes the emergence of the human spirit. After Memnoch's stint on Earth, God sends Raphael and Michael to bring Memnoch back to Heaven. *(MD 197, 200, 236)*

See also Angel, Archangels.

Rapunzel

Rapture   What the vampire's kiss promises. Upon surrendering to the swoon, mortals find themselves seduced by its sensuality. Vampires also look to experience this rapture from each other: upon sucking one another's blood, they can find great pleasure, as Lestat does with Marius and Akasha. Armand promises this rapture to Lestat and Gabrielle, if they only will surrender to him. He assures them that it is the end of all conflict. *(VL 200–201, 361, 486)*

See also Intimacy, Seduction, Sex, Surrender, Swoon, Vampire's Kiss.

Rapunzel   A character in a fairy tale about a beautiful woman imprisoned in a tower. Rapunzel's hair is so long that, if put out her window, it can fall all the way down and reach the ground. The witch who imprisons Rapunzel, as well as Rapunzel's eventual rescuer, use the hair as a ladder.

After cutting her hair one night, Gabrielle realizes that it will always grow back during the daytime to its former length. If she continues to cut it, she says, the tower would quickly fill up with as much hair as Rapunzel had. *(VL 182)*

See also Gabrielle, Hair.

Rat A symbol for the negative, disgusting part of the inner self, it also depicts something grotesque in appearance or some kinds of sexual perversion.

Lestat shows Louis that he can live off the blood of animals by grabbing a rat, slicing its throat, and drinking its blood from a wine goblet. This act reveals Lestat's acceptance of his vampire nature, but the act repulses Louis, foreshadowing how he will continue to feel about himself as a vampire. Yet, ironically enough, his revulsion for killing humans drives him to kill rats and other animals for a period of four years, until he finally targets a human victim. *(IV 32, 71)*

As they travel by ship, the vampires live off of rats to avoid suspicion. *(IV 163)* In other situations, rats also serve as nourishment. By the end of IV, Lestat is so weak that he is forced to live on rats to survive. He also lives on rats in his weakened state when he first emerges in 1985, until he has the strength to kill humans again. *(IV 329, VL 509)*

In the film *Interview with the Vampire*, Louis's insistence on drinking only animal blood involves many such scenes with rats. Lestat actually tells him he can easily be tracked just by following the dead rats. Some of the negative critical reactions to these scenes inspired Rice to write a poem she called "The Ballad of the Sad Rat."

Rat

I'm a lowly rat
in a vampire movie.
Oh, woe is me,
Who'll bite me first?

Will it be Tom
So cute and curly?
Or pretty Brad
Who looks so hurt?

These hunks from hell
Are all around me.
And how their fangs
Do make me squeak.

Sweet little Kirsten
Won't even pet me.
She just says Yuk,
Though she's very sweet.

Oh, thank you Larry.
Liz Smith, I love you,
And dearest Oprah
How good thou art.

I'm a lowly rat
In a vampire movie.
Your tender words
Do break my heart.

But don't you fret, folks
As you hear my story.
We want no tears
On your velvet and lace!

I'm a Hollywood rat
in a Hollywood movie!
What wouldn't you give
To take my place?

See also Animal Blood.

Ratcatcher   A derogatory term that Armand uses to goad a weak and broken Lestat, who is living on the blood of animals. It is derived from the term *harecatcher*, which referred to rural French aristocrats who had to hunt hares to keep from starving. *(VL 511)*

Raziel   The angel that pitied Adam and Eve when they were driven from Eden and gave Adam *The Book of the Angel Raziel*, which contained all knowledge of the universe. Before it was lost, according to lore, this book came into the hands of Enoch, Noah, and Solomon.

When Memnoch describes Heaven and the angels, Lestat mentions Raziel as one of the archangels. *(MD 206)*

See also Angel, Archangels.

Reading minds   An ability of the vampires, although it is limited in its scope. Generally, vampires can read each other's minds, the exceptions being the deliberate cloaking of one's thoughts, or the making of another vampire. In the latter instance, the minds of the two

involved in the process—the vampire and his victim—shut off from each other after the transformation. Lestat discovers this, to his chagrin, when he makes Gabrielle and Nicolas, and the loss of such an intimacy—which is achievable with other vampires—disturbs him.

Vampires can also read the thoughts of humans, and Armand utilizes this ability to make himself and Daniel wealthy. Through reading mortal thoughts, he locates lost treasures and stolen art. "If you can read the minds of men," Armand claims, "you can have anything that you want." (QD 98) Lestat reads human minds—or, rather, their dreams—to locate serial killers, his favorite type of victim. (BT 11)

Much to Louis's surprise, Armand claims in IV to be unable to read minds. Louis expects Armand to possess that kind of power, even though he himself has never experienced it. It may be that Armand merely did not wish to admit to it, knowing that Louis would be uncomfortable with possessing this information. (IV 257)

Armand is aware that there may be a greater single mind that transcends the vampires as individuals. This "mind" allows vampires to receive messages from one another and, to some extent, know each other's whereabouts. (QD 110)

When in danger, vampires like Gabrielle and Lestat take special pains to conceal their minds from the probing thoughts of pursuers. Akasha, however, always seems to know exactly where every vampire is, thus implying that she is the source of the mind that connects and transcends them all. (QD 250–252)

See also Cloaking, One Powerful Mind, Telepathic Powers, Vampire Powers.

Real estate   The vampires, particularly Armand, delight in buying real estate, and their subsequent transactions alert the Talamasca to their presence. For example, the Talamasca know Lestat bought Renaud's theater in Paris and started the Theater of the Vampires. Lestat's name is also associated with several properties in New Orleans, including a dozen mansions, thus giving Jesse the leads she needs to locate his town house. (VL 123, 508, QD 177, 179)

See Lestat's Houses, Materialism, Night Island, Pointe du Lac, St. Elizabeth's Orphanage, Town House.

Redemption   The act or instance of having sins forgiven and self-worth recovered, it is a central theme in both IV and BT. Louis and Lestat both search for redemption, but eventually Lestat realizes that it is just not available to vampires.

Actually, Louis just wants certainty and definition; he would be content with being damned so long as he knew *for sure* that this was the case. The situation, however, is quite different when it comes to Lestat, who had been in love with the notion of goodness even as a mortal. Thus, as a vampire, he has a difficult time accepting that he is trapped for eternity in a body that demands blood for survival. He fights against his vampire nature, at first trying to use his craving for blood to do some good; he attempts to kill only evildoers, but does not always accomplish this. Later he conceives of using his vampirism as a symbol of evil. As a rock star, he tries to get his mortal audience to eradicate all vampires, whom he views as creatures of evil, but this plan fails. And when Akasha offers Lestat a redemptive state of grace, which turns out to be a vast plan of destruction in order to achieve what she views as a greater good, he perceives in it no means of genuine redemption and so stands against her. Yet, as Akasha points out, he is still a killer. (QD 369, 371, 372, 392)

In BT, Lestat wrestles with the theme of redemption as well. When he begins to see that he is not really the vigilante he imagines himself to be, he decides to end his own existence by flying into the sun—an act that ends up making him into a more powerful vampire. When he reads *Faust*, he believes there is no such "happy ending" for him. He is Mephistopheles, and the Devil is not redeemed. But when he gains mortal form by switching bodies with Raglan James, he meets Gretchen, a nun, who believes there *is* a way: he can forget about recovering his vampire body and join her in the mission, saving lives. If he devotes his life to decreasing suffering, rather than causing it, he thus could wipe out his past transgressions. Gretchen believes Lestat came into mortal form for the same reason that Christ did: to achieve the redemption of his soul. Meeting her is his one hope. Nevertheless, Lestat cannot act on her suggestion, for he discovers he wants to be a vampire. As such, he turns his back on redemption and fully accepts the evil creature that he is. (BT 250, 424)

Only a year later, Lestat once again has reason to fear for his soul. He is being stalked, and he believes the Devil has come to take him to Hell. Indeed, the Devil has come, but with a different agenda. He calls himself Memnoch, and he wants Lestat's assistance. Claiming that he is not evil, nor interested in the things Lestat has done, he surprises Lestat by insisting that he is actually *against* evil. God is the source of evil, and if Lestat will help him, Memnoch thinks he may be able to turn the tide of evil before it destroys the world. This offers Lestat yet another chance for redemption. (MD 115–118, 129–137)

Lestat listens carefully to Memnoch's story, which includes a firm indictment against God for including death and suffering in His plan for humankind. Even God's plan to redeem human souls—done only at Memnoch's urging—involves blood, sacrifice, and violence, which, in God's name, i.e., the name of religion, continues throughout

history. Memnoch then shows Lestat what Hell is about—it is a place to educate souls in the art of forgiveness so they may enter Heaven. *(MD 302–318)*

Yet Hell is a place of such torment that Lestat cannot bring himself to be part of Memnoch's battle against God. He flees, uncertain whether anything Memnoch has shown him is true, and he never does resolve this issue. The state of his soul still rests in a void of uncertainty, particularly when his delivery of an icon infuses Christianity with new life. He does not know whether, with this act, he has served God or the Devil. *(MD 320–340, 350)*

See also Akasha, Christianity, Devil, Evil, Faust, Goodness, Gretchen, Hell, Lestat de Lioncourt, Louis de Pointe du Lac, Memnoch, Rock Star, Suffering.

Reeves   Jesse's family name. She is related to a South Carolina branch of the Great Family, and Miriam Reeves was her mother. It is not clear whether Jesse kept this name or took the name of her adopted parents. *(QD 146)*

See also Jesse.

Reeves, Miriam   Jesse's mother. She is one of a long line of women named Miriam in Maharet's Great Family, all of whom are descended from Maharet's daughter, Miriam. When pregnant with Jesse, she dies in a car accident. She thereafter appears to her daughter as a ghost that brings both comfort and warning. *(QD 145, 149)*

When Mael attempts to bite Jesse, Miriam appears and distracts him. She also beckons when Jesse is dying, trying to receive her spirit, but Maharet intervenes and makes Jesse a vampire. Miriam seems to be Jesse's guardian spirit, although she is impotent when it comes to truly protecting her. *(QD 239–240)*

See also Ghosts, Jesse.

Regina Maria   See Virgin Mary.

Reincarnation   The rebirth of a soul into a new body, after the old body has died.

Marius alludes to it when he discusses the existence of other immortals in the world. He mentions Ramses the Damned and others who do not act like vampires. Such immortals can walk in daylight and do not drink blood. Marius suggests that these creatures were once vampires who were burned to death by fire or sun and have returned in another form. He also shows belief in reincarnation by trusting the words of humans who claim to have once been vampires. Specifically,

the mortal Pandora tells Marius that she had been a vampire who had been burned when Akasha and Enkil were placed in the sun. Thus, she was able to seduce Marius into making her a vampire. *(VL 474–475)*

As part of her work for the Talamasca, Jesse goes to India to document cases of reincarnation—specifically, those reported by children. In four years of research, she documents over three hundred cases. *(QD 189)*

Memnoch tells Lestat that reincarnation is rare because souls soon figure out that going back into a body without taking with them the knowledge gleaned in their previous lives gains them little. The process may also necessitate the extinction of an infant soul, and only a small number of souls persistently reincarnate. *(MD 247, 251–252)*

See also Pandora, Soul, Stevenson (Dr. Ian).

Relationships The spiritual and mental bonding that occurs among vampires. The vampires are all connected through a common spirit and can read one another's thoughts, except for those of their own children. Their relationships are a mix of intimacy and loneliness, and are much like human relationships, except that any emotions involved are magnified. Vampires feel more deeply and are unconstrained by gender roles; male vampires fall in love with either males or females, and vice versa, adding to the erotic quality of their existence. Relationships between vampires of the same gender symbolize a locus for wholeness, for partners of the same sex can interchange roles rather than having to limit themselves to only one role. Through the subsequent balance and wholeness, they can access a fuller range of their inner powers.

"You're able to get to the deep, nongender things," says Rice, "like the unique nature of affection. Gender buries the issues, but nongendered relationships provide an opportunity for encounters to build hotly, for satisfaction to feed expectation, for patterns of sensuality to expand into realms where lovers fear to tread. The bisexual being is my ideal, because he or she cares about the one who is loved in an overwhelming way."

Vampires chose their companions because they have fallen in love and cannot bear to lose that mortal to death. Marius chooses Armand, Lestat chooses Louis, and Armand chooses Daniel for these very reasons. These relationships are subsequently strained by the increased intimacy and heightened sensitivity on both sides. Yet although there are separations and conflicts between the parties, the overriding emotional tone is one of great tolerance and affection, as well as physical appreciation and bonding. Emotional probing, physical caresses, and intense telepathy characterize the initial stages of such a relationship.

One of the most intense scenes of sensual union between males is that between Lestat and Armand when they meet at the Palais Royal in Paris. It is the first time Lestat has seen Armand clean and dressed in luxurious clothing. Armand stands against a wall, waiting, and Lestat claims that no one has ever been as alluring as the boy-demon Armand: "We were the sum of our desires . . . and it was time to be in each other's arms." *(VL 276)* They kiss and hold each other close, and Lestat tastes blood on Armand's lips. Then Armand drives his teeth into Lestat's neck. Lestat feels rapturous until it becomes clear that Armand is trying to suck Lestat's power out of him; the embrace ends in a battle for survival. *(VL 276)*

Armand and Marius also reveal sensual qualities when they re-unite after centuries apart. Marius walks into the Sonoma compound and feels the erotic sense of Armand's presence even before he sees him. They then embrace and touch one another, exploring as lovers. It is a highly charged moment. *(QD 273)*

As a mortal, Louis is enamored of Lestat, but he quickly grows tired of him when they are on an equal footing. *(IV 13–24)* He then falls in love with a mortal woman, Babette Freniere. She exhibits a strength of will that Louis lacks, but he realizes the tragedy of their relationship when she spurns him, goes mad from the contact she had with him, and dies at a young age. *(IV 66, 68, 131)*

His relationship with Babette foreshadows the nature and conse-quences of his relationship with Claudia, although when he tells the boy reporter about having had a former love, he is referring to some-one else entirely. *(IV 4)* In the first draft of IV, Louis ends his tale by saying that his greatest suffering as a vampire started with his falling in love with a mortal in New Orleans. And in the published version, he tells the boy reporter that he has only told his life story to one other; by this, he could mean Claudia, to whom he confessed his origins, or that mysterious person not yet revealed. This allusion is left a mystery; possibly Rice will clarify and develop it in a later novel.

Louis is entirely devoted to Claudia, although he wants her to remain a child. When she develops the mind of a woman, it disturbs him. However, he remains with her when she insists they go to Europe, and wants to continue being with her even when he knows that she hates him while Armand loves him. *(IV 264)* Armand is quite blunt about telling Louis that he wants him, loves him, and has been waiting for just such a vampire to cross his path. Louis comes to reciprocate these feelings, seeing in Armand an escape from his loneliness and the epitome of romantic love. "The wordless vision of our living together expanded and obliterated every other consideration in my mind," Louis claims. *(IV 284)* And just as can be typical of romantic love, Armand's need for Louis is so great that he manipulates circumstances to the point where he actually loses Louis. At the very moment when

Louis is preparing himself to let Claudia go, Armand's coven grabs her and kills her. The tragedy destroys the bond Louis had developed with Armand, and they drift apart. *(IV 284, 288, 306, 340)*

Louis then reunites with Lestat after Lestat publishes his autobiography. They reconnect in an erotic reunion and remain important to one another throughout the next two *Chronicles.* Louis, however, disappoints Lestat when he refuses to give him the Dark Gift after Lestat has become a mortal. It so sorely strains their relationship that Lestat contemplates destroying Louis in retaliation. Instead, he forgives Louis and invites him to live with him in their former abode—the New Orleans town house. *(VL 524, BT 264, 405–409)*

Lestat himself describes a number of significant relationships. He loves his mother, Gabrielle, and eventually makes her and his best mortal friend, Nicolas, into vampires. However, after their transformations, Gabrielle drifts away into nature and Nicolas goes mad. Lestat then meets a potential mentor in Marius, who tells him the story of the vampire origins and shows him Akasha. Yet Marius then turns Lestat away, so Lestat goes to New Orleans, which is where he makes and lives with Louis and Claudia for the next sixty-five years. *(VL 30, 158, 238, 363, 497–498)*

It is Akasha, however, who turns out to be the vampire with the most striking impact on Lestat. She rises and urges him to join her in creating a new world order. He participates briefly in the violence she demands of him because he loves her, but finally he rejects her ideas and stands against her. *(QD 249–263, 286–305, 353–377, 391–398)*

What Lestat really desires is a friendship with a *mortal* who knows what he is and accepts him anyway. David Talbot eventually develops unconditional love for Lestat, but Lestat still is not satisfied. He wants the two of them to be together as intensely as possible—and that can happen only if David becomes a vampire. David, however, resists, and Lestat has to face the possibility of losing him to age or accident. *(VL 337–338, BT 42–46)* Then, when Lestat temporarily becomes a mortal, he realizes there is an additional element to their relationship: David is also sexually attracted to him. Lestat wants to make love, to connect with David in a way he cannot achieve as a vampire, but David resists. He fears being overwhelmed by the immensity of Lestat's soul. Lestat eventually gets his vampire body back and forces David to join him as a vampire. This act threatens to end their friendship, but actually serves to strengthen it. *(BT 282, 314, 430–435)*

See also Community, Erotic, Estrangement, Fledglings, Intimacy, Love, Reunions, Sex.

Religion Religion, especially Catholicism, plays a strong part in the way the vampires think of themselves. Some are burdened by belief

structures in which they are deemed evil; others take on a new set of religious beliefs to give themselves purpose; still others view the freedom from their mortal beliefs as psychologically liberating.

Lestat and Louis were both raised as Catholics, but they differ in how this religious framework affects them. As a vampire, Louis does not want to give up his religion, although he recognizes how empty his beliefs and practices had been when he was a mortal, and he goes about seeking a means by which to be damned. *(IV 16)*

Lestat, on the other hand, dismisses his religious training as soon as he realizes that religious icons have no effect on him as a vampire. For example, he and Gabrielle take shelter in a church, beneath the altar, when Armand's coven pursues them. This upsets Gabrielle, who claims that the Blessed Sacrament is on the altar. Obviously, she is not as quick to shed her beliefs as Lestat, who insists this church is the safest place for them. *(VL 101, 189–193)*

Armand himself connects with the vampire establishment through religion. He becomes a zealous missionary for a satanic coven, believing that he should uphold and spread the rituals, although not personally believing in what they teach. He is like a priest who has no true faith but requires the structure of beliefs to function. When Lestat and Gabrielle shatter that structure, Armand is lost. Thus, he becomes vulnerable, two centuries later, to the power of Veronica's veil. *(VL 297–305, MD 334)*

The character of Marius observes that humanity is experiencing a loss of religion and suggests that this is a positive direction. The Christian religion replaced the gods of Rome, and now its own influence is diminishing. Marius believes that if no religious system replaces it in turn, then there may be something truly great on the horizon—even though it must mean that vampires become irrelevant. Other immortals agree with him, particularly Maharet, who believes that, throughout human history, religion has been responsible for war, persecution, enslavement, and other forms of brutality. She claims that the true enemy of the human species is any system of abstract belief (especially a belief in the supernatural) that has no compassion for life, or "the spiritual when it is divorced from the material." *(QD 448)*

Akasha, however, scoffs at Marius's belief that the world is moving away from religion. She claims that three fourths of the world is caught up with religious beliefs and it will always be so. She herself frames her plan for a new Eden in religious terms, and sees herself as a goddess coming to make the old myths of the Great Mother real. Her eventual death is symbolic of Marius's prediction that religious superstition, dominance, and cruelty must end so that moral progress can be made. *(VL 381–383, 465, QD 299, 365)*

Religion plays a strong role in MD. Roger grew up appreciating erotic mysticism and hoping one day to be a saint. He spent his life dealing drugs and killing for money in order to collect valuable religious artifacts, including the twelve books of the medieval mystic Wynken de Wilde. Wynken wrote about oneness with God through sexual union with women, and Roger wanted to found a cult on his ideas of love and sex. *(MD 66)* "Wynken was my saint," he says, "by virtue of his talent, and sexuality was my religion because it had been Wynken's and in every philosophical word he wrote he encoded a love of the flesh." *(MD 65)*

Roger's daughter, Dora, becomes a charismatic televangelist. He hopes she will appreciate Wynken's teachings, but she refuses them in lieu of more traditional religious writings. Because of Roger's lifestyle, Dora resists his attempts to give her some relic upon which to found her religious movement. She hopes instead for a miracle or a vision from the supernatural.

When Lestat kills Roger and Roger's ghost sends him to Dora, she views him as potential confirmation of her beliefs. He is given the opportunity to go with the Devil to Heaven and Hell, and Dora encourages him in this. In the process, he acquires a treasured icon, Veronica's veil, from the hands of Christ Himself. He realizes, nevertheless, that it proves nothing since what he had witnessed might have been a deception. Nevertheless, Dora grabs the veil and offers it to the church as evidence of God's existence. To Lestat's chagrin, she gets what she wanted. Lestat had never intended his actions to reinforce the destructive belief system based on Christ. When he later receives a note from the Devil thanking him for performing well, the implication is that strengthening Christianity in the apathetic twentieth century served the Devil. However, even that is uncertain. Yet the evidence is authentic enough for Armand, and he dies in the sun to affirm the miracle of the veil. *(MD 333–335, 350)*

See also Armand, Catholicism, Christ, Christianity, Devil, Eucharist, Flynn (Dora), God, Lestat de Lioncourt, Louis de Pointe du Lac, Marius, Memnoch, "Mystery Opposes Theology," Redemption, Religious Images, Religious Relics/Artifacts, Roger, Supernatural, Veronica's Veil, Wilde (Wynken de).

Religious images

Religious images Throughout the *Chronicles*, Rice uses themes, rituals, ideas, and doctrines from the Catholic religion in particular to enlarge and deepen the image of the vampire. Contrary to the tradition of the genre, which has vampires shunning churches, holy wafers, and crucifixes, Rice's novels have her vampires immersing themselves in religious traditions. Embued with a consciousness of their inherent spirituality (they have conquered death and gained powers of flight and

telepathy because a spirit has transformed the physical cells of their bodies), the vampires describe themselves as both angels and gods. Not only do they exhibit saintlike qualities—the ability to transcend time and gender, the striving for truth and intensity, and the gaining of immortality, in a sense—but some also act as priests, and all participate in a form of transubstantiation. Lestat and Magnus even offer up their bodies and their blood in a Christlike way. *(VL 89–90, QD 230)*

Conversely, Rice also employs darker religious images, especially that of the Devil. The Roman coven patterns itself inversely on the Roman Catholic Church, worshiping Satan as Christians worship God, and although the vampires more often refer to themselves as angels, they sometimes call themselves the Devil as well: "Am I not the devil in you all!" shouts Lestat to his mortal audience. *(QD 230)*

Rice was raised Catholic and, although she later left the church, she understood the literary value of its images. "I retain an appreciation for the power of the Catholic Church. Those images [the saints, the Eucharist, the death and resurrection of Christ] run all through literature."

See also Angel, Bible, Christ, Devil, Eucharist, God, Inversion, Memnoch, Religion, Saints, Transubstantiation.

Religious relics/artifacts

Statues and paintings—the material evidence of beliefs or religious practices—"are expressions of the human quest for truth." *(MD 90)* "Relic" often refers to part of the body of a saint or martyr, preserved after death for veneration. Some of the relics revered during the Middle Ages included a feather from Gabriel's wing, pieces of the true cross, a vial containing the last breath of St. Joseph, several heads of John the Baptist, and thorns from Christ's mock crown. There are two reports of a cloth with an imprint of Christ's face—Veronica's veil and the Holy Face of Edessa—and one of the burial wrapping of Christ, known as the Shroud of Turin.

Roger believes that an important relic like the Shroud of Turin should be at the heart of the religion that his daughter, Dora, preaches. Such an object would help her raise money, as it did in medieval times. He uses his wealth to collect such relics for her, but because his money was gained from criminal activity, Dora shuns his gifts. When Lestat decides to kill Roger, he sees an enormous number of relics in Roger's house. Among the artifacts are a thirteenth-century reproduction of Veronica's veil, pieces of wood said to be from the cross, and a lost *Book of the Hours. (MD 30–32)*

After his death, Roger returns as a ghost and implores Lestat to protect the relics for Dora. Lestat stores them in Manhattan's Olympic Tower, then brings Dora there to see them. Dora thinks she needs no such material proof to inspire a spiritual movement, but when Lestat

Rembrandt, Members of the Drapers' Guild

delivers Veronica's veil to her straight from the hands of Christ, she takes it and makes it the foundation of a new surge in her religious faith. She thanks her dead father for getting it for her. *(MD 88, 333)*

See also *Book of the Hours,* Flynn (Dora), Icon, Lestat de Lioncourt, Mandylion, Religion, Roger, Shroud of Turin, Veronica's Veil.

Rembrandt van Rijn   A seventeenth-century Dutch artist whose work was the pinnacle of the Baroque period. His abiding principle was to make his art true to nature and reality, and as his life changed from great wealth and happiness to tragedy and loss, his perspective became one of greater spiritual profundity. He considered the body to be an envelope for the spirit, which was touched by shadow. His work developed a quality of otherworldliness, revealing the inherent indestructibility of the human spirit.

In BT, David Talbot and Lestat share a deep affinity for Rembrandt's paintings. In fact, when Lestat first tracks David to Amsterdam, he discovers that David is there to locate a painting by Rembrandt stored in the Motherhouse. The painting is of the Mayfair

377

witch, Deborah, whose progeny cavorted with the spirit Lasher, the result of which is detailed in WH. The portrait reveals a fragile light in the midst of darkness, as if Rembrandt had foreseen for Deborah the possibility of salvation. David sends a photograph of the painting to Aaron Lightner in New Orleans. (BT 30, WH 286)

Shortly after both David and Lestat have purchased and read a copy of Goethe's *Faust*, they meet in the Rijksmuseum in Amsterdam in front of Rembrandt's *Members of the Drapers' Guild (The Syndics)*. The faces of the men it portrays are full of wisdom, gentleness, and patience, as if they possess the secret of great compassion and love. Lestat thinks they look like angels, and David inquires of him if any vampires have such faces that also reveal a knowledge of the true spiritual meaning of immortality. Lestat protests that this quality is only a projection from Rembrandt—for Rembrandt himself is immortal. Yet David's words still have a depressing effect on him: Lestat, along with all other vampires, is evil and, as such, cannot have the spiritual knowledge available to those mortals who truly strive for goodness. Although Lestat wants to believe that goodness and redemption are available to him, a darker side of him knows this is not an option. Upset and saddened, Lestat leaves, then writes a letter to David explaining his own theory about Rembrandt's art. (BT 35–38)

According to Lestat, Rembrandt sold his soul to the Devil in exchange for becoming a great painter. Since Rembrandt had seen the proof of evil, he became obsessed with the nature of goodness. He thus searched the faces of his subjects for the spark of inner divinity and used it to enhance his paintings, portraying spiritual "visions of what that person was at his or her finest hour." (BT 36) His own self-portraits, which reveal a man of progressive wisdom, were actually pleas to God to take note of his transformation. The Devil did not like the type of work Rembrandt was doing, so he brought disaster and tragedy into Rembrandt's life. Yet this only deepened Rembrandt's vision of love. On his deathbed, as the Devil was waiting for his soul, Rembrandt, like Faust, was redeemed by God.

It breaks Lestat's heart to look at Rembrandt's art and know that he, as evil incarnate, cannot be redeemed. This being the case, no vampires could ever have such faces. Although they are likened to saints and angels for other qualities they possess, they are killers and thus cannot know the purity of mortal love and compassion that God inspires in mankind. Lestat resolves at this point to stop tempting David with the vampire's version of immortality, for as a mortal with a soul attuned to the spiritual, David could achieve something greater, just as Rembrandt did. (BT 38)

Lestat's theory about Rembrandt is actually Rice's own theory. She had hoped to write a novel about it but instead gave the story to

Lestat, who claims that if he were mortal, he would write a novel about Rembrandt.

See also Angel, Faust, Mephistopheles, Religion, Saint.

Remiel According to the *Book of Enoch*, one of the seven archangels allowed to stand close to God's throne. Ironically, he is also possibly a Fallen Angel.

When Memnoch shows Lestat the angelic order, Lestat mentions Remiel. *(MD 206)*

See also Angel, Archangels, *Book of Enoch*, Fallen Angel.

Renaud The manager of the theater where Lestat and Nicolas first find work when they arrive in Paris. Lestat buys the theater from Renaud after he becomes a vampire, then sends him and his troupe to London to protect them when Nicolas becomes a vampire and threatens to turn all of Renaud's actors into vampires. *(VL 67)*

See also Renaud's House of Thesbians.

Renaud's House of Thesbians When Lestat and Nicolas run away to Paris, they find work in Renaud's, a small, run-down theater on the boulevard du Temple that seats three hundred. Lestat does odd jobs, waiting for his chance to get on stage, while Nicki plays the violin in its orchestra. When Lestat's opportunity to act arrives, he carries it off with great success and is signed on to play the part of Lelio, the aristocratic lover. *(VL 60, 67)*

As Lestat's fame spreads, however, Magnus abducts him and makes him a vampire. Lestat then uses Magnus's fortune to pay off the theater's debts and to send gifts to all its actors. Later he buys the theater outright, and gifts Renaud with ten thousand crowns so that he can stage larger productions. *(VL 121, 123)*

One day he decides to visit the actors. Everyone is glad to see him, until he goes out on stage and begins to perform acrobatics that defy human limitations and disturb the audience. When he sings so loud that he hurts people's ears, the audience starts to flee. A defiant old man shoots Lestat with a pistol, and it astonishes everyone when Lestat does not seem to feel it. Lestat explains it away as a stage illusion, but after his experience, never returns again to see the theater troupe. *(VL 132–141)*

Lestat eventually closes the theater and moves the actors to London. When Armand's disintegrating coven asks Lestat to assist them, he gives them the empty building and tells them to use their imagination. Renaud's then becomes the Theater of the Vampires. *(VL 143, 244–246)*

See also Lelio, Lestat de Lioncourt, Theater of the Vampires.

Renfield   A fifty-nine-year-old lunatic in Bram Stoker's *Dracula* who consumes flies, spiders, and birds. He is Dr. Seward's patient and one of Dracula's victims. Dracula uses him to get access to Mina, but when Renfield resists his authority one night, Dracula fatally injures him.

Lestat thinks that David Talbot ought to use this alias to book rooms in the Olympic Tower. *(MD 27)*

See also *Dracula*, Olympic Tower.

Reproduction   See Making a Vampire, Procreation.

Requiem for the Marquise   A melancholic music video that Lestat records about making Gabrielle a vampire. With its dark undertone of drums and cymbals, it is Khayman's favorite. *(QD 120)*

See also Music Videos, Rock Music, Rock Star.

Residual soul   See Soul.

Reunions   Because of the way vampires seek both isolation and community, they frequently separate and then come back together. Those bonded by love may also separate due to conflicts and misunderstandings. If they do come together after decades of separation, their reunion is often highly charged, and full of erotic overtones.

Louis and Lestat have been alienated from one another for over a century when Louis finally approaches Lestat's secret hideaway in Carmel Valley. Lestat senses Louis's presence in the dark; he can feel the beat of Louis's heart. He trembles with emotion as he reaches out and touches Louis. The moment is magnetic as they mentally probe one another. They both forget past injustices as they exuberantly embrace, for the immediacy of the moment is all that counts. Both are brimming with feverish satisfaction and delight, and the desire to try their relationship again is exciting but also somewhat excruciating because of its intensity. *(VL 524–525)*

Lestat's reunion with Gabrielle is just as stimulating, although it takes place in the midst of the chaos of Lestat's rock concert. Lestat has not seen Gabrielle for nearly two centuries, nor heard of anyone who knows of her. He believes she is lost to him forever. As he makes his way to his Porsche, Gabrielle pulls him into the car and they speed off together. He barely has a chance to react to her presence, for their reunion is short-lived: as Gabrielle goes off to make her bed in the hills that night, Akasha abducts Lestat. *(VL 543)*

During the gathering of the vampires in QD, many couples see one another again, including Mael and Marius, Marius and Pandora, and Louis and Armand. The most highly charged of these meetings is the one between Marius and Armand. Marius has dreamed of this reunion over the years. Armand comes up quietly behind him, and Marius feels the ache of his love. They touch, kiss, and hold one another. Armand yields easily to him. The presence of others waiting for them, and aware of them, adds to their erotic tension. They experience a moment of silent understanding and a complete awareness of each other and of what could have been, had they only remained together. (QD 265–274)

The most significant reunion at this gathering, however, is that between Mekare and Maharet. The twins had been separated six thousand years earlier after they had become vampires. Maharet's only physical clue since this time to Mekare's existence is the set of cave drawings in Peru. At the moment when Akasha decides to destroy Maharet and the remaining vampires, the twins are reunited. Mekare enters the room and kills Akasha. She then eats Akasha's brain and heart, thus taking into herself the vampire spirit. Although she cannot talk and seems to be more or less mindless, the twins are rejoined as two parts of a single soul. Maharet says that Mekare is her own self, and that when they come together, she experiences a great psychological and physical resolution. She then takes Mekare to a secret place so that they will never again be lost to each other. (QD 453–457, 464–465)

Across the span of a decade, Daniel has an on-again, off-again relationship with Armand. They are lovers, exchanging blood and developing deep intimacy. When Daniel's frustrated desire for immortality overwhelms him, he leaves Armand, only to find himself alone and dying from alcoholism. He needs Armand desperately but is unsure as to whether Armand can or wants to find him. When Armand does appear, they act as lost lovers, and Armand finally makes Daniel a vampire. (QD 104)

A more unusual kind of reunion is the one Lestat experiences with himself. After he switches bodies with the human Raglan James, he decides he does not like being mortal. He tracks James down and steals back his former body. When Lestat reclaims his physical body, he finally feels like himself again. The fact that he has chosen to experience this reunion forces him to realize that he desires to be a vampire. No longer can he comfort himself with the illusion that he was forced into this mode of existence. (BT 340)

See also Alienation, Erotic, Intimacy, Relationships.

Revenant   The name often used for vampires and other forms of the living dead, it means "one who returns." According to legend, some diabolical force is at work to animate these bodies. Revenants embody both the fear of death and the belief in reincarnation.

Armand uses this name in IV to refer to the mindless vampires of Eastern Europe who seem nothing more than animated corpses. When he uses the term to insult vampires in his coven, he gives the impression that there is a hierarchy in the vampire world, and the revenant is its lowest intellectual form. Revenant vampires are so low that they attack other vampires without provocation. (IV 247)

See also Making a Vampire, Old World Vampires, Reincarnation.

Rice, Anne   The author of *The Vampire Chronicles* who uses her own name as a pseudonym for Daniel, the boy reporter, when he publishes IV. Although Lestat makes no specific reference to Rice's name, he follows suit by adopting it as a pen name for the four *Chronicles* that he writes—VL, BT, QD, and MD. (QD 87, 173)

See also *Interview with the Vampire*, Lestat de Lioncourt, Molloy (Daniel), *The Vampire Chronicles*.

Rice, Stan   Anne Rice's husband and a poet whose work she uses to introduce different sections of QD; his poems emphasize the themes that run throughout QD.

"The thing that constantly interested me," Stan Rice says about his work, "is the difference between substance—stuff, material—and the brain that perceives it. There has to be a reciprocal relationship, but there's always this tug of war between what's there and what you personally *think* is there."

See also "Cannibal," "Duet on Iberville Street," "Elegy," "Four Days in Another City," "Greek Fragments," "Of Heaven," "The Offering," "Poem on Crawling into Bed: Bitterness," "Texas Sweet," "Their Share," "Tragic Rabbit," "Untitled" Poem, "What God Did Not Plan On," "The Words Once."

Rijksmuseum   The Rembrandt museum in Amsterdam where Lestat encounters David seated in front of Rembrandt's *Members of the Drapers' Guild*. They have a minor confrontation there about the true nature of spirituality, which inspires Lestat to impart to David his personal theory about Rembrandt's genius. (BT 34)

See also Amsterdam, *Members of the Drapers' Guild*, Rembrandt van Rijn.

"Rime of the Ancient Mariner, The"   A poem by Samuel Taylor Coleridge, quoted in IV and mentioned in QD.

See Coleridge (Samuel Taylor), Poetry.

Rio de Janeiro   A city in Brazil that is famous for its annual carnival.

As a young man, David Talbot had gone to Rio prior to a hunting expedition. There he had fallen in love with a young man and had become targeted by the spirits of a Candomble priestess. As a result, David became intrigued with her religion and returned to Rio to apprentice himself to that priestess. This introduction to the occult eventually had led to his tenure with the Talamasca and his life as a scholar. When as an old man he talks with Lestat, he expresses a longing to return to Rio. Lestat would make such a trip possible but is fearful of David's frailty. Once Lestat makes David into a vampire, however, they plan a trip together to Rio, where they will attend the carnival. *(BT 63, 430–435)*

It is in Rio that Lestat first notices he is being stalked. He thinks his stalker is the Devil, coming to claim his soul. *(MD 13)*

Rio de Janeiro is also the home of the archaeologist who discovers the cave drawings of the twins in Peru. *(QD 36)* (See Vampire Atlas)

See also Archaeologist, Candomble, Carlos, Memnoch.

Rio de Janeiro, Brazil

The Ritz

Ritz   A luxury hotel located in Paris, it was built in 1898 and over-looks the Place Vendôme in the heart of the city.

Lestat stays here, which reminds him of Versailles, while he waits to see if Raglan James can track him down. He does not have to wait long before he knows that James is there in Paris, attempting to contact him. *(BT 85)* (See Vampire Atlas)

See also Paris.

Rock concert   Lestat and his rock band have their live debut in San Francisco's Cow Palace on Halloween night. This concert draws the attention of mortals and vampires alike, and about thirty vampires attend with the intent to destroy Lestat.

During the concert, Lestat sings about the vampire history and origins, and experiences the concert as a Dionysian orgy. Although he

wants to confront the vampires who threaten to kill him, Akasha destroys them first and abducts Lestat. The mortal press downplays the events at the concert and soon the rock band is forgotten. *(VL 533–542, QD 197–231, 468)*

See also Cow Palace, Declaration, Dionysus, Halloween, Rock Music, Rock Star.

Rock music   When Lestat gets on stage, he finds that making rock music for a crowd is different from cutting records in a studio. Performing live is similar to the raw power of a Dionysian ceremony or a vampire Sabbat. Lestat feels the sound traveling through his body in an erotic "marriage of the primitive and scientific" *(VL 539)*, and he decides that rock music possesses a passion that can entwine the images of evil and death without embracing the reality of either. The music is barbaric and cerebral, shocking and inventive, brutal and defiant. There is something vampiric about it—something supernatural and "eloquent of dread." *(VL 6)* As an art form it dispenses with illusion, and as such exhibits an innocence akin to the work of saints. *(VL 535–536)*

See also Art, Dionysus, Music, Music Videos, Rock Star, Sabbat.

Rock star   The type of performer that Rice felt typified Lestat's attitudes. She felt that rock stars enthusiastically performed in a way that shocked and surprised audiences. Similar to the way she viewed vampires, Rice saw rock stars as symbolic outsiders and as possessing qualities akin to those of saints—most notably in their refusal to accept lies and their desire for experiential intensity.

When Lestat awakens in 1984, he hears the music of Satan's Night Out, a rock group that practices down the street from his house. He is enchanted by the way these singers scream in their art about good and evil. "Sometimes," he says, "they seemed the pure embodiment of madness." *(VL 5)* Lestat wants to join with this particular band and lead them to fame, for after reading IV, he is determined to use rock music to show the evil of the vampire. He then writes an autobiography in response to Louis's, and coordinates its publication with the release of his rock videos and albums. Satan's Night Out changes their name to The Vampire Lestat, and their first album sells four million copies. MTV shows their videos, and a tour, opening in San Francisco, is planned. As Lestat expects, his status as a rock star makes him conspicuous and draws the wrath of vampires worldwide, who flock to San Francisco in anticipation of annihilating him at his performance. *(VL 3–18, 519–542, QD 11–14)*

Rice looked to contemporary rock stars when she envisioned Lestat's music. "I based the voice on Jim Morrison," she says, "and the

music on 'L.A. Woman'—that one song. I wanted that engine-heating-up sound. That's what Lestat would have had. And I based the concert on general concerts I had seen." (Baby Jenks, however, thinks he sounds like Bruce Springsteen.)

See also Declaration, Music Videos, Rock Concert, Rock Music, Satan's Night Out, The Vampire Lestat.

Roger

A forty-seven-year-old international drug dealer, assassin, and art collector who becomes one of Lestat's victims. Lestat first spots him in New Orleans, then follows him to Manhattan. *(MD 13)* Intrigued with Roger's sophisticated criminal mind, Lestat stalks him for six months. "He's so intricately evil," Lestat insists. *(MD 14)* He sees Roger with his beautiful daughter, Dora, and decides to kill Roger in a way that will do Dora the least harm. *(MD 41)* Lestat's stalking and killing of this man reveals how his blood thirst has evolved. He reaches now for power and glory: he wants a malefactor who is supremely good at what he does. *(MD 212)*

On entering Roger's Upper East Side house, Lestat discovers a valuable collection of religious relics and artifacts. When Roger comes in, Lestat kills him, then cuts up his body, disposing of the parts all over the city. (This parallels Roger's vision of what had happened with his religious hero, Wynken de Wilde, whose female worshipers may have divided his body parts among them.) *(MD 86)* Lestat wanders as far as Lower Manhattan and goes into a Greenwich Village bar, where Roger appears to him as a ghost. Roger knows that Lestat is some kind of supernatural creature, and he wants to tell him his story.

Eccentric, brilliant, and clever, Roger bears a great love for beautiful and ancient objects. "I'm fervent and extremist and gothic and mad," he insists. *(MD 88)* He is an expert on medieval codex. With black hair and dark skin, Roger has an Asian face. The child of an alcoholic mother, he was raised in New Orleans, where he made the acquaintance of an antiques dealer named Old Captain. Through this man, Roger discovered some illuminated manuscripts of the medieval mystic Wynken de Wilde. He then set out to collect them all.

At age seventeen, Roger wanted to be a secular saint, to found a religious cult on the principles of "free love, give to the poor, raise one's hand against no one." *(MD 57)* Short of that goal, he wanted to commit a major crime. Wynken became his saint and sexuality his religion. He went to San Francisco to start his cult and ended up managing a rock group that planned, but failed, to put Wynken's ideas to music. To protect one of his group during a drug deal gone bad, Roger killed two men. Then he got into dealing drugs and killing for money. He became a killer spontaneously, in circumstances that demanded it, which is what made him so interesting to Lestat. *(MD 69)*

Along the way, Roger became attracted to the young nurse Terry,

who was caring for his dying mother. Roger got sexually involved with her and she became pregnant. Although he grew to despise her, he doted on his daughter, Dora. When Terry tried to take Dora away, Roger killed Terry and raised Dora himself.

Having learned to steal when he was young, Roger made a career of ransoming religious art, then got heavily involved in the international drug trade. He wanted to use the money to help Dora with her career as an evangelist, but she would not accept his "unclean" resources. Now Roger wants Lestat to convince Dora that his death cleansed his religious artifacts. "I ransomed it all with my blood." *(MD 91)* Roger asks Lestat to watch over Dora and keep the artifacts and Wynken's books safe for her. Then he fades out. *(MD 91)*

Lestat takes all of Roger's treasures, including the rugs that are stained with Roger's blood, to a safer place. Lestat calls these rugs his own relics. Then he goes to tell Dora that her father is dead. *(MD 103, 119–120)*

When Lestat accompanies Memnoch to Hell, he sees Roger there with Terry, along with Roger's other victims. Lestat wants to tell Roger about Veronica's veil, but Memnoch hinders him. *(MD 313–314)*

Lestat flees Hell and arrives in Manhattan to learn that Roger's death has been discovered: some dogs had dragged his head out from a heap of garbage. Lestat believes that Roger wanted it found and that Roger himself has gained entrance to Heaven. *(MD 330)*

After Lestat gives Dora Veronica's veil, she gives all of Roger's artifacts and books to Lestat, who stores them in St. Elizabeth's, although Louis takes Wynken's books back to the town house to read. *(MD 340–353)*

See also Flynn (Dora), Flynn (Terry), Ghost, Hell, Iago, Manhattan, New Orleans, Old Captain, Religious Relics/Artifacts, Roger's Mother, Upper East Side, Victims, Wilde (Wynken de).

Roger's mother   An alcoholic who ran a boardinghouse on St. Charles Avenue in New Orleans. Somewhat based on Rice's mother, she had a brother, Mickey, and a sister, Alice, and her own mother had been an Irish maid for wealthy families. She had also had a younger brother, Little Richard, who had died from lockjaw at the age of four. Unlike Rice's mother, however, Roger's mother dies of cancer. *(MD 59)*

The boardinghouse that she runs has special significance for Rice: "Roger's boardinghouse is based on a very specific house which lies directly across from 2301 St. Charles, where I grew up. The house is a Victorian built in the 1880s. I was in it several times as a child, but my principal love of it came from looking at it from across the street. In my childhood, it was an elegant boardinghouse for well-heeled elderly people. It was most beautiful and did not contain the dressing table in the front hall or an alcoholic owner. I remember it quite as described . . . dark red carpet, linen-draped tables in a large dining room, old gentlemen in seersucker suits and straw hats, ladies in flowered dresses and straw hats often sitting on high-backed wooden rocking chairs. One of these ladies was known to us as 'Blind Miss Stanton.' I recall a dress, a bit of flowered fabric, a bent back, a hat. She owned the black limousine that was garaged in our garage. Her driver, an elegant, lean, black man, sat on a stool at the entrance, whittling. We used to talk to him.

Roger's mother's boarding house in New Orleans

"A brilliant woman named Virginia Fortier lived there in my time. She worked tirelessly. She let me go with her one day through the house. . . . [This] gave me a sense of the carpets, the finery, and the many different boarders who lived there.

"The night before my mother's death, there was a fire at the Fortier house in the servants' quarters. My sister Tamara was in the hospital, and we were coming back to check on my mother, and we saw fire engines around the house. I saw them carrying out a man on a stretcher; his face was horribly twisted with pain. He had set the fire with a cigarette in the back bedroom. As it turned out, only his hands were burned. But the sight of him sent me into a panic. That the fire had happened in the Fortier house, that they were our friends, that Tamara was sick, that I had not slept in hours—all of this came together in that moment on the porch of the Fortier house as I ran into my father's arms. When we went home after the fire, I knew something had to happen because I couldn't take any more mentally. It was the strangest feeling. As the panic lifted, I remember feeling this near religious elation. Things were going to be all right; one could know happiness. I knew it at that moment. I knew a pinnacle of happiness.

"I actually saw the dressing table and the old woman in the hallway of another uptown St. Charles Avenue boardinghouse. That house was also filled with elegant people. There was, in its front hall, a beautiful dressing table, and the elegant old lady—the owner of the house—did sit there brushing her hair. The image startled me because she and the dressing table did not belong in the front hall near the stairs. I took that image and put it in Roger's house.

"Other elements of Roger's story stem from things I knew and saw in those days in both of those boardinghouses, but ultimately my work is fiction. Roger is a complete fiction; his mother is a complete fiction. Yet everything I write has tiny bits and pieces of reality to it."

See also Roger, Uncle Mickey.

Roget, Pierre   Lestat's first attorney, who is located in Paris. Roget is ambitious, clever, and willing to work at nighttime because of the vast sums of money that Lestat pays him. To disguise his vampirism, Lestat presents himself to Roget as the husband of an heiress from Saint-Domingue; as he "suffers from tropical fever," the lighting must always be dim when they meet. Through Roget, Lestat sends money to his family and friends and pays off Renaud's debts. When Lestat worries that he might himself make Nicolas one of his victims, he requests that Roget get Nicolas out of the city, but before Roget can take action, Gabrielle arrives. Roget makes her comfortable and urges Lestat to see her. Lestat makes her a vampire and, despite her mysterious disappearance, Roget never questions him and continues to serve his needs. (VL 118)

See also Agents.

Rogue vampires   On their journey on the Devil's Road, Lestat and Gabrielle see secretive, loner vampires who pretend to be human

and who live among mortals. They run from Lestat and Gabrielle as if they expect to be punished. *(VL 324)*

The Fang Gang also refers to themselves as rogues, to contrast themselves with those vampires who live in the coven houses. As rogues, they align themselves with Lestat. *(QD 46)*

See also Outcasts, Outsiders.

Roman coven   Led by Santino, the Roman coven calls its members the Children of Darkness. Rules of conduct, which are based on religious ideas and prohibitions, define it, and any vampire who does not abide by the rules is outcast and must be burned by fire. This coven invades Marius's studio in Venice, burns Marius, and abducts Armand, whom they introduce to their rituals.

Armand learns what he needs to do to survive: he becomes a zealous missionary of the Dark Ways that the coven practices. He then leaves Italy and takes over the coven that exists in Paris. There he hears that Santino has abandoned the Roman coven, leaving it in chaos. By the year 1700, there is no more word from that coven, although in the 1700s Lestat and Gabrielle encounter it (or another one) in Rome. But these vampires have changed with the times, and their Sabbat ceremonies are very elaborate. While they now mingle among mortals, they still exhibit superstitions about God by sleeping in graveyards and fleeing from any sign or symbol of the power of God. *(VL 296–303, 325–326)*

See also Covens, Dark Ways, Rules, Sabbat, Santino.

Roman Empire   The spread of Roman civilization across Europe, it stretched as far as Britain, the Middle East, Asia Minor, northern Africa, and Egypt. It lasted from 31 B.C., with the reign of Augustus Caesar, until A.D. 476.

Marius was made a vampire during the time of the Roman Empire, and just as Rome had taken over Egypt, Marius, a Roman, takes over from an Egyptian vampire the guardianship of Those Who Must Be Kept. When the Roman Empire falls, the Catholic Church increases its power and decrees that the pagan gods, including the gods who had fed on blood in Egypt (vampires), are actually demons. *(VL 382)*

See also Marius.

Rome   See Roman Coven, Roman Empire.

Royal Street   The location of the New Orleans town house in which Louis, Lestat, and Claudia lived as a vampire family. Rice modeled the town house on the Gallier House at 1132 Royal Street. *(IV 99)* (See Vampire Atlas)

See also New Orleans, Town House.

Rules The manifestation of the attempt by some to control others, by telling them what is and what is not permissible, as well as that which is punishable.

Santino's Roman coven devises a list of rules, which they call the Great Laws, to govern vampire behavior:

1. Each coven must have a leader to work the Dark Trick.

2. Mortals who are granted the Dark Gift must be beautiful, in order to insult God.

3. No old vampires should work the Dark Trick, for otherwise the powerful blood would make the young vampire too strong.

4. No vampire is allowed to destroy any of its own kind, except for the coven leader, who has obligations to destroy certain types of inappropriate and outlaw vampires.

5. No vampire should reveal to mortals his nature, name, coven locale, or history, and allow them to live. *(VL 301–302)*

Armand teaches these rules to covens around Europe and adds a few, called Rules of Darkness, for his own coven in Paris. They are to live among the dead in cemeteries, return to their own graves, shun places of light, honor the power of God, and never enter a church. *(VL 225)*

When Lestat and Gabrielle break these laws without suffering any consequences, it throws Armand's coven into confusion. Armand realizes that his framework is no longer effective, so he destroys as much of his coven as he can. Those who survive his destruction form a new coven based on a different set of rules, which are related to their new occupation as actors in the Theater of the Vampires. However, the rule concerning the prohibition of killing another vampire survives into the nineteenth century, and is used by the Parisian coven to judge, condemn, and destroy Claudia for her attack on Lestat. *(IV 249, 306)*

Marius, too, has some rules that he requires Lestat to follow. After Marius tells Lestat about Those Who Must Be Kept, he makes Lestat promise never to tell the story or to give away Marius's whereabouts. *(VL 477)* Lestat disregards these prohibitions in his autobiography, giving it all away. He also ignores other warnings and makes a child vampire just to see what would happen. "I want to affect things," he says, "to make something happen!" *(VL 522)*

Breaking the rules involves risk but it may also bring about a change in the vampire status, by creating a new meaning and rescuing vampires from irrelevance. Lestat wants to shake up old values and traditions, and pave the way for new possibilities. As Marius realizes, Lestat really betrayed no one in breaking the vampire rules, because no mortal believed him. Lestat had understood the faithlessness of the times perfectly, exhibiting truths in the guise of a rock star and publishing his autobiography as a novel—a work of fiction. *(QD 4–6)*

Yet the vampires who gather to attack Lestat and his sympathizers fail to understand this, and mount their attack *because* they are clinging to the old rules. They believe Lestat should not be disclosing the names and history of vampires to mortals, nor exposing himself as a vampire to mortal eyes. They demand that there be no exposure to cameras and no risk that could result in the capture or incineration of any vampire. Since Lestat ignored these strictures, he must be annihilated. *(VL 530, QD 11–14)* In addition to the rules stated above, these vampires also insist that there be no killing of mortals in a vampire bar. *(VL 529)*

Even the loose collection of vampires who survive Akasha's onslaught believe a few rules should still govern their actions. They are to make no more vampires, intervene no more in the mortal world, disguise the kill, write no more books, never wander off without leaving a trace, and leave the Talamasca alone. Lestat breaks these rules with glee: "I love to break the rules the way mortals like to smash their crystal glasses after a toast." *(BT 5)* Marius wonders if Lestat even could be happy without rules to break. *(QD 468)*

In MD, Lestat continues to ignore the "rules" when he freely tells Dora Flynn his name and what he is, with no intention of harming or killing her. In fact, she uses his appearance to her as confirmation of her religion, calling him an Angel of the Night. *(MD 127, 346, 348)*

See also Conformity, Covens, Forbidden Acts, Great Laws, Lestat de Lioncourt, Outcasts, Theater of the Vampires.

Rules of Darkness   See Rules.

Rummel, Isaac   One of Lestat's aliases, which he uses to book a room in the Manhattan hotel where he and David meet to discuss the Devil. He gives David his key to this room so that when David has rented rooms in the Olympic Tower, he can move Lestat's clothes there. *(MD 27)*

Rumpelstiltskin   A fairy-tale dwarf who could spin gold from straw and who used his power to help a princess. Dwarfs are symbols of ambiguous meaning. In their childish mischief, they personify primitive forces, but they also serve as protectors. Rumpelstiltskin appears to be evil because he demands that the princess give to him her firstborn child as his payment, yet he also offers her a treasure: gold.

In IV, Lestat is compared to Rumpelstiltskin when he stomps around, frustrated over Louis's reluctance to kill his (Lestat's) mortal father. However, in VL the image is used more positively, indicating that Lestat may be a Rumpelstiltskin in more ways than one, when he transforms Louis's drab, grief-stricken life into a sensory-enriched form of existence. *(IV 56, VL 182)*

See also Lestat de Lioncourt.

Rumpelstiltskin

Russell, Jeffrey Burton A history professor and a leading contemporary scholar on the Devil. His books include *Mephistopheles: The Devil in the Modern World*, *Satan: The Early Christian Tradition*, *Lucifer: The Devil in the Middle Ages*, and *The Prince of Darkness: Radical Evil and the Power of Good in History*.

Lestat mentions Russell as an author he reads. *(BT 101)* Russell is actually one of Rice's favorite authors and she looks to him as an authority on figures of evil.

See also Devil.

Russ In QD, one of the five members of the Fang Gang who ride motorcycles and dance in graveyards. *(QD 43)*

See also Fang Gang.

Russia The country where Armand was born. When Armand was a youth, Tartars abducted him from Russia, then sold him to a Venetian brothel, from which Marius rescued him. *(VL 290)*

See also Armand.

393

Sabbat A midnight assemblage of diabolists who hold licentious rites to renew their acquaintance with the Devil; it is what the vampires in Rome call their religious ceremonies.

Gabrielle and Lestat participate in a Sabbat as they pass through Rome on the Devil's Road. This Sabbat is a perversion of the Catholic Church's religious ceremony, which celebrates God's creation of the world, and the Jewish sabbath, a day of rest and religious observance. Lestat records his impression of the Sabbat in a music video when he becomes a rock star. *(VL 303, 326)*

See also Music Videos, Roman Coven.

"Sailing to Byzantium" A poem by William Butler Yeats that introduces BT, it is about the conflict of time and eternity.

In the poem, Yeats reflects on how art might be able to defeat time. Rice felt this poem was an appropriate backdrop for the unnatural form of a vampire, as it also is freed from biological mortality. However, for both vampires and art, timelessness may be gained only at the expense of vitality.

Initially, Rice had wanted to title BT *Once Out of Nature*, a phrase from this poem, for Lestat realizes that once he is out of nature and existing as a vampire, he really does not want to go back. "In the end," says Rice, "he's really in that mood: 'Once out of nature, I would not take my shape from any natural thing.' He's saying, I am a vampire and this is my nature."

See also Art, Poetry, Vampire, Yeats (William Butler).

Saint A person of great holiness, a saint is a symbol of divinity in humanity. Conferring sainthood upon a human being is the Catholic Church's way of recognizing purity, compassion, virtue, benevolence, and powers viewed as larger than life in members of its religious community. Once it also served the purpose of preserving the polytheism of old religions while still worshiping only one God.

In St. Louis Cathedral, Louis stares at the carved figures of the saints. Frozen and lifeless, they present a "cemetery of dead forms." *(IV 145)* To him, the statues represent the absence of God and the embodiment of the supernatural within himself. His body convulses, as if rejecting the death of his religion, but he then envisions himself desecrating the Host.

As a mortal boy, Lestat became enamored of the church. He wanted to be good, to be recognized as having the traits of a saint. When his family aborts his plan to enter a religious order, he then seeks out other ways to be good. In his case, he first sought to be an actor. *(VL 31)* Lestat viewed both actors and musicians as saints for they give and receive happiness, do not accept lies, strive for something better, and, with their art, repel meaninglessness and chaos. *(VL 52)*

Lestat does not abandon his quest for sainthood even after he becomes a vampire. He wants to use his evil to do some good, so he tries to kill only evildoers. He also becomes a rock star to present himself as a symbol of evil that might inspire mortals to reject such evil from their world. He believes that rock stars dramatize the battles against evil that individuals fight within themselves. *(VL 10)*

Akasha uses Lestat's desire to be a saint to manipulate him into becoming a "god" with her as she embarks on her bloodthirsty rampage. She demonstrates to him how the malleability of the concept "goodness" sanctions her plan. As a goddess, she makes what meaning there will be, and thus she decides what is good. If Lestat obeys her, he can be the saint he always wanted to be. Lestat, however, ends up being unable to abandon his ethics and eventually turns from her. *(QD 262)*

In BT, Gretchen, the nun, has statues of saints in her home, where she brings Lestat in his mortal form. He hallucinates that the other vampires are there with the saints, appearing as white statues. They are silent witnesses, refusing to help him. *(BT 225)* Gretchen tells him about saints she admires—St. Rose de Lima, St. Martin de Porres, and St. Rita—saying she sees in them the same urge for an extraordinary, heroic life that she wants for herself. Lestat recognizes parallels between what Gretchen desires and what he wants as a vampire. *(BT 242)*

Rice felt that many of her vampires shared qualities with the saints: courage, extraordinary powers, a sense of themselves united with the divine, heightened vision, and an urge toward the heroic. She viewed saints as people who would not accept useless lies, and who wanted to better themselves and affect things. They were willing to make major sacrifices to attain their goals. "It's obvious," Rice claims, "that these vampire characters are on a par with the saints. They can work miracles and transcend time. The vampire is one with the powers

Figure of a saint

that transcend the corruptible, and he represents the longing for immortality and freedom."

See also Art, God, Goodness, Gretchen, Joan of Arc, Lestat de Lioncourt, Religious Images, Rock Star, St. Anthony, St. Bonaventure, St. Dominic, St. Francis, St. Gall, St. Joseph, St. Lucy, St. Teresa of Avila, St. Thérèse of Lisieux.

St. Anthony   A thirteenth-century Franciscan orator who is the patron saint of harvests, barren women, and the oppressed. He is often depicted carrying the infant Jesus.

Lestat recognizes a statue of this saint among Roger's collection of religious artifacts. It ends up at St. Elizabeth's Orphanage (where it actually is today). *(MD 31, 345)*

See also Religious Relics/Artifacts, Saint.

St. Bonaventure   A thirteenth-century Franciscan bishop who wrote many theological works, including a treatise on holy poverty. He strongly supported education and the need for his order to provide buildings and books for the monks.

Lestat refers to this saint when he mentions the female preachers that Dora trains in her convent. *(MD 113)*

See also Flynn (Dora), Saint.

St. Dominic   The saint who, in the thirteenth century, founded the Dominican order of friars. This saint accompanies the Virgin Mary in visions to Louis's brother, Paul, and instructs him to sell the family plantation and do religious work. *(IV 6)*

See also Paul, Saint, Visions.

Saint-Domingue   The French name for Haiti, a former French colony.

Lestat claims to be married to an heiress from this island when he first becomes a vampire; the claim is part of his disguise while dealing with Pierre Roget, his lawyer. Two centuries later, Lestat is in this country when he sorts through his doubts about Akasha's plan. They argue and Lestat perceives Akasha's weakness: she needs an ally to confirm her vision. *(VL 118, QD 391–398)*

See also Haiti.

St. Elizabeth's Orphanage   A 47,000-square-foot, brick Catholic convent built in the Second Empire style during the 1860s on Napoleon Street in New Orleans. Originally a boarding school for girls, it became an orphanage for over a century beginning in 1870. Its

Front facade of St. Elizabeth's Orphanage

two long wings and four towers on each corner give it the appearance of a castle. On the second floor is a two-story chapel. The building surrounds a huge courtyard. In 1993, Rice purchased St. Elizabeth's, hoping to restore it to its original condition and to turn the courtyard into a magnificent garden. She has arranged her massive doll collection inside.

St. Elizabeth's is the home base for Dora Flynn's religious recruitment and the training base for her female missionaries. She lives in the northeast tower, on the third floor. Her plan is to use the building as a base for her religious movement. The house cost her father, Roger, $1 million to buy and an equal amount to restore. It is her piece of heaven on earth. *(MD 17–18, 87, 110–113)*

Lestat knows that Dora lives alone in St. Elizabeth's, and when her father urges him to appear to her, he goes straight to the former convent. Wandering around the huge building, he checks for "elementals" and admires the chapel and the religious art. There he encounters Memnoch the Devil, who explains that he is interested in Lestat's soul. Dora enters, interrupting their conversation, and Lestat flees from her to the main attic. She tracks him down and insists that he tell her what he is. He explains that he is a vampire and that he killed her father. Memnoch begins to approach, disturbing Lestat so that he leaves her there, intending to return later. *(MD 121)*

Only after he has been to Heaven and Hell with Memnoch does

Lestat come back to St. Elizabeth's. Dora has deeded the place to him—he calls it his "beast's castle"—and has sent Roger's religious artifacts there to be stored. Louis has unwrapped and arranged everything. Maharet then arrives with a shocking message from Memnoch. To prevent Lestat from damaging anything with his supernatural strength, she chains him and seals him into a windowless room. There he listens as David reads his own words back to him of the story about his journey with Memnoch. *(MD 340, 344–353)*

"St. Elizabeth's is deeply loved by me," said Rice. "My strongest personal thoughts on it are probably best expressed by Lestat when he first visits the building and imagines it as a European palazzo or a castle for Beauty and the Beast. Lestat's eyes see what I love about the building, and this is detailed in the novel [MD].

"The building means an enormous amount to New Orleans, and the orphanage has touched the lives of an unbelievable amount of people here. I have found numerous people who had visited St. Elizabeth's in years past. Many New Orleaneans remember taking the [orphan] girls for outings.

"My own strong feelings for St. Elizabeth's involve not only the

The chapel inside St. Elizabeth's Orphanage

fact that I visited it twice as a child, but also the fact that I have pretty good indications that my grandmother, Alice Connell, went to school in the central building (circa 1860), when it was called St. Joseph's Academy.

"I love the building because it reminds me vividly of several convents which I knew intimately as a little girl. One was the old St. Alphonsus Girls School on St. Andrew and Constance, now gone. It was a gorgeous old brick building with big stairways, much like St. Elizabeth's.

"The second convent was the home of the Little Sisters of the Poor on Prytania Street, near Amelia. It had a magnificent chapel. I spent one of the happiest summers of my life, between sixth and seventh grades, working there with the nuns to care for old people. I used to help the Sisters cut flowers to put before statues of the Virgin throughout the building. For a while, I wanted to be a nun and assumed I'd spend my life in a large brick building like the Home of the Little Sisters of the Poor.

"The third convent was St. Joseph's Academy on the corner of Ursulines and North Galves. I boarded there in a huge top-story dormitory during my junior year of high school. I described this building in detail in *The Witching Hour* as the boarding school to which Deirdre Mayfair went.

"St. Elizabeth's is so very much like these three great convents of my imagination that to have St. E's is to have them back again, to have again their beauty, their ambience, their glorious spaciousness, and their architectural detail."

On April 20, 1995, a team of clairvoyants (including a parapsychologist) investigated St. Elizabeth's for spiritual activity. They sensed impressions of the ghosts of children (just as Lestat had indicated), including a suicide. They also located a dark-haired caretaker in the attic where Lestat hid from Dora.

See also *Beauty and the Beast*, Crucifix, Elementals, Flynn (Dora), Lestat de Lioncourt, Maharet, Memnoch, New Orleans, Religious Relics/Artifacts.

St. Francis The son of a wealthy cloth merchant during the thirteenth century, he founded the Franciscan Order in Assisi, Italy. He lived as a hermit and a beggar and encouraged an attitude of love for all living things. He preached poverty, chastity, obedience, and repentance among his followers.

Lestat compares Dora's female preachers to the followers of St. Francis. *(MD 113)*

See also Flynn (Dora), Saint.

St. Gall A Celtic missionary during the sixth and seventh centu-

ries, he want to Gaul, then Switzerland. The monastery of St. Gall was established on the site of his hermitage.

Roger mentions St. Gall in the context of convent designs that contrast with that of St. Elizabeth's. *(MD 61)*

See also Saint, St. Elizabeth's Orphanage.

St. Joseph   The husband of the Virgin Mary and foster father to Jesus.

In the chapel at St. Elizabeth's, one of the life-sized plaster saints that Lestat sees is that of St. Joseph holding a lily. *(MD 114)*

See also Saint, St. Elizabeth's Orphanage.

St. Louis Cathedral   A massive Catholic church that lies near the Chartres Street entrance to Jackson Square, it is located in the French Quarter of New Orleans. It was named for the French king Louis IX, who led two crusades. The cathedral that now stands in this spot is actually the third one to be built there; a hurricane destroyed the first one in 1723, and a fire burned down the second in 1788.

Louis wanders into this church one night in a fit of shame and guilt over being a vampire. It is where his brother Paul's funeral ceremony was held, and Louis thinks about that as he watches people going to confession. He feels especially empowered when the religious artifacts fail to have the effect on him described in vampire legend and lore, and he even experiences a vision of himself trampling the sacred host. When he realizes that he is the only supernatural being in the church, he feels lonely. A priest comes over to Louis and invites him to confess, but when Louis claims responsibility for thousands of murders over the past seventy years, the priest believes that Louis is

The statue of St. Joseph that Lestat sees in St. Elizabeth's Orphanage

St. Louis Cathedral, New Orleans

taunting him. Becoming resigned to his evil nature, Louis kills the priest. *(IV 143–146)*

When Lestat comes to see Louis after his ordeal in the desert, he meets Louis at night in this church. And when Lestat regains his vampire body from the body thief, he again visits the church. This time he is angered at Louis's refusal to help him reclaim his immortal body, and he wonders if his temper will cause him to destroy Louis. When Louis arrives, they talk. Lestat swallows his anger, first inviting Louis to live with him, then denouncing him for his disloyalty. When Lestat leaves the church, he lights a candle in memory of his former self. *(BT 403–410)* (See Vampire Atlas)

See also Candle, Forgiveness, Superstitions, Visions.

St. Louis Cemetery   Established in the 1740s on the 400 block of Basin Street outside the French Quarter, it was the first cemetery in New Orleans.

Louis's brother, Paul, was buried in this cemetery, and Louis's tomb was erected here after it was believed that he perished in the fire at Pointe du Lac. The dates marked on Louis's stone are 1766 to 1794, although technically he "died" in 1791, when he became a vampire. After they recover from Akasha's death, Louis and Lestat wander here together. *(QD 479)*

St. Louis Cemetery also plays a part in the first draft of IV, the ending of which was later changed for the published version. It is in St. Louis Cemetery that Armand shows Louis how to find Those Who Want to Die, rather than taking victims at random. People who wander in cemeteries are often deeply grieved and do not want to continue with

St. Louis Cemetery, New Orleans

their own lives. Louis describes a scene between Armand and such a victim that takes place in the cemetery. (See Vampire Atlas)

See also Those Who Want to Die.

St. Louis Hotel   See Spanish Hotel.

St. Louis, Missouri   The location of the coven house where Akasha destroys Baby Jenks. *(QD 44)* (See Vampire Atlas)

See also Baby Jenks, The Vampire Connection.

St. Lucy   A Christian during the time of the persecutions of Diocletian, she was found out and her religion was revealed. A judge ordered her to be taken to a brothel. According to legend, however, the guards were physically unable to carry her there. Then an attempt to burn her failed. Finally, Lucy was killed by a sword thrust through her throat. Another legend holds that she tore out her own eyes to discourage a suitor, but they were miraculously restored. Venerated as a martyr, Lucy's relics are reportedly preserved in Venice.

One of Roger's artifacts that ends up at St. Elizabeth's is a statue of St. Lucy with her eyes resting on a plate. Rice is in the process of locating such a statue for the chapel. *(MD 345)*

See also Religious Relics/Artifacts, Saint, St. Elizabeth's Orphanage.

St. Margaret Mary   See Mission of St. Margaret Mary.

St. Patrick's Cathedral   The largest Catholic cathedral in the country, it is located in midtown Manhattan. Finished in 1878, with spires that rise three hundred and thirty feet, this Gothic Revival structure seats 2,500. The Stations of the Cross are carved inside in stone. Several events in MD are associated with St. Patrick's.

Roger always chooses a hotel across the street from the cathedral to meet his daughter, Dora. She cherishes the church and prays there. *(MD 5, 11)*

Lestat casually mentions St. Patrick's several times as he walks around the neighborhood, foreshadowing the impact the cathedral will soon have on his existence. He imagines that if the Devil catches up to him, he can run there and claim some sort of sanctuary. *(MD 26)* Lestat urges David to rent rooms in Olympic Tower across the street, with a view of the magnificent spires. Later, from the steps of St. Patrick's, he calls Memnoch to come for him there. *(MD 95, 161)*

After his journey to Heaven and Hell, on which he received the icon of Veronica's veil from Christ, Lestat watches Dora stand on the same steps to reveal the veil to the public. Her act infuses Christianity with new faith. Lestat also witnesses Armand's destruction in the sun in front of the cathedral to affirm this miracle. *(MD 335)*

St. Patrick's Cathedral

Rice set all this action at St. Patrick's because of her great appreciation for it. "All of my life, I have known and heard of St. Patrick's Cathedral," she affirmed. "Yet I never entered it until I first went to New York in my thirties. I found it breathtakingly beautiful and vital. Some years ago I visited it with [my son] Christopher and [husband] Stan. There was a choir singing and I cried. I became very emotionally taken with the moment. Later Christopher wrote a poem about his own visit to the Metropolitan Museum of Art, in which he mentioned

403

Mother 'crying' in St. Patrick's as he discussed the whole question of beauty and one's reaction to it.

"I returned to St. Patrick's on my last visit to New York, specifically to check out details for *Memnoch*, and prayed for awhile in the church. I was amazed to discover an altar to Veronica's veil on the left side of the church, set into the wall. I don't recall ever noting this before, but perhaps I did and it subconsciously inspired me. Anyway, I did not 'introduce' this altar into *Memnoch*. I simply noted it as very interesting.

"I suppose no church on earth has excited and inspired me as much as St. Patrick's except for St. Peter's in Rome. These churches are true churches." (See Vampire Atlas)

See also Armand, Flynn (Dora), Lestat de Lioncourt, Manhattan, *Memnoch the Devil*, Olympic Tower, Veronica's Veil.

St. Teresa of Avila A sixteenth-century Carmelite nun who experienced visions of Christ, had "interior" dialogues, and was even said to levitate on occasion. She founded many convents and wrote several books, such as *The Way of Perfection* and *Interior Castle*.

Dora Flynn reads the writings of this mystic. *(MD 82)*

As a child, Anne Rice was quite intrigued with this figure. "I loved St. Teresa and I read lives of her constantly. I have a statue of her in my house. I read a lot about mysticism when I was a Catholic girl, about meditation, about visions, about surrendering the mind to Christ. I believed I was going to be a Carmelite and a saint."

See also Flynn (Dora), Saint.

St. Thérèse of Lisieux A nineteenth-century Carmelite nun, she was known for the "little ways" of searching for simplicity and perfection in everyday tasks. She was also known as St. Thérèse of "the Little Flower."

In the chapel of St. Elizabeth's Orphanage, Lestat sees a plaster statue of St. Thérèse holding roses. *(MD 114)*

See also Saint, St. Elizabeth's Orphanage.

The statue of St. Thérèse of Lisieux that Lestat sees in St. Elizabeth's Orphanage

Salamander A groupie from New Orleans who travels to San Francisco with the rock band The Vampire Lestat to be with band member Larry. *(VL 523)*

See also Larry, The Vampire Lestat.

Salvation See Redemption.

Sampson, Eric The alias David Talbot uses to reserve a cabin on the *QE2*. Lestat hides in these quarters when he regains possession of his vampire body. *(BT 316)*

San Francisco, California

Sam Spade   A fictional detective created by Dashiell Hammett in the 1920s.

Lestat reads about Sam Spade and the Maltese Falcon in *Black Mask* magazine before he goes underground in 1929. *(VL 4, 7, 513)*

San Francisco   A city in northern California on the Pacific Coast, it is a leading center of avant-garde culture. Louis tells his story, which is published as IV, to the boy reporter in San Francisco. Louis returns to this city for his own safety after his book and Lestat's sequel provoke other vampires to seek him out to destroy him.

It is also the city where Lestat makes his live debut with his rock group, The Vampire Lestat, in the Cow Palace. The city charms Lestat; he finds it to be almost like Venice. Louis sees Lestat cruising down Divisadero Street in his Porsche looking for him, and joins him in time for the concert. *(VL 521)*

Khayman believes Lestat chose San Francisco for his debut because of its aura of goodness and escape from pain and deprivation. The residents there could easily be adequate combatants against evil, which is what Lestat wants. *(QD 203)*

Roger went to San Francisco to found a sexual-religious cult. He lived in the Haight district in the attic of the Spreckles Mansion on the edge of Buena Vista Park. While in the city, he managed a rock group, but when a drug deal endangered members of the band, he killed two people, then departed from the city. *(MD 66)* (See Vampire Atlas)

See also Cow Palace, Divisadero Street, Dracula's Daughter, Rock Concert, Roger, Spreckles Mansion.

Santiago   In IV, the vampire who follows Louis through Paris's

Latin Quarter when Louis is trying to find others like himself. Santiago is sinister, strong-willed, possessive, territorial, and suspicious of Louis, qualities that provoke Louis into calling him a trickster. In appearance he is tall and gaunt, and has black hair. Dressed in vampire drag—black clothes and a black cape—he mockingly repeats Louis's words and imitates his actions. Annoyed and frustrated, Louis sees this behavior as a challenge to his presence in Paris. He calls Santiago a buffoon and Santiago attacks, besting Louis until Armand's appearance puts an end to the scuffle. *(IV 213–216)*

Louis discovers that Santiago is a member of a vampire coven in Paris that resides in the Theater of the Vampires. On stage, Santiago plays the part of Death (although it is Armand who initiates the kill). Santiago remains suspicious of Louis and tries to probe him for answers about his origins. *(IV 242, 246)*

When the coven discovers that Louis and Claudia have broken vampire laws, it is Santiago who leads the coven to capture them. Santiago then orders Louis to be locked into a coffin, where he will starve for eternity. With Armand's assistance, Louis escapes. He then discovers that Claudia has been destroyed and sets fire to the theater in retaliation. As he is leaving the burning theater, he has one last confrontation with Santiago. Louis cuts off Santiago's head with a scythe, then leaves the corpse behind to be consumed by the fire. *(IV 296, 314)*

See also Coven, Theater of the Vampires.

Santino   A black-haired Italian vampire, he is the leader of the satanic coven in Rome when Marius lived in Venice. He was born to Darkness in the mid-1300s, during the reign of the Black Death, and his vision for vampires is that they be a "vexation without explanation" *(VL 301)*, which causes mortals to doubt God. Santino helps to form the Great Laws and see that they are carried out. He leads the attack on what they view as the heretic Marius, whom they are trying to destroy because he lives among mortals. Although the attack fails, it drives Marius from Venice and results in Armand's apprenticeship into the coven. Later Armand hears that Santino went mad and abandoned the coven, which subsequently dissolved in chaos. And when Lestat and Gabrielle meet the members of another Roman coven, there is no evidence of Santino. *(VL 300, 304–305)*

Santino shows up again in QD. Ironically, he accompanies Pandora to rescue Marius, the vampire he had once tried to destroy. *(QD 237, 253, 264)*

See also Gathering of Immortals, Marius, Roman Coven.

Saqqâra   A city in northern Egypt, just below Cairo on the Nile River.

This is where Queen Akasha's soldiers catch Maharet, Mekare,

and Khayman, who are attempting to flee after becoming vampires. Khayman ends up escaping but the twins do not, and Akasha condemns them to separation and entombment. *(QD 415)* (See Vampire Atlas)

See also Egypt, Khayman, Twins.

Sarcophagus   See Coffins.

Sariel   One of the seven premier archangels who stands by God's throne, he is responsible for seeing to the destiny of those angels who have flouted God's laws.

When touring Heaven, Lestat asks Memnoch if the angel Sariel is a real entity. Memnoch affirms that he is. *(MD 206)*

See also Angel, Archangels.

Satan   See Devil.

Satan's Night Out   Made up of Larry, Alex, and Tough Cookie, this is the band of rock singers who play down the street from Lestat's house and whose music awakens him in 1984. Lestat thinks the band looks like angels. He tells them that he can make them famous, then reveals his name. They laugh and hand him IV, the publication of which shocks him.

After he reads Louis's confessions, Lestat determines to use this rock group to make art for his own purposes. He changes their name to The Vampire Lestat—to coordinate their music with the title of his autobiography—and their live debut as a band takes place on Halloween night in San Francisco's Cow Palace. *(VL 5–6, 11–15, 536–542, QD 218–231)*

See also Alex, Cow Palace, Larry, Rock Concert, Rock Star, Tough Cookie, The Vampire Lestat.

Satie, Erik   A modern French composer particularly known for his piano compositions, he spent his career ignoring established musical conventions. His music is known for its harmony and melodic simplicity. His most popular works include the "Trois Gymnopédies."

In a Manhattan hotel bar where he meets David Talbot, Lestat hears Erik Satie's music being played on the piano. *(MD 7)*

Saul   The first king of the Jews, who sought assistance from the Witch of Endor to raise the spirit of the deceased prophet Samuel. This spirit then informed Saul that his battle with the Philistines would be disastrous. When Saul did end up losing the battle, as Samuel had predicted, he committed suicide.

Lestat believes that his distasteful reaction to Raglan James is

similar to what Saul must have felt toward the Witch of Endor. *(BT 154)*

See also Bible, James (Raglan), Witch of Endor.

Savage Garden   Another name for nature, it is what Lestat and Gabrielle call a world that would embrace exquisite monsters like vampires. For Lestat, nature itself is savage and ultimately its laws are based on aesthetic principles. He sees that in modern times, ethical truth is embedded in the physical. No one is safe from nature's savagery, not even the innocent. Only beauty is consistent. Gabrielle envisions a time when the Savage Garden will overtake civilization and destroy it. *(VL 131, 162, 334, 383)*

When Akasha takes Lestat on her rampage, she reminds him of what he believes about the Savage Garden and aesthetics. Death, she says, is everywhere in nature, but her new Eden will be a paradise, better than nature because it will redeem amorality. The survival of the vampires is the beauty out of which all other beauties will be born. *(QD 366)*

Lestat thinks that the final triumph of the Savage Garden is found in the South American rain forests. These forests contain the endless struggle of animal survival—hunger and satiation are fulfilled only through violent death. However, David Talbot points out that the botanical gardens in Barbados are full of "mad, savage" flowers that are also soft, tame, and safe. His perception reveals his more peaceful nature. *(BT 347, 382)*

Armand uses the concept of the Savage Garden to explain his attraction to Lestat: "You walk as if it is your garden to do with as you please. And in my wanderings, I always return to you." *(MD 147)*

Lestat tries to determine how God and Memnoch fit this concept of ruthlessness, beauty, and indifference to suffering. The garden in which he walks just outside of Heaven seems peaceful and perfect. *(MD 172)* Memnoch tells him, however, that his concept exactly describes God's plan for the world: "Your Savage Garden, Lestat, *is* His version of Perfection. It all evolved from the same seed." *(MD 301)* As Memnoch explains the story of Creation, Lestat begins to understand how beauty and brutality coexist, although he does not want to accept this as originating with the God of light that he has seen.

See also Akasha, Armand, Barbados, God, Memnoch, Nature.

Scent   Vampires often detect mortals through the scent of their blood. Lestat describes the scent as a blend of passion, roasted meat, water on a hot day, and new wine. In other words, the scent is intoxicating and generally irresistible. *(VL 110)*

See also Blood, Senses.

Scotch   A type of whiskey distilled from malted barley, it is David

Talbot's favorite drink. When David fails to order it in Miami, asking instead for a tropical drink, Lestat has his first clue that David is not who he presents himself to be. Soon thereafter Lestat discovers that Raglan James has taken over David's body. *(BT 201, 362)*

See also Talbot (David).

Scythe   An implement used for mowing, it has a long curving blade, which is attached, at an angle, to a long handle. This is the weapon with which Louis beheads Santiago when he incinerates the Theater of the Vampires. *(IV 314)*

In VL, two vampires close in on Lestat after his rock concert, wielding scythes. They fail to reach their target, however, as they go up in flames by Akasha's hand. *(VL 542)*

See also Rock Concert, Santiago.

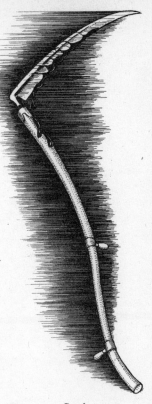

Scythe

Sebastian Melmouth   See Melmouth, Sebastian.

Secrecy   The need for this develops as a result of the intense intimacy of vampire relationships. Vampires have heightened senses, which allow them to instantly perceive when something is amiss, and their ability to read one another's thoughts (except for those of their own children) lets them anticipate what another vampire will say or do. Many vampires resort to cloaking their thoughts or deliberately confusing the thoughts of others in order to deflect such heightened awareness. Claudia does this when she plans to kill Lestat, and Armand does so when it comes to his involvement in Claudia's death. *(IV 134, 290–292, QD 18)*

See also Cloaking, Intimacy, Relationships, Telepathic Powers.

Secret Order of the Undead   How Jesse refers to the gathering of immortals at the Sonoma compound. *(QD 379)*

See also The Gathering of Immortals, Sonoma Compound.

Security   When Louis first becomes a vampire in IV, Lestat tells Louis that they should sleep in the same room for reasons of security. Having two rooms would require additional safety precautions and mean "double chance of notice." *(IV 33)* Yet Louis defies Lestat's caution and makes his bed in his brother's unused oratory.

The vampires also know that they must ensure their safety from mortals and from one another. The ones who need the most security are Akasha and Enkil, the Father and Mother, whose destruction would mean the annihilation of the entire vampire race. Thus, Marius takes great pains to hide them and moves them from place to place to keep their location a secret. What he does not anticipate, however, is

the possibility of one of them breaking out—which Akasha does. *(VL 462, QD 31)*

See also Coffins, Secrecy, Those Who Must Be Kept.

Seduction
The means by which vampires draw their victims to them. Vampires are sensual, subtle, and romantic; these qualities create a highly attractive allure. Vampires also represent rapture, immortality, dominance, and intense focus, which their victims find appealing. Vampires can also draw their victims close through mental manipulation. Armand does this with "those who wish to die"; he shows himself to them as the one who will gently and lovingly give them what they want. *(QD 303)*

Once the victim is physically close, the vampire seduces with the bite itself. The feeling of blood flowing out proves ecstatic for mortals. During this experience, Lestat feels great love for Magnus, despite the fact that he had fought against the contact with all his strength. Louis experiences the same overwhelming feeling, although he had actually chosen to become a vampire. And when Louis takes a "little drink" from Daniel, the boy reporter, he thereafter becomes obsessed with finding a way to become a vampire and achieve immortality. *(VL 91–92, IV 13, 16, QD 83)*

See also Dominance/Submission, Erotic, Intimacy, Making a Vampire, Rapture, Sensuality, Sex, Surrender, Swoon, Those Who Want to Die, Vampire.

Self-confidence
The sense of assurance about one's own powers and abilities, it is a pervasive theme in the *Chronicles*, especially when it is related to physical strength. *(VL 13)*

Louis experiences how a loss of confidence erodes his strength when he wrestles with Lestat, and when despair sets in, he is bested. He is weaker than he needs to be in part because he has confidence in nothing, and especially not in himself. Only when he forms a clear moral plan that he believes in—burning down the Theater of the Vampires—does he discover a source of inner strength. Afterward, despair and cynicism set in again, and he loses his newly discovered strength. *(IV 76)*

Self-confidence is also a factor for Lestat. He can engage his power of flight only when he believes he can do it; his confidence often needs to be bolstered with familiarity. After switching bodies with the mortal Raglan James, Lestat loses all faith in his ability to perform the simplest of psychic behaviors, such as astral projection. This reveals that his powerful vampire body is strongly connected to his positive sense of self. *(QD 286, BT 206)*

See also Body Switching, Flight, Hero, Lestat de Lioncourt, Louis de Pointe du Lac, Vampire Powers.

Self-deception   Human beings have the capacity to ignore parts of who they are or be so close to their situations that they fail to see them accurately. Vampires, having once been human, have the same capacity, and several vampires in the *Chronicles* suffer from self-deception.

Louis goes about looking for someone to either make his life better or condemn him, to take him to Heaven or bring him to Hell. He looks to Lestat, Claudia, and Armand to enhance his existence, all the while seeking a way to bring upon himself the damnation he feels he deserves. He is unable to see what Armand points out: that the power to create his own life lies within himself. Louis does, however, recognize this power in others. He knows that the Freniere women can allow themselves to be victimized by their brother's death, or they can take action to make their lives better. "You must take the reins of your own life," he tells Babette. *(IV 48)* He knows the power is within her, yet he seems blind to the same power residing within himself. His self-deception cripples him and makes him dependent on others. It eventually contributes to Claudia's death and to his growing sense of cynicism and despair. *(IV 309)*

Lestat, too, is deceiving himself. He takes on the challenge of using his vampirism to bring about good. He convinces himself that he kills only the "bad guys," and becomes a rock star to clarify to the world what being a vampire means. Yet Akasha shows him what his philosophy amounts to. She kills on a much larger and more brutal scale to achieve a paradise—being bad in order to do good, just as he has been doing. Then she tells him he is deceiving himself if he does not recognize the parallel between them. *(QD 259, 292, 392)*

Lestat resists this knowledge, but by BT, knows it is true. When he trails a serial killer and kills him, he satisfies his image of himself, but when he then goes on to kill the serial killer's intended victim, a frail old woman, he gets his first inkling that his evil cannot be redeemed (or even controlled), and that he loves the kill, regardless of who the victim is. Then, after he is given the chance to become mortal, he discovers that he would rather be a vampire. He finally recognizes the deception he has been perpetuating on himself and sees that he actually wants his vampire powers. *(BT 24, 418)*

Akasha, too, thrives on self-deception in order to make her plan feasible. She wants to be a goddess and to create a new Eden—a world run by women, where women can be safe. Yet she can achieve this only by redefining metaphysical concepts within a new value structure. She wants to transform her brutality into a vision of benevolence, and change dark to light, evil to good, vampire to god. So she relies on nihilism—the absence of meaning with the absence of God—to drain these concepts of their traditional meanings. Then she imagines that she can just create new meanings for them all.

Her self-deception also consists of believing she can achieve this alone, but in fact she needs someone to affirm what she is doing. She needs Lestat. When she does not admit this and tries to stand alone, she crumbles. The rest of her self-deception comes to light as her abstract ideas fail to play out in concrete, practical reality. She is attempting to place a structure upon human experience that does not fit. *(QD 396–397, 452)*

See also Akasha, Akasha's Plan, Lestat de Lioncourt, Louis de Pointe du Lac, *The Tale of the Body Thief.*

Senses/sensations   One of the key areas of change after a mortal becomes a vampire. Louis notices right away that he can see more vividly, to the point that he is so enthralled with bright colors that he stares at ordinary things, like buttons, for long periods of time. His auditory and tactile sensations are magnified as well, and he can smell the scent of blood and feel pleasure more strongly than before. As a vampire, Louis is now capable of deeper feelings of love and affection, despite possessing a greater degree of detachment. The drawbacks to this transformation, however, are that he no longer sees Lestat as a magical being, and that he feels pain more acutely than he did as a mortal. *(IV 19–20, 24, 88)*

Along with heightened sensations comes a change in visual perception. Lestat and Louis both describe how they see mortals as whirling molecules because now they can detect things that were too quick for their mortal eyes. Early in his vampire experience, Lestat also sees mortals as skeletons, and he describes his ability to see the entire process involved in a work of art when he looks at a painting. *(VL 114, 136, 568)*

After his exposure to the desert sun, Lestat finds that his bodily sensations are magnified. He feels intense pain, and when that subsides, he is more aware of temperature fluctuations and the insidious penetration of the cold and the wind than before. *(BT 48–49, 57)*

See also Extraordinary Life, Hallucinations, Hallucinogen, Vampire, Vampire Powers.

Sensuality   A trait vampires possess. Their heightened senses empower them to exploit, with finely tuned skill, the mechanisms of arousal. To victims (and sometimes to each other) they are seductive, charming, and irresistible, and move with feline grace. Some vampires exhibit the behavior of obsessive lovers, making the victim feel highly desired. Armand develops his own sensuality into an art as he blends together the carnal and the spiritual. *(VL 303)*

See also Armand, Erotic, Intimacy, Rapture, Seduction, Sex, Vampire, Victims.

Seraphim   In traditional Catholic systems, the highest of the nine

orders of angels. They are closest to God and have the most perfect understanding of Him.

When discussing the composition of Heaven, Memnoch describes this angelic rank to Lestat. *(MD 200)*

See also Angel, Nine Choirs.

Serial killer Murderers who exhibit a pattern of psychotic behavior known as episodic frenzy. They compulsively troll for victims who trigger memories in them of physical or emotional abuse, then stalk them relentlessly, often taking pleasure in torturing them before they kill them. Often they save a memento of the experience in order to relive it when the inevitable postmurder depression sets in. Consciously, they know little of what they do, and they often prove elusive to law enforcement authorities because they look and seem like ordinary people. Perversely, these killers often wish for death, for it will put an end to their uncontrollable behaviors.

In BT, Lestat stalks serial killers using his computer, breaking into FBI files to locate particularly compelling subjects. He also locates them through their violent dreams. "They are my brothers," he says. *(BT 12)* While he is in Miami, he is aware that a killer called the "Back Street Strangler" has struck six times, each time killing defenseless old women. Lestat takes particular delight in the fact that this one has been studied by twenty criminologists and yet no one has caught him.

The killer lives on Collins Avenue near South Beach, and it is his hallucinations that compel him to go out to seek out a victim. For him there is no boundary between fantasy and reality, and he possesses only a partial memory of the killing episodes. Lestat tracks this killer when he follows a potential victim, then loses interest as he realizes that the man is helpless to his compulsion, and not a crafty, cruel killer. In fact, the man does not even know what he is. Nevertheless, Lestat scares him away from the old woman's apartment, takes his life, then returns to the old woman and kills her. This second death precipitates in Lestat a depression over his evil nature and shatters his illusion of himself as a protector of the innocent. *(BT 10–21)*

In this scenario, Lestat himself acted like a serial killer. He, too, takes note of his potential victim (the killer), stalks him, becomes obsessed with him, and is compelled—albeit by his blood thirst and his need to do good—to kill him. When he dispatches one killer, he starts searching for another. The main difference here between Lestat and serial killers is that Lestat remains more conscious of his actions.

See also Back Street Strangler, Hunter, Lestat de Lioncourt, Victims.

Sex Vampire sexuality involves nongenital contact with their victims and with one another. Their primary pleasure comes through the bite and through sucking blood. Vampires sometimes experience sex

413

with one another by the sucking of each other's blood. Lestat describes his experience with Akasha—when they are simultaneously "kissing" each other—as unlike any pleasure he has ever known. Armand and Daniel engage in this kind of embrace while Daniel is still a mortal, although Armand only allows Daniel to drink his blood in limited amounts. *(VL 486, QD 92)*

When Claudia asks Louis what sex as a mortal was like, he tells her it was hurried and quick, and the "pale shadow of killing" *(IV 210)*, implying that the intensity and thrill of sucking blood supersedes that of human orgasm. Drinking blood from a mortal has sexual overtones for both vampire and victim. When Louis drinks from Denis, Armand's slave, he is caught in the throes of passion, just as Denis is. They rock together, as if having sex, and Denis has an erection from the overwhelming erotic sensations. Louis claims that the sexuality of the bite is one of intense intimacy and is amazed that any mortal can survive it. *(IV 231)*

Armand watches Daniel have physical sex with mortal women. He cannot do it himself, since as a vampire his organ is nonfunctional, but he is intensely curious about the union. *(QD 94)*

Lestat experiences mortal sex when he switches bodies with Raglan James. He rapes the first woman he meets—a waitress who invites him home. He enjoys conquering her, but then realizes he must hold back his appetites. He describes his human sexual desire as a localized feeling, but nevertheless it consumes all his thoughts. He finds, however, that he does not care for the odors or the tastes associated with sex. He is also annoyed by the sweat and stickiness, and the need for prophylactics. Overall, he thinks the experience is dismal, the subsequent pleasure minimal. *(BT 186–191)*

He finds sex with Gretchen, the nun who cares for him when he is sick, a little better. She desires to lose her virginity, and Lestat is gentle with her. Still, he feels that their physical union only increases their separateness. It is a blend of trust and menace, it is lonely and brief, and most significantly, it fails to make either person fathomable to the other. Moreover, her vulnerability invites violence and possessiveness. It does not compare with the union of a vampire and victim, just as Louis had told Claudia earlier. *(BT 239)*

Memnoch the Devil describes sex as the one glimpse of Heaven that God allowed humans. He describes his own encounter in human form with Lilia, a woman, and how other angels then followed his example. For doing so, they were almost cast from Heaven, but their contrition saved them. Not so Memnoch. He insisted that the human spirit participates in divinity and thus, after death, human souls should be allowed into Heaven. His arguments eventually encourage God to take on human flesh, and He admits that He, too, has experienced sex. *(MD 234)*

See also Dominance/Submission, Erotic, God, Gretchen,

Heaven, Incest, Intimacy, Lilia, Making a Vampire, Memnoch, Procreation, Rapture, Relationships, Seduction, Sensuality, Vampire's Kiss, Waitress, Watcher.

Shakespeare   A sixteenth-century poet and playwright, William Shakespeare and his work significantly influenced Rice. In the *Chronicles*, Lestat quotes from Shakespeare's *Hamlet*, *Othello*, and *Macbeth*, and the aura of literary sophistication this gives to him adds to Lestat's stature in Louis's eyes. He and Louis go often together to see Shakespearean drama.

Lestat claims to have learned the English language, in part, by reading Shakespeare. *(IV 100, VL 4)*

See also *Hamlet, Macbeth, Othello.*

Shaman   Someone who journeys into an altered state of consciousness for the purpose of enlightenment and the acquisition of spiritual powers, and consequently claims to see a different plane of reality. Rice was influenced by Carlos Castenada's *The Teachings of Don Juan*, a novel about being apprenticed to a shamanic guide, and the vampire experience in her *Chronicles* parallels that of the shaman in many ways.

Shamans claim to interact with spirits; the vampire race gets its start through an interaction with the spirit Amel. Shamans seek to establish contact with spirit guides for revelation and enlightenment, which is just what Louis hoped to find by following Lestat. Shamans are in control of their faculties and will. They can access nonordinary reality, such as hallucinations and visions, as clearly as others experience ordinary reality. They have adventures that they then relate to their community, as Louis does through his confession and Lestat through his four-part autobiography. Shamans often begin their spiritual journey with drumming, a sound that Louis describes when he hears his own heart beating in time with Lestat's, and shamans are fully aware and engaged in the moment, as Louis is when he wakes up to his heightened senses. He, like the shamans, recognizes the interrelationship among all things and the preciousness of life.

Shamans often practice at night—which is the realm of the vampire—to reduce stimuli from ordinary reality, and often gain their powers at the point of death in a terrible illness, just as Louis did. Shamanic powers are democratic, as is vampirism, and there is no need for a special guru to instruct. Each person's experience is the final authority for that individual. As Armand points out to Louis, the real power is within the individual's psyche. Lestat understands this and thus does not attempt to instruct Louis. Lestat's own first death was similar to a shamanic transformation.

Each of the *Chronicles*, but most clearly the first one, are shamanic invitations into another world. Rice's descriptions offer a form

of guided imagery that conveys to an interested audience what it is like to enter an uncharted realm of heightened awareness and raised consciousness. In this regard, Louis and Lestat are both a type of shaman; they offer the wisdom they have gained from an experience not normally accessible to humans. Yet seeing through these eyes does provide a unique new understanding of the human condition itself.

David Talbot learns to become a shaman when he apprentices himself to a Candomble priestess. It foreshadows his existence as a vampire. *(BT 66–67)* Interestingly, he also becomes Superior General of the Talamasca, a word that translates as *Shaman. (QD 201)*

See also Candomble, Outsider, Talamasca, Vampire.

Sheol   The ancient Hebrew term for the pit or gloomy realm of departed souls. It was not a place of punishment, but still it held no joy for the disembodied, confused souls who resided there. Many lost their identities and merged into other souls. Eventually, the idea of Sheol gave way to a division between Heaven and Hell (Gehenna).

Memnoch had once entered Sheol, and he describes his observations to Lestat. It was a wreath of human souls that surrounded the Earth. No light from Heaven penetrated Sheol, so Earth was all they knew, and many souls continued to focus on it. The souls had no knowledge of Heaven and no consolation of God until they saw Memnoch fall and learned about God through his prayers. Sheol, he says, was "a great sprawling replica of earth . . . a riot of imagination without Heavenly guidance." *(MD 248)* Many of the souls there failed even to realize they were dead. They remained attuned to the world they had left, their loved ones, or the affairs of their nations.

Some tried to become gods to mortals or to take possession of a mortal body. Others lost their hunger to endure, and they died and disintegrated. Those that endured had the power to project their imaginations and create an environment. They projected things like buildings and animals from Earth onto their landscape, seeking to reinforce their varied beliefs. The most enlightened even created gardens. *(MD 214–216, 235–236)*

After Memnoch pleaded his case for the human soul, God sent him to Sheol to find ten souls worthy of Heaven. Memnoch had to make up his own criteria, which he did as he walked among the dead. He noticed that souls seeking their kindred had created tiers. The most damned were closest to earth and their fleshly appetites, while those closest to Heaven were the most patient and loving. *(MD 246–248)*

Memnoch took millions of souls he deemed worthy out of Sheol, and God accepted them all into Heaven. But Memnoch was not satisfied. He wanted Heaven to be accessible in some way to *all* human souls. He challenged God to experience what it is like to be mortal, and for this, God cast him from Heaven a second time.

Nevertheless, God eventually came to Earth, where Memnoch was wandering, and devised a plan of salvation for human souls. Despite Memnoch's protests, He established access to Heaven based on His own suffering and sacrifice. God took all the souls in Sheol to Heaven, then gave Sheol to Memnoch to be his kingdom. In God's view, since Memnoch is so concerned for those souls that had failed to meet the proper conditions for getting to Heaven, he can provide an educational resource in Sheol to enlighten them. Renaming Sheol Hell, Memnoch collected many more souls than were present in Heaven and subjected them to the horrors of their earthly lives until they learned acceptance and forgiveness. He himself cannot return to Heaven until Sheol is empty of all such souls or until evolution is finished. He wants Lestat to assist him in his task, but Lestat is too horrified by the idea of meeting the victims he has killed since he became a vampire, so he declines. *(MD 291–292, 307–318)*

See also Christ, Gehenna, God, Hell, Human Evolution, Memnoch, *Memnoch the Devil*, Soul, Suffering.

Sheridan Blackwood   See Blackwood, Sheridan.

Sheridan le Fanu, Joseph   A nineteenth-century British writer famous for his vampire short story "Carmilla." Lestat mentions the story in VL, and David Talbot uses the author's first name, Sheridan, when he creates the alias Sheridan Blackwood for Lestat in BT. *(VL 500, BT 299)*

See also "Carmilla," Blackwood (Sheridan).

Shrine   A place in which devotion is paid to a deity.

Marius builds shrines for Akasha and Enkil all over the world. In them he keeps the Mother and Father safe from discovery by humans and other vampires. Two such shrines are described in the *Chronicles* in detail.

When he rescues Lestat from his first death experience, Marius takes him to the first of these shrines. Lestat is unsure of its location, but it seems to be an island in the Mediterranean or Aegean. They climb up a high cliff, then descend down into rock, where Marius has carved out a large fortress. Inside, he has created an exotic place filled with plants, incense, statuary, stuffed animals, and murals lighted by torches. Paintings depicting scenes from all over the world are vivid and vastly detailed, creating near-perfect illusions. He has also collected a huge library, and even has a guest room complete with a stone sarcophagus, which is where he puts Lestat.

The shrine itself consists of a bolted door, behind which is a golden tabernacle in which Akasha and Enkil sit as statues. Marius

brings them fresh flowers and incense daily, and sometimes places them so they can look out to sea. *(VL 370–376)*

The second shrine is embedded hundreds of feet deep in ice in a northern snow-covered wasteland. Again Marius has created an indoor paradise, but now he is aided by modern lighting, electricity, and computers. A satellite dish draws in news and entertainment from all over the world. He goes down to the marble antechambers via an elevator, rather than using a more primitive set of stairs. He also houses a giant aquarium and exotic birds, and outside he has a pen filled with pet wolves. He still burns incense, but he also exposes Akasha and Enkil continuously to the media or videotapes that Marius has brought. Akasha destroys this shrine when she rises. *(QD 23–28)*

See also Marius, Those Who Must Be Kept.

Shroud of Turin   The fourteen-foot-long sheet said to have been used in Christ's burial in the tomb, it is one of the world's most famous religious relics. It bears bloodstains and the double imprint of the image of a man prepared for burial in the manner current with the time of Christ: the body was laid lengthwise on the sheet and the cloth brought over the head and face, then down over the top of the corpse. Scientists and photographic experts have conducted extensive tests on this material, with no conclusive results. Radio carbon dating places its origins between A.D. 1260 and 1390, suggesting it is a clever fraud.

Roger mentions the Shroud of Turin in association with what he wants for his daughter, Dora. He believes she should possess an important religious relic as the heart of her religion to give it a sense of authenticity. *(MD 87)*

See also Flynn (Dora), Religious Relics/Artifacts, Roger.

Sibyl   A woman of antiquity in Greece, Rome, or Egypt believed to possess divine powers. In different accounts, their number varied from one to twelve. The most famous Sibyl, Cumae in Italy, led Aeneas in the Underworld. For centuries Roman priests guarded three books said to be the writings of Sibylline Oracles.

When Lestat wants to consult Dora about his decision to accompany Memnoch to Heaven and Hell, Armand insists, "It's like consulting the Sibyl." *(MD 146)* The phrase "a sleepless mind in his heart and an insatiable personality" comes to Lestat when he thinks of Memnoch. It turns out to be part of a description by the Sibylline Oracle of the Watcher angels, of which Memnoch was one. *(MD 188)*

See also "A sleepless mind in his heart . . . ," Flynn (Dora), Memnoch, Watcher.

Silver bracelet   Mael gives Jesse a silver bracelet after she leaves the Sonoma compound. On it are carved ancient symbols of the gods

and goddesses of the Druids. The bracelet disappears after Jesse's ordeal in New Orleans, then reappears again once Jesse has recovered from an illness and has gone to work in India. When Jesse finds the bracelet, she begins to sort out things about her visit to Sonoma that had previously been confused in her mind. At that point, she realizes what Mael is—a vampire. Her enlightenment leads her to Lestat, which results in events through which she becomes a vampire. Thus Mael's bracelet is a foreshadowing of what Jesse is to become. *(QD 161, 187, 189)*

See also Jesse, Mael.

Skin In mythology, skin is often associated with birth and rebirth. This is both because, when born, the infant passes through the skin, and because individuals, as they develop and grow, shed and renew their skin. As a mortal transforms into a vampire, his skin undergoes a similar transformation: the skin becomes an indestructible white substance and flushes only after the drinking of blood. It is sensitive to cold and heat, and is highly flexible. Louis first appears to the boy reporter as almost a cartoon character because of his white, unlined skin. *(IV 3)*

As vampires age, their skin grows harder: Akasha's skin, like that of the rest of the First Brood, feels as hard as marble. When exposed to sun, the toughest skin becomes bronzed, but the weaker skin of younger, less powerful vampires burns or disintegrates. *(VL 432–433, 448)*

See also Appearance, Vampire.

Slavery The exploitation of one person by another. Images of slavery in the film *Dracula* influenced Rice when she was writing IV. However, the idea of vampire slavery is not apparent in the rest of the *Chronicles*, for it is subsumed by the larger and more complex theme of dominance and submission in vampire relationships. "It [slavery] caught my attention at the time [of the writing of IV]," says Rice. "I may have been thinking of Renfield [a character in *Dracula* who is enslaved by the vampire]."

When Louis tells Lestat he wants to seek out other vampires, Lestat warns him that vampires are loners, and that in those instances where he finds several together, it is often the case that one will be the slave of the other. "That's how vampires increase," Lestat says, "through slavery." *(IV 84)* By this he means that one vampire makes another only if that other can serve his needs—and that the same situation applies to him and Louis, whom he made. Louis tries to discount this view of himself since in their relationship he does retain financial control, but he soon realizes that the monetary control—and, indeed, his entire sense of control—is an illusion. *(IV 123)*

The issue of vampire slavery revolves around the dynamic of dominance and submission. Louis is not forced to be a slave; he chooses this mode of existence. Although Louis does leave Lestat at Claudia's instigation, he continues his submissive pattern by becoming a slave to Claudia. He needs her to give shape and purpose to his life.

In many ways, Armand is like Louis in this regard. When he tells his story to Lestat and Gabrielle, it is clear that Armand easily falls under the spell, and thus becomes dependent upon anything or anyone that strongly attracts him. Thus his form of being enslaved derives from a personality trait that traps him in a submissive mode, one that provokes him into manipulating others to dominate him.

The relationship between Louis and Armand is extremely interesting, for both want to become a slave to the other. Armand wants to fall under Louis's spell and become connected to the age, while Louis wants Armand to guide him into deeper levels of vampire existence. Their relationship loses its spark when Claudia is destroyed, and Louis loses his passivity. Armand then just drifts along until he finds Daniel, whom he plays upon in the same manipulative way. *(IV 338–340, QD 83–92)*

Slavery is also significant in Louis's life in another way; he had been the master of slaves before he had become a vampire. He had operated a large plantation, Pointe du Lac, during the late 1700s, and he believed that his slaves were childlike savages. After he becomes a vampire, though, he realizes that many of his slaves are intelligent and astute, so much so that they suspect what his new nature is. Aware of Lestat's coffin, mysterious deaths in the area, and the facade Lestat and Louis put on, these slaves plot to destroy the vampires. In order to escape, Louis must set fire to the plantation and, with Lestat, flee to New Orleans. *(IV 27–29, 49–57)*

See also Armand, Daniel (slave), Dominance/Submission, Louis de Pointe du Lac, Pointe du Lac.

Sleep   See Death Sleep.

"Sleeping Beauty"   A fairy tale about a princess who is cursed by a witch to remain in a deep sleep until a prince comes to her and kisses her awake. The tale symbolizes dormant intuitions and passive potential. One of Rice's favorite fairy tales, she utilizes the image of the sleeping woman to describe Gabrielle in her vampire sleep, and Akasha's wakening from her trance by the call of her "prince," Lestat.

Lestat also refers to Sleeping Beauty when he first sees Armand at the Palais Royal. It is as if Armand has been kissed by a prince and has awakened to a beautiful new world. *(VL 275, 484, QD 2)*

See also Armand.

Snow   A symbol of purity, coldness, and penitential suffering, snow shows up in several key scenes in the *Chronicles*. When Lestat grows depressed over his compulsion to kill, he dreams of winters in the Auvergne when he killed the wolves, and he goes to see David, where it is snowing. Ice and snow cover his cold skin, mirroring his frame of mind. *(BT 39–40)* "Lestat kept remembering that last [mortal] winter," Rice said, "which was actually a terrible time. It was part of his penitential quest to go right back to that kind of pain and cold."

Akasha and Enkil are taken to a fortress of ice and snow, one which symbolizes their catatonic state. As vampires who take no blood, their skin is whiter and chillier than that of vampires who drink frequently. *(QD 23)*

After Akasha abducts Lestat from his retreat in Carmel Valley, she takes him to his childhood home in the Auvergne where it is wintertime. There she tells him that she intends to be a goddess of a new world. The cold climate there in the Auvergne parallels the coldness and desolation of Akasha's plan—which is to manipulate human evolution as if the members of the human race are just pawns to serve her purposes. *(QD 254)* Then she takes Lestat to slaughter Azim and his male worshipers. During and after this rampage, snow falls, covering the corpses and falling on Akasha as she illustrates her plan more fully to Lestat. *(QD 286)*

In BT, when Raglan James outlines for Lestat a plan for switching bodies, Lestat agrees to go to Georgetown, where it is cold, to make the switch. The low temperatures remind him of his childhood winters, and of the winter when Magnus carried him off. When he temporarily becomes a mortal there, two blizzards strike the town. These conditions provide the perfect setting for how Lestat's new heavier body feels to him: just as what happens to humans during a snowstorm, Lestat, too, is moving more slowly and experiencing a dimming of his senses. *(BT 199)*

Lestat makes his decision during the winter to go with Memnoch, and when he returns from Hell, he encounters Manhattan's worst snowstorm in fifty years. *(MD 29, 95, 324)*

See also Georgetown, Weather.

Solitaire   A card game—which is played alone—that Lestat enjoys on the night of Louis's first kill. It shows his lack of connection with Louis and makes Louis feel isolated from and resentful of Lestat. *(IV 30)*

Claudia, too, plays solitaire, on board the *Mariana* and in Paris—indicating that vampires are loners. After she is dead, Louis thinks it is ironic that while she is the one who played the game of solitaire, it is he who is ending up alone. *(IV 164)*

Sorcerer's apprentice   How Louis refers to himself when he tells Claudia that his role in making her a vampire was minor. He is reneging on his own responsibility by framing himself as a passive participant. *(IV 210)*

See also Claudia, Louis de Pointe du Lac.

Sonoma compound   Maharet's primary residence in Sonoma County, California, it is located outside Santa Rosa, at the end of an unpaved road. Here she keeps records of the Great Family. Maharet invites Jesse to visit her here for two weeks.

The location was based on a house Rice once owned in the redwood forest, near Mark West Creek. She used her memories of the place to get the feel of the woods and capture the right noises. "What was beautiful about the place," she says, "was the primal untouched quality of the creek. It was a blessed spot." The compound is much more elaborate in style than was Rice's home there.

As seen through Jesse's eyes in QD, the Sonoma compound is a rambling structure built into the foot of a mountain. Folklore typically views the hollow of a mountain as a "philosopher's oven," and psychologists see it as a symbol for the unconscious. Inside the house are spacious rooms, ancient art, and massive furnishings that have a medieval grandeur. In the cellar is a movie theater, and in the library are numerous volumes that trace family lineages. *(QD 152–153)*

Jesse first encounters vampires at this place, although at the time she is not aware of that fact. Only later, when she reads about Louis and Lestat in their respective autobiographies, does she realize that the "eccentricities" of Maharet and her companions match those of vampires.

The compound serves as a place of protection, where the vampires who have escaped Akasha's slaughter gather to form a plan of resistance. After listening to Maharet's story of how the vampire race began and of who Akasha is, they decide on a moral position that rejects Akasha and her vision. When Akasha arrives at the compound, she offers to make them her angels, then threatens to destroy them when they decline. Her last stand takes place at the compound, for it is here that Mekare destroys Akasha. *(QD 265–285, 454)*

The vampires remain at the compound after her death, until they feel strong enough to venture out to Armand's Night Island. (See Vampire Atlas)

See also The Gathering of Immortals, Jesse, Maharet, Moral Dilemma.

Soul   The sentient, immaterial part of a person that endures beyond the death of the body. It contains the thoughts, feelings, attitudes, hopes, and fears of the individual. In early civilizations, it was believed that the animating spirit, or soul, came from the body's blood, which was influenced by the cycles of the moon. "Heart's blood" was even another name for the soul. At that time, mothers were thought to be the givers of the soul, but in later patriarchal cultures, that power was attributed to semen.

One belief of early Christianity was that the soul had both a male and a female part. Christ had redeemed the male part, but since the female part needed a female savior, it remained unredeemed. In QD, Akasha attempts to be such a female savior and to create a new age based on matriarchy.

In folklore, vampires were believed to possess no soul because they were creatures of the dead. This is why they ostensibly showed no reflection in mirrors. The vampires in the *Chronicles*, however, are a fusion of spirit and flesh, and retain the emotions, memories, hopes, and fears of their mortal existence. Since there is no God to prohibit them from having souls, they do not lose that part of themselves with the physical death of their bodies, and continue to see their reflections in mirrors. Louis, however, does not realize this while he is still a fledgling. Tied to his Catholic beliefs and uncertain as to God's existence, he wonders if his eyes appear soulless to mortals, and whether he is drawn to the mortal Babette because the greatness of her soul is a complement to his lack of one. *(IV 64)*

The Druids tell Marius that when he is made into a god, his soul will remain trapped in this one form—his body—for eternity. They consider this a terrible fate because it will not allow him to experience the cycle of death and rebirth. This is why the burned vampire god Marius is replacing tells him to always scatter the ashes of vampires who go into the fire; only that action will free their souls. When Marius later sees the ashes of vampires burned in their crypts, he then wonders if their souls are still trapped in their ashes. *(VL 408, 429)*

Soul plays a central role in BT, when Raglan James approaches Lestat with a deal: he offers to switch bodies and allow Lestat to be mortal for a day. Such a switch is possible because the soul is composed of two parts. The higher, or astral, soul is able to leave the body, either to travel spiritually or to inhabit the body of another person. The residual, or primitive, soul remains anchored to the brain stem, keeping the body alive. It wants to reunite with the higher soul to complete itself, and will welcome its other half (or another higher soul) back into the body. Generally, the higher soul remains earthbound unless it sees a doorway to the Light, which will open only when the entire soul is released from the body. Ghosts who are earthbound either have not found or have not acknowledged this gateway. *(BT 122–123, 144–145, 157)*

"There's a long tradition of belief," says Rice, "that there are two or three different souls. In some form, Egyptian religion deals with it, but it was very popular with the English spiritualists at the end of the last century—the psychic investigators who studied astral projection. They talked about a cord connecting into the body and about different levels of the soul—an invisible soul and an etheric soul. I was basically trying to reason out my cosmology based on that evidence. The most compelling occult literature to me is the near-death experiences, the accounts of ghosts, and the accounts of astral traveling."

Rice took her research even further as she developed the cosmology of creation. *Memnoch the Devil* describes his experience of the creation of human souls and his horror of their abandonment by God. When Memnoch enters Sheol, he encounters all the human souls that have separated from their bodies. Some souls die, their essence dispersed. Others are strengthened by attention from the living. Still others become gods or oracles, demanding sacrifice and war, or go back to earth to possess human bodies. These souls remain closest to Earth. Those that have accepted their death and can forgive God for all that has been a part of their existence are closest to Heaven. *(MD 215–216)*

An Egyptian symbol of the soul

When Memnoch insists that human souls are worthy of Heaven, God sends him to Sheol to find ten worthy to stand in His presence. Memnoch wanders among these souls, realizing that they tend to gather according to like minds, forming tiers. "There was an order born out of the degree of each soul's awareness, acceptance, confusion, or wrath." *(MD 249)* Those closest to earth still have fleshly appetites, as was the case with the spirit Amel, who made the vampires. Most of them have some kind of preoccupation or obsession with their lot. "There is no such thing as a soul who loves nothing. He or she loves something, even if it exists only in memory or as an ideal." *(MD 249)* The brightest and most substantial souls are serene and accepting. They have let go of the need to comprehend mortal mysteries, and they have no resentment. Based on the criteria he formed from conversing with them, Memnoch takes these Illuminated ones to Heaven, and God accepts them. *(MD 248–257, 300)*

However, Memnoch feels that all souls should have the opportunity to gain access to Heaven, not just the most loving. If they were educated, they would understand and accept and become worthy. Eventually, God responds to Memnoch's concern by becoming a man and dying to redeem more souls. Memnoch, however, believes that, to be redeemed, a soul needs only an eye for beauty and should not have to endure suffering: "What did the suffering teach Job that he didn't know before?" *(MD 301)*

God assigns Hell (or Sheol) to Memnoch as an educational ground for the remaining souls who cannot accept His sacrifice. Memnoch shows this place to Lestat, who is horrified to realize that Hell is

a place where souls must confront their victims from their earthly life. *(MD 308–320)*

See also Amel, Astral Projection, Body, Body Switching, God, Heaven, Hell, Human Evolution, James (Raglan), Ka, Memnoch, Sheol, Suffering, Thirteen Revelations of Physical Evolution.

Soul switching   See Body Switching.

South Beach   Lestat temporarily stays in this area of Miami Beach, in the Park Central Hotel. South Beach runs for a square mile and is packed with 870 buildings. Many vintage-style hotels and restaurants make up this pastel and neon art deco district, which is an international mecca for the contemporary fashion crowd. The Park Central is a famous hotel specializing in nostalgia. Lestat loves South Beach for its art deco styles and colors. It is clean and thriving, with a drowsy but relentless atmosphere that is flavored by international cuisine and music.

Rice puts Lestat in South Beach because of her own affection for the place. She had stayed in one of the hotels on Ocean Avenue and loved the constant activity all around her. To her mind, Miami Beach—particularly the South Beach area—was a perfect vampire's city.

Here Lestat tracks and kills a serial killer who is stalking the back streets of South Beach. He then kills an elderly woman who was the killer's intended victim. As he goes out to the ocean to ponder his vampire nature, he spots Raglan James, who tosses a story by H. P. Lovecraft about body switching at him. (See Vampire Atlas)

See also Miami, Park Central Hotel.

Southern Comfort   Bourbon whiskey mixed with fresh peaches and peach liqueur.

This whiskey is Roger's favorite drink. He orders it in the bar where he appears to Lestat as a ghost and, despite the lore that ghosts cannot actually eat or swallow, drinks it. *(MD 50)*

See also Ghost, Roger.

Sow's ear   A reference to the quote, "You can't make a silk purse from a sow's ear," from Jonathan Swift's *Polite Conversations*. It is what Louis calls Lestat in contempt, implying that Lestat is inferior material, too vulgar to appreciate his vampiric state. *(IV 30)*

Spanish Hotel   Where Louis and Lestat stay during their first nights in New Orleans after fleeing Pointe du Lac. It is here that Louis seriously ponders the question of leaving Lestat. They have a fight, after which Lestat says they will talk. The next night, Lestat brings in two whores. He kills one and Louis finishes off the other when he tires

St. Louis Hotel in New Orleans

of Lestat's cruelty to her. That same night, Lestat brings Claudia to their rooms and makes her a vampire. *(IV 71, 90–95)*

In the first draft of IV, the hotel was the St. Louis Hotel. However, since at that time (1795) the city was in Spanish hands, Rice changed the reference. The St. Louis Hotel is located on 730 Bienville Street in the French Quarter. (See Vampire Atlas)

Spell-bind   How Lestat refers to the vampiric ability to confuse mortals by scrambling their thoughts. By spell-binding Lestat can obtain information or do something without invoking suspicion. *(BT 344)*

See also Seduction, Vampire Powers.

Spirits   Huge, seemingly invisible, whirling bodies of energy that hover over the physical world and play an integral part in the origin of

vampirism. "I'm developing my cosmology of what spirits are all the time," said Rice, "but it's primarily fed by things that were believed in the spiritualist movement in the nineteenth century."

Rice's spirits can move with the swiftness of thought, never age, possess distinct personalities, and are attracted to certain people, called witches. They have no moral code, and are thus morally inferior to humans, yet are still thought to be either good or bad. The good spirits want to give and receive love; the bad simply desire attention and play tricks on humans to get it. Giving them attention strengthens them.

While sharing the same DNA as humans, these spirits have a more complex makeup. Their double helix is twice the length of that of humans, contains ninety-two chromosomes, and has similarities to the DNA structure of lower life-forms. The spirits possess highly resistant immune systems, highly developed perception, and elastic cells that can die in intense heat or cold, leaving behind no residue.

Spirits respond to visible and auditory patterns, and are especially attuned to the rhythmical organization of music, which gives them a sense of order that both enchants and distracts them. Often witches deliberately use music to confuse and trap the spirits.

"If spirits exist," says Rice, "they respond to pattern and ornament. I once read about an idea—I think I got it from Henri Bergson—about how the brain would just dream endlessly if it didn't have the physical necessity to take care of the body. That's where I got the idea that the spirits drift around in unconcentrated form. When they're drawn together by a powerful emotion, then they can see and focus."

Rice's spirits can project themselves in several voices, thus making themselves heard either physically or telepathically, as an inner voice. Yet to achieve any form of self-awareness requires supreme concentration, and some desire the form of flesh in order to retain more easily whatever sense of self they acquire. Otherwise, they dream and drift about without self-knowledge, and most are unaware of time and/or purpose.

Although in VL Lestat hears about the spirit that entered the first vampires, Akasha and Enkil, the entire story is not told until the third *Vampire Chronicle*. Maharet, a witch who had lived in Egypt during Akasha's reign as a mortal queen, tells of how she and her sister, Mekare, attracted and manipulated spirits for good purposes. Mekare can actually see the spirits, and claims that they have a tiny physical core that allows them to interact with the physical realm. *(QD 150, 306–311, 316–321)*

These spirits are not to be confused with ghosts (who once had a physical body), although they are able to participate in poltergeist activity as well. As matter and energy in a sophisticated balance, the spirits can move objects and make wind and rain. Through their ability to communicate telepathically, they can tell secrets about the future.

Possessing no sense of right or wrong and no biological needs, they often act on whim, but what they really want is attention and love. Some of the spirits envy humans their fleshly form and the "bad" spirits lust after physical pleasures. Maharet hypothesizes that malevolent spirits may have been former ghosts who have forgotten they once lived; that may be why they envy the flesh so much. And their obsession with the erotic may be merely abstracted from the minds of humans who feel ashamed of sex. *(QD 157)*

The spirit Amel is known to both Mekare and Maharet. He is a bad spirit, powerful and envious. To get their attention, he brags that he has managed to pierce flesh and taste blood. They ignore these claims, but it is Amel who eventually initiates the spirit/body fusion that makes a mortal into a vampire. When Akasha and Enkil are wounded in an assassination attempt, Amel enters Akasha through her wounds. Amel's spiritual substance fuses with Akasha's cells and changes them. As Akasha's body is dying, the core of Amel merges with her flesh, and its energy with her soul. This spirit then finds a special organ, the heart (and/or possibly the brain), with which to join its own physical core. This interaction is possible because Amel's cells are made of DNA and amino acids, just like Akasha's are. As his spirit anchors itself in Akasha's physical cells, it gradually transforms those cells into immortal substance. Amel's blood thirst is then transferred to her and she drinks from Enkil, giving him in return the blood that Amel invaded. *(QD 319, 400–409, 422)*

When Akasha passes her blood to Enkil, then to others, they in turn pass it on to their own progeny. Amel's enormous form thus disperses through them all, making them as leaves of the same vine. They are interconnected by virtue of his size, and made immortal by the nature of his being, which has come to them through the blood. The vampires are thus a combination of spirit and body—like mortals—but Amel's spirit has transformed their bodies into a substance that can endure accident and disease and will resist change through eternity.

The new spiritual nature of their bodies gives them a lightness of step and the ability to jump high and even to levitate themselves or fly. As the spirit has an intuitive sense of direction and a lack of boundaries, vampires find that when the mortal habits of their minds let go, almost anything is possible. Their new bodies can now obey swiftly and completely whatever is willed, from lifting an object to exploding someone's heart. Vampires who want to fully utilize their power merely need to decide what it is they wish to do and then surrender to their power; their desire is then immediately accomplished. *(QD 336–348)*

The "good" spirits abandon Maharet and Mekare when they become vampires. Although as witches they had looked to the spirits,

Maharet comes to tell her daughter, Miriam, to stay away from them. She believes that spirits have no real value in the course of human evolution and that humanity is better off if it progresses away from spirit-based religions. *(QD 414, 422, 424)*

In MD, spirits are equated with souls of the dead. Memnoch mentions that Amel is one type of human soul that, after death, still possesses fleshly appetites. As he explains it, the human spirit evolved out of matter. This made the angels who were watching the process uneasy because they feared God might be replacing them, and they also questioned the wisdom of death and decay. They saw spirits of dying people surrounding the earth, "Souls drifting forever and ever." *(MD 202)* This place of hovering spirits was known as Sheol.

The angels perceive that the spirits or souls are individuals of differing degrees of intellect. Attention from living humans back on earth strengthens them, and some become as gods to their descendants. *(MD 201, 214–215)* Memnoch claims that the human spirit sets man apart from nature and puts him closer to divinity. As such, human souls should have a better quality of life than the suffering they are forced to endure on earth, and have access to Heaven. *(MD 262)*

See also Amel, Blood, Body, Human Evolution, Memnoch, Nature, Sheol, Thirteen Revelations of Physical Evolution, Vampire, Vine.

Spiritual, The   Sacred matters, such as those that Lestat and Armand discuss in VL. Armand tells how, after he became a vampire, a satanic coven of vampires apprenticed him to their Dark Ways. He became a missionary and perfected the act of killing by drawing only those victims to him who actually wanted to die. He felt that his way of being a vampire was spiritual because it was uncontaminated by appetite and developed through meditation and self-denial. When he killed, the spiritual and the carnal blended together. It seemed to him to echo the Christian communion, and put him on a par with the saints.

When Armand's way of life ends with Lestat's arrival in Paris, Lestat urges Armand to see that such spirituality can also be found in other types of visions, such as art. Armand eventually decides to continue with his spiritual visions through the Theater of the Vampires. *(VL 301–304, 312–313, 315)*

Two centuries later, Armand's thirst for the spiritual culminates in his self-destruction. Lestat shows him Veronica's veil and describes what he thinks he saw in Heaven and Hell. Although Lestat warns him that the veil proves nothing, Armand surrenders to it fully. To Lestat's astonishment, he goes out into the sun and allows himself to burn in a ball of fire to affirm the veil's authenticity. Armand wants to go to God. *(MD 335)*

Lestat also talks about the nature of the spiritual with David Talbot, when they look at Rembrandt's paintings together. David claims that only mortals possess true spiritual vision, such as that which is evident in the faces Rembrandt depicts. Lestat is upset that he, as a vampire, has no access to this special type of knowledge, and eventually he agrees with David. He thinks that Rembrandt sold his soul to the Devil in order to gain talent and fame, but because he was so spiritual and sought so hard to render a vision of goodness, God redeemed him. *(BT 34–38)*

See also Armand, Eucharist, Religion, Rembrandt van Rijn, Saint, Those Who Want to Die, Transubstantiation.

Spreckles Mansion   A mansion on the edge of Buena Vista Park in San Francisco, this was where a friend of Rice's lived during her early years in the city. "My friend Jack lived [there] in a big ballroom apartment attic," she recalled. "It was a squarish house, impressive in a simple way. I remember the red velvet cushions in the window seats and its views in different directions. How Gothic and strange it seemed, like a dreamy stage set for our emotional discussions." The house later became a bed and breakfast.

Like Rice's friend, Roger lives in the attic of the Spreckles Mansion. The rock band he manages rehearses in the mansion's ballroom. It was in this house that Roger launched his career as a killer. *(MD 66–68)*

See also Roger, San Francisco.

Springsteen, Bruce   A contemporary rock singer to whose singing style Baby Jenks compares Lestat's, although Rice actually modeled it on Jim Morrison's. *(QD 49)*

See also Rock Star.

Sri Lanka   A small island located south of India, it is the second place Akasha visits on her bloody rampage. There she shows Lestat the poverty of most third world countries, then urges the country's women to rise up and kill the men. The women see her as a goddess and savior, and do her bidding. *(QD 300–305, 379)* (See Vampire Atlas)

See also Akasha's Plan, *The Queen of the Damned.*

Stake   One of the superstitions in vampire lore, particularly since Bram Stoker's *Dracula*, is that a stake hammered through the heart of a vampire will destroy it.

Morgan witnesses this in a village in Eastern Europe and conveys the horror of this act to Louis. Louis has already told the boy reporter

that a stake's ability to destroy a vampire is a myth. However, in the first draft of IV, Louis admits that stakes could indeed have a deadly effect: driving a stake through the heart destroys it, and pins the help-less vampire to the coffin, where he can bleed to death. *(IV 23)*

See also Superstitions.

Stalker   See Memnoch.

Stanford Wilde   See Wilde, Stanford.

Stanhope Hotel   A small luxury hotel at 995 Fifth Avenue, across from the Metropolitan Museum of Art. Lestat claims that this is his favorite hotel in Manhattan. The public rooms here are adorned with French antiques. *(BT 128)*

Lestat tells David that he maintains rooms at this hotel. He loves the huge display of fresh flowers in the lobby. He wanders in one day to smell them and gets his first real glimpse of Memnoch. He has a vision of being surrounded by people who are laughing, talking, and crying, and he sees a frightening creature, "the worst thing I'd ever seen." *(MD 21–22, 102)* (See Vampire Atlas)

"Like many famous people," says Rice, "Lestat makes no secret whatsoever of where he lives. Most people assume he doesn't exist. He frequently slips into the Stanhope via its beautiful lobby late at night."

See also Lestat de Lioncourt, Memnoch.

Stanhope Hotel, where Lestat saw Memnoch

Stars   Seen as points of light in the night sky, they are associated with spirit, multiplicity, and destiny. The vampires often look up at the stars in moments of contemplation, wonder, and despair, such as when Louis crosses the Atlantic Ocean and when Daniel is made a vampire. *(IV 164, QD 113)*

"I don't like the stars," Rice admits. "They frighten me. Stars are a reminder of horrible things. They look beautiful but they have to do with the vastness and mystery of the universe. To Lestat, they signify the indifference of the Savage Garden where only aesthetics seem to matter: things are beautiful but nobody cares what you feel."

See also Pleiades, Savage Garden.

Starvation   The inability to get blood for survival. Some vampires use starvation as a means of punishing others, as when Armand seals vampires into tombs below Les Innocents. Louis believes this will happen to him when Santiago locks him into a coffin, but Armand rescues him the following night. Lestat starves himself when he goes into the ground in Cairo and later in New Orleans. Starvation can alter a vampire's temperament, as it does with Nicolas when Armand locks him up. Maddened, he slips into a long period of silence, then decides to commit suicide. *(VL 211, 342, IV 300)*

See also Blood, Entombed Vampires, First Death, Nicolas de Lenfent.

State of Grace   See Redemption.

Stations of the Cross   Also known as the Way of the Cross, these are depictions of the fourteen events Christ experienced on his journey to Calvary. They might be in the form of paintings or statues. Worshipers stop at each station, bow in respect, and say a prayer as they meditate on Christ's suffering. The sixth station features Veronica wiping Christ's face.

Roger owns a collection of paintings that Lestat recognizes as the Stations of the Cross. He also sees the religious series hung in the chapel at St. Elizabeth's, where Rice has placed her own collection. *(MD 99–100, 113)*

"I knew the story of Veronica's veil principally through the devotion of the Stations of the Cross," said Rice. "We often had them in church; the entire congregation would read aloud the prayers for each station. The priest and the altar boys would move from station to station. I always loved the station where Veronica wipes the face of Jesus."

See also Christ, Religious Relics/Artifacts, St. Elizabeth's Orphanage, Veronica's Veil.

Steam   In legends and fiction, vampires are said to have the ability to transform into mist or steam and go through keyholes. The boy reporter asks Louis about this myth, but Louis assures him there is no truth to it. *(IV 22)*

See also Keyholes, Superstitions.

Stevenson, Dr. Ian   A professor of psychiatry at the University of Virginia School of Medicine. He is mentioned in QD as a researcher who works in the field of reincarnation. His books include *Twenty Cases Suggestive of Reincarnation* and *Telepathic Impression*. His studies inspired the Talamasca to send Jesse to India, to document cases of children reporting past lives. She finds over three hundred such cases. *(QD 189)*

See also Reincarnation.

Stigmata   Marks on the hands and feet that suddenly appear, bleed spontaneously, can feel painful, and whose placement corresponds to Christ's wounds where he was nailed to the cross. The marks manifest themselves on exceptionally devout people—usually those who become saints—who often experience them during times of religious ecstasy. They are considered a brand of sorts, marking the believer as one of Christ's own.

Gretchen, Lestat's lover while he is in a mortal form, confesses that as a child she had prayed for such a miracle to happen to her. She had wanted to be extraordinary. When Lestat comes to her later in the form of a vampire, she is astonished, then repulsed. When she spurns him and prays to God, her hands and feet bleed profusely. The event shows how Lestat has become, ironically, a symbol of God; by showing himself as a devil, he inspires great faith in people, who recognize that if there is a devil, there must be a God. *(BT 357)*

As a child, Rice had read about the lives of saints who had experienced the stigmata, and she, too, had prayed fervently to be blessed with such recognition from God. She had wanted to be a saint, but not just an everyday, mediocre saint. She had wanted to be one of the special ones who are marked by God for being the epitome of religious devotion.

See also Gretchen, Saint.

Stoker, Bram   Author of *Dracula*. See *Dracula*.

Stoker, Dr. Alexander   The alias David Talbot uses to board the *QE2* with Lestat as they pursue Raglan James. He poses as a retired surgeon and pretends to the *QE2* crew to be Raglan James's personal

physician. The name itself is a reference to Bram Stoker, who authored *Dracula*. *(BT 299)*

See also *Dracula, Queen Elizabeth 2*.

Story of Creation   See *Memnoch the Devil*, Thirteen Revelations of Physical Evolution.

Stradivarius   See Violin.

Strasbourg   The site in the Alsace region between Germany and France where, in 1349, two thousand Jews were burned. They were blamed for the Black Death spreading through Europe at the time.

Memnoch mentions this event as part of the bloody history of Christianity. *(MD 287)*

See also Christianity.

Strength   See Aging, Self-confidence, Vampire Powers.

Substance   Physical material from which things are made, this is a central theme of *The Vampire Chronicles*. "One of the major themes in QD," Rice asserts, "is that the flesh teaches all wisdom. When we become unanchored and get into abstract thinking, that's where the real danger lies. Substance is its own great teacher; I feel a real connection with that idea. What the flesh desires is not necessarily bad, but requires exploration and attention."

Rice believes strongly that truth is derived from the physical world, and she selected her husband's poetry about substance to reinforce in her novels the importance of the material world. She wanted particularly to show that the "supernatural" realm of the vampires was really nothing more than an extension of the natural world, and emphasized that her vampires are anchored in their bodies.

For example, the Druids tell Marius that his soul will remain forever in the same form—his body. And as Jesse becomes a vampire, she sees the souls of the dead who have no form, which contrasts with her own feeling that the powerful blood has tied her to her physical substance forever. Maharet tells her to trust this feeling because all wisdom comes from the flesh. Similarly, Claudia urges Louis to put away his books and allow his "flesh" to instruct his mind. *(IV 122, VL 408, QD 41, 119, 241)*

See also Body, Poetry, *The Queen of the Damned*, Rice (Stan), "Texas Suite."

Subterranean room   Underground rooms in literature or folklore often represent the subconscious, and it is in just such a room that

Art from the Subterranean room: The Triumph of Death *by Pieter Brueghel the Elder.*

a vampire coven—creatures of the shadow—reveals itself to Louis and Claudia. It is a spacious ballroom beneath the Theater of the Vampires, which is carved out of an ancient cellar and shrouded in darkness.

Armand lights a candle, which illuminates a series of long mirrors and numerous paintings on the walls. The frescoes and murals are vivid and colorful, and Louis recognizes some, such as Brueghel's *The Triumph of Death*, *The Fall of the Angels*, and other paintings depicting hideous figures of death or instruments of torture.

Rice says, "I was very interested in the Northern European artists at that time—Brueghel, Dürer, Bosch—painters who I felt were absolutely grotesque in many regards."

Louis has the impression that the room is a cathedral of death. The juxtaposition of vampires with art of the most grim nature reinforces the fact that all derive from the same source inside the psyche— the shadow realm, which consists of primal fears and animal instinct. In this room Louis learns about Armand and realizes that the coven of vampires all wear black. It is here he is sentenced to remain for eternity nailed inside a coffin, while Claudia is condemned to die by exposure

435

Succubus, a female sex demon

to the sun. Claudia is destroyed, but Louis manages to escape. *(IV 228–230, VL 505)*

See also Art, Theater of the Vampires.

Succubus   A demon that assumes female form in order to have sexual intercourse with men as they sleep, the act of which manifests itself in their dreams.

Lestat views Armand as a sort of succubus in the way that Armand has invaded his private dreams and used them to attempt to seduce him. *(VL 201)*

See also Armand, Demons.

Sucking   See Bite, Vampire's Kiss.

Sudden death   One of the mortal fears that the vampires retain is that of instantaneous destruction. Louis claims that Lestat told him that there are people and types of things that can cause sudden death in a vampire, but he does not elaborate. Apparently these dark hints were only a ploy on Lestat's part to keep Louis with him, although the story, when told from Lestat's perspective, implies that Louis just interpreted this incorrectly. Only fire and the sun can cause sudden death in a vampire—and even the sun is not effective against the strongest vampires. *(IV 61, VL 498)*

See also Fire, Sun, Superstitions, Ways of Dying.

Suffering   Part of the vampire's lot as an immortal, suffering arises in many forms. For vampires, their experience of pain is more intense than that of mortals; because of their heightened senses, they "feel it like no other creatures." *(IV 88)* As an older vampire, Lestat says, "You'll know so much about suffering that you will go through rapid cycles of cruelty and kindness, insight and maniacal blindness. You'll probably go mad. Then you'll be sane again." *(MD 4)*

First they must experience the aches and pains of their body as it dies. They then must endure the psychological changes involved in transforming from mortal to immortal, especially those that involve loss: they remain the same as the world changes; they have to deal with monotony and boredom over centuries; they often grieve over mortals with whom they were once connected and who eventually die. Their conscience may also suffer, as with Louis and Lestat, who cannot tolerate that what they are compelled to do is evil. And there is also the agony experienced by those vampires, like Magnus and Claudia, who are destroyed in fire or sunlight. *(IV 21, 169, 285, 306, VL 96)*

The experience of suffering can either destroy or strengthen the vampires. It often inspires the first death or even the extreme of going into the fire. Yet those who endure it are deepened, gaining—as Lestat

describes it—a "greater luster" and "richer resonance." *(QD 3)* Lestat, however, also claims that he is meaner and more conscientious as a result of his ordeals, and that while they make him more clearly a vampire, the fact that he can still suffer profoundly also makes the human in him rise closer to the surface. *(VL 357–359, QD 1)*

Tracing suffering back to the beginning of creation, Rice explores it from the Devil's point of view. Memnoch fails to understand why God includes suffering as part of His plan for humankind, not even when God explains that it brings humans closer to Himself. The apparent necessity of suffering in God's creation is the major issue in Memnoch's resistance to singing God's praises. As humans evolve and suffering increases, Memnoch intercedes to urge God to find a different direction. He manages to persuade God to accept human souls into Heaven, but when only a fraction gain entrance, Memnoch continues to implore God on behalf of all the others.

God finally listens and comes to Earth to live as a man. He tells Memnoch He now knows what humans suffer, but Memnoch insists that he does not: all along He has known that He is the immortal God, so even in the material form of a man, He has not truly experienced suffering. God explains that He will die a horrible death on the cross, which angers Memnoch; to his mind, God's plan for the redemption of human souls rests on the worst and most bloody human superstitions. It can only engender more bloodshed and suffering—which it does. Memnoch shows the violent history of Christianity to Lestat and asks him to judge. *(MD 250–255, 272–280, 288–290)*

Lestat cannot endure what he witnesses, particularly when he sees the form of suffering inflicted on souls in Hell. Before they can be free, they must face their victims and learn forgiveness. Lestat has also witnessed the suffering of Christ. When Lestat visited Heaven, God showed Himself to Lestat in His suffering. This gave force to His plea that Lestat not be His adversary. *(MD 310–321)*

Lestat himself suffers from the ambiguity of it all, for he cannot tell if what the Devil has shown him is real or an illusion. He only knows that what he saw will haunt him forever and that he will never again feel safe. *(MD 350, 353)*

See also Christ, Christianity, Desert, First Death, God, Hell, Human Evolution, Memnoch, *Memnoch the Devil*, Senses, Sheol, Soul, Vampire, Thirteen Revelations of Physical Evolution.

"Suffer the little children to come unto me"

A phrase Christ used, quoted in Matthew 19:14, in response to one of the disciples who had been trying to prevent the children from approaching Him.

Claudia uses this quotation with Lestat when she presents him with the two boys through whom she wants to poison him. *(IV 134)*

See also Bible, Claudia, Victims.

Suicide   When immortality becomes a burden, some vampires contemplate, and some actually commit, suicide.

First as a mortal, Louis contemplates suicide. After his brother's death, he falls into a paralyzing despair. He wants to die and so puts himself into dangerous situations that make him vulnerable to a vampire, Lestat. Part of Louis's attraction to becoming a vampire is his wish to die, and he asks Lestat to kill him. When Lestat moves to do so, Louis fights him off, showing that he does not truly want to die. Instead, he becomes a vampire, yet even then he does not really live. He suffers guilt for two centuries over the fact that he must kill. *(IV 10, 16, 17, BT 104–105)*

In BT, after Lestat kills an old woman whom he attempted to save from a serial killer, he falls into a depression. Deciding it is time to end his existence, he flies to the Gobi to expose himself to the intense sun. The plan fails when he survives the exposure and, indeed, is strengthened by it. *(BT 46–48)*

In the first draft of IV, Armand agrees to mutually commit suicide with Louis by going into the sun, *if* that is what Louis really believes they should do; Louis's arguments have convinced him that what they do is evil. Louis, however, recognizes that he does not wish to end his existence, and demurs.

Those who do destroy themselves include Magnus, who jumps into a fire; Nicolas, who requests Armand's assistance in ending his life; and Armand and Mael, who both go into the sun. *(VL 96, 343, MD 335, 337)*

See also Armand, Desert, Fire, Lestat de Lioncourt, Mael, Magnus, Nicolas de Lenfent, Sun, Ways of Dying.

Sun   A symbol of divinity and spiritual enlightenment, it is a metaphor of grace. As such, vampires are unable to endure the rays of the sun. Vampire lore and literature says that the reason is because they cannot be in the presence of God, and the sun is God's closest earthly representative. As creatures of the shadow, vampires must reside in darkness. However, in QD, Rice offers a different rationale. Since there is no God in the supernatural cosmology of the first four *Chronicles*, the cause of the vampire's need to shun the sun is related to Amel, the spirit who enters Akasha and starts the vampire race.

Amel, as a spirit, fuses with flesh and changes it. Because Amel is using a lot of energy to achieve the fusion, he and the blood that carries his spirit "cannot endure the sun's heat coming down upon it." *(QD 405)* Thus, the vampires all know that to go into the sun is to be destroyed.

Mortals know that vampires must shun the sun as well, and in vampire history, worshipers of the sun god Ra opened up the crypts of many vampires to destroy them. When Claudia and Madeleine are exposed to the sun, it cremates them. And when the Elder who guards

Sun, a symbol of enlightenment

439

Enkil and Akasha (who is responsible for sustaining the life force of the vampires) exposes their bodies to the sun's rays, he causes death and damage to vampires worldwide. The youngest and weakest vampires disintegrate immediately, while the older ones are badly burned. Akasha and Enkil, however, suffer only a darkening of their skin, which fades over the centuries. Marius later predicts that drinking Akasha's blood may protect Lestat from the rays of the sun. It becomes clear, then, that the sun may not be the nemesis it originally seemed to be. The older and more powerful a vampire becomes, the less effect the sun can have on that vampire. *(IV 306, VL 433, 444, 473)*

Lestat discovers this for a fact when he goes to the Gobi. He flies directly into the sun, and while its rays reach into his every cell in an excruciatingly painful manner, they do not destroy him. His body saves itself by digging into the sand on the second day and he heals over time, with only a dark tan to show for his suicidal confrontation. *(BT 47–50, 54)*

Lestat is enabled to see the sun when he switches bodies with Raglan James and becomes mortal. It gives him a sense of optimism and well-being. He is impressed with the energy the daylight world seems to possess, where people walk around in safety and accelerated activity. He feels the chemistry of his own mortal body responding. "The world by light," he says, "was not the world by dark." *(BT 196)* No artificial light could ever duplicate the sun's effect. *(BT 195–197)*

Ironically, the sun becomes Lestat's ally when he battles with Raglan James to regain his former body. Knowing that the vampire's point of greatest weakness arrives with the rising sun, and knowing that he himself has already faced the sun and triumphed, he attacks James just before dawn, rattling him sufficiently to regain his body, and fleeing to a prearranged hiding place with his last bit of strength. *(BT 336)*

When Lestat brings Veronica's veil from the hands of Christ and Dora displays it at St. Patrick's Cathedral, Armand and Mael both step into the sun and burst into flame. They believe in the miracle and wish to use the shock of their deaths to bring attention to it. Before he goes to his death, Mael urges Lestat to do the same. *(MD 335, 339)*

See also Amel, Amon Ra, Armand, Calamity, Claudia, Death, Desert, Mael, Skin, Suicide, Ways of Dying.

Supernatural   As a phenomenon that exists beyond natural law, the vampires often view themselves as supernatural beings. Their understanding of the supernatural, however, involves viewing themselves as a higher order of consciousness that is merely an extension of the natural world. It was important to Rice to take the supernatural from its mystical realm and give it scientific possibility. In that way, vampire literature—Rice's, anyway—was freed of religious superstition and could explore new metaphysical territory.

The story in QD about the vampire origins reinforces this view. Amel, the spirit who invades Akasha, has a tiny physical core that enables him to merge with her; he is not something completely different in kind from the natural realm, but differs only in the degree of physical manifestation. The process of transforming Akasha's cells requires a great deal of energy, which the blood then feeds and the sun harms. *(QD 308, 321, 422–423)*

Louis wants to view vampires as supernatural creatures in a more traditional sense: he wants them to be related to the Devil in a Christian framework. Armand wonders why Louis needs to find answers about their vampire existence in such supernatural explanations; to his mind, God and the Devil are irrelevant superstitions, nothing more. Louis insists that the supernatural is real, but he eventually despairs of ever finding definitive evidence for this view. *(IV 240–241)*

When Memnoch takes him to Heaven and Hell, Lestat actually has the chance to experience the supernatural—to find out the things that he, David, Louis, and Armand want to know. He goes back in time to early civilization, sees angels, encounters God, and drinks from Christ. He also sees the making of Veronica's veil and gets a firsthand experience of the Fourth Crusade before he enters Hell. He realizes, however, that no matter what Memnoch shows him, it could all be a deception. He still has no certainty that the supernatural exists, although he believes he has had a profound experience. *(MD 331, 344)*

See also Demons, Devil, God, Gods, Memnoch, Superstitions.

Superstitions   Superstitions about vampires blend folklore and fiction, and are based on the Christian division of supernatural forces into God and the Devil. Vampires are creatures of darkness, and as such, many of the rituals that can harm them or ward them off involve religious artifacts. IV lays most of these unfounded superstitions to rest.

The boy reporter believes that vampires prefer darkness but Louis immediately turns on the light. While it is true that vampires cannot go into the sun, they do not abide only in shadows. The boy also asks about whether crosses can ward off vampires, if pounding stakes through the heart can kill vampires, and if vampires can become steam and drift through keyholes. Louis dismisses all of these. (However, in the first draft of IV, Louis admits that he can be hurt by a stake because it destroys the heart and he could bleed to death. Rice later changed this.) Louis explains that there is no supernatural magic involved in being a vampire. He can also see himself in a mirror and does not have to sleep in a coffin, although he adopts the habit despite his claustrophobia. *(IV 2–3, 22–23)*

Louis and Lestat both discover that holy relics have no effect on them when they enter churches. Louis goes into the church where his brother's funeral had been and even kills a priest. Lestat and Gabrielle

Killing a vampire with a stake through the heart is a popular superstition

enter a church in Paris and hide beneath its altar to elude Armand's coven. When Lestat first becomes a vampire, he picks up a crucifix and sees at once that it has no power against him. *(IV 143, VL 103, 189–193)*

In Eastern Europe, Louis and Claudia also demonstrate that garlic has no effect. The peasants hang it outside their homes to ward off vampires, yet Louis and Claudia blithely walk right past it. Louis even picks up a crucifix to adopt the pretense that he himself is a vampire hunter. *(IV 172, 185)*

See also Crucifix, Eastern Europe, Garlic, Mirrors, Religious Images, Stake, Steam, Vampire, White Stallion.

Surrender   To yield to the power, control, or possession of another, surrender involves the breakdown of the ego and allows for the attainment of greater inner power. In relationships involving dominant and submissive roles, surrendering to the dominant partner can result in spiritual transcendence; this imitates the relationship between God and a believer, who may gain union with the divine through total obedience. With vampires, victims who surrender to the bliss of the "kiss" achieve greater pleasure, and mortals who become vampires must continue to surrender to their nature, rather than resisting it, in order to develop it to its fullest potential.

Although Louis chooses to become a vampire, he cannot readily surrender to what it seems to mean. He watches Lestat, who can kill without apparent guilt and often does so, sometimes even wastefully. Yet Louis cannot give in to the demands of his nature, and so lives on the blood of animals for a while. Eventually he kills mortals, but this never ceases to bother his conscience. By the fourth *Chronicle*, he is still in the twilight world of a conscience-stricken killer, for he has never fully surrendered his humanity. Lestat constantly chides him for this weakness. *(IV 82–83, BT 104–105)*

Lestat surrenders to no one, mortal or immortal. His character has been formed by resistance and this insight makes him even stronger as a vampire. However, he does learn the value of surrendering to what he is. *(IV 84–85, VL 88–90)*

In QD, Lestat is abducted by Akasha similar to the way he had been abducted by Magnus. He had resisted Magnus, although he had eventually surrendered to the sheer pleasure of becoming a vampire. Akasha challenges him to make another such transformation—to find his inner power to do the things that she can do. She encourages him to defy natural laws: to join her across the room without walking to her, to fly into the air. He is frightened of such a step and she urges him to surrender. When he accepts, it seems to him like he is caught in a windstorm. His achievement, Akasha explains, is the result of gaining the strength of the "intangible thing that animates" him. *(QD 256)* He had preternatural speed before, so his increased powers are a simple matter of degree. *(QD 255–256, 263)*

Akasha also asks of him that he surrender his will and conscience to follow her. He tries, and the killing sprees that result are orgastic to him. In afterthought, however, he knows that he cannot just obey Akasha: to lose his moral integrity is to lose himself in a way he cannot tolerate. Unlike flight or killing with telepathy, it requires more of him than he can give. Surrendering for inner transformation and greater power means something different, Lestat discovers, than surrendering his essential moral nature and integrity. *(QD 356–361, 367–371, 394)*

The importance of surrender is made clear once again when Lestat observes Raglan James's erratic movements in his vampire body. James cannot easily work the bodies he possesses because he retains too much of his own ego; he cannot surrender to the body and allow his soul to anchor itself in its cells. This "gap" that exists between James's soul and the body he inhabits provides Lestat with an advantage in regaining his own body from James. *(BT 377)*

See also Akasha's Plan, Body, Dominance/Submission, Rapture, Swoon.

Survival   See Blood, Body, Security, Will.

Suspicion   A 1941 Alfred Hitchcock film starring Cary Grant and

Joan Fontaine. It is about a woman who discovers that her new husband is a liar—and perhaps even a killer who may be planning to
murder her.

In BT, this movie is playing on the television of the elderly
woman who had been the serial killer's intended victim. After Lestat
kills the killer, he returns to drink from the woman, despite his resolve
to strike only evildoers. As he takes her to the point of death, the
movie provides the imagery of a reverse parallel, when the character of
Joan Fontaine realizes that Cary Grant's character is not going to kill
her after all. This juxtaposition emphasizes the theme that appearances
are deceiving and that images are inverted. *(BT 23)*

See also Inversion.

Swamp   A symbol of spiritual decomposition, the swamp outside
New Orleans—called the Bayou St. Jean—is where Louis and Claudia
dispose of Lestat's remains after they have poisoned and stabbed him.
They also toss in the bones of the dead mother and daughter Claudia
has killed. As Louis watches the sheets in which Lestat is wrapped
submerge, he feels drawn to go down with them into oblivion. The
swamp may represent Louis's own subconscious, where Lestat can be
repressed but not killed. Lestat later reemerges, all the more powerful
for his experience. *(IV 139–140)*

See also Bayou St. Jean.

Swoon   A languorous drift into rapture, which both victims and
vampires experience throughout the *Chronicles* in the vampiric embrace. A swoon results from surrender and mimics orgasm. The victim
yields to the vampire's bite and the promise of ecstasy, while the
vampire surrenders to the bliss of taking a life by sucking the blood.
For vampires, this swoon is like the drunken swoon of an alcoholic,
and the compulsion to experience it over and over again is like an
alcoholic's addiction.

Rice thought of the experience as that of going out with the
tide—an image inspired by the poet John Keats. She imagined that the
experience would be gentle but too powerful to resist.

However, one of her characters, Roger, valiantly tries to do just
that. To Lestat's astonishment, Roger breaks through the swoon as
Lestat is killing him and tries to speak. He demands to know who
Lestat is and why he is drinking his blood. This maddens Lestat, so he
breaks Roger's neck. He has never before encountered a victim with
such power. *(MD 39)*

See also Addiction, Blood, Heart, Keats (John), Rapture, Sensuality, Surrender, Transformation, Vampire's Kiss.

Symmetry   The concept of two things being identical, or of one thing having identical halves, it embodies the principle of homogeneity and balance. Although symmetry is often imposed on the natural world, it is also an intellectual framework developed in accord with an aesthetic preference for purity and simplicity. Symmetry also represents static finality: it implies that there is no dynamic between opposing, nonsymmetrical forces—a dynamic that is necessary to produce life energy.

Akasha attributes the spiritual power of the twins, in part, to their apparent symmetry. Thus, she utilizes the concept of symmetry six thousand years later, to try to equalize moral concepts, so that she can be considered a benevolent goddess rather than a vampire killer. She attempts to dissolve all meaning, making the moral concepts of good and evil identical in their meaninglessness, then putting her own meaning into them so that she has a framework by which to declare a new Eden.

Symmetry, however, only works in theory. It is a simplified ideal, not a practical reality: the twins are identical only on the surface. One is assertive, the other cautious, and each has unique powers that the other does not share. Thus, Akasha can only make her plan work by deceiving herself about its applicability. She cannot utilize the abstract concept of symmetry to grasp and remold reality. As Maharet points out, Akasha has been dormant for too long in her own mind; she is out of touch with the world. Akasha wants to make Lestat mirror her, to create a symmetry of partners, but he does not share her obsession or ultimate nihilism. He shatters any potential symmetry between them, and in the end, her plan falls apart. (QD 311, 318, 323, 397)

See also Akasha's Plan, Mirrors, Paradox, Twins.

Talamasca   The organization introduced in QD that documents paranormal activity. The name derives from a Latin word meaning "animal mask," and was once used to denote witches and shamans. *(QD 201)*

"I found the word in a book on witchcraft by Jeffrey Burton Russell," Rice explains. "He was giving old words for *sorcerer* or *witch*, and one was *Talamasca*. When I saw the word on the page it inspired the whole idea of the organization. I thought that word was so beautiful." The organization itself was influenced by what Rice had read about English psychic research societies from the nineteenth century.

According to David Talbot, its Superior General, the organization came into existence in A.D. 758 to study vampires. Although its origins are shrouded in mystery, it holds vast wealth in antiquities, art, gold, jewels, manuscripts, and property. The Talamasca's motto is "We watch. And we are always there." *(QD 136, 162–193)*

The organization is introduced into the *Chronicles* through Jesse, Maharet's mortal descendant, who possesses extraordinary psychic abilities. She enters the order as an apprentice and finds in them a womb and a network that parallels not only the Great Family that she has learned about from Maharet, but also the worldwide network of vampires.

The Talamasca is a secret order. They require of their members confidentiality, honesty, loyalty, and obedience, but do not ask for belief in the supernatural. Their purpose is to document any manifestation of phenomena that seems out of the natural order. They have records of witch families, the witch trials of the Dark Ages, hauntings, sorcery, werewolves, and vampires. They also collect "vampire refuse"—possessions that vampires leave behind—and they have records dating back to the Dark Ages of vampire anatomy and its limitations.

To complete their collection and to resolve many mysteries, they desire a specimen of vampire tissue to study. *(BT 160)* Their method of acquiring knowledge is one of respectful, nonintrusive observation. Members are trained to memorize the details of an experience or apparition, no matter how great the shock of the moment. Most members possess some degree of psychic ability, and these are especially nurtured and protected by the organization.

Although members study the writings of other paranormal investigators, the organization does not embrace or offer any single theory to explain all the phenomena they study. *(QD 162–164)*

The Talamasca sets up Motherhouses in many major cities for the comfort and security of its members, and for storing records and artifacts. Most of the vampire collection is kept in the London Motherhouse. Its underground vaults remind Jesse of Maharet's Sonoma compound, for both house things of great mystery. *(QD 174–176)*

Many vampires are aware of the existence and activities of the Talamasca. Some are disturbed by it; others ignore it as having no importance. It intrigues Lestat, who has always fantasized about being a scientific specimen. Through the Talamasca's collections he is able to retrieve a locket he once owned containing Claudia's picture. *(QD 166–221, 227, 486–490, BT 419)*

In BT, David Talbot talks with Lestat about his involvement in the Talamasca, and about some of his concerns about living such a passive, scholarly life. David is also worried that the Talamasca may not be all that it seems. Even though he is Superior General, he believes that the elders who give him his directives possess motives for operating the organization that remain a mystery. (Rice will explore this mystery in future novels.) *(BT 61, 65, 78)*

The Talamasca provides a bridge between vampires and mortals. The members are not composed of spiritual substance like the vampires, but are more in touch with the spiritual realm, via their paranormal abilities, than ordinary mortals. As a form of continuous awareness, they parallel the vampires in the way they observe generations of activity. *(QD 174)*

The Talamasca unwittingly participate in David's plan to help Lestat get his body back in BT. Their man in Mexico, Jake, books passage for Lestat and David on the *QE2* and smuggles guns aboard. He is suspicious of Lestat but does not realize that he is a vampire locked in a mortal body. *(BT 298–300, 304–307, 316–319)* With his involvement in Lestat's cause, David is breaking the Talamasca's rule of noninvolvement, as well as ignoring his own directive not to talk with vampires under any circumstances. As a result of his actions, he is made a vampire—the very danger from which the directive tried to protect him. He then distances himself from the order.

Aaron Lightner, who invites Jesse into the order, describes the Talamasca in much more detail in *The Witching Hour*. And Rice further develops the origins of the Talamasca and the activities of its elders as a secret order in *Lasher* and *Taltos*, her sequels to WH.

See also Continual Awareness, Elders, Jesse, Lightner (Aaron), Motherhouse, Talbot (David).

Talbot, David   Superior General of the Talamasca, he is a cultured British gentleman with dark gray hair and black eyes who possesses a powerful ability to conceal his mind from others.

David assigns Jesse to investigate the vampires depicted in IV. After Jesse herself becomes a vampire, she tells Lestat about David Talbot and, intrigued, Lestat visits him at Talamasca headquarters in London. He offers David the Dark Gift, but David refuses it. Lestat finds himself powerfully attracted to this mortal who dispels his illusion that no one can refuse the gift of immortality, no matter what it involves. David continues to reject it, yet develops a friendship with Lestat; he even claims that Lestat is his only friend. Lestat loves David for his understanding and acceptance. He has always craved such a bond with a mortal, although he feels that he is a bad influence on David. He worries over David's health at the age of seventy-four and puzzles over the fact that David devoted his life to Talamasca activities. As a young man, David had been an adventurer, traveling the world and going on dangerous safaris. In Rio de Janeiro he apprenticed himself to a Candomble priestess and learned how to manipulate spirits. *(QD 172, 485, BT 51–80)*

Now, however, his quest is to crack the secrets of the universe. He has seen a vision of God and the Devil talking in a Parisian café, and the insights he gained from that vision give him hope that he may discover some important truths. On the other hand, he is disenchanted with his life, worried over his failing strength, and restless for something significant to happen. *(BT 74)*

He gets his wish when Lestat switches bodies with Raglan James and relies on David to help him get his body back. David devises a plan for knocking the soul of James out of Lestat's vampire body, so that Lestat can get in. In the ensuing struggle, Lestat gets his body back, but David's soul is knocked out of his. James steals his body, leaving him with the body Lestat had occupied as a mortal: that of a twenty-six-year-old physically fit male. David settles into the new body and allows James to meet with Lestat in his old one. Lestat damages David's former body in a rage, but David does not care; he has gained youth and a new chance at life without compromising his soul. *(BT 381)* He also gains immortality when Lestat forces him to become a vampire. *(BT 381, 417–422)*

The character of David Talbot held great significance for Rice. He represented to her the wise teacher; he also brought her face to face with issues of mortality. Rice expresses her concerns through Lestat. Whenever Lestat looks at David, he thinks of David's inevitable death. "I can hear it when I'm near you!" Lestat exclaims. "I can hear the weakness in your heart." *(BT 44)*

This statement foreshadowed a tragic event in Rice's own life: the death of her father, Howard O'Brien. Like David, he was seventy-four and had a failing heart. Although Rice had written BT before her father was actually ill, she had felt a great sense of darkness as she wrote. "It was an awful time," she said, "a black, black period."

This feeling was similar to the one Rice had just before her daughter had been diagnosed with a fatal case of leukemia, and the parallels between David Talbot and her father were just as uncanny. After BT was finished, Howard grew ill and died from degenerative heart disease. Later, when Rice read over an early draft of BT, she was amazed at how accurately Lestat's words to David predicted what happened with Howard.

"When I reread BT," she says, "I thought that anyone reading this book would think it was written *after* Howard's death. It was almost as if it had been written in a state of premonition." And just as Rice had resurrected her deceased mother by having Lestat make Gabrielle into a vampire, she saved David, a symbol of her father, in the same way.

Although Lestat made David to be his companion, from time to time David wanders off on his own or joins the other vampires. He has spent time with Armand, Jesse, and Maharet, yet he is always available for Lestat. David believes he actually may not survive long as a vampire because he cannot bear the killing, but Lestat insists he will get used to it. *(MD 5, 104–107)*

After Lestat kills Roger, David books rooms in Manhattan's Olympic Tower and helps Lestat move Roger's religious treasures there for safekeeping. Later David meets Lestat in New Orleans to hear about his first encounter with Memnoch the Devil. Recalling his own vision of God and the Devil, David thinks it is credible that Memnoch desires Lestat's assistance, but he advises Lestat not to ask Dora for advice on what to do. *(MD 140–148)*

Lestat decides to go with Memnoch to Heaven and Hell, and when he returns, David listens to the entire tale, then carefully records it. The possibility that it is all true tempts David to do as Armand has done: to go up in flames and join God. Lestat urges him not to because his entire experience could all be a lie or false vision. David and Lestat then travel together to New Orleans, where Maharet meets them. She instructs David to assist her in protectively binding Lestat before she

delivers to Lestat a note from Memnoch which indicates that Lestat has perfectly served him. While Lestat lies in chains, straining against this new horror, David goes over the story of his journey with him to make certain it is accurate. Since David cannot read Lestat's mind, Maharet helps him get the impressions right. *(MD 344, 347, 351)*

See also Body Switching, God, Olympic Tower, Talamasca, *The Tale of the Body Thief*, Veil of Silence, Visions.

Talbot Manor   David Talbot's ancestral home in the Cotswolds in England. Elizabethan in style, it has lead-mullioned windows; small, dark rooms; and a deep-pitched roof.

Lestat visits David here to tell him of his plan to fly into the sun. He also returns to Talbot Manor to heal when this attempt to destroy himself fails. *(BT 39, 49, 412)*

See also Cotswolds, Talbot (David).

Tale of the Body Thief, The   The title and story of the fourth *Vampire Chronicle*. The novel involves Lestat's adventure with a mortal, Raglan James. They temporarily switch bodies, but then James steals Lestat's vampire body with all its powers, intending never to return it to its original owner. Lestat initially agreed to this switch because he thought he wanted to be mortal again; however, once he is actually in a mortal body, he realizes he prefers being a vampire. *(BT 165, 291)*

In mortal form, Lestat must track his immortal body down and reengage his own soul with his body. Yet the mortal body which he is temporarily inhabiting is plagued with disease, loss of power, and vulnerability to death. When Louis and Marius refuse to help him, he enlists the aid of David Talbot. Together they succeed in retrieving Lestat's other half. David, however, gets more than he bargained for when he acquires the body of a beautiful young man and is then made a vampire by Lestat. *(BT 273, 277, 376, 422)*

The first edition jacket

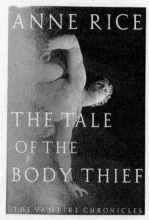

"*Body Thief* was a more intimate novel than *Queen*," says Rice. "I got inside Lestat again to speak about the seductiveness of evil. This novel is about self-discovery. It's a truthful statement about honesty and art. Evil is not beautiful. More and more, it [BT] seems to be an answer to everything raised in *Interview*."

BT is a tale of jeopardy and self-revelation that also possesses the emotional sensitivity of IV. Rice threads issues of good and evil, salvation and damnation, throughout. How far, Rice asks, are each of us willing to go to achieve excitement? Throughout the novel Lestat ponders his own ability and desire to make evil attractive. He loses some of his illusions about trying to be good, and that loss hurts him. In the end, he chooses vampirism over mortality and the possibility of redemption. He knows now that he is evil and that he loves what he is.

"To me," says Rice, "*Body Thief* has a deep meaning that has to do with selling one's soul to the Devil, and to what extent everyone does that. There's a bottom line of ruthlessness in almost every person where you decide what to do to make life exciting enough. That's what the whole book is about."

The idea for BT came to her the week she finished QD, but she put it on a back burner, to allow it to grow while she went to another novel that had been on hold for several years, *The Witching Hour*.

In the first draft of BT, Rice wrote fifty pages that she later cut because she wanted a more fast-paced opening. In these pages, Lestat recaps QD and describes what happened to various members of the surviving coven. He visits David Talbot in Venice and takes him to the Hagia Sophia. After he leaves David, Lestat finds himself in Hong Kong, taken there by Khayman on Marius's orders. Marius is still the stern teacher and demands that Lestat cease the antics that are making him conspicuous to the mortal world. As Lestat defies Marius and goes off into Hong Kong to hunt, it becomes clear that the old intimacy between them is gone. He then encounters a brown-haired man in Venice and in Hong Kong that later turns out to be Raglan James.

Rice thought BT could be the last book in *The Vampire Chronicles*; it certainly felt that way to her when she was finished. "I'll write another one if something comes to me," she admitted, "but this feels like a concluding book." A few months later, she knew she could write yet a fifth one, and did, calling it *Memnoch the Devil*.

See also Body Switching, James (Raglan), Lestat de Lioncourt, Redemption, Talbot (David), *The Vampire Chronicles*.

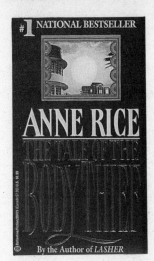

The mass market edition cover

Tammuz of Sumer   A vegetation god in Near Eastern mythology, he died each winter only to be resurrected with the spring. He was originally a sun god whose story was told in the poem "Ishtar's Descent into the Underworld," in which the goddess Ishtar betrayed his love when she offered him to be killed in her place.

Memnoch mentions Tammuz as one of the divinities from mythology who symbolized death, dismemberment, and regeneration. Primitive humans seemed to need the concept of sacrifice as a way to partake in their gods. When Memnoch hears God's scheme for a new religion based on His own sacrifice as Christ, he feels that God merely grafted Himself onto the worst human myths. (*MD 298, 300*)

See also Christianity, God.

Tapestry   A quilt that is hanging in the Sonoma compound of a colorful wooded landscape, in which images come and go, depending on one's perspective. From a certain angle, Jesse thinks she can see the

red-haired twins. The tapestry is a central metaphor of QD, which also weaves together diverse strands (the stories of the various vampires involved in confronting Akasha) to make a whole picture. And like the tapestry, there is no single character's perspective that yields the entire picture of QD. *(QD 140, 143–144)*

See also *The Queen of the Damned.*

Tax rolls   One method the Talamasca uses to document the locations and movements of the vampires across several centuries. Jesse finds the names of Louis and Lestat on tax rolls in New Orleans, and the dates and properties match those described in IV. She then goes into the town house where they lived with Claudia, which provides further proof of their reality. *(QD 144)*

See also Talamasca, Town House.

Teacher   A trusted counselor or guide who dispenses learning. The need for a teacher reflects a desire for one's parents to provide a voice of authority and a source of nurturing. Rice, however, feels that in the modern world, parents are no longer adequate to the task, and the child must become his or her own parent. This theme that such authors as Dickens and Dostoyevsky wrote about inspired Rice in her writing of the *Chronicles.*

Louis looks to Lestat to be his teacher after he becomes a vampire, yet Lestat seems to him to be uninterested at best, and bungling at worst. He dispenses information about living as a vampire in small, infrequent amounts. Louis views this as ineptitude, even cruelty. He feels that Lestat badly mishandles both Louis's first night as a vampire and his first kill, and that he could have learned much from a more caring and sophisticated teacher. He feels cheated and determines to attend to his own learning, although he claims that his ignorance about vampire ways binds him to Lestat in a dependent relationship for over half a century. Lestat plays on Louis's fears and desire for a teacher by withholding information and taunting him with his knowledge (at least, this is how Louis sees it). Later Louis looks to Armand as a teacher, but he experiences equally futile results. *(IV 21, 23, 24, 27–30, 32–35, 81–85, 316–319)*

Louis does not realize that Lestat is actually practicing a more Zenlike approach to teaching. Marius had instructed him to tell his fledglings very little—tell them nothing or, even, lie to them—because they would not be mature enough to be able to handle knowing the full scope of their vampire nature and history. So Lestat allows Louis to learn through experience, something Lestat considers to be the best teacher. In fact, Lestat had also become a vampire without the assistance of a teacher, and had searched for Marius in order to find a wise mentor. Although Marius taught Lestat the vampire history and ori-

gins, he insisted that Lestat go out and live the equivalent of a full mortal lifetime. If he were to accompany Lestat, he would stand between him and what he could learn. Lestat knows that he must become his own teacher and learn from his own mistakes, and he believes Louis should do so as well. Lestat also recognizes that Louis shrinks from all that he can be, and thus it would not be any use to teach him about the full range of his powers. (VL 470, 477, 498)

Armand wants a teacher, but one of a different sort. Made a vampire while still an adolescent, then robbed of his mentor Marius, he falls into obeying Santino's coven to save his life. Although he eventually leads the coven, he is ever on the lookout for others who could take him under their wing and link him to whatever age they live in. He asks it of Lestat, then of Louis, but both refuse to be what he wants. He eventually seduces the boy reporter, Daniel, learning from him the secrets of the twentieth century. Like Louis, Armand can never quite be his own master. (VL 282, 300–303, IV 288, QD 86–87)

Akasha realizes that Lestat has never had a teacher and wants to fill that void. She claims that she can show him things he has never imagined, although she first requires of him his surrender and obedience. Lestat becomes a mesmerized but reluctant protégé, and learns more about his powers. However, when Lestat glimpses Akasha's "new Eden," he is too repelled by its amorality to be a truly worshipful student. Although Akasha attempts to make him addicted to her, in the end he resists her allure. He does learn, but more as a result of seeing her for what she is than from absorbing her teachings. A teacher who needs disciples is not a true teacher.

In BT, David Talbot becomes the closest thing Lestat has had to a real teacher. When Lestat takes on the body of a mortal and loses his vampire powers, David must teach him how to cloak his thoughts, project his soul from his body, and knock another soul out of the body it is inhabiting. He is the experienced, older, and wiser being that Marius had been, and this time Lestat really needs a teacher. (BT 306)

Lestat becomes a pupil to the Devil in MD. Memnoch invites him to tour Heaven and Hell and to speak with God. In Heaven, Lestat tries to learn from the Great Books he sees there, but he forgets everything he reads. However, he does not forget the lessons of Hell as easily. There his victims wait for him. Memnoch wants him to be part of this school for souls, to be his lieutenant, but Lestat cannot do it. Nevertheless, Memnoch's teachings have made their mark: Lestat feels that humans are in the hands of supernatural madmen whose rules and schemes seem uninfluenced by human morality. He escapes from Memnoch and Hell but still feels unsafe. In the face of the ambiguity of all that he has witnessed, he knows he must remain his own teacher. (MD 166, 319, 324, 331)

See also Dickens (Charles), Knowledge, Memnoch, Quest, Shaman.

Ted   One of the three members of the rock band that Roger had managed in San Francisco. When a drug deal endangered them, the band split up and Ted went with Ollie to Los Angeles. *(MD 70)*
See also Blue, Ollie, Roger.

Teeth   See Bite, Fangs.

Telepathic powers   Vampires can project their thoughts onto mortals to confuse, hypnotize, and/or seduce them, and the more powerful vampires can manipulate the weaker ones through telepathy. Claudia claims that Armand has been urging her to die through telepathic means, although Louis does not believe this. Yet Armand had rendered her motionless as they talked, to the point that Claudia ends up wanting to leave Paris. *(IV 251)* Armand also protects his territory from other vampires by sending them warning signals to keep away. *(QD 101)*
Raglan James uses telepathy to convince the soul of the mechanic to switch bodies with him. He had gained the man's trust by plundering his memories and manipulating his obedience. He also uses telepathy to locate Lestat and to try to figure out what Lestat is thinking as he ponders the body-switching offer. *(BT 157)*
When he describes his first real conversation with Memnoch, Lestat allows Armand to see into his mind, as Armand had once done for him. The images are more immediate than the words. *(MD 143)*
After Lestat has been to Heaven and Hell, David decides to write all of Lestat's story down. But, due to the "veil of silence" between vampire and vampire child, to get the images right he must rely on Maharet's telepathic powers as she sees into Lestat's mind. *(MD 351)*
See also Cloaking, One Powerful Mind, Reading Minds, Spellbind, Vampire Powers, Veil of Silence.

Temple   In QD, the vampire Azim performs nearly continuous murders in a temple in the mountains of Nepal. Akasha chooses this place to make an example of him and to create a legend about herself as the savior goddess. She kills him in front of his worshipers, then slaughters all the mortal men there. While Akasha burns down the temple, the women go to their villages, claiming to have seen miracles. *(QD 62, 290–295)*
Lestat discovers another temple in BT. After Gretchen rejects him, he wanders through the jungle until he finds a temple hidden by overgrown vines and inhabited only by monkeys. There he grieves over the loss of Gretchen and realizes that he will have no more dreams of

Claudia. He has descended down a staircase into dark chambers, to the deepest pocket of his subconscious, and his self-honesty has shown him that there is no hope for his redemption. Now he knows what he is—a vampire—and that he has freely chosen this lifestyle. He decides to make this temple his secret place, although he tells David about it, in the hope that David will want to visit it with him. *(BT 358)*

See also Azim, Nepal.

Temptation of Amadeo, The The painting of Armand that Marius does as a metaphor for inversion. *(VL 292)* Done during the

The Temptation of
Saint Anthony *that may
have inspired Marius's*
The Temptation of
Amadeo

455

fifteenth-century Renaissance in Venice, the painting is of egg tempera on wood. Armand, a kneeling boy with auburn hair, is the central figure. Around him hover black-winged angels who wear expressions of bitter amusement. To one side lie human bones covered in dust. This painting presents a scene that contrasts sharply with the typical Renaissance paintings depicting demons tempting a saint. The angels portray Marius, the vampire, tempting Armand to join him in vampirism. *Amadeo* means "one who loves God," but in reality Armand is actually loving a vampire who just seems to be a god.

Marius did this painting when Armand was still mortal, only afterward making him a vampire. An emissary of the Talamasca retrieves the painting after Santino's coven burns down Marius's villa on the Grand Canal. Marius finds out later, from Jesse, that the Talamasca are in possession of his painting. *(QD 174–175, 277)*

See also Amadeo, Art, Talamasca.

Terry Flynn   See Flynn, Terry.

"Texas Suite"   A poem by Stan Rice that introduces the sections about Baby Jenks and Khayman in QD. It is about the nature of substance, and alludes to the experience of being anchored in the flesh. *(QD 41, 119)*

See also Poetry, Rice (Stan), Substance.

Theater of the Vampires (Théâtre des Vampires)
The theater on the boulevard du Temple in Paris where a coven of vampires perform onstage in IV. This theater performance was not part of the original version of IV, but was added when Rice was making changes for publication. Although she did not know it at the time, she was setting up a precursor for Lestat as a rock star onstage, thus linking him to Dionysus, patron god of the theater. *(VL 17)*

Once known as Renaud's House of Thesbians, which is where Lestat got his start as an actor, the building changes hands when Lestat buys it in 1789. He gives it to a coven of vampires who had followed satanic rituals, but whose illusions about the Dark Ways had been shattered by Lestat's appearance in Paris. They beg Lestat for protection and he advises them to become actors. He gives control of the theater to Eleni, hands Nicolas over to their care, suggests that Armand join with these vampires, and then leaves Paris.

Named by Nicolas, the Théâtre des Vampires becomes highly successful. The vampires perform as giant marionettes and the orchestra imitates mechanical musicians. Paris's lower classes accept this theater as a metaphor for the hated aristocrats when Nicolas writes plays that reflect the political unrest of the city. His themes involve death in the midst of life, and his intent is both to make a mockery of

An old theater on boulevard du Temple, similar to the Theater of the Vampires

all things sacred and to beguile mortals. One play is about a vampire who starves because he can get no blood from a puppet; another is about a girl forced to dance until she dies. Eleni predicts to Lestat that they could feast on victims onstage and get away with it—a prediction that later comes true. Vampires come from other parts of Europe just to be included in the productions. *(VL 245–246, 259–266, 312–315, 326–329, 340–341)* Attendance at the Theater of the Vampires is by invitation only, and the mortal ushers double during the day as guards. *(IV 217)*

Theatrical performances involve making fantasy appear real, and the vampires invert this concept to make reality an illusion. Eventually, they do kill onstage, but the mortal audience believes it is merely a performance.

Armand remains with the changing covens who perform in the theater, helping to perfect the theater's images but remaining scornfully on the edges. He is simply biding his time, waiting for a vampire to come through Paris with whom he will connect; he believes the theater is his best means of finding such a kindred soul. He must wait for over seventy-five years, as it turns out. *(IV 288)*

Louis and Claudia are invited to a performance of the vampires, which begins with the beating of a tambourine and the sound of a flute. The music is medieval and melancholic. The stage shows the image of a woods, and an old woman vainly pursues a figure representing Death. Death takes an interest in a young woman instead, and seven characters

who appear to be vampires gather around her. They strip her naked, thus exposing both her body and her fear, for she is a real victim. Armand seduces her, then passes her around until she dies. This scene was different in the original version of IV. The girl was brought to the mansion on the Faubourg St.-Germain and passed around to vampires standing in an oval and reciting Baudelaire's poetry. *(IV 218–227)*

After the performance, Louis and Claudia are invited below the theater to where the vampires reside, in a large ballroom. The room is decorated with long mirrors and gloomy, decadent murals of torment and death, reflecting a spirit of cynicism. Louis is not very impressed with the troupe of "actors," who all dress in black and seem rather superficial. *(IV 228–230, 247)*

The antics of the vampires attract the attention of the Talamasca, who collect a file on the theater through the years and who note Armand's uninterrupted association with it as evidence of his youthful immortality. David Talbot eventually shows the file to Jesse in QD.

Louis burns the theater down after the coven destroys Claudia. *(IV 312–315)* (See Vampire Atlas)

See also Armand's Coven, Eleni, Nicolas de Lenfent, Renaud's House of Thesbians, Subterranean Room, Talamasca.

Théâtre d'Orléans   A New Orleans theater that Louis and Lestat frequently attend, especially to see Shakespeare. *(IV 100)*

Theft   What some of the vampires do to acquire what they want or need. For example, Gabrielle takes the clothing off a young male victim so that she no longer needs to dress as a woman. Louis and Claudia both steal their coffins, and Lestat teaches Louis how to steal clothing and money from victims (although Lestat claims in BT that he never steals his clothing from victims). *(IV 24, 104, VL 171, BT 59)*

The greatest theft occurs, however, when Raglan James steals from Lestat: he not only takes twenty million dollars but also Lestat's preternatural body. James views being a successful thief as being like God, for both make something out of nothing. *(BT 127, 294)*

See also James (Raglan).

"Their Share"   A poem by Stan Rice about the presence of the dead, Rice uses it in QD to introduce the section about Jesse, who mingles with vampires and eventually becomes one. *(QD 136)*

See also Poetry, Rice (Stan).

Theodora Flynn   See Flynn, Dora.

Theophany   The appearance of a divinity in a form visible to humans.

Roger, David, and Lestat all use this term. Roger hopes that his

daughter, Dora, will one day experience a theophany, although he himself never did. Dora believes she has, in the form of Lestat, her Angel of the Night. *(MD 91, 334)*

See also Angel of the Night, Christ, Dionysus, God, Heaven, Osiris, Tammuz of Sumer, Tiamat, Vegetation Gods, Virgin Mary.

"They threw me off the hay truck at noon"   A line from James M. Cain's novel *The Postman Always Rings Twice*. Lestat quotes this line when he is mulling over how to begin BT. *(BT 2)*

"Thief in the night"   A biblical reference to 1 Thessalonians 5:2, where Paul is describing the sudden and surprising return of Christ.

Louis uses this phrase to describe Lestat's taking the life of the Freniere boy. *(IV 47)*

See also Bible.

"Thing on the Doorstep, The"   A short story by H. P. Lovecraft that Raglan James uses to convince Lestat he can perform the trick of switching bodies.

In the story, a man named Edward Derby marries a strange woman called Asenath who has access to dark secrets. When she stares at people, they experience the feeling of having exchanged personalities. They see their own bodies through her eyes, and some alien thing inhabiting their bodies is looking back at them. Asenath claims that consciousness is independent of the physical body, and that she herself wants a man's brain in order to surpass her father's mastery of unknown forces.

After Edward marries her, his personality changes, and he does uncharacteristic things. He confides to a friend that Asenath uses his body to explore unholy places, while she leaves his consciousness at home in her body. He is afraid that one day she will take him over permanently. Soon he perceives that she is not really Asenath but her father, who had taken over her body when he sensed death coming to him. Edward then tells his friend that he has now asked Asenath to leave his house, and she is gone. However, he can still feel Asenath attacking his brain and fears she will eventually triumph. He is then taken to a sanitarium, where he undergoes a metamorphosis of his personality, and his friend, the narrator, knows that Edward is no longer in his own body. The friend kills the impostor body-soul, then is visited by a dwarflike, smelly thing that he cannot quite recognize, but which gives him a letter of confession. The thing turns out to be the decomposing corpse of Asenath, whom Edward had actually murdered. The soul had clung to the dead body until it could attempt to crowd Edward out of his own.

Lestat and David discuss this story in the context of Raglan James's proposal to trade bodies with Lestat. David is skeptical, but Lestat is intrigued, and begins to believe that body switching actually can be achieved. *(BT 28, 46, 92–93)*

See also Body Switching.

Thirst (blood thirst)   The impulse that drives vampires to drink blood, even when it is no longer necessary to take in blood to survive.

In young vampires, the thirst is a means of survival, for it helps them to overcome their revulsion about killing. And the oldest vampires claim that, for them, the thirst gets worse because they are closer to the source of it—the spirit Amel, who first entered a human being (Akasha) because he thirsted for blood. When Akasha and Enkil were first made, they found the resulting thirst to be unbearable, and were only able to decrease its intensity by making more vampires. *(QD 406)*

In the first draft of BT, in a scene that was later cut, Marius and Lestat discuss how their thirst remains unquenched. This is symbolic of their deeper desires: the more they experience of the mysteries of the universe, the greater their longing for profound answers. Lestat also wants love, and his thirst for blood symbolizes this need. He craves understanding and acceptance from a mortal mind.

Burdened by the immorality of killing humans, however, Louis survives exclusively on animal blood for a period of four years until the lack of satisfaction it brings finally drives him to take a mortal. *(IV 74, 82–83)* Khayman, one of the First Brood, experiences no need for blood, but his desire is so overpowering that he can drink from three or four mortals each night. *(QD 120)* And Armand, whom Lestat calls the "embodiment of thirst itself," seems to be as much a psychological vampire as a physical one. He wants to live his life through others and utilize their powers rather than develop his own. *(VL 512)*

Vampires choose to satiate their thirst at different points in their nightly existence. Lestat kills immediately upon arising; he "drank a little from one [victim], and more from another, and then took the grand wallop of death itself from the third." *(VL 122)* Louis, however, allows his hunger to grow for hours, until finally he is absolutely driven to seek a victim. The thirst—sometimes called hunger—becomes a knot in his stomach and a fever in his veins, which throb as if they are contracting. *(IV 113, 126)*

Claudia's thirst is connected to an unconscious psychological drive to find something that seems ever to elude her. Louis thinks it may be a search for her mother, especially when she becomes obsessed with killing families, and mothers and daughters in particular. *(IV 125)*

One image that horrifies a vampire is the thought of being prevented from satisfying the blood thirst. Both Lestat and Louis hear the screams of vampires sealed into walls who are not allowed to drink,

and Louis experiences this overwhelming fear for one night, when Santino seals him into a coffin. *(IV 300–301, VL 211)*

See also Addiction, Amel, Blood, Entombed Vampires, Rapture, Swoon, Vampire.

Thirteen Revelations of Physical Evolution

The successive stages of God's creation of the world, as witnessed by the angels. Memnoch describes them to Lestat as "the thin outline of all you'll know once you die." *(MD 204)* They are as follows:

1. God changed inorganic molecules to organic, which first appeared in water.

2. The molecules organized themselves into three forms—cells, enzymes, and genes—and single-cell forms evolved into multicellular forms. There was some spark of life and a crude sense of purpose. Green life forms took root on land.

3. The spark of life present in animals was similar to that in the angels, but unlike immortal angels, animals were dying and decaying. At this point, some of the angels began to question the plan. They discovered a punitive quality in the suffering they observed. God explained it to them as the interchange of energy and matter in nature: death feeds life.

4. In the Revelation of Color, extravagant beauty took form in the diverse flowers and sea creatures. The songs angels sang in Heaven began to change to include all that the angels were observing.

5. In the stage of encephalization, nervous systems and heads with brains formed on the animals. The angels were confused by the fact that God's creatures in the physical world were becoming more like them.

6. Those animals with heads had faces, as angels had faces, that expressed their intelligence.

7. Some animals emerged from the sea onto land. Dinosaurs evolved, and killing became more vicious and dramatic. When the angels questioned Him again, God still insisted that killing and death were all part of the energy exchange that kept nature in balance. There was no waste.

8. In this stage, warm-blooded birds made their appearance. Their feathers, like the wings of angels, inspired pride among the angels, and then minor rebellion, which God immediately quelled with more reassurances.

9. The coming of mammals frightened the angels. The suffering and mammal cries of pain were as yet unequaled. They showed the hideous fulfillment of the promise of death present from earlier stages.

10. When apes walked upright, the angels viewed it as a mockery of God.

11. The upright apes began to treasure beauty and bury their

dead, showing evidence of caring and kinship. Thus commenced modern man, coming closer than any creature heretofore to the affection angels could feel.

12. The human spirit evolved from matter, and its similarity to them startled the angels. They watched as the female differentiated from the male and became beautiful and alluring, like the angels themselves. They feared God might be trying to replace them. The angels also saw the souls of the dead surround the Earth.

13. Mate selection diversified and improved the stock, and both genders increasingly seemed to be angels split in two. *(MD 185–204)*

Memnoch goes into a rage, demanding to know what God has in mind. "I considered it a disaster!" he tells Lestat. *(MD 200)* Yet God insists the scheme is balanced. The two remain divided on this issue.

See also Angel, God, Human Evolution, Nature, Soul, Suffering.

"This is my body, this is my blood"

The words of Christ at the Last Supper with His disciples, they indicate that His followers are to share in His holy essence. Magnus quotes Christ's words when he gives his blood to Lestat, and Lestat quotes the same line when he offers himself as a sacrifice to mortals and as a way to achieve immortality. *(VL 274, QD 211)*

See also Bible, Blood, Blood of Christ, Eucharist, Transubstantiation.

Thomas

The disciple who doubted Jesus's resurrection and had to touch Jesus's wounds to believe.

When Mael first sees Khayman, he, like Thomas, touches Khayman's skin, as if he cannot believe its hardness otherwise. *(QD 212)*

See also Bible, Khayman, Mael.

Those Who Must Be Kept

The first two vampires made, Akasha and Enkil. Akasha was the first vampire and she came into being when a spirit, Amel, passed into her mortal body through a fatal wound and fused with her heart and blood. In turn, Akasha made Enkil a vampire as he lay dying. As immortals, they were soon worshiped and envied. They did make other vampires, but they contained the process so that Egypt would not become solely a race of Blood Drinkers. They mythologized what had happened to them with the tale of Osiris, believing they were meant to be gods. A cult grew up around them to try to use their power for good, although some priests wanted to steal from them the secret of immortality.

Khayman, Akasha and Enkil's court steward who was the third vampire made, was largely responsible for the spreading of vampirism. Among these early Blood Drinkers there were often battles for supremacy. Some of them imprisoned Akasha and Enkil beneath heavy stones in order to steal the powerful blood, but eventually Enkil and Akasha broke free. As the centuries passed, the king and queen grew silent and immobile, taking victims only occasionally and changing their position when no one could see the movement. Legend grew that all vampires were connected to Akasha and Enkil, the Mother and the Father, and that their destruction would mean the end of the whole vampire race. Thus, the priests who worshiped them began guarding them, and eventually these two came into the care of the Elder, an Egyptian who reluctantly took on the burden of protection. (VL 433–461)

In QD, some of the vampires surmise that Akasha's and Enkil's silence is a result of their being overwhelmed by the noise of all the voices—the endless cries of the world—which come to them by virtue of their magnified sense of hearing. Vampires have to learn to screen out these voices or go mad. Akasha basically confirms this supposition when she tells Lestat of the trance that came over her and how only his voice came over all the rest to wake her and motivate her to rise. (QD 260)

The Elder comes to dislike Akasha's and Enkil's silence and lack of response. He begins to doubt the legends, so he decides to place them in the sun. He wants them to react, to move to save themselves. He also desires to see if anything would happen to him and the other vampires if these two were harmed. The legend proves true. In the sun their skin turns a deep bronze, while all other vampires are either disintegrated or terribly burned; only the oldest ones survive without calamity. The Elder then removes them from the sun.

After the burning, Marius is made a vampire. He is drawn to Egypt, where Akasha comes to him to ask him to become the new guardian. Shaken by the knowledge that what happens to these vampires happens to him, he takes her and Enkil out of Egypt and erects temples of secrecy and protection for them all over Europe. (VL 462)

After Lestat searches for Marius for ten years, Marius comes to him and brings him to an island where he has built a fortress of stone on the cliffs. In a chilly room deep inside the cliff he shows Lestat Those Who Must Be Kept. The vampire progenitors sit silently on thrones, dressed in fine white linen. In three hundred years they have not taken a drink, although Marius has drunk from them. They seem like stone, simultaneously dead and alive. Marius admits he does not know whether they are at peace or simply locked in silence, but he keeps things in their room beautiful for them in case they can see. The room is full of flowers and torches, and he has painted on the wall a mural of Egypt. A huge gold tabernacle engraved with Egyptian designs dominates the room. (VL 360–396)

Lestat is upset at the thought of becoming like them one day and urges Marius to leave with him. But Marius tells him to talk to them, and Lestat tells Akasha she is beautiful. The next night, Lestat goes to

them and plays a violin in the hope of waking them with music. Akasha awakens and urges him to drink from her. He does so and she bites him, drinking from him at the same time. Enkil intervenes, almost killing Lestat in the process, and Marius sends Lestat away, extracting from him the promise never to tell anyone about what he has seen or heard. *(VL 483–490)*

However, two centuries later, in 1984, Lestat writes about this adventure in his autobiography. He also records the images, legends, and names in his music videos. Marius, who has taken Those Who Must Be Kept to an ice fortress in the north, plays the music videos for them. In response, Akasha rises, kills Enkil, traps Marius under ice, and abducts Lestat from Carmel Valley. It becomes clear to the vampires that the vampire spirit resides only in her, and that Enkil was irrelevant all along, except to be her companion. *(QD 11–23)*

See also Akasha, Calamity, The Elder, Enkil, Marius, Voices.

Those Who Must Be Kept   One of Lestat's rock music videos detailing the myth of Akasha and Enkil. *(VL 520)*

See also Music Videos, Rock Music, Rock Star, Those Who Must Be Kept.

Those Who Want to Die   What Armand calls his victims, those mortals who are enthralled with what he is and who respond eagerly to his call.

People who desire death are portrayed onstage in the Theater of the Vampires in the form of a crippled old woman. She seeks the figure of Death, but Death avoids her and pursues instead a beautiful young woman. *(IV 219–220)*

In QD, Armand shows Daniel how to find these people and call them; he tells Daniel that Louis had been reluctant to do this. *(QD 198)* Although there are no published accounts of such an interaction between Louis and Armand, it had taken place in the first draft of IV, and happened as follows:

Louis first hears of victims such as these in the mansion in Paris, where the vampires bring in girls who look forward to being sacrificed to their blood thirst. Later, Louis realizes that Armand gravitates to such victims as well. It is the perfect union—one of the killer and the person who wants his or her life to be taken. In fact, it is the only kind of kill that fully satisfies Armand. Louis learns from Armand to perform this act in cemeteries, because that is where people who have despaired of life go. Louis describes one encounter with a woman who brings flowers to the grave of her child, who has been dead for only a year. The woman has also lost her mother. Armand steps out to her and she does not fear him. Rather, she explains her unhappiness to him: "I expected the death of one, but I never expected the death of the

other. And I'm lost now with a great gulf of darkness on either side of me and I don't feel as if I want to remain here alone." Armand's perceptiveness and gentleness with such victims moves Louis, but he himself claims (in this draft, at least) to prefer those who struggle for life.

When Lestat warns Armand not to go after Dora, Armand insists that Dora is safe. He does not have to go after victims because they come to him and surrender: "I can stand before a house as always, and out of the doors will come those who want to be in my arms." (MD 147) There are enough victims for him from among Those Who Want to Die.

Another group of victims who want to die are those described in QD—the worshipers of Azim. They move toward Azim's temple in long lines, despite the fact that they know no one returns from his temple alive. (QD 63–64)

See also Armand, Azim, The Spiritual, Victims.

"Through a glass darkly" An allusion from 1 Corinthians 13:12. The Apostle Paul uses this phrase metaphorically to contrast the imperfect knowledge of unenlightened people with the fullness of the knowledge one experiences while in God's presence.

Lestat describes the perception of mortals in IV in the same way. Only "vampire eyes" provide a god's-eye-view of life. This is because vampires possess greater awareness, heightened sensitivity, and the possibility of achieving greater spiritual truths than mortals, who can live out only one short life span. (IV 82)

See also Bible, Senses, Vampire Eyes.

Tiamat A primordial divinity in Near Eastern mythology. Before the earth was differentiated from the sky, only the abyss (Apsu) and chaos (Tiamat) existed. Together they gave birth to gods, among them Ea and Marduk. When Apsu threatened to kill their offspring, Ea seized him. Tiamat retaliated by giving birth to monsters. Marduk then intimidated Tiamat's army and destroyed her. From the blood of her consort, he created the first man.

Memnoch mentions this divinity as one of the representations in human mythology of divine regeneration via dismemberment and death. He scorns God's imitation of such primitive and unnecessary violence. (MD 298)

See also Christ, God, Gods, Theophany.

Tiger A symbol of strength, wrath, cruelty, and darkness of the soul, it is also associated with Dionysus, for it, too, indicates an unbridled expression of the instinct's base powers.

Lestat sees himself as a manifestation of Dionysus, so he is clearly linked to the tiger that he dreams about in the fourth *Vampire Chronicle*. Quoting a line from William Blake's poem "The Tyger," he sees himself as a vicious predator who might harm David Talbot, the hunter in the dream. That dream is based on one of Rice's own dreams, but she, rather than David, was the participant. The tiger had approached her and put his paws on her shoulder. "I thought it was going to kill me," she says, "but it only ate the necklace I was wearing. There's no question but that I'm as influenced by a dream like that—in terms of feeling, mood, and symbolism—as by [the] things I read and see." (BT 5–6)

In the dream, the tiger approaches, its fangs at the ready. It licks David's throat, but instead of ripping it open, the tiger simply eats a gold chain hanging from David's neck. David then kills the tiger. Lestat wonders if the dream forebodes David's death. Yet as the tiger is also related to Dionysus, the half-god who died and was resurrected, its appearance could mean rebirth for David as well. And, in fact, the tiger is Lestat, who brings David both death and immortality.

The image of the tiger is repeated when Lestat finds himself lying in David's house, on the skin of a Bengal tiger, after his dangerous exposure to the sun. "It [the tiger] feasted on children," David had told

Tiger

him earlier. *(BT 44)* Lestat recalls how he, too, had feasted on children—Claudia, whom he had made into a child vampire. *(BT 49,
143–146, 179, 253, 326)*

See also Blake (William), Dreams, Lestat de Lioncourt.

Tillich, Paul   A contemporary American theologian known for
merging depth psychology and existential themes into Christian doctrine. With Kierkegaard, he believed that faith was man's ultimate
concern, that God is the ground of the self, and that people should
strive for "new being" instead of salvation. He rejected the notion of
a personal God that would sooth ineradicable human anxieties.

As part of her religious education, Dora reads Tillich's writings.
(MD 81)

See also Flynn (Dora), Religion.

Tim   In QD, one of the five members of the Fang Gang, who ride
motorcycles. Akasha destroys him, along with the other vampires,
when he is on his way to Lestat's rock concert. *(QD 43)*

See also Fang Gang.

Time Bandits   A 1981 British comedy about six dwarfs and a little
boy who steal the Map of Creation from the Supreme Being. The map
pinpoints holes in the space-time continuum, and the characters subsequently travel through these holes from one place in time to another,
only to wind up in the Devil's den. This movie is a favorite of Armand's, and he watches it over and over. His favorite part is where the
dwarfs sing "Me and My Shadow" for Napoleon. *(QD 95)*

Tolstoy, Leo   A nineteenth-century Russian writer, famous for
his novels *War and Peace* and *Anna Karenina.*

Lestat refers to the first line from *Anna Karenina* when he is
searching for opening lines for BT, and Gretchen says that Lestat, in his
mortal form, reminds her of an angel who came to earth in a short story
that Tolstoy wrote, "What Men Live By." *(BT 232)*

See also "What Men Live By."

"Tomorrow and tomorrow and tomorrow . . ."   A line
from Shakespeare's *Macbeth.* Macbeth says this in despair after he
hears of Lady Macbeth's suicide.

Lestat, who loves Shakespeare, quotes this line as he leaves a
theater where he has just watched a Shakespearean play, and when he
insists to Louis that they will have time to talk together after his rock
concert. *(IV 129, VL 526)*

See also *Macbeth,* Shakespeare.

467

Tough Cookie The female member of the rock band Satan's Night Out.

Lestat hears their music and comes out of the ground in 1984 to join them. After he shows them that he can lead their band to greatness, they change the band's name to The Vampire Lestat. *(VL 13)*

See also Satan's Night Out, The Vampire Lestat.

Tower A symbol of spiritual elevation, it links earth with Heaven. Towers denote height and the act of rising above the ordinary and going in the direction of magical energy. Towers with windows correspond to the eyes, or sight, and being on the top floor implies residing in the mind, or reason.

For Magnus, Lestat, and Louis, towers are testing grounds for their vampire powers, a symbol of the greater spirituality available to those who can accept it.

In IV, Louis first discovers a Transylvanian vampire in the ruins of a monastery. The old building has a tower with a window, and its unused, decrepit condition indicates that this vampire does not have the spiritual quality that Louis and Claudia possess. This proves to be the case when they discover that he is no more than a mindless corpse. *(IV 188)*

Later in Paris, Armand takes Louis up a tower so they can talk in private. Louis is hesitant to climb up it, but Armand insists that he possesses the power to do so. Armand is symbolically urging Louis to accept the spiritual aspects of his existence as a vampire. Louis, however, is afraid; he has not yet entirely accepted the idea that he is a devil, so he is trying to cling to his humanity. In a reverse echo of Bram Stoker's *Dracula*, who descended the outside wall of his castle, Louis and Armand ascend together to the top floor. *(IV 281)*

The tower possesses a window, and the two vampires look out over the roofs of other buildings as they talk. Here Armand appears to Louis to be an angel, which is especially significant in terms of where they are. That they are in the reflective mode—the aspect of mind closer to divinity, according to Aristotle—is emphasized by the presence of books in the room. Armand attempts to seduce Louis, to fuse with him and draw him into fully accepting his vampire nature, with all its powers. Yet Louis refuses to relinquish his life with Claudia, even though he is somewhat aware that what he had with her is over. *(IV 292)*

Lestat, too, climbs a tower with Armand, but with more catastrophic results. It is the tower he inherited from Magnus, in which he was made a vampire. He had been taken to its heights to be given the gift of immortality, even as corpses of young men rotted in the dungeon below. Lestat lives in Magnus's tower until he leaves Paris. He then gives the tower to Armand, who had come out from his crypt

below Les Innocents and who has begun to read books for enlightenment. When Lestat is in need of assistance many years later, he returns
to Armand, who pushes him from the tower room. Lestat "falls from
grace," breaking all the bones in his body as he hits the ground below.
(VL 83, 508)

When Akasha arises from her silent sleep, she takes Lestat to his
old castle in the Auvergne. She moves toward the old tower and
beckons to him, symbolically urging him toward her form of enlightenment. She wants him to move as she does, and poses a test to his new
powers by flying to the top room. As there are no steps, he, too, must
fly as she has done. He hesitates, because he wants to comprehend this
power, but Akasha tells him he must let go of his need to think it
through and should just do it by the force of his will. He then moves
to join her, and succeeds. *(QD 256)*

In the tower room Lestat is confronted with his past. Akasha uses
his former weapons as a metaphor for what he will do for her. He will
kill for her, and it will be justified by her new world order. She then
tells him he will be a god before she takes him from the tower.

See also Flight, Vampire Powers.

Tower of Babel   Mentioned in Genesis 11:1–9, it is the Babylonian tower that the people of Earth were building to try to reach into
Heaven. To humble them, God altered their speech, making them
unable to communicate with one another in the same language. He then
scattered them over the face of the Earth and the tower was never
completed.

Lestat compares the buildings along Manhattan's Fifth Avenue—
particularly Olympic Tower—to the Tower of Babel. He mentions it
just as the Devil is coming for him. *(MD 162, 321)*

Town House   Louis owns several town houses in New Orleans,
and he places his mother and sister in one when he can no longer run
the plantation after his brother's death. However, the most significant
town house is the one he lives in with Lestat and Claudia.

He moves with Lestat into this residence on New Orlean's Royal
Street after they must flee Pointe du Lac. Rice based her description of
it on the Gallier House at 1132 Royal Street in the French Quarter of
New Orleans (despite the fact that the Gallier House was not built until
1857). The vampires' town house has a hidden courtyard with a garden
and fitted wooden shutters. Lestat imports chandeliers, carpets, vases,
statuary, art, and tapestries to adorn the interior of his new home, and
commissions a mural of a magical forest for Claudia's room. Louis
feels that the town house is even more secure and luxurious than the
plantation. *(IV 99–100)*

Louis and Lestat live there with Claudia for sixty-five years in a

*Gallier House, New
Orleans, model for Louis's
town house*

second-story flat until Claudia's actions—her attack on Lestat—result
in a fire that drives them out. Just prior to the fire, Louis had signed the
town house over to Lestat in preparation for his leaving New Orleans.
Over a century later, this documented transaction is helpful to Jesse's
investigation for the Talamasca about the vampire's existence. (*QD*
179)

Jesse locates information that the house is currently operated by
a rental agency, which receives payment from a Parisian attorney. She
rents the home so that she can explore it thoroughly. There she discovers the old wallpaper and the mural described in Louis's confession.

Jesse also finds a door that opens a secret compartment; inside it she discovers one of Claudia's dolls and a diary containing several entries written by Claudia. *(QD 179–180)*

In BT, Lestat returns to this town house with his dog, Mojo. He hires craftspeople to restore it to its original condition, and refurbishes it in a French style. He wants the present to eclipse the past. He realizes that his living there again may aid readers of *The Vampire Chronicles* in locating him, but that amuses, rather than worries, him. He also knows that Louis has noticed the renovation, and, when it is finished, he asks Louis to move in with him. After Lestat returns from making David a vampire in Barbados, he finds Louis there. To his surprise, David is also there, and David urges Lestat to join them on a trip to Rio. *(BT 396, 430)*

After Lestat first meets with Dora, he goes to the town house to find safety from his brief yet startling encounter with Memnoch. However, Memnoch is there at the town house—no place is safe from the Devil—and he implores Lestat to listen to what he wants. They struggle, but then Lestat agrees to hear Memnoch's plea.

Lestat agrees to accompany Memnoch to Heaven and Hell. After his ordeal, he returns to New Orleans, to St. Elizabeth's, his new home. Louis invites him to return to the town house and even takes Wynken's books there, but Lestat prefers his castle. *(MD 129–139, 353)*

The Gallier House in New Orleans is open to the public. (See Vampire Atlas)

See also Diary, Fire, Jesse, Magical Forest, Memnoch, New Orleans, Real Estate, Royal Street.

"Tragic Rabbit" A poem about a painting of a rabbit. Stan Rice both did the painting and wrote the poem. The poem introduces QD and is a response to the theme of life versus art in William Butler Yeats's poem "Sailing to Byzantium" (which introduces BT). This poem emphasizes a theme that Anne Rice wanted to bring out in QD: that wisdom resides in the material world and in the flesh. In other words, art is not superior to life, nor can it entirely imitate life.

"I look upon art as a kind of addiction," Stan Rice says. "In other words, making art is dangerous. You'd better watch out because it requires you to go all the way. There's a war going on between the world of real things and the ideal world of art, and if you're ever goaded into thinking of yourself as a thing as pure as a painted rabbit, you'd better watch out for the true flesh, which contains death itself."

See also Poetry, Rice (Stan), "Sailing to Byzantium," Yeats (William Butler).

Traini, Francesco A fourteenth-century Italian painter who was

famous for his depictions of violence and brutality in paintings like *Inferno* and *The Triumph of Death*.

Louis sees reproductions of his work in the subterranean room of the Theater of the Vampires. *(IV 230)*

See also Art, Subterranean Room.

Transformation   What happens to those who are chosen to become vampires. Drained of blood, to the point of death, they then find that the demonic blood animating their seducer takes hold in their hearts. *(VL 442)*

The first transformation scene is Louis's, and he describes the experience in detail in IV. The transformation begins for him when, as a mortal, he is overwhelmed by his first glimpse of Lestat. "I was reduced to nothing," he says. "I forgot myself totally." *(IV 13)* He is seduced by, then gradually addicted to, Lestat's description of his personal vampire experience. In comparison, everything in Louis's life seems trivial, and he realizes how empty his own routines, beliefs, and aspirations are.

And after he experiences what it is like to kill someone (the overseer), Louis tells Lestat to just kill him. Lestat moves to obey, but Louis then finds himself struggling with Lestat. He realizes he does not want to die, and so yields to Lestat's desire to make him immortal. Lestat, urging Louis to will himself to remain alive, drains him of blood nearly to the point of death. As Lestat moves his lips erotically against Louis's neck, the subsequent feeling of sudden paralysis terrifies Louis. Lestat then bites his own wrist and gives it to Louis to suck. In the resulting swoon, Louis hears their hearts beating together, as two drums. When Lestat withdraws his wrist, all things appear different to Louis. *(IV 17–20)*

He sees as a vampire and the effect is hallucinatory. He becomes entranced with such simple objects as Lestat's buttons; he is overwhelmed by the magnified noises of the night; and he falls in love with the moonlight. Then his body begins to ache and Lestat explains to him that his mortal form is dying. As his new senses take over, his human fluids leave his itching, tingling body. By the next evening, Louis's transformation is complete. He is more powerful, faster, and more sensitive than he had ever been in human life. To his consternation, however, he realizes that Lestat has now lost his magical appeal. They are equals, and thus Louis is able to see Lestat's flaws. *(IV 20)*

"The whole thing [about the transformation]," Rice explains, "is to learn your nature. It's to look at a tree until you see its true self."

For Louis, the transformation involves a breakdown of the ego. He emerges from a limited point of view that was informed by empty beliefs, and moves into a vast realm of infinite possibility. His new perception overwhelms him with its beauty. *(IV 20)*

Lestat, too, experiences this transformation, although he fights longer and harder against it, and, when it does occur, is less intimidated by it. Like Louis, he also is caught up in its ecstasy: "I was nothing but pleasure," he later describes about Magnus sucking his blood. *(VL 88)* He finds that he is unable to speak, and he experiences an unendurable thirst with the loss of his blood. He believes that something else is breathing for him, and is overwhelmed by a loud noise, the sound of a "deep gong." As Magnus continues to drink, Lestat sees hallucinations and visions of his own past life, and of how Magnus became a vampire. When Lestat is offered blood from Magnus's wounded neck, he drinks ravenously. As he does so, a feeling of numbness, that is laced through with rapturous sensations, creeps through his body. He feels an incredible love for Magnus—a bond unlike any he had felt as a mortal—and he also feels loved, for all his cravings are satisfied. The blood feels like a light passing through him, and brings him great clarity, weightlessness, and calm. As his waste leaves his body, fear and disgust also become distant experiences (although a hot pain does move through his chest). *(VL 88–92)*

Jesse, Daniel, and Marius all describe their transformation experiences as well. Marius tells of a vision of Those Who Must Be Kept. His maker gives it to him, while also feeding him a command to serve the Mother. With every exchange of blood, Marius learns more about the vampire mythos. He experiences the draining of his blood as the draining of his self. His maker tells him that he is now a servant of the Mother, and that the moon gives him his strength. *(VL 418–420)*

When he makes Daniel, Armand gives him a dream of a garden paradise that Armand calls the gateway of life and death. It replicates the Villa of the Mysteries in Pompeii, where the two of them had become "secret lovers" years earlier. Daniel also connects with other vampires through visions in which they are aware of his joining them. Specifically, he sees both Louis and Lestat looking back at him. He also experiences a stomachache, feels immense pressure from the blood flowing out of his body, and perceives a host of unconnected images and sounds. Then he falls asleep. *(QD 112)*

Jesse adds a sense of weightlessness to her description of the transformation experience. She sees the souls of other dead people leaving the earth as they die, and hears music. Maharet instructs her to beware of ideas that have no "flesh." For Jesse, receiving the blood brings heat and a sense of being anchored forever to her body. She also feels the sensation of becoming nothing, of being emptied. She envisions the lost twin Mekare looking at her, and the connection seems to give the real Mekare the direction she needs to find the other vampires. *(QD 241)*

Lestat experiences a further stage of transformation from drinking Akasha's blood. To him it seems a rebirth, or a second transforma-

tion. He awakens her from her trance and they lock together, deliciously sucking blood in a seemingly eternal circle until they are forcibly separated. Two centuries later, when Akasha comes to make Lestat her prince, she passes on to him new powers through her blood. Even vampires older than Lestat now believe Lestat may be more powerful than they as a result. *(VL 249, 486)*

When Lestat makes Gabrielle, the transformation process is offered through his eyes, as the vampire bringing it about. He feels great love for Gabrielle and great thirst for her blood. He offers her the Dark Gift, and she takes it. She represents to him a blend of mother, lover, victim, peer, and companion. It is everything he can do to push away from her just before she dies, for he experiences an intense ambivalence: one part of him wants to crush her, the other to draw her to him. When she drinks, he feels the blood coursing through his veins like molten metal, but he also feels numb. He pushes Gabrielle away without any sense of a decision to do so: it is his body that instinctively saves him, not his mind. The experience exhausts him, and builds a strange wall of silence between him and his child. *(VL 158)*

The transformation process is a metaphor of self-reinvention and redemption. "My work is filled with those moments," says Rice, "where people are scattered and broken and have to reinvent themselves—and do! I think that's a very important vision for our age. As religion loses its hold on people in a magical way, people have to reinvent themselves in terms of new ideas."

See also Making a Vampire, Vampire Powers.

Transubstantiation   The Catholic doctrine of the mystical transformation of the Communion wine and bread into the physical flesh and blood of Christ.

The vampires mirror this sacrament as the spiritual power of Amel works on their blood: "It worked not merely to animate the tissue but to convert it slowly into something else." *(QD 128)* This connection with religious symbols adds spiritual depth to the vampire archetype.

See also Eucharist, Religion, Religious Images.

Transylvania   The region of Romania, near the Hungarian border, that was the setting for Dracula's castle.

Louis and Claudia travel through this area on their quest for Old World vampires. Here they encounter several vampires who are mindless, animated corpses. Discouraged by their encounters, they leave Transylvania. *(IV 188–197)*

See also Eastern Europe, Old World Vampires, Quest.

Tree Grows in Brooklyn, A   A 1943 novel written by Betty

Smith about a young girl, Francie Nolan, who reaches for happiness despite her poverty and an alcoholic father. The book is bought by the intended victim of a serial killer as Lestat watches. He comments that he, too, has read and enjoyed this book. *(BT 16)*

Trial   The vampires at the Theater of the Vampires hold a trial for Claudia, whom Lestat has accused of trying to kill him. The rules of this coven demand capital punishment for such a crime. Armand wants to get Louis away from Claudia, so he is the one responsible for setting up the trial. He then forces Lestat to testify against Claudia, and oversees her punishment himself. He then falsely tells Louis that he had no power over Claudia's fate.

Armand engineered the trial to manipulate Louis into loving him, but it proved to be a farce. It backfired for it drained from Louis the very spirit with which Armand had fallen in love. *(IV 304–306, VL 506)*

See also Armand, Capital Crime, Claudia, Deception, Madeleine, Rules.

Trinity Church   Located at the foot of Wall Street, this Gothic structure was built in 1846. Many famous people, such as Alexander Hamilton, are buried in its cemetery.

After depositing the last of Roger's dismembered corpse in a trash heap, Lestat sits on the steps of this church and looks over the gravestones. Some people disturb him, driving him away. *(MD 46)*

See also Wall Street.

Triumph of Death, The   The name of a painting by Pieter Brueghel that Louis sees reproduced in the ballroom beneath the Theater of the Vampires. Replete with hideous images, it reinforces the idea of the vampire's dark lair as being a place of evil and death. *(IV 229)*

See also Art, Brueghel (Pieter), Subterranean Room.

Truth   A transcendent and fundamental spiritual reality. Several vampires seek truth and much of the debate in QD revolves around the concepts of goodness and truth.

If there is a God, then God defines truth. However, since the vampires can find no evidence for God, they realize they must make their own truths. Akasha takes this idea to an extreme. She believes that, in the absence of an Absolute Being, she can proclaim herself a goddess and define truth within her own framework. Even as a mortal, Akasha had found the concept of truth to be malleable. She decided what she wanted to do, then proclaimed it a great truth that her people must follow. She and Enkil had "spread" these "truths" through wholesale slaughter, forcing others to believe and obey. As the Queen

of Heaven—a title borrowed from the goddess she had once worshiped as a mortal—Akasha would continue this approach. She wants to remake the world according to her own vision, and selects certain human events—like war and genocide—to support her theories and reduce truth to merely a matter of abstract ideals. *(QD 303, 440–452)*

Marius points out to Akasha that she is failing to see the whole picture; her truth is a subjective point of view that should not be the basis for what happens with humanity. He uses the metaphor of a tree, which, from one perspective, can be described as an agent of destruction and vampirism. However, there is more to the tree than just being a part of the cycle of nature. It is also a thing of beauty, which makes its own contribution. *(QD 403, 442)* Marius's plea echoes the notion that while truth may not be entirely clear or absolute, its principles are to be found in the material world, and not in abstract, simplistic ideas that disavow parts of life for its own purposes. Yet Akasha discounts Marius and his theory.

David Talbot also wrestles with questions of truth, and with the difficulty of never knowing ultimate answers. In BT, Lestat claims to seek truth only in the physical world and in aesthetic principles, because God cannot be known. The truth of the vampires, he adds, is that they are a mystical experience without any revelation of truth. And encountering a vampire, without acquiring through the experience a clear explanatory frame of reference, can actually drive mortals mad. *(BT 66–71, 230, 254)*

When he encounters the Devil, Lestat thinks he may discover ultimate truth. He goes to Heaven and reads from books that seem to contain all the answers, but as soon as he leaves Heaven, he forgets what he has read. He also sees a balustrade from which he realizes that he will understand everything about the Earth's history, but God stands there, preventing him from looking. *(MD 166, 168–169)*

Memnoch then tells Lestat the story of creation and how Christianity evolved as God's plan for humankind. As a result, God also created and perpetuated evil, which Memnoch wants Lestat's help in diminishing. Memnoch also shows Lestat what Hell is really like—a place of educating and purging—but Lestat finally has had enough. He escapes and returns to his life, realizing that nothing he has witnessed with Memnoch proves anything, for it could all be an illusion. The loss of one of his eyes seems to symbolize his inability to see the real truth. When Memnoch's note arrives, hinting that Lestat was duped, he realizes he cannot even be sure of the truth of that. *(MD 350)*

See also Akasha's Plan, Deception, Knowledge, Memnoch, Queen of Heaven, Quest, Savage Garden.

Twain, Mark   A nineteenth-century American writer and humorist, famous for novels like *The Adventures of Tom Sawyer* and *Huckle-*

berry Finn. Also known as Samuel Clemens, he is one of the writers from whom Lestat claims to have learned the English language. *(VL 4)*

Twilight The time of day when night begins to take over. As a mortal, Lestat hates this time because twilight precedes darkness and he fears what darkness portends. *(VL 65)*

See also Dark Moment, Darkness.

Twins Symbolically, twins are the synthesis of dual aspects of one person, or the wholeness of the psyche. Not only do they portray a pull in contrary directions, but they depict apparent symmetry, and also paradox, for two are as one. In addition, twins represent complementarity and counterbalance among such dualities as life/death, passive/ aggressive, masculine/feminine, and finite/infinite. Twins often carry an aura of the exotic and unusual, and are thought to be blessed with a special energy.

The twins in the *Chronicles* are Maharet and Mekare, red-haired witches who live in a Palestinian tribal society while Enkil and Akasha reign as King and Queen in Egypt. The twins' mother was a witch, and, as twins, they are able to enhance her powers to attract and communicate with spirits.

This power attracts Akasha's attention, but they refuse her invitation to come to her court. She then sends soldiers, who kill their people and force the twins to the Egyptian court. After the witches answer her questions about the spirit world, Akasha imposes a death sentence on them. However, she lifts this when the spirits protecting them demonstrate their power. Instead, Enkil orders Khayman to rape them before the court, to prove that the twins lack power.

Assisted by Bedouins, the twins then travel back to their own land, where Maharet has, from Khayman's rape, a mortal child.

After the twins' release, one spirit, Amel, remained behind at the court on Mekare's command. Through a series of events, this spirit transforms Akasha and Enkil into vampires. Akasha brings the twins back to explain what has happened and what must be done. They advise Akasha to destroy her body, for otherwise she will be driven by the spirit within her to make other blood drinkers. She denounces the twins and demands, as punishment, that Maharet's eyes be poked out and Mekare's tongue cut off, and that they be tied together overnight and burned alive the following day. Just before this sentence is carried out, Mekare prophesies that she herself will eventually be the agent of Akasha's demise.

While the twins are imprisoned, Akasha makes Khayman a vampire. In a rage, he gives the Dark Gift to Mekare, who then gives it to Maharet. The twins escape, but are then caught, sealed into stone coffins, and set adrift in opposite oceans. Even the spirits desert them

now. Once released, Maharet searches for, but fails to find, her twin. They only reunite centuries later when Akasha rises, and Mekare moves forth and fulfills her prophecy. *(QD 306–348, 381–389, 399–426, 455–457)*

See also Akasha, Akasha's Plan, Dream of the Twins, Legend of the Twins, Maharet, Mekare, Witches.

Typhon In Greek and Roman myth, Typhon (also known as Set) is the brother of Osiris. It was he who tricked Osiris into a coffin, then sealed it. He is also responsible for cutting Osiris into pieces after Isis had rescued him.

Armand mentions this name in his stories about Marius, because Marius had hinted enigmatically about the vampires' connection with the tale of Osiris. Gabrielle tends not to believe Armand's tale about Marius, although she admits that it is unlikely he could have made up the reference to Typhon. More willing to explore the possibilities, Lestat reads the old Egyptian myths seeking clues about Marius and about his own vampire nature. *(VL 295, 330–331)*

See also Osiris.

Uncle Mickey Roger's mother's brother, he has only one eye. The true story of how he lost it has been a family secret for years.

As a sign of his credibility, Memnoch tells Lestat to mention to Dora her uncle Mickey's eye. Dora is surprised when Lestat says this but tells him how her uncle Mickey was beaten up in Corona's Bar in New Orleans. He had held back a bet on a horse that ended up winning, so the bookie had sent some men in to teach him a lesson. He lost his eye in the fight, and the men beating him deliberately stepped on it. Dora adds that because the family had hidden the shameful truth, her own father had always thought Uncle Mickey had lost his eye playing with fireworks.

The story proves to Lestat that Memnoch knows secrets. It also foreshadows the loss of Lestat's own eye, and that loss becomes a symbol of being unable to see all the consequences of one's actions. (MD 74, 138, 153)

Uncle Mickey is based on Rice's own mother's brother. The incident she describes in the novel was real. Rice dedicates the novel to her uncle Mickey, his descendants, and to another uncle who was in Corona's Bar that night.

"My uncle Mickey did have his eye kicked out of his head by gangsters in Corona's Bar in the Irish Channel," said Rice. "My uncle Marian Leslie witnessed the dastardly deed and told my father of it. My father said that my mother never believed it. Like Roger's mother in *Memnoch*, my mother always believed that her brother had suffered an accident with a firecracker.

"My aunt Pat Harberson repeated the whole story of Uncle Mickey's eye to me and told me that Marian had said, 'If only they hadn't stepped on the eye, the eye could have been saved.'

"The story of Uncle Mickey suffering at the hands of gangsters

is like all the material a writer pours into a work: everything you use comes from somewhere, and everything is there to use."

See also Eyes, Lestat de Lioncourt, Memnoch.

Undead Another name for vampire. *(MD 334)*
See also Vampire.

Underground What vampires call the activity of ceasing to drink and then going into a form of hibernation or suspended animation, when they bury themselves deep in the earth. They then move into a dream state, and become too weak to resurrect themselves. It is usually brought on by despair or boredom, and Lestat experiences going "underground" twice.

The first time it happens to Lestat is after he has been searching in vain for Marius. Not only does Lestat begin to despair of ever finding Marius, but he also hears that Nicolas has jumped into the fire and that his own mortal brothers have been murdered in the French Revolution. To make matters worse, he discovers that Gabrielle has finally tired of his love for mortals and has left him. Lestat sinks into oblivion, but Marius, surprised that this condition has happened to Lestat so soon, comes and pulls him out of it. Marius explains that vampires must go into the ground from time to time to help them endure the passing of centuries, although Maharet claims she has never lost consciousness in all her six thousand years. *(VL 358, QD 426)*

The second time Lestat goes underground is in 1929, in New Orleans. After suffering a number of wounds and losses, he is too weak to endure the swift changes in the world around him. Lestat goes into the ground under his own house, and awakens in 1984 from the sounds of a rock band playing down the street. His self-consciousness breaks through the dream state he is in and he feeds on underground creatures, then rats and cats, until he has the strength to lift himself out of the ground and go drink from humans. *(VL 4–7)*

See also First Death.

Understanding the Present Subtitled *Science and the Soul of Modern Man*, this 1992 book by columnist Bryan Appleyard argues against relying on science for solving problems concerning value and meaning. He claims that science has been so culturally pervasive that it is buried within us and determines our modern perspective. Since science is mobile and ever-changing, it moves us into an aimless, arbitrary relativity that makes no provision for who we are. As a result, we have abandoned our true selves. Unrelenting pessimism, skepticism, despair, and uncertainty indicate our state of spiritual fatigue. Since science divides knowledge from meaning, it fails to address our inner needs. We long for reassurances from nature, but as we are fundamen-

tally different from the rest of nature, we cannot find our purpose by achieving harmony with it. Humanity can only be saved by an act of absolute assertion of the inner self, by taking the risk of being accountable in a spiritual context. The human condition demands religion, and science cannot provide answers to our most fundamental quest for purpose.

Dora Flynn agrees with Appleyard's premises, so she urges her father to read the book. He does so, later mentioning it to Lestat as a valuable statement on the spiritual impoverishment of modern times. Lestat knows the book and agrees that theology must come from within the self, from "a totality of human experience." He decides to read the book. *(MD 32, 90)*

"*Understanding the Present* is one of many such books that I read on the state of religious thinking in our times," says Rice, "which is one of my fields of constant study."

See also *Memnoch the Devil.*

"Untitled" poem   A poem by Stan Rice, used in QD to introduce the section describing Lestat's rock concert. It is about the limitations of the flesh. *(QD 195)*

See also Poetry, Rice (Stan).

Upper East Side   An area of Manhattan located between Fifty-ninth and Ninety-sixth streets and from the East River to Fifth Avenue; this is where the wealthy reside.

Roger owns a house here, between Madison and Fifth avenues, in which he stores his religious artifacts. Hirelings live on the lower and upper floors. Roger's own rooms are accessible only from a rear entrance and are stuffed full of trunks, statues, icons, crucifixes, and books. When Lestat enters the house, he senses that a young man whom Roger had loved had recently died there. He sees a black granite statue of a demon that reminds him of his stalker, and it turns out that Memnoch is indeed there with him. In these rooms, Lestat kills Roger and cuts him apart, then later returns to the house to retrieve the relics and put them in a safer place. *(MD 29)*

See also Manhattan, Roger.

Uptown   In BT, the location in New Orleans of Louis's house. Lestat describes this area when he visits Louis. Large Victorians and small cottages line the streets, and some of the yards are so overgrown that it feels like a place in the country. Currently, Uptown is known primarily for its universities—Loyola and Tulane—and Louis's choice to reside in this area seems appropriate in view of his love for books and his emphasis on exploring intellectual questions.

Louis lives there in a small cottage behind a huge, deteriorating

Louis's Uptown house

Victorian mansion. The trees are so overgrown that even the moonlight cannot penetrate through their branches. Some of the cottage's windows are broken. Louis owns only books, paintings, and a few prized possessions, and Lestat keeps a favorite chair there for himself. Lestat dislikes the way Louis chooses to live, like some ghost in a dusty old place, but Louis will not be dissuaded from his simple lifestyle. Lestat is often tempted to clean it up for him, and after one especially disheartening visit there, Lestat destroys the cottage. Louis then moves in with Lestat in the French Quarter. *(BT 103–104)* (See Vampire Atlas)

See also Louis de Pointe du Lac.

Uriel One of the chief angels named in noncanonical writings, he is variously called a cherub and a seraph as well as the archangel of salvation. As an angel of prophecy, he serves as a muse to writers and teachers. Since he is the angel in charge of natural forces, he may also have been the angel who warned Noah of the flood and the one who

wrestled with Jacob. In Milton's *Paradise Lost*, Satan tricked Uriel into giving him directions to Eden.

At one point during the evolution of God's creation, Uriel accompanies Memnoch to question God. *(MD 206)*

See also Angel.

Uruk   Also known as Erech, this was an ancient city on the Euphrates River in Mesopotamia. It was ruled by the Sumerian king Enmerkar, and historians consider Uruk to have been one of the greatest cities of Sumer. Anu and Inanna were its patron deities.

When he is seeking a queen, King Enkil brings Akasha from Uruk to Egypt. *(QD 314)* (See Vampire Atlas)

See also Akasha.

Vagabond monsters   The name Claudia uses for the mindless vampires she and Louis see in Eastern Europe. *(IV 199)*

See also Old World Vampires, Revenant.

Valley of the Shadow of Death   A phrase from the Twenty-third Psalm of David, it describes a frightening place of evil and darkness. David claims that God's presence guides him through it.

Memnoch uses this phrase to describe the gloom of Sheol. *(MD 248)*

See also Bible, Sheol.

Valois, de   The alias Lestat uses when, as a mortal, he goes to Paris to become an actor. *(VL 66)*

See also Lestat de Lioncourt.

Vampire   A preternatural, malignant creature transformed from a deceased mortal and sustaining itself on the blood of the living. Having once been human and in possession of consciousness, vampires are closer in kind to human beings than any other monsters. They exhibit the reality of an asocial inner life, and embody the horror of sociopathic conduct. As a symbol, vampires are typically associated with the Earth, darkness, the moon, and the abyss, all of which are identified as feminine. Shunning the sun involves losing the male element, thus making male vampires androgynous and female vampires doubly powerful.

The connection between vampires and their victims is through that of blood: both need it to survive. Blood symbolizes life and kinship, and gives rise to many sexual connotations. It pumps just as hot when its owner is terrified as when sexually aroused, giving the vampire a double-edged allure. Although vampires threaten with death, their bite promises ecstasy and the possibility of immortality.

In folklore around the world, the vampire image evokes terror and inspires a wide variety of rituals mortals superstitiously practice to ward off or kill the vampire. Tales of vampires date back to ancient times, and are found across most world cultures. Among the earliest vampire images are the bloodthirsty goddess Kali; the Egyptian deity Osiris; and Yama, the Tibetan Lord of Death. Other names for vampires include Nosferatu, Verdilak, and Lamia.

The vampire myth originated before the development of monotheistic religions, and before the idea that the mind was separate from the body. Many ancient cultures believed in the human being's capacity for alternate mental states and that there were several types of souls. Often the creation of a vampire was believed to have occurred as the result of the soul leaving the body after death: the higher soul departs for celestial realms but a lower part of the soul reenters the body at some point before decay sets in. The reanimated body, an image of the unchecked, imbalanced subconscious, thus was free to pursue its evil course.

Vampire mythology has many universal features, although the most familiar to Western culture comes from Eastern Europe, where vampires developed from residual souls that returned to, or remained (depending on the version of the myth), with the corpse. The superstition that the soul wanted to reanimate the body to live again filtered into vampire fiction. Christianized, this animating soul then became a demonic force. Beginning with *The Vampyre*, Dr. Polidori's story of Lord Ruthven in the early nineteenth century, vampires tended to be aristocrats who lived in desolate places and whose bodies had been invaded by an evil spirit that animated them.

Bram Stoker's *Dracula* was the most famous of these early stories, and most film versions of *Dracula* stamped contemporary vampire fiction since the 1930s with stereotypical expectations of what the vampire should be like: vampires cast no reflection in a mirror, have razor-sharp canine teeth, dress in black (often wearing a cape), are repelled by garlic and crucifixes, and can be destroyed by decapitation, fire, exposure to sunlight, or a stake (made of the same type of wood as Christ's cross) through the heart. Count Dracula could transform himself into a bat, wolf, or mist, and many vampire stories picked up on that image. Vampires in genre fiction also sleep in coffins (which are often filled with earth from their native ground), and rise nightly to drink blood from their victims. Sometimes vampires drain the victims of blood slowly; other times, they kill them instantly. Sometimes the bite of a vampire means certain immortality for each and every victim; at other times, the vampire performs a ritual with the bite, choosing only special mortals to become vampires.

Rice found this preternatural creature compelling: "I always thought the vampire was the most charming, magnetic monster of the whole supernatural pantheon." When she set out to write her own

version of the vampire story, she was already aware of both the legends and the available fiction surrounding the vampire.

"When I was a child," she says, "there was a story going around in my family called 'The White Silk Dress.' [Actually, "Dress of White Silk" by Richard Matheson.] It was told from the point of view of a child vampire. I thought it was quite wonderful and never forgot it. I wanted to get into the vampire. I've always been interested in the point of view of the people right in the center of it all."

Although Rice never finished Stoker's *Dracula*, she had read enough to realize that his presentation was different from the way she understood vampires. He emphasized the vampire's foul, animalian qualities, while Rice viewed vampires as sharing some traits with angels and saints. She felt they would—and should—have a refined spiritual aura about them: "I always saw vampires as sort of romantic and abstract. I saw them as angels going in the other direction. They had become finely tuned imitations of human beings imbued with this evil spirit, and the spirit was not material. I think they were presented that way in some of the old movies—in *Dracula's Daughter*, in particular."

As a result, Rice's vampires retain few of the typical genre trappings (except for those, like Armand's coven, who cling to empty superstition). While they can be destroyed by fire, some can and do survive exposure to the sun. A stake through the heart cannot destroy them. They can see themselves in the mirror, because they take up physical space and there is no God to prohibit their reflection by denying them a soul. Many of them sleep in coffins, but it is not necessary, and none worry about getting the "right" dirt. They grow sharp teeth with which to drink blood, but they have no fear of churches, crucifixes, or other religious artifacts.

Although Rice's vampires represent the maximum proximity between human and monster, they possess certain features that reveal right away what they are: luminous white skin, gleaming fingernails, seemingly impossible speed, incredible flexibility, exaggerated facial expressions, and an unnatural gleam in the eye from reflecting too many colors. *(VL 124)*

Victims are attracted to Rice's vampires because they also possess the special allure described in earlier vampire fiction. They offer intimacy, power over death to those they choose to make immortal, and sensual rapture. Sinking their teeth into a victim's neck provides immensely erotic sensations to both parties (although vampires like Louis, who feel guilty over this pleasure, take their victims more quickly). Armand believes that the victims who surrender most easily are Those Who Want to Die.

The vampire mythos Rice developed in the *Chronicles* is inspired by the fact that vampire lore can be traced back to early gods and goddesses like Osiris and Dionysus. Their ritual practices used blood sacrifices to symbolize mastery over life. Yet, with the rise of Christianity, the priests transformed these vegetation gods (and vampires along with them) into demons, proclaiming that since blood held the magical quality of life that only Christ could sanction, stealing it was an act of sacrilege. Thus, the vampire became an evil creature of the night.

But through associating the vampires with ancient gods and goddesses, Rice links the Egyptian mythologies (Osiris) to the Greek and Roman (Dionysus or Bacchus), both of which foreshadowed the life, death, and resurrection of Christ. The vampire progenitors, Akasha and Enkil, are Egyptian royalty who align themselves with the worship of Osiris. They are not invaded by the Devil but by a spirit who wants to experience the movement of flesh; it enters them through their bodily wounds. As an entity of vast dimension, it urges Akasha and Enkil, via an unquenchable thirst, to make other vampires to share in the burden of getting blood for it. The spirit then invades whoever is given the blood, changing their body's cellular structure and joining all vampires together into a single network. In Rice's version, vampires are not satanic, then, but merely the result of an accidental fusion of a spirit with flesh that provides extraordinary powers along with immortality, and craves blood for self-renewal. *(QD 422)*

Unlike the purely evil monsters of nineteenth-century fiction, Rice's vampires possess human qualities. They experience their own unconscious compulsions, and feel lonely, anguished, guilty, compassionate, angry, bored, sad, and more. They seek love and companionship, and some desire to find ways to do good with their powers. They are able to love whomever they choose without the restrictions of social propriety, because they are outside society's boundaries. Their senses are magnified to the point where all of life takes on a precious glow. In short, the vampires of the *Chronicles* retain the romantic image of the vampire as a dangerous creature of the shadows, but add to it the power of transcending gender and of retaining human emotions and psychological conflicts.

For example, David Talbot fears that vampires lose their humanity by losing the balance between their intellect and their moral sensitivity. Their moral development stops while their intellect continues to grow. He fears that this will cause his own demise. *(MD 107)* These latter qualities are the result of Rice's personal intrigue with the figure of the vampire. Familiar with films that allowed the potential for vampires to embody more (and less) than pure evil, she probed the vampire image for its deeper layers. *(IV 37, 43, 44)*

"That is what interests me: the idea that these characters are tragic heroes and heroines, that they have a conscience. They have hearts, they have souls, they suffer loneliness, and they know what they're doing. They don't want to be doing it [killing], and yet it's their nature. I wanted to put myself in the vampire's skin and see through the vampire's eyes, and ask the questions I felt were inevitable for a vampire to ask.

"The horror of the vampire is that they're locked in the physical. They can't hearken to the lessons of the physical because they have to kill—and that betrays the lesson that life is meaningful. The vampire is outside life and sees the beauty of life, yet he has to kill to survive. I think that is a powerful metaphor for the compromises we make every day."

See also Amel, Appearance, Blood, Clothing, Hawthorne (Nathaniel), Insects, Moral Dilemma, Outsiders, Rapture, Shaman, Superstitions, Swoon, Thirst, *The Vampire Chronicles*, Vampire Eyes, Vampire Nature, Vampire Powers, Vampire Tales, Vegetation Gods, Victims.

Vampire abilities   See Vampire Powers.

Vampire bars   Clandestine meeting places for the vampires, which lie in the back rooms of bars frequented by mortals. Bars are places of secrecy on the fringes of society where outsiders gather for companionship, entertainment, information, and the freedom to express themselves. They are generally associated with night life, as are vampires.

While writing VL and QD, Rice lived in the Castro District in San Francisco. She observed all around her how leather and gay bars served as hubs of the community. The "invisible" subculture came to life in bars; people considered threatening by society at large met here on neutral territory, where social judgments that alienated them and made them outcasts were suspended. Inside the bars, they formed a complex culture, similar to the way poets and writers of the fifties and sixties met in bars for community, support, and relaxation.

In Rice's novels, the vampire bars are located in large cities around the world and, along with coven houses, are part of the Vampire Connection. They are considered safe places where no vampire is permitted to harm another, and become central sources of information on vampire activities. While mortals drink and carry on with the excesses of life in one area, the vampires, who also drink (albeit not in the same manner), gather in another. (Lestat does mention that vampires always order hot drinks to stave off the cold and to keep in touch with human sensibilities. [MD 7, 15–16])

While the vampires do not drink alcoholic beverages, it is significant that they meet in places where alcohol is served. Alcohol is a mysterious liquid that burns when lit. Known as "fire water," it represents a union of opposites that parallels the "living dead" nature of the vampires. It is also associated with Dionysus, the god of uninhibited, insatiable desire, whose orgies involve both the heights of euphoric creativity and the threat of destruction. Lestat refers to himself as a Dionysus. *(VL 501)*

The vampire bars are first mentioned in VL, when Louis tells

Lestat about them in San Francisco. "There is Dr. Polidori in London," he says, "and Lamia in Paris. There is Bela Lugosi in the City of Los Angeles, and Carmilla and Lord Ruthven in New York." (VL 528–529) In QD, Khayman visits one in Athens called Lamia, and another in New Orleans is mentioned but not named. (QD 131)

San Francisco's vampire bar, based on a composite of the gay bars in the Castro District, is called Dracula's Daughter. "Vampires transcend gender," says Rice, "so where else would they go but to the Castro?" In her mind, the bar was located on Castro Street and Market, where in reality a building housed a gay bar and The Elephant Walk restaurant. It was a significant corner, Rice points out: police raided the real bar the night that members of the gay community stormed City Hall because Dan White had been sentenced to only eight years for murdering the mayor and gay city supervisor Harvey Milk.

In the front room of Dracula's Daughter, where mortals drink Bloody Marys, posters of cinema vampires like Bela Lugosi hang on the walls. The bar also shows vampire films and plays Lestat's rock videos, while its patrons dress in wild costumes. Ironically, vampires pass through the crowd unnoticed, going to the back to angrily debate the meaning of Lestat's book and songs. On one wall of the back room is a mural of a deteriorating castle and graveyard; on the ceiling, images of devils and witches dance. Black velvet hangings, black tile, and brass fixtures complete the decor: "It was the cliché reinvented as if it were not a cliché." (QD 14)

Written in black on a red wall is a declaration of the various offenses that the "outlaws" Louis and Lestat have committed through publishing their books and revealing vampire names, traditions, and origins. The declaration calls on the "Children of Darkness" to attack Lestat while he performs his rock concert on Halloween.

When Akasha rises, she burns down vampire bars and coven houses all over the world, transforming these "wombs" into arenas of death. What had once been declared places of security prove as transitory as everything else in a world where vampires can exist and absolutes seem to vanish.

Interestingly, after QD was published, fire damaged the actual building on Castro that inspired Rice. (QD 11–16, 20, 48–49, 52, 130–31, 202)

See also Akasha, Bela Lugosi, Carmilla, Coven, Declaration, Dionysus, Dracula's Daughter, Dr. Polidori, Lamia, Lord Ruthven, Mortals, Theater of the Vampires, The Vampire Connection.

Vampire Chronicles, The
The five novels in the vampire series written by Anne Rice.

The first, *Interview with the Vampire*, is a confession by Louis, a vampire, to a boy reporter, who publishes the story under the pseudonym Anne Rice. In it, Louis explains that he became a vampire under

the inept direction of a vampire named Lestat, and details what it was like to carry the subsequent burden of guilt and remorse for two centuries.

Using the same pseudonym, the vampire Lestat writes the rest of the *Chronicles*. He describes his own experience of being a vampire and how he used it to become a rock star. As a result, he shakes up the vampire world by calling forth the vampire progenitor Akasha. She enlists him in her plan to change the mortal world as well, and is eventually dispatched, to the great risk of the vampire race. The fourth *Chronicle* is an adventure in which Lestat agrees to switch bodies with a mortal con artist. His next book takes him to Heaven and Hell with the Devil. He meets God, hears the story of creation, and returns to Earth more afraid for his soul than before. (Lestat actually dictates this book to David Talbot.) All of the novels involve themes of good and evil, free will, immortality, and redemption.

As a corpus, the *Chronicles* involve a cosmology of the spiritual and supernatural world that shows it to be on a continuum with the natural world, although it still retains an eternal mystery.

Although Rice created her own vampire mythos, she changed and evolved some of its facets through the four books. For example, when Louis describes his transformation, he mentions hearing a drum, which turns out to be his heart beating with Lestat's. Lestat, however, adds to this experience by describing visions of Magnus, his vampire maker, and then Daniel sees Lestat and Louis acknowledging him as he makes the change. Others even hear voices during their transformation. Thus, the more involved Rice became with her characters, the more nuances she added to the most sensual and dramatic aspects of their experience.

Also, in the first novel, Rice had viewed the vampires as a bit more sinister. Injected into various parts of Louis's confession are allusions comparing vampires to insects; these were inspired by a science fiction story from the fifties about a man who was really a giant insect.

"That has always been part of my image of the vampire," Rice says, "that tall, dark man in that story who was camouflaged. I'm fascinated by the whole idea of the thing that looks human but really isn't. Tranvestites and drag queens and all forms of illusion—it's all linked together for me."

As part of that theme, Lestat seems more callous and vile in IV than he turns out to be in subsequent novels. While the apparent discrepancies may be confusing, they are easily attributable to the divergences of a story told from two perspectives. Louis has a dependent, passive personality and he rages against the one who will not take him by the hand through the most unique experience he has ever had. Lestat, however, is a tough, independent character who knows better than to do such a thing. Although he knows that he is evil, his motives

and actions are not as despicable as how Louis, within his embittered perspective, presents them to be. *(VL 498–499)*

An evolution of ideas, characters, and cosmologies is inevitable in a series of novels that spans so many years and so much mythological material, and stories that Rice has not yet told may hold keys to even deeper mysteries of the vampire nature.

"For me," she explains, "the philosophical meaning of being a vampire has been fully explored. It's time for a mutation. I feel that all my novels mutate toward the end into something else. They end with the butterfly stretching its wings. *The Vampire Chronicles* have mutated."

See also *Interview with the Vampire, Memnoch the Devil, The Queen of the Damned, The Tale of the Body Thief, The Vampire Lestat.*

Vampire cities   Lestat names several cities that he describes as perfect for vampires to inhabit. They are Amsterdam, for its late nights; Miami, for its color and restlessness; Paris, for its complexity; and New Orleans, for its sinisterness. In a part that was cut from BT, he also views Hong Kong as a good place for a vampire. *(IV 40, BT 9, 33)*

See also Amsterdam, Hong Kong, Miami, New Orleans, Paris.

Vampire comics   Khayman reads comics about vampires to get an idea of what blood drinkers are thought to be. *(QD 126)* Ironically, he himself ends up being in a vampire comic because Innovative Corporation serialized *The Vampire Chronicles* in graphic novel form.

Vampire Connection, The   Vampire bars, coven houses, and other meeting places around the world are referred to in the declaration against Lestat as the Vampire Connection. This physical connection is a metaphor for how the vampires are interconnected by a spiritual web. A sophisticated communication system that seems to operate by the power of a single mind joins all the vampires; thus they are aware of one another and able to telegraph their thoughts to each other telepathically. *(QD 14)*

See also Coven, One Powerful Mind, Telepathic Powers, Vampire Bars.

Vampire covens   See Covens.

Vampire drag   See Clothing.

Vampire eyes   Louis uses the phrase "vampire eyes" to tag the new vision he acquires when he is made into a vampire. This sort of "third eye" or "mind's eye" indicates superhuman abilities, which

Louis describes in IV: "I saw as a vampire," he says. "It was as if I had only just been able to see colors and shapes for the first time." *(IV 20)* He is captivated by the physical environment, which blossoms forth. Mortals appear to him as whirling, vibrating creatures, full of blood, and he stares at simple buttons or flagstones, watching their minuscule changes in the shadows and moonlight with awe and reverence. He learns that he can also see aging and change among mortals more clearly, and for this he mourns. Lestat informs him, however, that, no matter how much they may have helped him to appreciate it, these new eyes prevent him from ever returning to the mortal world. *(IV 82)*

Louis teaches Claudia about her "vampire eyes," urging her to drink up the world, and to hunger for whatever their expanded sensory experience offers. He sees life as too precious to waste. Savoring that which mortals take for granted, he understands this is possible only because of his new perspective, which allows him to be detached. *(IV 114)*

Not only does Louis see more vividly with his heightened, almost hallucinogenic, perception, but he can see easily in the dark. He also views his milieu in a different time frame: what mortals perceive as movement too quick for the eye, Louis perceives as slow and almost languid. The material composition of his eyes has been altered with the metamorphosis of his body cells.

The eyes of a vampire appear to mortals as flames: hypnotic, beautiful, and alluring. They can mesmerize at random, so vampires who mingle among mortals often wear dark glasses. Lestat's eyes remain wild and alive even as his body deteriorates after Louis and Claudia attempt to kill him. Thus the eyes are the last part of the vampire's body to lose their substance. *(IV 3, VL 3)*

Lestat also uses the phrase "vampire eyes" when he looks at another vampire and sees the difference in substance between vampires and mortals. He believes that vampires possess the vision of God, and that this perspective provides his sense of detachment. Vampires can take life without the moral overtones of murder, just as God can and does. Vampire eyes allow him to see human life in its entirety, thus connecting him to the divine plan that rules the lives of men. *(IV 83)*

From the physical descriptions of each of the vampires, it follows that they would possess special sight. Their eyes stand out from their smooth white faces like "demonic fire" or "flames in a skull." The eyes are variously described as extraordinary, incandescent, and hypnotic to mortals, and reflect moods of coldness, hunger, power, vulnerability, mindlessness, independence, and maturity. When Claudia ages inside her child's body, the change from innocence to sensuality is evident in her eyes: "Yet more and more her doll-like face seemed to possess two totally aware adult eyes." *(IV 102)* Lestat says that his own gray eyes absorb color and light from surfaces but are not themselves the source of light, indicating the absence of the sun in a vampire's existence.

Traditionally, eyes symbolize the inner spirit or soul. Thus, seeing becomes a spiritual act. One of the first vampires from the Egyptian era, Maharet, loses her physical eyes, yet she still can see by using the eyes of a mortal, showing that a vampire's vision transcends matter. *(QD 267, 411)* Lestat also loses an eye when he visits Hell with the Devil, but he gets it back, along with an altered perspective on life and death. *(MD 320, 350)*

When Lestat first sees through the eyes of a mortal again after switching bodies in BT, he adds one more dimension. He says that seeing with vampire eyes gives the immediate vivid impression of meaning. "All sounds to us are rich and translucent," he says, "all colors dazzlingly vibrant, all textures intimate and sensual." (BT unpublished section) By contrast, mortal vision is dim and lifeless. *(BT 169)*

See also Eyes, Senses, Vampire Powers.

Vampire films   The vampire bars exhibit posters from vampire films like *Dracula* and *Dracula's Daughter*. Khayman actually watches some of these films, noting the stereotypes about vampires they perpetuate but taking consolation in the fact that he belongs to a group with an identity. *(QD 125)*

See also Dracula's Daughter, Lugosi (Bela).

Vampire Lestat, The   Lestat joins the rock group Satan's Night Out and makes plans to lead them to fame. After he reads IV, he decides to coordinate their music with an autobiography he intends to write and changes the name of the group to The Vampire Lestat. *(VL 15)*

See also Rock Concert, Rock Music, Rock Star, Satan's Night Out.

Vampire Lestat, The   The title of the second *Vampire Chronicle*, which details Lestat's transformation into a vampire and his consequent quest and adventures.

When Rice first contemplated her sequel to *Interview with the Vampire* (as early as 1982), she included a female character named Sandra, who worked at the radio station with the boy reporter (named David, who later became Daniel). David had disappeared, so Sandra went to New Orleans to find the house that Louis mentioned in the tapes. She located it and found herself enchanted by a weakened Lestat, who gradually grew stronger with her help. They fell in love and Sandra became a vampire. Rice eventually wrote a different story.

"I knew when I finished *Interview with the Vampire*," says Rice, "that I wanted to write a sequel, but I wasn't ready. It took me a long time to get back to those characters and to feel that I had anything to say. When I wrote the first book I was Louis. When I wrote the second

one I was Lestat. I was going back and rewriting the first one in a much fuller way."

The second *Chronicle* is inspired by Lestat's emergence into the 1980s and his subsequent discovery that Louis has published their story via a reporter. Lestat feels that Louis distorted what happened, and did not really know the whole story. He tells his side to set the record straight, to show how much more there is to being a vampire than Louis was able to convey.

The Vampire Lestat was a difficult book for Rice to write. "It was very hard to get into. I never found a way to compress Lestat's childhood into a tight form. I was never satisfied with descriptions of the village and his life there, or even of Magnus or the tower. The 'Devil's Road' chapter, where Lestat goes all over Europe, was one of the hardest to write. I broke off the novel at that chapter and didn't resume until a year later. It was an utterly defeating chapter. It just drove me crazy." Eventually she found the voice she wanted to use for Lestat by developing a similar voice for the male character, Elliott, in *Exit to Eden*, an erotic contemporary novel. This helped her to break through her block.

The chronological tale of Lestat's life, taking place over a decade before the events in Louis's story, goes as follows: As a young man Lestat escapes the poverty of his ancestral home and finds fame in Paris as an actor. His courage and beauty attract the vampire Magnus, who forces the Dark Gift on Lestat, then abandons him. Lestat manages to deal with this dramatic change in his existence, and even flourishes with it. He then makes his mother, Gabrielle, and his best friend, Nicolas, into vampires. He also scatters a coven in Paris run by Armand, and goes off in search of a mentor, Marius.

After ten years, Lestat meets Marius and learns about how the vampire race got its start in Egypt. He is shown Enkil and Akasha, the king and queen, who silently and catatonically preserve the vampire spirit in their own bodies and thus must be kept safe. Lestat awakens the queen, Akasha, and they drink from each other until Enkil forces them apart. Marius then sends Lestat away for his own protection. Lestat ends up in New Orleans, where he spots Louis and makes him, then Claudia, into vampires. A brief chapter offers his version of the events surrounding his life with Louis and Claudia, Claudia's subsequent attack on him, and his recovery. He then offers his perspective about being a vampire through the publication of VL, and prepares for his rock concert. Louis, who has been estranged from him, joins him, fearful that other vampires, who resent the way Lestat has publicized them all, will destroy Lestat. Yet Lestat performs his concert without a hitch, and the novel ends when Akasha, awakened by Lestat's music, abducts him. The book is left unfinished and requires a sequel.

That sequel is QD, in which the publication of VL plays a significant part. VL's presence in bookstores angers most vampires, and also

The first edition jacket

spawns a new vocabulary and awareness for vampire covens. The book is denigrated in the declaration that is written on a wall in the vampire bar in San Francisco. *(QD 11)* Khayman sums up VL's theme as, "And this and this and this, and it means nothing." *(QD 204)*

More significantly, however, the publication of VL results in one character becoming a vampire. After she has already investigated Lestat and Louis from what Louis provided in IV, Jesse reads VL and decides that Lestat can provide answers for the mysteries in her own life. Through Lestat's autobiography, she learns about her friends, Mael and Santino, and recognizes that her aunt Maharet may be a vampire, too. The book even makes Jesse recall a repressed memory of having seen Mael and Maharet in their daytime, deathlike sleep. *(QD 190–191)* She goes to the concert and is fatally injured, so Maharet makes her a vampire.

In BT, Lestat refers to VL by name, and cites images in dreams that are from his mortal boyhood before he killed the wolves. These dreams feed into a sense of despair that sends him into the desert to expose himself to the sun. *(BT 4, 6)*

See also Akasha, Armand, Auvergne, Devil's Road, Gabrielle, Lestat de Lioncourt, Magnus, Marius, Paris, Rock Concert, Rock Star, Those Who Must Be Kept, *The Vampire Chronicles*, Wolves.

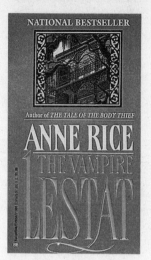

The mass market edition cover

Vampire limitations
Although the vampires receive extraordinary powers when they make the transformation, there are boundaries to their new experience, some of which are self-imposed. Louis, for example, cannot surrender to what he is, so he never experiences the fullness of what it means to be a vampire. Among other things, he does not allow himself to fly or to read the minds of his victims. *(BT 104)*

And when vampires lose confidence, they lose strength. Lestat experiences this when Akasha teaches him to trust himself to levitate and fly through the air. He can do this, but when he doubts himself he nearly falls. *(VL 13, QD 286)*

Vampires are also able to read each other's minds, except for when targeted vampires cloak their thoughts, or when one vampire has been made by another. The children of vampires are cut off from their makers by a veil of silence. *(VL 249, QD 18, BT 2)*

Generally, vampire powers increase with age and awareness, so it is the younger vampires, and those who refuse to open up their minds, who prove more limited than those with curiosity and experience. *(VL 7)*

See also Cloaking, Self-confidence, Vampire Powers, Veil of Silence, Victim Psychology.

Vampire nature
The physical constitution and inner force that compels vampires to drink blood. The spirit Amel created this need by transforming the vampires from mortal to immortal substance. This

transformation provides vampires with detachment, heightened senses, telepathic powers, and a different perspective on life to aid them in their predatory activities.

Louis and Lestat argue over the idea that Louis must do what his vampire nature dictates—kill humans. Even drinking from animals, as Louis resorts to for mere physical survival, will not really satisfy him. If he would only surrender, Louis would be filled as he was "meant to be, with all the life that you can hold." *(IV 83)* At first Louis resists, but eventually he gives in to it, although he continues to feel guilty over what he is. *(BT 104)*

See also Blood, Humanity, Killing, Moral Dilemma, Vampire, Vampire Powers.

Vampire powers (abilities)

The vampires in the *Chronicles* possess many of the attributes of traditional genre vampires, but with their additional powers also defy the stereotype. Vampires' powers increase with age, and an older vampire who makes a child passes on his or her power (although making more than one child over a brief period of time results in successively weaker children). In fact, Armand's satanic coven has rules against older vampires making children for the very reason that a young vampire could thus be more powerful than members of the coven who have been in existence longer. *(QD 301)*

The powers Rice's vampires possess fall into one of three categories: physical, mental, or emotional.

PHYSICAL POWERS   Physically, the vampires are strong: Lestat claims he can bend a copper penny double; Khayman can walk through plaster walls or hurl a car. *(VL 7, QD 123)*

As part of their strength, they can project the sound of their voices to an ear-shattering level, as Lestat discovered onstage at Renaud's. Vampires can also speak too low for the human ear to detect. *(VL 138)*

They possess great speed of movement. The boy reporter thinks Louis's arm is abnormally long due to the quickness of his reach. Louis also uses his speed when he talks with Babette; he wants it to seem like he actually disappears at the end of their conversation, so that she will think he is a guardian angel. *(IV 25, 48)*

As the vampires age, their body cells harden and whiten; they seem like marble to the younger ones. Nevertheless, their bodies remain flexible, light, and dexterous. They can jump to great heights, and some can even levitate and fly around the world. A few of the vampires also practice astral projection, although Lestat does not enjoy this activity, for it makes him feel unconnected to the Earth. *(VL 7, 138, QD 135, BT 2)*

Vampires also have the ability to heal very quickly. Khayman discovers, after sticking a knife into his hand, that the wounds close so

fast that he has to open them again just to pry the knife out. Akasha's blood heals Enkil, when his arm is cut off by the conspirators, and Lestat, when he is left for dead in the swamps. The Fang Gang use their blood to heal the puncture wounds on their victims. Lestat also heals after an exposure to the desert sun that would have turned less powerful vampires to ashes. *(QD 120–123, 125, BT 47–49)*

MENTAL POWERS Vampires possess metanormal perception, a heightened sense of pleasure and pain, and hyperdimensional consciousness: they can hear mortal voices of anguish from around the world, as well as listen in on one another's thoughts. This experience of the sensory world increases their appreciation for life, and magnifies the sensual aspects of the kill, making it an orgastic experience. When vampires look at art, they can see the entire process that created it. Similarly, they perceive how insubstantial life is because they can see bodies as particles of heat and light. *(IV 20, 44, VL 114)*

Their powers of concentration allow them to experience the sensory qualities of any given moment to a degree beyond that of any mortal. These powers also allow them to read with great speed, pick up other languages easily, and mimic sounds. Lestat learns to read without being taught, and he can imitate the sounds of the instruments that Satan's Night Out plays. Possessing extremely acute vision, they can see in the dark and perceive the spiritual depth that is buried in mortal flesh. Primarily, it is the will of each particular vampire that determines the extent of their mental powers; those who have more confidence and a willingness to explore their powers develop them the most. *(VL 12, 127, 497, BT 104)*

Vampires can read minds to a fairly accurate degree, except for those of their own children or minds that are skillfully cloaked against them. Being able to read the minds of mortals allows them to manipulate their victims and, in Armand's case, acquire great wealth. They can also hypnotize and scramble the thoughts of mortals, as when Marius takes a drink from a victim and makes it so that she will not remember it. After Jesse stumbles upon Mael and Maharet in their daytime sleep, Maharet gives her instead a vision of falling asleep by the stream; it is only years later, with Jesse's attempts to remember, that the illusion wears off. Armand also gives Daniel an illusory vision of the Villa of the Mysteries in Pompeii, to give a highly sensual context to Daniel's transformation. When speaking with one another and when giving their powerful blood, they can provide full-blown images of their past experiences, as Armand does when he shows his story to Lestat and Gabrielle. Lestat does the same when telling Armand his experience of talking with Memnoch. *(VL 293, QD 22, 98, 111, BT 2, MD 143)*

Vampires can move objects at will, such as when they open doors or locks, or when shoving another vampire away without touching him. *(VL 265)*

Because the vampires are so intimately connected via the spirit

497

Amel, they possess joint awareness of one another. Their sensitivity to this increases with age, although it is not always consistent nor easily controlled. Since she is aware of all of her children, Akasha knows exactly where to go when she wants to kill them. Armand can perceive the mental impulses of other vampires, although the meaning behind them is not always clear. The vampires can also cloak themselves and their whereabouts from the prying minds of others, as Louis, Lestat, and Gabrielle sometimes do to protect themselves. *(QD 110)*

One other mental power, that only Khayman mentions, is the ability to superimpose into contemporary photographs images of people from other eras he has known. "In his [Khayman's] photograph from Rome, there were Roman people in tunics and sandals superimposed upon the modern versions in their thick ungraceful clothing." *(QD 120)*

EMOTIONAL POWERS   Able to participate in transgender love, the vampires can bond more intimately than they could as mortals. Lestat and Gabrielle, for example, become more than mother and son: they are also lovers, peers, and companions. Yet vampires also feel loneliness more keenly, as a description of Khayman illustrates: "He could feel human pain with an eerie and frightening perfection. He knew what it meant to love, and to be lonely, ah, yes, he knew that above all things." *(QD 121)* For Louis, too, loneliness and despair are magnified with the feeling that his "life span" now stretches out into endless nights of guilt and need: eternity seems a cold, dark wasteland.

Yet while pain is more intense for vampires, so also is ecstasy. They love their victims intensely: they can see the precious life with greater appreciation than they did as mortals, because their experience of it is so sensual and provides the greatest physical and emotional satisfaction they have ever known. Louis claims that sex as a mortal is a pale shadow compared to the experience of the kill. *(IV 210)*

While vampires can blend easily among mortals in cities like Paris or New Orleans, they also feel the isolation of their invisibility: they are outsiders to the human race. Nevertheless, as outsiders, they possess a unique perspective that allows them to appreciate life more than they did as mortals. They can see everything as more vivid, evocative, and spiritual. Indeed, Lestat thinks that vampires possess a God's-eye-view and thus a deeper understanding of life. *(IV 20)*

See also Aging, Androgyny, Cloaking, Extraordinary Life, Love, Outsiders, Rapture, Reading Minds, Senses, Suffering, Superstitions, Telepathic Powers, Vampire, Vampire Eyes, Vampire Limitations.

Vampire psychology   See Addiction, Androgyny, Beliefs, Boredom, Conformity, Dark Moment, Detachment, Dominance/Submission, Dreams, Endurance, Estrangement, Extraordinary Life, Hallucinations, Intimacy, Inversion, Love, Outsiders, Paradox, Rap-

ture, Senses, Suicide, Vampire Nature, Vampire Powers, Victim Psychology, Violence, Visions.

Vampire's kiss   The description of a vampire sucking blood, usually from the neck, wrist, or breast of a victim. Since the vampire's teeth sink into erotic zones of the mortal's body, the mortal's subsequent pain mingles with pleasure, making the experience highly sensual and seductive. Although the vampire is stealing the victim's vitality via the kiss, the victim is often aroused enough to want to surrender. If not, the bite can paralyze the victim and force the surrender.

In traditional genre fiction, this kiss is most often heterosexual, from male vampire to female victim or vice versa. However, the first vampire kiss described in the *Chronicles* is from Lestat to Louis, and continues to be free of such gender-role biases. *(IV 19)*

See also Bite, Fangs, Rapture, Swoon.

Vampire tales   Fiction about vampires was popular in the nine-

An erotic depiction of the vampire's kiss

teenth century. Lestat mentions the most prominent of these stories in VL, when he describes how he and Louis epitomized the vampire of those times. The first one published was *The Vampyre*, written by Dr. Polidori, Lord Byron's physician. Even more popular was the serialized *Varney the Vampire*, about Sir Francis Varney. Then came J. Sheridan le Fanu's "Carmilla," a short story, and Bram Stoker's *Dracula*. In each of these tales, the vampires are strangers among mortals, and bring evil that must be eradicated. *(VL 500)*

See also "Carmilla," *Dracula*, Dr. Polidori, Sheridan le Fanu (Joseph), Stoker (Bram), *The Vampyre*, *Varney the Vampire*.

Vampyre, The Written by Dr. John Polidori and published in 1819, this is the first substantial vampire tale in the English language. Polidori was influenced by, and wrote it after, Lord Byron's attempt at a vampire tale while he visited with Mary Shelley and John Keats. The narrator, Aubrey, tells the story of a man, Lord Ruthven, who entices English society with his mysterious, unique manner. Aubrey becomes Ruthven's traveling companion and is witness to atrocities he believes Ruthven has committed. He suspects Ruthven of being a vampire, but then Ruthven is fatally wounded. Ruthven binds Aubrey to an oath: that he must not tell of Ruthven's crimes and must keep his name clean for a year and a day. Aubrey complies with Ruthven's dying plea. After Ruthven dies, his body is placed in the moonlight—at his request—and disappears. Aubrey returns to England and tells no one of these events, although Ruthven's disappearance disturbs him. Soon, Aubrey's sister becomes engaged. He discovers her betrothed is Lord Ruthven—he *is* a vampire!—but Aubrey is bound by his oath not to tell what he knows, even though his sister is planning to marry before the year is up. He begs his sister not to go through with the wedding ceremony but she ignores him, believing, like everyone else, that Aubrey merely has spells of madness. She marries Ruthven and becomes the vampire's victim, while Aubrey dies a madman.

Lestat mentions this story as one of the nineteenth-century vampire tales that gave the vampire its contemporary stereotype. *(VL 500)*

See also Dr. Polidori, Vampire, Vampire Tales.

Van Kindergarten, Baron An alias Lestat uses to book a room at the Ritz Hotel in Paris. It was inspired by someone Rice knew who had also used this name to hide his identity. *(BT 85)*

Varna The Bulgarian port where Louis and Claudia disembark to enter the land where they believe they will find answers about their vampire nature. *(IV 70)*

See also Eastern Europe.

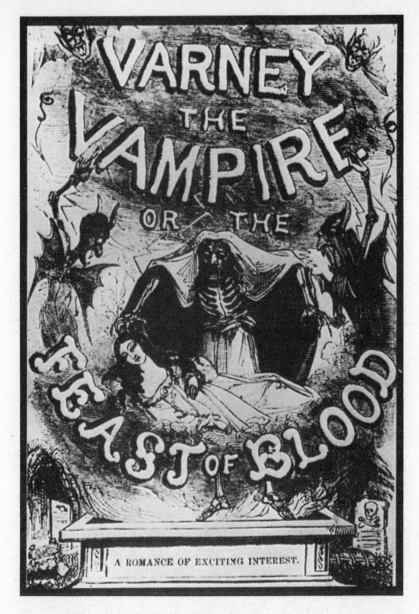

Frontispiece for Varney the Vampire, *a nineteenth-century vampire tale*

Varney the Vampire, Or, The Feast of Blood   A nineteenth-century vampire tale about the character of Sir Francis Varney. Written in 1845 by John Malcolm Rymer, it was published over a span of two years as one of the serialized "penny dreadfuls" to which Armand makes reference in QD. When collected together, it became the first English vampire novel. In this book, the vampire is presented as a

501

loathsome creature: gigantic, powerful, bloodthirsty, and ferocious. His eyes are described as metallic and, since he destroys himself in the end, he possesses a degree of self-awareness.

This is one of the vampire tales to which Lestat refers at the end of VL. Louis also mentions it in the first draft of IV as a fanciful story that holds no truth for him. Nevertheless, Claudia, who has also read it, insists they visit Eastern Europe to find other vampires. *(VL 500)*

See also Penny Dreadful, Vampire Tales.

Vegetation gods Deities from ancient times, like Osiris and Dionysus, who were worshiped in relation to crops like corn and grapes. As fertility gods, their function was to ensure the cycle of foods grown from the earth. The ceremonies for these gods often involved blood and sacrifice, giving them an obvious link to vampires.

"The vampire as we know him today in myth," says Rice, "is a disguised image of a vegetation god that's been inverted and misunderstood. The figure [of the vampire] that rises with the moon—the Mother Goddess symbol—that draws to himself the blood so that he's renewed, is a dim echo of the vegetation gods that were once worshiped."

Rice did not deal with this connection in IV, but when she wrote about Lestat, she began looking for deeper mythological roots. "I was reading Sir James Frazer and thinking, somewhere in this mythic lore is something perfect for the vampires. It's all going to click. [The link came] from Frazer and [Joseph] Campbell and books on myth by Robert Graves. I happened upon the Osirian myth, and I felt such an attraction to this Egyptian lore that it was almost like a physical buzz. It took me almost halfway through the second novel before I hit on that connecting link, but it was like turning something over and seeing the other side; it all fell into place. I think if you mine the subconscious, if you constantly drive for that feeling of intensity and connection, those things get discovered. Only after it was all rolling did I see that Lestat was a Dionysian figure. And then I saw the way to make the mythology of the vampires. To me it was sort of a joke: Lestat finds this ancient Roman Marius, and Marius tells him, well, guess what, we're vegetation gods." *(VL 330, 408–409, 433, 536)*

God, as Christ, refers to the vegetation gods as a symbolic foreshadowing in human mythology of His own incarnation. His suffering, death, and resurrection echo the stories of these deities. Memnoch believes that such stories represent the worst human fears and superstitions and that when God grafted Himself onto them, He made a terrible mistake. *(MD 272–273, 300)*

See also Christianity, Dionysus, Osiris, Tammuz of Sumer, Vampire.

Veil of silence   An inability to know another vampire's thoughts. Vampires experience this situation between themselves and their children, despite the fact that they can read the thoughts of other vampires, and despite their strong desire for intimacy with their progeny. Armand tells Lestat that this is the lot of all vampires. *(VL 249)*

Despite the veil of silence, vampires who are thus estranged can locate one another via the impressions left in the minds of mortals or other vampires who have seen them. When Lestat needs to speak with David, the other vampires who hear his message deliver it to David. *(MD 8, 140)*

After Lestat describes his experiences in Heaven and Hell, David decides to record it all. Because of the veil of silence between them, he is limited to Lestat's words until Maharet assists him by scanning the impressions in Lestat's mind. *(MD 351)*

See also Children, Estrangement, Fledglings, Telepathic Powers.

Venice   A city in northeastern Italy known for its canals and romantic settings.

Marius's art studio is on the Grand Canal in Venice. He fre-

The Bridge of Sighs, Venice

quently is frustrated by his attempt to re-create in fine detail the beauty he sees as a vampire. He finds Armand, makes him an apprentice, then brings him into the realm of darkness to be his companion and lover. Marius has to flee Venice when Santino's Roman coven destroys his studio and sets him on fire. *(VL 291–296)*

Lestat encounters David Talbot in Venice in the first draft of BT (which was later cut). Lestat's concern for his mortal friend, who appears healthy but is aging and frail, is echoed in the city's facade: Venice appears to be solid but is in fact slowly sinking into the ocean. Lestat and David enter the Basilica San Marco together, a magnificent church of mosaic art, which also will one day perish.

Lestat refers to this meeting with David when he remembers seeing Raglan James in Venice near the Piazza San Marco. *(BT 26, 93)*

See also Grand Canal, Marius.

Vera-icon   The Latin term for "true image," some scholars claim it is the source for the name Veronica, the woman on whose veil Christ left an impression of His face. Others dismiss this association, claiming Veronica as the Latin form of Berenice.

The phrase is often used in reference to Veronica's veil, and Lestat uses it when he mentions the images made when another cloth touches the veil. By one count, seventy-three new icons were made while Lestat was in Manhattan. *(MD 337, 339)*

See also Icon, Veronica's Veil.

Veronica   See Veronica's Veil.

Veronica and Her Cloth   A book by Ewa Kuryluk (1991) on the phenomena of iconography. The emphasis is on Veronica's veil, an icon supposedly made when, on the way to His crucifixion, Christ left an imprint of His face on Veronica's cloth. Kuryluk describes the history and symbolism surrounding this legend, linking it to the symbolism of menstrual blood.

When Dora displays the veil to the public as a miracle, Lestat sees this book in piles in the bookstores. *(MD 338)*

See also Blood, Christ, Veronica's Veil.

Veronica's veil   The religious relic that reputedly bears an imprint of the face of Christ. According to legend, as Christ dragged His cross to Calvary, a woman stepped out to offer her cloth to wipe His face. She reminded him that she was the *hemorrhisse*, the woman He had cured of a twelve-year-long issue of blood. He accepts the veil, but when He returns it, His face has been imprinted on it. The veil was preserved by religious authorities in St. Peter's Church in Rome, al-

though there is some evidence that the real veil (if there was one) was lost in 1527 during a Protestant attack on Rome. It showed up again afterward in several processions, but this may have been a copy. Most skeptics claim that the Veronica was merely a painting done on cloth to perpetuate a fraud that encouraged worshipers to give to the church.

The Veronica legend derives partly from the biblical story of the hemorrhaging woman, from apocryphal texts circulating during the first century, and from a fourth-century account of a woman named Berenice. Mythologically interpreted, it adds feminine aspects to the masculine spirituality of Christianity.

This icon was most famous from the fourteenth through sixteenth centuries. As a way of raising money, church officials would display it to the crowds. One person who claims to have seen the Veronica in this century at St. Peter's says it is a white cloth with a reddish-brown stain, but with no clearly distinguishable facial features.

The Veronica is often confused with another icon, the Holy Face of Edessa. According to legend, this cloth also bears Christ's face but was imprinted for a dying merchant in Edessa who was subsequently cured.

Roger owns a series of pictures of the veil and a fake Veronica from the thirteenth century. These paintings supposedly represent early copies of the veil itself, but there is little consistency among them. (MD 99)

When Christ invites Lestat to witness His crucifixion, Lestat actually sees the making of Veronica's veil. He is amazed by the miracle. When Christ gives it to him, he tucks it into his shirt and flees. However, he cannot escape Memnoch, who takes him on a tour of the bloody imprint of Christianity on the history of humankind. All the while, Lestat keeps the veil safe. Even in Hell, he keeps assuring himself that he has it, but when he flees, Memnoch insists that he not be allowed to escape with the veil. Nevertheless, he does, possibly because it is actually what Memnoch wanted. This is what David Talbot thinks. (MD 284–287)

Lestat returns to Dora and, with the veil in his shirt, drinks from her menstrual blood, linking her to Veronica. In this way, he is nourished without harming or killing her. He tells her his story and presents the veil. Dora is amazed at its legitimacy, having previously scoffed at the idea of basing her religion on the physical evidence of such an icon. Her father, Roger, had once offered her his thirteenth-century fake, but she had refused it. Seeing the true veil transforms her, although Lestat warns her that it means nothing; it could all have been an illusion concocted by God or the Devil. Nonetheless, Dora claims that Roger got it for her through an Angel of the Night, and she takes it to St. Patrick's Cathedral to show the church authorities. Standing on the steps, she shouts that she has the veil. Interestingly (and unbeknownst

Roger van der Weyden,
"Saint Veronica"

to Rice at the time), there is an altar dedicated to the veil inside this church, linked to the sixth Station of the Cross. *(MD 35, 330–335)*

Although Lestat had originally accepted the veil "because Christ gave it to me!" he never meant to give it to Dora for such purposes—to reinforce a religion he despises. *(MD 341)* He realizes later, via a note of thanks from Memnoch, that he may have served as a pawn in the Devil's attempt to bring the veil to the twentieth century to perpetuate the evils of this bloody religion. *(MD 350)*

The media picks up Dora's claim, and people flock to see the veil. Some gain an imprint from it onto their own cloth, others are physically healed, while many more experience a renewal of faith. Some of the vampires, like Armand and Mael, sacrifice themselves to the veil, dying in the sun to affirm that it's a miracle. Disgusted, Lestat thinks about using his vampire powers to destroy it. David wonders why he hesitates, and Lestat says that he cannot bring himself to do it. He decides instead just to return to New Orleans. There is nothing he can do now to undo what has happened. *(MD 337, 339–344, 346–348)*

"The story of Veronica's veil has always captured my imagination," Rice admitted. "I knew it principally through the devotion of the Stations of the Cross. I loved the little pictures on the walls of churches which showed Veronica holding up the veil with the face of Christ on it. I thought it vivid, tragic, sensual, and spectacular. I adored it! In my opinion, Veronica was always an exceptionally beautiful name that connoted only romance. It was one of those ornate, glamorous names. I would love to have been called Veronica.

"The story has a special appeal for me because I wanted to be a painter when I was a child, and this scene has been painted many times and, of course, involves a painting within a painting—the veil.

"While writing *Memnoch*, I thoroughly researched the veil. But before that I had treasured every reference to the veil I had ever found in the history of Catholic art, the history of the Shroud of Turin, and various histories of relics.

"I did not know that Veronica was the *hemorrhisse* until I got deep into my deliberate research. I was inspired and charmed by the connection. I did not set out to plot it. I was delighted that Veronica had been the woman who had touched Jesus' hem and was healed of her bleeding. I loved that Christ's church had embraced women held by others to be 'unclean.'

"I was also much enthralled with legends of where the true veil went, who had it, where it surfaced, and where it was lost. The Talamasca, only mentioned briefly in *Memnoch*, has a treasure trove of relics and manuscripts. I imagine many such things in their possession as potent as the veil."

See also Armand, Blood, Christ, Christianity, Flynn (Dora), *Holy Faces, Secret Places*, Icon, Knowledge, Lestat de Lioncourt, Mael, Mem-

noch, *Memnoch the Devil*, Religious Relics/Artifacts, Roger, St. Patrick's Cathedral, Vera-icon, *Veronica and Her Cloth*.

"Vexation without explanation"   Santino's vision of what a vampire was meant to do: to cause humans to doubt the existence of God as a force of order in the universe. Santino formed the Roman coven based on this idea. *(VL 301)*

See also Roman Coven, Santino.

Viaticum   See Eucharist.

Vice Versa   A 1988 film starring Fred Savage and Judge Reinhold. In it, a man and his son touch an ancient Tibetan skull just as each is wishing he were the other person. Their personalities switch bodies, and they then have to deal with their new perspectives.

Raglan James gives a videotape of this film to Lestat in Paris, to communicate to him the idea of switching bodies. *(BT 91)*

See also Body Switching.

Victim psychology   The complex motivations and behaviors of those who desire to be dependent upon, or submissive to, an idea, a force, or another person. The victim can be a mortal from whom a vampire sucks blood, a vampire who is a victim of his own addiction to the swoon, or a vampire who wants to be submissive to a mortal or another vampire. Armand and Louis typify this latter attitude.

While typically, between vampires and mortals, the victim is thought to be the one who submits and surrenders to domination, the vampire's need for blood, and the swoon he experiences while drinking, weakens the vampire. He submits and surrenders as well, thus giving the victim a fleeting sense of control. The most prolonged victimization scene is that between Armand and Daniel in QD. Daniel pursues leads to Lestat's house, where he encounters Armand. Armand follows him around the world, watching him and playing with his mind, but refusing to give him what he wants: immortality. They eventually become companions, but Daniel never stops asking for the Dark Gift. Armand has never made another vampire and does not want to. He continues to lure Daniel into frenzies of activity in order to have someone through whom to understand the era, and Daniel initially submits because Armand is the only vampire he knows who might grant him immortality. But as Daniel continues to experience the strained ambiguity over whether he will eventually become a victim or a vampire, he knows he cannot go on. Armand finally gives in, and makes him a vampire. *(QD 112–114)*

This dominance/submission aspect of a relationship is even more pronounced when it is played out between two vampires, who often

take turns being the dominant and the submissive party, sometimes in unexpected ways. When Armand wants Lestat to take him on the Devil's Road journey, Lestat retains control by refusing to grant his request; later, when Lestat needs help from Armand, he discovers that he is the victim as Armand pushes him off a tower. *(BT 265, VL 508)* Similarly, Lestat controls Louis for sixty-five years, but by the end of IV, and again in BT, Louis is the one in control: he withholds from Lestat that which he desires and needs—assistance in getting his immortal body back. *(IV 335, BT 264)*

See also Addiction, Armand, Dominance/Submission, Louis de Pointe du Lac, Mortals, Seduction, Slavery, Swoon, Those Who Want to Die.

Victims   In the *Chronicles*, most of the vampires' victims are anonymous, but a few are mentioned in more detail, for they have added significance beyond that of merely ensuring the vampires' survival. Plus, the way in which individual vampires kill their victims indicates what kind of personality each has.

In terms of mortals, the first victim mentioned is the overseer whom Lestat utilizes to get Louis used to death and to test his commitment to becoming a vampire. Louis watches as Lestat kills the overseer slowly, then helps Lestat get rid of the corpse, an act that nauseates him. Louis is not yet prepared to kill. *(IV 15)*

In fact, his need to kill horrifies him. It paralyzes him so much so that, after he becomes a vampire, Lestat must take a man originally meant for Louis. Then Lestat captures another man and holds him for Louis to drink. This victim is a runaway slave, which provides an interesting foreshadowing of Louis himself: he later realizes that he is a victim and a slave to Lestat. Louis drinks from the slave until the heart stops, at which point Lestat warns him to discontinue or else he will endanger himself. *(IV 29–30)*

Although Louis soon learns he can live off the blood of animals, and thus appease his conscience, he eventually returns to the greater pleasure of drinking from humans, although he never gets used to being the harbinger of death. To really know a person, Louis claims, is to take his or her life, because the soul of the vampire becomes one with the heart of the victim and is nourished by it. *(IV 63)* Much as Louis despises his need for human blood, he also loves the act when he is in the midst of doing it. His next significant victim is Claudia, a five-year-old child. Although Louis means to kill her, he does not finish the job. Lestat then makes her a vampire. When she later learns of how Louis victimized her, she is horrified, and her bond with him becomes contaminated by her hatred. *(IV 74–75, 92–93)*

Claudia's own search for victims embodies her inner drive to find her mother. One pair of victims, a mother and daughter, prefigure

Claudia's eventual destruction in the arms of Madeleine, her surrogate mother. *(IV 106–107, 306)*

Claudia also uses victims to trick Lestat. She lures him with a pair of beautiful seven-year-old boys whom she has drugged and poisoned. They are metaphors of her own lost innocence. When Lestat drinks from them, he is incapacitated enough to be vulnerable to the mortal blows Claudia inflicts on him. *(IV 134)*

Another significant victim is the beautiful girl who is killed on-stage at the Theater of the Vampires. The mortal audience believes she is only acting, but her fear is real. The vampires strip her naked and suck her blood until she dies. *(IV 220–226)* In the first draft of IV, this girl is passed around to vampires living together in a mansion in Paris. She is just as helpless, but the scene is more violent and erotic because it depicts something closer to a pack of wolves biting her all over. This scene was especially poignant for Rice: "All my life, I've thought it would be horrible to die with people looking on who had no compassion, whether they were doctors and nurses, or people in the Colosseum in Rome."

Armand has the most unique approach to the taking of life. He looks for the type of victims he calls "Those Who Want to Die," whom he finds through their dreams or in cemeteries. They are ready for what he offers, because they are self-destructive, deeply grieved, or have despaired of life. To him, this is a more spiritual way of being a vampire, for he is giving as much as taking. *(VL 303)*

The greatest number of victims are Akasha's. Although she claims to be appalled at the suffering that vampires and mortal men have caused, she herself is guilty of the most violence. When she joins forces with Lestat, they slaughter thousands of mortal men in the space of just a few nights. She also tries to annihilate most of the vampires. Akasha frames her slaughter as a means that is justified by a benevolent ending: the building of a new Eden full of peace and prosperity. The three male victims she gives to Lestat on Lynkonos, and his taking of them, are symbolic of the very male violence she intends to eradicate. *(QD 292–295, 375–376)*

In IV, Louis describes Lestat as having no respect for his victims and even as showing downright cruelty to them. Lestat brings two whores into their hotel rooms in New Orleans one night and pretends to seduce them. But he kills one and slits the wrist of the other, draining her blood into a wineglass to drink. He then puts her in a coffin. Louis grows exasperated and kills her to end her suffering. Years later, Lestat defends what he did in VL: he says the whores had drugged and robbed many seamen, and possibly even murdered them. Thus, his actions were not cruel, merely just. *(IV 77–80, VL 499)*

In fact, the same motivation prompts his killing in BT. Lestat's favorite victims are serial killers, because by doing some evil he is thus,

in a way, doing some good by wiping them out. He describes how he tracks, then kills, the Back Street Strangler in Miami. *(BT 11–21)*

As Lestat's bloodthirst evolves, he turns to more sophisticated prey, "someone with the mentality of an Iago." *(MD 12)* He settles on the forty-seven-year-old racketeer and assassin, Roger. (Roger, however, is one victim from whom Lestat cannot walk away, as he returns as a ghost to tell Lestat his story and urge him to help his daughter, Dora.) *(MD 48)*

Despite this claim to vigilantism, Lestat does slip at times and take innocent victims. After he saves an old woman from the strangler, he returns to her for a "little drink." He has read her life through her memories and finds her irresistibly interesting. He cannot stop himself, however, and kills her. This makes him wonder if there is any way to stem the tide of evil in him; accepting defeat, he decides to end his existence. This same sense of despair makes him vulnerable to being victimized by Raglan James. *(BT 22–23)*

Vampires can be victims of one another as well, as Lestat is when Claudia drugs and stabs him, and then dumps his body in the swamp. Her intent is to kill him, but she does not succeed. Nevertheless, some vampires do succeed in killing others of their kind. Armand kills younger vampires wherever he goes, and Louis sets fire to the Theater of the Vampires, which is filled with vampires, to retaliate against the coven for destroying Claudia and Madeleine. Akasha can kill telepathically, and she does, nearly annihilating the world's population of vampires in QD and saving only a select few, in the hope that they will aid and abet her plan. One of her more spectacular kills involves Azim's demise in his temple. *(IV 137–138, 313–314, VL 529, QD 109, 291)*

Lestat himself becomes something of a victim. The Devil approaches him and asks for his help. Calling himself Memnoch the Devil, he takes Lestat to Heaven and Hell, insisting that together they can resist the tide of evil perpetuated by Christianity. Lestat listens and observes. To his shock, he discovers that in Hell, his victims will confront him because they must learn to forgive in order to get into Heaven. *(MD 317–318)*

In the end, Lestat decides he can serve neither God nor the Devil, but when he gives Veronica's veil to Dora straight from the hands of Christ and inadvertently infuses new faith into a violent religion, he receives a note from Memnoch congratulating him on a job well done. Although he does not believe it, he realizes he may well have been duped by the Devil all along, merely to increase the force of Christianity and its destructive consequences. *(MD 318, 334, 350)*

One of the effects on Lestat of the knowledge he has gained is that he vows he will never again take another victim. He drinks from Dora's

menstrual blood in order not to harm her, but he repeats his vow to the other vampires that he cannot kill anymore. *(MD 320, 348)*

> See also Akasha's Plan, Armand, Artist, Back Street Strangler, Claudia, First Kill, Killing, Killing a Vampire, Lestat de Lioncourt, Louis de Pointe du Lac, Memnoch, *Memnoch the Devil*, Moral Dilemma, Roger, Serial Killer, Talbot (David), Theater of the Vampires, Those Who Want to Die, Vampire.

Vienna   A city in Austria where Louis and Claudia stop after traveling through Eastern Europe. Here they piece together their theories about what they have seen of the Old World vampires and form a plan about what to do next. Claudia suggests they try to make another vampire to see what would happen, but Louis shuns the idea. They decide to go to Paris next. *(IV 199)* (See Vampire Atlas)

> See also Old World Vampires, Quest.

Villa   See Night Island.

Villa of the Mysteries   A former residence outside the Herculaneum Gate of Pompeii. Much of the city of Pompeii was destroyed when Mount Vesuvius erupted. When Rice visited Pompeii she was impressed by the eerie quality of the ruins. "I walked down this long avenue at the edge of town at sunset, to the villa. I passed the graves and memorials to all the Pompeiians, and the sunlight was that incredible golden that it gets in Italy. I tried to get that feeling of the loneliness of the ruins with Daniel. I remember feeling very haunted and having nightmares that night. I could almost feel the ghosts of everybody out there. It imprinted itself on me emotionally." Daniel visits the villa when he is traveling around the world to get away from Armand.

A classical villa built in the second century B.C., it has a rotunda that looks toward the sea. Originally owned by a priestess of the cult of Dionysus, the villa is famous for its paintings, which stretch into two rooms. In one room, the paintings depict twenty-nine different figures performing a Dionysian ritual—the initiation of a woman into the Dionysian cult. She is terrified by the flagellation scene of a black-winged creature about to strike another initiate, but then seems to recover from her fear and dances in ecstasy, preparing for her divine marriage into the cult. The dominant theme of this group of paintings is about the torment and deliverance of the soul.

The villa is a particularly appropriate place for Armand to approach Daniel, since they are engaged in a relationship of dominance and submission. Daniel has not seen Armand for several months and wonders if he is free of Armand's tormenting presence. Armand has hounded him for four years, asking him to explain his motivations for what he is doing in every kind of activity. When Daniel approaches the

*Villa of the Mysteries,
Pompeii*

villa, Armand appears and leads him in. He bites Daniel, then by allowing him a brief drink of his own blood, seals Daniel as his lover.

When Armand finally decides to make Daniel a vampire years later, he re-creates a vision of this Villa with its lush gardens. *(QD 91–92, 111)*

See also Armand, Dominance/Submission, Flagellation, Molloy (Daniel), Pompeii, Victim Psychology.

Vine   A common symbol the Christian faith uses to express the interconnectedness of creation. In John 15:5 Christ says to his listeners, "I am the vine; you are the branches," to indicate how they are connected to him, the source of their spiritual power. Similarly, Marius describes the relationship of the vampires to Those Who Must Be Kept as that of a vine (and also a web), since what befalls Akasha and Enkil befalls all the vampires. "It was the vine, this thing, and we were the flowers . . . connected by the twining tendrils that could reach all over the world." *(VL 445)* For example, when Akasha and Enkil are placed in the sun, most of the vampires existing at that time either disintegrate or are horribly burned as a result. "Cut them and you cut us," says the Elder to Marius. "Burn them and you burn us." *(VL 435)*

The vampires are mentally as well as physically connected to one another through this web. The spiritual substance of Amel had fused through Akasha's blood with her body, and the vampires are often aware of each other's thoughts, dreams, desires, and physical location, although there are qualifications to this awareness. In QD, vampires

the world over receive through the vine the chaotic dream images of Mekare, and many become aware of the destruction Akasha is wreaking in other countries. *(QD 105)*

As her soul rises from her burning corpse, Baby Jenks actually sees the vampires' web of entangled souls. Radiating out from Akasha in all directions are silvery threads of dancing light. The threads seem to make a net over the world, and caught in the net are vampires, which appear as pinpoints of light. They are a multitude of souls "locked in indestructible matter unable to grow old or die." *(QD 57)*

See also Akasha, Amel, One Powerful Mind, The Vampire Connection.

Violence   All the vampires have their own style of killing, but some are more brutal than others. Armand prefers to draw out his victims seductively, while Khayman kills them in a savage frenzy of thirst, breaking his victims' bones and sucking out the marrow. Lestat likes to prolong the experience, while Louis kills quickly because he feels guilty about what he is doing. The most violent vampire of all, however, is Akasha. She uses her spiritual powers to ignite the blood of her vampire brood and to explode their hearts. She also kills thousands of mortals in the space of just a few nights in this same manner. Her violence, she feels, is justified by her righteous cause and by the new world order she wants to establish. Using violence to end violence is the paradox within which she operates, and it ends up destroying her—quite violently. *(QD 437–454)*

For Lestat, violence is an addiction he conquers. When first he rushes mindlessly to complete the task of killing men as Akasha has instructed him, he is unable to stop until Akasha steps in. "I loved it, loved it beyond all reason, loved it as men have always loved it in the absolute amoral freedom of war." *(QD 295)* However, he does resist the urge to do this again and actually takes a stand against what Akasha wants him to do.

Rice does not condone Akasha's form of violence. She believes evil truly happens when people are hurt or killed for an abstract idea. Although she thought Akasha's logic made sense, she did not believe her plan was the best way to achieve peace. Rice is attracted to other forms of violence—those that inspire the emergence of heroic qualities, such as when Lestat fought the wolves. "I love to see one heroic person against the odds, or many heroic people."

After he accompanies the Devil to Heaven, Lestat witnesses the ironic violence of Christianity. Memnoch has told him the story of creation and how God's plan included death and suffering as part of the energy cycle. Even God Himself died on behalf of the salvation of human souls, spawning a religion based on the bloodiest human superstitions. In case Lestat needs more proof, Memnoch exposes him to the

horrors of the Fourth Crusade, then offers him a litany of other violent events inspired in the name of Christ. Lestat is horrified by all that he sees. Then Memnoch takes him to Hell. There Lestat discovers that human souls are tormented by their victims until all learn to forgive. Lestat cannot bear the relentless barrage of gruesome images, and when he returns to his normal existence as a vampire, he vows never to take another human victim. *(MD 289–290, 310–322, 348)*

See also Akasha's Plan, Evil, Fourth Crusade, Killing, *Memnoch the Devil, The Queen of the Damned,* Wolves.

Violin Nicolas's playing of the violin entrances Lestat. He thinks the sound is powerfully affected and extremely human, although he is aware that the finest players have been accused of being possessed by the Devil because their music had such magic. Nicolas studied with Mozart, ignoring his father's insistence that he go into the family business. When he and Lestat go to Paris, Nicolas plays in Renaud's theater and on the boulevards to make money, expecting that he and Lestat will soon fail in their venture and be swallowed by darkness and ruin. He intends his playing, which speaks of his own inner emptiness and despair, to hurt others. However, Lestat's talents lead them instead to triumph. *(VL 59–60, 64)*

After Lestat becomes a vampire, he sends Nicolas a Stradivarius and spies on him one night. Nicolas senses his presence and tries to lure him with the violin. Lestat resists, while perceiving that Nicki's music shows the depths of his despair. Nevertheless, once Nicki is a vampire and fails to respond to anything, Lestat gives him the violin, hoping it will wake him from his stupor and make him vital again. *(VL 119, 130, 259)*

Nicolas then plays forcefully, in a manner that tells the story of what has happened to him. He shows his rebellion against all things, and that the music is the darkness of his soul. His playing draws out the surviving members of Armand's coven, who dance as marionettes, and Nicolas proclaims the start of the Theater of the Vampires. *(VL 259–260)*

When Nicolas deliberately goes into the fire, Eleni returns his violin to Lestat. He carries it with him, and when he joins Marius, he finds the violin in the guest room, as if Marius understands its significance to him. One night Lestat decides to try to awaken Akasha; he believes that the violin's music has the power to do it. He imitates what he remembers from Nicolas's playing and before long, Akasha sings a high note that threatens to shatter his eardrums. She rises up and steps on the violin. Although it is crushed, it has achieved its end. The playing of it prefigures what Lestat will do two centuries later with his rock music. *(VL 342, 484, 485)*

Rice herself was once obsessed with the violin. "I wanted to be

Violin

a great violinist," she claims. When that did not seem probable, she gave up her lessons. She had wanted to develop a skill that would ensure that her life would not be one of mediocrity. She tells a fictionalized version of this story in the first draft of IV: Louis describes how he once saw a little girl crying. She wanted to play the violin, but her mother would not pay for the lessons and denigrated the girl's ambition. Her parents tried to convince her that mediocrity is her only hope in life. That attitude, Louis claims, is the essence of egotism: the refusal to believe that greatness can occur in our midst.

See also Nicolas de Lenfent.

Virgin Mary   The mother of Christ, she is enshrined in the Catholic religion as a sort of deity.

Lestat and Baby Jenks both compare Akasha to the Virgin Mary. In her white gown, she, too, looks pure and beautiful, and has the ability to make them feel as if they are in the presence of a holy figure. Lestat recalls that his childhood memories of the crowning of the Virgin ceremony are like the adulation Akasha receives after her first massacre in Azim's temple. Her actions fill him with enchantment and religious fervor, which is the same way he felt as a child at that ceremony. News reports of Akasha's slaughters indicate that survivors also view her as the Virgin Mary and as a worker of miracles, the Queen of Heaven. (QD 57, 303, 379)

In his books, Wynken de Wilde compares the beauty and purity of his sister-in-law and lover, Blanche de Wilde, to that of the Virgin Mary. (MD 65)

See also Akasha's Plan, Queen of Heaven, Religion, Religious Images, Wilde (Blanche de).

Visions   Manifestations to the senses of something immaterial or imaginary, visions play an important role in the *Chronicles* by showing that the vampires' heightened senses are intensely vivid and pervasive—and even enhance their imagination. Their visions are sometimes caused by another vampire, which indicates how strong their telepathic connection is to one another. And some of them have significant visions first as mortals.

It is a vision that starts into motion the chain of events that results in the story told in *The Vampire Chronicles*. Louis's brother, Paul, claims to have seen St. Dominic and the Virgin Mary in a vision; they instructed him to sell the plantation Pointe du Lac and go to France. Louis scoffs at this vision and the next moment, Paul, who is walking away, falls to his death from the gallery. Louis's subsequent despair, which involves visions of himself hurtling down the steps after his brother, makes him vulnerable to Lestat.

Shortly after he and Claudia believe they have destroyed Lestat, Louis enters St. Louis Cathedral and has an extremely detailed vision of Lestat's funeral. In a state of despair he sees a procession that includes Claudia. Lestat is inside the glass coffin. Claudia reads from scriptures about the curse God placed on Cain after Cain killed his own brother, Abel. Louis reacts violently to his vision. He now understands that he has killed his brothers: Paul and Lestat. As if to add to his self-condemnation, he then kills a priest. *(IV 145–149)*

Armand has visions of Marius after he believes Marius has been destroyed by fire. He sees Marius burned by the fire, and pleading with him to come help him, but these visions fade as he gets involved with the satanic coven that abducted him. Only later, when Lestat shows up in Paris and moves freely among mortals in red velvet clothing as Marius had done, do the visions return in force. *(VL 300, 305)*

Armand also uses visions as an effective technique for luring to him the type of victims he likes best: Those Who Want to Die. He draws them to him by giving out visions of himself as the one who can make their wish come true. *(VL 303)* He also uses visions to manipulate other vampires.

One night, shortly after he becomes a vampire, Lestat sees the possibility of grace, restoration, and healing—but he can have it only if he comes to Armand. Lestat rejects this vision because he knows that Armand, the source of it all, is a leech on the passions of others, "the embodiment of thirst itself." *(VL 512)* When Lestat is about to go underground for the second time, in 1929, Armand hangs around his house, projecting into Lestat's mind more visions to try to lure him out. And while still underground, Lestat also sees visions of Marius in a twentieth-century red velvet suit, showing motion pictures to Akasha and Enkil. Akasha then speaks to Lestat, beckoning him to her. He thinks the visions cannot be true, but later realizes that what he has seen actually may have been sent to him from Akasha. *(VL 514–516)*

Lestat has other visions as he feasts on Akasha's blood after she arises in the twentieth century. He sees how other vampires died, witnesses the burning of the coven houses, hears voices, and sees himself fighting the wolves as a young man. Akasha also gives him a view of the vampires she has saved so that he will not worry about their survival. *(QD 250–251)*

David Talbot also describes a vision he had as a young man. He saw two people in a café on the Left Bank in Paris conversing in a language he did not know, yet understood. He determined that they were illusory beings, for they were illuminated by a light that seemed to come from an otherworldly source. It occurred to him that God was one of them, the Devil the other, and that they were discussing the Devil's discontent with his job: he no longer wanted to do it, but God insisted that he continue, for his job was important. David cannot recall exactly what they looked like and despairs over the fact that this

vision has no immediate effect on him. He has gained from it no real illumination, although at the age of seventy-four, he is returning to a belief in God. *(BT 73–75)*

Lestat associates his stalker with David's vision, although he is not sure why. Neither he nor David can clarify the connection. *(MD 15–16)* However, Memnoch, the stalker, confirms that David's vision in the Parisian café was accurate. He is the Devil from that vision, and he *is* tired of his job, as he had indicated. God had taken an interest in David, so David's seeing the vision had been planned on His part. *(MD 133, 212)*

Dora Flynn had asked for a vision from the supernatural, and Lestat came into her life. Although she knows that he is not human, she is unafraid because she believes his appearance is one of a series of miracles that will confirm her religious convictions. Lestat wants to help her, so he gives her Veronica's veil. She insists that he is an Angel of the Night, sent to her from God to provide what she needs to make a spectacular religious impact on the world. *(MD 158, 334)*

See also Dreams, God, Hallucinations, Memnoch, Telepathic Powers, Waking Dream.

"Vision without revelation" What Lestat believes to be true about the vampires. They are a miracle without meaning, supernatural creatures whose existence is linked to a nonexistent devil. Consequently, they reveal the emptiness of the concept of God. *(BT 254)*

Voices Those who drink from the blood of the old ones, particularly from Akasha, thereafter hear the voices of mortals all over the world. Many of these voices are crying plaintively or moaning in pain. Akasha thinks they are praying to her and the sheer numbers of them, and their great volume, force her into silence. *(QD 254–260)*

Other vampires hear these voices as well, especially those whose heightened senses are the sharpest. Several vampires mention the necessity of learning to control the voices by blocking and screening them out; otherwise, the continual din might cause madness. In fact, Akasha believed that the voices that spoke of the legends about her had dismissed her as being dead and locked her into the unreality of myth, making her doubt her own existence. These voices overwhelmed her and she lost all sense of herself until she learned to pay attention to only one voice at a time—one that said things that she wanted to hear. *(QD 20, 62, 259–260)*

Several vampires mention these voices when they are given the Dark Gift: Jesse hears them when she drinks from Maharet, and Lestat hears them when he receives Akasha's blood. *(VL 249–50, QD 240, 250)*

See also Transformation.

Voison, Katherine La See La Voison, Katherine.

Waitress   A young woman who gives Lestat his first meal when he is human again, and unwillingly, his first experience of mortal sex. He rapes her and thereafter she demands that he leave her apartment. He regrets his impulsive act and later returns as a vampire, giving her an antique rosary as a gift to make up for his treatment of her. *(BT 178–193, 401)*

See also Sex.

Waking dream   A trancelike state that Louis engages himself in when he is deep in thought. Louis describes it in the first draft of IV: his thoughts are so intense that they give birth to visions, which is what happens to him in St. Louis Cathedral when he dreams of Lestat's funeral procession. *(IV 144–147)* He believes this type of rumination is as essential to his well-being as night dreams.

See also Visions.

Wall Street   An area in Lower Manhattan, it is New York's financial district. One of its famous buildings is Trinity Church, built in 1846.

After killing Roger and distributing parts of his body around the city, Lestat wanders around the Wall Street area. He sits on the steps of the church and looks over its cemetery, noting stones that date back as far as 1692. *(MD 46)*

"I have been in that cemetery and in the church," said Rice. "I was taken there by a reporter for *The New York Times* for a story that appeared during the publicity tour for *The Tale of the Body Thief.* I loved the church and the cemetery." (See Vampire Atlas)

See also Roger, Trinity Church.

War   Symbolically, the struggle of light with darkness, and/or of good with evil. The idea of war often involves liberation or protection, and represents freeing the person from inner enemies. However, this presentation does not necessarily match or justify the reality of war, which can often be one of unrestrained aggression and exploitation.

Armand questions Daniel about the nature of war: why do men desire to clash violently against one another? He fails to understand this desire of mortal men, since he was made a vampire when he was only an adolescent. He himself kills only because of the allure of blood. *(QD 89)*

The most powerful vampire, Akasha, wants to eliminate war. She believes, along with Armand, that war originates because of men. Her logic goes on to propose that if she were to eliminate most men, leaving women to run the world, she could achieve a peaceful paradise on Earth. Ironically enough, to accomplish her goals, she must first declare war on men. *(QD 259)*

See also Akasha's Plan, Paradox, Violence.

Washington, D.C.　Lestat wanders around the nation's capital the day he becomes a mortal man again. He walks along the Potomac, and looks at the monuments and Arlington Cemetery, in love with the way they honor the principles of the Age of Reason. *(BT 196)* (See Vampire Atlas)

See also Georgetown, Jefferson Memorial.

Watcher　A member of a high order of angels, also known as the "grigori," whom God sent to instruct humans. They lusted after the

Trinity Church on Wall Street

women and cohabited with them. For this, God cast them from Heaven and they became the Fallen Angels.

Memnoch claims that many angels watched the creation. Some were as mirrors, reflecting each step, while others questioned it. Only about two hundred coupled with women, and these angels were contrite enough to be allowed to remain in Heaven. They were fallen in the sense that they had corrupted themselves before God, but were not barred from His presence. *(MD 182, 208, 240)*

Memnoch also points out to Lestat that a phrase that describes him, "a sleepless mind in his heart and an insatiable personality," was used by the Sibylline Oracle to describe the Watchers. *(MD 188)*

See Angel, Fallen Angels, Memnoch, Sibyl.

Ways of dying   In IV, Lestat controls Louis by hinting that Louis does not know all the ways a vampire can die. After they battle in the swamp, Lestat says he should drive Louis's horse into the swamps, for when Louis would have to dig a hole for himself there when the sun came up, he would end up smothering in the mud. Yet vampires do not die this way, since Lestat himself is tossed into the swamp and survives. In addition, Lestat digs himself deep into the earth twice and never smothers. As Louis, however, does not know this, his fear of death makes him reluctantly compliant to Lestat's wishes. *(IV 33, 45, 77, VL 502)*

Later, their apparent inability to die troubles both of them. When Louis realizes that Lestat has survived the swamp, he feels that immortality may be a trap of endless nights. Lestat does not feel quite as anguished, but he is somewhat concerned, after centuries have passed and he has exposed himself to the sun, that he might be truly immortal, with no way out. *(IV 165–166, BT 47–50)*

Armand comes to inform Louis that only fire and the sun can kill vampires, nothing else. (He does add dismemberment to this list, but this part of the cosmology dropped away in later *Chronicles*.) Although Claudia and Madeleine die in the sunlight, the sun seems to be effective only on these weaker vampires. Akasha, Maharet, and Lestat all survive exposure to the sun. Fire, however, can destroy even the strong, devouring Magnus and Nicolas so that there is nothing left but ashes. *(IV 292, 306, VL 96, 343)*

Armand and Mael both choose to die in the sun. When Lestat delivers Veronica's veil from the hands of Christ into Dora's, she makes a public display of it. Armand and Mael are so moved by the authenticity of this miracle that in honor of the veil, they step into the sun to make a public display of their destruction. *(MD 335, 337)*

See also Akasha, Armand, Claudia, Death, Dismemberment, Fire, Immortality, Madeleine, Mael, Magnus, Nicolas de Lenfent, Suicide, Sun, Superstitions.

Weather   Aspects of weather in literature are often analogous to the state of a character's soul. "The use of weather is instinctive with me," Rice admits. "I'm aware that it has great meaning, but I don't think about what I do with it; I just let it happen."

See also Darkness, Snow.

Web   See Vine.

Webber, Andrew Lloyd   See *Phantom of the Opera*.

Webster, Daniel   A nineteenth-century American statesman and orator who was made a prominent character in Stephen Vincent Benét's popular 1937 short story "The Devil and Daniel Webster." Webster's eloquence before a demonic jury saves a farmer from paying the debt of his soul to the Devil.

When it becomes clear that he might be able to bargain with the Devil, Lestat refers to Daniel Webster. *(MD 129)*

See also Lestat de Lioncourt, Memnoch.

Webster, John   A seventeenth-century English poet and dramatist who wrote about the disasters of moral degeneracy. Lestat quotes one of Webster's poems to Claudia, and she then writes the quotation in her diary: "Cover her face; mine eyes dazzle; she died young." *(QD 136, 184)* The lines are taken from Webster's poem "The Devil's Law Case," and Lestat thinks they are appropriate for Claudia, who is a vampire child.

See also Poetry.

Weightlessness   The feeling of lacking gravitational pull described by both Louis and Jesse as they transform into vampires. Louis also uses this term to describe the experience of drinking blood. *(IV 88, QD 241)*

See also Swoon, Thirst, Transformation.

"What God Did Not Plan On"   A poem by Stan Rice, one of three that opens MD. The subject is God's underestimation of how much suffering human consciousness can bear.

See also Poetry, Rice (Stan).

"What Men Live By"   A short story by the nineteenth-century Russian writer Leo Tolstoy, which Gretchen thinks of when she talks with Lestat. It involves an angel coming to earth. *(BT 232)*

A poverty-stricken shoemaker finds the angel and invites him into his home, to learn his trade. Neither the shoemaker nor his wife knows what to make of this mysterious young man, who looks human

yet seems so different from them. All they know is that he needs help, and they give him what they can. The angel lives with them for several years, bringing them prosperity, until one day, he announces that he is leaving. He then reveals that he was an angel sent to Earth to learn three things: what dwells in the human heart (charity); what is kept from men (knowledge of their needs, which otherwise would isolate them in self-centeredness); and what they live by (love).

Lestat's presence in Gretchen's life has similar implications. He looks human yet talks like a mysterious, alien being. He inspires in her compassion and generosity, and helps her to explore other dimensions of love. He repays her charity by strengthening her faith in God, although this is not intentional on his part. Like Tolstoy's angel, Lestat, too, discovers that many human beings are motivated to help others, and that he has been the recipient of that charity.

See also Angel, Gretchen, Tolstoy (Leo).

White chrysanthemums   To Claudia, they are a symbol of death. She puts these flowers in a vase just before she attempts to kill Lestat. *(IV 130)* She also places some on what she believes to be Lestat's corpse. *(IV 139)*

See also Death, Flowers.

White roses   What Maharet sends to Jesse just before Jesse attends Lestat's rock concert. Jesse believes that white roses are for funerals, and does not realize how truly appropriate the gift is, on this, her last night as a mortal. The gift of these flowers makes it seem as if Maharet had guessed what would happen to Jesse. *(QD 138)*

See also Flowers.

White stallion   The animal the peasants in Eastern Europe use to locate the resting places of vampires. The Englishman Morgan describes such an event to Louis in IV.

The peasants take the horse to a cemetery, where they whack it with a shovel. It gallops up a hill, but then returns to where the newest graves have been dug, coming to rest on top of the grave of a young woman dead only six months. When the peasants dig up the coffin, they discover that the corpse is still fresh and flexible, which the peasants take as proof that the body is that of a vampire. *(IV 180)*

See also Morgan, Superstitions.

Whores   See Victims.

Wilde, Blanche de   Wynken de Wilde's sister-in-law and lover, she participated with him in his religious orgies. Blanche was one of a secret circle of five women who met together at her castle to enact

White stallion

sexual mystical rites in the garden. Wynken called her his patron and dedicated his books to her. Hidden within his poems were responses to correspondences about the abuse she suffered from her husband.

When Blanche's husband discovered what was going on, he killed Wynken and ended the ceremonies. He buried Wynken's books with his corpse. Blanche and her friends seem to have dug up Wynken's books and perhaps even distributed his body parts among themselves as relics of their saint. (MD 64–65, 84–86)

See also Diana, Diane, Eleanor, Religion, Wilde Castle (de), Wilde (Damien de), Wilde (Wynken de).

Wilde Castle, de   The home of Damien and Blanche de Wilde, it was where Wynken and his five women performed secret sexual rituals to gain mystical experiences. Their orgies took place in the garden, as depicted in most of Wynken's miniature paintings. After Damien killed Wynken to end the rites, he buried Wynken and his books near

the fountain. Since the books turned up later, Roger suggests that Blanche may have unearthed them.

In the First World War, de Wilde Castle was obliterated. *(MD 64–65, 85)*

See also Religion, Wilde (Blanche de), Wilde (Damien de), Wilde (Wynken de).

Wilde, Damien de Blanche de Wilde's husband and Wynken de Wilde's brother, who caught Wynken practicing sexual rituals with his wife. Enraged, he stabbed and castrated him, then buried him with his illuminated books in the castle's garden. *(MD 80, 85)*

See also Wilde (Blanche de), Wilde Castle (de), Wilde (Wynken de).

Wilde, Stanford One of the aliases that Lestat uses for legal purposes. It is both a reference to the author Oscar Wilde and the architect Stanford White. *(BT 139)*

Wilde, Wynken de The author of the illuminated manuscripts that Roger owns, he was a medieval Rhineland Catholic influenced by German mysticism. Forced into the Benedictine Order, he secretly practiced his own rites. During the twenty-five years before the invention of the Gutenberg printing press, Wynken wrote a set of prayer books on parchment, illuminating them by hand. "He was scribe, rubricator . . . and also the miniaturist who added all the naked people frolicking in Eden." *(MD 84)* His books—a theology of love and a celebration of sex, "filled with lascivious invitations and suggestions and possibly even some sort of secret codes for clandestine meetings"—were considered blasphemous and profane. *(MD 64)* In many of his poems, he covertly responded to his lover's secret correspondences about her abusive husband. The scenes he depicted were always in a castle garden and always featured one naked man with five naked women dancing together around a fountain.

Old Captain, a boarder at Roger's mother's boardinghouse, first shows Roger one of Wynken's books. Roger becomes enthralled and sets out to collect them all, ending up with twelve. He believes Wynken designed them as a secret communication with his lovers. Further research reveals that Wynken was considered a heretic in love with his brother's wife, Blanche de Wilde. He was organizing orgies with her and four of her female friends. Wynken loved the flesh and claimed to find oneness with God via sexual rites. However, his brother, Damien, discovered what he was doing and, accusing him of practicing the rite of the goddess Diana, executed and castrated him. Damien buried Wynken, along with his books, by the fountain in the garden.

The books, however, survived intact, possibly rescued by

Blanche. Although Roger was advised to sell them to get funds for college, he valued them more for their content than their monetary worth. Wynken de Wilde's writings inspired him to consider forming his own religious cult, based on contemporary sexual practices. He loves the idea of mystical rites involving sex and love.

After Lestat kills Roger, Roger returns as a ghost and tells him about Wynken's books. He makes Lestat promise to keep them safe and to give them to his daughter, Dora. Dora, however, eventually gives them to Lestat. Louis reads them and tells Lestat how much he enjoys them. *(MD 58, 61–65, 80–85, 340–341, 352)*

"Wynken de Wilde's name was compiled by me," said Rice, "from the names of several artists of the period. I liked the sound of it. In some future books, perhaps I can tell the full story of Wynken and his love for Blanche de Wilde. Maybe I can devote an entire novel to it, within the framework of *The Vampire Chronicles* or the Talamasca files. I'm not finished with Wynken; that I do know.

"Wynken de Wilde's books are not based on anything real. They were inspired by the scholarship on Bosch, Grünewald, and other painters—[the] scholars insist they were members of some sort of cult and that their work is replete with blasphemous symbols. Though I have not accepted any of the theories I've read, I do feel that we have many Northern German Renaissance painters—Cranach, Grünewald, and Bosch—who have left us very disturbing 'sacred works.' The idea that a sensualist 'code' may exist in someone's work is very enticing. I do not know of any miniaturist, though, who has left us disturbing work.

"I have studied and handled many illuminated manuscripts. I have numerous books on these manuscripts and have referred to them throughout my writing career. Tonio Treschi seduces the Cardinal in *Cry to Heaven* while the latter is reading a beautifully illuminated prayer book. And, of course, Ashlar was taken with the Celtic style of illumination in creating his history of the Taltos. I believe that Lestat describes loving to work in the monastery library when he was a boy.

"I have personally handled [these manuscripts] at the Newberry Library in Chicago, thanks to the kindness of people there. I collect facsimiles of prayer books, Books of the Hours, etcetera. Even when I was a penniless, struggling author, I laid down a huge sum of money for a facsimile of a Book of the Hours. It was my treasure. I still have it.

"Obviously, the whole theme of manuscripts, scribes, monks, and the preservation of sacred and important work in fine manuscript form is key in my imagination, and I have not finished with it by any means. Later novels will include more on this subject, which I study all the time."

See also Diana, Diane, Eleanor, Father Kevin, Flynn (Dora), *Gar-*

den of Earthly Delights, Old Captain, Religion, Roger, Wilde (Blanche de), Wilde Castle (de), Wilde (Damien de), "Wynken, Blinken, and Nod."

Will   Mental powers manifested in behavior. The will assists mortals in becoming vampires, and is a central factor in the activities of cloaking and astral projection. David Talbot tells Lestat that, even in sleep, the will is operative, and Lestat in turn claims that his entire life has been shaped by his will. *(BT 311, VL 497)*

The will is what Lestat urges Louis to use to survive being drained of blood to the point of death. *(IV 18)* Claudia uses her will in the same way, first when she survives Louis's initial attack, and then when Lestat makes her. *(IV 74, 93)* Her strong will is evident to Lestat later on; he believes that when Claudia attacked and almost killed him, it was her will, as much as the knife itself, that overcame him. *(VL 501)*

The will physically moves a vampire, when necessary, to sustain and protect the body. If a mortal stumbles upon a sleeping vampire, it is the will that, without waking the vampire, moves the arm to strangle the intruder. When Lestat first becomes a vampire, he vomits blood. His will moves him to lap it up off the floor, because it is what he needs to survive. *(VL 105, 108)*

The vampire with a seemingly stronger will than Lestat is Akasha—or so it appears at first. She devises a plan to create a new Eden on Earth, at the expense of mortal men everywhere, and urges Lestat to be her apprentice. He goes along with the plan a few times, participating in shocking slaughters, even though he has doubts about their actions. However, eventually he realizes that Akasha needs him and that therein lies her weakness. She has an iron will but only if there is one other person to ratify it. In short, her will is nearly indomitable, but it is flawed. Its vulnerability leads to her downfall and destruction. *(QD 397, 452)*

The person whose will Lestat struggles most against is David Talbot's. David claims that he will never ask for the Dark Gift. Lestat simply cannot comprehend why anyone, particularly a man of David's age who could die at any time, would refuse it when offered. David insists that he will never compromise his moral integrity when it comes to this point. Finally, Lestat forces the Gift on him, offering him a way to be immortal without having to compromise. *(BT 43–46, 422)*

See also Body, Choice, Hero, Transformation, Vampire.

Wilson, Ian   See *Holy Faces, Secret Places*.

Winter   See Snow.

Witches   In their mortal lives, the twins Maharet and Mekare are

known as witches, or seers. In such primitive cultures as theirs, witches are revered because they are perceived as being beneficial to the tribe. They attract and manipulate spirits to offer advice and make rain.

The twins' mother, Miriam, is a powerful witch, but her daughters, as twins, have double her power. Their fame as rainmakers spreads as far as Egypt, which lies a full ten-day journey from their home on Mount Carmel. Because of the power the twins possess, the Egyptian rulers, Akasha and Enkil, invite them to come to their court. They decline, bringing ruin upon their tribe when the king returns with his soldiers to force them into compliance.

As witches, Mekare and Maharet are loved by the spirits, who attempt without success to free them from Akasha. And after the twins are raped, one spirit, Amel, retaliates. He attacks the king's steward, who had done the deed, and it sets into motion a chain of events that leads to Akasha becoming the first vampire and, eventually, the twins becoming vampires. *(QD 402–409)*

Six thousand years later, Jesse, a descendant of Maharet's and a seer of spirits, discovers documentation of witch families during her work for the Talamasca. Their power appears to be hereditary in nature. To Jesse, the pattern of the witch families is similar to the pattern of the Great Family that Maharet had shown her. *(QD 169)*

One of the witch families the Talamasca documents is described in detail in *The Witching Hour*. A young woman, Rowan Mayfair, is the recipient of healing powers that make her a skilled neurosurgeon, but she also knows that she can use her powers to kill. The Talamasca, through Aaron Lightner, introduces her to her family records, which date back to witchcraft persecutions in Scotland, when her ancestor Suzanne was burned at the stake in 1659. Rowan learns that she is the descendant of both a witch and a member of the Talamasca, who together produced a long line of witches.

See also Maharet, Mekare, Miriam, Spirits, Twins.

Witches' Place
An area in Lestat's village in the Auvergne, where people had been burned at the stake as witches. As a boy, Lestat hears stories about the witches and also sees the blackened stakes. He cannot endure visiting the place, for he feels that the accused were victims of absurd superstitions.

An image of the Witches' Place enters Lestat's mind when Magnus jumps into the fire. Lestat cringes at the thought of flesh and bone being burned to a crisp. Later Nicolas taunts him with the image, and then Nicolas, too, goes into the fire. *(VL 47, 56, 97, 235)*

When he visits Hell with Memnoch, Lestat sees an image of the Witches' Place. *(MD 312)*

See also Fire, Hell, Magnus, Nicolas de Lenfent.

Witching Hour, The   The title of Rice's supernatural novel involving the Talamasca and a family of witches called the Mayfairs.

The point at which this novel interconnects with *The Vampire Chronicles* is when Jesse reads the research done on witch families in the Talamasca files. Also, when Lestat seeks out David Talbot in Amsterdam, he discovers that David is attempting to locate, at Aaron Lightner's request, a portrait by Rembrandt of Deborah, one of the earliest of the Mayfair witches. *(QD 169, BT 30)*

The Witching Hour adds dimension to Rice's cosmology in its description of the physical characteristics of the spirit Lasher, who may be similar to Amel. Rice also describes in the novel the Amsterdam Motherhouse, and gives a more detailed portrait of Talamasca investigator Aaron Lightner.

See also Lasher, Lightner (Aaron), Spirits, Witches.

Witch of Endor   A figure from the Old Testament whom King Saul consults when he faces the Philistine army. He asks a sorceress to conjure up the ghost of Samuel the prophet. When she does so, Samuel accurately predicts Saul's defeat and death.

Lestat thinks that his distaste for Raglan James must have been what Saul felt when he saw the Witch of Endor: "It was absolutely base to have to deal with him." *(BT 154)*

See also Bible, James (Raglan), Saul.

Wolfkiller   The name Magnus repeatedly uses to refer to Lestat. He sends the name telepathically to Lestat after Lestat has spied his white face in the audience at Renaud's theater. *(VL 79)*

See also Lestat de Lioncourt, Magnus, Wolves.

Wolves   Symbols of violence, chaos, and destruction, wolves represent a threat to life and order but, almost paradoxically, they are also a symbol of valor.

Lestat begins his story of how he became a vampire with an incident involving wolves. As a twenty-year-old man, he sets out to kill a pack of wolves that have been killing sheep on his father's land. Lestat takes his mastiffs and several weapons along to aid him. A pack of eight wolves attacks him, killing his dogs and his horse. After a life-and-death struggle, Lestat manages to destroy the wolves and return home the victor. The villagers make a cloak for him of wolf skins. When Lestat dons it, he becomes a symbol of valor.

The wolf fight is a metaphor for Lestat's inner conflicts. He has no real life on his father's estate, and this threatens his inner vitality. His empty existence in the Auvergne is as deadly to him as the wolves potentially were. And just as he had fought the wolves, so must he fight

Wolf pack

off malaise and poverty. "But whatever I had learned or felt when I was fighting those wolves went on in my mind even as I walked." *(VL 28)*

Lestat triumphs over both, but his strength, courage, and resilience draw the eye of a vampire, Magnus, who is seeking a worthy successor. He targets Lestat for immortality. Thus, the wolves become for Lestat a symbol of both destruction and rebirth, and he often thinks back to that episode to fortify himself. *(VL 74)*

Lestat compares vampires to wolves when he refers to the vampire's predatory nature. Like wolves, vampires are hunters; similarly, like wolves, vampires should be run out of the world. *(BT 234–235)*

Marius also keeps a pen of wolves at the shrine he builds for Akasha and Enkil in a snow-covered wasteland in the north. *(QD 253)*

See also Lestat de Lioncourt, Magnus, Predators.

"Words Once, The"   A poem by Stan Rice that introduces the section in QD about Pandora. It is about the brutal clarity of language in times past. *(QD 59)*

"The poem addresses a sentiment from the sixties that I opposed," explains Stan Rice. "It was a tendency to define things by

changing their names with euphemisms. New terms tended to get us farther from things."

.See also Poetry, Rice (Stan).

World of Darkness   A phrase the old queen vampire uses in Armand's first Parisian coven to describe the vampire realm. *(VL 218)*.

See also Queen Vampire.

"Wynken, Blinken, and Nod"   A children's poem by Eugene Field about three fishermen named Wynken, Blinken, and Nod who sail off in a wooden shoe. Their adventure is likened to the sleepy dreams of a child.

When he sees the name "Wynken" on Roger's passport, Lestat thinks of this poem. *(MD 45)*

See also Roger, Wynken (Frederick).

Wynken de Wilde   See Wilde, Wynken de.

Wynken, Frederick   The alias Roger uses on his passport; it refers to Wynken de Wilde. *(MD 42)*

See also Roger, Wilde (Wynken de).

Yeats, William Butler　An Irish poet active in the late nineteenth and early twentieth centuries who utilized the conflicts of opposites—like art and life, body and soul, eternity and time, and intellect and emotion—to structure his poems. He employed these pairings to test moral and aesthetic values, and to convey the complexity of experience.

Rice used his poem "Sailing to Byzantium" to introduce BT, because it captured the idea of being outside natural law, which is the vampires' case. To introduce the second part of BT, Rice used Yeats's poem "The Dolls." In it, the dolls express their contempt for human life, in the process forgetting that they themselves are mere imitations of life. Their beauty and changelessness may be attractive, but they are sterile, stagnant, and uncreative. *(BT 394)*

"That poem ["The Dolls"] is about mortality and immortality, and the human versus art," Rice explains. "It's a gruesome poem, saying that's what we are—we're accidents—and the dolls are something perfect. So at the end [of BT], what does Lestat do? He goes back and does a terrible thing to David: he takes him out of nature and makes him a doll, whether he wants it or not. That's the final kicker of just how bad Lestat is."

In the first draft of BT, Rice had included Yeats's poem "The Cold Heaven" but ended up not using it in the published version. In that work, Yeats regrets opportunities missed and wonders if ghosts are submitted to purgatorial memories of their past life. The poem forces readers to confront the fact that there is no escape from the self, which often strips away any and all illusions. Although Rice did not feel the poem was necessary to the novel, it does capture the new wisdom Lestat attains by the end of BT.

See also Art, Dolls, "The Dolls," Poetry, "Sailing to Byzantium."

"You can always count on a murderer for a fancy prose style"

A line from Nabokov's *Lolita*, which Lestat quotes when he is pondering opening lines for BT. *(BT 2)*

See also Nabokov (Vladimir).

Zagzagel   The angel that tutored Moses, his name means "divine splendor" and he knows seventy languages. He is the angel in the burning bush and chief guard of the Fourth Heaven. When Moses died, Zagzagel accompanied God to receive his soul.

When touring Heaven, Lestat mentions this angel to Memnoch and Memnoch acknowledges his reality. *(MD 206)*

See also Angel.

Zeitgeist   The moral, intellectual, and cultural state of a given era.

Armand believes that vampires need to be anchored in the zeitgeist in order to survive the malaise of boredom that can claim so many. For that reason, he had been involved in the satanic coven that formed the vampire "dark ages." When the coven dissolves, he begs to be allowed to join Lestat, the "vampire for a new age." Lestat refuses, so Armand waits at the Theater of the Vampires for someone like Louis. But then Louis ends up fading into cynical despair when Claudia is killed. It is not until the twentieth century, when Armand meets Daniel, that he finds someone to link him to the age. He follows Daniel around for nearly ten years, observing and asking him questions until Armand feels ready to actually engage with society himself. *(IV 285, VL 303–308, 311, QD 86, 97)*

See also Armand, Boredom, Change, Endurance, Molloy (Daniel), Nineteenth Century.

Zombie   A mindless corpse that is animated by voodoo magic.

The vampires of Eastern Europe are compared to this type of creature, because they seem to have no cognitive abilities. The term is also used in the first draft of IV to describe Louis's self-absorbed, reflective trances. *(IV 51, 197–199)*

See also Old World Vampires.

Zoroaster   An ancient Persian prophet and visionary who believed that good and evil are absolutes, engaged in constant struggle. His sayings are collected in the *Avesta*.

Roger refers to this religious figure to indicate the extent of his daughter Dora's spiritual ambition. "Dora knows that that's what's required." *(MD 88)*

See also Flynn (Dora).

TIME LINE

Around 4000 B.C. *(before the fall of Jericho)*

Akasha brings the twins to her court; Khayman rapes them, and Mekare then asks the spirit Amel to avenge them.

Amel fuses with Akasha and makes her a vampire; she in turn makes Enkil a vampire.

Maharet has a mortal daughter, Miriam, who starts the Great Family; Khayman takes Maharet and Mekare back to Egypt.

Akasha makes Khayman a vampire.

Khayman makes Mekare, who makes Maharet.

Maharet and Mekare are separated and sealed into coffins; both escape but fail to find each other.

Akasha and Enkil make other vampires; they are worshiped, then trapped for many years so other vampires can steal their blood. Finally, they free themselves, but gradually begin to withdraw from the world.

Khayman makes vampires who war with the vampires Akasha and Enkil made.

Around 3000 B.C.

Akasha and Enkil go into their trance.

Around 1000 B.C.

Maharet makes Eric a vampire.

Roman Empire *(after 49 B.C.)*

The Elder places Akasha and Enkil in the sun, causing vampires everywhere to be burned or destroyed.

Roman Empire (*after 49 B.C.*) *continued*

The God of the Grove (the Druid's vampire) makes forty-year-old Marius a vampire.

Mael becomes a vampire.

Marius takes Akasha and Enkil out of Egypt to Antioch.

Maharet goes to Antioch and puts a dagger in Akasha's heart to establish the truth of the legend that Akasha must exist for all other vampires to exist.

1300s

Santino becomes a vampire.

1400s

Marius makes Armand a vampire when Armand is seventeen years old.

Magnus becomes a vampire.

1760

Lestat's mortal birth.

1766

Louis's mortal birth.

1779

Lestat goes with Nicolas to Paris, to become an actor.

1780 (*winter*)

Magnus makes twenty-year-old Lestat a vampire, then goes into the fire.

Lestat makes Gabrielle a vampire.

Lestat encounters Armand's coven.

Lestat makes Nicolas a vampire.

Lestat gives Renaud's theater to four vampires who, with Nicolas, turn it into the Theater of the Vampires.

1780 (*May*)

Lestat and Gabrielle begin their journey on the Devil's Road; Lestat writes his first of many messages to Marius.

1789

Nicolas goes into the fire.

Lestat's mortal family is killed during the French Revolution.

Gabrielle leaves Lestat to go into the jungles.

Lestat goes underground.

Marius comes to Lestat and takes him to the island where Akasha and Enkil sit as statues. Lestat awakens Akasha, but Marius then sends Lestat away.

Lestat arrives in New Orleans.

Claudia's mortal birth.

1791

Lestat makes twenty-five-year-old Louis a vampire.

1794

Slaves drive Lestat and Louis from Pointe du Lac.

Lestat makes five-year-old Claudia a vampire.

1795

The three then settle into the town house in New Orleans.

1862

Claudia attacks Lestat and throws his remains into the swamp; when Lestat survives and returns, Louis burns the town house and he and Claudia flee.

Claudia and Louis travel by ship to Eastern Europe, to seek out Old World vampires.

Claudia and Louis go to Paris.

Louis meets Armand and his coven at the Theater of the Vampires.

Louis makes Madeleine a vampire.

Armand's coven destroys Claudia and Madeleine.

Louis retaliates by burning down the Theater of the Vampires.

After 1862

Louis travels with Armand, then returns to New Orleans, where he claims to have seen Lestat again.

Armand leaves Louis.

1917

David Talbot's mortal birth.

1929

Lestat goes underground in New Orleans.

Armand takes over New Orleans as his own territory.

1950

Jesse's mortal birth.

1955

Daniel's mortal birth (or possibly two years earlier).

1975

Louis tells his story to the reporter in San Francisco.

The reporter, Daniel, seeks out Lestat but encounters Armand.

1976

The publication of *Interview with the Vampire* under the pseudonym Anne Rice.

1984

Lestat rises from his coma, after hearing the music of Satan's Night Out; upon reading IV, he decides to become a rock star.

1985

Killer makes fourteen-year-old Baby Jenks a vampire; she is destroyed later that same year.

The publication of *The Vampire Lestat* under the pseudonym Anne Rice.

Jesse, as a member of the Talamasca, investigates the New Orleans town house and documents the vampire activities there.

Lestat's rock concert is scheduled on Halloween in San Francisco; other vampires plot to annihilate him.

Louis reunites with Lestat.

Armand makes thirty-year-old Daniel a vampire. (He may have been thirty-two.)

Akasha awakens from her trance, destroys Enkil, buries Marius in ice, and begins her worldwide slaughter of vampires.

Mekare sends dreams to vampires worldwide about the twins and their story.

1985 (continued)

Khayman remembers who he is after a long period of amnesia, and follows Akasha to San Francisco, where he attends Lestat's concert.

Pandora and Santino rescue Marius and accompany him to Sonoma.

Vampires gather at Lestat's rock concert; Akasha kills most of them.

Gabrielle reunites with Lestat.

Akasha abducts Lestat and with him begins her slaughter of mortal men.

Maharet makes thirty-five-year-old Jesse a vampire.

The vampires who survive Akasha's destruction gather at Sonoma.

Marius reunites with Armand.

Akasha and Lestat arrive at Sonoma.

Mekare destroys Akasha and becomes the new Queen of the Damned.

Lestat records the aforementioned events.

Lestat meets David Talbot.

1988

The publication of *The Queen of the Damned.*

1991

Lestat tries to end his existence.

Lestat meets Raglan James and switches bodies to become mortal again; James absconds with Lestat's vampire body, but Lestat retrieves it and kills James.

Lestat makes David Talbot a vampire. David is seventy-four, but currently has the body of a twenty-six-year-old man.

Louis and David agree to live with Lestat in the New Orleans town house.

1992

The publication of *The Tale of the Body Thief.*

1992–1993

Louis, David, and Lestat part ways.

Lestat returns to Rio and senses his stalker.

Lestat sees Roger and starts to stalk him.

1994

Lestat discusses his stalker with David.

Lestat kills Roger, then speaks with Roger's ghost; he meets Roger's daughter, Dora.

Lestat's stalker introduces himself as Memnoch the Devil, and asks for Lestat's help.

Lestat accompanies Memnoch to Heaven and Hell. He meets God, hears the story of creation, and sees Christ's passion and the making of Veronica's veil. He visits Hell but decides against helping Memnoch. In leaving Hell, he loses his left eye to Memnoch.

Lestat gives Veronica's veil to Dora; Dora uses it to fan the flames of Christianity.

Armand destroys himself in the sun to affirm the veil's authenticity; Mael similarly destroys himself.

Dora gives St. Elizabeth's to Lestat. Maharet returns his eye and chains him to restrain him. She gives him a note from Memnoch, which thanks him for aiding him. Lestat dictates his experience with the Devil to David.

Interview with the Vampire is made into a movie starring Tom Cruise, Brad Pitt, and Kirsten Dunst.

1995

Publication of *Memnoch the Devil*.

VAMPIRE ATLAS

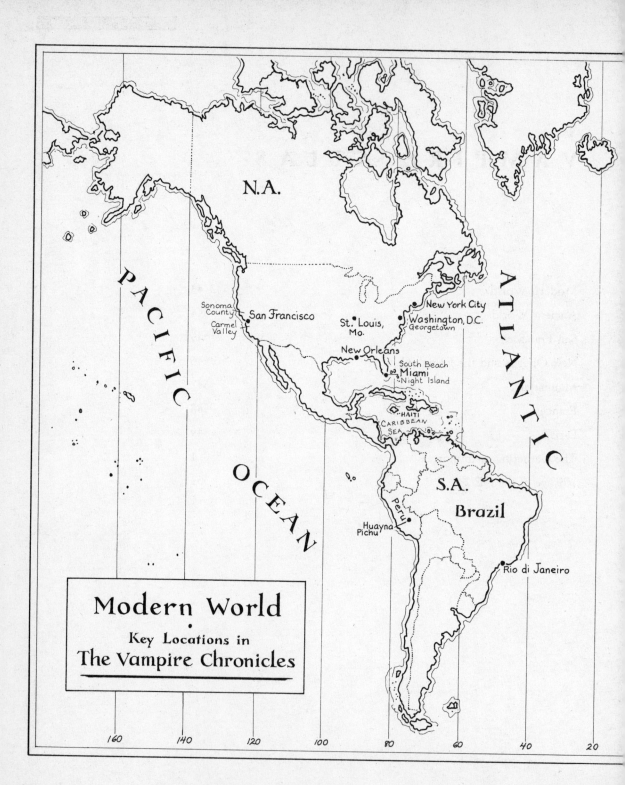

Modern World

•

Key Locations in

The Vampire Chronicles

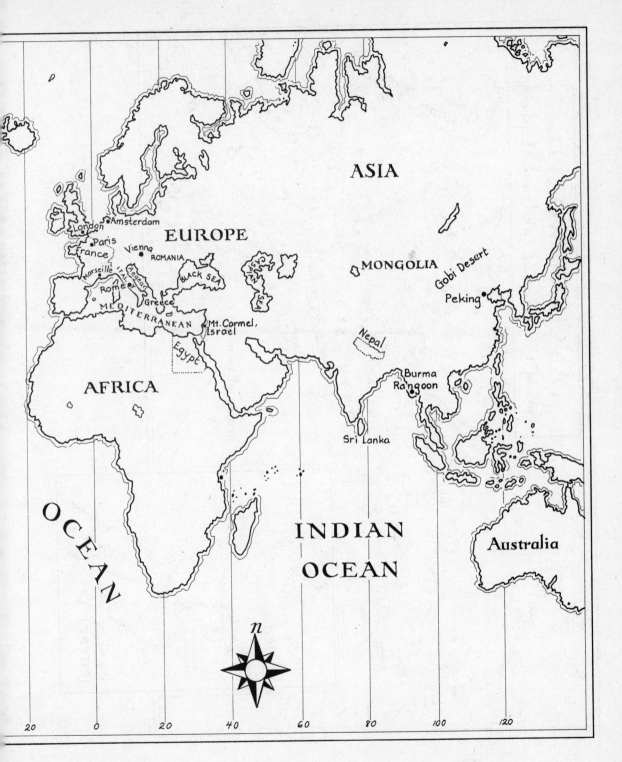

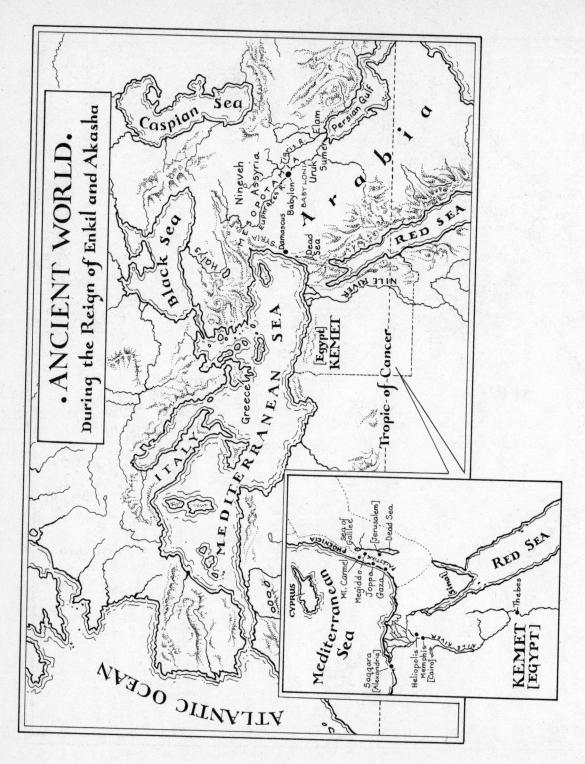

ANCIENT WORLD.
During the Reign of Enkil and Akasha

Caspian Sea

Black Sea

ATLANTIC OCEAN

MEDITERRANEAN SEA

ITALY

Greece

Halys

Nineveh
Assyria
MESOPOTAMIA
Euphrates R.
Tigris R.
Damascus
SYRIA
Babylon
BABYLONIA
Uruk
Elam
Sumer
Persian Gulf

Arabia

Dead Sea

RED SEA

NILE RIVER

[Egypt]
KEMET

Tropic of Cancer

Mediterranean Sea

CYPRUS

PHOENICIA

Sea of Galilee
[Jerusalem]
Dead Sea
PALESTINE
Mt. Carmel
Megiddo
Joppa
Gaza

Saqqara
[Alexandria]

Heliopolis
Memphis
[Cairo]

NILE RIVER

[Sinai]

RED SEA

Thebes

KEMET
[EGYPT]

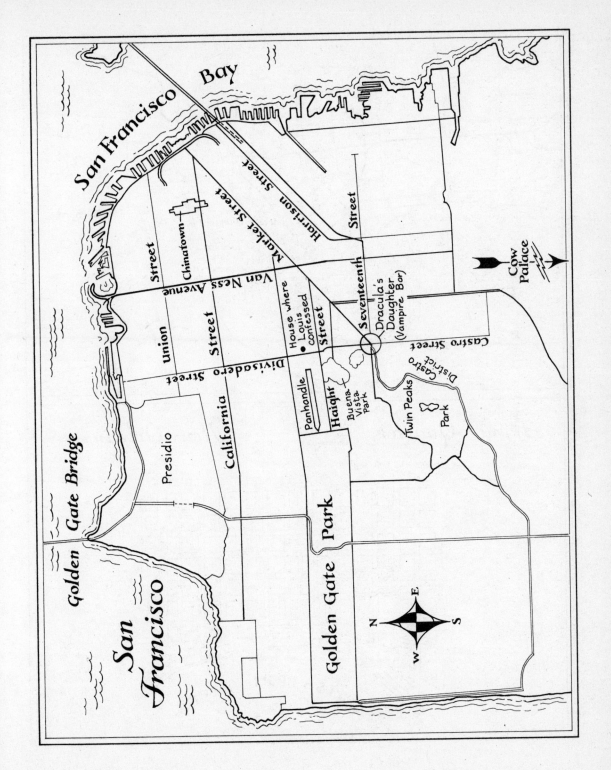

San Francisco Bay

San Francisco

Golden Gate Bridge

Presidio

Chinatown

Union Street

Street

California

Street

Divisadero Street

Van Ness Avenue

Market Street

Harrison Street

House where
● Louis confessed

Street

Seventeenth

Panhandle

Haight

Buena-
Vista
Park

Twin Peaks
Park

Castro
District

Dracula's
Daughter
(Vampire Bar)

Castro Street

Street

Golden Gate Park

Golden Gate Park

Cow Palace

N E
W S

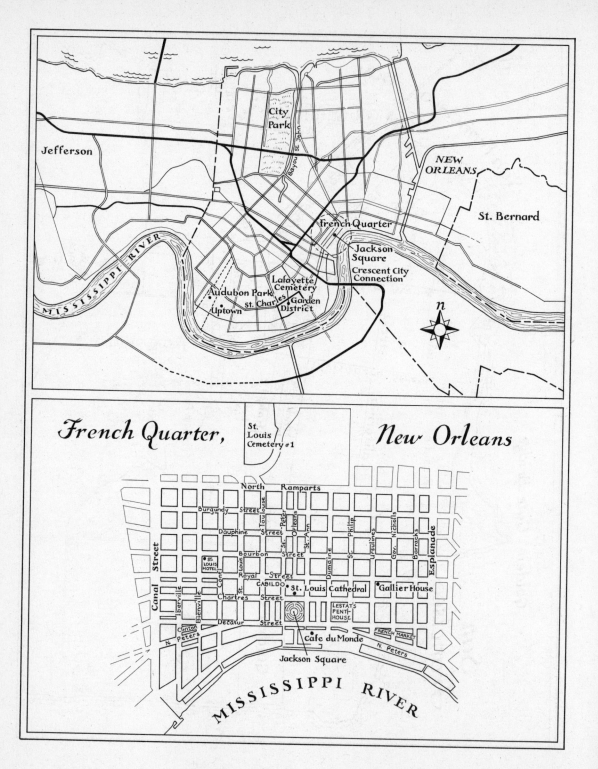

French Quarter, New Orleans

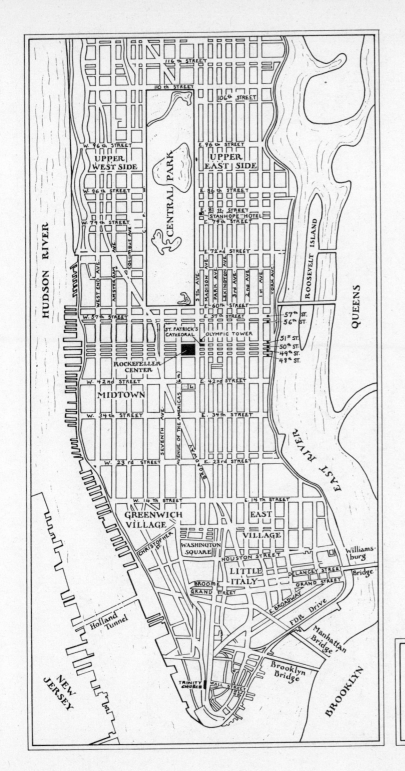

UPPER
WEST SIDE

UPPER
EAST SIDE

CENTRAL PARK

HUDSON RIVER

ROOSEVELT ISLAND

QUEENS

116th STREET
110th STREET
106th STREET

W. 96th Street
E. 96th Street

W. 86th Street
E. 86th Street
E. 81 St. Street
STANHOPE HOTEL
W. 79th Street
E. 79th Street

E. 72nd Street

W. 57th Street
E. 60th Street
E. 57th Street

57th ST.
56th ST.

ST. PATRICK'S
CATHEDRAL
OLYMPIC TOWER

ROCKEFELLER
CENTER

51st ST.
50th ST.
49th ST.
48th ST.

W. 42nd STREET
E. 42nd STREET
MIDTOWN

W. 34th STREET
E. 34th STREET

W. 23rd STREET
E. 23rd STREET

W. 14th STREET
E. 14th STREET

GREENWICH
VILLAGE

EAST
VILLAGE

CHRISTOPHER ST.

WASHINGTON
SQUARE

HOUSTON STREET

Williamsburg
Bridge

DELANCEY STREET

LITTLE
ITALY

GRAND STREET

BROOME
GRAND STREET

E. BROADWAY

FDR Drive

Holland
Tunnel

Manhattan
Bridge

Brooklyn
Bridge

TRINITY
CHURCH

WALL STREET

EAST RIVER

NEW
JERSEY

BROOKLYN

5th AVE
MADISON AVE
PARK AVE
LEXINGTON AVE
3rd AVE
2nd AVE
1st AVE
YORK AVE

WEST END AVE
AMSTERDAM AVE
COLUMBUS AVE

SEVENTH AVE
AVENUE OF THE AMERICAS
BROADWAY

New York
City

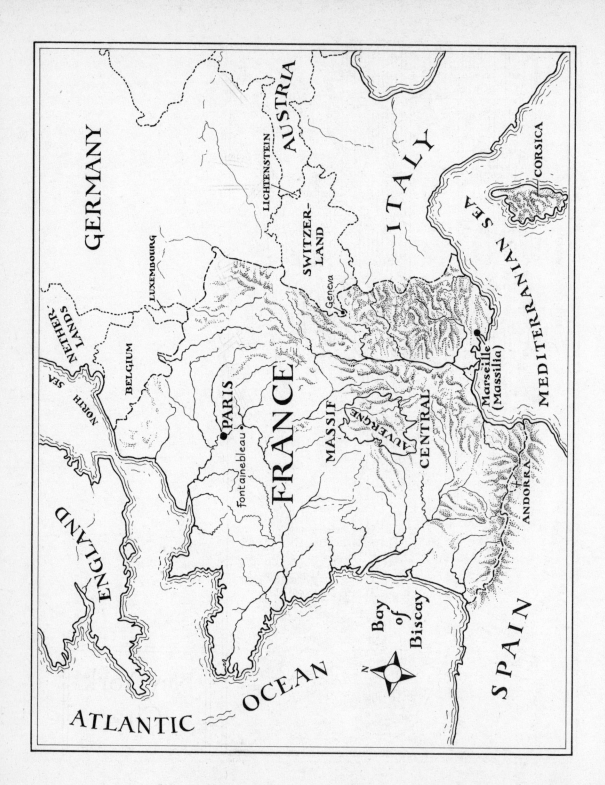

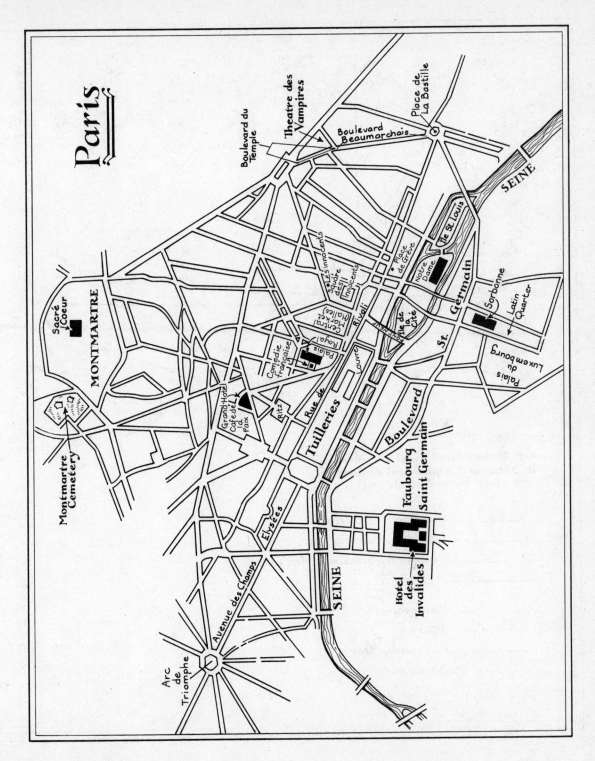

Paris

Montmartre Cemetery

Sacré Coeur

MONTMARTRE

Montmartre
Cemetery

Boulevard du
Temple

Theatre des
Vampires

Boulevard
Beaumarchais

Place de
La Bastille

SEINE

Île St. Louis

Place
de Grève

Notre
Dame

St. Germain

Sorbonne

Latin
Quarter

Les Innocents

Square
des
Innocents

Les Halles

Central
Hotel

Rivoli

Rue de la Cité

Pont Neuf

Palais du
Luxembourg

Comédie
Française

Palais
Royal

Grand Hotel
Café de la
Paix

Ritz

Louvre

Rue de

Tuilleries

Boulevard

Faubourg
Saint Germain

Hotel
des
Invalides

Élysées

Avenue des Champs

Arc
de
Triomphe

SEINE

549

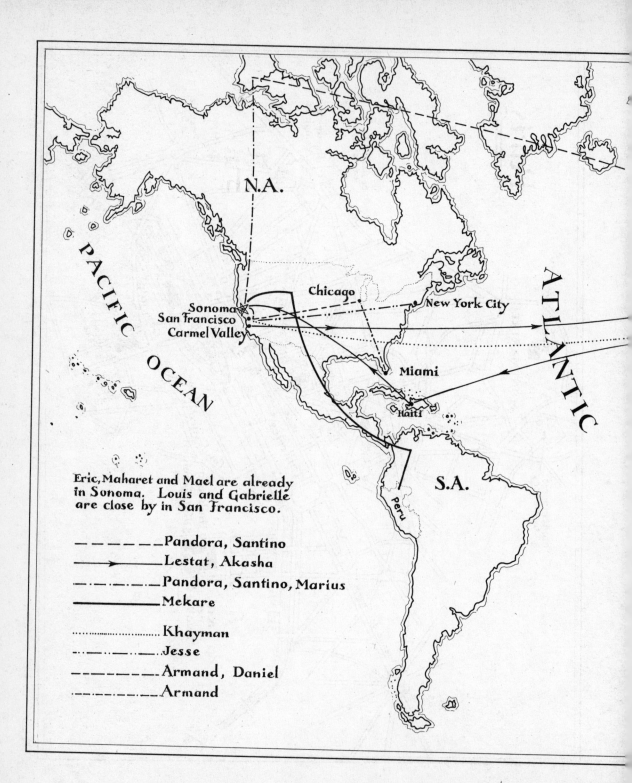

N.A.

PACIFIC

ATLANTIC

Chicago

New York City

Sonoma
San Francisco
Carmel Valley

OCEAN

Miami

Haiti

Peru

S.A.

Eric, Maharet and Mael are already
in Sonoma. Louis and Gabrielle
are close by in San Francisco.

— — — — — Pandora, Santino

———▶ Lestat, Akasha

—·—··— Pandora, Santino, Marius

————— Mekare

············· Khayman

—··—··— Jesse

— — — — Armand, Daniel

—··—··— Armand

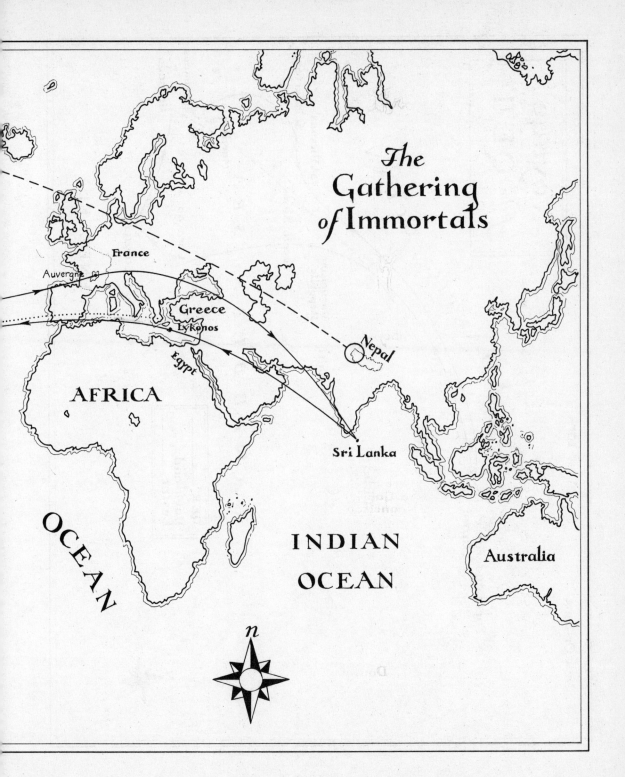

The
Gathering
of Immortals

France

Auvergne

Greece

Lykonos

Egypt

AFRICA

Nepal

Sri Lanka

INDIAN

OCEAN

Australia

OCEAN

n

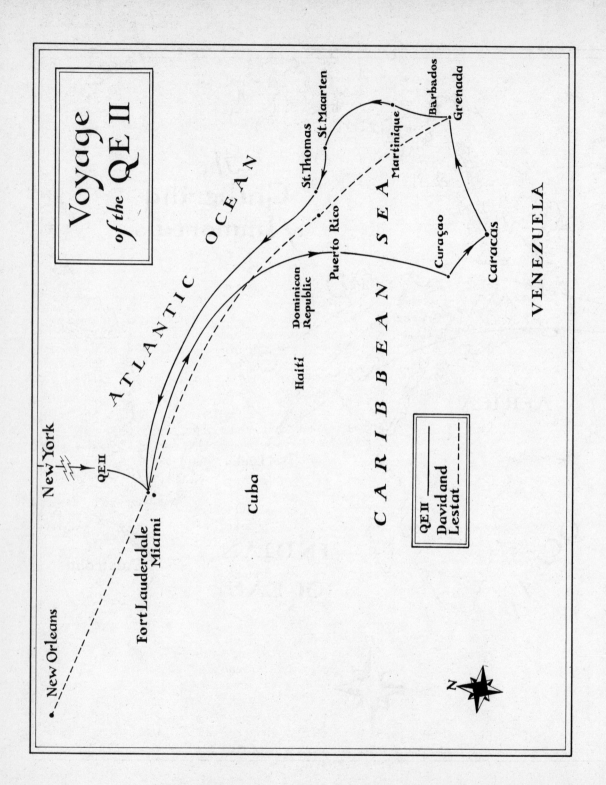

Voyage of the QE II

New Orleans

New York

Fort Lauderdale
Miami

ATLANTIC OCEAN

Cuba

Haiti

Dominican
Republic

Puerto Rico

St. Thomas

St. Maarten

Martinique

Barbados

Grenada

CARIBBEAN SEA

Curaçao

Caracas

VENEZUELA

QE II
David and
Lestat

N

INTERVIEW WITH THE VAMPIRE

A short story by Anne Rice, August 1973 approx. Later became a novel completed January 1974.

"Do you wish to record the interview here?" asked the vampire.

The boy had drawn the small tape recorder timidly from his briefcase. He hadn't expected this response. "You don't mind . . . that I record the interview, possibly broadcast it on FM radio throughout San Francisco?"

"I haven't the slightest objection," said the vampire. "I was referring to the room." He gestured now to the small round oak table, the straight-back chairs. In the rhythmic flashing of a neon sign beneath the window, the boy saw these, and a door that was not the hall door, partially open.

"O, it's fine," said the boy, and quickly he checked the batteries of his recorder, lifted its clear plastic lid to start the tape, and looked timidly at the vampire. "Is this . . . your room, then?" he asked.

"No," the vampire smiled. "Just a room." He was standing at the window and the red light shone on him at intervals of three seconds. Then there was only the dim light from Divisadero Street and the passing beams of traffic. The boy could see a washbasin and a mirror, and again he stared at the partially open door.

"Do you want the light on?" asked the vampire gently.

"You mean you don't mind?" asked the boy.

"No, of course I don't mind," said the vampire, walking slowly and silently to the center of the room. His long cape flared around him. "I know that you did not have a close look at me in the bar. It was very dark. I don't want you to be nervous, frightened."

"Thank you," said the boy. And then the vampire reached above the center of the round table and pulled a cord, flooding the grim narrow room with harsh light. He looked down at the boy, and the boy

could not repress a gasp. His fingers danced on the table, backward, to grasp the edge. The vampire was utterly white and smooth, as if sculpted from bleached bone, but in his handsome and seemingly inanimate face burned two magnificent green eyes. He smiled at the boy and the chalk-white flesh moved with the infinitely flexible but minimal lines of a cartoon.

"You *are* frightened," he said gently. "Don't be."

"No," said the boy, clearing his throat and loosening his tie. "Only amazed." He studied the vampire's high cheekbones, his long slender nose. The clothes, as he had seen in the bar, were magnificent, a tapered coat of the last century, collar stiff and white as the vampire's flesh, the large silk tie perfectly folded and knotted, the cape velvet. He lowered his hand now slowly from the light cord and the cape fell gently over his arm. On the hand with which he barely touched the table now he wore an emerald ring, the only color in his total makeup other than the brilliant green of his eyes. Now he sat down in the chair opposite the boy and the boy could see no evil in his face, no menace. He might have been a man of thirty-five if such a man could have ever existed.

"Shall we begin, then?" asked the vampire in the same gentle manner. He laid one hand over the other.

"Yes, yes, of course," said the boy, his voice hoarse as if he were out of breath, and he punched the button of the recorder. He set the microphone on the table between them and he said, "One, two, three," adjusting the dial until the light on the recorder gave an even glow. "Well," he rubbed his sweating palms. "We're ready. Shall I ask you . . . anything?"

"Absolutely anything."

"Well, then, I'll just ask you anything at all."

"Yes, anything." The vampire laughed. "Anything at all." And he smiled at the boy as a father might smile at a son, the laugh lines like pen strokes at the corners of his eyes.

"All right. . . . right!" said the boy. "Well." And then he swallowed and stared at the plastic lid of the recorder and only slowly lifted his eyes again to the vampire's. "Ok. Are you really a vampire?"

"Yes," said the vampire, with just a touch of a frown.

"When did you start being one?" the boy asked.

"In 1791," said the vampire.

"What were you doing then?" asked the boy, as if the precise date had surprised him.

"Running an indigo plantation in Louisiana," the vampire explained. "I had come there from France."

"Oh, then you were born in France?"

"I was born in France," said the vampire. "Of a noble family tracing its ancestry to the time of St. Louis. Now, except for me, the

family has entirely died out. The name would mean nothing to you."

"Did the whole family move to Louisiana?" asked the boy.

"No. There was a tragedy," said the vampire, his speech suddenly a little slower. "My brother died then and I felt responsible for his death. I was not a vampire then, of course, and did not dream of ever becoming one. I loved my brother and when he died . . . I felt it was my fault."

"Would you like to elaborate on that?" asked the boy. "I mean if you'd like to go into it."

"I don't particularly mind now," said the vampire. He put one of his beautiful white hands out flat on the table and looked at the hand thoughtfully.

"It's not painful . . . ?" the boy asked.

"No, it's merely something I haven't discussed in so long," said the vampire. "I couldn't say the story brings me pain anymore at all. My brother saw visions," he said and he looked off when he spoke now as though he had become absorbed in memory as he spoke. "He'd always been different, unlike the rest of us, unlike other boys his age. But I had always been very fond of him. As a matter of fact, I protected him. I remember I wouldn't allow the others to make fun of him, and if he didn't want to do certain things, I insisted he be left alone. He was gentle, loving by nature. He wasn't any older then than you are now." He looked up at the boy. His eyes were huge and serene. "But something happened. I'm not sure when it began, but my brother began to see himself as a saint with a mission. He saw a vision in his oratory in which St. Dominic and the Virgin Mary both appeared to him and told him to sell all our property and to use the money for God's works. He was to be a great saint and save France from the rising tide of atheism." The vampire stopped, extremely thoughtful. "I haven't discussed these things in years," he said softly.

"But did you believe him?" asked the boy.

"No," said the vampire, gazing off again. "I thought he was mad. The day that he came and told me about the vision, I laughed at him. But actually, I was bitterly disappointed. I thought he was mad."

"But that's understandable," said the boy agreeably. "Who would have believed him?" he asked.

"Is it so understandable?" asked the vampire. "I think perhaps it was vicious egotism. Let me explain. I loved my brother as I told you, and at times I did believe him to be a saint. I fully expected him to ask for my permission to enter the priesthood. I had wanted this since he was a small boy. And if someone had told me of a saint in Ars or Lourdes who had had this vision a hundred years before, I might well have believed that. I was a Catholic, not such a bad one for the times. But I didn't believe my brother. Not only did I not believe him, I never even entertained for a moment that he might be telling the truth. His

faith I never doubted, nor his love for God. I was simply convinced that no brother of *mine* could be a saint. That's egotism. Do you see?"

The boy thought about it before he answered that yes, he thought he did. "He might well have seen this vision," said the vampire.

"So you never found out?"

"No. He died within minutes after telling me. He just walked out of my study, stood for a moment at the head of the stairs and then he fell. He was dead when they found him at the bottom, his neck broken, and I was suspected of having told him something that made him fall. Everyone blamed me."

"But how could they?" asked the boy. "Had anyone seen him fall?"

"Yes, two of the servants saw him fall. And they said that he looked up as if he had just seen something in the air. Either that or he had something on the tip of his tongue. He was about to speak and then he fell. But this didn't matter. It was indirect, all that was said against me. I was blamed for not having understood him, for not having cared for him. He was very much loved and people wanted to blame someone. No one said to me to my face that I had killed him. And of course I never told anyone his story of the vision. But I couldn't bear to be in that house after that. I was a very emotional young man, then, you see. And I, too, had loved him. I sat in his room for two days and two nights after he died just staring at him. I was obsessed."

"This must have been dreadful. But you did find out finally . . . didn't you?"

"Find out what?" asked the vampire, with a slight rise of his eyebrows.

"What made him fall. I mean, after you became a vampire, weren't you able to know?"

"No," the vampire shook his head. "Nor did I ever find out if he truly saw visions. I'm a creature of this world, not the next."

"Not the next!" the boy repeated, astonished. "You mean there is a next?"

"I don't know," the vampire smiled. "As I said, I'm a creature of this world." He studied the boy for a moment, then smoothed a rough place on the table with one of his white fingers. "But we were talking of Louisiana, how I came to be a vampire, weren't we?"

"Yes, how did it happen?"

"Well, I wanted to get away from my family estate. I sold it to a cousin and brought my sister and my mother to Louisiana. They were furious about it, but they didn't have any choice and when they discovered we owned an immense plantation and three houses in the city, they were satisfied. I saw little of them then and could think only about my brother. I went out up the river to see the plantation about twice a week, left the slaves to an overseer and spent my time walking about

town. I thought constantly of my brother, about his body rotting in the ground in France. I could think of nothing else."

"How awful for you," said the young man.

"Yes, it was," said the vampire. "And it inclined me to be careless. I walked in alleys and black streets at night; I drank too much in cabarets; I cared about nothing, really. And consequently, I was attacked. It could have been any type of person really, a sailor, a thief, anyone. But it was a vampire. He caught me just a few steps from my door one night and left me for dead in the mud."

"You mean . . . he actually sucked your blood?" the young man asked.

"Yes," the vampire could not repress a slight laugh. "He sucked my blood," he nodded. "That is the way it's done."

"But you lived," said the young man. "You said he left you for dead."

"Quite right. And I remembered nothing, only that a man had approached me, caught me about one arm, and then blackness. I was weak and dazed and lay in bed unable really to answer the doctor's questions. Then a priest came. I told him about my brother. I told him for the first time about my brother's visions, how I had not listened and how my brother must have seen something before he took the fatal step at the top of the stairs. I remember I was feverish and it was important to me that the priest understand my guilt and my love for my brother. I remember I made everyone else leave the room and I clung to his arm telling him everything, even the details of the vision, such as the color of the Virgin Mary's veil."

"Did he believe it?" asked the boy.

"No," the vampire made a short laugh. "As a matter of fact, he scoffed at it. He said my brother was probably possessed of the devil, if he'd seen anything at all, and might even be in hell. As a matter of fact, he said the French Revolution was proof of it. France was possessed by the devil as a country. Probably all of Europe was possessed. There would be another great plague."

The vampire shook his head, his lips forming a slight smile, his eyes moving over the surface of the table as if he were seeing these things spread out before him. "Remarkable," he mused. "But of course at the time, I was furious. I went wild."

"Went wild? What did you do?"

"Well, I wrecked the room for one thing and nearly killed the priest. I think it took two men to tie me down. Then my sister kept trying to feed me soup, and some doctor suggested they bleed me. The fools. I nearly died. But I didn't care. I said life was over for me and death was what I wanted and they didn't dare to bring the priest back to my room. Had they bled me again, I very probably would have died, but that night the vampire came. It was after my sister had fallen asleep

and I remember he laid a silk shawl over her face right where she sat at the table with the damp cloth for my forehead and a basin of water. She never once stirred from under that cloth and by morning, I was greatly changed."

"How did he change you? Did it happen that night?"

"No, not that soon. I remember that sunrise distinctly, as a matter of fact. It was the last one I ever saw. And I knew it would be. I can remember it so distinctly, better than any sunrise before it ever. I remember seeing the light at the tops of the French windows, a gleam behind the lace curtains, and the gleam grew brighter and brighter in great star patches among the leaves.

"Finally the sun came through the windows themselves and the lace lay in shadows on the stone floor, and all over the form of my sister who was still sleeping, shadows of lace on the shawl over her shoulders and head. As soon as she was warm, she had pushed the shawl away without awakening and the sun began to make her eyelids tighten. Then it was gleaming on the table and in the water in the basin. And I could feel it on my hands on the counterpane and then on my face. I lay in the bed thinking about all the things the vampire had told me and then I made up my mind that I would do it, become a vampire. It was the last sunrise I ever saw." The vampire was looking at the window now. And when he stopped, the boy heard the noises from the street. It seemed unnaturally quiet in the room suddenly and the sound of a passing truck was deafening. Then it was gone. The tape rolled.

"Do you miss it?" the boy asked timidly. "The sunrise."

"Not really," said the vampire. "There are other things. But where were we? You wanted to know how it happened."

"Yes."

"I left New Orleans and went upriver. The other vampire had a house in St. Jacques Parish. A huge house, as I recall, built by his own slaves. They did excellent brickwork, I remember, and the place was kept by the vampire's blind brother who never knew he had a vampire for a brother. He was the strangest old man, he talked to slaves who'd been dead for years, and kept telling us to eat everything on our plates. I became a vampire there in that plantation house and was fully experienced in killing swamp animals before summer. I remember the first human. It was a runaway slave; he was massive, the man, and wild with fear. They'd been hunting him with dogs and when I came on him at the very middle of the night, he had just fallen asleep. I remember my friend, Lestat, was telling me I had to kill him, no way out of it, a human being at last. I had hardly become accustomed to the swamp myself; the snakes, the stench, all these things aroused in me fear for which I no longer had any real use; I was like a man with a lost limb who insists he feels the limb, feels pain in it or cold. And then, with Lestat just a few feet away, I bent over the sleeping man. He was still

wet with perspiration, his torn pants drenched, and when my teeth went into his throat, the throat tensed like a massive arm muscle. I can remember that well, and those eyes glinting for an instant as the breath went out of him."

"My God," the boy said.

"Don't be frightened," the vampire turned away from his thoughts and looked at the boy. "I should imagine this is difficult for you, interviewing a vampire. You've never done such a thing, have you?"

"No," said the boy. He stared as if he'd lost the power to speak. His face was drained and he couldn't take his eyes off the vampire's eyes. "And you mean it . . . every word of it," he murmured.

"What did you say?" the vampire leaned forward politely.

"It's a completely new experience," the boy stammered quickly. He checked the tape and the light on the recorder. The tape turned and turned as it did all the time. "Did the black man die?" he asked, clearing his throat and repeating the question again immediately in a stronger voice. He looked up at the vampire.

"Black man . . . O, you call them blacks again. I forgot this. They were blacks then. Then they were Negroes. And now they're blacks." The vampire laughed. "Yes, he did die. As a matter of fact, I rather overdid it. He had more blood than I really needed and I wasn't particularly comfortable after the feast. But it was the first one, and I could feel him dying as I drank, and with my new vision, my new awareness of things, I simply couldn't pull away from him. I think Lestat forced me finally to go back to the house. It was as close to morning as we dared stay out."

"Your new awareness?"

"Yes, things looked considerably different," said the vampire. "I haven't thought about the difference for years. We become accustomed to things so easily, don't we? I remember that first night when the vampire, that is Lestat, of course . . . when he came to me in New Orleans and I told you we talked the whole night. I was on the other side of the world then. I could only dimly imagine seeing the world as he described it. And now if I speak to you about it, you can only dimly imagine you see what I see. I remember Lestat told me the whole history of the world that night, or so it seemed to me as a human. Time stopped. The night was infinite as if the span of hours had begun to curve, to encompass the entire shape of recorded time like a balloon, swelling slowly without end. World without end . . ." the vampire's voice trailed off, and then he looked at the boy. "Do you understand?"

"I'm trying," said the boy. "You said you see things different now."

"Yes, completely different. But it's no real use trying to tell you about this. It's the story you're after for this radio station, isn't it? You

want to know what happened, how I came to be here."

"Yes," said the boy, but he said it so softly he might have said it to any comment the vampire made.

"Well, I stayed on that plantation for years. Lestat left after a while. He really always wanted to be in Europe, and I cared nothing about Europe at all. I saw Louisiana in my new vision and New Orleans was becoming a metropolis. It was a reckless, charming city and I could roam it for hours every night never causing the slightest bit of unwanted attention. I liked the crowds after the opera, the women getting into carriages, and the slaves . . . they were always easy when I had to feast and was ready to go home. They had to stop for me, show me some humility simply because I was a white man, and I had them without the slightest struggle, usually leaving them dead. One did live once and went crazy. They called her Loony Lucy Locket all her life after that, and whenever she saw me she'd scream, but she screamed at all kinds of gentlemen and no one paid her the slightest attention."

"Did anyone put two and two together? Figure out that you were around?" the boy asked.

"I beg your pardon? Oh you mean talk of vampires, suspicion. Not for a long time. There was so much voodoo then, and so many unexplained murders. The fleet was always in there, sailors roaming the streets, women for any price to a fortune. Even when I took young men of property, the victims were often buried without anyone noticing the marks. Of course, I might have made my presence known just for the fun of it. But then I was watching things, seeing things, experiencing my new vision, and I had no desire for personal fame whatsoever. I still have little, really. I don't think I've ever even considered an interview of this type before for that reason. I prowled New Orleans and the swamps around it for years without there ever being a whisper of vampire. And when Lestat's brother died, I buried him in the night and let the old plantation house go to ruin. I liked watching it go to ruin. Some evenings, I sat for hours in one spot and watched it decay. I could hear the termites eating, watch the spiders in the moonlight. I could hear the water rising around the foundations. There was no darkness that wasn't alive with sound, or impenetrable to my eyes. And occasionally I had the opportunity to frighten someone there and that delighted me. I chased two men for a mile through the swamp one night and one of them nearly drowned. And not long after that a group of Negroes came out there at sunset just to see the haunted ruin and I could hear them as I was getting up. I came out on the upper gallery and they went wild. I wish more people had come. But no, there was no talk of vampires. And I decided to go back to France in 1863."

"But how could you do that? How could your friend do it? You can't stay up in the daytime, can you? That's what I've always heard . . ."

"And you've heard correctly," said the vampire with a nod. "But I travel the way vampires always travel. I have my body shipped. I made all the arrangements one evening at the Hotel St. Louis through an agent. Bought his dinner, gave him an enormous dinner, and had him arrange to pick up my coffin in a suite I had rented the following night. I believe I shipped myself as myself that time, my deceased 'uncle' by my own name. My family was long dead, of course. I was sending myself home for burial at the family estate. And I had no intention of staying around to watch the South lose the war."

"You knew the South would lose?"

"My dear boy, everybody knew the South would lose. On the ship home, I dined on rats, and finally awoke one evening as planned in a Paris apartment I'd rented months before. Everything had gone perfectly. If Lestat had been around, I might have had an easier time. But I'd lost Lestat. I never saw him again."

"Do you suppose he's still alive?" the boy asked, and then he swallowed as if the vampire might be angry.

"I imagine so. There are so few people who even believe in vampires, I can't imagine anything really happening to him. But then that depends on where Lestat went. And Lestat was theatrical. He liked people to know he was about, to frighten ones he had no intention of killing, and acquire a reputation. But even so . . . the truth is, I just don't know. I wanted to see the whole world then, and Lestat would have only been a bore. I'd been a vampire for only a few months when I knew how little Lestat had used his powers, how little he cared about what he could come to know with immortality and vision. He was a prankster, and if I had told him the things I saw or wanted to do, he would have laughed. I suppose the type of vampire a man becomes depends on the man really; it's the way it is in life. I remember, for example, that I was still completely fascinated with animals after years. When I fed upon a new animal, it was a new experience. I worked up from rats, which had never much bothered me, all the way to magnificent horses. Of course, I enjoyed occasional people then for a variety of reasons, but there was so much to be experienced just with animals. I can remember the first time, for example, when I killed a panther in a zoo in Germany. What an experience that was, lying beside that enormous cat, sinking my teeth into the back of its neck—which was by no means easy—and hanging on to the beast as I fed. It was still heaving with breath afterward. And I lay there warm and full beside it—why, it was as long as I am when it stretched out—and I lay there just resting as it died. And the smell of it, such a smell."

"Then you do smell things," asked the boy, after a slight pause.

"Ah . . . yes, but not as you do," the vampire commented. "I mean I am not repelled by odors as you might be." Then he touched his chin with one of his long fingers and his brows met for an instant,

making two fine lines in his smooth forehead. "Of course, I'm not attracted by fragrance as you would be either. But I am certainly aware of an odor."

"Did you . . . finally become interested in people? The way you were in animals?" the boy asked. And now he could not help doing what he had almost done several times in the past—that is, looking more carefully at the vampire's mouth. He could see the white lips were of a different texture, like silk, and now as the vampire smiled and said nothing, he glimpsed the white teeth. He swallowed, trying not to show his reaction, because he couldn't see the tips of the upper teeth, and he looked down. When he looked up again, he was aware of the vampire's fine eyelashes, like fine black wire in his lids, curling just slightly at the ends. The boy was staring blankly at the top of the tape recorder at once and he could feel his heart against his shirt.

"Yes, I did," the vampire was laughing. "But I was patient, moving up to it slowly, more slowly than most. And seeing the creations of people all the while. Greece, for example. I spent years in Greece just roaming the ruins. Night after night I went alone to the Acropolis, not caring if I was to feed on field mice afterward. But there were always people, and I came finally to think only of people, to meet the greatest richest part of my experience. I think the first real person I truly appreciated was a young woman in Greece. She was unquestionably the most beautiful woman I'd seen at that time. Mortal men would turn and stand dumbfounded when she passed. And she was reckless. She had a little bit of English money and she cared about nothing, really, an unusual Englishwoman for those times. In her youth, she'd known Keats, I believe it was, and she always carried a little velvet volume of his poems with her. She wrote herself then, too, and kept everything locked. I remember one evening I persuaded her to read a poem to me and I thought it was rather good. She said it was shocking and I believe she was right."

"You knew her . . . as a friend?"

"Well, I told her what I was," said the vampire. "But she didn't believe me. I'd come late in the evening, never see her in the day, and I didn't drink tea. But I don't think she believed me even for an instant. Until the night I killed her."

"You . . . killed her?" the boy asked.

"Yes," said the vampire simply. "I told her I was going to do it. She said I was the most peculiar man she'd ever met, and she couldn't have felt any safer on the Acropolis in the moonlight with anyone else she knew, even her own father. Then I showed her my teeth and I prepared to kill her. It was the most thrilling kill I'd made up till that time, easily the most thrilling kill. The experience with the panther was nothing compared to it."

"But she must have gone crazy!" said the boy.

"No," the vampire said calmly. "She was too surprised. 'Then you've been telling me the truth,' she said with amazement. Then she simply closed her eyes. If I hadn't felt her heart beating, I would have thought her dead already. She never opened her eyes. I know she didn't suffer at all. I must have held her there for the better part of an hour and when I left her, she looked as if she'd been made of wax. She was like an enormous old doll. I put one of her gloved hands into the other, arranged her parasol right beside her, and her little velvet book, and smoothed her petticoats and her skirts just as she wanted them. It was as different from the panther as it would have been to have spoken with the panther. How else can I say it to you so you'll understand? And your FM radio audience, so they will understand?"

"O, you're doing beautifully," said the boy, but it was time to change the tape. The vampire rose and walked on the creaking boards to the window, and the boy hurriedly replaced the cassette with another, his hands wet and trembling so that he had to fumble with it, which made him all the more nervous. From the back, the vampire looked quite ordinary; and the boy swallowed and drummed his hand nervously when the vampire turned around, stepped into the light again, and looked down. He could see the Adam's apple move slightly under the smooth white skin of the throat above the vampire's stiff collar. "She was a very old woman," the vampire said, just touching the boy's shoulder now with a firm hand as if he meant to calm him.

"I'm sure," said the boy, clearing his throat and shifting in his chair as the vampire sat down. The vampire sat back now and crossed his right knee over his left and rested his long slender arm on the table.

"Was it . . . was it always people after that?" the boy asked, his voice barely audible to himself. He leaned over his own little microphone and started to ask again, "Was it . . . ?"

"They became the main interest," the vampire nodded, glancing just for a second at the recorder's light. "All manner of people. All manner of emotion. I spent considerable time in all European countries, before I came back to Louisiana. And, of course, I was disappointed but not at all surprised to see how it had changed. My mother's and sister's graves were still being tended by a niece there of whom I'd never even known. My sister had apparently married quite late, had two daughters and one of them had left this young girl. She was the only one of my family that I was able to discover and she kept the graves beautifully, even though her husband made almost no money as a grocer. I started a romance with her on the evenings when she ran the little store. He did something those nights, bowled or played cards or some vulgar thing, leaving her alone with the cash register and the late customers who wanted liquor. So I began to come in on those evenings and buy magazines. I bought cigarettes once and she saw me throw them away. I had to tell her then that I came to see her. And she fell

completely in love with me. Of course, I never told her what I was or who I was, but I did give her money, a good deal of it, and the last time I saw her, I told her to leave that husband of hers for good. She wouldn't. It was the Church, she said, she went to Mass every morning at five A.M. So I took care of it for her. Of course, I never told her. And I loathed the man. I could hardly bear being around him on general principles, let alone locked to him for fifteen minutes, sucking his sap and listening to him curse. He was drunk, the blood was what you'd expect from a lizard. I was infuriated by him. And then he lay there in the alley breathing like a snoring dog. I had to break a bottle, and cut his throat with a piece of glass. Then I took his wallet so she'd think it was a robbery. I threw that away in a field and put all the money in a poor box outside a church. Of course, she never knew I was her ancestor. . . ." he sighed.

"Did you ever see her again?"

"No, there was no reason for that. It was just a family obligation. All I could do for her. I had some other things to do which were fun. Somebody had restored Lestat's plantation house, put screen porches on it and rebuilt the old cistern and cemetery. I wanted to see who these people were and have a talk with them."

"You mean you went to see them at night?"

"Exactly, and what a bunch they were. They had faked everything, including a name that no one would have known in Louisiana in two hundred years, and a completely false coat of arms. They had old land grants they said came from Louis XIV and a map of the original plantation which almost made me laugh in their faces. There wasn't a mention of Lestat's family, of course, and a phony monument, cracked and distressed to make it look real, had been put over the grave of his old blind brother whom I had buried myself before I left. They wined me and dined me, though I never really touched anything of course, and told me all of this while I talked of visiting the house in my childhood, of the ruins, and of the old story of ghosts. Yes, they'd been in the North then, aunts and uncles living here apparently or in New Orleans, they lied, and they wanted me to know that their oldest girl, who was at the Sorbonne, was to be the Queen in one of the Mardi Gras clubs this spring. I hated them. The air conditioners were droning and the children were brats and the woman's accent was utterly false, and the husband didn't know what to do with his fork or his knife and never blotted his lips once before taking his wine so the glass was murky and ugly before the meal was half over, and I could see it was all lies. Finally, when they got to talking more of their times in Brooklyn, New York, it was clear they'd come from there, and were trying desperately to hide it, and the family money was invested in a chain of dry cleaners, and the great old house was an obligation, something to live for, the past not allowed to die, the great South they

must desperately try to preserve. You get the picture?"

"Yes," said the boy. "What did you do?"

"I killed them all," said the vampire with a smile. He showed more of the teeth now than ever before, and the boy just stared at him, his own mouth slack, his hand fluttering for a second by the recorder.

"One by one," said the vampire. "I was furious. Besides, I sensed something else about them, but this is hardly something I can use to explain my actions to you. I know you'll be glad to hear it, though, when I'm finished. Death is something so different to you, I would imagine. Unless, of course, you've been a soldier."

"No, nothing like that . . ." the boy nodded weakly.

"Well, to be quick about it, I killed one of the men first. I told him who I was, what I was, and just how I had left the house in 1863. I told him who was buried in the cemetery and demanded to know how he had gotten the house, the stack of forgeries and what he was up to. He went through the gambit of emotions from A to about M and then emptied a gun into me. After that, he was quiet. He offered me everything, deeds, money, even said he would care for me himself, my coffin if I wanted it, and see I was safe. He said he had connections, he could do things I didn't even know about. I killed him. But what he'd said intrigued me. All this happened in his study. I was supposedly in bed for the night, and I just took him out with me and got rid of him on the way home. The next night, he was just 'missing' and I had ample opportunity to kill the woman. I frightened her deliberately and she also went for the gun, but couldn't get a grip on it. Apparently, when they found her in the morning and didn't find their 'guest' in his bed, the police were called. But it was a quick examination, I must say, considering the state in which I left her, blood all over the room; and that was when I began to see there was something strange. There weren't any police around the next night when I came back, but all sorts of other men. And such men. They all came from Brooklyn, New York, or some place like it, and they prowled around as if they could see in the dark. The children were absolutely gone, of which I wasn't glad really, as I didn't see why they should have been involved in the first place . . . that's something we haven't spoken of yet, children . . . you won't forget to ask me . . ."

"No . . ." the boy shook his head, his eyes wide, his lower lip slack as he stared absorbed at the vampire.

". . . and the man was alone in his study, with two of these creatures from Brooklyn, New York, outside the door wearing their hats as if they were walking about in downtown Manhattan. They had found the body of the other man in the swamp where I left him, and the only fellow I had left was saying into the phone that something was very wrong, and the man to whom he was talking wasn't going to live till tomorrow night if something wasn't done. At least, I *think* this is

what he was saying. When he saw me in the room with him, he dropped the phone and fired at me with a small handgun. Then the two New York fellows came in, firing at me, and all three men just fired for quite some time.''

"What did you do?" the boy asked anxiously when the vampire stopped.

"I was trying to describe it. I suppose it's best to say I picked one of the men and approached him steadily until he was forced to drop his gun and to stare into my eyes, unable to move. He could have avoided this, had he known what to do. But then people rarely do. I then went for his jugular vein at once to kill him. The blood was of no consequence, I wasted it. When he fell on his knees, the other men had already run away. I was alone then with the owner of the house. 'You killed my wife!' he shouted as if it had never occurred to him. I told him I had, indeed, and I told him precisely why . . . about the house, about my living there and all his papers being fake. But he was frantic. I doubt he heard or understood what I was saying. The strange thing was, he was not really frightened for himself. He was trying to make a deal with me. The fellow I'd bitten was completely dead now, and he bent down to check his heart two times. Then he told me that he and I could make millions of dollars.

" 'For what?' I asked. But he was so thrilled with this plan of his that he had forgotten all danger. He asked if I minded if he had a drink and said I could have the house, the house was the least important thing in the world, and then he poured himself a glass of Wild Turkey bourbon.

" 'Not to me, it's not,' I said indignantly, explaining that though I had no intention of confiding anything to such a person as he, *this was the house* in which I had become a *vampire*. But he was like a person possessed of a grand passion. He was mumbling to himself about the opportunity of a lifetime, and he kept looking at the dead man and laughing. Then three of his other New York friends stormed the room, emptied their guns, and tried to back out, nearly knocking each other down. I killed one of these in the hallway while the others watched, then fled, and the owner just sat there at his desk laughing. 'This is marvelous,' he kept saying. 'No one can stop us,' and this sort of thing.

" 'What do you mean no one can stop us!' I demanded, thoroughly annoyed at this point. I wanted to kill him and I wanted him to know why and be frightened. I wanted him to realize what a vulgar stupid man I thought he was with his false documents and coat of arms; but he didn't even care. He said that I had to listen to him, it was only fair. He had listened to me, after all, when I told him a long and preposterous story and I owed it to him. 'You bored me for two nights as your guest,' I said. 'I nearly went mad. I owe you nothing. And look what you've done to the house,' but nothing upset him. He was con-

vinced that when I heard what he had to say I would be as delighted as he was. He checked the new body now and clapped his hands like a child. 'This is fantastic!' he whooped, and when I reminded him I had killed his wife in the same way, he just brushed that off, saying this was business.

"I think I listened to him for about a quarter of an hour before I finally understood. He was a gangster which didn't surprise me or mean anything to me one way or another. I read the papers. These things have little interest for me at all. But when I realized that he wanted me to be a gangster with him, I was dumbfounded. And I haven't been dumbfounded in a century. But he had it all planned. And he meant every word of it. We were to be partners and I was to kill people simply when he pointed them out. No one would ever catch me. They wouldn't even know who sent me or why I had committed the murder. And through this, he, my partner, would become the richest man in the world. He could ask as much as one million dollars for a single murder; and there wasn't a 'contract' as he called it that we couldn't handle. I could even kill the present premier of Soviet Russia, or Red China, he pointed out. It would be a 'snap.' You understand I'd heard all these words before and could follow him completely; I just could hardly believe he meant it. I could hardly believe that he knew what I was, had seen what I was, believed it, and still wanted to make this proposition. But it was the only thing on his mind. When I said I had no interest in it at all, he just stared at me. For a moment, I thought his heart had stopped.

" 'Why not?' he asked. Now he was dumbfounded.

" 'Why should I?' I asked.

" 'But you can have millions, anything you want! Don't you believe me, haven't you been . . .'

" 'I don't need them. Of course, I've been listening. What would I want with anything you've mentioned?' I asked.

"He shook his head. But I could see he was beginning to understand. But then his eyes brightened. 'You need someone to take care of you!' he said. 'Your coffin. You need a partner to look out for that thing in the day,' he cried. 'You never thought of that, did you?'

" 'I take excellent care of it, myself,' I told him. 'And you would be the last person I would trust it to, besides.'

" 'But we could be partners,' he said. 'I got men working for me, and I wouldn't let anything happen to you any more than I'd kill the goose that laid the golden egg!' he pleaded. He went on and on about what a nice room I could have, and how he'd get me whatever vampires want. 'You can't shop around in the day, for instance. I could go to stores for you, get you stuff,' he said.

" 'Thank you, but I can get everything I need at night,' I said. He was reaching the end of his rope. Finally, he began to threaten me. His

men wouldn't let this happen. They'd find me, kill me, no matter where I tried to hide, New York, Paris, Rome . . . the whole world was nothing to them, they had men everywhere, did I know what they were called in the underworld, would I like to hear it with my own ears?

" 'Why don't you call them now in one of these places and give them a description?' I suggested, handing him his phone. It was making noises on the carpet. 'Just tell them that I'm a vampire with a coffin somewhere in Louisiana. Tell them how I dress, how tall I am, and that when they find me, it ought to be in the day, and they can find out what to do from any twelve-year-old boy who's been to the pictures.'

"He was enraged. 'You're crazy to do this!' he shouted, hurling the phone across the desk. He swept papers and glasses and guns to the floor. He began to curse. 'A cross!' he shouted suddenly and began to look around.

" 'That's foolishness!' I scoffed. 'Children make that up when they're frightened at night.' I couldn't help but laugh."

"Is it foolishness?" the boy asked, now leaning over the table.

"Yes," the vampire shook with laughter. "So is the nonsense about mirrors," he shook his head, and just smiled for a minute before going on with his story. "Where was I? He was properly frightened and outraged, as I'd wanted it. But he wouldn't give up this scheme. He kept insisting there must be something in the world I wanted, something worth it for me to become his partner. And then came his final plea. Did he have to die? Why couldn't he be a vampire like me?

"Well, this was the last straw!" said the vampire. "I was exhausted, it was nearly morning, and the man had alternately infuriated me and bored me for hours. I personally detested him. 'You become a vampire like me!' I almost spat in his face. 'It would take more than that to close the gap between us!' I was trying to restrain myself. I dragged him by the collar down the hall and into his wife's bedroom where the blood still stained the wallpaper and the chair. 'Don't you have a particle of feeling for your own wife!' I demanded. 'For your own men? They tried to save your life and you stare at their bodies and clap your hands . . . and you're asking me to make you immortal, to have a thing like you around until the end of time?' I was thundering at him as he hung there by his collar. 'I can't stand having you around for another five minutes!' I told him. 'I'm not even going to drink Drop One of your miserable blood!' I rammed him neatly in the throat with both teeth, withdrew and watched it flow over his open shirt. He just stared at me for a few minutes and then passed out. When I dropped him on the bed, I knew he would be dead in a matter of seconds and I had to hurry to get back to New Orleans. But then he said something. As spent as he was, he managed to ask me one favor. 'If you like to kill people,' he was moaning '. . . there's this guy in Jersey. I wish you'd

get him . . .' Then I slammed the door on him in disgust.''

He folded his fingers now and looked at the boy. "Don't you think that's remarkable?" he asked. "The idea!"

"But what about the henchmen?" asked the boy. "The other men in the hats? Did they try to stop you when you had to get back to New Orleans?"

"No, not a one. As a matter of fact, there was no one around outside the house at all. I took one of the cars, a Cadillac, I believe it was, and taught myself how to drive on the way home. I almost always hire a chauffeur, you know, but this time I was really in a hurry. And I wanted to do it. Cars had begun to interest me. It was fun."

"But what about the newspapers? Did they say anything about the man?"

"Yes, apparently they said things which had to do with the things the man had been saying, these people he knew in other cities, gangs, mobsters. It was all blamed on them. I remember it distinctly, because I was in a bar the next night when I read that he had been stabbed with an ice pick and I laughed out loud. People were staring at me. An ice pick, can you imagine? They were searching the grounds for the murder weapon until dark." The vampire smiled. "I don't often read the papers really, but that whole family had been so remarkable. And the children. I wonder what became of those children."

The vampire stopped. He was looking off out the open window. The neon light was flashing at the same regular interval. And now, at the mention of children, there was a pause, the boy apparently on the verge of moving his lips several times, but not doing it. Finally he said, "You said . . . not to forget to ask you . . . about children."

"O, I did, didn't I?" said the vampire, and now he studied the small cassette. "But this is all the tape you have left, isn't it? And I don't know the time for sure . . ."

Quickly the boy drew back his shirt cuff and looked at his watch. "It's after nine!" he volunteered.

"And I have an appointment . . . we don't have much more time," said the vampire. "Perhaps you should ask me now what is most important to you, best for your interview," he said graciously.

"Well," the boy coughed and shifted in the chair. "This family you mentioned in Louisiana . . . all this happened not so long ago, right? Then you came to California shortly after?"

"Yes, just after. I like California," said the vampire. "I like San Francisco, in particular."

"Yes, it's my favorite town, too," said the boy. "I came here one summer right out of school and I just can't leave it."

"It's beautiful," the vampire agreed, smiling as if he saw the pleasure and sincerity in the boy's face when he spoke of San Fran-

cisco. "You relaxed there for a moment," he said. "I wish I could put you at ease. You've only relaxed when you were thoroughly absorbed in my story."

"O, I'm all right," the boy said at once. "But how do you live in San Francisco?"

"I have a house," said the vampire. "And a suite at a downtown hotel. It's no problem really. I get home before sunrise. My coffin locks from the inside. There are messages there for my houseboy, or the maids. I've had many houses since I came, it's the simplest thing in the world. There's nothing that can be done in the day that one cannot do at night. It's a matter of persistence."

"But what if . . . ?" the boy hesitated, looking down at the turning tape and up at the vampire . . . "but what?"

"But what if what?"

"But what if I do take this tape right to the studio and broadcast it here in the city?" he asked.

"But what if . . . why, young man, that's why I granted you the interview. You told me you were going to do just that when we met in the bar," said the vampire. He shrugged. "You puzzle me. I thought that was your purpose."

"But then everyone will know," said the young man, amazed.

"But no one will believe you," said the vampire as casually as before.

"But I have it . . . all here on tape."

"Still," the vampire shrugged again, "who is going to believe you?"

"You're right!" the boy's face colored. He stared helplessly at the cassette. The tape continued to turn. "Quick. Tell me anything. What you do here. How you kill people. Now," he said, flustered, his hands moving wildly in the air.

"I roam around as you saw me tonight, visit bars like the Pink Baby on Chestnut and Union Street and talk to young men and women who go to bars alone. Then I go home with one of them, a man sometimes, other times a woman, and then I kill them. I don't always kill them, you know. It's possible to feed without killing. Killing is more of . . . well, should I say, an event?"

"But how do you get them to go with you? What's your pitch? What do you say, romantic things? What do you say to the men?"

"Pitch? I don't follow you."

"I mean, what do you tell them to get them to invite you home?" the boy asked.

"That I'm a vampire," said the vampire.

"But you're not serious. You don't tell them that!"

"Of course I do," the vampire gestured with his open hand. "I just answer the questions they ask me about it, tell them things they want to know about living forever, what fun it is to wear a long black cape, the places I've traveled, whatever they wish to talk about. Generally, we're on our way 'home' in a matter of minutes. And then I feed upon them. They rarely remember anything in the morning, if they live."

"But they don't believe you," said the boy.

"Of course they don't. They don't believe me at all," said the vampire. "I tell them the same thing I told you tonight in the bar, and they don't believe me any more than you did when you came here."

The boy stared at him, aghast. It was as if he were frozen, that his hands could not move off the table beside the recorder and he couldn't ask any more questions.

"Well, you didn't . . . did you?" asked the vampire, folding his arms.

"No," the boy confessed, his eyes fast on the vampire's eyes. "It must be simple for you, very simple."

"Simplest thing in the world. They're all egotists, just as I was when my brother told me he was an elected saint. They might believe in me if some good friend of theirs told them with his hand on a Bible he'd seen me roaming a Transylvanian woods, but no man or woman out there in San Francisco tonight is going to believe I'm a vampire simply because no one *they know* in San Francisco could possibly be one!" he smiled.

The boy smiled slowly, tensely. "You're right."

"Is there anything else?"

"Yes," the boy said, with a glance to see that the tape was nearly out. "Is there anything you regret?" He studied the vampire more intently now, his own eyes narrow as if he were trying to see through the vampire's calm. The other did not change, however.

"Regret?" His eyes moved slowly over the dreary little room. "Not really," said the vampire. "I don't think the world's about to end. I can't imagine boredom. I suppose that will be when I begin to regret. If such a time comes, a time of boredom," he said. But he looked as if he wasn't telling the boy everything and the boy saw this. "I suppose I could say something about love now, something 'good' for your radio audience, edifying, you know . . . but when I think of how much I love what I see and hear and understand now, I can't say I truly miss 'love.' I suppose I'd have to say that as a human I did miss it, then. Never knew it, then. But that was another world," he said.

"Would you have it over, if you could?" the boy ventured. The tape had only a few more minutes.

"There's no way," the vampire said quickly as though he had thought this out a long time ago. "And if you mean would I take that miserable life I had then for this again, the answer is no. I want this. I like being immortal, to put it in your terms, though it makes me laugh.

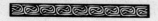

But we have to go now. The owner of this room will be coming back, and I don't want you to be seen here or get into any trouble," said the vampire, rising.

"I don't know how to thank you," said the boy. He pushed the button. The tape was finished. He was keenly aware of the vampire's towering height, of his white fingers barely touching the top of the table. A breeze stirred from Divisadero Street. "I don't know what to say . . ." He realized that he was backing away from the table.

"I don't think it's going to be much use. They won't believe it," the vampire said calmly. "But I've enjoyed it as much as you have."

"I'll go right now and put it on the radio," said the boy, reaching behind him for the doorknob.

"By all means," said the vampire.

"Do you think . . . we'll meet again?" The boy felt the knob and turned it slowly. The door opened with the pressure of a draft.

"Look for me in the Pink Baby, where you saw me tonight," said the vampire with a gracious gesture of his outstretched hand. It was as if he were waving good-bye. "I'm frequently there. And I'll look for you."

"Great, great . . ." said the boy. "Are you coming?" he said awkwardly as he stood in the hallway, his eyes glancing at the dim red lightbulb over the stairs.

"No, I'm going to wait for the owner of the room," said the vampire.

"All right, then. Thanks again," said the boy. "I'll look for you."

"Fine!" said the vampire.

The boy took one last look at the white-faced figure smiling at him across the table and ran down the stairs and out of the building, across the pavement to his car. Then he drove full speed to the FM radio station with his tape, nearly running a red light.

BIBLIOGRAPHY

Appleyard, Bryan. *Understanding the Present*. New York: Doubleday, 1992.

Armstrong, Karen. *A History of God*. New York: Ballantine, 1993.

Broderick, Robert C., ed. *New Catholic Encyclopedia*. Vol. VI. New York: McGraw-Hill, 1967.

Burnham, Sophy. *A Book of Angels*. New York: Ballantine, 1990.

Campbell, Joseph. *The Power of Myth*. New York: Doubleday, 1988.

Carus, Paul. *The History of the Devil and the Idea of Evil*. La Salle, Ill.: Open Court, 1974.

Chopra, Deepak. *Unconditional Life*. New York: Bantam, 1991.

Cirlot, J. E. *A Dictionary of Symbols*. New York: Philosophical Library, 1971.

Cohen, Daniel. *The Encyclopedia of Monsters*. New York: Dodd, Mead, 1982.

Crisp, Tony. *Dream Dictionary*. New York: Dell, 1990.

Davidson, Gustav. *A Dictionary of Angels*. New York: The Free Press, 1967.

Dickstein, Morris. *Keats and His Poetry*. Chicago: University of Chicago Press, 1971.

Ebert, Roger. *Roger Ebert's Movie Home Companion*. New York: Andrews and McMeel, 1989.

Edinger, Edward F. *Goethe's Faust*. New York: Inner City Books, 1990.

Eliot, Alexander. *The Universal Myths*. New York: Meridian, 1976.

Fodor's New Orleans. New York: Fodor's Travel Publications, 1988.

Frazer, Sir James. *The New Golden Bough*. Edited by Theodore H. Gaster. New York: New American Library, 1964.

Gibson, Walter S. *Hieronymus Bosch*. New York: Praeger, 1973.

Glaiszer, Geoffrey Ashall. *An Encyclopedia of the Book*. New York: The Word Publishing Company, 1960.

Goethe, Johann Wolfgang von. *Faust.* Translated by George Madison Priest. New York: Knopf, 1957.

Hall, James. *Dictionary of Subjects and Symbols in Art.* New York: Harper & Row, 1979.

Hill, Geoffrey. *Illuminating Shadows: The Mythic Power of Film.* Boston: Shambhala, 1992.

Huber, Leonard. *New Orleans: A Pictorial History.* New York: Crown, 1971.

Joshi, S. T. *The Weird Tale.* Austin: University of Texas Press, 1990.

Kuryluk, Ewa. *Veronica and Her Veil.* Cambridge, Mass.: Basil Blackwell, 1991.

Lass, Abraham, David Kiremidjian, and Ruth Goldstein. *The Facts on File Dictionary of Classical, Biblical, and Literary Allusions.* New York: Facts on File, 1987.

Licht, Fred. *Goya: The Origins of the Modern Temper in Art.* New York: Universe Books, 1979.

Magill, Frank. *Master Plots.* Englewood Cliffs, N.J.: Salem Press, 1976.

Margolies, Morris B. *A Gathering of Angels.* New York: Ballantine, 1994.

Marinez, Elsie, and Margaret Le Corgne. *Uptown/Downtown: Growing Up in New Orleans.* Lafayette: Center for Louisiana Studies, 1986.

May, Rollo. *The Cry for Myth.* New York: Norton, 1991.

Milton, John. *Paradise Lost.* Edited by Merritt Y. Hughes. New York: Odyssey Press, 1962.

Norris, Joel. *Serial Killers.* New York: Doubleday, 1988.

O'Connor, Peter. *Understanding Jung, Understanding Yourself.* New York: Paulist Press, 1985.

Pirie, David. *The Vampire Cinema.* New York: Crescent Books, 1977.

Poole, Susan. *Fromer's New Orleans.* New York: Simon & Schuster, 1989.

Ramsland, Katherine. *Prism of the Night: A Biography of Anne Rice.* New York: Dutton, 1991.

Redgrave, Michael. *Venice.* New York: Spring Books, 1961.

Rice, Anne. *Interview with the Vampire.* New York: Knopf, 1976.

———. "The Art of the Vampire at Its Peak in the Year 1876." *Playboy,* January 1979, pp. 385–390.

———. "The Master of Rampling Gate." *Redbook,* February 1984, pp. 50–58.

———. "Playing With Gender," *Vogue,* November 1983, pp. 434, 498.

———. *The Vampire Lestat.* New York: Knopf, 1985.

———. *The Queen of the Damned.* New York: Knopf, 1988.

———. *The Witching Hour.* New York: Knopf, 1990.

———. *The Tale of the Body Thief.* New York: Knopf, 1992.

———. *Memnoch the Devil.* New York: Knopf, 1995.

Ronner, John. *Know Your Angels*. Murfreesboro, Tenn.: Manne Press, 1980.

Russell, Jeffrey Burton. *Mephistopheles: The Devil in the Modern World*. Ithaca, N.Y.: Cornell University Press, 1986.

Russell, John. *Paris*. New York: Abrams, 1983.

Ryan, Alan, ed. *The Penguin Book of Vampire Stories*. New York: Penguin, 1987.

Seidel, M. *Brueghel*. New York: Putnam, 1971.

Shepard, William R. *Historical Atlas*. New York: Barnes & Noble, 1964.

Starr, S. Frederick. *New Orleans Unmasked*. New Orleans: Edition Dedeaux, 1985.

Stauffer, Donald. *Selected Poetry and Prose of Coleridge*. New York: Modern Library, 1951.

Turner, Alice K. *The History of Hell*. New York: Harcourt Brace & Company, 1993.

Vermilye, Jerry. *Five Hundred Best British and Foreign Films*. New York: William Morrow, 1988.

Walker, Barbara G. *Women's Dictionary of Symbols and Sacred Objects*. San Francisco: Harper San Francisco, 1988.

Wesler, Allan. *Images Encyclopedia*. Surfside, Fla.: Enterprises Publishers, 1990.

White, Kristin. *A Guide to the Saints*. New York: Ivy Books, 1991.

Wilson, Ian. *Holy Faces, Secret Places*. New York: Doubleday, 1991.

Wolf, Leonard. *The Annotated Dracula*. New York: Ballantine, 1975.

Wright, William Aldis, ed. *The Complete Works of Shakespeare*. New York: Doubleday, The Cambridge Edition Text, 1936.

Zee, A. *Fearful Symmetry*. New York: Macmillan, 1986.

p. 8. Kali from Vijayanaqar (15th century), Madras, National Museum/Giraudon Art Resource, NY

p. 14. Amenhotep III as Amon-Ra (18th Dynasty). Paris, Louvre / Alinari Art Resource, NY

p. 31. Joe Cornish

p. 32. Courtesy Department Library Services, American Museum of Natural History

p. 41. © 1982 Warner Brothers

p. 42. Tate Gallery, London/Art Resource, NY

p. 51. Hieronymus Bosch, *Death and the Miser*, Samuel H. Kress Collection, copyright © 1993 National Gallery of Art, Washington, c. 1485/1490, oil on panel

p. 52. Erich Lessing/Art Resource, NY

p. 53. Isabella Stewart Gardner Museum, Boston

p. 57. Permission of Café du Monde

p. 60. Caravaggio, *Amor Vincitore*. Berline, Gemaeldegalerie Dahlem / Foto Marburg Art Resource, NY

p. 62. Joe Cornish

p. 67. Katherine Ramsland

p. 68. The leading hotels of the world

p. 80. Katherine Ramsland

p. 82. Courtesy of the Cow Palace, San Francisco

p. 95. Courtesy Department Library Services, American Museum of Natural History

p. 100. Michelangelo, *Last Judgment* (detail). Vatican, Sistine Chapel / Alinari Art Resource, NY

p. 104. Young Bacchus. Naples, Musco Nazionale/Alinari Art Resource, NY

p. 106. Frank Corey

p. 107. Katherine Ramsland

p. 111. Universal, 1931

p. 112. Universal, 1936

p. 116. Culver Pictures

p. 119. Peter Paul Rubens and Jan Brueghel the Elder, *Paradise*. The Hague, Mauritshuis / Scala Art Resource, NY

p. 135. Pieter Brueghel the Elder, *The Fall of the Rebellious Angels*. Brussel, Musee des Beaux-Arts / Giraudon Art Resource, NY

p. 136. Hammer Film Productions Ltd.

p. 143. Alinari-Scala

p. 149. Four Seasons Hotel, Washington

p. 155. Benvenuto Cellini, *Ganymedes* (restoration of antique sculpture). Florence, Museo Nazionale / Alinari Art Resource, NY

p. 170. Goya, *Los Capricios, Ya eshora*. The Metropolitan Museum of Art, Gift of M. Knoedler and Co., 1918. [18.64(80)]

p. 171. The Bettmann Archive

p. 179. Erich Lessing/Art Resource, NY

p. 188. Scala/Art Resource, NY

p. 190. Erich Lessing/Art Resource, NY

p. 194. Courtesy Department Library Services, American Museum of Natural History

p. 199. *Daedalus and Icarus*. Rome, Villa Albani / Alinari Art Resource, NY

p. 210. George Kerrigan

p. 223. Cover of Ramses III sarcophagus: Isis. Paris, Louvre / Alinari Art Resource, NY

p. 226. Katherine Ramsland

p. 230. Photo courtesy of the Washington, D.C., Convention and Visitors Association

p. 236. Cinerary urn with the celebration of Neviane. Rome, Museo Nazionale / Alinari Art Resource, NY

p. 244. Katherine Ramsland

p. 264. Steven Ramsland

p. 268. Universal, 1931

p. 303. Karen O'Brien

p. 306. Katherine Ramsland

p. 319. UPI/Bettmann

p. 325. Steven Ramsland

p. 332. Katherine Ramsland

p. 334. Orpheus and Eurydice, Roman relief. Naples, Museo Nazionale Alinari/Art Resource, NY

p. 336. Osiris (late period). Berline, Aegyptische Sammlungen Foto Marburg/Art Resource, NY

p. 339. Steven Ramsland

p. 344. Katherine Ramsland

p. 352. Katherine Ramsland

p. 357. Jan Cossiers (1600–71), *Prometheus Carrying Fire*, Madrid, Prado / Bridgeman Art Resource, NY

p. 359. Courtesy of Cunard

p. 360. George Kerrigan

p. 377. Rembrandt, *Syndics of the Cloth Guild*. Rijksmuseum, Amsterdam.

p. 383. UPI/Bettmann

p. 384. Steven Ramsland

p. 397. Katherine Ramsland

p. 398. Katherine Ramsland

p. 400. (Top Left) Katherine Ramsland

p. 400. (Bottom) Katherine Ramsland

p. 401. Katherine Ramsland

p. 403. Katherine Ramsland

KATHERINE RAMSLAND has a Ph.D. in philosophy and a master's degree in clinical psychology. She has contributed to *Psychology Today, The Writer,* and *The New York Times Book Review.* Among her eight books are *The Witches' Companion: The Official Guide to Anne Rice's Lives of the Mayfair Witches, The Anne Rice Trivia Book, The Roquelaure Reader,* and *Prism of the Night: A Biography of Anne Rice.* Dr. Ramsland teaches philosophy at Rutgers University and lives with her husband in Princeton, New Jersey.

Also available by
Katherine Ramsland

_____THE WITCHES' COMPANION: The Official Guide to
Anne Rice's Lives of the Mayfair Witches   345-38947-6
$29.95
     This volume provides exclusive supplementary material to
the Mayfair Witches trilogy. With character bios, genealogies,
maps and hundreds of illustrations and photos, no visitor to the
world of Anne Rice will want to be without this unique and
comprehensive guide.

_____ANNE RICE TRIVIA BOOK   345-39251-5 $5.99
     Who was the groupie who traveled with Lestat's rock band
to San Francisco? Who was Yuri Stefano's friend in the
Talamasca in Amsterdam? Sharpen your pencil and prepare
yourself for these and over 1,000 other tantalizing questions to
test your devotion to the universe of Anne Rice.

Published by Ballantine Books.
Available in your local bookstore.

To order by phone, call 1-800-793-BOOK (2665) and use your
major credit card. Or use this coupon to order by mail.

Name_____
Address_____
City_____State_____Zip_____

Please send me the BALLANTINE books I have checked above. I
am enclosing $.................. (Please add $4.00 for the first book
and $1 for each additional book for postage and handling and
include the appropriate state sales tax.) Send your check or
money order (no cash or CODs) to:
Ballantine Mail Sales, 400 Hahn Road, Westminster, MD 21157.

Prices and numbers subject to change without notice.
Valid in the U.S. only.
All orders subject to availability.   RICE

581